"The Chameleons' dark, thrilling music is treated like a religion in their hometown, where they command the same devotion as their fellow travellers Joy Division. They were on the verge of breaking internationally when it all unravelled, and at last the whole story is told, in a compelling writing style and with a unique pop culture perspective that reveals who, how, and why they are such a key band. View From A Hill is the last great untold story of the Manchester post-punk era."

John Robb, Louder Than War

MARK BURGESS

VIEW FROM A HILL

PUBLISHING

Published by Mittens On Publishing
145 - 149 Cardigan Road, Leeds LS6 1LJ, UK.
www.mittenson.com

Written by Mark Burgess
Edited by Jaz Long and Karren Ablaze!

First published by Guardian Angel, 2007
Second edition published by Metropolitan Press, 2010
Revised third edition published by Mittens On, 2014

© Mark Burgess, Jaz Long, Karren Ablaze! 2014

Typeset by Chris Brereton
Front cover illustration by Christopher Ramsey
Back cover photo by Tony Skinkis
Cover design by Shaun Central: shaun_central@hotmail.com
Family tree by Jaz Long, typeset by Adam Wright and Chris Brereton

All rights reserved. No part of this publication may be reproduced or transmitted in any form by any means, electronic or mechanical, including photocopying, recording or any other information storage or retrieval system, without the prior written permission of the publisher. This book is sold subject to the condition that it shall not, by way of trade or otherwise, be lent, resold, hired out or otherwise circulated without the publisher's prior consent in any form of binding or cover other than that in which it is published and without a similar condition being imposed on the subsequent purchaser.

All copyright remains with the authors, photographers and artists.

British Library Cataloguing-In-Publication Data
A catalogue record for this book is available from the British Library

ISBN 978-0-9574270-1-3

Printed by Graficas Cems, Spain

Dedicated to my father Albert,
and my mother Doreen.
Thanks for a wonderful life.

I'd like to especially thank Fenella Stefaniuk,
James Oakes, Simon Lawlor, Paul Fallon, Rob Brown,
Mark Kennedy, Steph Wilcox, Yves and Sally Altana, Carlo
van Putten, Tini and Gerhard, Jytte and Daniela Haug,
for their love, friendship, understanding and support
through the years.

I'd also like to thank the team at Mittens On Publishing
for all their hard work and dedication in making this
edition happen.

Finally, in loving memory of Bryan Glancy,
and Richard and Mandy Horne.

CONTENTS

	Introduction	ix
1.	Childhood	1
2.	God Save The Queen	27
3.	Years And The Clichés	55
4.	Rock Of Ages	80
5.	Wonderful Radio One	100
6.	Angels And Devils	119
7.	Shot By Both Sides	150
8.	Men Without Hats	172
9.	Another Great Rock 'n' Roll Swindle	196
10.	A Tale Of Two Tonys	214
11.	Signs Of The Times	229
12.	Jacob's Rest	237
13.	The Devil's Dam	248
14.	The Road To Damascus	260
15.	A Stranger In The Dark	275
16.	In The Footsteps Of Saul	292
17.	The Dead Can Dance	299
18.	The Sun And The Moon	317
19.	The Great Adventure	336
20.	Tripping Dogs	349
21.	Heaven And Hell	377
22.	Zima Junction	393
23.	Venus On The Rise	413
24.	Splitting In Two	427
25.	Resurrection	435
	Epilogue	449
	The Chameleons & Mark Burgess Discography	471
	The Chameleons Family Tree	476

INTRODUCTION

View From A Hill is a many-faceted thing. Mark Burgess renders four decades of pop culture vivid by his participation and communication, taking us round the world on musical and spiritual quests. Highlights include the best ever way to get kicked off your record label[1], a poignant definition of success[2], and the psychological terror of a close encounter with evil[3]. These moments, as well as his reports of supernatural phenomena, make this a remarkable rock memoir that rewards the reader time and again.

One element of Mark's story - and the one we can hardly be unaware of - is that he was the vocalist, lyricist and bassist of The Chameleons. For many of us, The Chameleons are a mythical band. One that, should Scroobius Pip hold up a copy of *Script Of The Bridge* and then cast it aside with a shout of "just a band!", we would protest mightily, and never stop protesting as to their profound musical value and chimerical status.

In this introduction I want to explore something of The Chameleons' strange and shimmering nature. The starting point has to be their output: the oceanic guitarscapes crafted by Reg Smithies and Dave Fielding, John Lever's innovative percussion, and Mark's extraordinary lyrical and vocal abilities. The first incarnation of the band, emerging from the same kind of wonderful historical accident that produced groups like The Smiths or The Beatles, sent forth three albums' worth of faultless material. While it's easy to imagine a world without The Chameleons, I feel that the question to ask is *how did this miracle even happen?*

The history that Mark recounts here takes us part of the way towards an answer. A child who could sing before he could speak is forced through an education system that sometimes succeeds - but in the end grossly fails - to nurture a soul yearning to play, to create new worlds through the joyful adventures of art. Condemned through class prejudice to an engineering school at the age of fourteen, his energies blast out sideways into typically teenage escapades. Careering around, with the safety net of education no longer there, he is caught in the empowering arms of punk rock. Punk - art

---

1. Read about Mark's sudden departure, for the noblest of reasons, from Geffen Records in chapter 18.
2. Chapter 18.
3. Chapter 13.

in its truest form, the most explosive impetus to creativity many of us have ever known - takes his heart and sets it on fire, and in those rapturous and often dangerous times he finds solace and forges new connections. Then, bouncing on punk's aftershocks, he cannot fail to release what has been growing within him. It's just a matter of time, those aforementioned accidents of history, and a shedload of drugs.

In these pages we can glimpse the forces that brought Reg, Dave and John to these same coordinates in space/time - otherwise known as right place/right time, and how they adopted Mark as the singer of their new, unnamed band. We're treated to heart-stopping recollections of their LSD-fuelled meanderings on Tandle Hill, where they discovered that a bridge could have a script, and where they first heard the hypnotically eerie whistling sound that would become the ethereal motif of their early songs. Mark retraces the exciting steps that led to their first Peel session, and then to the release of their debut single, 'In Shreds', a thunderous anthem of disaffection and alienation that placed them firmly on the post-punk map.

Of course, such serendipity was purely artistic. The Chameleons had all the dark intensity of Joy Division combined with the power and presence of early U2 (and a whole lot more besides), yet they were never to penetrate the mainstream. Their habit of getting robbed blind by managers and record labels, like innocent babes lured to the wolf's lair, was to ultimately to take years - and albums - off the band's life. From the moment their first drummer, 'Scoffer', pocketed most of the fee from their very first gig, through to the elaborate heists performed by a succession of managers and record labels, they were manipulated by cunning thieves who understood that all The Chameleons really wanted to do was play music, and who held this youthful passion to ransom. You'll read, in heartbreaking sequence, how they were betrayed almost every step of the way. Those three pristine studio albums emerged despite it all; you can't help wondering what they would have achieved without the leeches.

The resultant under-exposure is one element of their enduring cult status, but a bit of punkthropology might reveal more. As a child of the same city as this group, I can't help enquiring why the potential familiarity of geography didn't, for me at least, dilute their mystery.

I grew up in south Manchester allied to a youth culture that would now be described as post-punk, but which, back then, was called Alternative. I was part of a variegated gang that went to goth nights but danced to The B-52s, Killing Joke, Wire, The Only Ones. We didn't call ourselves punks but would happily hang out with '77-style punks and chicken-dancing psychobillies. If this was a tribe ill-defined from within, we were solidified by the revulsion of those outside of our world: casuals, flick'eads, thus called for the fringe that rested horizontally across their foreheads, went around wearing tracksuits, Fred Perry tops or v-necked jumpers. To us they were the mainstream we were wired to avoid. They yelled at us in the street, accusing us of heroin consumption: "Smack'ead," they'd shout. Attired in black clothes, with pale faces and scruffled-up hair, I guess we resembled nothing more than the images on the anti-heroin adverts the government placed in music papers in the early eighties[4].

One of the bands we loved to dance to was The Chameleons. 'In Shreds' would cause The Ritz's bouncy dance floor to rise and fall with the pounding of our monkey boots. I knew all the songs on *Script Of The Bridge* without ever having had the money to buy it; those tracks permeated our lives, they were just there, in the air - and on the airwaves. When Mark Radcliffe[5] announced Tony Fletcher's death, I was sad. I hadn't even known who he was, but he was connected to The Chameleons and that was enough to make me cry as Radcliffe played 'Tears', an incredible piece of twinkly heartbreak pop, in tribute. I bought that single, and a cassette of *What Does Anything Mean? Basically*, and when *Strange Times* came out I met a boy who enticed me round to his house to listen to it, accompanied by a refreshing tab of acid. There, whilst admiring the carpet's undulations, I heard The Chameleons become both poppier and wilder. It's a massive, furious album - so passionate, it's the sound of someone's soul coming out. This *is* Northern Soul, dynamic and poised, vulnerable and knowing; the jagged sound of a troubled land.

Eventually, I got to see them. They were playing the Free Trade Hall at the culmination of an all-dayer that they had curated. As the day wore on I felt less comfortable, and when they played I was propelled to the back of the room by a strange force. The place was full of casuals! Loud, drunk, football boys with flick'eads, singing along to the keyboards and the guitar riffs and hurling themselves around ferociously. I stood forlornly at the back as the musical moments that I had expected to be precious, delicate and emotional were given the football terrace treatment.

Nearly thirty years later, I meet Mark[6], and ask him what was up with that.

"I loved the band but I was alienated by the fans," I tell him.

---

4. The disincentive to heroin use that they proposed in this campaign was that it would make you look like a post-punk rockstar. Propaganda fail!
5. On his *Cures For Insomnia* show on Manchester's Piccadilly Radio.
6. My co-interviewer was Simone Ivatts, the originator of this project.

"Yeah, me too!" he laughs. "It was a real mixture of people. We had a lot of real hardcore Mancs, a lot of goths, and some punks - a whole mishmash of different people. We were quite hard to figure out, I suppose. When we started there wasn't a goth scene. That came later, like 1984 and '85, and they kinda discovered us. We were kinda atmospheric, big-sounding, and that struck a chord. You know, we certainly weren't goths, we were never goths!"

"You never looked like it!"

"No, never!"

So, what in the hell had happened? They were making our kind of music but they attracted people who looked like they wanted to kick our heads in. How could we both love the same music? Did it mean they had secret, inner depths and hidden sensitivity? Did they, like us, scrawl teen angst poetry in moments of despair? I can't leave it alone. "I'm thinking about what you just said about you having punk and goth fans, or maybe proto-goths, and then locals who were into football..."

"Football is very ingrained in the culture here [in Manchester]," Mark concurred. "We were all brought up with it - my generation was, anyway. So it's not surprising that all the hardcore Mancunians were into football. I grew up with them, but it reached a point where things diverged. I was running around with a bunch of football hooligans, basically - then punk happened."

And there was another, crucial element in the equation. "At the time," explains Mark, "we were all taking the same drugs. A lot of the songs came directly from our experiments with psilocybin mushrooms and LSD, and everyone was doing it at the time. We weren't just dropping this stuff and going to clubs like happened later. We were getting out of the towns and going 'Fucking hell, what's this like?!' It was turning us inside out..."

In nature, chameleons change colour according to their environment - but not these Chameleons. They stayed true to theirs, with a level of integrity that only served to rub journalists up the wrong way. Sartorially, too, they also refused to compromise: "They were not exactly camera-ready," a friend observed. "That was another thing that set them apart; they just dressed how they dressed."[7] Here's an excerpt from chapter six to illustrate their approach:

> *We were each given a sum of money [by CBS] and told to go out into London and buy some new clothes. One*

---

7. An observation made by DIY activist Justine Wolfenden in conversation.

by one, we drifted back to James' flat, burdened with our assorted carrier bags, and then proceeded to nosey through each other's purchases. "What did you get?"

"A couple of shirts and a jacket. What did you get?"

"Some jeans and this shirt."

Finally, Reg came back carrying a small, single, plain white plastic bag. Everyone stopped to look at him.

"Is that all you got, Reg?" Dave asked him.

"Yeah," replied Reg, "I couldn't find anything I liked, so I just got this."

Again, there was a moment's silence.

"What is it?" Dave asked.

Opening the bag, Reg pulled out an antique Rupert Bear annual.

"We weren't interesting enough people," Mark explains, to a clamour of protest. "No, I mean from a media point of view. Everyone's perception of what The Chameleons should be bore no relationship whatsoever to who we were. We had more in common with The Fall than The Cure, or Sisters of Mercy, in the way that we looked, and the way that we were as people: we looked like the fuckin' Undertones. Our audience would hear our records and expect us to present ourselves in a certain way. They're going 'Wait a minute, he's supposed to be thin and wiry! He's not supposed to look like a lumberjack'. We didn't, you know, 'present' it. We were just like Oasis were when they started – just Mancs. They wore Adidas tops, and that was us, we were in jumpers and Doc Martens boots and spiky hair, cos we came from round here. But we were making music that people thought should be presented in a different way."

They put their records in some pretty unusual outfits too - Reg's sleeve artwork had a psychedelic vibe to it which was out of step with the sharp lines and garish colours of the 80s. Their refusal to play the game in any way led to them being either slated or overlooked by the snobbish London-centric music press who dismissed them as merely a Northern phenomenon. This was a few years before those same papers developed a fixation on everything Mancunian that they haven't yet grown out of. But in the 80s, England's North-South divide was real and ferocious; there was a cultural ravine between Manchester and London. The capital was the home of traitors and industry sell-outs, while Manchester's streets buzzed with an electricity that bestowed increased stature, magical powers, and, usually, a considerable arrogance on those who had risen from them. Of course, Mark

E. Smith, Morrissey and Ian Brown channelled this arrogance in a way that benefited their careers, but not The Chameleons...

"From reading the book," I say to Mark, "it seems like you suffered a combination of getting shafted by the music industry, and something approaching a conspiracy on the part of the music papers."

"Well, we didn't endear ourselves to people, we had a real 'fuck you' attitude." He goes on to reveal a profound innocence of PR and a true punker's allergy to schmooze: "If you talk to a journalist, and they ask you all these questions and you give them your answers, and they're not liking what they're getting, your attitude is like 'fuck off then'. Why are you talking to me? Why do I have to justify it anyway? And 'oo the fuck are you?"

Despite this refusal to submit to the mainstream, The Chameleons were to have a spellbinding effect on the ears of musical cognoscenti everywhere. They were irresistible to listeners in Spain, Germany and America, and in their hometown the power of their music was enough to draw members of rival tribes toward them in a way that only The Who had previously managed. The football casual element did not beat up the gothy post-punkers, and the latter were too fey to take on their enemies in this way, thus a mods-and-rockers type conflict never did materialise.

So it's clear that The Chameleons' mythical status is truly, essentially, down to their music. Any band can possess attitude and idiosyncrasy, and fall foul of misfortune and prejudice, but few can muster such original output. The Chameleons manifested their glorious post-punk symphonies seemingly without effort, conjuring arrangements that are frequently breath-taking, and their hypnotic, dreamlike songs refuse to be forgotten. They were perfect for their time and place. It wasn't them, you know - it was the world that missed out.

View From A Hill is replete with vivid descriptions of the strange times that produced this legendary band, the (road and acid) trips that bonded them, and the moments that gave rise to their sonic hallmarks and their language. Mark's adventures and misadventures intertwine in this extensive yarn; reading it feels like sitting with the author in an isolated bar - perhaps in the Shetlands - and being transported through time, space and a few other dimensions to boot. He doesn't deceive us with a happy-ever-after ending, but is realistic in his assessment of how the band finally disintegrated, and honest about a personal tragedy that is sadly still a taboo in our supposedly enlightened society. The energy that makes him a seeker and a seer emanates from this book as evocatively it does from our most treasured Chameleons' records.

THE ORIGINS OF THIS EDITION

View From A Hill has been published twice before, and I was intrigued when I heard of its existence. The early '00s internet wouldn't let me buy it; I tried the local library which didn't have it either, so I filled in a reservation card, paid my 60p, and waited three weeks for a postcard that implied that there was not a single copy in the entire British library system. Apparently you could get it on eBay for anything up to £95, if you were lucky to have those kind of disposables. Eventually a friend (Pete Harrison) of a friend (Simone Ivatts) acquired a copy, and it was passed around our city. Following this, and an extraordinary Chameleons Vox gig in Leeds, Simone struck up a dialogue with Mark and offered to prepare the book for reissue in electronic form. I'd just brought out a book of my own and was in the mood for a bit more publishing action[8]; Jaz Long and I then met up with Mark after a show, and he gave us the go-ahead to do whatever we wanted with his manuscript. A crazy honour!

Mark is living a big life. He has an enviable ability to communicate his experiences, and his storytelling is rich and loquacious. The text we started work with had a jungle-like quality to it. Before wading in, Jaz armed himself with a tonne of research, boosting his prior knowledge as a keen fan of Mark's work by assembling the discography and the family tree you can find in the appendices. Thus prepared, he took a deep breath and went in with a machete to clear some paths. I ventured after him with the garden clippers, pruning the prose till its beauty was inescapable. We know as readers the joy of losing oneself in a work, so we operated like forest rangers, dedicated to preserving the book's natural variety and complexity[9].

Mark, for his part, offered us absolute trust, which we hope we have repaid with dedication and loyalty to his vision, and without sacrificing his distinctive voice.

And here it is - for all you tricks of the light.

Karren Ablaze!
Andalucia, November 2014

---

[8]. I'd been dreaming of producing a series of book on mythical bands, starting with this shortlist: The Chameleons, Huggy Bear, Joanna Newsom, Scritti Politti, Josef K.
[9]. Thanks also to our team of proof readers: Jerome Smith, Gavin Bradbury, Ian Cockburn, Declan Kelly, Keah Whittaker, Bela Emerson and Paula Farr.

1. CHILDHOOD

Both my parents worked full time from the age of around fourteen until their eventual retirement. For the first few years of my life, when he wasn't lifting coal from wagon to cellar, my father worked for a housing construction team as a labourer, before finally becoming a project manager for a fire protection company. From what I can gather, in his late teens and into his early twenties he'd been something of a local hard case and was constantly getting into fights. Eventually he joined the army as part of his National Service and was recruited into the regimental boxing team, and this seemed to calm him down.

My father was an all-round athlete, one of those guys that would excel in any competitive arena. In the late 1950s he'd been a star apprentice with Manchester United Football Club after talent scouts had spotted him playing for various factory football teams around the region, as well as for Manchester Boys, where quite a few notable professionals had started out. Back then, anyone who was any good could earn a few coppers turning out for amateur teams on a Sunday morning, and so my father would top up the meagre allowance the army gave him by playing for any team prepared to pay for his services.

Great things were forecast for him - so much so that he eventually came under the eye of Sir Matt Busby himself, who at the time was busy building the squad that history would remember as The Busby Babes, the blueprint for Busby's famous European Cup challenge of 1959. Shortly before my dad was due to sign for Manchester United, he was riding pillion on a motorcycle in North Manchester when another motorcycle, having swerved to avoid an oncoming bus, ploughed into him, instantly ending any possibility of a career in professional football. Something of this nature would have crushed a lesser man, but my father was philosophical about it. He'd been rather blasé about playing for Manchester United anyway, having been a supporter of their rivals Manchester City all his life, and would much rather have played for them. In any event, had the accident not occurred, it is highly likely that he would have been on the aeroplane that crashed on leaving Munich airport on 6th February 1958. The ill-fated Flight 609 was carrying the United team back from a European Cup match in Belgrade, but failed to take off and ploughed through a fence at the end of the runway, killing twenty-three of those on board. Of these, eight were members of the

Manchester United first team squad, many of whom were my dad's friends. Had this been the case, I would never have been born.

Subsequently, I became a ray of hope, the focus of his lost opportunity, and I would often wake up to find my bed cluttered with footballs, cricket bats, or tennis rackets. I would, so my mother used to tell everyone, invariably pick up the tennis racket and attempt to strum it.

Before she became a hospital administrator, my mother began her working life as a trainee typist until I came along - unplanned - in 1960, whereupon she left work for a while to wean me out of nappies before returning to employment at the Cromer Cotton Mill where she remained for many years. Not much music there - just the continuous, thunderous roar of machinery from six in the morning until six in the evening. My mum and her colleagues learned to lip-read so that they could hold conversations over the horrendous din. No ear protection of any kind was given to any of them, so it's a miracle that they weren't all rendered stone deaf.

However, the Cromer Mill did provide me, unappreciative wretch that I was, with a somewhat contrasting environment. The majority of the workforce was made up of young married mothers, and so the Mill provided a nursery for the children of its unfortunate captives, and at around the age of two I was duly enrolled. Here, I would star as a Lollipop Man in a nursery production that would have been worthy of Andrew Lloyd Webber, and I would also be introduced to the music of The Beatles.

One of the few tortures that never varied at the nursery was the appalling lumpy porridge breakfasts, which were enough to drive the sweetest of angels into having demonic fits worthy of *The Exorcist*. That was until one of the youngest staff trainees, whose name was Irene, hit upon the bright idea of revealing The Beatles' music to some of the worst cases, of which I was one. After that, the task became much easier. "You want to hear The Beatles, don't you? Well then, eat your porridge!" John, I suffered for you, mate.

People have said and written a lot about John Lennon over the years - the vividly surreal imagery of his writing style, his hilarious quick wit and cruel sense of humour - but my love of Lennon stemmed simply from his natural charisma, the power of which, for me at least, was at its peak when he'd been a member of The Beatles in the early 1960s. I still hadn't learned to speak by the age of three and a half, although I would happily prattle on for hours in my own, incomprehensible language. My mum - by now concerned with my apparent lack of development - says that I came home one day singing 'I'm A Little Aeroplane'. My version is that it was 'Please, Please Me', but whatever the truth, it wasn't long before the Cromer

Nursery had me singing like a lark, and in so doing, introduced me to the wonderful world of the English language, which I continue to desecrate to this day.

The nursery staff comprised women in their late twenties or early thirties, most with children of their own, along with a few trainees in their late teens. This being 1963, Beatlemania was in full swing and so, in the corner of the nursery, there was a Beatles record player along with the first couple of Beatles albums, or LPs as they were known in those days. The chairs had Beatles cushions, four different ones, naturally, and where the annexing walls met, Beatles wallpaper.

Very soon I knew all of the songs on that first Beatles album by heart, and at the age of four I made my first-ever public appearance, at the Cromer Mill Christmas Pantomime. To my great excitement, it was decided that the nursery would purchase an entire set of Beatles instruments, complete with Ringo Starr drum kit, and the grand finale of the pantomime would be four Baby-Beatles all in matching suits and wigs, miming to 'Twist and Shout'. I eyed the plastic, toy Rickenbacker guitar hopefully and successfully passed the audition.

The difficulty lay in choosing the drummer. Our head Matron, and the show's guiding light, got it into her head that whoever was chosen for this role ought to be able to perform a little drum solo. The only problem was that we were all three or four years old, complete amateurs with absolutely no experience of playing drums in a world famous pop group. One by one, we were placed before the drum kit. Some tried to eat it, others kicked it over (obviously years ahead of their time), until finally it was my turn. A combination of showing off and beginner's luck saw me get the solo right and that, as they say, was that. To my utter dismay, the beautiful toy Rickenbacker was handed to someone else and I got landed with the drum stool.

The Cromer Nursery Christmas Beatles Tribute was a roaring success, not at all ruined by the moment when, in sheer desperation, I ran from the stage holding my groin and yelling, "Wee-wee! Wee-wee!" I'm told my dad wept openly.

Once the extended family got wind of my new obsession, there was no end to the humiliations I was subjected to by way of bribes. At the annual Christmas gathering, my nana - my grandmother on my father's side - made me a present of a Beatles album, but only if I agreed to stand up in front of the entire family and sing 'All Things Bright And Beautiful'. Well, it was a small price to pay. At least I had it better than my cousin Wayne, whose father Derek constantly bullied him into performing George Formby impressions. It seems that music ran in the family, because Derek possessed a rich, operatic voice, which he would take out and dust down whenever the family celebrated a wedding. In the late 1950s he'd been offered a contract by Cliff Richard's manager, but had turned it down when he discovered that he would be expected to undergo extensive cosmetic dental surgery.

Daryl, the son of my nan's sister, played keyboards in a 1960s pop group called The Powerhouse and he would often give me Powerhouse gig posters to put up on my bedroom wall. They'd recorded one or two singles and had once shared a stage with Jimi Hendrix. I always looked up to Daryl over the years. I had no brothers or sisters of my own, so Daryl became something of a mentor. Later in the 1960s, when practically every male over the age of eighteen had grown their hair down to their waist, cultivated beards and followed the hippy trail to India, Daryl had greatly resembled George Harrison, which impressed me no end. He bought a beautiful red sitar, which he would often take out and play whenever I called round. He even tried to teach me to play the organ for a while but, not owning any keyboards of my own, it had been impossible for me to practise at home and so he hadn't been able to sustain my interest. Daryl knew a great deal about a great many things and, as I grew older, we would talk for hours. He was never patronising and wouldn't talk down to me, as many adults are prone to do when they communicate with children.

My nana kept a large, upright piano in her back room and I would spend hours hammering away at it, although I never heard her or anyone else in the family actually play it. Eventually she decided to get rid of it and, knowing how much I loved it, she offered it to me - but my mother was adamant that it was far too big for the tiny house we lived in and refused to let me have it. I was upset about this when I found out, but my mum was probably right. A guitar took up far less space and would have been a welcome compensation, but it would be years before I would finally lay my hands on one, so in the short term I had to make do with the tennis racket.

Another of my dad's brothers, Brian, along with his wife Ethyl, managed a pop group in the early 1960s, and sometimes they would take me along to a few of the band's local gigs. One of those gigs had been on a Saturday afternoon at the Palace Cinema in Manchester, where the band had found itself sharing the bill alongside solo singing sensation, Frank "I remember you-hooo" Ifield.

Quickly capitalising on my triumphant debut at the Cromer Christmas Pantomime, my auntie Ethyl and uncle Brian whisked me off to another show the following Easter where I was propelled onto the stage to perform 'Please, Please Me', while strumming my cardigan button. Following this, I was given an Easter egg, which until recent years was the only time I was ever paid in hand for a performance.

The following year, my parents took me to the Odeon cinema in Manchester for the opening of *A Hard Day's Night*, the first Beatles movie. Outside the cinema were hundreds of screaming girls and I was more than a little freaked out as I was led into the dimly-lit screening room, but was then very pleasantly surprised when, as four giant Beatles magically appeared on the screen in front of me, it gently began to rain jelly babies. I was rather disturbed by the scene in which John Lennon seems to disappear down the plughole, however, and it was a while before my mum could coax me back into a bathtub.

Family Photograph, 1968.

'I Am The Walrus' is one of the greatest and most original records I have ever heard, and I believe that the many hours I spent listening to it in my Nana's back room (with the record player arm extended so that it would play repeatedly) was time well spent. I quickly developed a passion for records, and one Christmas morning I came downstairs to find a Dansette record player - one of those that resembled a suitcase when it was packed away - and I was taken down to Central Records in Middleton to choose my first batch of records. These included discs by The Beatles, obviously, another Liverpool beat group that I liked a lot called The Searchers, and - to illustrate my varied taste at that time - Ennio Morricone. Over the next few years, I would add records by Cilla Black, Procol Harum, Thunderclap Newman, John Barry and James Brown.

Those first few years, we lived in a house that today would be described as "a small townhouse oozing Victorian charm," but back then the single word 'slum' was sufficient. It was situated on Gilmore Street, behind the Brunswick pub in Middleton, a suburb on the northern outskirts of Manchester. I can remember that my mum hated the house almost as much as she seemed to hate the landlord, but for me, the memory is a happy one. The house stood in the midst of a maze of alleys and rickety wooden doors framing black stone walls, bridged by endless rows of damp sheets fluttering from washing lines - a scene that in later years could easily have graced the sleeve of at least a dozen Smiths records. I was never short of toys, my favourite being an old Lambretta scooter that had been left to rot in our back yard by a former tenant, and my object of ultimate desire was a bright pink bubble car that was always parked in the alley at the rear of the house.

My main hobby was wandering off, and I would indulge in this at every opportunity, no matter how vigilant my mum tried to be; some of my more spectacular escapes would have made Harry Houdini proud. Our house was situated only five minutes' walk from where Middleton railway station once stood, and the whooping sound of the steam whistles was a constant, irresistible attraction. More often than not, my mother would be alerted by the noise of screeching brakes as I tried to negotiate the main road, but sometimes I would make it all the way across to the railway station only to be escorted home by the fat controller to a mother on the edge of a nervous breakdown.

One drizzly afternoon, my mum made the mistake of blinking once again and I clicked into wandering mode. Climbing onto the seat of my Lambretta, I managed to find a way of prising open the back gate and I set off down the alley - on foot, as the Lambretta had no wheels. As I walked along the pavement, I noticed that the door to a large building was ajar and so, squeezing through the gap, I entered, at which point the door slowly and ominously closed behind me, and I was shut in. The building was St Peter's Church and the echo of even my tiny footsteps reverberated around the chapel as I walked along the central aisle between the wooden pews. Eventually my eyes rested upon a huge, stained glass window high above me and, silhouetted against the light, I saw the figure of a man with his arms outstretched. As my eyes became accustomed to the gloom I continued to stare at him, fascinated, until I realised to my horror that blood was pouring from a number of wounds on his body and that he appeared to have been nailed in place. In a panic, I turned and fled the way I'd entered and saw that the door was once more ajar. Darting through into the light rain, I could hear the sound of my mother calling my name. She found me a few moments later, drawn by the sound of my singing. After that, I gave St. Peter's a very wide berth.

I was taken out of nursery at the age of four, and eventually, our number came up at the local housing office and we were finally granted a plusher council house - complete with hot running water, inside toilet and a garden - on the Hollin housing estate. By this time, my dad had been forced to find work in other parts of England and I only saw him on occasional weekend visits home. One big advantage of his working away was that he was nervous that I might forget him in his absence, and so always bought me the most spectacular presents when he came back.

Around the time of my fifth birthday I was enrolled at the local school, Hollin Infants, and on my first day there I entered a classroom filled with frightened, crying children who were all freaking out because their mothers had gone off and left them. The only kids who were not crying, interestingly enough, were those that I recognised from my time at the Cromer Nursery, and I suppose it was because we were now veterans when it came to being left in the care of others. Having said that, when the bell rang out at 10am, I waited by the main gate for my mother, as I'd been instructed, only to be told by a member of staff that this had simply been the bell that had sounded the morning break and that my mum wouldn't be back to collect me until much later. On learning that I was expected to spend the whole day there I grew just a little depressed, but I didn't cry.

I proved to be a fast learner and, by way of a reward and further motivation, I was the first child in my class to be allowed to progress to more interesting and colourful books by the likes of Dr. Seuss and Hergé. My favourite book by Dr. Seuss is called *Because a Little Bug Went Ka-Choo!!*, which remains one of the most astute illustrations of chaos theory, in relation to cause and effect, that I have ever read. I grew to love books almost as much as I loved music and, at quite an early age, was put in charge of the school library, which ensured that I got to read the best of the new books as soon as they came in.

Eventually I progressed to Hollin Primary School for Juniors, which was situated directly next to the infant school. The only decent teacher I ever had was Miss Entwistle, and it was she who planted in me the idea of becoming an actor, after she'd been particularly pleased with some of my improvisational performances during class - so much so, that I would often be called upon to repeat the improvisations at school shows. The idea of being an actor appealed to me because I loved play more than anything else. What's more, it seemed to be a vocation that completely negated the need for proficient mathematical skills, maths being a subject I hated intensely - a hatred that stayed with me for most of my academic life, until a growing fascination with the subject of physics gave me the motivation to work harder to improve my grasp of abstract mathematics. For some strange reason, the teacher who really lit my fire, although I was never actually taught by her, was Miss Elbourne, or Miss Hell-Born as she was referred to by many. Miss Elbourne was a giant of a woman with close-cropped black hair. She seemed extremely stern and only ever dressed in black clothes, and most of the other kids were terrified of her. The sound of her stilettos snapping against the tiled floor of a deserted corridor would echo endlessly in the darker portions of my heart and, whenever I would hear her coming, I would dart, rabbit-like, for the nearest hiding place and peek from behind a curtain of hanging coats as this strange creature passed by. Sometimes, if I found myself out of class early and was feeling particularly brave, I would sneak along the side of the building until I was level with Miss Elbourne's class, and then carefully peek through the window and watch her strolling up and down between the regimented rows of desks as she sensually stroked her snap-ruler. On one such occasion, I came almost nose-to-nose with the wide grinning face of a small boy with a strange haircut and funny, stuck-out ears. This was the first time I ever remember seeing Reg Smithies, whose destiny would ultimately become so closely entwined with my own.

By September 1970, I'd been transferred to Hollin Secondary Modern for Seniors, more commonly referred to as Hollin High School, or simply "the big school". Hollin High was situated in the middle of farmland on the edge of nearby Hopwood. This was Middleton's green belt, an area protected from any kind of urban development.

Having to wear the school uniform was the worst thing about Hollin High for me. Out went the Chelsea boots and Paisley shirts, and in came the grey. Grey or white shirts, grey jumpers, grey or black pants, grey socks, black shoes and black blazer. The idea went beyond the notion of instilling discipline. The education gods reasoned that introducing school uniforms into state schools would blur economic disparity between the pupils and reduce the likelihood of bullying or victimisation. This being the era of glam rock, the annual school parties were an explosion of colour. Kids, free of school restrictions at last, took the opportunity to reflect what was, it has to be said, a fashion culture embarrassingly devoid of the slightest semblance of taste, with its striped tank-top pullovers, flared pants flapping in the wind, embroidered flowers and patch-sewn slogans, plastic imitation leather jackets of purple and blue with huge penny-round collars, yellow, green, black or silver platform shoes that elevated the wearer about six inches off the ground, two-tone shirts or trousers of yellow and green, or purple and violet that shimmered in the light, glitter under the eyes, and top hats! It's a shame the kids weren't allowed to wear whatever they chose during the normal course of school, because school photographs could have been truly hilarious.

My new English teacher was a most unpleasant woman named Miss Abrahams, and every first and second year pupil came under her personal supervision. As I was soon to discover, she was a bully, and often alarmingly out of touch with reality. Miss Abrahams was a particular thorn in my side because of my spectacles which, due to a very slight defect in my right eye, had been forced on me at an early age on the advice of eye surgeons. As my young ego and libido developed, I refused to wear them - in fact, I grew to loathe them, and my mother's constant nagging would have little or no effect. In an effort to get me to conform, my mother offered to buy me a pair that were identical to John Lennon's, complete with tinted lenses, and this proved more successful for a while, but gradually the novelty wore off and I'd often deliberately neglect to take them to school. Miss Abrahams knew that I had to wear them, of course. In fact, I think she had our house wired for sound because she seemed to know everything. Whenever she caught me not wearing my spectacles, she would bellow and shout and shake me quite violently.

This problem was compounded by Mr Hill, who taught Rural Studies. Mr Hill had spent six months at the South Pole, studying penguins. He knew what life was all about. Stomping about the corridors in his tweed jacket, khaki trousers and Dr Martens shoes, and sporting a great, bushy brown beard, he was a foreboding figure. Mr Hill didn't like The Beatles, least of all John Lennon, and he refused to believe that my spectacles, with their tinted lenses, were truly necessary. Whenever he would see me wearing them, he'd also bellow and shout, and shake me even more violently than Miss Abrahams did. With Mr Hill at one end of the school and Miss Abrahams at the other, my days became a trial of bellowing, shouting, being shaken all about-ing, with one teacher demanding that I put the spectacles on and the other demanding that I take the spectacles off. Consequently, I became a nervous wreck.

Reg Smithies moved to Hollin High at the same time as I did, but we never shared the same classes as we were streamed differently, Reg being six or seven months older than I am. However, we shared a great interest in pop and rock records and were talking regularly by this time. I remember we both loved The Alice Cooper Band, who were then creating a lot of controversy in the wake of their album *Killer*, which had featured a track called 'Dead Babies' and its follow-up, 'School's Out', an anthem for teen rebellion which became a number one hit single in the UK that summer.

Dave Fielding, the other founding member of The Chameleons, moved to Hollin High from Boarshaw Primary School, and I noticed him almost immediately whenever we gathered in the schoolyard to play football during breaks from class. He caught my attention mainly because of his long, shoulder length red hair. We used to play with a tennis ball, rather than a football. I don't remember why this was, but it did wonders for our skills and Dave, in particular, was an excellent player who made the school team. He was also streamed differently from me, being slightly older, so away from the football, our paths wouldn't cross very often, but when they did the one thing we invariably discussed was music. He would often hand me cassette tapes of albums and tracks that he'd heard through his older brother, Alan, and so I got to hear a lot of interesting music that otherwise would have passed me by. Unlike Dave and Reg, I didn't have the advantage of having older siblings who bought interesting, obscure records, but I would watch *The Old Grey Whistle Test* religiously every week, a late night live TV show that featured many artists from the UK underground scene. Additionally, every Wednesday morning I'd deliver the *New Musical Express* along with the usual morning papers and would read it from cover to cover as I worked my paper round, so I could usually hold my own in those conversations where the aim is to name-drop as many obscure sounding bands as possible. And if I did find myself getting out of my depth, I'd simply make them up: "Heard that new Greasy Bear album yet? No? Where've you been, man?"

Dave Gedge and Peter Solowka also attended Hollin High. They went on to form The Wedding Present in 1985, a band which would ultimately score eighteen Top 40 hits. I remember Dave Gedge vaguely, but didn't have that much to do with him. I remember Pete Solowka better because, like me, he also loved T. Rex. I recall both of us sitting either side of the hi-fi speakers in Mr. Wright's dinner-time disco, going crazy as we listened to the T. Rex single 'Twentieth Century Boy' just hours after it had been officially released, our ears wedged firmly against the speaker cones.

Another kid told me that Gedge and Solowka would ride around on bikes, hunting street dogs with sticks, and that there was one dog that would always escape them, which earned it the nickname 'Foxy The Sly'. I remember thinking that if I ever caught them beating my dog with sticks, I would shove said sticks firmly up their arses and swivel them both around in a very narrow alley. My dog's name was Sandy, but I quickly abbreviated this to San, which, after graduating to Ian Fleming novels and reading *You Only Live Twice*, I discovered was a Japanese word that denoted "honourable". His arrival had been recompense after I'd taken in a stray Alsatian pup, only to have him taken away again when his original owner had seen me leading him to my Nan's house to proudly show him off. I'd been heartbroken, so my mother had agreed to allow me to choose another, and she took me to Collyhurst Dogs' Home - a sanctuary for strays - one afternoon, to pick one out. I was extremely lucky to find him, although I prefer to think of it as fate, and we went everywhere together. At lunchtime I'd dash home from school to feed and exercise him, but as he got older, when the weather permitted, I began taking him to school with me. During class, he'd wait patiently outside until, on hearing the bell that marked break time, he'd go and sit by the school doors. He was a very smart, streetwise dog and I never had to use a leash, not even while walking together alongside busy main roads, which we did every morning, just ahead of rush hour, when I delivered the morning papers. San's favourite thing was to sit and watch passing thunderstorms. Whenever we were inside and we heard the sound of distant thunder, he would gently nudge me until I opened the front door, whereupon he'd sit on the mat by the open door, looking up at me until I joined him. Together we would silently watch the storm pass, his head darting from left to right as the lightning flashed overhead. Everyone at school took a liking to him, even the teachers, and so he never had a problem with any of them and I was never instructed to keep him away.

I found most of the lessons boring, to be honest. A female teacher began teaching guitar during lunch breaks, but my father always made some excuse whenever I asked if I could have a guitar, so I could never join the class. It seemed all I ever had to do was ask my father for something and, if it were within his power, he'd grant it - except when it came to the one thing I wanted the most.

I wasn't that bothered about missing out on the guitar classes though. The tunes Miss Bromley forced the other kids to learn were as dull as dishwater, and lunch breaks spent learning to play guitar in class would have allowed me less time to spend with San. I much preferred being with him than stuck in a stuffy classroom learning to play 'Kum Ba Yah'.

One of the mandatory subjects at Hollin High was Religious Studies, presented by a very eccentric looking individual who resembled a genie in western-style clothing. I would irritate him by raising all sorts of awkward questions concerning mankind's origins, drawing my inspiration from Darwin's *Origin Of The Species* or Eric von Däniken's *Chariots Of The Gods*. The more wound up he got, the more research I would do, and so the more forceful my arguments became. Had it been a science or archaeology class, I probably wouldn't have had a leg to stand on. However, this was Bible class, so anything the old fool countered with sounded even more ridiculous than the outlandish proposals I threw at him, and gradually other pupils would join in and support my arguments. Ironically, Religious Studies, which might have seemed the most irrelevant subject on the school curriculum, became one of the most interesting.

I did learn some things at Hollin High, though. For example, I learned that true courage was standing by your own convictions, even in the face of brutality, and that the truly brave were seldom to be seen swaggering and beating their chests around the school yard. I learned that a boy's Achilles heel lies in his budding sexuality and that girls realise this before boys do. I learned this from my girlfriend Tracey Bassnet, or Brassneck, as she was nicknamed. All the girls at Hollin High were named Tracey, Lindsey, or Julie. I learned that 'necking' was like trying to kiss girls that had very large mouths and no teeth. I learned that one must never, ever, ever drink too much sweet cider - that little gem came courtesy of Dave Barnes and Steve Brackenridge, my best mates at school. Together with Barney and Brack, I also learned how to sneak through other people's gardens unseen, which was always good for a laugh or two. I learned, after having been examined by a doctor during a legitimate case of grumbling appendicitis, that if you feigned appendicitis, all he could do was take your word for it because no-one could tell if you were faking or not. That did come in useful from time to time. I'd then spend the day tucked up on the couch watching Trade Test Transmission Films produced by the oil industry, used throughout the day to test broadcasting equipment - back then television broadcasting didn't begin until 4pm. With their wide and varied subject matter, they offered far more to retain my attention than any of the lessons at school.

As my three years at Hollin High drew to an end, it was constantly drummed into us that the rest of our lives (and the future of civilisation as we knew it) depended upon our academic performance over the final two years of school. Consequently, we were encouraged to spend all of our waking hours during the last year at Hollin High reading, rereading, and memorising everything they'd crammed into our heads over the previous seven years.

I'd never really had a problem with exams. I could usually amble through the preparations without much effort, confidently doing my own thing. After some quick reading and revision in the run-up to the exam I'd be able to walk away with at least a 'B' grade pass, while most of the academic snobs would be nervously puking in the playground. It was simply a matter of being able to suss what it was an examiner was looking for in a test paper and then focusing on these aspects during the revision. Examiners were not looking for fresh or original interpretations. Instead they were testing a pupil's ability to remember facts within specifically defined parameters, so if you knew what they wanted and gave it to them - which that could be determined by reading through previous exam papers - they gave you a pass. Despite outward appearances, I was sure that, given the opportunity, I could achieve anything I wished to. I'd developed a kind of jungle sensitivity in the playground, to the degree where I knew which teachers or which kids were dangerous and how to avoid confrontations with them, and I could usually bluff my way through most tricky situations. Overall, I believed that despite the fear-mongering and the hype, the final two years would present few problems. What I hadn't reckoned on, of course, was the insanity of the education system, coupled with a slice of divine justice.

Halfway through my second year at Hollin High, the Labour government introduced the comprehensive system in an attempt to eradicate barriers to academic progress caused by social and economic inequality. It resulted from a series of studies that seemed to suggest that children from middle-class households started school with certain advantages over their working-class counterparts. It wasn't that middle-class children were inherently more intelligent, it was argued, but rather that certain linguistic and cultural differences caused by contrasting home environments were having an impact, due to the quality of the reading material left lying around the home, for example, or the more sophisticated way in which middle-class parents related to and communicated with their children. In an attempt to eradicate these disparities it was decided that children would be streamed differently - not on ability, which had previously been the case, but rather by their chosen career path. A child would therefore be expected to choose a career by the age of fourteen and, having made that decision, the remainder of the student's academic life would be structured accordingly. Additionally, pupils were to be amalgamated in larger numbers for their final two years of study, which meant that Hollin High School would no longer house fourth, fifth and sixth year students, but rather they would be transferred to a larger school more able to deal with the increased class sizes.

During the final months of our time at Hollin, we were each summoned to attend an interview with a senior member of staff from the school to which we were to be transferred. In an enactment of what later came to be something of a cliché, my mother had hissed to me on the way to the interview that she would personally brain me if I embarrassed her by replying with 'pop-star' or 'actor' when asked what I wanted to do when I left school, so when the subject was broached, I simply shrugged my shoulders. The interviewer turned to my mother for guidance and, to my horror, I realised that I was being streamed onto an engineering curriculum. Afterwards, none of my protests cut any ice with her. She openly ridiculed my notions of a career in the arts, arguing that I'd need to secure a proper job when I left school. Although this infuriated me, in light of the times - an era of rising unemployment and dwindling opportunities - it was understandable, but despite her best intentions I don't think she was ever truly able to understand the impact of such an attitude on what remained of my academic career.

As if this setback wasn't enough, there was the reality of getting used to a new school. Having had the importance of our final two years endlessly repeated to us at the very time we needed to feel the most secure and confident, we were then moved to a totally new environment, with new rules, hierarchies, dangers, and hundreds of new faces. Kids we'd seen every day for years suddenly vanished into the sprawling mess that was Moorclose Senior High, a cold, characterless, ugly, concrete bunker of a school. The rug had been pulled from under our feet, effectively forcing us to start over again.

Backing onto the wasteland that had once been the Dingle were a row of detached houses and bungalows, homes to the mildly affluent, and in the garden of one of these bungalows lay an apple orchard tended by a six and a half foot ogre. We would raid the orchard just for something to do. The crab apples were sour and inedible, but the fun lay in the raid, and the fruit made handy missiles to throw at the pursuing monster, along with the usual kinds of insults. The Ogre, whom we nicknamed 'Lurch' after the character in *The Addams Family*, was a bullying clod of a creature, facially resembling a demented caricature of Kirk Douglas, complemented by a pair of heavy, thick-rimmed black spectacles. I knew he was a bully because, for a brief time, I'd struck up a friendship with his only son, John. He proved to be a rather sad, dispirited little boy with blond - almost white - hair, who, happily, bore absolutely no resemblance to his father. He did greatly resemble a teacher at Hollin High School, and after pointing this out to John one afternoon, he told me that this was his uncle, and that his father was also a teacher at another school across town.

After a while I stopped calling around to see John, solely due to the tyrannical nature of his father, who I soon grew to loathe. John was never allowed to read anything that was illustrated, especially *Knave*, *Penthouse* or *Playboy*, and any books he did wish to read had to be vetted by his father first to gauge their suitability. The only TV shows he was allowed to watch were the regular Saturday morning reruns of Laurel and Hardy. John was terrified of his father and never seemed to entertain even the slightest notion of rebellion - a very unhealthy situation, in my view. Eventually, his father forbade John to have anything more to do with me, or any of the other kids John had got to know through me. The Ogre didn't feel that kids from the local housing estate were suitable company for his son, believing that we might lead John astray or encourage him to stand up for himself, which was probably true. He also began to suspect that our gang had been responsible for the raids on his orchard, which was also true, a fact that was confirmed when, on the resumption of hostilities, he almost caught me one night. I was only just able to scramble back over the fence in time and, knowing that The Ogre couldn't follow as there wasn't an easily accessible gate to the fields from his garden, we turned on him and once more pelted him with his own apples. The Ogre, dodging the missiles, shouted threats and insults from the far side of the fence, but I wasn't particularly worried by any of them. He didn't know where I lived exactly and it wasn't as if he was a teacher at my school.

The date of my transfer from Hollin High to Moorclose Secondary Modern finally arrived, and that first morning I boarded the school bus with a sickening feeling in the pit of my stomach that I shall never forget. Moorclose was everything that I'd dreaded it would be; it was worse, in fact, and I began to make enemies at once.

The first step was to report for tutorial, which was held twice a day when the attendance register was taken. It was wise to get on with your tutorial master or mistress, because you came under their special charge, and this would remain the case for the remainder of your stay at the school. I walked into my tutorial that first morning, praying that this was as bad as I was going to feel for the rest of the day and telling myself that things couldn't really get much worse, when suddenly they did. Sat behind his desk was my tutorial master - The Ogre! Oh shit.

Even now, I still believe that The Ogre was dangerously psychotic. Not only was he my tutorial master, but he was also my metalwork teacher, which was a very important subject for any aspiring engineer, apparently, and so I had the subject about four times a week. Each hour in his company seemed like a day.

The Ogre thought he was the most wonderful of all of God's creations. Once employed as an engineer, he had been bullied by colleagues who had taken him for a half-wit, and so he eventually left that profession and worked hard at night classes, where he achieved a diploma and became a teacher. This tale was supposed to inspire us to work hard, so that one day we might become the shining example to the world that he obviously was. It didn't cut much ice with me, though. What he was too stupid to realise was that his experiences, far from giving him an abhorrence of bullying, had caused him to become an oppressor of the worst kind.

The Ogre bullied anyone who would let him, and most of us did. This monster had chips on both shoulders. The first one stemmed from his fate at the hands of his fellow engineers, who obviously knew a dick when they saw one. The second stemmed from a crueller act of fate. The Ogre had missed his true vocation and should really have become a world famous opera singer, of which he would never tire of reminding us. Sometimes the metalwork would be dispensed with altogether in favour of Puccini. At other times, it would simply be playing in the background while we all stood at benches filing metal, in rough time with the music, at The Ogre's insistence, presumably so that it wouldn't disturb his enjoyment too much.

Often, he would creep up behind you and you wouldn't know he was there until he started softly singing an operatic stanza two inches from your right ear. This happened to me many times, and the wild desire to break into laughter was only tempered by the knowledge of what would happen if I did. I was to learn that The Ogre was a violent individual, and every day he would try to bait me by reminding me of what my future had in store. "You're nothing, Burgess," he would say. "The Cromer Mill, that's where you'll end up." Of course, I was never able to let these taunts go by without comment, to which his reaction was always the same. The Ogre would grab me by the hair until my feet were barely touching the ground and I would be dragged away from the bench, much to the amusement of the rest of the class. "Thick and stupid!" he would bellow into my face, so close that his hot breath would be all over me.

Finally, the day came when I decided that I'd had enough. I'd been to see the Headmaster that morning, because I was unhappy about many of the classes I was being forced to take. Other streams had drama classes and were regularly being taken to the theatre. I knew this because I'd heard other kids moaning about having to go. I'd hoped to be allowed to swap courses but the Headmaster, who was so gentle and unassuming that I don't even remember his name, told me that unfortunately the system wasn't geared to making such a drastic administrative change for such an average student, and that I would just have to work hard and simply make the best of it.

Angry and disappointed, I reported for afternoon tutorial and joined the queue of boys outside awaiting the arrival of The Ogre, who eventually appeared and immediately approached me with his usual banter. "What's this I've been hearing about you wanting to change classes? What does a no-good bum like you ever hope to achieve, son? I think you're a queer, Burgess. Is that right? Are you a queer?"

A young boy standing next to me started laughing. The Ogre immediately turned on him. "What are you laughing at, Dixon?" he said and, clenching a full fist, punched him low in the stomach. Dixon gave a violent wheeze and immediately collapsed onto the floor. Totally unprepared for the assault, he'd been seriously winded and was unable to get his breath, and the boy's face quickly began to turn blue. I backed away as a crowd gathered around him and another teacher from the room opposite, seeing the commotion, rushed over and started to administer first aid. I glanced away to see The Ogre looking on, a harsh, gnarled expression on his crimson face. To my knowledge, no investigation of this incident ever took place. I was never asked to provide a statement of what I'd seen that afternoon, despite the fact that I'd been at the very centre of the incident.

Another even more dramatic incident was to suddenly bring my life into sharp focus. As often as I could, I would skip school dinners - they were universally awful - and along with a few other boys, I would eat at a local café away from the school. Sometimes, a boy called John, who was a couple of years older and who was preparing for his final exams, would join us there. That day, he wasn't at the café and we were just asking each other if anyone had seen him, when there came a loud honking sound from outside the café. Going out to investigate, we saw John grinning broadly with a crash helmet in his hands. He was sitting astride a brand new 50cc motorcycle that his parents had just bought him for his sixteenth birthday. He would be dead a week later; a car pulled out in front of his bike and killed him instantly. Naturally, everyone was deeply shocked, and I remember thinking to myself, what if that had been me? What would the last year, or the last week, or the last day of my life have been like? The answer was - miserable. All my life I'd been doing what other people told me to, and I didn't even know why. Older people, my parents, teachers - what did any of them know about anything? What the fuck was I doing at

Moorclose? I certainly didn't want to be there. Most of the kids didn't want to be there. Most of the teachers didn't want to be there. Fuck it! From now on, Moorclose was going to see a lot less of me.

The most common method of playing truant was to stroll into school in the morning, get your attendance mark at tutorial, and then casually stroll out again. You had to be careful, because it meant having to come back again later in the day for afternoon registration, which in turn meant that you had to make damn sure that a teacher whose class you should have attended during the morning didn't see you while you were getting your attendance mark in the afternoon. By this method, however, I would still have to endure The Ogre because he was my tutorial master. Collecting my mark and then skipping his metalwork classes was out of the question. I'd been giving the matter a great deal of thought, but in the end, considering his psychotic episode with Dixon, I ceased to care about getting caught and simply stopped turning up for school at all.

One big problem was where to hang out during the day. Adults would often report a couple of young kids wandering around a small town like Middleton to the local truant officer, or the wag-man, as he was known, so for the most part I would end up hanging around central Manchester, where my fellow truants and I would be rather less conspicuous. One of our regular haunts was the Virgin Records shop, which in those days was a poky little place just off Piccadilly, and was rather more progressive than your average record shop, very different from the Virgin Megastores that evolved over the following decades. The guy that worked behind the counter would obligingly let us listen to new records for most of the day. Alternatively, we would sometimes stroll over to the Granada Television studios, and watch television celebrities going in and out, usually Coronation Street soap stars, annoying them for autographs and laughing at their posh accents.

I remember one afternoon, a few weeks before Christmas, we saw Frank Carson, a famous TV comedian, outside a city centre store with a Granada film crew, asking people what they were intending to buy as part of their Christmas shopping. As we stood and watched him entertain the crowd with jokes, big, stupid grins on our faces, he said suddenly. "And here's a couple of young lads, what are you wanting for Christmas?" The cameras came towards us and we stood there beaming. Then it dawned! TV! Granada Reports was a regional news programme that showed at 6.30pm. Our parents watched Granada Reports in the evening and here we were bunking off school. We suddenly sprinted off through the middle of the film unit, almost knocking the cameras over. We could hear the comedian shouting after us "Whoa! Lads! Come back and be on television," and I remember my mate Barney yelling back over his shoulder, "Not fuckin' likely, mate!"

Still secretly skipping school, I began hanging around with a slightly older kid named Gary, who had left school a year earlier and was signing on the dole. When we weren't wandering around Manchester, we'd hide out at my mother's house during the day while she was at work. Eventually, the neighbours noticed and, sure enough, having provoked one pair of twitching curtains too many, we discovered that a neighbour had alerted the local truancy board and the situation came to a head when the truant officer turned up. Once rumbled, we went for broke and emptied the dustbin of its banana skins, soggy tea bags, and other debris and pelted the official with them, as he attempted to shield himself with his clipboard. It was a highly entertaining afternoon, but I knew then, with a heavy heart, that my days of freedom were numbered.

You could never describe Gary as a criminal in the truly serious sense - more a kind of likeable rogue. One fateful night, he was caught breaking into domestic gas meters in order to steal the small change and, subsequently, he was sentenced to six months in a correctional facility. By the time I saw him again, I'd been forced, if only temporarily, back into the system.

The letters to my parents started to arrive shortly after the siege of Kirkstall Road, and they came as something of a bombshell to my mother. Of course, my father was still working away from home during the week, so she was the one who had to face the flak. When my father found out I hadn't been going to school, he exploded, screaming that I was the biggest disappointment of his entire life, before delivering a left hook to the jaw. This was all the more shocking for the fact that it was the only time in my life my father had ever hit me.

Meanwhile, the consequences of my truancy continued. I was brought before various education committees. I recognised some of the faces as teachers from Moorclose, but none of them had ever taken me for any subjects. They threatened to have me placed in state care, or sent away to a correctional facility, but by this time I couldn't have cared less. Finally, I was summoned before a magistrate and again, it was my poor mother who had to accompany me. However, just before we went into the courtroom, the truant officer took me to one side. He explained that a new rule had been introduced, decreeing that if a pupil reached the age of sixteen before 28th May of that year, they would be entitled to leave school legally without having to stay for the exams. My sixteenth birthday fell on 11th May and the process of getting me into a courtroom had taken so long that, by the time I got there, my birthday was only three weeks away.

There were about thirty people in the courtroom, including the magistrate, who then proceeded with a total character assassination of my mother, and all eyes were on her as she sat weeping. I suspect they knew that the only way they could get to me was to get to her, but although I was raging inside, I refused to be baited or show the slightest sign of remorse or regret. Interestingly, during the whole process of tribunals, meetings and court proceedings, not once did anyone ask me why I wasn't going to school. They only threatened me with what would happen if I didn't.

Having now received the good news that my legal departure from that mad house was imminent, on my return to school I found The Ogre gone. Only two weeks before, another boy - a rather hard-looking gypsy kid, who'd also been forced back into class by the truancy board - had been the victim of some of The Ogre's bullying, but instead of putting up with it the kid had risen from his chair and given the bastard an almighty kicking. I wish I'd been around to see that. At any rate during the whole three-week probation period and beyond, I was never to see The Ogre again. There is an Italian proverb, "Revenge is a dish that gentleman of taste prefer to eat cold." I always took some satisfaction from the fact that I never did become the deadbeat that The Ogre insisted I was, nor was I ever forced into the Cromer Mill. On the contrary I became the very thing that he had desired to be the most, a professional singer.

I remember during my final week watching a group of kids, who having reached leaving age, were dancing across the schoolyard to freedom and as they did, saw the assistant headmaster approaching his car. "Hey Newton, fuck off!" one of them yelled. "We're free now, so fuck off you old bastard!" With an amusing degree of dignity Mr Newton turned gracefully from his car and in his usual upper-middle-class drawl he shouted "Yes, you fuck off too, and don't fucking come back!" Some of them did come back though. Not to study, but rather to stand at the school gates, hovering like ghosts, totally unsure of what they were supposed to do next, until finally they'd be shooed away by patrolling teachers, only to return the following afternoon. Others walked immediately into the Cromer Mill, lured by the promise of a regular pay packet. I saw sixteen-year old boys turn into haggard old men in the space of a month.

The big day came and I walked out of the gates, never to return. I wish I could say that I remember feeling happy and elated, unfortunately I was too deeply disturbed by the whole ordeal, and I don't remember feeling anything other than a burning resentment and anger towards everything.

The rage that I felt as a result of the Moorclose experience took a long time to abate. I spent most of this time running around with some seriously psychotic people, usually to football matches where I spent most of the time actually being the football. I started to go to Maine Road, the home of Manchester City Football Club, on a more regular basis with one or two kids I knew from school. My father had taken me to a few home games as early as 1967 when, after coming home from work one weekend, he found me ready for bed in a pair of George Best pyjamas. George Best was probably the finest football player I've ever seen in my life and the only reason I think he isn't universally recognised is because he never had the opportunity to shine on a world stage, playing as he did for Northern Ireland, who never qualified for the World Cup. He was as famous for his social antics as he was for his football, and was constantly being disciplined on and off the pitch. George Best was a star of Manchester United however, and my father, being a devout City fan, was having none of it. He had my mother swap the George Best pyjamas for ones depicting Colin Bell, a star of Manchester City and England. Then, in a panic, he immediately resolved to take me to see a City game. It worked, and from the moment I saw the stadium and the crowds cheering as the team walked out I was hooked. I'm so grateful to my Dad for steering me away from Manchester United. I shudder to think how I might have turned out had I been allowed to develop such a hideous perversion.

Eventually I grew out of attending football games with my Dad, and so I bade farewell to the Main Stand at Maine Road and the relative tranquillity, pipe smoke, flat caps and rosettes the size of dinner plates, for the more intense tribal experience of the old Kippax Street stand. The Kippax was unusual in comparison to most other standing terraces in that it was constructed from solid concrete and steel rather than wood, and it ran the whole length of the pitch, as opposed to being placed behind the goals at either end. The terracing was exceptionally steep, which meant that despite the many thousands of people that flooded into it, you could always see the action on the pitch. I never did see or experience any danger, I might add, despite some very high attendances and some extremely frenzied goal celebrations.

Many people find it hard to understand the attraction of football matches and I respect that. For me it's the entire experience, not just the action on the pitch and I've yet to experience anything in terms of a social gathering that's as satisfying as a home match day at Maine Road, win or lose. Attending a match is a complete onslaught of the senses: the banter with mates over a few beers before the game, walking amongst the teeming throngs of fans towards and around the stadium. In those days, the aroma of fried onions would permeate the air, rising from dozens of hamburger carts that littered the route. Above all, there's the single unifying explosion of joy that transcends age, race, or gender when the goal finally comes. In what other social situation would you get upwards of 35,000 people gathered together and collectively focused on one aim, to will their side to victory? How it feels to be in the midst of it can only be understood by direct experience. I've been to games with people who previously haven't had the slightest interest in football, having seen the odd match on television, only to see them converted into Maine Road regulars by the experience of actually going. One or two Americans have asked me how I can be so passionate about a game that might only provide a single goal over a ninety minute period, or worse still, no goals at all, as opposed to basketball for example, which seems to yield a goal a minute. They seem to feel that more goals equal more excitement. Nothing could be further from the truth. After all, the longer you go without an orgasm, the more intense the orgasm is when it is finally achieved.

Of course, back in the late seventies, a dark shadow hung over British football terraces. I don't know when football violence started, or how it came about. Perhaps it had always been there, but I know from direct experience that in the late seventies it was rife. I can honestly say that I've never swung a fist or lashed a boot in all the days I've been going to City. However, I did see scenes of violence that I shall never forget. I also received my fair share of bruises during my travels to away matches while trying to avoid getting my head kicked in by home supporters at stadiums such as Anfield in Liverpool, Elland Road in Leeds, or Upton Park and Highbury in London. After a while, the high adrenaline of being confronted by opposing fans or escorted through town centres by squads of police as we chanted our tribal songs of support became the chief attraction. It certainly wasn't the football. Back then Manchester City had the worst away form in the old First Division.

While regularly attending away matches, usually by way of the football specials that were laid on by British Rail, I discovered that many of the worst elements of Manchester City's travelling hooligans had attended Moorclose Secondary Modern and were only a year or two ahead of me. Consequently, I came to develop more than a nodding acquaintance with many of them.

Violence is the most striking impression I have of the mid-1970s. It seems that suddenly it was everywhere, everyday, and it became an unpleasant fact that was simply accepted. For my part, I was on the periphery rather than an active participant, more a witness to it than an instigator. We were like packs of roving dogs, attacking en masse and running when outnumbered. For a while it seemed like just some savage game, but it became all too real one night in a small suburb called Heywood.

We'd been mooching around looking for trouble, but the streets had been empty all night and the worst elements amongst us were beginning to grow restless and dangerously bored. As we walked back toward the town centre, a lone figure walked up the road toward us. I was only half aware of what was going on and I vaguely remember one kid, a particularly vicious little shit, veer off, walk up to the front door of a house, stoop down and then quickly rejoin the pack. The figure drew closer and under the streetlights, I could make out some kind of uniform. I knew it wasn't a policeman because they never walked around alone at night anymore; they'd long since taken to cruising around in cars. Suddenly as the figure passed us the kid lashed out. The object he'd picked up was an empty milk bottle, which he then smashed over the guy's head without warning. The victim, I could now see, was Asian, and a security guard, probably on his way home from work. He fell to the floor at once and, even in the dim glow of the streetlight, I could see he was bleeding. The whole pack sprinted away with the culprit at the head of it, laughing like a lunatic.

As we ran to the bottom of the hill though, I just stopped. Most of the others continued but Gary, only recently released from his stint in borstal, stopped too and stared back at me. I turned around and walked back to where the guy was sitting in the road, holding his head. He hadn't seen his attackers in any detail, just that it had been a group of boys. I had an old, silk Manchester City scarf around my neck and so I used it to try to stem the flow of blood. I looked up to see that Gary had followed me back and we both helped the guy to his feet. "Bloody bastards hit me with a bottle," the guy kept crying.

"Yeah I know, I know," was all I could say, feeling like the biggest shit in the world.

We walked him towards the centre of town and flagged down a patrolling police car. We told them what had happened, leaving out one obvious detail. No, we hadn't got a look at them, they were away too fast, and it was too dark. Eventually the police seemed satisfied and they began to organise some medical attention. From the look of it, the guy was going to need quite a few stitches to the head. The police didn't question us any further and the guy kept thanking us, which just made me feel a hundred times worse. We hopped a bus back home and neither of us spoke for the duration of the journey. I never hung around with any of those animals again, but there is a postscript.

Every Sunday morning without fail, we'd meet at our old school, Hollin High, to play football. Not long after the incident with the security guard, I turned up for a game as usual, but the regular crowd was in a sombre mood. One of them told me that someone had attacked an old man in Jubilee Park in Middleton with bicycle chains the previous evening. They'd left him battered and unconscious, and needing over sixty stitches to his face and body, having robbed him of all he had. This amounted to about £2 as he'd not long fallen out of the pub.

I got back home later that afternoon to find my father waiting for me. Most of the older generation in the town knew the old man and were determined to find out who'd carried out the attack. He grilled me for about an hour and it was with a great sense of relief that I was honestly able to tell him that I didn't know who was responsible. Had I known, would I have told him? In all honesty, I don't know. As it turned out the police didn't have to work too hard to catch the bastards; it was the kid that had bottled the security guard that night, along with his closest sidekick. They were both charged, and after confessing to a number of other, similar offences they were each sentenced to five years in jail.

In the mid-1970s, many of the boys who left school early with few or no qualifications either went straight onto the dole or ended up in one of the few factories that had survived closure. The dreaded Cromer Cotton Mill was one, and another, possibly worse, alternative was McBride's, a chemical detergent factory on the edge of town.

I was more fortunate. After a relatively short period on the dole, my father found me work as an apprentice fitter with the industrial fire protection company for whom he worked, a division of EMI called Minerva Sprinkler Systems. The novelty of working for a living and earning a wage compensated for the boredom of the work, although I found it hard to make friends amongst my workmates. My father was the foreman and so the others were somewhat wary of me and kept their distance. They could hardly complain about the boss in front of the boss's son, not that I would have told tales or anything. Consequently I could have a laugh with one or two of them, but most of the guys I worked alongside tended to be rather tight-lipped whenever I was around.

For the most part, I'd be working at lathes preparing material for installation, or filling out the week's timesheets for my dad who hated doing them himself and who never seemed to feel comfortable unless he was up a ladder. Working with my dad gave me the opportunity of seeing a whole different side to his nature, and although we would often fight, the disagreements were never serious. In some ways we were able to catch up on all the times we'd missed while he'd been working away from home. The experience also highlighted the distinct differences between us, and I was determined from the outset that I wouldn't spend the rest of my working life in a pair of overalls. However, in the short-term I was content to bide my time and wait for inspiration. It was as if I expected it to arrive one morning on the doormat along with the morning post. The job meant I spent weeknights away from home and on reflection, being away from Middleton for long periods was probably the best thing that could have happened to me. The basic wage was only fourteen pounds a week, aye lad, and for that you could have a weekend in Blackpool, do a spot of serious gambling, travel in style, go to loads of football matches, home AND away, hang out in nightclubs, buy designer clothes, upgrade your hi-fi and still have a bit left over.

Well, at least I could, because working away from home meant that the amount of weekly expenses we were able to claim could sometimes boost my take home pay to around £300 a week, which in 1976 was worth about five times what it is today. With that sort of money at my disposal I was having some great times on my weekend visits home to Manchester - as were my closest mates - but it was all a bit of a waste, as I didn't really have anything to focus on. Leaving school when I did after all that had happened was a bit like being released from prison, and accordingly I went a little barmy for a while.

After the initial novelty of working for a living and having money to burn wore off, spending most of the week in another town and only getting back to Manchester for the weekends became a bit of a drag. At first, I'd found the task of adapting to life in the small Welsh town of Denbigh strange and intimidating. The main source of employment in the town was a kitchen assembly plant, and it was here that we spent six or seven months upgrading and installing fire protection systems. The town really seemed to be little more than a collection of pubs, about fifteen of them, all within a few minutes walking distance of each other. Being a visiting sixteen year old in a town like that could potentially have been quite dangerous for me - I'm sure it would be today - but I enjoyed my time there for the most part. The people I got to know were a great bunch of characters, warm and humorous. All they really liked to do, though, was drink gallons of beer and throw darts at the wall. So many pubs in such a small area and every one of them had a first rate darts team; it was all they did. Still, I have to say that they did it very, very well.

Back in Middleton, my best mate was a younger boy called Ken Grimes. Ken was exceptionally bright. He attended Bury Grammar school, and was expected to take the Oxbridge exams. Each weekend we'd bluff our way into one of the local pubs and get drunk. I never did get asked for proof of my age, which was just as well, because there wasn't much else for a sixteen year old to do in Middleton in 1976; it was rather like existing in some kind of social limbo. There really wasn't any kind of youth culture to speak of - but all that was about to change dramatically.

2. GOD SAVE THE QUEEN

Despite all the ups and downs, problems at school, the violence of the seventies, the general absence of my father during my early years and the often lonely experience of being an only child, I don't recall being particularly unhappy. In a sense I must have been, I suppose, as my chief interests were music, books, television and, later on, cinema, all of which could be interpreted as escapist, or at the very least transcendental. Within each medium was a particular taste for the fantastic or surreal. The first books to have an impact on my psyche had been those of Dr. Seuss, considered by the more progressive child psychologists of the time to be vibrantly healthy and highly educational to the fledgling mind, yet quite surreal in terms of themes. From there I moved on to Lewis Carroll, C.S. Lewis and J.R.R. Tolkien, whose book *The Hobbit* had been introduced by an English teacher during my second year of high school, only to be abandoned after three or four chapters in favour of Graham Greene. The teacher held a vote as to whether or not to continue with it, and only two of us opposed the switch. As a result, the teacher made a present of the book to both of us. Years later after discovering Tolkien had written a sequel, the gargantuan *The Lord of the Rings*, I took it on with relish and have continued to reread it every few years.

I was also drawn to science fiction, chiefly H.G. Wells, Robert Heinlein, Philip K. Dick and John Wyndham. I came to love Heinlein because of his ability to challenge our most profound beliefs - religion, marriage, the nature of conjugal relationships - in a wildly imaginative way. Dick's paranoid, mind-bending visions took root in my young, fertile imagination, while Wyndham also provoked a philosophical re-evaluation of values, but did so by framing his fantastic scenarios within a more commonplace setting - not some far-flung corner of an unknown universe, or a century or two into the future, but rather the more familiar environments we all inhabit daily. *The Day of the Triffids* tells the story of a world that was suddenly rendered blind by a mysterious, celestial event, forcing the remaining population into a struggle for survival in competition with a carnivorous life form that had already evolved without the aid of a visual cortex. In *The Kraken Wakes*, Wyndham ponders what might happen if another life form, living in the deepest regions of our oceans, attempted to colonise our planet by melting the polar ice-caps.

Even the poetry I favoured was otherworldly, rejecting Wordsworth's allegorical frustrations stemming from his desire to fuck his sister, and Oscar Wilde's literary reactions to a sexually repressed society, in favour of darker glimpses of an underlying reality offered up by the likes of William Blake:

> *Every night and every morn, some to misery are born. Every morn and every night, some are born to sweet delight. Some are born to sweet delight. Some are born to endless night.*[1]

Similarly, the work of W. B. Yeats:

> *The darkness drops again but now I know*
> *That twenty centuries of stony sleep*
> *Were vexed to nightmare by a rocking cradle,*
> *And what rough beast, its hour come round at last,*
> *Slouches towards Bethlehem to be born?*[2]

I belonged to the first TV generation, and can't ever recall not having a TV set in the corner of the room. Here I developed my taste for the fantastic and surreal. I became an avid fan of *Star Trek* when the BBC first started screening it in 1969. What the show lacked in budget, it made up for with a cast that shared a genuine and unique chemistry, and while some of the stories were undoubtedly silly, many of them were truly challenging and made for great science fiction. *Star Trek* was the vision of its creator, Gene Roddenberry, and he was to be commended for trying to present a vision of the future that was wholeheartedly optimistic. In the *Star Trek* universe, poverty, starvation and war had been eliminated on earth and humanity was reaching out, seeking new life and new civilisations. At the height of the Cold War, the bridge of the U.S.S. Enterprise had a Russian lieutenant. When all the other science fiction of the day consistently presented aliens as a threat, the bridge of the Enterprise boasted a part-alien, part-human first officer in the form of the Vulcan Mr Spock. When African Americans were marching in the streets of the US demanding equal rights and an end to segregation, the ship's communications officer was an African American woman. Indeed, the first ever interracial kiss on American TV occurred in

---

1. Auguries of Innocence by William Blake.
2. The Second Coming by W. B. Yeats.

an episode of *Star Trek*. The importance of Lieutenant Uhura's presence on the bridge of the U.S.S. Enterprise was personally acknowledged by the Rev. Martin Luther King, Jr., and Nichelle Nichols, the African-American who portrayed her, went on to become a senior recruitment executive at NASA.

Towards the end of the 1960s, the independent television company Rediffusion commissioned a show with the curious title, *Do Not Adjust Your Set*, which consisted of surreal comedy sketches and satirical skits, and featured a resident band called The Bonzo Dog Doo-Dah Band, featuring Neil Innes and Vivian Stanshall. So it was that I became familiar with the work of Eric Idle, Terry Gilliam, Michael Palin, and Terry Jones. Not surprising, then, that I made such an easy transition to the team's follow-up project for the BBC, the equally curious *Monty Python's Flying Circus*. I didn't know in advance that it was largely the same team. Having read the TV schedule, I believed it would be exactly what it said on the tin, some kind of bizarre circus, so I nagged my mother to allow me to stay up to watch it. Imagine her consternation when she walked into the room to find her twelve year old son laughing and giggling at animated pictures of a naked Adolf Hitler with huge tits, a baby's pram that went around eating people, and a man with a tape recorder stuck up his nose.

By far my favourite TV show of all was *The Prisoner*, a surreal tale of a man who, after resigning from an unspecified, highly placed role in society, is abducted by forces unknown and held prisoner in a weird, mysterious parody of an English country village. He's unable to discern the warders from his fellow prisoners, and the chief guardian of this village is Rover - a giant balloon that roars like a beast and seemingly has a mind of its own. Having had an irrational, and inexplicable, dislike of balloons from an early age, I found this slice of surrealism particularly disturbing. Each week, our hero would attempt to escape by a variety of means, or thwart his captors' attempts to force him into revealing the reasons for his resignation. He is stripped of his identity - we never did learn his true name - and instead he is only ever referred to as Number Six. The chief administrator of this creepy little village is Number Two, and so the series poses the question: who is Number One? The show was the most provocative and original slice of television drama in the history of the medium and went unchallenged until the arrival of *Twin Peaks* some thirty years later.

Many came to view *The Prisoner* as little more than a pretentious and silly manifestation of 1960s' paranoia, but I think of it as so much more. The series deals with the illusions of democracy, the insidious nature of the education system, social manipulation and control, the erosion of individuality, the pressure to conform to the body politic, and the onset of global surveillance and the cashless economy. When it was over an outraged nation, dissatisfied with the series finale, hounded the show's star and guiding light Patrick McGoohan, forcing him to flee the country, vowing never to return.

Television would play a profound role in what I still feel is the single most important event in the history of mankind. On 20th July 1969, the astronaut Neil Armstrong, commander of Apollo 11, became the first human to set foot on the moon. Due to the time difference the event occurred in the UK during the early hours of the morning, and I remember being lifted from my bed by my mother and whisked downstairs to watch it as it happened. The primitive, blurred, black and white images did little to dampen my enthusiasm and excitement, and I'm very grateful to my mother that she had the insight to ensure I bore witness to it.

Occasionally, my parents would take me to the cinema, usually on a rainy day when it had been too wet to go to the beach during a family holiday. Typically we would see war films such as *Where Eagles Dare*, *The Battle of Britain* and *The Great Escape*, or westerns such as *The Alamo* and *How The West Was Won*. My parents also loved James Bond movies, which is how I developed a love of film soundtracks, particularly the work of John Barry, after being taken to see *You Only Live Twice*.

My favourite movies also had science fiction themes, but in the main I was forced to watch them on television because, on release, they'd often been classified with an X-certificate, restricting admittance to those who were eighteen years or older. Such titles included *It Came From Outer Space*, *Invasion of the Body Snatchers*, *Forbidden Planet*, and *The Day The Earth Stood Still*. As the 1960s progressed, science fiction films became more sophisticated, and I remember being completely overawed by Kubrick's *2001: A Space Odyssey*, which I saw in a suburban cinema in the neighbouring town of Oldham. I'd spent most of my school summer holiday staying with my grandmother and had gone in the company of a few older kids. I loved it so much that when the others rose to leave, I elected instead to keep my head down and remain in the cinema for a repeat showing. The other kids dutifully grassed me up to my grandmother, who turned up at the cinema searching for me, but she couldn't see me in the darkness. When I eventually got home I was met first with abject relief, followed by anger for putting them all through so much worry, but this didn't prevent me from returning to the cinema for repeat viewings at least three more times during that summer.

I saw my first ever adult film, or X-rated film as they were known then, by mistake. I went to the cinema intending to see something else but had got the date wrong, and found that the Palace Cinema in Middleton was actually showing something called *Taxi Driver*, starring some guy named Robert De Niro, who I'd never heard of, having been too young to see *The Godfather Part II*. Not wishing to waste the trip, I decided to try my luck and bluffed my way past the cashier, not really expecting much more than perhaps a tacky soft porn movie. What I saw was probably one of the best movies I've ever seen, and I found myself returning to the cinema every night that week to watch it again.

Over the next couple of years spending hours in a cinema became a regular habit, and during a brief period on the dole after leaving school I'd visit the city centre cinemas every Wednesday, bouncing from one to another to take in as many movies as I could. After being totally captivated by *Close Encounters Of The Third Kind*, I went to see it every Wednesday afternoon for six weeks, after which I'd cross the street to another multi-screen and see something else. Thus it was that I saw *Star Wars* for the first time, although I wasn't initially impressed by it, feeling it was inferior to Spielberg's effort by a couple of hundred light-years. Not until I saw the vastly superior *The Empire Strikes Back* did I become a fan of the *Star Wars* saga, although I was never quite able to get past the appalling dialogue.

For most of my early life, however, pop music dominated my interest. Although I'd been too young to truly appreciate the influence of acid on the 1960s generation, I did treasure the resulting surrealism displayed by the acid generation's chief acolytes, The Beatles. The media bombast aimed at the Fab Four in the wake of *Magical Mystery Tour*, their televised Christmas special, had been little short of frenzied. If the film appears a tad silly now, to my seven year old eyes it was nothing short of wonderful, and I rolled around the floor in stitches at the sight of John Lennon dressed as a restaurant waiter, shovelling spaghetti onto the fat lady's plate.

My mother and father would often hire babysitters at the weekend so they could socialise. Once I'd turned ten years old, if they couldn't find a babysitter, they would go anyway and I'd spend the odd Saturday night alone. Until the eventual arrival of my dog, San, my only company was a transistor radio, and I'd huddle beneath the covers of my bed with the radio glued to my ear. The only late-night radio station that played music that even remotely interested me was Radio Caroline, a pirate radio station that operated from a ship miles offshore, outside British jurisdiction, and it was Caroline that introduced me to records by The Doors, Led Zeppelin and a rather curious sounding guy called Mark Bolan.

I liked The Doors, and I'll even admit to quite enjoying some of the early Led Zeppelin records, but to the ears of this particular ten year old,

Marc Bolan sounded altogether fresh and different. His voice was unlike anyone I'd ever heard, and initially his sound was very original, being based around acoustic guitars and hand percussion. Some of his earliest themes reflected an obvious love of Tolkien which, naturally, I appreciated. Before the year was out, he'd broken into the mainstream with a huge hit called 'Ride a White Swan', and his career took off from there.

Bolan subsequently gave birth to what became known as glam rock, a cultural phenomenon that was to define an era for millions of British kids, and so it was that the first real live concert I ever attended was by T. Rex in 1973. Marc Bolan, besides being one of the most genuinely exciting figures of seventies glam rock, was also shrewd when it came to pitching his ticket prices. Knowing that the majority of his audience were very young kids, he kept the cost of the tickets down to £1 plus 35p booking fee. The prospect of attending the gig alone made me nervous at first, but when the big day came I headed into Manchester and, as I turned the corner and approached the venue, I walked into absolute pandemonium. I'd never seen so many girls in one place in all my life and they all began screaming whenever they caught sight of anyone who looked even vaguely like Marc Bolan. I ran into a barrage of ticket touts and pirate tack salesmen, and had my first encounter with a character I came to know as Spivey. He was a large, overweight individual with greasy blond hair, and he had a habit of talking out of the side of his mouth. As I approached him he greeted me with what was to become a familiar refrain over the years: "Tickitsh! Tickitsh, al buy anyee shpare tickitsh! Tickitsh! Tickitsh, al buy aneefin shpare!" After failing to part me from my ticket or sell me one of his tacky, satin Marc Bolan scarves, he gave up and gliding past him I entered the venue.

Inside the air was filled with the heavy scent of incense, and above me paper aeroplanes, launched from the higher balconies, performed aerobatics. I took my seat and eventually the lights dimmed until we were in absolute darkness, and the deafening sound of hysterical screaming erupted all around the hall. After a few moments, a star-shaped platform at the centre of the stage was illuminated and on it lay Marc Bolan, clutching the Gibson Les Paul sunburst guitar that featured in all the photos I had of him, and he began playing the opening riff to 'Twentieth Century Boy'. The platform was elevated until it was almost vertical, and Bolan suddenly catapulted himself into the air, landing deftly on the main stage precisely as the rest of the band kicked in, all of which was timed with the loudest bang I have ever heard. The backdrop, which until that point had simply been a huge, black drape, fell away to reveal the band's name in illuminated letters about 30 feet high. Over the next few years the spirit of T. Rex would diminish to an embarrassing degree, but on the strength of that night they remain the most exciting rock and roll band I have ever seen. What's more, the gig gave me a moment that I shall treasure for the rest of my life: eye-to-eye contact and a sign of acknowledgement from the man himself. When it happened, a girl next to me laughed joyously and gave me a huge hug as Bolan then skipped to the opposite side of the stage to continue his flirting. He left my head reeling - I'd touched souls with a young god.

It later became very trendy to play down the early 1970s, but despite the nightmarish sense of fashion, I look back at the young pop music of the day with great fondness. As a thirteen year old in 1973, I would much rather have T. Rex, David Bowie, Roxy Music (then featuring Brian Eno), Queen and Slade, than 1980s pop icons such as Midge Ure's Ultravox, Duran Duran, Blancmange, Spandau Ballet and the rest of the dross. As we get older most of us still regard the music of our youth as the real deal, while dismissing the music that's turning our kids on as rubbish. Show me an ageing father who says he loves techno and I'll show you a liar.

I was fortunate enough to get to see many of glam rock's luminaries during the early seventies, most notably the fledgling Roxy Music, supported by an unknown, underground band with a strangely camp and charismatic lead singer, collectively called Queen, and a curious group featuring two brothers from California, Ron and Russell Mael, who called themselves Sparks. Ron Mael was, and still is, one of the most strangely eccentric and original pop artists I've ever seen, with his slicked black hair, pencil-thin ties, zany waistcoats, pencil moustache and an unwavering stare that blends a stylish weirdness with the comedic. He was the main composer for the band as well as the keyboard player, and his style reflected his outward eccentricity, often fusing a powerful pop sound with highly unusual percussive timing and intelligent, almost operatic lyrics. His brother Russell, who sang mainly falsetto but who had an incredible range that seemingly spanned three or four octaves, fronted the band. After hearing the single that broke them into the mainstream, 'This Town Ain't Big Enough for the Both of Us', I grew to love them with a passion, even following their UK tours around the north-west of England. Sparks were one of the few bands that managed to transcend the glam tag and continued to evolve in a fresh and interesting way, going on to more or less invent the disco sound of the mid-1970s in the form of the single 'Beat The Clock', something they've never really been given credit for. I'm talking about them in the past tense, but Sparks continue to make great albums to this day and their live gigs are as interesting, humorous, and dynamic as ever.

The Free Trade Hall was a great venue in Manchester and a place that I would visit often over the next couple of years. It was more suited to classical concerts or opera, with its high balconies and superb acoustics, and was the permanent home of Manchester's Hallé Orchestra. Despite a capacity in excess of two thousand, it was still somehow able to maintain an intimate atmosphere. Sadly The Free Trade Hall is no longer a venue, but recently I was happy to see that some of my graffiti, scrawled discreetly on the wall by the stage doors one afternoon whilst hunting autographs, was still there. On that occasion the band had been a Glaswegian outfit called The Sensational Alex Harvey Band, solid favourites of mine. Alex Harvey was a very original artist and writer in his own right. He'd been around the music scene for a very long time, playing jazz and blues in Hamburg in the late 1950s and early 1960s. The band didn't come to public attention until well after his forty-second birthday, proving that you can still be cool and perform in a rock and roll band at that age. I saw The Sensational Alex Harvey Band play the Free Trade Hall a couple of times, but on this particular occasion they'd managed to have a chart hit and were playing two sold-out nights.

At the second of these shows I managed to get right down to the front, and climbed onto the stage to embrace Alex as they were playing their closing song, 'Faith Healer'. The stage security rushed over to carry me off, but at seeing a fourteen-year old with his arms outstretched and dressed clothes identical to his - a black and white striped rugby shirt, Levi jeans and blue suede shoes - Alex just smiled and waved them away. He took me by the shoulders and brought me over to the microphone as he sang the final chorus. I looked out across the audience, all of whom had their arms in the air, as powerful searchlights panned back and forth. I felt another hand on my left shoulder and turned to see the band's guitar player, Zal Cleminson, and with the last chord ringing out, the rest of the band came forward to take a bow, all of them pausing to give me a hug. It was one of the best moments of my life. I'll never forget the sight of that audience from the stage, thousands of arms raised in the air, the searchlights panning to and fro, and the rush of adrenaline I felt as I stood there trying to take it all in. Years later I learned that one of those pairs of arms belonged to none other than John Lever.

By the mid-70s, as I came near to the end of my penal sentence at Moorclose Senior High School, the excitement of glam rock was most definitely on the wane. By this time the adoration that had been heaped upon Marc Bolan over the previous few years - T. Rexstasy, the press had labelled it - was taking its toll, and the alcohol and drug abuse was obvious.

David Bowie had made some fabulous albums – he was about to enter his *Station To Station* period – but I found his more recent flirtation with fake, plastic American soul music rather uninspiring. By this time he'd quit Britain for America, and as much as I loved listening to records, for me the real excitement now from seeing and hearing music performed live. Sparks had turned to disco, which, though innovative for the time, I found rather tame and hard to relate to. Alex Harvey, having sustained a mild heart attack, was out of circulation. Roxy Music made some fine records too, but I'd lost interest quite early on following Brian Eno's departure from the band. Bryan Ferry, despite having a great voice, was simply a fashion statement as far as I was concerned, and I was too young to appreciate his Cole Porter covers. As for The Beatles, I'd lost Lennon's thread at the beginning of the seventies during his fight with heroin addiction, and Paul McCartney's Wings just wasn't my thing at all. My main source of sustenance had been The Doors, but Jim Morrison was five years dead by this time, and I was just hearing the echoes. I quite liked Queen early on, and one night a friend and I travelled over to the Liverpool Empire to see them, coincidently bumping into Dave Gedge and Pete Solowka on the train. Queen had come a long way since those early support gigs with Roxy Music and delivered a massive performance that lasted the best part of three hours, which impressed us no end. This was to be Queen's last British theatre tour and soon after they too quit the UK for America, the land of stadium rock.

The big rock album at the time had been Bruce Springsteen's *Born To Run*, which was passable, but I found his themes of a romanticised, nomadic biker's lifestyle rather hard to relate to, and it was all a little too American for my taste. As for the rest, it seemed to me that the scene, such as it was, centred on a tribe of washed-out, clueless hippies, lost without a compass, droning endlessly on about hard-loving women, adrift in a late-sixties afterglow like it was the only orgasm they'd ever had. What's more, the few bands that were able to retain even the bluntest of edges seemed to be lumbered with embarrassing lead singers, content for the most part to strut around in tasteless costumes, opening fish-farms and moaning about their income tax. Roger Daltrey? Mick Jagger? It was more than any sane sixteen year old could stand.

The arrival of The Sex Pistols may have got up many people's noses, but to my ears they were a breath of sweet fresh air during a particularly suffocating period of my life. Yes, we were manipulated. Yes, we were sold a pre-packaged cultural identity, but it was a new wave that threw up, if you'll pardon the expression, some extremely talented and original writers: Mark E. Smith, Mark Perry, John Cooper Clarke and Pete Shelley, to name just a few. The Mods had had it better, they were certainly better dressed, but for the first time it seemed that punk gave us the latitude to express our teenage angst in a unified and artistic way, and provided a more positive alternative to the blind aggression of the football terraces. A lot of lives changed after punk came along, including mine; in its wake, nothing would ever be quite the same again. Sadly, the initial excitement of punk would prove to be short-lived. In the wake of 'Frigging in the Rigging', The Lurkers, The Members and other sad cases, the raging sea of angst would become a mere boating lake, leaving only an army of washed-out, clueless punks, lost without a compass, droning on about life in the suburbs like it was the only orgasm they'd ever had.

I remember seeing these strange, stark ads that had been fly-posted around town for the 1976 Sex Pistols gig at the Lesser Free Trade Hall in Manchester, but only noted them for the weird and untypical style of graphics. Knowing absolutely nothing of who or what they were, and spending all but the weekends in a far-flung corner of North Wales, I didn't go.

However, with Christmas fast approaching I awoke one morning to find that The Sex Pistols were the inspiration I'd desperately been waiting for. I picked up the freshly delivered morning paper and saw that they were plastered all over it, and read through the story, laughing as I scoffed my toast down. Apparently they'd appeared on some London regional TV programme and caused a national outrage during a live interview littered with foul language during peak-viewing time. This was much more like it, I thought to myself. Everyone around me was talking about it for days, and judging from the media reaction most of the older generation had immediately wanted to converge on London and publicly lynch the four members of the band. I decided to hunt down a copy of the Pistols' 'Anarchy In The UK', and it was lucky that I did because not long after its release EMI Records, panicked by the outrage the band had stirred up across the nation, threw them off the label and promptly deleted the record. I played that single repeatedly, driving my mother mad - it was the most wonderful thing I'd heard since 'Children of the Revolution' some four or five years before. In its wake, as 1977 dawned, the music scene began to get seriously interesting.

It was around this time that I was temporarily moved onto the night shift at work, and as I laboured through the small hours in the deserted building, I'd listen to Radio Caroline. During my break one night, while sipping coffee, I heard another punk record on the radio. It was by The Damned, and the song was 'Fan Club'. I remember thinking it was the sexiest track I'd heard in years, and set about trying to find out everything I could about the band. As it turned out, I didn't have to search any further than the radio dial. John Peel, a veteran of Radio Caroline before being poached by the fledgling Radio One, where he would establish himself as something of a guru for the underground music scene over the years, also embraced the new sound on his regular evening slot, fuelling the gradual momentum. The sessions he commissioned from these new bands are arguably the best recordings of their day, and each night I'd sit there, cassette recorder paused, ready to capture them.

It wasn't long before I realised that punk was something I wanted to be part of, and catching my usual Friday night train back to Manchester I made straight for one of my regular haunts, The Ranch, situated behind Piccadilly and owned by Manchester's famous drag artist, Foo Foo Lamar. The Ranch had always been one of the more interesting hangouts and was frequented mainly by Bowie freaks and members of the local gay scene. This particular summer, though, the Ranch was already changing, as a new look began to emerge that was so radical it was scary. Black PVC and leather, swastikas and raincoats draped in painted graffiti denoting phrases like 'WHITE RIOT', 'THE WORST', or simply, 'FUCK OFF', worn by people sporting some of the maddest haircuts I'd ever seen. 'Anarchy in the UK' boomed from the club's PA, and gradually I discovered more great records: The Damned's debut single, 'New Rose', which was the first punk single to be released, 'White Riot' by The Clash, and a fantastic single entitled 'Boredom' by some local Manchester band called Buzzcocks.

I cut my hair, bleached it, raided my grandfather's closet for old suits, attacked them with scissors, invested in mohair, took loads of amphetamines and, diving into the throng, proceeded to have a great time. I was a punk. However, I was about to have a rather contrasting experience that would, in the long term, also have a massive impact on my way of thinking.

One night I went with a friend to another club we'd discovered called *Waves*, which was a bar for biker types situated around the back of Shude Hill in central Manchester. My mate went off into the crowded club to buy some amphetamines - 'whizz' we called it - from one of the club's regulars, and when he eventually came back he ushered me into one of the toilet cubicles to partake. I expected him to hand me the usual wrap of paper containing white or yellow powder, slimming pills which were known as Dexys, or small capsules referred to simply as French Blues. Instead, he held out a tiny piece of cellophane that contained two tiny, round, black pills. I looked at him, feeling more than a little cynical. "This is IT!" he said, grinning like a loon. I was dubious to say the least. What I didn't know was that he held in his hands two tabs of the finest microdot acid. I placed it on my tongue as he instructed, causing it to slowly dissolve. Down the rabbit hole I went, and was changed forever.

Although it would be years before I would experiment with LSD on a regular basis, this first foray into Wonderland was significant in that, in the wake of the experience, my way of thinking was completely changed. The shift wasn't immediate but gradual, as I became increasingly dissatisfied with what I was doing with my life.

This being my first acid trip, I broke a fundamental rule of etiquette and allowed the guy I was with to run off on his own. I was to learn in the fullness of time that the golden rule regarding LSD is that you should only take it with people that you absolutely trust, in which case you can have a fun and a very interesting experience in just about any situation. I spent the entire trip inside the club, only briefly venturing outside with my mate when he suffered an attack of acid-induced claustrophobia. The sights and sensations of the outside world were too much for me however, so when my mate said he was going to walk home I decided to go back inside until the effects of the drug had diminished enough to enable me to determine up from down. I remember the kaleidoscopic sensations of colour and sound; records I'd heard a hundred times suddenly sounded fresh and exciting. A club regular who always brought bongo drums so he could jam to the records, recognised me as a kindred spirit. He invited me over and together, laughing and sharing beer, we banged out rhythms for hours.

Fortunately my mate made it back to Middleton - albeit at a slow pace - without coming to any harm, and eventually I found him sitting in the park as I made my own way home. Together we went back to my parents' house, drank coffee, and talked about our experience until finally I pulled out the headphones and played him some tracks from my copy of the new Damned album. Under the diminishing influence of the acid the band sounded even more exciting and alive, at least to my ears. He was less than impressed though, and decided to stick with Bob Dylan.

If the Bill Grundy incident had brought the Sex Pistols to national attention, perversely it had made them impossible to see. Local authorities, the British Government, even some members of the Royal Family denounced them as the antichrist. In their wake, however, a whole string of imitators sprang up, and suddenly we had a scene. My favourites at the time included The Clash, The Jam, The Stranglers, The Adverts, Buzzcocks, and the original Damned.

The first time I saw The Damned live, they were supporting some dodgy pub rock band at a venue called the Electric Circus, which stood on the edge of Collyhurst on the outskirts of central Manchester. I'd discovered the venue after dropping by some months earlier to see an Australian rock band called AC/DC. The Damned lasted about ten minutes before flying bottles and abuse from supposedly peace-loving progressive rock fans drove them off the stage. The second time they were treated with a great deal more respect, supporting T. Rex in what were to be Marc Bolan's final shows before his death. It was a shrewd move on Bolan's part. Having staged a comeback, looking and sounding better than he had in years, he'd booked one of the elite punk bands as support because he knew that everyone wanted to see them. The Damned were absolutely electric, relishing the big stage, and I was so impressed that I travelled to the Hanley Hall in Stoke to see the show a second time, only to find when I got there that it had been cancelled. As a last resort, I caught the last show of the tour at The Rainbow Theatre in London, and found myself seated next to the musician John Miles. I wasn't a fan, but it was an interesting encounter nevertheless. After the show I made my way around the building to the backstage door and waited for Marc Bolan to emerge. By now the hysteria around T. Rex had long since dissipated so it was somewhat easier to catch a glimpse, and I was even able to get an autograph. Later I found my way to another club called The Roxy, which was pretty much the centre of the punk universe, before finally catching the overnight train from Euston back to Manchester.

Later the same year, in September 1977, Marc Bolan attended a party and was subsequently driven home by his girlfriend, Gloria Jones. During the journey she lost control of the couple's Mini 1275GT and ploughed into a steel-reinforced fence post, killing Bolan instantly. I was deeply shocked when it happened, but I was glad that I'd been present at Marc Bolan's last ever gig and that he'd looked and sounded as good as ever. Those of us who loved him knew that this is precisely the way he would have wanted it, to die young and beautiful like his hero Eddie Cochran.

With the coming of spring 1977 it seemed as if we faced a rock and roll future for the first time in ten years. My love of music had never really waned as such, but over the previous couple of years I'd been buying a lot fewer records as the lure of the football terraces had taken hold. With the onset of punk, however, buying records and going to gigs reinstated themselves as my main passion in life, although I was still going to Maine Road on a regular basis. I even managed to see Manchester City win a trophy at Wembley when they beat Newcastle 2-1 in the League Cup Final, fielding a team that only just missed out on the league championship by a single point to Liverpool. Happily the violence of the football terraces began to recede as a regular presence in my life and, after witnessing two Liverpool fans almost getting kicked to death in a shop doorway behind the Kippax one night, I stopped going altogether for a very long time, although I never lost my love for the club.

Aggression was channelled instead into something fresh, something vital and culturally dangerous - or so it seemed. Violent music? Well, yes - in a sense I suppose it was, but given the ambience of the times, that was to be expected. And yet despite all the 'get pissed/destroy' type slogans, punk's aggression was expressed mainly through fashion, music and dance, as a new generation kicked against an apathetic, boring establishment. Britain had been in a cultural coma for over ten years, but now a shocked nation was sitting bolt upright, and, if anything, the violence flowed in the other direction. It wasn't punks who were going around attacking other people; it was the average working man, armed with sticks or razors, jumping on anyone who dared to look and behave differently. This behaviour was in direct response to the outpourings of a hysterical media, erupting in the face of this new and sudden threat to the Moral Fabric Of Society. Now youth had its own voice, its own heroes (or rather anti-heroes), its own identity, clubs, venues and fanzines. In retrospect, none of it was real, except for the shift in attitude - but attitude was everything.

For one thing, the tired notion that you had to spend years mastering your instrument before you could form a band and play was shattered. Punk took rock and roll music back to its roots. Marc Bolan had been the first of the mainstream pop stars to recognise how fresh and vital the punk scene was. After his death, someone asked his producer Tony Visconti whether it was true that Bolan only knew five chords. Visconti thought for a moment then replied, "Well, yeah, but how many do you need?" This sums up the spirit of the times perfectly.

Punk demystified the whole process of making records. Traditionally you formed a band, wrote and rehearsed songs and played gigs - all in the hope of being spotted by a record company talent scout. Alternatively, you sent tapes and photographs off to them in the hope of securing a record deal, the chances of which were thousands to one against. Suddenly, the accepted wisdom changed - the concepts of stardom and success became of little or no importance, and making an exciting record became an end in itself. Punk's democratisation of the creative process taught bands and performers how easy it was to achieve these goals for themselves. Although born of The Sex Pistols, The Clash, The Stranglers, and others - most of whom were recording for major labels - punk suddenly took on a life of its own. Many of the best records of the era were self-financed, and then independently distributed as the scene became better organised. A cartel of independent distributors was set up, and bands suddenly found an outlet for their records. Meanwhile, John Peel continued to host his programme five nights a week on Radio One and he'd make a point of playing every record he was sent at least once, and repeatedly if he was suitably impressed. Thus independently-made records could conceivably get airplay on the UK's only national radio network. Peel also invited bands to London to record specially commissioned, four-song sessions for his programme, two of which would be featured each night. In this way, ten new bands a week would be introduced to a national audience - an unprecedented statement of intent that has never been equalled to this day. All the rules and notions of what constituted great records and interesting music were thrown out as high adrenaline merged with the seriously weird. It was suddenly a case of 'anything goes'.

Until this time, though, the only places you could see and hear these new bands around Manchester were in the city centre. Middleton, however, was about to play host to some of the best of them. Middleton Civic Hall first opened its doors in the mid-1970s, but it had struggled to attract the patronage of the town's youth and thereby justify the enormous amount of ratepayers' money that it had cost to erect. Initially it had housed the annual Christmas Pantomime, the occasional hearing aid exhibition, and a twice-weekly ballroom dancing session for the town's old-age pensioners. I'm tempted to say that demand for the hearing aids rose dramatically amongst the older generation over the space of the following six months, but that would be pure speculation. In any event, Middleton Civic Hall's only concession to teenage angst up to that point had been a Monday night disco hosted by a curious chap named Sam Shrouder.

Sam, as resident DJ, with his long blond hair, huge spectacles, white frilly shirt and stars and stripes trousers, was a seriously gruesome sight as he danced back and forth across the stage to the rebellious sounds of The Stylistics and vintage soul music. His disco nights were always packed for the simple reason that there was absolutely nothing else in the town for a teenager to do. Too young to drink in bars, a Middleton teenager would normally have a tantalising choice between the local community centre, with its table tennis - usually with only a single remaining bat - street corners, or burglary.

Due no doubt to Sam's apparent ability to pack them in at the Civic Hall, he was appointed chief booker, given a substantial budget, and sent off to find fresh material to feed to Middleton's culturally starved youngsters. Surprisingly, old Sam, to the delight of many - but to the horror of the local council – came up trumps. Late in 1976, Sam set off on a talent-spotting mission to London and began dishing out Civic Hall contracts to a whole host of new bands eager to find gigs up north. These bands included The Damned, The Jam, The Slits, X-Ray Spex and The Adverts, months before punk rock became a household name. By the time the gigs came up the following year, the punk scene had exploded out of London and these obscure, strange-looking bands were all the rage. Sam's contracts had to be honoured, and Middleton Civic Hall consequently became a Mecca for all those hungry for the new scene, finally making some money into the bargain. Of course for those more used to the wholesome, soothing sounds of The Stylistics, the sight of Dave Vanian of The Damned dressed as some kind of vampire grave digger was a bit of a shock to the system, but once they realised that these colourful characters weren't actually going to vomit on them they began to get the hang of it and started enjoying themselves, and for those of us already familiar with the scene, it provided a considerable saving on bus and train fares.

I remember the excitement that I felt when I read in the local paper that The Damned were due to play at the Civic Hall. I'd been exalting the merits of this band, amongst others, to my mates over the previous six months, but they were seemingly unimpressed. That said, hardly anything of note ever happened in Middleton, so I was able to persuade quite a few people to check them out; all of them subsequently spiked their hair within the year. Sadly, the local authority's response to Sam's shrewd entertainment coup was to sack him, in order to appease the multitudes of outraged parents who had come after them with gnashing teeth.

The best venue in Manchester for punk gigs was without question the Electric Circus. Once punk arrived, it was the Circus that came to fill the void in Manchester, and very soon the prog rock brigade vanished altogether and it became an exclusively punk hangout. Tony Wilson, who was credited with getting the Sex Pistols their first-ever television performance the previous year by way of his weekly TV show *So It Goes*[3], managed to get regular live gigs on the air featuring many of punk's premier bands. What was particularly cool about this was that the tickets for these shows were distributed free because the TV company was paying the bands anyway. All that was required was to pick up the tickets from places like Virgin Records on a first-come, first-served basis. So, it wasn't unusual to be able to go along and see The Jam, The Clash, Buzzcocks and Siouxsie And The

---

3. 28th August 1976. *So It Goes* also handed debut TV appearances to other punk luminaries, including John Cooper Clarke, Buzzcocks, Elvis Costello and Blondie – JL.

Banshees, all on the same night, for nothing. The Electric Circus was home to many of these kinds of shows, as was Middleton Civic Hall on a couple of occasions.

I became a frequent visitor to the Electric Circus that year and saw more bands than I can remember. The Jam were regular visitors, and I saw them there two or three times. They were without doubt the most exciting trio I've ever seen, and to be only a few feet away from those powerful AC30 amp stacks was an indescribable experience. I was spoilt in a way by this intimacy, and when they finally graduated to the larger, seated theatres, I found it hard to connect with the band in the same way. Other bands were able to make the transition, though, and chief amongst them were The Clash, who, until heroin got a grip of them in the early eighties, were never anything less than absolutely dynamic. The Stranglers too, by crossing a punk feel and attitude with a slight Doors influence, were able to take a much more mature and interesting direction than many of their contemporaries, and always seemed more comfortable on a larger stage.

1977 was also the year of the Queen's Silver Jubilee, and the Sex Pistols decided to commemorate this occasion with a new single, 'God Save The Queen', aimed directly at the hypocrisy surrounding the celebrations and voicing opinions that many young kids had toward the monarchy - all delivered in typical Sex Pistols style. Promotional posters for the single featured the now-iconic image of Queen Elizabeth II sporting a safety pin through her nose, and these were fly-posted the length and breadth of the country. The record was to be released on 7th June, the date of the Jubilee celebrations, when the majority of the country would be crowding into suburban streets littered with Union Jack bunting and images of our beloved ruler, to sit at long tables, eat celebratory buffets and drink specially-commissioned Jubilee beer.

Retailers refused to stock the record on that day, and most radio stations banned it. That left only advance orders. You could pay for the single in advance, but you couldn't collect it until after the celebrations were over. The advance orders alone took the single directly to number one, although the establishment denied this, claiming it had been, at best, a number two single, and to this day pop history reflects this. No-one could get hold of a copy or even hear it, and yet on Jubilee day 1977, 'God Save The Queen' was Britain's best-selling single. The record shops all displayed the chart placings for that particular week, but the spot that should have been occupied by the Sex Pistols was simply left blank.

In a counter-celebration of their own, the Sex Pistols, under the fresh patronage of Virgin Records, chartered a river boat and, before a specially invited audience, cruised up and down the River Thames blasting out the single. When the boat docked, an army of baton-wielding police officers were waiting, and they immediately ran at the party attempting to identify and arrest members of The Sex Pistols. Photos of the police beating the revellers began to circulate around the music press. Malcolm McLaren, the band's manager, was apprehended, but because the police hadn't the faintest idea what The Sex Pistols looked like, the band managed to escape, although some of the guests were not so lucky.

After the incident was reported in the national newspapers, punk-bashing became much more widespread, and if the police didn't actually sanction it, then they certainly turned a blind eye. Hordes of vigilantes took to the streets intent on beating any punks they happened to find walking around. In fact, it was reported that John Lydon, lead singer with The Sex Pistols, was attacked in the streets of London by a mob wielding razors.

The Teddy Boys - known simply as Teds, who used fifties rock and roll to define themselves as a movement - also joined the fray. They'd declared war on punks from the very beginning, seeing punk rock as a rival youth culture. I fucking hated Teddy Boys. They looked ridiculous, even by seventies standards, and besides - how on earth could you have a youth cult with a name like that? I used to taunt them with that: "Hey! Where's your fuckin' bear?" Or, pointing at their girlfriends: "If that's your Judy, does that make you Punch?" Gangs of Teds often waited outside the Ranch at turning out time, so they could ambush us as we emerged.

The number of attacks on punks escalated throughout 1977, fuelled mainly by the tabloid media and perpetuated by gullible morons and football hooligans, who now felt they had public sanction to go around attacking people. Although Sam Shrouder's contracts continued to ensure that some of the best bands on the scene passed through Middleton, the violence eventually resulted in the crowds staying away from the gigs. Attending a gig at Middleton Civic Hall meant running the gauntlet of knuckle-draggers waiting outside to kick your head in. I was generally exempt, because most of them were people I knew from the football terraces; so despite being a known punk I was apparently untouchable, but anyone unfamiliar or from out of town was a target.

The most savage illustration of this came on the night The Boomtown Rats were scheduled to play. As the band were leaving the venue they saw one unfortunate punk under attack, and it quickly transpired that he'd been hit on the head with a hammer. The band were able to disperse the hooligans and, not risking the wait for an ambulance, they carried the injured kid to their van and rushed him to hospital, probably saving his life in doing so[4].

Although I'd managed to see almost all of punk's leading lights many times during 1977, the one band that had always eluded me was the Sex Pistols. Their sudden rise in notoriety had meant that they were banned practically everywhere, and by the summer of 1977 it was almost impossible to see them. In order to circumnavigate this problem, the band would book gigs under an assumed name – for example, SPOTS, which stood for Sex Pistols On Tour Secretly - and the details would be spread by word of mouth only. For those of us isolated in the suburbs of northern England it became nearly impossible to find anything out.

In December 1977, my luck changed when I discovered that the Pistols would be playing on Christmas Day at a venue called Ivanhoe's in Huddersfield. The gig was definitely on, but the problem lay in how to get there. Nothing moves on Christmas Day, no buses, no trains. I didn't own a car, and my Dad would definitely have missed his, should I try and slyly borrow it. I would have to hitchhike. At the Christmas Eve party, no-one else was particularly interested in accompanying me. Everyone seemed to think it would be a waste of time, that we'd spend most of Christmas Day getting up there only to find the gig cancelled. Nevertheless, I saw it as possibly my only chance to see the Sex Pistols, so I was determined to go.

Very early the following morning I made my way up to the junction of the motorway. During the night it had been snowing quite heavily, so I augmented my usual leather and mohair Punk attire with a borrowed hippie Afghan coat turned inside out against the freezing cold. Little was moving on the motorway, and the clothes certainly didn't help, but eventually a car stopped and I got in.

The elderly man driving the car got it into his head, for some reason I was never able to fathom, that I was a soldier making my way home on Christmas leave - perhaps he thought only soldiers desperate to get home to their families would be mad enough to hitchhike on Christmas Day.

"So where are you going?" he asked me.

"I'm on my way to Huddersfield to see the Sex Pistols."

"Oh that's nice. So where are you stationed?"

"Pardon me?"

---

4. The hooligan that had been responsible for this attack was fated to receive some divine justice. About a year later, he and his cronies were scouting Blackpool Pleasure Beach looking for trouble and found it, when he himself received a similar hammer blow to the head and was instantly killed, thereby proving the old maxim that he who lives by the sword, dies by the sword, or in this case, the hammer.

"Where is your unit stationed?"

"No, I'm not in the forces, I'm going to see the Sex Pistols."

"My son's in the Air Force, you might know him."

"It's unlikely. I'm not in the Air Force."

"Oh you're in the Army then are you?"

"No, I'm on my way to see the Sex Pistols."

"Oh yes? So how long is your leave then?"

"Erm, I'm on a forty-eight hour pass."

This kind but dim gentleman took me all the way to Huddersfield - "No I'll take you all the way in, I insist, I mean if you have to report back to your C.O. in forty-eight hours that doesn't leave you with much time to choose your next pistols," - and I arrived outside the venue at around 10am. I'd made better time than I'd dared hope, but then was left with the rather puzzling dilemma of what to do in Huddersfield on Christmas Day. And then a miracle happened: after hanging around the venue for about an hour, a pub opened nearby.

Having to listen to 'Mull of Kintyre' on the pub jukebox over and over again was a small price to pay in return for warmth and the constant stream of whiskey that came my way for the remainder of the morning. Finally, the landlady called last orders as the aroma of Christmas dinner began to drift from the kitchen and, reluctantly, I returned to the venue intending to hang around until something happened.

Back at the venue, something was already happening. The whole of the outside of the building had been covered with *Never Mind the Bollocks - Here's the Sex Pistols* posters. I strolled over to the venue just as a coach pulled up outside. The coach was full of kids of all ages, and they immediately disembarked and started filing into the building. A chap at the door ushered them all in, and on seeing me he assumed that I'd just climbed from the bus with the rest of the kids. "Yes, that's right, go straight in," he told me. At the entrance to the main hall another man stood with a number of huge sacks, and as each child approached he gave them two Christmas parcels. When it was my turn, he looked at me for a second and said, "Well you're a bit big for a main present but you can have one of these," and he gave me a small parcel. Totally bewildered I walked into the main hall. Ahead of me were a number of long tables, and a huge buffet had been laid out. In the centre of the room was a cake bearing the words 'Merry Christmas From The Sex Pistols.' I opened my parcel and saw it was a gift-wrapped *Anarchy in the UK* promotional handkerchief. The small boy in front of me opened a large Christmas parcel and pulled free a brand new skateboard. I think I sort of blinked a few dozen times and looked back at the gift-giver in total confusion. He laughed and told me that Virgin Records were throwing a party for all the kids whose parents were local striking firemen. The fire brigade had been on open strike, due to low pay, and had consequently gained a lot of public sympathy.

Meanwhile on stage, the band's equipment had been set up, and a DJ was playing records and chatting to the children. Someone at my shoulder put a very large whiskey in my hands before waltzing off into the throng. The DJ told us that we were all very lucky boys and girls; that many people around the country would give their back teeth to be where we were. Happily I still had mine, but had I known what was in store I probably would have pulled them at the door if asked, because the Sex Pistols were going to play a special gig just for us. My mouth fell open and I heard a voice shout, "The band's here!" I rushed outside to see a second coach pull up and, yes, the destination sign on the front of the bus really did say 'NOWHERE'. The doors opened, and the first person I saw was John Lydon. He was holding a paper aeroplane and, as he climbed from the bus, he launched it over the heads of the waiting crowd. Sid and Nancy climbed down next, followed by the rest of the band and its entourage. I went back inside, and someone placed a plate of food in my hands and topped up my glass. I stood at the back of the room, unable to take in what was happening. The band entered, spread out, and started chatting to the children. Sid Vicious picked up one giggling child by the ankles and was spinning him round before placing him gently back down.

The band walked over to the cake. Sid picked up the knife and everyone seemed nervous for a second, but then he flipped it casually into the extremely large cake and someone else started dividing it up. Everybody got some. Finally, the band was called onto the stage and they began to play.

Needless to say, it was a brilliant moment and I noticed that there were a few movie cameras filming. The band played three or four songs, ending the short set with my personal favourite, 'Bodies', as John crawled along one of the long tables towards the remains of the cake. Suddenly, on impulse, I leapt forward and, grabbing a handful of cake, I rubbed it into John Lydon's hair. John couldn't scream the lyrics for laughing and fell headlong into the rest of the cake and, as if on cue, a mass of giggling children rushed forward, and they too began picking up huge dollops of cake and throwing it all over him. When the set was over the band began milling around playing with the kids again.

I became aware of someone standing directly next to me, laughing. "That was fuckin' great with the cake, man," he said. We started chatting, and he told me he was the band's tour manager. He said that, as far as he knew, tonight's gig was already sold out, but he took my name and promised to get me in on the guest list. He led me over to a corner where there was a whole stack of promo stuff, posters and badges, things like that. "Take as many as you want," he said, and I grabbed a huge pile of posters and badges to take back as Christmas presents for friends, even managing to get a few of them signed. I walked out and hid them beneath a derelict truck standing on flat tyres on some waste ground opposite the venue.

As the afternoon wore on, the party ended and everyone began to make their way out. The band had left, but I continued to hang around. A couple of lads who'd also travelled up from Manchester for the gig struck up a conversation. They didn't have tickets either, so the three of us waited in the venue for a while trying to keep a low profile so that the security staff wouldn't throw us out, until at last we found a small room upstairs. I was telling them about the events of the afternoon and handed them some Sex Pistols badges that I'd picked up. We could hear that the band had returned and begun soundchecking, but we didn't dare go out to watch in case the security staff caught us. Eventually, boredom got the better of us and we went out front to see. We watched the band's soundcheck for about fifteen minutes until some burly security guys insisted we leave the building.

The pub I'd visited that morning was open again and so we killed some time there before making our way back. By this time, the queues were huge and the venue manager was saying that if anyone didn't have tickets they might as well go home. In desperation I walked up to the guy and explained I'd been put on the guest list, not really expecting much. "Oh yes," he said, "I remember you from this afternoon, but I don't remember you two." My companions showed him the badges I'd given them, offering them up as proof that they'd been with me earlier and the guy just walked us in. Unreal.

Anyone who tells you that the Sex Pistols couldn't really play doesn't know what they're talking about. The band was raw - savage even - but they sounded great and they were accomplished and tight. Overall, I can honestly say it was one of the best Christmas Days ever. What we didn't know was that we were witnessing the end of an all-too-short era. This was the last time the Sex Pistols would ever perform in the UK, and it was gratifying to read many years later that John rated this as one of the best gigs they ever did.

No-one believed my story once I returned home. Not even the gifts of Pistols promotional posters and badges seemed to convince them, and one guy who lived across the street went around telling people I'd made the whole thing up.

The following year I went into a shop in central Manchester called Paper Chase. In the basement of the shop you could buy all sorts of obscure posters and photos of film stars, rock stars performing, things like that. This particular day I happened across some of the classic photos taken by Kevin Cummins, who used to sell his prints through the shop. On the wall was a photo of John Lydon wearing a beret and pulling open his jacket to reveal a shirt that read 'Never Mind The Rich Kids, Here's The Sex Pistols', and in the audience, slightly hidden behind another guy, was me looking on.

When The Sex Pistols' movie *The Great Rock 'n' Roll Swindle* was released, I was disappointed that the film of that day hadn't been used and often wondered what had become of it. This question was answered in the year 2000 when, following the release of another Pistols documentary, *The Filth and The Fury*, I finally saw the footage, and there I am, quite clearly rubbing cake into John Lydon's hair. I now have the ultimate souvenir[5].

Once the music industry came to fully embrace punk, the rot quickly set in, and it wasn't long before the entire scene became a watered-down parody of itself. It seemed that the New Wave would instantly embrace any wanker that happened to don a leather tie and an oversized suit. The sense of danger and anarchy slowly drained away, and instead the scene became a PVC limbo of bland music and bad singers. The record industry, in conjunction with the NME, tried to forge a new direction for the scene by promoting what became known as Power Pop, fuelled in part by the massive chart success of The Jam and drawing on the Mod scene of the late sixties as its main source of inspiration.

Outside the mainstream, however, the original punk scene had created a healthy UK-wide independent underground with a strong Do-it-Yourself ethic, and it was from this source that the most interesting music over the next couple of years would emerge. Rough Trade, which had begun life as a record shop in Ladbroke Grove, expanded into an adventurous, pioneering independent record label which even managed to establish its own independent distribution network. Liverpool's Zoo Records released an EP by Big in Japan, before eventually giving us The Teardrop Explodes and Echo And The Bunnymen. Meanwhile, in Manchester, a plethora of independent labels emerged, ranging in resources and philosophy from the tiny New Hormones imprint (who released the first Buzzcocks EP), through the Manchester Musicians Collective label, Object Music, to Factory Records, most notably the home of Joy Division.

---

5. More footage from the Ivanhoe's gig finally surfaced in Julien Temple's 2013 documentary about the day's events, entitled *Never Mind the Baubles* – JL.

Sadly, though, Manchester was soon to lose one of the crucial, early focal points for those wishing to experience punk in a live setting. Urged on by conservative parents and elements of the media, the Electric Circus was issued with a closure notice, and the building was condemned and subsequently demolished.

The last two nights of the Electric Circus were a brilliant, unforgettable, yet extremely sad affair. The event took place over the weekend of 1st October 1977 and featured The Fall, John Cooper Clarke, Buzzcocks and Warsaw, along with a host of other bands[6].

The Fall's Mark E. Smith is one of the most enigmatic, charismatic and genuine performers Manchester has ever produced. The Fall's performances were always darkly sinister and intense; they immediately became big favourites of mine. Manchester's very own punk poet John Cooper Clarke cut a striking figure with his anorexic frame, black suits, white shirt, black tie, mad beehive black hair and a pair of black Ray-Ban sunglasses that seemed to be permanently glued to his nose. Inevitably hilarious, he recited poems with titles like 'You Never See a Nipple in the Daily Express' and 'I Married a Monster from Outer Space' in an exhausting rant that suited his thick, Salford accent. The first time I ever saw him at the Electric Circus he recited his ode to Heinz baked beans as two transvestites danced around him, continuously pelting him with cold baked beans as they performed a striptease, with John barely able to continue through fits of laughter.

Buzzcocks would eventually go on to enjoy a string of hit singles, but they really had to be experienced live to be fully appreciated. While their records were undoubtedly good, they were never really able to capture the raw energy of their live performances, and the bootleg recording of their set at the last night of the Electric Circus, *The Best in Good Food*, remains the greatest album they never released. The first time I ever saw them I'd turned up at the Circus to see The Stranglers, but I'd mixed up the dates and was a week early. On being told that the featured band that evening was a local band called Buzzcocks and having already bought their excellent debut record, *Spiral Scratch*, I paid my 50p and went inside. I recognised Pete Shelley immediately as one of the regulars at the Ranch, and the band simply blew me away.

Other small venues came and went around Manchester, but none really captured the essence of the scene quite like the Electric Circus had. The organisers even tried to establish the New Electric Circus in another

---

6. A compilation album documenting this event, *Short Circuit: Live at the Electric Circus*, was released by Virgin Records in June 1978 – JL.

building closer to the city centre, but a venue is more than just its name, its soul resides in the walls of the building, its context and its ambience, and so the New Circus only managed to stay in business for a short time before apathy forced it to close its doors permanently.

The vacuum in Manchester was eventually filled, and when it came, it was in the wake of what was to become another musical phenomenon. The band in question was Joy Division, and the place was the Russell Club, a reggae haunt in the heart of Hulme taken over each weekend by the post-punk modernist movement, and re-christened The Factory.

I first came across Joy Division at the Electric Circus when they were still operating under the name Warsaw. I remember them very clearly: they struck me as a rather static, unhappy-looking bunch of characters and they sounded terrible, but they had a charged presence, there was no denying that. The gaunt, uncommunicative lead singer looked most uncomfortable on stage, and so the guitarist became the main focal point. Dressed in the style of a 1940s German army officer, he'd shout out things like, "You all forgot Rudolf Hess!" The bass player, the most visually striking member of the band, looked like a refugee from the Polish ghetto complete with cloth cap and beard. After the Electric Circus closed I didn't see them again until they turned up on the closing slot of Granada Reports, a regional news and arts TV programme. By this time, they'd changed their name to Joy Division and had metamorphosed from Warsaw's undisciplined punk thrash into something altogether darker, more introspective and experimental. Their first album, *Unknown Pleasures*, produced by Martin Hannett, would help to define the sound of the post-punk era.

I found the sudden transition from the highly charged atmosphere of punk to one of alienated, brooding depression too sharp a contrast at first, which is ironic considering the body of work I was later to produce as a member of The Chameleons. It may have been that I wasn't open to the changing mood of the times, although I think it was more a case of my unwillingness to celebrate or wallow in my own feelings of alienation. My brief flirtation with drugs had come to a temporary halt; I wasn't taking as much amphetamine as I had the previous year, I didn't smoke dope, hadn't the slightest interest in heroin, and had dropped acid only once, so I suppose I may have been out of step with the mood of the moment. Having said that, I quickly came to think that Joy Division's 'She's Lost Control' and 'Atmosphere' were among the greatest recordings of their day.

Over time, Joy Division's ideas became more refined, and the fresh intensity of the band's live performances was truly something to behold. Yet their live sound was often inconsistent, and on one occasion was so bad I'd been forced to abandon my place down at the front and seek refuge in the bar. The band grew stronger with every gig they played, however, and were far more sophisticated than anything else happening in the British alternative music scene at that time. This didn't stop me from referring to them as Joy Depression though.

My most memorable experience watching Joy Division was at one of the last shows they ever did on 8th April 1980[7], after I'd become re-acquainted with the other founding members of The Chameleons. By this time we had formed bands of our own: Ken and I were playing together as The Clichés, while Dave and Reg were part of Years. We met up one night at a Fall gig and, as we all made our way back to Middleton, they told me they were struggling to find somewhere to rehearse. Ken and I had a regular rehearsal room but very little equipment, and so it was suggested that we pool our resources. Our relationship built gradually from there, and evolved to the point where we'd jointly put on gigs. We were keen to support local venues, especially the Derby Hall, having already played here with Years and The Clichés respectively, so when the venue announced a season of local talent nights we dutifully attended them all. Each Monday night we'd catch the bus to Bury, but more often than not the gig would consist of a group of hopeless throwbacks, resembling characters from *Asterix the Gaul*, presenting faithful reproductions of Pink Floyd songs. Thankfully, the finale to the season was a major improvement, as Factory Records had taken over the venue for the evening, and accompanying Section twenty-five and A Certain Ratio were headliners Joy Division.

On our arrival we - Reg, Dave, me and a couple of others - were greeted by the most unfamiliar sight of queues at the front door and 'Sold Out' signs. We were kicking ourselves for not anticipating this, and in desperation we turned to the promoter Adrian, who we'd now come to know quite well. We reminded him of all the dross we'd paid to see over the previous six weeks, making the long journey in all weathers, and told him we weren't trying to get in for nothing, we just wanted to get in. Finally, he relented and said that, if we agreed to help clear away a few beer glasses after the show, we could come in, which seemed fair enough.

Once inside I noticed that the audience had evolved somewhat since the last time I'd seen the band, and they were now a rather curious crowd, dressed in Fred Perry shirts, Slazenger sweaters and sporting side-parting haircuts - we were being treated to an early glimpse of where Manchester's fashion culture was heading. As Joy Division took the stage we jostled our

---

7. The band would play only three more shows after this - JL.

way to the front to get a better view, but I was immediately struck by something odd. The lead singer performing the band's opening song was not Ian Curtis.

I said nothing for a while, trying to make sense of this situation, but the longer the set went on the more confused I became. Glancing around the room, it seemed that either most of the audience hadn't noticed or didn't care. How could that be? It was obvious from the way they were dancing around that the Fred Perry brigade now represented the band's regular following. How could they not notice that it wasn't Ian Curtis up there? At the end of each song, the whooping and cheering of the crowd erupted, as if this was all perfectly normal. After some time I turned to the guy standing next to me and said, "That's not Ian Curtis!" He gave me a puzzled look. "What are you talking about? Course it is!" I patiently repeated the statement and he looked again at the singer, who was now in the midst of an Ian Curtis dance routine, whereupon the guy told me I was full of shit. We argued for a minute or so until finally he grew irritated, saying that he'd seen Joy Division dozens of times over the previous two years and did I not think he'd know Ian Curtis when he saw him? I replied that I too had seen Joy Division numerous times and he obviously didn't recognise Ian Curtis when he saw him because that wasn't Curtis up there. About half an hour into the set, the singer[8] glanced stage right and promptly walked off, to be replaced immediately by Ian Curtis. I looked around at the audience, laughing at their bewildered expressions. The guitarist walked over to the keyboards and Joy Division performed two or three songs from their forthcoming album, *Closer*. Throughout that performance I was mesmerised; it felt and sounded fantastic. Once those songs were finished, the band walked off the stage and that was it. The gig was over, and the room erupted into violence.

Not expecting the evening to end quite like this, the Derby Hall management had been allowing the audience to carry glasses of beer into the venue all night. I don't think they got any of the glasses back, because they now began to rain down onto the stage along with a torrent of abuse, as the stage crew valiantly tried to dismantle the band's equipment. Some of the worst elements of the audience tried to climb onto the stage and attack the crew, only to be hit with microphone stands and anything else that came to hand. A stack of folded chairs, which had been lying unused around the venue, were seized, and these too were thrown in the direction of the stage and lay broken and splintered on the floor amongst the piles of smashed

---

8. Alan Hempsall of Crispy Ambulance – JL.

glass and blood. I remember thinking to myself that our promise to help clear up would see us at the venue until dawn. At long last the handful of security staff managed to clear the hall, and eventually Adrian showed up, his face as white as a sheet. He explained that the management hadn't been able to get Curtis onto the stage, and what we'd seen had represented something of a compromise.

As I was finally getting ready to leave the venue, I walked into the front lobby and saw another familiar face - Paul, a staff writer for the Bury Times. He had reviewed both Years and The Clichés at the Derby Hall earlier that month, and we'd got to know him quite well. Sitting with him at the table was Ian Curtis. I walked over, said hello and pulled over a vacant chair to join them for a few moments. Ian didn't look at all well. His face was very pale, and he seemed extremely unhappy. "What the fuck was that all about?" I asked him. Curtis was distant and said that he just hadn't felt up to performing, and that he'd been ill for some time. I told them about the arrangement we'd made with the promoter to get through the door, adding that all the clearing up I'd just had to do had been worth the short time he'd been on stage, because what I'd just seen and heard from them had been truly awesome. At that, he cracked a smile and thanked me. I asked him what their plans were, and he told me that they had a new album about to come out and a US tour planned. "America, eh?" I joked. Curtis just looked very sad and didn't reply.

Not long after this, Reg and I were at my place listening to John Peel when he featured a track that at first had us scratching our heads trying to figure out who it was. At first we thought it was some lost demo by The Doors. After the final strains of the song had faded away, Peel told us it was from the new Joy Division album, and that he was playing it in memory of Ian Curtis, who had committed suicide on 18th May 1980, at just twenty-three years old.

3. YEARS AND THE CLICHÉS

The Factory club opened its doors in 1978, and it was here I spent most of my weekends along with one or two friends. During the rest of the week it was known as The Russell Club, serving up reggae to the local Afro-Caribbean community. It was situated in Hulme, a mile or so from Manchester city centre.

We saw more bands play there than I can remember, but I do recall seeing Psychedelic Furs, and a drummer-less Echo and the Bunnymen. The rather flat dynamic of the drum machine didn't really endear the band to me, and I was far more impressed by their label mates The Teardrop Explodes fronted by the brilliant and enigmatic Julian Cope, who was also the band's bass player[1].

I became an admirer after buying their first single 'Sleeping Gas', and I occasionally travelled to Liverpool to see them play. The band featured a brilliant guitar player by the name of Michael Finkler, and I was very disappointed later on when the band, having signed to a major label, replaced him with the rather bland style of Troy Tate. Cope eventually abandoned the bass to focus on lead vocals and theatrics and, while I found his pogo-stick microphone stand a bit over the top, there was no doubting the man's charisma, talent and highly-developed sense of humour.

My friend and bandmate Ken was a couple of years younger than I was, and lived around the corner from my parents. He was one of the guys I'd dragged along to see The Damned at the Civic Hall the previous year. We'd been companions at many of the punk gigs ever since, though he'd declined to come with me to the Pistols show in Huddersfield. Despite this blunder, he was an incredibly bright, intelligent individual with a quick, dry wit that was as endearing as it was funny. Ken didn't suffer fools and could be extremely sarcastic, causing him to get up a lot of people's noses - never mine though, despite its not inconsiderable size - which reminds me of one

---

1. I met him years later outside a venue in Los Angeles where he was due to perform that evening. He turned up naked except for a pair of red Sooty and Sweep shorts, seemingly blitzed out of his head, riding in the back of a Cadillac convertible that had been completely covered in floral wallpaper. "You have to make the scene man," he kept saying. Yeah Julian, right! It had rained that afternoon in LA, which was very unusual for the time of year. From the stage he asked the audience if they'd enjoyed the rain. "Yeah," they shouted back. "I did it to freak you out," he said.

of my favourite Ken-isms. One night we were both on the prowl around town. "Where are we going, exactly?" Ken had asked.

"Oh I don't know," I mused, "I'm just following my nose."

"Let's face it," Ken retorted. "This could turn out to be a long walk."

As the punk scene grew increasingly crass and, in our eyes at least, rather embarrassing, we began to lampoon the movement by way of a series of gags and sketches that we promised ourselves we'd write up one day, but never did. Gradually this idea grew into the formation of a mock punk band that would ridicule all the truisms that were now typical elements of the scene, and we called our new band The Clichés.

There were two major problems from the outset. First, there were only two of us, and two did not a punk band make. Second, neither of us could play. Not that this mattered in the grand spirit of the times, but we couldn't even fret a note, and we thought we should at least be able to do that. We set this minor detail aside for now, promising to give it some serious thought. In the meantime, as Ken correctly pointed out, it was all in the marketing, so we launched our own promotional campaign. This consisted of two cans of spray paint which we used to spray the name of the band on every empty wall we could find around Middleton, and a few blank sheets of paper and some crayons, which we used to create cartoons of an anti-hippy nature. We then inserted the cartoons discreetly into the dust sleeves of various hippy albums on display at Central Records in Middleton. The cartoons would be signed with the words, 'THE CLICHÉS - HANG A HIPPY', or, 'BORING FARTS - GREATEST SHITS!'

As we had absolutely no equipment, we'd often go to the A1 Music store in Manchester on a busy Saturday afternoon with the mock intention of stealing some, and this became something of a ritual. Each time we'd leave the shop, we'd feign whispers to each other out of the sides of our mouths. "What did you get?"

"I got a plectrum. What did you get?" "I got a plectrum too."

"Ah yeah, but look! Mine's a Gibson."

We soon realised, however, that accumulating equipment two plectrums at a time would probably take an eternity. By this time I'd quit my job with my father - mainly so I could spend more time in and around Manchester - and had ultimately been forced to sign on the dole, so I no longer had vast sums of money to throw around. When my father had initially asked me why I was quitting I retorted that if The Sex Pistols weren't good enough for EMI, then neither was I, but really I'd been increasingly disenchanted with the general pattern of my life since I'd dropped acid eighteen months before. The wage packet ceased to be important to me; deep down inside something had changed profoundly, but it defied clear definition. Despite being cash-strapped, Ken and I did eventually acquire a couple of instruments. I opted for bass guitar, having developed a fascination with the instrument after becoming a devoted worshipper of Gaye Advert, who played bass for The Adverts. I was able to pick up a similar looking guitar to hers in a local junk shop for £25, along with a small practice amp to play it through, and I spent hours playing along to their records, learning all her basslines. Eventually I graduated to J.J. Burnel of The Stranglers, and would often play along to the album track 'Goodbye Toulouse', playing it at 45 rpm to develop a faster technique. I also became a massive fan of Public Image Ltd bass player Jah Wobble. I'd seen their debut shows in London and Manchester that year, and was inspired. In an *NME* interview, Wobble had attributed his rich bass sound to placing the face of his speakers three inches away from the studio wall. I immediately seized on this brilliant idea and, within the confines of my tiny bedroom, proceeded to do the same thing. By this time I was experimenting with four eighteen-inch speakers, in two huge cabinets, set up in stereo, and the sound was awesome. Unfortunately I lived amongst a row of terraced houses, and after jamming along to Public Image for a few minutes there came a loud rapping at the front door. Sheepishly, I opened the door and saw a neighbour, who lived about three doors away and who now seemed a bit agitated. "Mark!" he pleaded. "Just come with me a minute, will you?" I followed him to his house, and on entering his living room I noticed a large number of brass ornaments scattered about the floor that had been dislodged from various shelves and crannies around the room. "For fuck's sake," he laughed, "turn it down a bit, eh?"

Ken began learning the electric guitar, bought from a disenchanted cousin for £20 and, despite the more complex fundamentals involved, he was as fast a learner. Ken ultimately discovered the holy grail of punk guitar playing - the bar chord - and although he'd play his guitar as though he were sawing it in half, this seemed totally in keeping with the statement we were attempting to make.

Any punk band worth its salt obviously had to play at deafening volume, and so we set about finding some rehearsal space. Luckily, the very reasonable (or very deaf) local priest agreed to let us use the community hall one night a week. Each Wednesday, Ken and I would hump what little equipment we had to the church hall at St Agnes', and blissfully hammer out our cacophony for hours.

Mark and Ken: The Clichés.   Photo: Tony Skinkis

After a while, a second short stint with my father in Scotland provided the extra funds I needed to upgrade our equipment, and we added a rather nice bass amp, a PA amp and a couple of PA speaker cabinets, along with two microphone stands. Ken proved equally proficient when it came to providing backing vocals, which meant that we were able to include the obligatory punk chant choruses. Meanwhile, in the absence of any other members, I took on lead vocals. Our microphones were Beyer Dynamics, the best, and came courtesy of Jack George's mother, although by way of very tragic circumstances.

Jack was a few years older than we were and had lived in our street. He'd been the butt of many jokes due largely to his terrible taste in contemporary pop music, and his massive porn collection, which he always boasted about. Jack also played guitar, but had chosen a dubious, albeit more financially secure, road to fame: working class cabaret. He called his band Strawberry Pie, and they'd bang out cheesy cover versions of classic songs in the many pubs and working men's clubs up and down the country. The pay was very good, and the band played nearly every night of the week, but the lifestyle took its toll on Jack. Playing so many pubs and clubs meant that he drank a great deal. With Jack, that meant pints and pints of cider, which is one of the worst things you can drink in large quantities due to its high acidic content, which wreaks havoc with the stomach lining. He went from being a slim, attractive blond man, to being a very fat and bloated blond man, although he never lost his youthful good looks. He'd already survived one burst stomach ulcer - "They wheeled me off to join the jossers," he'd joked, recounting how the doctors at the hospital had written him off, and wheeled him out of the ward to a quiet corner where he could die without distressing the other patients. Semi-conscious, he'd overheard their dark mutterings and had suddenly sat bolt upright, insisting that he wasn't going anywhere, celestial or otherwise, and demanded that they take him back to the main ward immediately.

Sadly fate had other ideas, and a year or so later he developed a second lacerated stomach ulcer and was rushed back into hospital. Worse still, the doctors diagnosed the advent of lung cancer - although Jack had never smoked cigarettes in his life. As if this were not enough, x-rays revealed a mysterious shadow on the brain, and Jack was never to recover. His mother, hearing that Ken and I had just formed a group and being aware of our friendship with her only son, made us a present of his microphones. "What do you think she did with his porn collection?" Ken asked, tears welling in our eyes as his mother walked away[2].

Once I'd grasped the basics, I began writing my own songs. I remember one Sunday afternoon I'd just finished my very first composition, and I was so excited that I immediately dashed across town, bass guitar and practice amp in hand, to visit my cousin Daryl. Accompanying myself on my bass, I played him the song. When I'd finished he looked at me for a few seconds, quietly blinking, then said "Hey our Mark, that's really good is that." He immediately whisked me off to one of his local haunts, The Brunswick in Middleton, where I found myself playing songs I'd never heard before in my life. In addition I performed my newly written tune, accompanied by Daryl on the organ and his guitar-playing friend Jimmy, to a boozer rammed with semi-drunk hard cases - a true baptism of fire.

Egged on by this, I feverishly began writing more songs which I'd then play to Ken, and if he approved he'd work out the chords. Before too long there were half a dozen songs and we decided it was time to bring in fresh recruits in the form of a lead singer and a drummer. We approached a local character called Mark to be our frontman. He seemed to fit the bill, being

---

2. It might seem rather callous or heartless to laugh or joke about such circumstances but this is often the nature of humour in the north of England amongst the young, especially around Liverpool and Manchester. For example when asked about Ian Curtis' death and its contribution to the spread of the Joy Division myth that ensured the band's fame and reputation, the other members replied, looking at each other with deadpan expressions, "Yeah, I'm glad he agreed to it actually, aren't you?" It's just one of the ways we tend to deal with the darker aspects of life.

eccentric and intelligent, with a suitably surreal sense of humour, but it quickly became apparent that he was almost completely tone deaf and that listening to him was unbearable. He was intensely keen though, and came to believe that being in a punk band was his true calling. To this end, he switched to drums, but he was only marginally better a drummer than he was a vocalist. I genuinely liked Mark and tried to encourage him in every way I could, even donating my bedroom as rehearsal space for a couple of weeks while my parents were away on holiday. I remember sitting on the front step in absolute anguish as Mark pounded away on a newly acquired, very expensive drum kit, sounding more like a steam train than a percussionist. "He'll have to go," lamented Ken and so, sadly, he did.

We were eventually able to find a replacement drummer - well, sort of. Carl, from across the street, owned something that vaguely resembled a drum kit and so we recruited him. Initially, he had a tendency to turn every arrangement into either a bossa nova or a waltz, but this was an endearing contrast to Ken's power chords, and at last we had a full complement of guitar, bass, and drums. Consequently, rehearsals became a distorted cacophony of driving, distorted rhythm and fits of laughter. Amazingly, none of the neighbours ever stormed in to complain.

In the weeks following The Fall gig at Rochdale College we'd forgotten all about our little arrangement with Dave and Reg's band, Years, until they unexpectedly turned up at the community hall one night. Years were also a trio, featuring Dave on guitar and occasional vocals, Reg on bass and occasional backing vocals, and their drummer, Sid, who, for the most part, was also the lead singer.

From the outset, it was obvious that they'd been heavily influenced by The Who, and they'd constructed a very powerful sound - although some of the lyrical content was even dodgier than ours. We dutifully surrendered our rehearsal room and sat back to listen, very impressed by their competence. By this time they'd played quite a few gigs and really had their shit together, and we declined to play when it was our turn, so embarrassed were we by our relative ineptitude. Eventually though, as the weeks progressed, we did play in front of them and were pleased to get a very positive reaction. Shortly after, I began to hear rumours that Dave, in particular, had been so impressed that he was now considering disbanding Years and inviting me to join them in forming a brand new band. Naturally I was flattered, but at the time didn't really give it much credence. Dave was very serious about his music, so much so that Years were already on the brink of releasing their first single. On the other hand, Ken and I didn't take it very seriously at all. The Clichés was just something to do to ease the boredom while we worked out what to do with our lives. Ken was planning to sit the entrance exams for Oxford University, whereas I was gravitating toward studying drama, which is why I'd returned to the classroom to sit O-level exams. My plan was to go on to study at A-level, and then apply for a place at Manchester Polytechnic, which boasted one of the best drama, TV and film production departments in the country.

Now that our two bands were firmly reacquainted, Ken and I began checking out Years gigs whenever they were playing around town, even accompanying the band when they began to find gigs further afield in Liverpool or Leeds. Reg's bass playing was impressive - the epitome of cool - and Dave's performances on guitar were truly electric. Despite Sid's appalling lyrics - and I've never been able to get my head around lead vocalists who also play the drums - his playing was brilliant, and his banter between songs was often hilarious. Sid had a very nasty streak to his personality though; he seemed to enjoy humiliating people and could be really condescending. I liked him well enough and we never had a problem, but it was another reason why I was loath to join them for a long time.

Our circle of friends grew to include some of the people that followed Years around on a regular basis. Tony Skinkis was a regular at these gigs. A straight-talking Clash fan with a very dry wit, Tony would use his van to drive Dave, Reg, and Sid to the venues, and it was Tony who had turned me on to Alternative TV. Mark Perry - an early Sex Pistols fan and editor of perhaps the best-known punk fanzine *Sniffing Glue* - had formed the band, and for me they were one of the most original outfits to emerge from the punk scene.

Tony and I, along with a kid named John Mather on drums, formed a side project which we named The Most Uncontrollables and, although we never played a gig, we'd get together to jam occasionally and cover our favourite ATV songs, 'Why Don't You Do Me Right', 'Action Time Vision' and 'Splitting In Two'. John was a fine drummer, and also something of an eccentric. I remember calling round to see him one day, just after he'd been paid a visit by a couple of Mormon missionaries. John had immediately grabbed his 8mm camera and, without saying a word to them, had opened the door and silently filmed them as they valiantly tried to deliver their message. Finally, faced with only a silent John Mather and the sound of the whirring camera, their nerve broke, and they beat a hasty retreat down the path. John followed them, and a chase ensued with the Mormons running down the street and John running alongside, leaping hedgerows and garden paths, keeping them in frame the whole time. He then gleefully showed the film to everyone who called round to see him.

Dave Gedge and Pete Solowka, neither of whom I'd seen since my days at Hollin High School, would attend Years gigs whenever their university schedules permitted. Dave Gedge studied at Leeds University, while Pete had opted for Liverpool, and they'd formed a band together. I knew that Dave Gedge played, because Dave Fielding told me that they'd learned to play together very early on[3]. Gedge's band was called Mitosis and they weren't bad either. 'Thatcher The Snatcher' was my favourite tune of theirs.

Forming bands became the vogue in Middleton. The town has always enjoyed a strong musical tradition, and so I feel I have to mention the great, unsung, undiscovered Shy Talk, a band that was the brainchild of another childhood friend of ours, Steve Minakovich. Dave, Reg and I decided that Shy Talk's debut in the lecture amphitheatre at Leeds Polytechnic, where Steve attended a media studies course, was something we just couldn't miss. Steve was a very big, awkward hunk of a guy. He was part-Austrian, part-Czech, but had been brought up in England. His father was a very competent jazz guitarist with a regular gig at the Midland Hotel in Manchester, and he taught Steve to play from a very early age. I could never take Steve very seriously though. For one thing, as a kid, he was a massive fan of The Osmonds, and thought that Donny in particular was the best thing to happen to pop music since the Partridge Family. By 1979, he would declare that REO Speedwagon was the greatest rock and roll band in the world. His favourite song of all time was 'Jingle Jangle' from the movie *The Dirty Dozen*. The guy wore a bright red baseball cap the right way round and his instrument of choice was a Sunburst Ibanez. What can I say? I liked him a lot, but he was a total dork.

Steve had booked the amphitheatre and posted hand-made advertising bills all around the college. When we got there - "Don't worry, you're on the guest list," he told us - he'd set up a merchandising stall, and he presented Dave, Reg and myself with large, round, sew-on patches depicting a very badly drawn bird of some kind and the words SHY TALK in ugly, fake Olde Worlde type script. I remember Reg saying to me, "Ohhhh! Shy Talk! I thought they were called Shite Hawk."

As the tension failed to build around the amphitheatre and the lights dimmed, all six people in the audience grinned in anticipation. The stage, now completely plunged into darkness, was set. A door opened at the rear allowing a little light to spill across the stage, and three musicians rushed out. Steve was easily identifiable in his red baseball cap, despite the

---

3. Daves Gedge and Fielding, along with Chris Seddon and Kevin Rosbottom, had actually been in a band together – Sen – while still at Hollin High in 1974 – JL.

atmospheric lighting. He ran to his guitar only to trip over some unseen obstacle and went flying across the stage in a very undignified manner. Laughter carries a long way in an empty amphitheatre and I'm ashamed to say that Dave, Reg and I not only laughed loudest, but also longest; I don't think we stopped until the set was over. They even treated us to an encore. It was one of the best gigs I've ever seen, but for all the wrong reasons. Poor Steve, he wanted rock stardom so very, very badly, and he never forgave us our modest destiny.

After months of rehearsing at St Agnes' church hall, our time finally came when Ken walked in one evening to announce that he'd secured the band's first gig. We were to support a band from Bury called Jackson Cooker, at Holkenbrooke Tennis Club. Like Ken, the band also attended Bury Grammar School For Boys and they'd privately rented the prefabricated clubhouse hut as a venue for the gig. Initially I was apprehensive. I hadn't been taking our rehearsals all that seriously, and it hadn't really occurred to me that we'd eventually launch our tirades on an unsuspecting public, but gradually Ken talked me around, and finally I agreed.

When the big day arrived, an uncle of mine who owned a camper van offered to drive our equipment to the venue. We set up for the soundcheck and immediately hit our first snag. My beautiful new valve amp, which until that point had been working perfectly, started blowing fuse after fuse, forcing me to ignominiously borrow an amp from the headline act. As it turned out, that wasn't the only thing we were forced to borrow from them. The second problem was a little more serious, although the solution proved easier to solve than one would imagine. Carl, our rock-solid drummer, didn't bother to turn up, and we were debating what to do about it when suddenly the drummer from the headline band offered to sit in. I think I said something stupid like, "You don't know any of the songs."

"You're a punk band aren't you, what else is there to know?"

I was forced to admit that he had a point.

Dave Fielding turned up in the company of Dave Gedge and Pete Solowka, and I recall that Dave Gedge in particular was taken with our specially made 'I Am A Cliché' t-shirts, and demanded to know where he could buy one. The place was packed in the end, which was surprising when you consider that Jackson Cooker, being nice law abiding lads and not having a license to sell beer, could only sell soft drinks at the bar. I was nervous to the point of nearly puking, but in the end we got it together and ambled onto the makeshift stage. I still tingle now when I think of that night. Everyone went absolutely ape, and the vibe was pure spirit. The drummer bluffed his way through the entire set, even grasping some of the more subtle dynamics on the fly, and he sportingly threw in a mock drum solo as I introduced the band, getting a massive cheer. Gedge later told me it was the most exciting set he'd seen since The Clash, and as Dave, Ken and I laughed wildly outside the venue, steam rising from our soaking shirts, a girl I'd never seen before was attempting to steal my bootlaces. The whole thing was totally surreal.

As word got around Middleton concerning The Clichés' triumphant debut on the world stage, Carl turned up, very apologetic and vowing to be there for the next one. Having enjoyed our debut so much, it was inevitable that we'd want to play again. Dave suggested Cleworth Road Youth Club as a venue, and we immediately set it up. Years agreed to play too, but insisted that we play last, which worried me a little because they were obviously far more competent than we were. However, our enthusiasm and humour always saw us through and so, in the true spirit of the times, we shrugged off the doubts, and with our regular drummer now in tow, continued to have as good a time as possible.

Eventually Dave suggested that Years should play gigs with The Clichés on a regular basis, and we went on to play another couple of shows around Middleton. We began to earn a local reputation for great songs, despite the fact we couldn't play our instruments properly. The Clichés made their final performance to a full house at Bury Derby Hall. The gig was in no way marred by the moment when Carl, in a fit of zeal, threw in an improvised, energetic drum solo and, catching the rim of his glasses with his drum stick, accidentally hurtled them into the audience.

Some time later we were having a coffee in one of our regular haunts, when Dave suddenly asked what we were planning to do with the group. We didn't take any of it seriously and I told him so, but added that I thought it would be great if we got to make a record one day. Years had just produced their first record, a self-financed single called 'Come Dancing', so these things were obviously possible. I had about three or four copies of it, because every time I bumped into Dave he'd talk me into buying another. I'd probably have owned even more copies had it not got to the point where I'd dive out of the way whenever I saw him carrying them. "They'll be worth something one day," he kept saying, prophetically as it turned out.

The idea of making a record was exciting, obviously, but by this time I had exams coming up, and was living on a student grant. Ken continued working hard toward his Oxbridge exams, so he didn't have much money either. As for Carl, he wouldn't even contribute to the meagre cost of rehearsing in the church hall. Getting money from him would be like trying to draw water from a stone.

Dave told us that he had the answer. All we needed to do was raise the money for the actual recording, which wasn't as expensive as we probably thought it was. Years would then take the money they made from the sale of their first single and press a joint single featuring Years on one side and The Clichés on the other. The single could then be released on their Tuff Going label, and distributed locally as well as through the independent network. The more we thought about it, the more we liked the idea, so we eventually agreed, provided that the other members of Years also gave their blessing. Dave assured us that this would present no problem.

So it was that I, along with Ken and Carl, walked into a recording studio for the first time to record three tracks for the proposed joint single. The tracks we chose were 'Rock Of Ages', inspired by the movie Hollywood Boulevard, 'Leaving Town', a song about how desperate Ken and I were to get out of Middleton, and an ode to a wasted life titled 'Whole Wide World', which culminated in me, Ken, Carl, Tony Skinkis, and the three members of Years laughing, clapping out of time and singing along on the track's fade-out to the gospel tune, 'He's Got the Whole World in his Hands'.

A press release was sent to the Middleton Guardian, which featured an early photo of Years as we still hadn't got around to having any promo photos taken. Our three freshly recorded tracks, along with Years' contributions, were sent for review to the Rochdale Alternative Press. I remember buying my copy from the news stand outside the shopping centre feeling very nervous. "There's only one way to describe this demo tape by The Clichés," the review read. "Oh-oh," I thought, putting down the paper. Picking it up again, I read on. "Fucking brilliant!" it continued. Sadly for The Clichés, this was to be our zenith.

Term ended and, having sat my exams, I awaited the results and tried to decide what to do with the summer. I was completely broke, so finding some temporary work seemed like a good idea, but the thought of working away from home with my father again was an unbearable one.

Reg and I had taken to hanging out with each other a lot, and we were talking about our situation one afternoon when he told me that Dave's father, who was a manager at a local vinegar bottling plant, took on casual workers in the summer. "Let's do that then," I suggested. "At least we'll earn some money." Reg was less keen; he had worked there before and wasn't too happy about doing it again. In my naïvety, though, I managed to convince him. After all, how bad could it be?

The demand for vinegar increases tenfold in the summer, apparently, and so the factory would temporarily employ students or part-time employees to help pack the increased output onto wooden pallets, which would then be transported to all the retail outlets. The work wasn't hard, just monotonous. Reg and I would stand at the end of a conveyer belt that ran from the production plant downstairs and lift the packs of bottles as they came streaming up. We'd pack them onto crates, which would then be taken by forklift truck to the waiting wagons. To ease the daily monotony we'd collect the crossword puzzles from all the morning papers and struggle to solve them for most of the day, with the help of some of the characters we worked alongside. Their humour, wit and ability to help solve the hardest crossword clues helped keep us sane. Well, relatively sane. Two blokes I remember with great fondness were Stan, who drove one of the fork-lift trucks and was the crossword king, casually barking out the answer after we'd spent hours trying to work it out, and Big Harry, a giant of a man just short of sixty years old, who sometimes helped us stack the packs of vinegar. The conveyor line would often become clogged or break down for short periods, allowing enough time for a conversation and a smoke, and Harry had a very dry sense of humour, so that practically everything he'd say would induce tears of laughter.

    One afternoon, as Reg was working alongside Harry, Reg let out a huge fart. By coincidence, Harry chose this exact moment to have a heart attack. He was off work for many weeks before he was pronounced stable enough to return to work. That morning, as he took his place on the conveyor line, his first words to Reg were, "For fuck's sake Reg, if you're going to do that again, warn me! You nearly fuckin' killed me!"

    The worst thing about working at British Vinegars was the acrid smell of the vinegar itself which, no matter how many times you showered or washed your clothes, always seemed to permeate your body. Reg and I were on the top deck of a bus, each of us carrying a cardboard box filled with products we'd bought from the factory shop. Eventually two very pretty girls got on and sat a few seats in front of us and we got an encouraging smile from them. All looked good, until the moment when one of the girls turned to the other and said, "Is someone eating chips?" "I don't think so," said the other, "why?" "There's a really strong smell of vinegar up here," remarked the first girl. We looked at each other and then desperately tried to cover up the black lettering on the boxes - British Vinegars. They turned around and spoke directly to Reg. "Can you smell it?" they asked him. Reg, his face turning bright red, feebly denied it. "No, I can't smell anything," he blustered, while I just burst out in hysterics.

    One morning Reg and I were walking along the road to work and, as usual, we were having a conversation about paranormal phenomena. This time the subject had been spontaneous human combustion, and as I prattled on, relating what little I knew on the subject, I suddenly noticed a great amount of smoke emerging from Reg's coat pocket. "Reg!" I shouted, "You're combusting! You're combusting!" Reg, in total confusion as he hadn't even been smoking, just held the outside of his pocket away from him, on the edge of panic as smoke continued to pour out of it. "Water, that's the answer." I shouted, laughing, "We need to get your body temperature down." I pretended to try to throw him into the nearby river, but he was too strong for me. Neither of us has any idea what caused this.

During a similar, conversation I asked him where he would go if he had the opportunity. "The Himalayas!" Reg answered immediately. "I'd go and try and find the Yeti. Where would you go?" I thought for a minute and then said, "Loch Ness, to find the Loch Ness Monster." As we worked that afternoon, the idea wouldn't leave me alone until finally I said, "Well, the Himalayas are halfway round the world, but Scotland is only five or six hours north of here, why don't we go up there?" We explored the practicalities and in the end decided that, were we to have the opportunity, we'd definitely go. I didn't think too much about it until I was with Tony Skinkis a few days later, smoking a joint. "Oh, by the way," I croaked between tokes, "Reg and I are mounting an expedition to Loch Ness to find the Loch Ness Monster." Tony looked at me for a moment with the comical, mock-serious expression he always has in such moments and said, "Great, I'll come with you." We started to plan the expedition in earnest. We'd take tents, sleeping bags, camping stoves, cameras, obviously, and Tony would find a cheap car-hire company and drive us up there. I told Ken about our expedition and he wanted to come too. That made four. We would all share the expenses and head up there for a week that coming August.

By this time, Carl's lack of commitment and enthusiasm, and his constant failure to turn up for rehearsals or get involved in any of our madcap schemes, resulted in his sacking, and so The Clichés were once again without a drummer. John Mather offered to step in, but he was just a little too weird to be around, although he did drum for us one afternoon when we decided to borrow a generator and set up the gear in the town's public bandstand. The assembled throng were so enraptured by the sight and sounds of The Clichés that someone eventually phoned the police and they turned up to investigate before sending us packing with a flea in our ear.

Eventually I began to get discouraged about not being able to find the right people to augment our band. Not only had we failed to find our front man - my role in this regard was still temporary as far as I was concerned - but we were also struggling to acquire a new drummer. The whole thing had begun as a lampoon to temper the boredom of living in Middleton, but now that we'd played a gig and were planning a record release, I was enjoying it more than ever. Ken enjoyed it very much too, but he was feeling the pressure of his impending exams. All his hopes and plans for his future were at stake and so he had less and less time to mess around in a joke punk band. Consequently I was seeing much less of him, and came to spend more and more time with Dave and Reg, along with a new face, Alistair.

Ali was a quiet, charismatic individual and one of a new generation of punks who had begun to spring up from around 1979 and into the early 1980s. The bands on which this new generation focused drew their inspiration and identity from a sort of fringe political anarchy, an ideal that was embodied by bands such as Crass. These bands were, typically, fiercely independent, and their ideas generally tended to lean toward left-wing extremism. Their audience wore what I came to regard as a kind of uniform, which consisted of a ragged leather motorcycle jacket, usually with 'Anarchy' and 'Peace' symbols painted on the back, lots of heavy silver studs, black, ragged Levi jeans, heavy boots and dyed, spiked, slicked hair. Ali had one of the most amazing record collections I've ever come across, and a meticulously varied taste. He was one of those guys who did everything beautifully and gracefully and was a very cool individual. He was also one of those people who could have smoked a ton of cannabis without ever seemingly falling victim to its adverse effects. Nothing ever seemed to fuck him up, except perhaps his upbringing, but then that can be said for most people.

We'd all occasionally travel to Liverpool together to spend the weekend with our old Hollin mate Pete Solowka. Pete was a student at the University, and during his first year he lodged in the halls of residence. He would always have crates of home brew beer in his cupboards which we would invariably empty before taking cabs into town to a venue called Eric's. Eric's was on Matthew Street, just opposite the spot where the Cavern Club used to stand before Liverpool City Council, in their wisdom, levelled it to make way for a municipal car park[4].

Those Friday night train journeys to Liverpool were always a laugh. Loaded with sleeping bags and cheap speed we'd board the train at Victoria station in Manchester and be in fits of laughter for the entire journey. One night we climbed off the train at Liverpool Lime Street station and walked

---

4. An exact replica of the Cavern Club now stands in exactly the same spot, much to the delight of the Japanese tourists.

down the platform toward the exit with the rest of the passengers. At that moment, a copy of Knave fell out of Reg's sleeping bag onto the platform behind him, revealing the centre spread in all her natural glory. A young girl, who'd been walking along behind us, picked up the magazine and ran up to Reg in order to return it to him. Reg, his face now glowing bright red, frantically denied that the magazine was his. "Oh yes," the girl said, "I just saw it fall out of your sleeping bag." Reg, however, was sticking to his guns. "No, no," he kept saying, "it's not mine," while the rest of us howled with laughter.

Once in Liverpool, we would head for Eric's regardless of who was playing. On that particular Friday night we saw Gang Of Four, reputedly one of the most exciting post-punk bands around, and it wasn't hard to hear why. Eric's had the somewhat unusual policy of putting the headline act on first, while the lesser known support bands went on later. Support bands would therefore be forced to make an extra effort to be noticed, which nine times out of ten was a positive thing. The following night the headline act was Spizz, who changed the name of his band every year. Originally, it had been Spizz Oil, the following year when I'd seen them alongside Joy Division in Leeds it was Spizz Energi, and, this being 1980, the band's name had become Athletico Spizz '80. His set was hugely entertaining, and I remember thinking that they were going to be a very tough act to follow. Next came a collection of four curious looking individuals, a drummer, a bassist, a guitarist and a singer who called themselves The Frantic Elevators. From their accents it was obvious to us that they were Manchester lads, which confused us because we'd never heard of the band before. They played an absolutely brilliant set that was a mixture of punk satire with song titles such as 'I Feel Like The Hunchback Of Notre Dame', as well as one of the most soulful ballads I'd ever heard, 'Holding Back The Years'. The singer was a comical-looking individual. He had short, curly red hair, and wore a raincoat over a too-small jersey which stopped just above his navel exposing his belly. In his hand was a plastic shopping bag containing odd percussive instruments or whistles, which he'd pull out and use mid-song. His voice was fantastic, and he displayed a tremendous wit and humour in his banter with the audience, winning them over immediately despite his bizarre appearance. I remember thinking that he looked more like a character from the Beano or Charlie Brown than a singer in a punk band. Mick Hucknall would go on from these inauspicious beginnings to enjoy a twenty-five year career with Simply Red, selling some fifty million albums along the way.

Eric's was a great club to hang out at, brimming with characters of every description. One night I met and talked with Pete Wylie, whom Dave and I had seen with his band Wah! Heat some time previously. His album, *Nah=Poo - The Art Of Bluff* became a big favourite of ours later on.

I remember one comical character that we used to see milling about Eric's, whom Dave and I referred to as Robert Mitchum because of his striking resemblance. One evening, while we were sitting at a table drinking our beer, we observed him as he walked around the club wearing a raincoat and a porkpie hat. At the next table sat a small group of student-looking types, and we watched Mitchum stroll over to them. One of the guys sitting there had a pint on the table in front of him, whereupon Mitchum immediately took out his penis and placed it in the beer. The others gaped at him. After a few seconds, Mitchum withdrew his penis from the glass. "Are you going to drink that?" he asked one of the guys sitting at the table.

"Well, I'm not going to fuckin' drink it now am I?" the guy shouted back.

"Okay," said Mitchum, "if you're not going to drink it, I might as well have it," and he walked off with the pint glass in his hand.

August arrived at last, and we set about organising our expedition to find the Loch Ness monster. Tony, Reg, Ken, and I were still very keen, and so Tony sourced a cheap car from a local rent-a-wreck car hire company and, equipped with an RAC road atlas, we set off for Scotland.

The journey proved too far to complete in a single day, and we found ourselves just north of Perth on the A9 as the evening shadows began to lengthen. A campsite was marked on the atlas at a place called Dunkeld, and it was agreed that we would camp there for the night. The tent area lay in the grounds of a large, beautiful Scottish house, which had been converted into a hotel and was situated close to the banks of a wide river. Once settled, fed, and watered, we set off to explore the area, taking a long path by the riverbank where we eventually rested as the sun began to set, directly opposite one of the most beautiful stately homes I've ever seen. Tony rolled a couple of joints and we sat there, getting pleasantly stoned and enjoying the tranquillity. Little could be heard save for the gurgling river, the occasional splash of a feeding trout as it leapt from the water, and the echo of moorhens calling to each other across the vast expanse of river. We were all dyed-in-the-wool city boys, but we were rapidly beginning to appreciate the qualities of the Highland countryside.

The following day we arrived at Inverness by way of the A9 and, as we took the A82 along the western shore, Loch Ness gradually came into view. We pulled the car over at one of the large lay-bys that are placed every few miles along the road and stood gazing out across the water and the surrounding mountains, bathed in bright summer sunshine beneath a cloudless sky, mesmerised by the mysterious beauty of the loch. For me, it was love at first sight, and this was a love affair that was to last a lifetime.

When we had been at Loch Ness for about ten minutes, I saw something small and dark moving across the water. I watched for a few seconds before dashing back to the car to retrieve my binoculars. I scanned the surface and relocated the mysterious object as it moved slowly across the loch. "What can you see?" asked Tony.

"There's something out there," I shouted back excitedly.

Tony reached for the binoculars; "Let's have a look." He followed my mark and picked up the mysterious object.

"What is it? What is it?" I kept asking urgently.

"It's the legendary Loch Ness Boat," Tony replied dryly.

Fifteen miles further on we came to the small town of Drumnadrochit and beyond that, the hamlet of Lewiston, situated in the Glen of Urquhart. We'd already seen the ruins of Urquhart Castle in the distance and had intended to head straight for it, but as we drew nearer we saw a large sign by the roadside: 'BORLUM FARM: CAMPING, CARAVANNING, BED AND BREAKFAST, HORSE RIDING'. We decided this would be a good place to set up camp, and resolved to explore the ruined castle later. We made camp and then decided that, rather than take the road to the castle, we'd climb the remainder of the hill and descend on the other side to where we estimated that the ruined castle lay. The higher we climbed, the more spectacular the view was across the glen, and the only sound we could hear was the distant bleating of the sheep that grazed on the hillsides. We were so high above the glen that the sound of passing traffic on the road far below was carried away on the gentle breeze.

Eventually we were able to see Urquhart Bay, the deepest part of the loch, in the distance. The view down to the castle from high on the other side of the hill was also spectacular and, using bridleways and hidden paths, we were eventually able to negotiate our way down the slopes. We crossed the road to the castle and walked across the parking area to the front gate. At this point the road is high above the Loch and the castle lies directly on its banks[5].

We came across a small green hut where, during normal business hours, you pay an entrance fee. Business hours were over by now and the

---

5. The site has recently undergone major development, bringing the parking area further down the hillside and altering the access to the castle, which is now via an underground visitors' centre.

hut was empty and locked up for the evening. We looked at each other and in silent agreement, climbed over a second small locked gate, and continued down the hill toward the castle. For the next couple of hours we had the castle to ourselves as the sun set over the western slopes of Loch Ness. We were disappointed to discover that the castle tower had been barred with an impenetrable black, iron portcullis, so we wouldn't be able to climb it that evening. Still, we had the run of the rest of the castle, and we made the most of it.

Directly beneath the tower was a narrow path leading down to a stony beach. Wisely ignoring the sign, which read 'DANGER: NO ACCESS,' we clambered down and found ourselves directly at the water's edge. The water was flat calm, a natural mirror without so much as a ripple on the surface. The beach was littered with dry wood, and as the night grew darker, we gathered some and lit a small campfire. Tony rolled another joint and we lay there by the fire, in silence, gazing out over the mysterious waters. It's difficult to describe the ambience of Loch Ness at such a moment. Gradually, the high slopes of the far bank faded from view until they became a grey silhouette against the darkening sky, almost resembling a huge tidal wave. Occasionally the distant beam of car headlights could be seen on some lonely road on the far bank, and the silence was only broken by the gentle lapping of the water against the shore.

We'd been sitting there for around an hour when something quite spooky happened. As we stared out at the water, the flat calm suddenly gave way to a wash of violent waves that hit the beach, as if a huge boat had just passed - yet on the water nothing moved. The wash gradually intensified and began to make us feel rather uneasy, so with the campfire now mere embers, we gathered ourselves and made our way back to the campsite along the narrow pedestrian walkway that runs parallel to the A82. As far as I was concerned, our first night by the shores of Loch Ness had been perfect.

We spent the following day in Glen Urquhart and, paying our £1 entrance fee this time, we climbed the castle tower. The day was warm, bright, and clear, and I remember thinking that such a moment, gazing out over such an idyllic view, was worth £1 of anybody's money. Later on we drove further up the A82 and, about three quarters of the way along the Loch, we discovered another campsite which lay directly on the bank of the water's edge, this time situated in the district of Invermoriston. We pitched our tents on grass that was flat and even, with a row of trees separating the tents from the rocky beach at the Loch side, providing natural shelter from the breeze that was beginning to blow in off the water.

The first CBS photo shoot with Anton Corbijn.   Photo: Tony Skinkis

On closer inspection we saw that the campsite had a couple of rowing boats moored to a wooden jetty, and we asked about hiring one of the boats for a couple of hours. The campsite manager was a grey-bearded, wise old Scot and he pulled out four bright orange life jackets, which he instructed us to put on before allowing us to take the boat out. We looked at each other sceptically. He seemed to notice this, and went on to say that the water can change from flat calm to a rough current in less than ten minutes. "You either wear the jackets or you don't take the boat," he told us. We dutifully put the jackets on and he led us down to the water's edge. Pointing north toward Inverness, he told us to keep an eye in that direction, and if we noticed mist or cloud lower than the surrounding slopes we were to bring the boat in immediately.

With Tony on one oar and me on the other, we rowed out onto the water and tried to entice the monster to the surface using crisps and cannabis roaches, but nothing seemed to work. After about twenty minutes I happened to gaze north up the Loch where, sure enough, mist was forming at the Loch mouth. We were three quarters of the way across the Loch toward the far shore and so, reluctantly, we turned the boat around and headed back. The old man had not been exaggerating. Reg and Ken had to help me and Tony with the oars just so we could maintain our position against the powerful current and not get swept down the Loch. It took all four of us, heaving and puffing, to bring the boat back in.

The evenings were as tranquil as our night beneath the castle tower had been, except on the last night when we were invaded by a battalion of midges and were forced to retreat to the car. We sat there getting stoned with the windows wound up but the midges were obviously experienced in tourist warfare and knew how to get in. When we could stand their incessant feeding no more, Tony started the car and drove at about sixty miles an hour down the A82 with all the windows open in attempt to blow them all out of the car. This seemed to do the trick, albeit only temporarily, and later we found that our tents were thankfully midge-free. The common belief is that the Roman legions were deterred from conquering the Scottish Highlands because of the fierceness of the Scottish hordes, but I think it was the midges that sent them packing. Imagine armies of Romans marching through the heather in their heavy, leather armour, probably soaked with rain because it's nearly always raining in Scotland - and to compound their misery, they're being eaten alive from inside their armour by thousands of tiny midges. That's probably why they built Hadrian's Wall so high above the surrounding marshlands.

By the fourth day we'd exhausted the immediate possibilities of Invermoriston campsite. I wanted to stay longer as the peace of Loch Ness, especially at night by the water, had stirred something deep inside me. Besides, we had yet to explore the Loch's far shore. Tony, however, was visibly restless, and the hire car was due back at the end of the week, so we decided to return by way of Fort William and Oban, taking in the district of Glen Coe and Loch Lomond. This route would eventually bring us, by way of Glasgow, to the A75 that led back to England.

Loch Ness lies along the Great Glen fault, a crack in the earth that was filled with water when the ice barriers melted away at the end of the last ice age, forming a string of Lochs that run from the sea estuaries of Scotland's west coast to Inverness and the North Sea beyond. Aside from these natural, glacial developments and the blasting out of roads, the area has remained practically unaltered ever since. The Lochs have been artificially joined by way of the Caledonian Canal, which provides access to the North Sea for the fishing fleets that harbour to the Southwest. The A82 snakes its way through the mountain passes, criss-crossing this series of Lochs until it meets the sea at Fort William and the fishing port of Oban beyond, and from there it's possible to catch a ferry to the Western Isles. I have to say that the Highlands possesses some of the most beautiful landscapes I have ever seen, and the route we took home can be truly spectacular at the right time of day and year, especially around the foothills of Ben Nevis. It has rained heavily every time I've passed through Fort William and I wouldn't have it any other way. It's as if the brooding ambience of a rainstorm perfectly suits the mood of the place, with its narrow estuary flanked on either side by granite hills of yellow and purple heather and fast flowing mountain streams. Even the tacky souvenir shops and fast food bars lining the town's narrow streets are pleasurable to experience. Walking around Fort William in a heavy downpour, taking all of this in, never fails to instil in me a feeling of deep calm.

By the time we reached Oban the rains had passed, and the single night we spent camping there was a fitting end to the trip. Again we were able to climb high above the fishing port, and as night fell one of the giant sea ferries came gliding up the estuary and gracefully sailed past us out to sea, her lights blazing in the dusk.

We were so impressed with our first expedition that the following September we decided to mount another, and this time, in addition to Tony, Reg, Ken and myself, we were joined by Dave, Ali, my girlfriend Fenella and Tony's girlfriend Jackie. We piled into the back of a hired transit van with our quilts and sleeping bags along with Reg's ghetto blaster, and took the long route to Loch Ness. This time we arrived by way of Glen Coe, intending to return via the A9 and Edinburgh. The weather was mild, despite the onset of the first signs of autumn, but the Highlands were by this time blissfully free of midges. Having returned to the campsite at Borlum Farm, we once more crept over the small, wooden gate at the castle after closing hours, and built another campfire under the tower on what we came to regard as our secret beach.

Sadly, we found the site at Invermoriston much changed. The wise old Scot was now gone, to be replaced by a couple of obnoxious Englishmen from Birmingham who came running across to us shouting and waving their arms after Tony inadvertently drove over a plot of freshly planted grass seed. Their first priority on taking over the campsite had been to clear away all the trees, which had served as a windbreak to the stiff breezes that blew off the water. We were quite upset about it, feeling that the ambience of the place had been ruined, and during the general arguments over the grass seed, we raised the matter. "Oh, we just felt it would be nicer if people were able to see the Loch from their tents, you know, without having to get out of them."

"They were living things," Dave protested.

The two men shot each other a sarcastic glance. "They were trees!" the bigger of the two exclaimed.

We made our way to the water's edge, and I noticed that the rowing boats had now gone and in their place were a number of small, round, plastic pedal boats with cartoon bug-eyes painted on the front, like those you would expect to find on a boating lake at a public park. "What's that about?" I asked one of the men who was working nearby.

"They're for the kids!" he said, in a tone that suggested he was talking to an idiot. "You know, so they can play on the water."

"Play on the water?" I laughed. "You can't send little kids out on Loch Ness in those, they'll drown!"

"Well, obviously if it's raining or something we won't let them take the boats out," he reasoned.

"Do you plan to give them lifejackets?" I asked him.

The man looked at me blankly.

We quickly abandoned these madmen, and drove around to the eastern part of the shore. There we discovered what Tony and I came to regard as our favourite stretch of road. It ran flat and straight to the distant horizon, flanked on either side by a forest of fir trees and isolated mountain lochs and, beyond in the far distance, the Hebrides mountain range, rendered in soft hues in the sunlight so that the entire scene was like driving into an oil painting. Down by the Loch side in the village of Foyers we met Frank Serle, an old, retired soldier living alone in a caravan parked by the water's edge, who spent all his time trying to photograph the Loch Ness Monster. In an effort to support himself through the tourist industry, he had constructed a makeshift exhibition in an adjoining caravan, and we laughed at his sad attempts to fake photographs of the monster using what appeared to be papier-mâché models. At first, he didn't realise that the girls were with us, and so, taking them for backpackers, he tried to persuade them to move in with him. In addition, there were a few advertisements in the exhibition inviting any potential Girl Fridays to join him full time in his exploration of Loch Ness' murky depths, although it was obvious to us that the only murky depths that really interested him were in a woman's pants.

By 9pm the following night we were back in Middleton, and it was hard to believe that such a swift change of scenery and ambience was possible. Loch Ness had made a profound impression on us all, although our most amazing experience - the one that would galvanise the idea of Loch Ness as the band's spiritual home - was still ahead of us. Over the years I've been back there many, many times, and I still dream of buying a house overlooking the water.

Meanwhile back in Manchester, in the wake of The Fall, who were continuing to evolve, and Joy Division, who were hurtling toward the tragedy that would eventually see them metamorphose into New Order, hordes of new bands began springing up across the city. Most of them, it has to be said, represented little more than variations on these two main themes, but there were a few that were original in their own right. Amongst them was a band that Dave introduced me to called Grow Up. They were definitely in my top five, although sadly I never got the chance to see them play. Grow Up was the brainchild of John Bisset-Smith, a member of the band Spherical Objects, and a fellow student at Rochdale College. I love Grow Up's debut album, *The Best Thing*, to this day, and was gratified to hear that when John Peel received his copy, rather than pick out a couple of tracks to feature on the programme over time, he chose instead to play the album in its entirety during a single broadcast.

Post-punk Manchester had spawned more than its fair share of talented musicians, yet there were few venues where they could play, and even fewer opportunities for them to reach a wider audience. In response, a collection of local luminaries set up what became known as The Manchester Musicians Collective. Alerted to this new development, we went along to the general meeting that was held at The Cyprus Tavern, a bar, club and venue in the centre of town. The Collective came about as a result of the efforts of Trevor Wishart and Dick Witts, who'd both been involved in similar enterprises elsewhere. Witts sometimes fronted an arts programme on local television[6] and had become a bit of a local celebrity. He also had a three-piece band of his own, The Passage, who were also definitely in my top five, and their single 'Taboos' remains one of my all-time favourites.

An elected committee ran the Collective, and local bands were invited to join. Joy Division and The Fall had already done so and, consequently, whenever these two bands were due to play in Manchester, the much-coveted support slots would be offered exclusively to the Collective, which would then vet the membership and decide who should fill them. In addition, bands were encouraged to invite each other to play at gigs they had organised for themselves, and the Collective itself ran a regular gig night in the basement of The Cyprus Tavern. All of this sounded very noble and interesting, but we decided against joining. Ken was still focused on his efforts to secure a place at Oxford or Cambridge, so we were hardly rehearsing at all by this time. In any event, it all seemed too grand and serious for the likes of us. As for Years, I remember Dave and Sid being particularly cynical about the whole thing, and we just went to the meetings for something to do really.

Mark Hoyle fronted Vibrant Thigh along with a guy called Martin Coogan, and had initially introduced us to the Collective. They'd been

---

6. The Oxford Road Show, BBC2 – JL.

members from the outset, having featured on the Collective's compilation album with the track 'Wooden Gangsters'. Although originally from another part of town, Hoyle had an apartment on Hollin housing estate, not far from where Dave and I lived. He was a witty, highly intelligent, strange individual with a very unique talent, seemingly limitless amounts of energy and enthusiasm and an unquenchable optimism. I don't remember exactly how I came to meet him for the first time, I just vaguely recall him turning up one night at a pub I often drank in back then - the Old Boars Head in Middleton - and being introduced to him by Dave. Subsequently we'd go along to hear Vibrant Thigh on a regular basis.

One day Mark and Dave came around to see me. Vibrant Thigh had been invited to play with a couple of other Collective bands at Brannigan's, a venue in Leeds, but the rest of the band weren't able to do it. Mark would never pass up the opportunity to play a gig, so after first recruiting Dave, he then asked me to play bass. With only a day to rehearse, we wrote a short set of about four or five songs, a prolificacy unequalled by Dave and me in all the years since. We piled into the van with the other two bands, a guitar pop outfit called The Units fronted by a guy called George, who it transpired had played all the instruments on the Jilted John records, and IQ Zero, whose singer, Mick Duffy, later went on to write for the *NME*.

We arrived at the venue and already I felt dubious. Outside we bantered with three or four heavy looking skinhead punks as they inhaled glue from inflated crisp packets. By the time we were due to start, the room was only sparsely occupied, and right at the front of the stage, sat at a table and staring menacingly, were the skinheads. We played three or four of the hastily improvised songs we'd prepared, but I could tell Mark was growing edgy and, totally unexpectedly, he thanked everyone and said that he'd now be playing drums on the next couple of songs and immediately retreated behind the kit. Mark was a bit of an all-rounder instrumentally and I was relieved to hear that he could play drums quite well, but it meant that I was now expected to take over the lead vocals. I had nothing prepared, no lyrics, no melody ideas, nothing - so I was forced to improvise. When it was over there was a rapturous response from everyone in the room. "I told you it would be fine," Mark said happily, and the skinheads made a point of coming over to tell us how much they'd enjoyed it, but it was a couple of hours before my nerves had stopped jangling. So it was that I shared a stage and played bass alongside Dave Fielding for the very first time.

In the end Dave and I stopped going to the Collective meetings altogether after growing increasingly cynical about the whole enterprise. It seemed to us that all the best support slots were being snapped up by the people who formed the committee, all of whom had bands of their own, while everybody else had to content themselves with playing to an empty Cyprus Tavern on a Tuesday night. We continued to see a lot of Mark Hoyle - that is, until he got into hot water with some very unsavoury characters, forcing him to disappear from Middleton for a while. Vibrant Thigh, alas, came to naught, but he did eventually go on to form Dub Sex (and, later on, Dumb) and made some very fine records, the most notable being the underground hit, 'Swerve'. Guitarist Martin Coogan went on to form Judge Happiness, later changing the name to The Mock Turtles and scoring a top twenty hit in 1991 with the single, 'Can You Dig It?'

Dave and I would sometimes go to watch Judge Happiness before they made the transformation, and later invited them to open a few of our shows. I remember one particular night we went to hear them at a small venue just outside Middleton. By way of a support act, Martin's brother came on and did a thirty-minute stand-up comedy routine. The man was an absolute riot, and afterwards I made a point of telling him how much I'd loved it. He thanked me and explained that he'd just graduated from Manchester Polytechnic in drama, and that the comedy was just a means of earning an Equity card. Since then he'd been offered work doing voice-over impressions for a satirical puppet TV show called *Spitting Image* and so was seriously considering sticking with the comedy. I told him that, judging from what I'd just seen, that would be wise; I hear Steve Coogan has gone on to do quite well since then.

4. ROCK OF AGES

Not long after our first expedition to Loch Ness, Reg dropped a bombshell in the form of an invitation to join his band, going on to tell me that Years were splitting up. This was a real shock because they had been together for, well, years. But Reg explained that he and Dave had been drifting apart from Sid for quite some time, and things had finally come to a head. Reg would move from bass to guitar, which he said was his preferred instrument anyway, and I would take over the bass.

By this time my affection and admiration for both Dave and Reg ran deep, but I was hesitant because I felt that Dave in particular took the whole idea of playing in a band far too seriously and that he had genuine aspirations for success. I still felt I had to find a serious direction of my own and was continuing with my plan to study drama. Having successfully passed the first round of exams at Rochdale College, I'd immediately enrolled for the one-year A-level course which, if successful, would give me the minimum entry requirement for Manchester Polytechnic. Consequently, I didn't feel I was able to dedicate the time and focus required, and the last thing I wanted to do was to let them down. I told them I'd give it some serious thought.

Over the next few weeks, as I worked my final week at British Vinegars, Reg and I spoke a lot about forming a new band together. I remember thinking that there was no reason why I couldn't rehearse with Dave and Reg in the evenings whilst working at my studies. There wouldn't be a conflict of interest unless the band suddenly got a break, and while I wasn't exactly cynical, I didn't think it very likely. What swung the decision in favour of joining the band was a conversation I had with Dave one evening on his parents' front doorstep. I'd told him that I was worried about how seriously he took a prospective career in music, that I doubted I'd be able to live up to it, and that ultimately I had other plans. He told me that I was worrying needlessly. "We're all mates and we have a really good time together, so we just carry on having a really great time together and the music will take care of itself. It'll just come naturally."

A couple of days later I walked down to the telephone box during my lunch break, called Dave and told him I'd join his band. I then phoned Ken and explained the situation. Ken was disappointed that our regular Wednesday night rehearsals were finally ending, but he understood.

Surprisingly, quite a few of the guys that followed Years around were incredulous that I was disbanding The Clichés to join Years. Similarly, Dave and Reg were getting the same kind of grief. One former teacher from Hollin High, who'd subsequently become a big fan of Years, on hearing what Dave and Reg were planning to do exclaimed, "What have you asked him to join for? You won't get anywhere with him in the band!" We met again to talk about the finer points. "Who are we going to get in as lead singer?" I asked.

"You're the lead singer," Dave said, "and the bass player."

We jammed along with each other for a couple of hours and, when it was time to pack our stuff away, I hesitantly asked him whether I had passed the audition.

"Oh yeah," he smiled, "I think so."

Despite the end of The Clichés I still hadn't cancelled our rehearsal room booking, so I kept it on as it seemed like a good place to start. We had yet to write any songs together, so I suggested that we jam out something we already knew, and nominated The Beatles' 'Tomorrow Never Knows' as the whole song is played on a single chord - although, as we jammed, we added a second chord. This was to be our one and only rehearsal in St Agnes' Church, as it was simply too much hassle for Dave and Reg to get their equipment up there every week. What was needed was somewhere more convenient where we could rehearse more regularly, and permanently store the bulk of our equipment. After some searching, with the help of my cousin Daryl, we were able to find a room that suited our purposes above the Railway Inn, a pub on the corner of Townley Street in Middleton. For most of that first year this suited us very well, and we wrote and arranged most of our early songs there, rehearsing three nights a week.

By now Dave and Reg had left Rochdale Art College, and Dave had found himself a job in central Manchester as a graphic designer with an advertising company. Reg, in the meantime, had finished his temporary summer job at British Vinegar and was signing on. Consequently he had lots of free time and, on the days when I wasn't in college, he'd come over and we'd jam out ideas together in my bedroom. The outline of 'Monkeyland' was one of the first things Reg and I came up with.

Our main problem revolved around finding a drummer, and it proved as difficult for us as it had been for The Clichés. John Mather came along once or twice with his kit but, as I say, John was too weird, unreliable and difficult to communicate with. Even Reg, who'd known John the longest, seemed ill at ease, and so it ended there.

Finally, Dave hit on a solution. He happened to know an excellent drummer who might be willing to sit in with the band as a favour, until we could find someone permanent. Brian Schofield had taken drumming lessons from an early age and, by this time, was as near to a professional drummer as I'd ever heard. He would augment the £200 a week he earned at the Senior Service cigarette factory by sometimes as much as £60 a night drumming with cabaret duos in various working men's clubs around the region. He made no effort to hide the fact that he didn't care for our music, and regarded us all as weird, scruffy, pot-smoking layabouts. I don't know why he bothered to turn up at all, but he did. More often than not, anyway. 'Scoffer' would never allow us to forget what a HUGE favour he was doing us by agreeing to fill in on drums. Sometimes he'd bring his girlfriend to rehearsals and then, as she sat there admiring him, he'd throw in some additional snare or tom rolls to impress her, then nod and wink in her direction, causing Dave and me to discreetly break out in hysterics.

It was around this time that magic mushrooms became the vice of choice, especially for Dave and me, although I could never quite get used to eating them raw. We discovered them through a work colleague of Dave's named James, who also sat in on rehearsals occasionally, having given Dave a lift to the Railway Inn directly from work. James was an advertising executive with a passion for drugs, and seemed to know everything about every high going, legal and illegal. He was a gentle, unassuming guy with a warm smile, a genuine wit and intelligence and a rather posh, well-educated accent, and he soon became a close friend of the band.

We'd barely begun when I got a phone call from someone at Rochdale College who was putting together an event featuring some very respectable local bands. Having read the review that The Rochdale Alternative Press had given The Clichés, the guy on the phone was asking if he could book the group to appear. To my surprise, Dave immediately said we ought to do the gig. Consequently, our first ever show together was under the name The Clichés. We arrived to soundcheck on the evening of the gig to find that the whole event had been very professionally organised, something we weren't used to at all. They even had a lighting rig, alongside one of the biggest PA systems I'd ever seen.

James came along with a friend of his - a huge guy named Roger, who had once played semi-professional rugby - to add moral support. It was just as well that Roger came with him because the hooligans of Rochdale, typically three years behind the times, decided that the gig was a punk gathering and tried to kick anyone entering the college who wore so much as a leather jacket. They'd tried to kick James as he neared the main entrance but then, on seeing Roger, had thought twice about it and slunk away[1]. We played an unremarkable set, early in the evening, but we all felt the experience had been good for us, and we got paid - or at least Scoffer did. He'd demanded most of the fee on the basis that he was the only professional in the group.

The experience only served to whet our appetite, and before long Dave found us a gig at another pub, also called The Railway, in nearby Royton. We were to play two sets with a thirty minute break in the middle. Everything was going well until a major fight started, and we took refuge behind some upturned tables. The landlady tried to blame us for the fight and initially refused to pay us, but Dave argued quite forcefully with her and finally we did get paid, albeit ten quid less than had been agreed. Once again, Scoffer claimed most of it.

Dave found us another pub gig, in Oldham, and this was to be our last foray onto the pub circuit for quite some time. We met at our rehearsal room to collect the band's gear and, due to limited space in the vehicle, were forced to take it in stages. Dave and Scoffer went ahead with the first wave, but returned very quickly with a sombre expression. Dave told us that when he and Scoffer had arrived at the pub two very large, very heavy looking blokes had met them at the door and had intimated that they'd wanted to fuck Dave over the pool table. Amid further, similar remarks, Dave and Scoffer had both turned right around and drove directly back. We all looked at each other, and in the end decided it would probably be best if we pulled out.

It wasn't solely from a desire to play live that we put ourselves in these situations, but rather on the advice of others, mainly ex-musicians who had played in bands during the sixties. "Play anywhere!" they told us. "Play anywhere that'll have you, any shit-hole that books bands, get the experience."

Of course, the sixties were long gone and good venues willing to book and pay bands they'd never heard of were rare. What's more, the few venues there were didn't provide the kind of experiences that we wanted. And when

---

1. Roger was rather intimidating to look at, but he seemed gentle enough to talk to. Unfortunately, we didn't get to know him very well because he disappeared not long after we met him. James told us that Roger was also partial to magic mushrooms and took them on a regular basis. One night though, after taking a relatively small number, around a hundred, he completely freaked out and vanished from the scene. James was finally able to track him down at the house of Roger's parents and was told that Roger had moved back in, that he never came out of his room anymore and that he always slept with the light on. The news startled me - Roger was not a soft guy - so I always approached the magic mushrooms with a degree of caution after that.

we thought about it, it was impossible to say what we hoped to achieve. Far better, we decided, to concentrate on our songwriting and try to push that, rather than playing in shit pubs to people who didn't give a fuck whether you lived or died on the spot, or indeed, to people that might be eager to determine that one way or the other.

So that was what we decided to do. Scoffer wasn't too happy about it because not playing gigs meant no money for Scoffer. He scaled down the number of times he was prepared to turn up, and from that point on we saw him one night a week. The rest of the time Dave, Reg, and I would work on getting songs together.

This was a prolific period for us, and although we discarded many of our early songs, we did accumulate a few that we quite liked. 'Monkeyland' was finally completed after I had the idea to give it a soft verse with a loud, powerful, chorus dynamic. 'Here Today', inspired by the murder of John Lennon, evolved from an idea of Reg's, who'd been playing around with the tremolo settings on his guitar amp. There was a meandering tune titled 'Dear Dead Days' which, although we didn't continue to develop it at the time, came in useful many years later. Another, 'Turn To The Vices', was written in about two minutes when we were on mushrooms one night. 'Falling From Grace With Myself Again' contained one of my favourite choruses, while 'Singing Rule Britannia - While The Walls Close In' was meant as a diatribe against Thatcherism. Finally, there was another of my favourites, 'Less Than Human', which is about someone being racked by guilt. These were a few of the early songs that survived in one form or another, after having titles, lyrics, and arrangements modified.

Our Friday nights would usually be spent in Ali's flat where we'd indulge in the delicacy known as 'hot knives'[2]. The recipe was one small lump of cannabis, preferably of the black variety, two metal butter knives heated on the stove until the tips were glowing red, and one bottle - preferably glass - with the base rim removed. This was quite tricky and involved heating the bottom of the bottle on a stove and then running it under a tap, whereupon the base would crack and fall away. Then, holding the neck of the bottle to the mouth, the chef took the knives and used one of them to hold the piece of cannabis resin while the other was placed

---

2. I'd discovered this delicacy at the Deeply Vale Free Festival, where there'd been a large tent with a sign outside reading: 'HOT KNIVES - 50p', and outside a large queue had formed that included Dave. Suddenly, Dave saw Reg coming out of the tent with a huge smile on his face. Shouting him over Dave had asked, "What are they like Reg?" "Alright!" answered a smiling, very-stoned Reg. "Great!" Dave exclaimed, rubbing his hands together, "I'm getting two. I'm starving!" He'd expected them to be hot buns of some kind.

directly on top of it. The heat of the knives then smelted the resin, and the resulting smoke would be inhaled through the neck of the bottle. It was worth all the hassle, and we would usually spend around an hour doing this before hitting the pub.

That summer we were all sitting around when the subject of acid came up. "You've taken acid, haven't you Mark?" they asked. I told them I had, a long time ago, that I rated the experience as life-changing, and did my best to describe it. Everyone decided they wanted a taste, and Dave suggested that he ask James to give us a ride to Deeply Vale to buy some. James agreed, and we roamed around the festival site for about half an hour until finally someone pointed out a long-haired, bearded gentleman in black clothes and a black top-hat with feathers stuck into the brim. We bought the LSD, which this time came on tiny squares of blotting paper, and James dropped us off in Middleton, before heading off to London where he was planning to relocate.

We sat in the flat, eyeing the small squares and each other, and then we each swallowed some of the tiny slivers of paper. An hour later no-one could feel any effects and we began to think that we'd paid good money for nothing. "Perhaps we didn't take enough?" someone said, so we all swallowed more. Another thirty minutes passed by and still nothing was happening, so we decided to give up and go for a beer instead. As we walked down the main road toward the pub, however, we noticed that something was most definitely happening. For one thing, the outside world seemed to be turning into a Walt Disney cartoon and, for another, the pavement on which we walked seemed to be made from soft, quilted cushions. This rather curious development was followed by around six hours of unequivocal, riotous hilarity. It was still daylight, this being a summer's evening, so we spent most of that time in Jubilee Park in the centre of Middleton, laughing, clowning around and talking absolute gibberish. At one point, Dave had to be physically restrained from storming into the Old Boars Head, swinging an old lavatory ball cock that he'd found somewhere. I became aware that our general behaviour might seem somewhat odd to other inhabitants of the town, and so I suggested we escape into some nearby woods to avoid drawing too much attention to ourselves. For me, taking LSD in the great outdoors offered a far more interesting experience than being confined to a club or bar.

Our first acid trip together only whetted our appetite for more, so we decided to do it again. This time we would be accompanied by Tony Skinkis, who'd taken LSD a number of times before. We elected to avoid the town centre altogether in favour of Hopwood and the paths beyond. The plan was to then head out along farm tracks and bridleways to the cenotaph monument at the summit of Tandle Hill, situated in the middle of Tandle Hill Park on the edge of Royton.

Tandle Hill and the immediate surrounding area had been gifted to the people of Royton in 1919, along with certain conditions forbidding its ruination by any sort of development or other exploitation. As a result the spread of urbanisation had bypassed Tandle Hill completely on every side so that the hill resembled an island in a sea of neon lights, and by this time the area had been designated as a country park.

Standing at the summit and looking out, the view was impressive at the best of times, but with LSD-enhanced sensory perception it was truly awesome. Eventually we entered the rather dense wood that backs onto the hill. There was an almost total absence of light, and we were only able to negotiate our way by feeling for the tarmac path with our feet. Gradually, though, as our eyes became accustomed to the darkness, we found a park bench, and Ali, who didn't need his eyes for such a task, began rolling a joint. I can clearly remember the stillness of the wood, broken only occasionally by the rustle of the leaves in the cool night breeze. After a while we made our way back to the bridleway, and eventually back into the town and home. "That's what I call a Saturday night," someone said. "Same time next week?"

Sure enough, the following weekend we all met up again at Tony's flat. Our merry company was augmented yet again when Ken, having heard all about the adventures of the previous week, fell in. Our destination was again Tandle Hill, but this time we chose an alternative route to the previous weekend. Rochdale Road splits two areas of land that separate the estates of Hollin and Hopwood from that of Boarshaw. On the Boarshaw side is an area of wasteland with a river running through the middle of it. The river continues under the main road and into the wood itself on the opposite side, via a huge aqueduct. We decided to follow the tunnel under the main road to the woods on the far side, but some were unnerved by the darkness and the prospect of rats, and turned back to cross the road by the conventional route. By this time the effects of the acid were beginning to kick in, and our wild laughter echoed deafeningly in the darkness all around us. Those who had turned back were waiting on the far side and were laughing wildly at our efforts to reach the bank without falling in. Fortunately the water level wasn't very high, and we were able to skip from stone to stone without coming to grief.

The next task involved climbing to the top of a steep, sandy bank that rose high above the river, and running, full flight, down again, making sure to stop before our momentum took us over the edge of the riverbank and into the water. Under normal circumstances this would have presented no problem, but, due to the disorientation and lack of co-ordination in our limbs, it was touch and go. One by one, we took our turn and collapsed at the bottom in hilarity, all except Dave, who just sat there laughing, refusing to come down. We all stood in a line and promised to catch him and he took us at our word, but we then moved at the vital moment and he was only just able to prevent himself from hurtling headlong into the shallow water. From Hopwood we walked into adjoining Deadwood, although it's far from that in the summer. As we ploughed through an area thick with giant ferns, I remember thinking that I'd never seen the woods look so beautiful in all the years I'd lived there. The colours of the forest seemed sharp, yet muted; soft, yet vibrant. These contradictions confounded the senses - it was as if I was seeing nature for the very first time.

By now it was getting dark, so we left the woods and walked across the neighbouring North Manchester Golf Course. Over the years I've walked over by the golf course in all kinds of weather - sunshine, rain, sleet, and snow - and there would always be at least two idiots out there pulling golf trolleys. Once I even saw a guy playing as I sheltered from a thunderstorm. Darkness seems to be the only condition that defeats them, and so we found the golf course completely deserted. We spent at least twenty minutes on our hands and knees on the putting green, unable to believe that grass could be cropped that short, running our hands along it to savour the texture. "I feel like a nit on a skinhead's scalp," said Dave, and, not for the last time that night, we fell about laughing. In the interests of science, I had decided to record my impressions in the notebook that I always carried around with me, but it took all the focus and concentration I possessed to write down Dave's statement, along with similar meaningless comments. In the end, all I was left with was a string of abstract nonsense that seemed to make perfect sense at the time.

We rejoined the path and walked alongside the golf club grounds, passing the lightning tree that had stood there ever since I can remember. I stopped to look at it, as I always did, and promised myself that I'd photograph it one day. I couldn't imagine the ferocity of a lightning bolt that could do such a thing to a fully-fledged English oak. We reached the main road and, instead of crossing it and following the canal to the bridle way, we stayed with the road a little further and then took the farm track up towards Tandle Hill Tavern. The tavern lies about two miles along this track, and behind the tavern is a public footpath that takes you past some farm buildings and across a field to the cenotaph on Tandle Hill.

Reg, Mark and Dave, 1980. Photo: Tony Skinkis

Before reaching the hill, a farm-track crosses the motorway that slices a path directly through the farmland by way of an iron and concrete bridge painted in municipal blue. I'd seen busy motorways many times, of course, but I'd never seen them under the influence of LSD. It was like gazing down on a life-sized model village. The speeding cars and trucks resembled giant toys as they glided along the tarmac below, and the futuristic curves and illuminations of the motorway itself were spectacles worthy of Steven Spielberg. It was all in the lighting, I suppose, and the way in which the acid enhanced it. The hallucinatory effects of the drug were only now dawning on Ken it seemed, and I heard him say, "What's the script with this bridge?"

Tony, again with his characteristic mock-serious expression, echoed "What's the script of the bridge, News?"[3]

Then Reg chipped in, imitating a TV announcer, "FEATURING LIVE ON SCRRRIPT OF THE BRIDGE TONIGHT..."

I was laughing so hard I could hardly stand, and taking my little notebook I scribbled it down: SCRIPT OF THE BRIDGE, TV PRO-GRAMME.

Continuing up the track, we finally arrived at the Tandle Hill Tavern. We had no idea of the hour - Wonderland being a timeless state - but it had to be quite late as the tavern was locked for the evening and there were no

---

3. News at Ten was Tony's rhyming slang for Ken.

vehicles parked on the track outside. We made our way through the yard at the rear of the inn, stumbled noisily over the stile, and crossed the field to the hill. Looking across the field I could see the silhouettes of cattle grazing on the slopes. One lifted its head to watch us, but didn't seem unduly disturbed. "The field's full of cows," someone whispered.

"Er, young bulls actually," I answered. We all stopped and looked at each other, before continuing on at a brisk, comical walk rather than a run, as we didn't want to provoke them into chasing us.

In the darkness we somehow missed the stile that provides access over the iron fence running around the perimeter of the hill, so we patrolled around until a gap was found through which we could all squeeze. Some of us knew what to expect from the view, but for Ken this was going to be a new experience, so I asked him to keep his eyes fixed on the ground until I told him he could look. He gamely did as I asked and we approached the cenotaph with our backs to the view. We stood there side by side facing the cenotaph. "Now!" I said, and we both turned around.

"Fuckin' 'ell!" he exclaimed when he saw the view. His words were not lost on the rest of us. Even though I'd stood there in the same state the previous week, the impact of all that neon, as far as the eye could see, was still mightily impressive. The hill was an island in a sea of lights.

The evening was warmer than the previous week. The sky was clear, with only some thin scattered cloud, and the stars shone brightly. The noise of the passing traffic from the motorway below was carried away from us on a light breeze and could barely be heard. The only discernable sound was a faint, musical drone that was reminiscent of those plastic tubes that you whirl around your head to create musical notes from the air. When I mentioned it to the others they said that they could all hear it too.

The profound nature of the entire experience is something that is very hard to convey. We were all aware of it, to varying degrees, despite the hilarity and nonsense. Tony was saying that he'd taken acid many times during the course of his life - he was six or seven years older than the rest of us - but he'd never experienced anything like this. Consequently, he told us that this would be the last time he'd ever take acid; that there wouldn't be any point, as he felt that this particular trip could never be bettered. This proved to be a very wise insight. Although I was to take acid often over the following eighteen months, I was never able to capture the perfection of this night and, in the end, resigned myself to that fact. In our conversations that night, Ken and I both felt that it really was the end of one era and the beginning of another; that we were somehow finally saying goodbye to our childhood. The entire world was spread out before us to the far horizon and we were about to step into it, to embrace and experience it - and things would never, ever be the same again.

God only knows how long we sat there. We'd reverted to some kind of mid-childhood state, rolling sideways down slopes with our arms tucked into our sides, or lying on the grass in a line with our heads on the edge of the slope surveying the view upside down. "Check out the panoramic," Tony kept saying. Inspired by the inverted panoramic, I spent at least twenty minutes lying with my head at the base of the cenotaph, staring upwards along its length into the star-filled sky, marvelling at the perspective. Somewhere along the line we formed the Planet Earth Society, dedicated to expanding the frontiers of human knowledge and understanding.

Eventually we decided it was time to explore the woods. As they had the previous weekend, the dense trees screened out most of the light. Giggling softly, we fumbled our way down the main path. From the midst of the wood we were all startled to hear the hoot of an owl, and in response someone immediately lit a disposable cigarette lighter, swinging it from left to right and back again in an attempt to ward off this unseen creature of the night. This ridiculous spectacle had us howling with laughter once again. The path led through the centre of the woods to a picnic area, where a group of wooden trestle tables had been constructed for that purpose. We sat above them on a makeshift bench at the top of a high, grass slope before rolling, roly-poly fashion, down to the bottom. Someone said something concerning the return of the roughnecks and I liked the phrase so much I immediately reached for my notebook and pen. "I've lost my pen!" I exclaimed suddenly. Everyone immediately stood up and began twitching their heads, eyes to the ground, like hens. "It must have been when I rolled down the hill," I reasoned, and began climbing the slope in an attempt to find it. One or two came with me to help, seriously believing that we had a chance of finding it in the pitch darkness. As I stood there at the summit of the slope, though, I looked out again at the vast expanse of orange neon toward the horizon and the city of Manchester. In the sky, I saw the lights of an aeroplane as it circled the city awaiting its landing instructions. I counted another, and another. They numbered six in total, all in various parts of the sky.

I began to descend the slope again when I heard Reg's voice ring out. "What's that?"

He was pointing to the sky above our heads at a very strange, oddly-shaped object drifting silently overhead, very low in the sky. Its underside was illuminated, and we could see three large discs arranged in a triangular fashion. We watched, fascinated, before finally losing sight of it over the tree line. As we continued to gaze up at the sky, clouds drifted over and veiled the stars, except that the layers of cloud approached each other from opposite directions, rather like a curtain coming down after a performance.

"What sort of clouds can do that?" I asked, but no-one said anything. Suddenly, all the birds in the park broke into the dawn chorus for about twenty seconds before lapsing into silence again. We just stood there for a moment, not saying anything, on the brink of laughter. "Mm," someone murmured, before the laughter broke out.

We took one last look at the view before following the main path down, not wishing to push our luck with the bulls in the field. We climbed over the iron fence and pondered over which direction to take. "What about that way?" someone suggested, pointing down the path toward the district of Royton.

"No, we don't want to go that way," I said, "That just leads back to suburbia."

"Well, all the paths lead back to suburbia," retorted Reg. "It's what happens in between that counts, innit?"

We all looked at him for a second, blinking in the moonlight.

"Fuckin' 'ell Reg," Dave said, laughing. "I think that's one of the most profound things I've ever heard."

Finally, we decided on a direction and made our way back to the underpass that runs beneath the motorway. By the entrance, a rickety wooden fence separated the path from a grassy hollow that led to the grass verge beside the motorway. A bright orange light illuminated the area, but due to the warmth of the evening and the dampness of the grass, the hollow had filled with a fog that beautifully reflected the orange light. We climbed over the fence and each of us vanished into the fog in various directions. Within it none of the others could be seen, and I wandered around giggling, occasionally bumping into one of them, as they too emerged from the fog. We would then pass each other, and disappear back into the fog in opposite directions. At last tired of the game, we rejoined the path and made our way back into town.

The effects of the acid, although diminished, had not ceased entirely, and so Tony invited us all back to his flat for coffee and a joint while I read out some of the nonsense I'd written in my notebook. At some point we hit upon the idea of drawing little cartoons to accompany some of the phrases I'd written down during the course of the evening. At last, one by one, we each made our way home. Ken and I walked the road to the Hollin housing estate, until finally we stopped to say goodnight. "What a night!" Ken said. I gave him a huge hug.

"Yeah," I laughed, "what a night!"

Tony, it transpired, fancied himself as an amateur photographer and so later that week, when we met to rehearse as usual, he came along with us and offered to take what would be our first stab at some promotional photographs. Scoffer was absent that night, but that didn't deter us in the slightest. While we were grateful to him for helping us out, as far as we were concerned, the band still needed two things: a permanent drummer, and a name.

Picking the right name for a group, as anyone who has ever been in a band will tell you, is one of the most difficult tasks you can face. We must have written down hundreds, and each person's contributions reflected a certain mindset. Reg's ideas were by far the most original, The Rabbit Hutches, The Gnomes Of Dullwitch - which we used once when we'd been stuck for a name after Adrian at Bury Metro Arts had invited us back for a gig at Bury Derby Hall - and The Burning Curtains, which I liked a lot but Dave didn't.

At the rehearsal that night, in between songs, we were having a discussion about how best to promote the group and determine our immediate aims, now that we had a hatful of songs. "What you need to do, right, is get some fuckin' songs recorded and send 'em to John Peel," volunteered Tony, and everyone agreed that this was a very good idea. Scoffer was due to be at the next rehearsal, so we decided that Reg would bring his ghetto-blaster - which served us for many years after - and we'd record some of our songs onto a cassette and send it to John Peel. However, Scoffer failed to show up; it transpired that he'd arranged an audition for himself with a local cabaret group called The Trend, a band we despised. "We'll do it without him, we'll just record the songs without drums," Dave decided.

I think we recorded four songs onto the tape, the last of which was 'Monkeyland'. "What do you think about that then, John?" Tony said into the microphone, before switching the recorder off. The next day Dave mailed the tape, along with my address and phone number on a hastily scribbled note, to John Peel at Radio One in London.

Late one Saturday morning I came leaping down the stairs, gathered up the mail from the mat and put the coffee on. As I glanced through the mail, which contained the usual assortment of brown envelopes and prize-winning notifications from the Reader's Digest, I came across a large white envelope with the instantly recognisable logo of BBC Radio One emblazoned all over it. I ripped open the envelope and found a hand written note from John Peel. It read:

> *HEARD THE TAPE, SOUNDS LIKE SOMETHING VERY WORTHWHILE IS GOING ON. IF YOU DO A STUDIO TAPE MAKE SURE I GET TO HEAR IT. FORGIVE BREVITY, BUT I HAVE OVER 1,000 TAPES TO LISTEN TO. THIS IS TRUE! JOHN PEEL.*

Laughing to myself I immediately phoned Dave. "Meet me at Ali's as soon as you can," I told him, "Peel wrote back."

I quickly dressed, not even bothering to shave, and dashed down to Ali's flat. By the time I arrived it was around noon and Ali was already up and about. I immediately handed him the letter and he read it. "Cool!" he said, smiling. Peel had been a favourite with all of us for years, and lately it had become almost a ritual for us to gather at Ali's over a smoke and listen to his programme.

Dave arrived and read the letter, more than once. "Right!" he said, "We've got to go into the studio: Cargo!" The matter of finance raised its ugly head. Dave fell silent for a moment, lost in thought, and then reminded us that we had loads of gear left over from Years and The Clichés that we didn't use, spare microphones, microphone stands and PA amps we no longer needed. He suggested we take the lot down to A1 Music in Manchester and take whatever we could get for it, surmising that it would be enough money to get us through the door at Cargo Studios. "We'll ask Tony to give us a lift in his van," he said. This seemed like a good plan.

"When?" I asked.

"Now!" Dave said and went off in search of a phone box.

Tony was as excited as the rest of us at the news, and so we emptied everything we didn't need from the rehearsal room and loaded it into his van. A1 Music was notoriously mean when it came to buying second-hand equipment, and this day proved to be no exception. Despite this, Dave was most persuasive and used all his bargaining skills to squeeze the guy for every penny he could. "It isn't much for all that gear," I observed ruefully.

"It'll be enough," Dave said as we drove back to Middleton.

The following week Dave booked us into Cargo. By this time he'd got to know the owner and chief engineer, John B, quite well, and so John cut us a lot of slack. We recorded at least three tracks that day: 'Turn to the Vices', 'Falling from Grace with Myself Again', and our newest song, 'Things I Wish I'd Said'.

The first ever picture of The Chameleons, by the canal in Middleton.   Photo: Tony Skinkis

After weeks of rehearsing in the room over the pub, it was a revelation to hear the results of a studio recording. Scoffer was frequently a pain in the arse, but he was a tight drummer. Unfortunately, he was also a tight something else. We ran over the allotted time and were desperately emptying our pockets of change to make up the shortfall so that we'd be able to take the tapes away with us. Scoffer stood there eyeing the ceiling. "Come on Scoffer," I said to him, "You're on good money, get your wallet out." Scoffer looked indignant, clutching a huge and extremely silly Valentine's Day card he'd just bought for his girlfriend that played the theme from *Love Story* whenever it was opened. He had been boasting all afternoon that this tacky item had cost him ten quid, yet he stubbornly refused to contribute anything towards liberating the tapes.

"Listen!" he said, "I'm doing you a favour drumming on this you know, I'm a session drummer, me!"

We were about five quid short but John, knowing that this was to be more than a normal demo tape, kindly waived the shortfall, and we dashed off to Reg's house to play the cassette. To our dismay, it sounded totally different through Reg's music centre than it had on the studio's JBL monitors. Dave phoned John B at the studio and naïvely told him that something must be wrong with his equipment. John B patiently explained that it was bound to sound different on a domestic hi-fi system, but conceded that as the engineer, it might have been wise to warn us of this, and so he graciously agreed to allow us to remix the tracks that week at a reduced rate. What's more, he offered us a free recording session for reasons that involved some sort of local community grant, so we went back in and recorded a version of 'Here Today' and as much as we had of 'Dear Dead Days'. This coincided with one of our regular rehearsal nights, so Scoffer didn't complain too much when he found out it wasn't going to cost him anything.

Later that week, having remixed the tape, we met again at Ali's flat and contemplated our next move. I assumed that we would simply mail the tape back to John Peel, but I was wrong. Dave felt that it would be better if we went to London and handed it to him in person. That way we'd also be able to hawk the tape around to one or two record companies. We made some copies of the cassette, mailed one to Factory Records (who never bothered to reply), and Dave took the others. Finances being what they were, it was decided that only two of us should make the trip. Reg wasn't interested in going to London anyway. I thought it was all a bit mad but I was willing to go for the craic. Dave's eldest brother Alan had moved to London, so Dave arranged for us to stay with him overnight, and Ali rolled us a few of his finest joints for the journey, which I placed carefully in a little tin that I carried around for such things.

On our first day in London, we sauntered over to Cherry Red Records and were actually ushered into someone's office whereupon the guy immediately loaded the cassette. "It's rock 'n' roll," the guy sang, smiling. He told us he quite liked it, but said that overall he felt that we should approach major labels. I told him I was cynical about major labels, and preferred an independent label. He asked if he could keep the tape, and we left.

Next stop was Virgin Mansions, home of Virgin Music publishing, although at the time we just assumed that the recording division would be in the same building. The reception area was chaotic, with lots of people sitting around in suits awaiting appointments, motorcycle couriers coming and going, and three rather gorgeous receptionists who never seemed to be off the phone. Eventually we were able to steal a few words with one of them, but she told us that it would be impossible for us to see anyone without a prior appointment. We left a package behind the reception desk and, looking at us as if we were something that had crawled out from between the radiators, she reluctantly promised to hand it to their A&R Department. Judging from her distinct lack of enthusiasm however, I didn't really expect her to.

Our last port of call was the BBC at Portland Place, and we sat ourselves down on the stone steps at the foot of the church which stands opposite the BBC buildings, having been told by the doorman that John Peel had not yet returned from lunch. Our plan was simple: we'd wait there until John Peel walked past on his way to work and then put the tape in his hands. This seemed like a good moment to open my tin and enjoy one of Ali's special joints. I sat there getting mildly stoned, casually watching all the comings and goings, and this evolved into a game of Who's Who, as various BBC celebrities filed in and out of the different buildings. Sir Robin Day strolled right by us, as did the actor Patrick Troughton, who'd been my favourite Doctor Who. A couple of presenters from the children's magazine programme Blue Peter walked by, as did Dave 'Kid' Jensen, who we instantly recognised - he hosted a nightly Radio One show that was nearer the mainstream than Peel's. On seeing Jensen, Dave and I shouted his name and rushed up to him. He smiled, obviously pleased at being recognised, but all we could think of to say was, "Er, have you seen John Peel?" He didn't seem too happy about this though, and politely told us that he hadn't, before walking off.

The afternoon wore on without any sign of our target and we began to resign ourselves to leaving the package for him at reception, when I happened to glance up and saw him walking past. We immediately rose again and ran in pursuit shouting his name. When he realised that he wasn't being attacked, he relaxed and we hurriedly explained why we were there, showing him the note he'd written to us as proof. He seemed a little bemused to be accosted in the street, but on reading the note - during the course of a single month he must have written hundreds just like it - he took the tape and asked us if we could leave it with him for half an hour. He promised to listen to it, and then let us know what he thought that day. "I don't want to listen to it while you sit there staring at me," he said, and we told him that we completely understood.

Dave and I went off to a nearby coffee shop to kill thirty minutes before returning to our place on the church steps. After a while, sure enough, Peel emerged and called us over. "Is this really you? I mean, it isn't a wind up or anything?" This confused us for a moment, until we realised that Dave had re-used an old cassette box which still bore the name of another band - Fast Cars - on the side of it. Dave explained this, and Peel nodded and said, "Well I think it's rather good, what's the name of the band?" This stumped us and we just blinked at each other for a few seconds before telling him, somewhat embarrassed, that we hadn't thought of one yet. This made Peel laugh, "Well it's rather good in my view, I'll play it to my producer and see what he thinks of it. Is there a contact phone number?"

"Inside the box," Dave replied, "It's Mark's home telephone number. I work most days."

"Right!" said John, "Well, as I say, I'll play it to our producer before we go for a few pints tonight, and I'll let you know."

"Maybe you should play it to him after he's had a few pints?" I suggested.

Peel laughed, and we said our goodbyes.

In high spirits, we dashed to Euston station to catch our train back to Manchester. I didn't honestly expect much, reasoning that this sort of thing must happen to Peel all the time. However, in the media he'd always had a reputation for being very sincere, so I was pleased that he'd said that he liked our tape. It later transpired that, amongst all the hundreds of new bands Peel had featured and the thousands of bands he hadn't, and all the different methods they'd dreamed up to try to get his attention, not one of them had hit upon the simple plan of waiting outside the BBC, introducing themselves and handing him a tape. This had really struck a chord with him.

Two days later, I was roused from my sleep by the sound of the telephone ringing, and I dashed downstairs to answer it. Somewhat blearily, I spoke into the telephone. "Hello?"

"Hello, is that Mark?"

"Yes."

"This is John Peel here."

"That's good, Tony," I yawned, "That's brilliant, you should go on the television with impressions like that."

"No, this really is John Peel."

I stood bolt upright. Now that I was a bit more awake, the voice was unmistakable and, besides, I remembered that Tony was on a camping holiday in the South of France.

John continued, "I played your tape to my producer and we both love it. We want you to come down to record a session."

I stood there unable to take it in. "I don't know what to say, I mean... brilliant, I just don't know what to say," I blustered.

"Well, my producer is here so I'll hand you over and you can sort something out, and I'm looking forward to it."

Then he was gone. The new voice on the phone told me that they both loved the tape. "I've been playing it non-stop in the car all weekend," Peel's producer enthused. "When would you like to come down and record it?"

Rather on the hop, I just said, "Well, as soon as possible really."

The producer explained that we had a choice. We could record it within the next few weeks at Langham House, the old BBC eight-track studio that they'd been using for years, situated in a basement building at Portland Place; or, we could wait a while until they'd completed the conversion of a new twenty-four track, state-of-the-art studio at Maida Vale. "The eight-track!" I blurted.

"Are you sure?" he asked.

"Yes!" I said without hesitation, "We don't want to wait!"

"Okay then good, I'll send up a contract today, it'll include the date of the session and all the details you need for coming down. Thanks again, and the best of luck."

"Thanks! Great! Great! Thanks," was all I could think of to say.

Once again I phoned Dave and Reg and told them to meet me at Ali's flat, although this time I didn't say why, as I wanted it to be a surprise. When everyone was present, I just said, "the Peel session, we've got it! There's a contract on the way today!"

Everyone was quiet as they tried to take it in, except Dave who was just staring into space and nodding his head. "Brilliant!" he kept saying, staring away into space. "Brilliant!"

Later that afternoon, Ken called round to Ali's, and he had some news of his own. He'd finally been notified that he'd passed his exams and was due to attend Oxford University for the formal interview. I was so proud of him. I knew that many privileged people, regardless of IQ or exam results, strolled into Oxford or Cambridge on status alone, but Ken had worked hard and had earned it. He was just as excited to hear our news, of course, and immediately offered to come along as a roadie, as did Ali. After all, Peel sessions were a big deal and it wasn't every day you got the opportunity to stroll into the BBC.

During the week, Tony phoned from the south of France to ask how everything was going. I told him what had happened, and he immediately offered to hire a van and drive us down to London. The entire Planet Earth Society would be in on it. That only left Scoffer. At rehearsal, Scoffer was his usual, grumpy self. "John Peel? Radio One? I've never heard him on Radio One."

"It's a late night programme," we patiently explained.

By this time the contract had arrived and we were amazed to discover that Peel sessions paid quite well. What's more, should the session be repeated at any time, which did happen occasionally, the band would be paid all over again.

As the big day approached, though, Scoffer continued to irritate. "I hope you're going to get some decent clothes, you lot," he barked one night, "I'm not going to London with you dressed like that, bunch of scruffy bastards." Dressed as he was in a white turtleneck shirt and fake leather jacket, it struck me that he was hardly a guru of fashion himself.

"We're going on the radio, not the television. What does it matter?" Dave said.

"It matters to me!" Scoffer continued, "And another thing, those two that are coming with us," meaning Ali and Ken, "are they chipping in with petrol money too?" Scoffer was annoyed because we'd asked him to contribute toward the van hire and the fuel to London.

"They're coming as roadies!" I said, shouting now, "You don't charge your roadies petrol money, we should be grateful to them for helping us out, and they haven't asked for anything for doing it. You're being paid for it, so what the fuck do you care?" I was seething. "He's got to go," I blazed on the walk home.

"What, and cancel the session you mean?" Dave said. As much as I hated to admit it, I knew that he was right. Sacking the drummer and pulling out of the Peel session was unthinkable.

We still had to overcome the problem of finding a name for the group. In desperation, Dave suggested that we all write ten suggestions down on a list and then compare notes. I was a big fan of the *Spider-man* comics as a child and had been particularly struck by one of his lesser-known adversaries, who, having a metal head, was able to change his face and identity at will. I don't know why this character struck such a chord with me, but it did, and taking my list, I added his name. When I got back to the rehearsal room later that week we all took our lists out to compare them. It transpired that Dave had also written down the same name. We thought this a very odd coincidence, and everyone else seemed to like the name, so we decided to use it. From now on, we were The Chameleons.

5. WONDERFUL RADIO ONE

The night before the recording of the Peel session, we slept on Ali's floor in order to ensure an early start for our journey. So great was the level of excitement, though, that I don't think any of us slept much, and as the grey light of dawn filtered down through the jungle of cannabis plants, we shook ourselves, drank some tea, and began carrying the equipment to the hired van. Practically sleepwalking, we loaded the amps, guitars and drum cases into the back. Grasping quilts and sleeping bags against the morning chill, we were prepared for the long journey ahead, and that's when we found out that the van wouldn't start. We tinkered and sprayed it with lubricant, but it still wouldn't start. It was far too early in the morning to phone the van hire company, so in the end we unloaded all the gear and pushed the van down the road in an attempt to bump start it. This time, thankfully, the recalcitrant vehicle coughed into life, and by 6.30am we'd loaded up again and were on our way to the motorway. Three of us, including the driver, sat along the bench seat in the front, while four crouched precariously amongst the equipment in the back. Tony made very good time, and by 10.30am on 8th June 1981, we were at the BBC studios at Langham House.

We were greeted by the session producer Tony Wilson[1] and his engineer, who looked very much how you might imagine a 1960s BBC boffin to look, complete with thick-rimmed spectacles, but minus the white coat. They both had frightfully posh accents and were a little stiff at first, but they gradually became friendlier as the day wore on. They worked methodically and quickly, and it was immediately obvious that they knew exactly what they were doing. The studio itself looked like a television set from an old episode of Doctor Who, which it might have been once, who knows? For those of you interested in the technical aspects of the recording process, there were lots of red buttons and switches, large glass meters with bouncing needles that seemed to measure sound levels, and brightly coloured bulbs that blinked on and off.

We were told we'd be playing the songs live and that I'd be required to record a guide vocal, though they'd only be keeping the drum and bass tracks. The guitars would be replaced later and the vocals would be recorded last. Finally, all four songs would be mixed. We decided to record the most

---

1. Not to be confused with the late, great Manchester impresario.

recently-written song first, 'The Fan And The Bellows', lyrically inspired by the opening speech from Shakespeare's *Antony and Cleopatra*. The remaining songs were 'Here Today', 'Things I Wish I'd Said', another of our earliest tunes which, for absolutely no reason I could fathom, dealt with the situation I believed would exist between Dave and me one day, and 'Looking Inwardly', which didn't then have finished lyrics. The boffins seemed a bit nervous when I told them this, but I assured them that it would be fine.

The session got off to a slow start because of Scoffer, whose nerves got the better of him whenever he saw the red light come on. He had been droning on all morning about how he was the only serious musician in the band, and the irony was not lost on our producer and engineer. Once he started to get it right the frosty atmosphere began to dissipate, and we all started to relax. By lunchtime we'd recorded the bass and drums to all four songs, and stopped for a bite to eat. We were told that we could use the BBC canteen - 10p for a cup of tea, £1.50 for meat and two veg - very nice. The presenters from *Blue Peter* sat at the next table, but we politely pretended not to notice.

We returned to the studio, whereupon Dave and Reg began the process of recording the guitars, while I lay under the grand piano with a sheet of paper and a pencil, writing lyrics. Reg recorded his guitar parts immediately and without fuss, leaving Dave lots of time to be creative. I never ceased to be amazed by Reg's guitar playing - it seemed to flow so effortlessly from him, yet he was consistently the most original guitar player I've ever encountered, bar none. And no matter how often you rehearsed a song with Dave, when it came to putting it down on tape he'd always spontaneously throw in something totally unexpected and brilliant, and this day was no exception. He created fresh parts for every song on the session, elevating them to a new level.

Finally it was time to record the vocals and, to be honest, I don't remember that much about it, except for the moment when, not being used to the freshly written words for 'Looking Inwardly', I tossed them away mid-take: "I don't need these lyrics, what am I doing here?" Tony was laughing, and the producer, grinning, gave me the thumbs up.

The last stage was the mixing. The session was due to end at 10pm, but the boffins were still hard at it three hours later. It was now very obvious that they were enjoying this and, given the number of sessions they'd recorded - which they told us was in the hundreds - we felt very proud that they were keen to continue well past their deadline.

We were disappointed to learn that we wouldn't be allowed to take a copy of the session home with us, as the recordings now belonged exclusively to the BBC. We were told that we would have to wait until the session was broadcast the following week, and then tape it off the radio. We said our goodbyes, piled everything back into the van, and headed for our mate's flat in Notting Hill before making our way back to Manchester the following day.

We decided to back up the broadcast with a gig, so we contacted our friend Adrian at Bury Metro Arts and secured another date at the Derby Hall. In the local paper the advert for the concert read: 'LIVE: THE CHAMELEONS - FEATURED ON RADIO ONE, JOHN PEEL'.

The night before the broadcast we were listening to Peel's programme in Ali's flat, and at the close of his show Peel stunned us all. I can't remember his exact words, but he was telling his listeners not to miss the following night's programme, as he was featuring a very special session by a new band, and went on to tell the story of how Dave and I had collared him outside the BBC. He said that the session was quite wonderful. We just sat there beaming proudly at each other. The following night we all gathered again, cassette tape at the ready, our nerves jangling. Peel repeated the story, and after each track he would heap praise upon the band. "The Chameleons!" he exclaimed following one of the tracks, "Unheard until tonight on Radio One."

We were all impressed by how well our tracks sat amongst the programme's other content, which featured records by some very respectable bands, like The Cure and Siouxsie And The Banshees. Our music leapt powerfully from the speakers, and it was one of the most unforgettable moments I ever had with the band. Practically anyone who was anyone had recorded early sessions for his programme - so many great artists and bands - and here we were, taking our place amongst them.

The very next day a man with an American accent introduced himself on the telephone as Danny Goodwin, and said he was with Virgin Music Publishing. Danny and his boss Richard had heard the session and wanted to know if they could see the band live. I told them that the only gig we had scheduled at present was at the Derby Hall in Bury the following week. He had trouble pronouncing Bury and wanted to know where it was, and then asked if I could arrange to get them in.

By the day of the gig the band's reputation had spread, and we were surprised to find ourselves playing a sold out venue. Scoffer, in typical fashion, refused to pick up Dave and Reg in his car, so they had to make their way to the venue on the bus. Sure enough, the Virgin boys showed up and Danny Goodwin introduced his boss, Richard Griffith, and we exchanged a few words before the show. The band was on form that night, and we all felt it had gone well. Our instinct was confirmed later when Danny and Richard came backstage and told us that they were seriously impressed, and wanted to sign the band to Virgin Publishing and bring us down to London. Not having a manager, we had little or no understanding of how the business worked, so they had to explain to us what a publishing deal was. They would buy up the rights to all songs we wrote, in return for a royalty. We were rather confused by this. "Yeah, but it's a record deal we want," Dave said.

Danny explained that getting a record deal for the band would become their responsibility, and that it would present no problem to them.

"What about money?" a voice boomed from the back of the room. We turned to where Scoffer now sat with his young girlfriend on his lap. "Well, obviously," Danny continued, "we'll negotiate something by way of an advance against your publishing royalties."

It was a fair and valid question of course, but inside I was seething. It seemed to me that what we were talking about here were advances on songwriting royalties. Dave, Reg, and I wrote and arranged all the songs. We would then take Scoffer through these loose arrangements during rehearsals, step by step, telling him exactly what we wanted him to do. Scoffer had no creative input and despite his relative affluence, when it came to contributing financially, his attitude left a lot to be desired. If he hoped he was going to receive a quarter of the band's songwriting royalties then he was sadly mistaken, I thought to myself, but said nothing for the time being. Later that week we arranged to travel to Virgin Mansions in London to talk about the publishing deal. It hadn't dawned on us until that night that finding a regular drummer hadn't been the only necessity, and that we'd neglected another role, arguably the most important - that of manager.

Our shift in fortune had been so swift, it hadn't even occurred to us that we'd need one. Danny and Richard had come to Virgin from Island Records, and Richard had originally been the manager of Ultravox when John Foxx had fronted the band before being replaced by Midge Ure. During the John Foxx era I'd loved the band and had seen them perform a few times, including one gig at Middleton Civic Hall. By that time the escalating violence deterred people from attending the venue, and Foxx walked on stage to perform the band's opening song, 'I Want To Be A Machine', to about thirty or forty people. I was one of them, standing directly in front of the stage singing along to every word. Amazingly, Danny not only remembered the gig, but also remembered seeing me at the front mouthing the words, as I seemed to be the only person in the room who was familiar with the band's songs. I thought he was having me on at first, but he'd remembered everything down to the last detail: "You were outside at the back of the venue talking with Stevie Shears," he correctly recalled. Later that month Danny introduced me to John Foxx, whom they still managed on a professional basis since he'd gone solo, and he was a nice, approachable, unpretentious fella.

The first order of business was an awkward one. They immediately picked up on the tension that existed between Scoffer and the rest of the band, and asked us what the situation was. We explained that we'd asked Scoffer to play as a temporary measure and that, in the minds of Reg, Dave and me, he wasn't a full member of the band in the true sense. His attitude had been steadily driving us all mad, and he wasn't part of the song writing process anyway, but things had been moving so fast, we hadn't had an opportunity to resolve the situation. Richard seemed somewhat relieved to hear this. I don't suppose Virgin Music would have relished investing time, money, and effort into signing us, only to see a change of line-up further down the road because we couldn't get along. The one and only question Scoffer had asked concerned money, and in my more cynical moments I came to think this was why they seemed wary of him. In any event, we resolved to deal with the problem directly on our return to Manchester.

In later years, Scoffer was to tell people that we fired him from the group because of his looks. Such a statement was typical of him in some ways and, at the time, it made Dave and me in particular quite angry, but I mellowed with the passing years. It is true that the man had a face like a Mexican pizza, which was due to an unfortunate blood condition[2]. However, if he'd believed in what we were trying to achieve, if he'd pitched in and pursued our aims as energetically and as passionately as the rest of us, then he would truly have been one of us, and no power on earth could have split us up. But this simply wasn't the case - Scoffer was as different from us as salt is from sugar.

At the time I was so fed up with him that I didn't give it a second thought, but later I came to regret how we'd treated him. Two wrongs do not a right make, and I've never been a vindictive or vengeful person. Every budding musician dreams of being signed, and it's no small thing to snatch the dream away from someone, but my main regret is that we allowed the situation to come to this.

---

2. One evening at rehearsal during a quiet moment, Scoffer asked Dave, "So what about my spots Dave, what do you think?" Dave was just about to say, "Yeah Scoffer, they're pretty bad, have you seen a doctor?" when Scoffer cut him off. "Yeah," he continued, "they cost a fortune but I think they look really snazzy." He'd been referring to the new set of spotlights he'd just had fitted to the front of his car.

Dave, Reg, and I sat in Richard's office, and listened to a phone conversation between Danny and an A&R rep at CBS, during which he told her he'd found the best band since U2. It took a good five minutes to realise that Danny was talking about us. The hype had begun, and suddenly everything became increasingly ridiculous and unreal.

At the end of the conversation a youngish man with long red hair and a beard, wearing a T-shirt featuring a photo of Lady Diana Spencer emblazoned with the words 'IF IT AINT VIRGIN IT AINT WORTH A FUCK', entered the room grinning like a lunatic, arms spread wide so that we could all read what was on the shirt, and asked us what we thought of it. We just sat there staring at him, not really knowing how to react. Finally, he left the office, giggling. "Oh," said Richard, casually, "that was Richard Branson." I'm willing to bet he didn't wear that shirt for his knighthood ceremony.

Over the next month, there were quite a few meetings of this kind and, after consulting with a lawyer, a publishing deal was negotiated and signed. Virgin granted us a small, yet adequate, advance, so we were able to think about buying some serious equipment. Danny and Richard then set about organising what were to be our first gigs in London, while we got on with the process of finding a permanent drummer.

We had become quite friendly with Mike Sweeney, a DJ at Piccadilly Radio[3] in Manchester, and he agreed to make an announcement on air without naming the band, along with a few likes and influences, and a phone number. Auditioning drummers was an embarrassing and unpleasant experience; we'd usually be able to tell within five minutes of meeting someone that they were wrong for the band. Not just from the way they looked, I hasten to add - although with the guy that walked in with hair down to his arse and Quo patches sewn into his denim, this was certainly a factor - but we could ascertain a lot from the general tone of conversation. Not wishing to show them the door without at least giving them a chance, though, we'd sadistically allow them to spend thirty minutes setting up their drums and play along to a few bars before telling them that we'd let them know. This would be followed by another thirty minutes spent making light conversation as they took it all down again. I don't recall how many people we put to the test in our little room above the Railway Inn, but the search seemed endless.

I'd long since discarded my old £20 Arbiter bass from The Clichés days, having damaged it during a gig, in favour of a slightly more expensive

---

3. These days it's called Key 103 – JL.

and worse-sounding Ibanez. On the day, with only around £75 in my pocket, it had been the best of a poor choice. With Richard Branson's money burning a hole in my pocket I was now able to pick out a Fender Jazz bass. The auditions were in full swing when I lumbered into the rehearsal room that evening, struggling with my rather heavy purchase, and first laid eyes on John Lever. I knew right away that he'd be the one.

When it came to playing the drums, Scoffer was a hard act to follow - after all he'd been having drum lessons from an early age - but John seemed to have the songs pretty much down, and the chemistry felt good. Regardless of how technically proficient a musician is, if the chemistry isn't there, nothing is going to happen. At first Reg was a little doubtful. "His bass drum's a bit sloppy," he grumbled, but after a while even he agreed that John was the last piece of the puzzle, and The Chameleons were fully formed at last.

John hails from Tameside, which was on the opposite side of the county from us. Some found his sense of humour difficult to follow, but he frequently had us all in stitches. He would keep us entertained for hours with his stories. During his first driving test John knocked an old man off his bicycle. "So," he said, turning to the driving instructor, "I suppose that means I've failed, does it?" He did eventually pass, though, and bought himself an old yellow Ford Escort van, the like of which I've never seen before or since. Whenever he would give us a ride in it he'd always apologise for the horrid smell that permeated the inside, explaining that, no matter how hard he tried, he could never get rid of it. "Something's died in here," he'd say, "I just can't find it."

One of my favourite stories was of the time when, while working as a postman, he'd found himself in dire need of a piss while out on his round one morning. Being in the middle of suburbia and somewhat desperate, he went into a public telephone box, leaving his sack of mail outside, and began urinating. As he did so, he turned to see a middle-aged woman standing outside waiting to make a phone call, so he immediately grabbed the telephone and pretended to have a conversation as a torrent of urine flooded the floor of the phone box.

He told us of his previous band, The Politicians, fronted by a man who seemed intent on getting inside John's pants, and who wrote strange songs about office stationery. John and the band were playing support to the Bootleg Beatles on the night of John Lennon's assassination. "So," John had asked the Lennon clone, "what are you going to do now, then?"

I have to say that I found John's drumming style very odd indeed. At first we thought he was left-handed because of the way he set up his kit, but he explained that he had bought the kit without having the slightest idea how to set it up. Being a Genesis fan, he studied a poster of their drummer, Phil Collins, and set up his kit according to the picture, not realising, of course, that Collins is left-handed. Consequently he taught himself to play open-handed on a left-handed drum kit with his left foot on the kick drum, which probably explained the slack technique that had disgruntled Reg during his audition. By the time he realised his mistake it had been too late to rectify it, but his unusual technique gave him a distinctive and individual style, and with time his bass and snare drum work tightened up considerably.

Not long after John had been welcomed in to the fold, we were forced to vacate our room over the Railway Inn. The couple that ran the pub didn't ask us to leave - instead they squeezed us out gradually, putting more and more furniture in the room so that in the end it became almost impossible to work there. My cousin Daryl came to the rescue when it transpired he'd gone into partnership with Mike Harding, a well-known comedian and folk singer. They were building a recording studio about ten minutes away from the Railway Inn and he offered to rent us regular rehearsal space at the new complex, and so Moonraker Studios became our new home.

Following Peel's glowing endorsement of the band on Radio One, we suddenly found we were attracting local media attention. First came the *Manchester Evening News,* which ran a feature on the band in their pop music section. We met the journalist as arranged and related the story of how we'd landed the Peel session despite not having found a name for the band, and gave him a tape of the session along with a publicity photo that Tony had taken. The following Friday the paper ran the story around a photo of The Boomtown Rats above the caption: 'THE CHAMELEONS: FAME WITH NO NAME'. The article took the line that we were attracting a lot of attention without doing anything to earn it, barely mentioning the music at all. The idea that a band could secure a Radio One session and a major publishing deal based purely on the quality of their songwriting seemed hopelessly beyond the writer in question.

We fared a little better with the *New Musical Express.* Mick Duffy, who Dave and I had gotten to know following our little adventure in Leeds with Mark Hoyle and IQ Zero, was now a freelance writer for the *NME,* and he phoned Dave and asked for an interview. Kev Cummins, who'd taken the photograph of the Sex Pistols in which I can be seen in the audience all those years ago, was commissioned to do the photo shoot for the article. After spending a few hours wandering around Manchester, he chose a shot of us sitting beneath a Warhol screen print of Marilyn Monroe that used to hang in the Whitworth Art Gallery.

During the shoot I asked him about a set of live photographs he'd taken in 1973 of David Bowie during his final *Ziggy Stardust* tour. I was interested to know how he'd managed to get such clear, unhindered shots, as they are amongst the best photos of Ziggy that I'd ever seen. "You must have been getting jostled about by the crowd, surely?" I asked. He told us that, on the contrary, during the tour he'd gone to Leeds specifically to photograph Bowie, having learned that there was to be a matinee performance at around 5pm that evening. All the regular shows had sold out months in advance and, knowing that many of his audience were in their early teens, Bowie's management had added the matinee performances to accommodate them. When Cummins had turned up at the early performance in Leeds, there hadn't been more than fifty or sixty people in the room. Bowie did the show anyway and Cummins was able to get his shots unhindered.

A London journalist who was in the process of producing a compilation album featuring up-and-coming bands for a London-based label called Statik Records, read of The Chameleons in the *NME* and approached us about contributing a track. This gave us the first real opportunity to record with John for the first time. We booked ourselves into Cargo Studios and decided to record 'Here Today'. The album was to be titled *Your Secret's Safe With Us*, and we were all excited about being on vinyl at last.

After rooting around the studio I found a plastic whirly tube gathering dust in a corner. This was a child's toy that had been very popular for a while in the seventies. The idea is, you swing the tube around your head and the wind rushing through it causes a musical drone that varies according to the speed of rotation. It reminded me, in a minimalist sort of way, of the sound we'd heard the night we'd dropped acid on Tandle Hill, and I decided I wanted to use it on the track. Over the years, the sound would become a regular feature on our albums.

Sometime after the *NME* article appeared, I received a phone call from a man I'd never heard of, who claimed to be the manager of Echo And The Bunnymen and founder of the Liverpool label Zoo Records. He sounded a bit irate on the phone and it took him a while to get to the point, but it seemed that along with another producer he also had a band of his own called Lori and The Chameleons; furthermore he told me that the two of them had produced the first Bunnymen album as The Chameleons. "You must know that!" he barked. I told him that I didn't know that, as I didn't have any records by Echo And The Bunnymen, which at the time was true. He remarked sarcastically that he found that hard to believe but, at any rate, we would have to change the name of our band. I sympathised and said it was unfortunate, but explained to him that changing our name at this point would be rather awkward as our John Peel session had been broadcast only a few weeks earlier, and we'd already had national coverage in the *NME*. Changing the name now would really fuck things up, I thought to myself with a heavy heart. However, what sympathy I had for the guy suddenly evaporated when he said, "Well put it this way, if you don't change the name I'll get a few guys I know here in Liverpool to come over to Manchester and fuck you up." I shouted back at him to go ahead, telling him what I thought of him in no uncertain terms before slamming down the phone.

Later, Danny and Richard told me that this guy had been on to them too, once he'd learned we were signing with Virgin Publishing. He had initially threatened to sue, but had then offered to drop the matter if he could produce the band. We declined his offer and never heard anything from him again. Over the years, I would occasionally be asked if we were the same Chameleons that had produced the first Bunnymen album. "Oh yeah," I'd invariably reply, tongue firmly in cheek, "we taught them everything they know."

Meanwhile, in London, Danny and Richard were putting together three showcase gigs for The Chameleons in order to hype the band to major record companies. As things developed, it dawned on us that we lacked a great deal of experience when it came to live performances. I think we'd only played about five gigs - none of them with John - and as the dates drew nearer Dave, John and I grew increasingly nervous. Reg, though, never seemed to get ruffled. Outwardly, he was the epitome of cool and calm. Inwardly, of course, he was bricking it just as much as the rest of us.

The first two shows were to be as support to other up-and-coming acts. I don't remember the band we played alongside on that first night, but suddenly the idea of what a showcase gig was became painfully clear to me. The audience was mainly made up of record company representatives with names like Ashley or Rupert. A few of them engaged me in conversation before the gig, but most of them were less than interesting to talk to, and I'd brush them off - possibly not a wise attitude to have when you're trying to secure a record deal, but an honest one nonetheless.

The most irritating encounter I had by far was with a very senior executive from CBS. He was an American, in his late forties, dressed in what was obviously his gig-suit. This consisted of a pair of black and white baseball boots, dark blue denim jeans with matching jacket, and a red baseball cap, none of which sat too well with his thick rimmed spectacles and great, brown, bushy beard. Beside him, at the end of a leash, was a large brown bloodhound. "Do you like The Clash?" he asked me.

"Yes, of course," I replied.

"The great thing about The Clash, in my view..." he began and then went on to talk the biggest load of tripe I'd ever heard.

"Where are you from?" I asked him, cutting him off.

"CBS," he replied.

"No, I mean where are *you* from?"

"Oh excuse me, Cleveland."

"Ah!" I murmured knowingly, nodding my head. "Of course you are." Pausing to enjoy his puzzled look, which now perfectly matched the expression on the face of his dog, I rejoined the others.

Danny was in the middle of his umpteenth pep talk, telling us that everyone out there understood that we weren't very experienced, but not to let that bother us and we should try to relax and enjoy it. I told him that I'd already devised a way of illustrating my lack of experience and stuck an 'L' plate on the back of my jacket. It just seemed to suit such a ridiculous situation. In any event, the show seemed to go quite well, although our nervousness and dissatisfaction at playing to an industry audience was obvious. Danny came in and told us that many of the label reps were quite impressed, and would be returning to watch the band over the following two nights.

The show went much the way of the first, but afterwards we were graced by the presence of, as far as we were concerned, a genuine VIP. During the run-up to the gigs Danny and Richard had asked us, given the choice, whom would we like on board as producer for our first album. After debating amongst ourselves, we decided that, given such a choice, it would have to be Steve Lillywhite. We'd all been impressed with the work he'd done on U2's debut album and, judging from their early singles, he'd crafted the sound that had come to define the band. John, in particular, was a huge fan of his and would buy records simply on the basis that Lillywhite had produced them. In addition to the U2 records, I had particularly enjoyed the second, rockier Ultravox album, *Ha-Ha-Ha*. Imagine the look on our faces, then, when Danny walked into the dressing room and introduced us to our favourite producer. The meeting was relaxed, with everyone laughing and joking, and we were proud when he told us that he'd been impressed by the band, and was definitely interested in producing us. Not for the first or last time, I was struck by the completely surreal nature of the situation, given the pace of recent developments.

The final showcase gig was by far the best. The venue was in the basement of one of London's central colleges, and we immediately noticed a big improvement in the band's drinks rider, which consisted of an entire crate of imported beer. By this time all the bullshit was beginning to get to us, so we were determined that we were going to distance ourselves from the hype, loosen up and just try to enjoy it for what it was. We were fed up with being paraded in front of London's music business elite. As far as Danny and Richard were concerned, the objective had been to provoke a bidding auction, which seemed to me to be a long way from what I thought we were about. Additionally, I'd been disappointed to learn that Island Records, the only major label I'd been remotely interested in signing to, had officially passed on the band, and I seem to recall I was in a sulk about it. From that point on I lost all enthusiasm for impressing record companies. Despite everything that was happening around me since we'd secured the Peel session, I'd retained a rather naïve, punk attitude and sense of integrity and was openly cynical about major record labels, feeling we'd be far more at home with the likes of Cherry Red or Rough Trade. We had approached these companies early on, of course, but although they told us they liked the music they felt that we were very much a major label concern and had advised us to go with the present flow.

We took the stage feeling more relaxed and blasé than at any other time during the whole charade, and as a result we turned in a blinding set. I could tell from Danny's reaction during the show, and afterwards, that it had been exceptional and we'd delivered precisely at the right time, albeit inadvertently. Every label rep in the place wanted to sign the band immediately, and we were told afterwards to turn up at Virgin Mansions the next day for a couple of very important meetings.

The following morning we arrived to discover that the first of those meetings was with Miles Copeland, who then was managing a band called The Police. Copeland was one of the most powerful independent players in town. I liked The Police very much and knew one or two things about the band and about Miles, including the fact that he'd once worked for the CIA. A man by the name of Jeremy Pierce accompanied Miles at the meeting, and was introduced as Miles' business partner. Over the space of the next two hours or so, Miles told us that he wanted to be involved in the management and development of The Chameleons. Pierce would handle the day-to-day business of the group, while Miles himself would act as consultant, and we would sign to their own independent record label - although the label wasn't truly independent as it ran under the auspices of A&M Records via their distribution outlets.

Miles had a very hypnotic manner about him; in fact, I was reminded of Kaa, the cartoon boa constrictor in the movie Jungle Book. "If you sign with us," Miles concluded, "I'll guarantee that you'll all be millionaires within two years." He paused for a moment to allow this to sink in. Suddenly the silence was broken a sound not unlike a chorus of chainsaws. Reg, exhausted by the previous nights' exertions, had been lying on one of the office couches and, having fallen asleep during Miles' sales pitch, was now snoring his head off. The room erupted into laughter, with the exception of Pierce, who shot irritated glances at Miles as we all laughed hysterically.

Had such an offer come from Miles Copeland alone, I dare say we would have considered it seriously, but there was something about Pierce, something I couldn't exactly put my finger on, that I didn't trust. The thought of him managing the band made me shudder, and I was relieved to find that the others shared my misgivings. Hoping to strike while the iron was still hot, Pierce followed us to a nearby pub for a drink, while Miles said his goodbyes and left. Our conversations with him only served to reinforce our doubts, and in the end we just told him we'd think about it. "Don't think too long," he said, "you're riding on the crest of a wave at the moment." I felt I understood what he was saying. The excitement around the band was very much due to the PR talents of Danny and Richard. The Chameleons were good, but we weren't that good - not yet. I hadn't fallen into the trap of believing our own hype; I knew that we had to capitalise on the excitement surrounding the band before it dissipated, whereupon all the sharks would move on to feed on the Next Big Thing.

"By the way," Pierce said on leaving, "I understand you're meeting with CBS this afternoon. I work in their business department. I'll be leaving soon to work with Miles full-time, but until I do, I'd rather that they didn't hear of our meeting. It isn't done for a person who works for a company to approach an artist on behalf of another company. It could get me into a lot of trouble."

One of the first people we were introduced to in London had been Annie Roseberry, who had just moved to CBS from Island Records, for whom she'd signed U2. In fact it had been Annie at the other end of the phone that first afternoon when Danny had been singing our praises, and she'd been around the group ever since. We were all very fond of her; she was by far the most likeable of all the record executives that we'd met. Annie was extremely keen to sign the band, so we headed for the offices of CBS in Soho Square for a meeting with her and her boss, Muff Winwood, head of the A&R department.

Muff Winwood was a curious character, more like a school teacher than a record company executive. He'd started out as a successful musician with the band Traffic (fronted by his brother, guitarist Steve Winwood) before moving on to record production. I knew that he'd produced Sparks in the early seventies, and that later he'd produced the debut Dire Straits album, which I also loved. Winwood told us he genuinely liked The Chameleons, and that he wanted to sign us to the Epic label. Epic was owned by CBS and operated out of the same building. They outlined a deal that would run to five albums. My chief concern, given the rather large investment that was being contemplated here, was that they'd expect us to have immediate chart success. I'd spent some time looking around the offices, and all the acts - with the arguable exception of The Clash - were mainstream, middle-of-the-road pop acts such as the newly signed Altered Images and the now horridly-evolved Adam And The Ants. Granted, they'd supported and developed The Psychedelic Furs - and this seemed to carry some weight with Dave and John in particular - but I wasn't impressed, because by this time I disliked that band and resented the comparisons that came later from the media.

Winwood assured us that there would not be pressure to deliver instant chart success, and that singles were merely promotional tools for albums these days. He went on to explain that the cost of marketing singles was so great that it was rare for anyone to make money from them, and that he saw The Chameleons as a long-term albums band in much the same vein as U2. He outlined our development as a gradual build over three albums, by which time they hoped that we'd be firmly established. Winwood struck us all as a very straightforward, honest individual. However, such discussions were incredibly complex and I realised very quickly that we were well out of our depth. Danny Goodwin, who seemed to have developed some affection for us, was doing his best to act as a guardian angel and steer us through the mire, but the absence of a personal manager - someone we could trust to have our best interests at heart - meant that we never really stood a chance from the beginning.

We discussed Steve Lillywhite's apparent interest in producing our first album, and Winwood told us that if we were able to agree terms and signed with Epic, we could conceivably be in the studio working with Lillywhite within a few weeks of putting pen to paper. He knew, of course, that this would be a great incentive to us. He was quickly able to suss that our music was the only aspect of all this nonsense that we truly cared about, and that the prospect of working with someone who at the time we all regarded as the best record producer around was tantalising.

The subject of personal management eventually came up and we ruefully admitted that we didn't know anyone who fitted the bill. They told us that they knew quite a few people, professional managers with lots of experience, who might be interested in taking the band on, and offered to put us in touch. Naïvely, we told them we were open to the idea.

Over the next couple of months we had quite a few meetings of this sort with a whole host of music industry luminaries, and all the time I had the feeling that I was walking through some kind of hallucination. This seemed like a dream come true, but it was happening too fast. Only months before, Reg and I had been humping vinegar in a warehouse and now here we were, sitting at large tables in corporate boardrooms discussing sums of money and resources that were undreamed of, even by our ambitious standards. I'd read enough rock biographies to know that, usually, if such things came at all it was only after years of relentless effort spent in ignominious obscurity, which at the very least made for a good story once success came. Where was our story? It was extremely hard for me to see the situation with any degree of clarity.

I wasn't happy about the prospect of signing with CBS, though. I knew that much. Every visit confirmed my worst fears. I had little or no respect for the acts on the label, either artistically or for the way they'd chosen to market themselves, and in this assessment I would have to include The Clash. As a teenager I'd loved them with a passion, but had since come to regard the band as a total sell-out. Walking around the offices visiting the various departments I found the label to be staffed with airheads, bullshit merchants and accountants, and every encounter would leave me more cynical and depressed. Gradually however, Dave, Reg, and John came to favour CBS/Epic, which defied my understanding. Having said that, all the major labels - with the exception of Chris Blackwell's Island Records - had credibility problems as far as I was concerned.

Following that initial meeting, Winwood took us all to lunch at a rather plush restaurant in Soho. Beneath the surface, it was little more than a trendy burger house, and Ali, who was the only vegetarian amongst us at that time, was bemused when he was served what appeared to be a large bowl of raw cauliflower. During the meal we made small talk until Winwood finally asked how we'd spent the earlier part of the day. I told him of the meeting with Miles Copeland and almost mentioned his partner, Jeremy Pierce, when I remembered his parting words, so hesitating for a moment, I just said that I wasn't able to recall his name. "Jeremy Pierce!" said a voice from down the table. Dave and I shot nervous glances at each other and all eyes fell on Reg.

"Nah, Reg," said Dave, leaping into the fray, "that was last night at the gig, you're getting mixed up."

"No, it was Jeremy Pierce," Reg said again.

I glanced over at Winwood, who was now holding his fork motionless in front of his mouth, a look of total surprise on his face. I desperately tried to get Reg's attention in the hope of shooting a warning glance at him, but his eyes never left his plate. "No, Reg you're wrong," I insisted, "the guy's name was Julian something or other."

"It was Jeremy Pierce!" Reg exclaimed, now visibly irritated. Winwood suddenly looked at his watch and apologised, saying something about being late for another meeting. He rose abruptly, settled the bill, and left so fast that the only thing missing was Roadrunner's beep-beep.

"Reg!" Dave asked, exasperated, "Didn't you hear what Jeremy said before he went?"

"Nah," said Reg, "I wasn't listening."

The upshot was that Pierce left CBS earlier than he'd planned, but we reasoned that he only had himself to blame. After all, how could he be trusted to manage the band when he couldn't even manage his own affairs properly?

With each passing day, the others, just as I feared, gravitated toward CBS as the label of choice. Danny and Richard tried valiantly to steer us away - their only reason for courting CBS in the first place had been to add momentum to the hype. But Annie, seriously impressed with the band, had come to believe in the band's potential, and with her we seemed to share the same language when it came to taste and aspiration.

When we weren't in London being shunted round from pillar to post, we'd lock ourselves away in Moonraker Studios, and in the midst of all this excitement the new tunes came thick and fast. This was the period that 'Second Skin' began to come together, and a rather rocky song called 'Don't Fall'. We had performed an improvised version of the song at the showcase gigs, and the hastily scribbled lyrics, penned the night before the first of these shows in my hotel room, reflected to some degree the desperation I was feeling about our general situation.

We then retreated to Cargo Studios in Rochdale to record some fresh demos. John B, the owner of Cargo, had recently taken on a resident house engineer, Colin Richardson, who was able to bring a lot of good ideas and enthusiasm to what we were doing. By the time the recordings were finished, it had been more or less decided that, despite my protests, CBS/Epic was to be the label of choice. Annie had called into the studio to see how things were progressing, and it was encouraging to see that she loved the songs, although a few of them would ultimately fall by the wayside, only to emerge years later on dodgy retrospective albums.

During our negotiations we also met with quite a few candidates for the role of manager. Record companies don't usually like to deal directly with bands; artists can be temperamental, idealistic and unrealistic, and so they prefer to see someone at the helm with whom they can relate and communicate. All the candidates had come with quite impressive CVs and prior high-level management experience, but for one reason or another they were all rejected. I can't for the life of me remember how we came to decide on the successful candidate, who, for the sake of this narrative, I'll refer to as Moz.

Moz lived in the Midlands and, in previous years, had been the manager of a well-known and quite successful chart band that we'd all had a great deal of respect for. After this band's inevitable disintegration, he hovered on the fringes of the music business for a while looking for his next gig, so to speak. He seemed very straight by our standards, but he was generally well thought of, and obviously experienced. It was decided that we'd work together on a trial basis, and if all parties were happy at the end of this, we'd sign some kind of management contract.

At last, the lawyers were satisfied with their negotiations (and the size of their invoices, no doubt) and we were told that everything was ready and awaiting our signatures. Steve Lillywhite had agreed to spend a week with the band at RAK Studios in central London to produce a single, and the signing of contracts was scheduled to coincide with that. In the meantime, he was to come up to the rehearsal room in Middleton to hear us play some of the songs that were being considered.

Lillywhite told us that his favourite contender for a single was 'The Fan And The Bellows', which was no surprise as it was also the favourite choice at CBS. He also homed in on a new song we'd written called 'Nostalgia', which they'd earmarked for a possible follow-up single, although it's probably my least favourite song that we did, chiefly because I felt I could never sing it properly.

Finally, we ran through the outline of an idea still very much in development, but one that we found sufficiently exciting to want to pursue. The song had only the barest of arrangements and hardly any melody or chorus, but Steve told us that if we agreed to his two initial suggestions then we'd be free to record the new idea, and that pleased everyone. Later I saw my second cousin Daryl, and happened to mention that Steve Lillywhite had dropped by his studio the previous day. His face was a picture, and the sound of his jaw hitting the floor reverberated for miles.

In an alley by the churchyard where the sleeve photo for 'As High As You Can Go' was taken.
Photo: Tony Skinkis

We returned to London to sign the CBS contracts and begin work on our debut single. Everyone's spirits were high, though I couldn't dispel the nagging doubts at the back of my mind. CBS/Epic had just released a single by Altered Images, from Glasgow. Ali had bought the record, 'Dead Pop Stars', in the wake of their very impressive Peel session. It was produced by Siouxsie And The Banshees' bass player Steve Severin, who managed to inject just the right amount of dark tension to counterbalance the rather sweet and unique talent of the band's singer Clare Grogan. The result was a great and powerful debut single. Naturally, the band had wanted Severin to produce the album too, but Epic had insisted on a tried and tested mainstream producer. Martin Rushent had found considerable success producing the once brilliant, but by this time rather bland, Human League. There was no denying that he had been instrumental in turning this pioneering, underground electronic combo into a veritable hit machine, so Epic persuaded Altered Images, in the interests of commercial success, to hire Rushent instead.

On hearing the results of Rushent's involvement with Altered Images, I was mortified. He'd managed to turn what, initially, had been an interesting and unusual new band into little more than pop fodder. Having said that, it was a ploy that worked, much to the irritation of many who had to listen to it on heavy rotation on the radio. Their third single, 'Happy Birthday', was now riding high in the charts, while the smiling face of Clare Grogan, adapted by the record company to a palatable and marketable sweet-little-girl look, complete with pink hair ribbons, graced all the leading glossy pop magazines.

The night before we were due to sign the contracts, I sat beside Tony in my hotel room with a very heavy heart. By rights, it should have been the proudest and happiest night of my life thus far, but in reality, I had become quite depressed about it. CBS/Epic were about as mainstream as it got, and I knew that if we resisted that, if we didn't fit in with their view of what a young rock group should be about, we were going to have serious problems and perhaps blow the best and only chance we might have to establish ourselves. I felt that The Chameleons were selling out before we'd even started. Tony did his best to reassure me, "Don't worry, Queens Park[4], you're not going to lose it. We'll look after you, have a drink." The two of us then proceeded to drain the hotel mini-bar.

---

4. Tony's rhyming slang for Mark.

6. ANGELS AND DEVILS

The next morning we gathered in the CBS boardroom with our new manager to sign on the dotted line. Danny was present too, and I could tell by the look in his eyes that he also felt we were making the wrong decision.

Over the course of the previous months, both he and Richard had tried to steer us in another direction, but this plan too had been flawed in my view. The very respectable music business figure that they had wanted us to sign with, having been instrumental in building Island Records alongside Blackwell, was now striking out on his own - but he still hadn't sorted out fundamental aspects of his organisation, such as distribution and major backing. Going with him would have meant that we'd have had to wait before starting work on a record, and after all these months of negotiations and discussion we were eager to make a start. After the signing, Danny stayed for a celebratory drink before saying his goodbyes. I think I saw him about three times over the following three years.

We stayed at the Sherlock Holmes Hotel on Baker Street, which was a step up from what we were used to on the Bayswater Road. Moz had used it a lot during his managerial career and it looked impressive, although it wasn't quite as grand as the plush reception area suggested. The hotel was used to having rock bands stay there and knew exactly where to place them, ignoring some of the wilder antics that young bands can get up to away from home. In our case, this amounted to little more than water fights up and down the corridors in the early hours of the morning, and filling ashtrays with spent roaches.

Despite the relatively posh lodgings, however, we'd still scoot across town and spend time with our mate James at his new flat in Notting Hill. James was the rather mad son of a wealthy industrialist and had a great sense of fun. While our class differences were obvious, he was never a snob, always treating everyone with respect and exhibiting a great generosity and a stylish sense of humour. We often stayed at his flat, getting very stoned together and listening to his interesting and richly varied record collection. James had a house rule that you could only play a single side of any album at any one time; I was thus introduced to a whole range of artists and records that I would never have otherwise discovered: Tuxedomoon for example, The Penguin Café Orchestra, Was Not Was, Throbbing Gristle, and the brilliant Cherry Red compilations of Morgan Fisher. My favourite record in James' collection formed part of a box set by Godley And Creme, formerly of 10cc, entitled *Consequences*, chiefly because it featured a specially commissioned play, *The Hurricane* by Peter Cook, whom I adored.

Despite a reputation to the contrary - Peter Hook from New Order used to refer to us as 'the Christian band' - we could party with the best of them, thanks largely to James' tutelage. One particular evening James invited me onto the back of his motorcycle, intent on riding over to Tottenham to visit a friend. The fact that we were both off our faces on acid at the time didn't daunt us in the slightest. That night John Peel had decided to repeat the session that we'd recorded for him earlier in the year, and the others were listening to the programme at the flat. Growing rather worried about us, as James and I were now considerably overdue, they phoned Peel at the studio and, after explaining the situation, John relayed a request on the air for us to phone them and put their minds at rest. Unfortunately, we didn't hear it.

James had taken me to meet a Hells Angel friend of his called Ed, a rather intimidating guy until you got to know him. As I sat there smoking some particularly strong weed and getting mellow, I scanned the walls of the sitting room, which had been decorated with every kind of sword known to man, including an antique Samurai sword. Suddenly my eyes rested on a framed photograph depicting the burnt out foundations of a house while a couple of police officers stood by raking the damage. "What's the story with that photograph, Ed?" I asked him.

"Oh that," he replied not even glancing at it. "That was a party we went to once. 'Course it didn't look like that when we got there."

Later that week we arrived at RAK Studios to start work on our first single, and were greeted by Steve Lillywhite's regular engineer, Phil Thornalley, who would later become The Cure's bass player. However, the first day proved to be rather a trying one and, before long, I was questioning our decision to choose Lillywhite to produce the record.

Having decided to begin with 'The Fan and the Bellows', Steve started programming a drum computer rather than setting up John's kit. Computerised drum machines had become all the rage following Martin Rushent's chart success with Human League, and when I questioned the wisdom of this, Lillywhite actually mentioned Rushent as though he were a shining example. "How many hit records have you had?" he finally snapped.

"None," I admitted.

"Well then!" said Lillywhite, and continued to programme the machine.

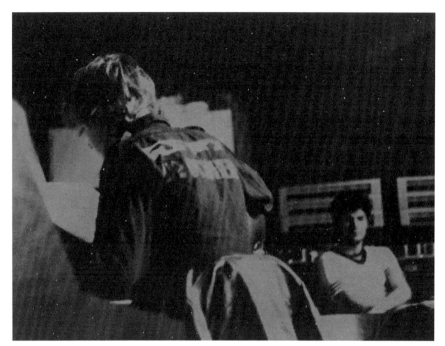

'In Shreds' session, with Steve Lillywhite in the U2 t-shirt.   Photo: Tony Skinkis

I just couldn't get my head around this at all. The Human League were a synthesiser band, drum machines sat well with them and always had done, but we were a guitar band. Besides, if we'd wanted a record that sounded like Martin Rushent had produced it, we would have hired Martin Rushent. Steve Lillywhite was renowned for his live drum sound, and yet here he was spending hours hooking up a drum computer. Dave, too, had his doubts and said so. "Look, I'm only going to use the bass drum and snare," Lillywhite retorted. "Let's just try it my way, okay?"

What this meant in practical terms was that after the computerised bass and snare pattern had been recorded, John was expected to record his high-hat beats, snare rolls and symbol crashes as separate overdubs without being able to play his full kit. This would have proved difficult for the most experienced drummer, but for a young man on his first recording session, wracked with nerves under the watchful eyes of a producer who he'd idolised for years, it was a long and laborious process. Both the approach and the finished result felt completely wrong to us, and we said so - but no-one was listening.

Then there was the actual tuning of the instruments. In the past we'd always tuned our instruments by ear, but Lillywhite had said, wisely, that we'd have to use electronic tuners. "I don't work with bands that don't use tuners," he said. The problem with this was that none of us had perfect pitch, so we'd gradually been tuning the guitars higher and higher, and now we didn't sound right when all the guitars were tuned down to concert pitch. We eventually realised that by tuning the guitars down, we'd lost many of the natural harmonics generated by the reverb channels on our amps. As a compromise, we tuned the guitars two semitones higher, lower than they had been, but still high enough to get the harmonics ringing again. One positive side-effect of this was that we suddenly found we were snapping less strings during performances.

The next problem stemmed from a disagreement over the lyrics to the song. The label was adamant that 'Bellows' would be the band's first single, but they had a problem with the words 'Cupid masturbates'. "You can't say that on the radio," they kept insisting.

"It's a perfectly acceptable word, it's in the dictionary and everything," I protested.

"That's beside the point," they said. "It's offensive and no-one will play it. You can use the original lyric on the album but we'll need another line for the single."

I continued to argue against this, but I was fighting a losing battle. Mainstream radio airplay just wasn't at the top of my list of priorities. The offending line summed up the entire spirit of the song for me and, of course, this was precisely the kind of thing I'd been afraid of - I just hadn't expected it so soon. In the end, after heated discussions between ourselves, the label and the producer, I agreed to try to compromise - but I was cursing everyone.

Next up was 'Nostalgia'. Thankfully, Lillywhite had abandoned all notions of using the drum computer by this time, and John's confidence was beginning to return. The huge drum sound that was Lillywhite's trademark began to crystallise, and we all felt a little better. I still didn't like the song much, although I was stunned by the quality of the production on the backing track as it came together. However, it was a boring song to sing from my point of view, and the huge sound of the new backing track failed to inspire a vocal worthy of it.

Finally it was time to lay down the brand new idea. The bass and drums were already arranged. Reg, John, and I improvised and recorded a guide arrangement without any kind of vocal melody or chorus to hook onto. Reg and Dave continued working on the backing track, refining the guitars, while I went off on my own with a tape recorder to work on the vocals and lyrics. I know that Lillywhite was dubious about the track, believing that at best we'd come up with an option for an additional B-side for the single. The whole thing was especially interesting because no-one had yet heard any of my vocal ideas, and had no clue what to expect. The idea was so fresh that each of us inspired the other, including Lillywhite, who together with Dave and Reg, managed to build a backing track of epic proportions.

I ran through the song about five or six times, growing more confident with each take. I knew we definitely had something, because I could feel the electric atmosphere emanating from the control room. I heard Lillywhite's voice on the intercom: "No lyrics? You've got to be joking," he laughed.

I was particularly proud to hear Dave's voice in the background. "The Rolls-Royce of Mark Burgess performances," he quipped. "What's it called, by the way?"

I thought for a second, and replied: "In Shreds."

The song reflected all the fears, the doubts, and the cynicism I'd been feeling over the previous month. "The whore in my bed" was CBS: "It seems to me we're becoming part of the machinery."

'In Shreds' session, RAK Studios, London. Photo: Tony Skinkis

As we were now almost at the end of the year, only the actual recording of the songs was to take place that week. Mixing was scheduled for January 1982. To provide us with a reference point, Lillywhite decided to rough-mix 'In Shreds' there and then, which took him about fifteen minutes. We finished the work on the other two tracks and, in good spirits, cassette tapes in hand, we left for home and the Christmas holidays.

Back in Middleton, a cheque for the first part of our advance from CBS arrived, and a meeting was set to determine what to do with it. Moz was present, naturally, along with Ali and Tony. I'd assumed that the cheque would be split four ways, and that we'd each contribute to the band's overall expenses. As Moz had not been instrumental in securing or negotiating the deal he didn't expect a commission, which was just as well. He did, however, have plenty to say about how the money should be used, and how the business side of The Chameleons should be organised. The band would be classed as a business partnership for tax purposes, and the money would be used to open a business account at a local bank. The four of us would draw a modest, weekly wage, as would Tony and Ali. Moz was against us buying a vehicle of our own, arguing that we'd save money by hiring a vehicle as and when we needed one, but we wanted a vehicle at our constant disposal. Reluctantly, he agreed to look into it. I think he hoped that, with time, he'd persuade us to think again, but he was wrong. We put in an order with a Ford dealer in Manchester for a nine-seater minibus with a fitted bulkhead at the back, allowing us to safely stow all the equipment.

All thoughts then of a windfall - which would have enabled me to move out of my parents' house and set up on my own - were banished, but we did distribute some money to everyone by way of a Christmas bonus, so at least we all had a good time.

My mother's attitude had changed somewhat over the previous six months. At first, she'd rolled her eyes as if to say "Here we go again," as I told her that I was leaving college to concentrate on the band. But once she saw that I was earning a wage, she relaxed. My father also had a shift of attitude. He hadn't been all that impressed by The Clichés, but after hearing The Chameleons on the John Peel show and learning that we would be putting out a record the following year, he was rather impressed. Life at home became easier; it was certainly more affordable, and so moving out and finding a flat of my own seemed less of a priority, at least in the short term.

For myself I invested in the latest gadget, a Sony Walkman. The sound quality was unbelievable, and I'd walk around listening to the tracks and making reference notes ahead of the final mixing sessions. I called round to see Ali, and found Dave already there. He was listening to the tape practically non-stop too, especially 'In Shreds', and we got into an excited discussion about it. As far as we were concerned, the fifteen-minute rough mix had it all. "What do we need to mix it again for?" Dave kept asking. I knew what he meant, it sounded great to me as it was, but we had nothing to lose by letting Lillywhite try a more polished mix. After all, he was arguably one of the best and most accomplished rock producers in the world.

1982 began with one of the heaviest snowfalls England had seen in twenty years. We were invited to play at the ICA in London as part of an event marking the new year, so the mixing sessions with Lillywhite were scheduled for later that week. Our spirits were soaring as we drove through the early morning in heavy snow to meet Moz at a service station on the M6, and I remember how good it felt to be away from Middleton and on the road again. Edgbaston, where Moz was based, seemed like a very boring place and, as if to emphasise this, Moz told us rather proudly that it was the hometown of the band UB40.

After spending an hour at Moz's office we went to a café, and over breakfast he told us that after a great deal of thought he'd decided that he didn't want to be personal manager to the band, but would instead act as business manager on a salaried basis. It seemed to me that what he was saying was he didn't want to look after the band, just the money. Consequently, my initial feeling was to tell him to stuff it. As we left the meeting, Dave noticed my mood and I told him how I felt, but the others didn't seem unduly bothered. The arrangement negated the need for a complicated management contract so, as they rightly pointed out, if he failed to impress us we weren't obliged to continue working with him. Satisfied with this reasoning, I fell in.

Just down the road from the venue in central London, the hire van broke down and, laughing hysterically, we were forced to push it through the thick snow down the royal mile to the ICA building. When we walked out onto the stage that night, we were surprised and pleased to hear a cheer rise up in the audience. It was the first time this had happened, and indicated that our reputation was beginning to spread beyond Manchester.

The mixing of the tracks proved a tedious affair, and I spent most of the time playing darts in the recreation room. Having spent many hours playing darts in Wales a few years earlier, it didn't take me long to brush off the cobwebs and I began to hit the treble-twenty with two out of every three darts I threw. "Not bad," said a voice from behind me. I turned to see a rather beautiful blonde girl in a black Crombie overcoat and matching Doc Martens boots. She took the darts from the board and we had a game in which I was only able to beat her by a narrow margin. Just then, the studio manager came in and told her it was time to go, and she smiled and said goodbye as Ali and Tony walked into the room. "I know that girl from somewhere," I remarked after she'd left.

"You should do," said Tony, "that was Kim Wilde."

Kim had just had a couple of huge hit records and had become something of a sex symbol in the media. I'm glad that I hadn't recognised her as it might have dangerously affected my aim.

My favourite moment during that week came when Tony walked into the control room during a break in the mixing and announced to Lillywhite that they had his next production job lined up. The cassette he thrust into the machine consisted of Ali on Les Dawson-style piano[1] playing the country and western song 'El Paso', while Tony sang his own version of the lyrics, which had something to do with a horse that had no legs. Lillywhite looked at Tony in total, blank confusion while the rest of us fell about laughing.

We took away cassette copies of the mixes to play and discuss amongst ourselves, and our feelings were unanimous: 'The Fan and the Bellows' was a washout. John had done his best overdubbing the rolls, but the track, despite a powerful sound and huge mix, just didn't have the feel we'd hoped for, and the Peel session version, recorded and mixed in a single day on antiquated eight-track equipment, was, in our view, superior.

'Nostalgia' had a great backing track, and Lillywhite's idea of running the fade-out vocal backwards to create an additional backing vocal was inspired, but the lead vocal was lacklustre. Now that we'd taken the tuning of the guitars down the key was too low, and I just hadn't been fired with enough enthusiasm to give the track the close, melancholic feel that it had needed.

By far the best track of the session was 'In Shreds', but we felt that Lillywhite's attempt at a polished mix had suppressed much of the excitement and brashness that the rough fifteen-minute mix contained. The harmonics bouncing off the guitar reverbs had almost resembled a male voice choir on the rough mix, but they were barely audible on the finished product. Repeated playing of the new mixes alongside the original served to strengthen our resolve, so we decided that we wanted 'In Shreds' to be the debut single, using the rough mix from the previous December.

This was news that CBS, and Steve Lillywhite in particular, didn't want to hear. CBS were insisting that 'The Fan and the Bellows' should be the

---

1. Les Dawson was a particularly brilliant British comedian who would often perform a routine in which he played famous, instantly recognisable tunes on the piano, but so slightly off-key as to render them hilarious, which I'm told is a very difficult thing to do even for the most accomplished pianists.

single, but contractually we had full artistic control over our music, so I made a point of insisting that if they were determined to release this track, then it had to be the uncensored version. Checkmate! Of course this didn't mean that CBS would have to play ball and release 'In Shreds' as a single: persuading them to do that was more of a struggle, and Dave was getting pretty vocal about it. "I don't understand what their problem is," he would say. "It's a great record."

Unfortunately, our criteria for what constituted a great record were very different from CBS' corporate thinking. A great record in their opinion was Altered Images' 'Happy Birthday' or Adam and the Ants' 'Prince Charming'. Why? Because these records were sufficiently bland to be guaranteed airplay on Radio One - all day, every day - and had subsequently gone on to sell tens of thousands of copies. Despite what CBS had said during our early discussions, they were investing a great deal of money and they wanted a hit single immediately. Nothing that was happening was a surprise to me but, of course, nobody likes a know-all, and my efforts to point this out began to create a bit of tension, especially between Dave and me. In the end though, I think it was largely due to Dave's passionate, persuasive arguments that CBS finally agreed to put 'In Shreds' out. It was decided that Reg would design the front sleeve, and CBS would handle all the promotional artwork.

Next, we had to get Lillywhite to agree to us using the rough mix, and he was harder to convince. He told us that, in his view, the December mix was technically substandard, and that he had his reputation to consider. We were incredulous because, to us, the track sounded wonderful. "In what way is it substandard?" I implored him.

"Well just listen to the high-hat cymbals," he laughed in exasperation. "There's far too much compression on them."

I don't think we laughed in his face but it was a close thing. He suggested another remix, but we just didn't see the point. He couldn't match the rough mix after spending over seven hours on it, so why waste more time and money? "It's great, Steve," I assured him. "It really is a great record."

"Come on Steve," chipped in Tony. "Are you a punk or a New Romantic?"

In the end, Lillywhite agreed.

We didn't want to use either of the other two tracks we'd recorded as B-sides to the single, so we decided to record another song. Having spent a fortune on the redundant RAK tracks, we recorded the new track in the same studio we'd used to record our demos: Cargo, in Rochdale.

Surprisingly, Lillywhite offered to come up to Cargo and produce the B-side solely for expenses. Colin Richardson, the house engineer at Cargo, was understandably thrilled at the prospect of working alongside Lillywhite, and this rare opportunity served him well for a long time to come. Lillywhite didn't really know what he was letting himself in for, however. Cargo still enjoyed an underground reputation, but as far as equipment went the place was beginning to have a run-down feel to it.

Steve's first task was to completely empty the live room of everything - including the carpets - and to record and mix the song in a single day. He worked very, very hard. I was pleased that he liked the idea of including the whirly tube on the recording, and he engineered the drone of the pipe so that it was in tune with the track. By overdubbing the sound many times, he was able to create a whirly-tube orchestra.

The strain of the day began to take its toll, however, and I remember him and Dave having a stormy argument at one point. We eventually finished the track at around two in the morning, by which time the atmosphere had grown very tense. Having finished the mix we sat back to hear it for the final time, and we all felt that the result was quite amazing. After it had played out, Lillywhite rose from his chair and, slinging his jacket over his shoulder, said his goodbyes and left. We'd pushed him fairly hard in the relatively short time that we'd worked together, and I knew in that moment, deep down, that we'd lost him.

A few days later I received a phone call from Moz. "Who's going to have a hit record then?" he sang down the phone.

"What are you talking about?" I asked, confused.

"I've just heard 'Less Than Human'," he said. "It's fantastic."

"It's the B-side," I said, still confused.

"Well, maybe we could make it a double A-side instead," he suggested.

I told him I didn't think so but, in the interests of diplomacy, I said it was an interesting idea. I was pleased, though, because up until then it was the first time I'd ever heard him say anything positive about our music. It would also be the last.

Reg unveiled his illustration for the front sleeve, a drawing of a woman wearing a crash helmet, stood in a bath holding a baby with crazy, staring eyes. We all thought it was brilliant, except for Moz who, for reasons I was never able to fathom, got it into his head that the baby in the drawing was his own daughter, Sophie, and he freaked out. We all assured him that this wasn't the case - I think we'd only met the child once - but I definitely got the feeling he didn't believe us.

Muff Winwood's doubts about the sanity of releasing 'In Shreds' multiplied ten-fold once he saw the proposed sleeve, but our A&R contact Annie, bless her, really liked it and was able to persuade him to give it the green light. So as not to alienate their art department completely, we agreed to allow them to work on an adaptation of the drawing, as well as providing additional ideas for promotional posters. To be fair, they didn't skimp at all when it came to providing promotional material. They manufactured a large number of black T-shirts with the baby's face on the front, and it remains the most popular Chameleons T-shirt. They also came up with a set of postcards featuring the illustration from the poster, and hundreds of button badges. Less good was the fact that we wouldn't get to make a promotional video for the single, and that they were only intending to press 5,000 copies. This was the minimum number that they were contractually obliged to press and we knew then that, despite all the gimmicks, they intended to bury the record and continue to pressure us into releasing 'The Fan and the Bellows' by way of a follow-up. The press department did their bit though, and gradually, mixed reviews began to appear in both national and regional papers.

We'd wanted to use the press photograph that had been taken the previous year in front of the fountain in Piccadilly, but CBS vetoed this in favour of a new photo session that they'd arranged using one of their regular photographers. Additionally, we were each given a sum of money and told to go out into London and buy some new clothes. One by one, we drifted back to James' flat, burdened with our assorted carrier bags, and then proceeded to nosey through each other's purchases. "What did you get?"

"A couple of shirts and a jacket. What did you get?"

"Some jeans and this shirt."

Finally, Reg came back carrying a small, single, plain white plastic bag. Everyone stopped to look at him.

"Is that all you got, Reg?" Dave asked him.

"Yeah," replied Reg, "I couldn't find anything I liked, so I just got this."

Again, there was a moment's silence. "What is it?" Dave asked.

Opening the bag, Reg pulled out an antique Rupert Bear annual.

Now we had some nice, shiny photographs to bandy around and a new record coming out, the next task was to find a good agent and get some live experience in readiness for a promotional tour. The agency to be with in those days was a company called Wasted Talent, and we were introduced to Ian Wilson, who had been instrumental in breaking U2. Wasted Talent represented just about every decent left-of-centre band around, so we were pleased when we were told they wanted to take us on. We were then thrown right in at the deep end and booked to support U2 at the Sheffield Lyceum. By this time U2 had released their second album, *October*, and were in the middle of what would be their last sold-out theatre tour before migrating to America and the dizzy heights of stadium rock. For The Chameleons this would be our third or fourth show with John on the drums, so as you can imagine, we were a little bit nervous.

We arrived at the venue for the soundcheck and found it to be unexpectedly relaxed and unhurried. Annie knew U2, having signed them to Island a couple of years earlier, and introduced us. They were extremely polite and pleasant to chat with, and I was pleased that they seemed so grounded. As they prepared to soundcheck, however, their road manager ordered everyone to clear the room. Our disappointment was obvious as a security guard began approaching. "Oh no man, not them, they're the other band," said Bono, and we were left alone. The rest of the hall was now completely empty except for the technical crew, so the four of us picked out places in front of the stage to listen. They played 'Fire', and never in all my life had I heard a band sound that great. It was at this point I remember thinking that we really needed to get our own sound engineer. Next up was 'Celebration', and, again, it was astounding. Their entire soundcheck had taken less than fifteen minutes.

I don't remember much about our set that night except that the theatre was filled with around 2,500 people and, by the time we walked out, despite a great audience reaction, I was trembling with nerves. I was exhilarated after the set, though, and walked around in a daze until eventually I made my way to the front of house to watch U2. Most of the songs I'd hoped to hear from their debut album, *Boy*, were present, along with one or two songs from their latest album, which came across much better live than on record, and overall I really enjoyed it.

One proud moment came after the show, as I was making my way back to our dressing room. A group of young guys had recognised me and told me they'd seen our set. "We thought you were brilliant," they enthused. Smiling, I thanked them. "Better than the other lot," one of the lads continued, and they all nodded emphatically in agreement. I looked at them for a second thinking that they had to be joking, but they were deadly serious.

"Well, I don't know about that," I laughed, "but thanks."

As we gathered our things and walked out to the front of the empty stage, it was nice to see Bono sitting on the edge of the stage, chatting to fans and signing autographs. Annie told us we'd been invited back to the hotel to have a drink with the band, but, once there, Bono and Larry retired to their rooms for the evening, leaving Adam, Edge, Annie and Steve Lillywhite, who had driven up for the show.

Adam struck me immediately as the rock star of the band. He was dressed in a skin-tight black leotard that had a leopard skinned heart on the front of it, while his hair had been cut in the style of an Afro and bleached blonde. "He looks like a bottle of Guinness," I whispered to Tony. Adam was hitting us with every cliché in the book, and he kept badgering us to go with him to a club in town, but we were more interested in speaking with Edge. In the end, fed up with his constant nagging, Tony and I agreed to go and followed him to the lift. He pressed the ground floor button, but Tony and I jumped out as the doors were closing, sealing him inside. He was then carried down to the lobby alone, leaving us free to return to the party.

Edge was a shy, gentle, softly-spoken bloke, and at one point, after someone ordered a plate of sandwiches and seeing there was now only one left on the plate, he quietly asked Dave if we thought anyone would mind if he ate it. We both looked at him for a moment and told him we didn't think so. He took the sandwich and, just as he popped it into his mouth, we bellowed, "EDGE! Have you just taken the last sandwich? You greedy bastard." He turned bright red and began laughing hysterically, spluttering bits of sandwich everywhere.

He asked me what I thought of the new album, *October*, and I told him that, in all honesty, I was a bit disappointed after their great debut, but that I loved the band and had really enjoyed hearing them close up. Nodding, he agreed that he felt the same way, and explained that they hadn't had much time to write it with everything that had been going on around them in the wake of *Boy*, but that their label had been pressuring them to record a new album for the American market. "Bands have their entire lives to write their first album," chipped in Lillywhite, "and about six months to write their second."

There was silence for a moment. "Aye!" Tony said, with a nod of his head.

Later that month, we were booked as support to our label-mates Altered Images on what was to be their first national tour. Those gigs were a real baptism of fire, as Altered Images, now enjoying their second hit single with a debut album imminent, were about as mainstream as it got. Dealing with Dave and me proved to be a bit of a trial for John who, whenever he committed some error on the drums, would suddenly find one or both of us, cranked-up on speed, screaming at him across the stage.

Despite the contrast in styles, we found that we generally went down very well with their audiences. Altered Images seemed ill at ease with the live concert experience, though, and they had the worst road crew I think I've ever encountered. From what we could gather, most of them had been recruited from Glasgow and were close friends of either this band member or that, and didn't seem to have a clue what they were doing. The same could be said for us, of course, but at least our crew had mastered the basics and had everything under control, although we were sharing the same sound engineer. Curiously, Altered Images were selling out the venues each night but were consistently sounding awful. Due to what I suppose could be described as an overly aggressive attitude, we didn't share their fate. "If one person out there tells me we sounded shit tonight, mate, I'm going to wrap this guitar round your fuckin' neck," Dave had threatened the sound engineer one night and, as if he suddenly had something to prove, he seemed to make the extra effort. One of Altered Images' guitarists had overheard this exchange and collared me backstage one night. "Why does your guitarist have to be so arrogant?" he demanded.

"Ask yourself this," I replied. "Why is your support band consistently getting a better sound out front than you are, when we're both using the same engineer and you're the ones that are paying his wages?"

On the morning after the show in Brighton, they came out of the hotel to find that their bus had been broken into and a number of items had been stolen, and it became obvious that most of their party, with the exception of their drummer Titch and singer Clare Grogan, believed we were responsible. This may have been because our bus, as luck would have it, was untouched.

Being on the same label as Clare Grogan, I also noticed how insidious CBS could be when it came to manipulating their acts, and more than once on that tour we'd seen Clare break down in tears. When the media backlash came, it was swift and cruel. A *Melody Maker* journalist, whose name I forget, went along to review one of the shows and it was published under the headline 'DON'T CALL ME SCARFACE'. This journalist then continued to relate how, while at the gig, he'd been in the men's toilet and had overheard some guys talking about the scar that ran along Clare's cheek. For the remainder of the review, he then scornfully focused on her scar in a perverted and ill-considered attempt at humour. When we read the review, we were as horrified as everyone else and when we went into the CBS offices that week, everyone was talking about it. What the editor was thinking when he approved it, I can't imagine. The same journalist had written a glowing article on The Chameleons only a few weeks earlier and so I, for one, felt a kind of guilt by association, even though I was as disgusted as everyone else seemed to be. CBS had been hiding copies of the review from Clare all morning, but eventually she read it and was distraught. The sight of her weeping broke my heart.

Over the next few months I witnessed the gradual disintegration of Altered Images with sadness. Their sessions for Peel, along with their debut single, had been inspired, fresh, and original, but since joining CBS they'd been victims of corporate and media manipulation and plain bad advice. I felt for Clare especially. She seemed such a sweet, trusting talent, who worked extremely hard for no other reason than to do her best for those around her. But once the media tide turned, everyone - or so it seemed to me - abandoned her.

February 1982 saw us booked to support Killing Joke over two consecutive nights in Leicester and Manchester. We turned up at the venue in Leicester in plenty of time, but Killing Joke still hadn't arrived, and when they did eventually turn up, they were five and half hours late. To compound the problem, a third band, The Sinatras, had also been billed, and were due on first. Killing Joke's late arrival left very little time for a soundcheck, but at last we were summoned to the stage. I immediately plugged in my bass and fretted a couple of notes to make sure that everything worked properly. "That's great, thanks a lot," boomed a voice from the stage intercom.

"That's it, is it? That's what I've hung around all day for?" I shouted from the stage.

Dave, who'd been busy setting up his own gear across the stage hadn't noticed this exchange, and once he was ready to go he did the same thing.

"Great, thanks!" boomed the voice of the sound engineer again.

Dave and I just looked at each other in disbelief. John tapped a few beats of his bass drum and one on the snare.

"Great, that'll do!" said the engineer.

As I was looking at Dave, I noticed a few members of Killing Joke standing at the corner of the stage, laughing at the situation.

"What are they laughing at?" I shouted, getting seriously angry, the amphetamine combining dangerously with adrenaline.

Dave glanced over his shoulder and they were still laughing. "I don't know!" he shouted sarcastically.

I repeated the question, aiming it directly at them. Their singer, Jaz Coleman, tried to fix me with an intense stare, but when it comes to intense stares I'm the master, especially when I'm pumped-up on speed. I returned his glare briefly, then un-hooked my bass, grasped it by the neck and ran at them. Dave, similarly fired up, did likewise and the members of Killing Joke fled to their dressing room and slammed the door. Dave and I were kicking the door and cursing them, but they stayed put. Eventually, their tour manager turned up with about half their crew, and attempted to calm the situation down, but by this time we were furious and far from ready to be placated. Sensing that we were being stitched up, and not wishing to face a hyped-up Killing Joke audience with only the barest of line-checks, we decided to pull out. As we were gathering our things, The Sinatras came into the dressing room. They explained that they hadn't even had a line-check, but some bigwig agent had promised to come down to see them and they didn't want to pull out and blow their chances. We wished them luck and packed the gear back into the bus, although we did decide to stay and watch the gig.

Shortly after all this excitement, Killing Joke's tour manager found us again and said the band wanted to apologise, and were hoping that we'd turn up and play Manchester the following night. We refused, and I phoned Moz to tell him what had happened. He told me that he thought we were being very unprofessional, which was true, but not what I wanted to hear. I'd hoped for something a little more supportive. I replied that if he'd been there doing his job like he was supposed to then perhaps the whole thing could have been avoided, and we left it at that. But then I had to remind myself that he was a business manager, not a personal manager. The man simply didn't know how to handle such an obvious band of freaks.

The Sinatras took the stage and, from the first song to the last, they were showered with beer and saliva. What's more, they'd suffered these indignities for nothing, because the agent that had promised to come and see them never turned up. We watched some of Killing Joke's set, which came complete with an occult worshipping fire-eater, but we left well before the end, seeing it for the bollocks it was.

Another memorable date from that period was at Northwich Memorial Hall in May 1982. Our support band had one of those irritating lead singers that seem to think they are, in actual fact, Jim Morrison, but who are, in actual fact, invariably naff. This was his band's first ever performance, and he got a little carried away, screaming "Go to church, go to church," whenever he ran out of lyrics. We'd completed our soundcheck and retreated to the dressing room when suddenly the door opened and in walked around twenty young girls and a rather large woman, and they immediately began to undress. In utter confusion we just stood there staring at them; none of them, it seemed, had seen us. "Excuse me?" I said, and the large woman gave a startled jump and whirled around.

"What are you doing in here?" she barked.

Taken aback by this sudden reversal - this should have been our question, after all - I quickly recovered. "This is our dressing room," I replied, stifling a laugh.

"Oh no," she assured me, "it's ours."

"Who are you?" Tony asked her.

"We're booked to appear here tonight." she informed us.

Our confusion deepened. "What are you, a band or something?" he asked.

"No, we're a dance troupe, a Morris dance troupe."

"Morris dancing?" exclaimed Tony, smirking, "Who booked a Morris dancing troupe as a support act?"

"The main group," she said, in a tone that suggested that they obviously had more right to be there than we did.

"I don't think so, love," said Tony.

"Oh they did. They asked us earlier today while we were doing a routine in the town centre, but if you don't believe me ask them, they're on the stage now."

"We're the main group!" Tony told her, unable to contain his laughter any more. "That's the support band."

We all marched out to investigate, and it turned out that the eccentric singer in the support band, having seen the troupe performing in the town centre, had indeed invited them along to perform at the show. We were pondering what to do when Tony whispered in my ear. "We're sharing a dressing room with twenty nubile young girls, do we *really* want to chuck them out?" We thought about it and decided no, we didn't, so by way of a compromise we segregated the dressing room as best we could and allowed them to perform first - not on the stage, but directly in front of it. They didn't go down too badly, either. Certainly better than the support band, who were unequivocally awful.

Most of the audience consisted of young women; Tony, in particular, seemed to be getting plenty of attention, and he got a little carried away. After flirting shamelessly with some of them as he packed away the band's gear, he handed out his phone number, never dreaming that anything would come of it. The following Saturday night, however, he was at home watching a movie with his girlfriend when there came a tremendous knocking on his front door. The young girls had looked up his name and number in the North Manchester phone directory, crosschecked it with an address, and had decided to pay him a surprise visit. Tony dealt with the situation in his customary fashion, i.e. he pretended it wasn't happening, and refused to answer the door, grimacing as the girls shouted his name through the letterbox. "Who are those girls?" his girlfriend demanded angrily.

"I don't know, do I?" Tony lamely insisted.

"Well, they know you - how did they get your address?"

Tony spent the rest of the week in the doghouse, but he learned a valuable lesson that night.

I remember our gig at Aston University chiefly because it was the first time we met a young girl who called herself Angel. She was a very tall, thin, striking girl with bleached blonde hair, a vague gothic-punk look, and high cheekbones. Angel was an aspiring singer, and she engaged us in conversation before the soundcheck in the college refectory, promising to return for the gig that evening along with a friend, so we dutifully offered to put them both on the guest list. Another reason I remember the show is that Steve Lillywhite turned up and bought some hash from a Rastafarian guy who was hanging around the lobby. He returned to the table where we were all sat and unwrapped the silver foil only to find he'd just spent £35 on a black wine gum.

Angel returned that night with her friend Julia, who I couldn't take my eyes off the whole night, not even as we said goodbye. I turned without breaking her gaze and walked directly into the front of a parked car, while everyone laughed wildly from the van.

By this time I'd been going steady with Fenella for a couple of years. She was a naturally beautiful woman with flaming red hair, who lived with her parents on the family farm, along with her three younger brothers (her mother would adopt a fourth, Daniel), and for the most part our relationship had been great, until I started experimenting with drugs. She'd tried mushrooms with us, and had even enjoyed it, but hadn't wanted to go any further than that. We began arguing more, and gradually drifted apart. I realised that I preferred to spend my time with the others, getting stoned and having laughing fits, rather than sitting in a Middleton pub surrounded by fake brass tack, having conversations that went about as deep as the ice in a rum and black.

Having met Julia, the realisation that my relationship with Fenella had to end struck me like a thunderbolt. This was a situation I was extremely ill-equipped to handle. Fenella had been my first proper girlfriend and I adored her, believing that she understood me on a deep level. She had little in common with the others, who didn't really understand what we saw in each other. no-one knew Fenella like I did, though, and breaking up was a real wrench for me. But I'd fallen in love with another girl - what was I to do? Fenella took it very calmly, actually, giving nothing away. It was as if, deep down, she knew it was only a matter of time before I came crawling back, which is pretty much how things panned out.

I started seeing much more of Julia, who shared a house with Angel in Birmingham, until I was spending most of my time there. I remember the weekend Julia and I finally got it together. We'd been invited down to London by our mate James who, having now bought a bass guitar, was jamming for fun in a band he'd formed with some other friends, and they were throwing a party at their rehearsal room in Greenwich. Tony hadn't wanted to go, and no-one else felt confident enough about driving the van, so John stepped in and offered to take the others in his car, while Julia and I opted for the train. John was still driving around in his weird Ford Escort, which was proving to be even more unreliable than usual, and I remember having grave misgivings about it at the time. Sure enough, when we arrived at the party we found that the others still hadn't turned up.

Time passed, and still there was no sign of John and the others. By now, we were all growing seriously worried. Finally, at around midnight they strolled in. John's car had chosen the worst possible stretch of the M1 on which to break down, an area where extensive repairs were being carried out. Consequently, all but two lanes - one of them being the hard shoulder of the motorway - had been closed down. John had no breakdown cover, nor was he able to diagnose the problem. Additionally, it had been raining heavily and visibility was exceptionally bad. Huge lorries had been thundering down the lane of the hard shoulder, but due to the appalling driving conditions, they hadn't been able to see John's car until they were bearing down on it, which had led invariably to loud, blaring horns and dangerous evasive action by the trucks. They'd spent around two hours huddled together with blankets over their heads, hiding from the situation like a flock of ostriches. Eventually they were able to sort it out and get moving again.

John, in particular, was extremely pissed off, and we had to stop him from dumping the car in the Thames. James, always trying to impress, made the mistake of telling John that he knew someone that would happily pretend to steal the car and get rid of it, leaving John free to claim on the insurance. "What insurance?" John asked, in all honesty. Of course James, thinking that John would never take him up on such an offer, promptly forgot about it. On the day of our departure, however, John suddenly threw James the keys to the car, thanked him for helping get rid of it, and left. Poor James was forced to drive the car to North London and discreetly dump it. By the end of that weekend, Julia and I were together and we spent every spare hour at her house in Birmingham.

I soon learned that I wasn't the only one to be making a significant change in their domestic circumstances. I was visiting Ali one afternoon when Dave arrived and announced that he and John were moving out of their respective parents' homes, and were planning to move into a house together. From their descriptions, the suburb they were moving to sounded very dodgy indeed, and Ali, Tony, and I glanced at each other doubtfully. "Are you sure about this, John?" Tony asked him.

"When you take a big step like that it's important that you get it right, and it sounds far from idyllic," I added.

"It'll be all right, don't worry," he assured us.

On seeing the place, the rest of us seriously doubted the sense of it. The house was off-kilter, showing obvious signs of subsidence. I don't think it had a single straight wall, and judging from the location, staring at the walls would be the only source of entertainment. They were to share the house with three other people. John had taken the larger, ground floor room while Dave had a smaller bedroom upstairs. A strange girl in her early twenties had one of the remaining two rooms, and a large, hairy, overweight medallion man who looked about fifty and never seemed to change out of his bathrobe, occupied the other room. The third other resident was Medallion Man's sixteen year old live-in girlfriend. All told, they were a seriously gruesome trio.

By this time, John had spent far too many weekends at James' flat in London, and was now rolling joints that were - and this is no exaggeration - about a foot long. He'd buy cigarette papers that came on small rolls and would tear off long strips and place them between two Chinese tablemats made from straw, enabling him to build huge reefers, which he would then sit and smoke by himself. Dave didn't partake because he never smoked tobacco. Accordingly, John's consumption rose to around an ounce of cannabis a week, and this was strong, high quality cannabis, pure black resin smuggled out of Afghanistan. Nor was he eating properly; John's diet consisted exclusively of Pot Noodle, and over the next few months his physical and mental condition deteriorated rapidly.

John's already parlous mental state took a dramatic turn for the worse the night that he decided to try LSD with Dave. We often talked about the previous summer's acid trips to Tandle Hill, and he eventually decided he wanted to try it for himself. Dave phoned me one Saturday night and, against my better judgement, I agreed to go with them. I'd expected another hike up to the hill away from the masses, but John had decided that romping round the countryside wasn't for him, and wanted to go to the regular Saturday night piss-up in the bar at Manchester Polytechnic instead.

I didn't have much money on me that night; before Dave's phone call, I'd envisioned a quiet Saturday night in the local pub, then home in time for *Match of the Day*. These days you can simply nip to a cash-point, but back then debit cards and cash dispensers were practically non-existent. John and Dave didn't have much money on them either, so I argued that the cost of getting there, plus the entrance money and the cost of a few beers, wouldn't leave us with enough money for a taxi home. "We'll walk back," Dave argued. "We'll be tripping, loads of things will happen, it'll be an adventure." Walking six miles back to Middleton, zapped on acid, on a Saturday night, with every drunken idiot in the city hitting the streets at the same time? Oh, it'll be an adventure all right!

The night began well enough. The music at the Poly suited the mood, the beer was cheap, and we even bumped into a few familiar faces. One of them offered us more acid. I declined, bracing myself for the journey back, but John and Dave split another tab between them. At around 2am the bar began to empty and I found them both sitting outside, admiring the architecture[2].

We sat talking for a while, allowing the crowds to disperse before making our way home when, suddenly, I began to feel a growing ache in the pit of my stomach, which was steadily growing worse. What I was experiencing was the onset of poisoning - the acid had been diluted with strychnine as a cost-cutting measure. This wasn't the worst of it, either. While we were experiencing the effects of the LSD within the confines of the bar John had been fine, but now that we were on the streets, the full effects of the acid were kicking in and he was struggling to handle it. Meanwhile, we faced the six-mile walk back to Middleton.

How we managed to complete that journey without getting arrested or into a fight I'll never know, but we did made it in just over three hours. I was coherent enough to be able to steer them through the maze of back streets that enabled us to reach the main route home without having to negotiate the centre of Piccadilly or Oldham Street, where most of the drunken violence was apt to occur. In all that time, not a single night bus passed us on the road and we had to walk every inch of the way. On finally arriving back in Middleton, we stopped to rest in the park. Dave was trying to calm John down by reassuring him that the effects would soon wear off, but by this time John was in pieces and didn't think he would ever reach normality again. Thankfully, the pain in my stomach, which at one point

---

2. Admiring seventies architecture is a symptom of LSD abuse; I reckon those concrete monstrosities were designed by people who dropped too much acid in the sixties.

mid-journey had caused me to double over onto the pavement, was beginning to abate. After a brief rest, I took them back to my parents' house, and tried to bring John down as gently as we could. Eventually Dave accompanied John home. This was the first time I'd seen the flip-side of the LSD experience, and not only was I shaken by John's reaction to it, but I felt a little responsible as well.

John's nightmare experience with LSD didn't seem to halt his other habits in any way, and he continued smoking his phallic joints day after day and eating dehydrated slop. The physical demands on a professional drummer are heavy at the best of times but, combined, all of these things took their toll on John that summer. The change was obvious in some ways, but I don't think any of us truly realised how fucked up he really was until the first afternoon of rehearsals for our first national tour, when he collapsed onto his drum kit, sobbing.

By this time, I was only coming back from Birmingham when work demanded it. Consequently, the change in John seemed more sudden and dramatic to my eyes. I'd often nagged him to start looking after himself a little better, to stop smoking so much dope, and to eat properly; I think I even suggested that he move out of that crazy fucking house and go back to his mum's for a while. That said, I was consuming a lot of dope too, as well as amphetamines, so I was hardly in a position to give John advice. But my role in the band was a lot less physically demanding and, like Dave, my recreational habits didn't seem to impair my ability to perform, at least not at that stage.

We all seemed to be paralysed by what was happening to John, and felt powerless to help. We were too young to realise that ultimately, in these situations, no-one can help in any practical sense. While others can lend support, it's up to the individual to climb out of the chaos resulting from prolonged substance abuse. In the meantime, we continued to write and rehearse as much as we could in preparation for the release of 'In Shreds' that coming March, and for the promotional tour which would start in April.

That Easter weekend we decided to take another road trip to Loch Ness, although John couldn't be persuaded to join us. James offered to drive a few of us there, and Ken was on a break from Oxford so he decided to come too. Angel was by this time going steady with Reg, and she too joined our merry band. I was sad that Julia wouldn't be able to come with me, but she had a family commitment she couldn't get out of. Along with Ali and Tony, we numbered eight in total. James took Dave, Reg and Angel with him in his father's rather nifty Saab Turbo, and Tony hired another car from

Rent-a-wreck and took me, Ali and Ken. We arranged to meet up at the campsite on the bonnie banks of Loch Ness.

The weekend didn't go well for the most part. James, Dave, Reg, and Angel would disappear each evening into Inverness to eat in restaurants, while the rest of us huddled around a camp stove, dining on the usual kind of slop. We felt that the others weren't really getting into the spirit of things and an attitude of rivalry began to develop, with Tony in particular becoming irritated by James' constant need to be at the centre of things. Another problem was the rain. Ken shared my tent, which was relatively new, but Ali had borrowed an old one which he was sharing with Tony. It leaked quite badly, which did nothing to improve Tony's mood. Ken and I were rather dispirited by the whole thing and I remember saying to him, as we walked along the road to a nearby pub one night, that this would probably be my last trip to Loch Ness. I was feeling too nostalgic about our first couple of trips there, and for me the magic had gone. He told me that he felt the same way. My words were to prove somewhat ironic considering what followed.

We explored our usual haunts around the Loch but, by Easter Sunday, it had started raining again, and this proved to be the most miserable evening of the whole trip. James and his posse shot off to Inverness without telling anyone, and by half past ten that night they hadn't returned. Much to Ali and Tony's irritation, James had taken the entire supply of weed with him so we couldn't even get stoned. Consequently, as the evening wore on, we just sat in the car in silence, listening to the gently falling rain outside. I sat in the back of the car with Ken, both of us trying not to giggle at the ridiculousness of the situation, as that would have only worsened matters. Ali and Tony sat in the front, staring out of the windscreen and feeling totally dejected.

We were parked facing a bank of trees that shielded the campsite from the main road. Hoping to lighten the mood, I suggested that if we were going to sit staring out of the window all night, the least we could do was turn the car around and face the water.

"Why don't we just fuckin' turn the car round and go home?" Tony barked, and again Ken and I had to fight hard not to burst out laughing.

"We can't do that Tony, we can't just fuck off without a word and leave the others here wondering where we are."

"We could write them a note," suggested Ali, obviously sharing Tony's sentiment.

"Have you got a pen and paper with you?" I asked. Of course, no-one had. I always carried both, but I wasn't letting on. "We'll just have to wait until they come back," I reasoned. "We can't just take off without a word."

Once again, a dejected silence fell in the car, so as soon as I noticed that the rain had stopped, I wasted no time in suggesting that we make the best of our last night by driving up to the castle for a mooch around. This idea wasn't greeted with a great deal of enthusiasm, but anything was better than sitting there staring into the trees, so we set off up the Loch along the A82, to Urquhart Castle.

As we pulled into the car park area that overlooked the castle we saw James and the others sitting in the Saab, so we drew alongside. The windows rolled down and immediately a fresh joint came over, and once mildly stoned, Ali and Tony's mood improved and everyone lightened up. We clambered out of the cars and, making our way down the snaking path, climbed over the gate and entered the deserted castle. As we always did whenever we climbed down there after dark, we reverted to early childhood and spent some time running around, laughing, and joking. As we stood in the castle grounds taking in the moment, I heard Reg ask, "What do you think that is over there?"

Turning around, James and I gazed down the Loch in the direction that Reg indicated. From our position high on the slope, facing the tower, we looked at the horizon toward Inverness and strewn across the mouth of the Loch were a series of thin, vertical strands of white light. I had never seen anything like it, and I remember turning to James and asking "the Northern Lights?", though I doubted it. The lights resembled distant gas jets, strung out across the Loch in a uniform manner rather than scattered across the sky.

"I suppose it must be," replied James, grinning.

"Far out!" I exclaimed. "I've never seen them."

As we continued to watch, the string of lights across the water grew intensely brighter and by now everyone had stopped what they were doing to look. Suddenly, above our heads, thin strands of purple and blue light appeared. They were fanning out, giving the impression they were refracted downward at an angle just above the horizon where each one met with one of the white lights on the water. These new strands seemed to end at a single point above our heads, creating the illusion that we were gazing out from behind the bars of a giant, illuminated cage. Looking up I noticed that, apart from these thin slivers of purple light, the sky was relatively clear - the rain clouds now having blown away - and there were only occasional banks of scattered cloud over the water. Above us the Plough was clearly visible amongst the other stars, and from the midst of them, as if suddenly emerging from some invisible point and with an audible whoosh, a burst of colour erupted. Almost like red smoke, it swept in a perfect one hundred and eighty degree arc from right to left above our heads, leaving a trail of red haze in its wake. Halfway through its course another colour erupted, this time green, and swept across the sky in a similar fashion in the opposite direction, crossing paths with the red, and this in turn was followed by a burst of gold. As these colours traversed the sky, I could hear the rippling effect caused by some obvious displacement as the colours followed their course. "Oh fuck, someone's dropped an atom bomb!" I heard myself say in the midst of it.

"Nah," someone else said. "If it was an atom bomb we'd all have been blinded."

"Well, what the fuck is it?" I heard someone else say.

I was vaguely aware that I was grasping the shoulders of James' motorcycle jacket as my eyes snapped back and forth across the sky. The scattered cloud that I'd seen earlier over the Loch now seemed to be illuminated from within. Bursts of white light, as quick as lightning, yet unlike any kind of lightning I'd ever seen before, began shooting in short spasms across the sky, away from us down the water. We ran further up the grass slope to try to get a better overall view and, as we stood gazing out toward the distant orange haze that was Inverness, at the point where we'd seen the first of these unusual lights strung out like beads across the water, I noticed that they were still there, bright as beacons.

Above our heads, I saw that another source of white light was unfolding itself. I use the term unfolding because that is the best way I can think of to describe it, although it is barely adequate. This point of light seemed to be emerging from within the very fabric of the sky. I watched, fascinated, as it continued to unfurl and steadily grow in size. The intensity of the light was the purest and brightest I can ever remember seeing, yet it didn't dazzle the eyes in the slightest and I was able to look directly into it without squinting. Eventually this light fully unfolded to reveal a human figure, with arms outstretched. I remember noticing the folds and pleats of what appeared to be some kind of dress, but I was unable to lift my gaze higher than the chest area - I couldn't summon the will to gaze upon its face. As I stared at the figure in utter disbelief, I felt a tremendous sense of elation and euphoria, without the slightest trace of fear. The only voice I remember hearing was that of Angel, who was ironically exclaiming, "It's an angel! My God! It's an angel! Can you see it?"

As we continued to watch, the figure began to collapse in on itself until finally it disappeared into a single finite point and winked out. The sweeping colours were gone, as were the bursts of light within the cloud over the Loch, and the thin strands of purple light running down to the horizon were quickly growing dim. All that remained were the vertical strands of white light strung across the mouth of the Loch, which were now also diminishing. I remember looking at each of the others in stunned disbelief. Everyone was just standing around, huge grins on their faces. We climbed back down the steep bank and eventually decided that it was time to go, although I had to practically drag James. "It might come back," he said.

"Trust me, James. I don't think it'll be back," I said, and reluctantly he followed me toward the main entrance.

As we arrived back at the car park, a pair of headlights emanating from a parked vehicle - one that hadn't been there when we arrived - suddenly illuminated us on full beam. We quietly debated what to do about it. Unbeknown to the rest of us, Tony and James had identified the headlights as belonging to a van of some kind and, fearing it might be the police, started feeling very paranoid. Beyond the car park, the road vanished into a bend and we now saw another pair of headlights slowly emerge, followed by another, which in turn was followed by yet another. I was used to seeing cars coming along this stretch of road late at night at very high speed, but what struck me about these vehicles was how slowly they were going. They couldn't have been driving much faster than ten or fifteen miles per hour.

Now it was my turn to be gripped by paranoia and apparently, I wasn't the only one, because I heard someone suddenly shout "Go!" This broke the spell, and we piled into the cars to make good our escape. James' powerful Saab was gone in a flash, and we followed as quickly as we could. The pair of lights that had held us transfixed was quickly in pursuit, and as Ken and I peered out of the rear window we saw that the vehicle was dangerously close. It was indeed a van of some kind but the glare of the headlights, still on high beam, made it impossible to discern any details. Still, there were no flashing blue lights or sirens - whoever it was, they weren't the police. Tony was unable to accelerate away from the mysterious van, and was swearing and cursing into the rear view mirror. I remember him saying something about wanting a better look at them, and so he told us all to hang on to something and then slammed on the brakes. To avoid a collision our pursuers were forced to swerve to the other side of the road. Fortunately, there was no oncoming traffic. In coming to a sudden halt, the van's engine had stalled, and the driver was having difficulty restarting the engine, but we couldn't see anything of the occupants. Tony threw the car into gear and took off, leaving them stranded.

Throughout the drive back, Ken and I kept looking out of the rear window searching for the pursuing headlights but could see no sign of them. Soon we pulled into the campsite, and climbing from the car we all waited by the side of the road, expecting the van to hurtle past but it never came. We stood there laughing nervously, debating what to do. Most of the others decided they'd had enough excitement for one night and opted to retire. Meanwhile, James, Ken, and I decided we wanted to go back and try to find the van. The way I looked at it, our paranoia had prevented an opportunity to discover whether its occupants had seen the lights in the sky, and I suddenly became eager for some kind of verification. We drove all the way back to the castle but saw no sign of any other vehicle. I tell myself I missed an opportunity that night, but I also remember the deep feeling of dread that had come over me as I saw those other cars come creeping slowly around the bend in the road. This was a feeling I was to experience again in the future, and I often ask myself whether something altogether more sinister was happening that night.

Looking back, I regard 1982 as one of the most profoundly strange periods of my entire life. The experience at Loch Ness was still very much in the forefront of my mind, although no-one around me, except for Angel, who was there, and Julia, who had heard our numerous accounts, would talk about it. Well, that's not entirely true: when Dave and I were on close terms, he'd seen it, when we weren't, he hadn't. For the most part, the others shrugged their shoulders and got on with their lives, which was probably the most sensible way of dealing with it. The consensus seemed to be that what we had seen had merely been the phenomenon known as Aurora Borealis, more commonly referred to as the Northern Lights. Ali refused to discuss it at all, while Reg put it down to smoking too much dope; "Life's weird enough on its own without all that," he muttered. I wasn't prepared to dismiss the incident so casually, though. Whatever its nature, I'd had some kind of vision, and was convinced that I'd been given a glimpse of something bigger, beyond what the author Colin Wilson describes as "the triviality of everydayness". Maybe it was a vision that I needed to have, and the others didn't? But I know that I wasn't the only one of us who saw it.

Overall, I put the others' reactions down to fear: the fear of confronting an experience that turned set paradigms concerning the nature of reality on their head. I wouldn't say that this experience changed me. On the contrary, if anything my drug abuse increased. Life, in the wake of this experience, came to seem more trivial and mundane than ever. It was as if in the hallucinatory experiences of LSD or psilocybin mushrooms, I could find some compensatory factor for having to endure a reality where, generally speaking, celestial angels don't appear above our heads. As for hallucinations, I've never had any. What I mean is I've never, while under the influence of drugs or otherwise, ever seen anything that isn't actually there. I've seen things that have taken on the appearance of something else, but that isn't the same thing at all. Assuming a person hallucinates, perhaps we can say that the experience is due to some kind of trick of the mind. What about a shared hallucination, though? What the fuck is that?

One evening I was at Julia's house in Birmingham, engaged in a conversation with Angel, when I turned to look at Julia and saw she was smiling, silently transfixed, staring into a space in the far corner of the dimly lit room. Angel and I looked at each other for a moment before asking her if she was all right. "I'm fine," she said softly. "I'm just wondering what on earth that is on the hi-fi speaker."

We followed her gaze and looked at the speaker, which had a black cloth covering fixed onto the front of it to protect the cones. The covering, however, was no longer black. Projecting out of it was a scene so surreal that to relate it will sound like complete madness, yet the three of us saw it clearly and unambiguously. On the front of the speaker were outlines in purple and blue depicting a forest glade of some kind. I continued to stare with my mouth wide open and what appeared to be a swarm of butterflies rose up suddenly into the air, as if disturbed by something, and flew off amongst the trees. At that precise moment, I heard Angel's delighted exclamation. "My God! Butterflies! Did you see them? What's going on?"

We continued to stare into the black cloth. The forest dissolved away to be replaced by a high mountain range. Cut into one of the mountainsides was a long, winding stairway and descending the stairway was a small group of individuals, all wearing hooded robes. "Are you seeing this?" I quietly asked the others.

"Yes, they seem to be monks, or something." I heard Julia reply. The hooded figures continued their descent until, suddenly, they seemed to halt and turn to face us. The strange figures were now looking directly at us, and one raised his arm and pointed at us, as if he had noticed us watching and was alerting his companions. My heart was pounding in my chest as I desperately tried to take stock of what was happening. It was obviously a hallucination of some kind but how on earth could three people hallucinate the same thing? There was no question of suggestive interpretation. For the most part, we all watched in silence, comparing and confirming what we had witnessed immediately after, and when Julia or Angel did speak it was only to confirm something that I had already seen with my own eyes. The moment the figures had seemed to notice us, the vision faded out and we were left stunned, staring at an ordinary hi-fi speaker, which was once again black and featureless. This is absolutely true, and it is one the strangest things I have ever seen.

Other synchronistic events occurred that would compound my feelings of confusion. One afternoon I was with Dave, when he suddenly handed me a copy of *The New Scientist* that had been lying on the coffee table at James' flat. "Read that!" he said. I forget the actual context of the article, but one short paragraph was particularly relevant. I can't quote it exactly, although I think Dave cut it out of the magazine and still has it somewhere. To summarise, the article was discussing Loch Ness, and it said that there was something peculiar about the region that seemed to cause hallucinations. Additionally, it went on to say that these hallucinations could often be shared by a group of people at the same time. In my paranoia, it was almost as if the paragraph had been planted in the magazine for our benefit, which was, of course, ridiculous, but it illustrates my state of mind at the time. I have yet to hear of any elaboration of this theme worthy of publication in *The New Scientist* that seriously supports such a notion, which would by definition constitute a psychic or telepathic experience.

Meanwhile, the release date and promotional tour for the new single crept ever closer, and suddenly the pressure was on. Moz decided he would organise a couple of local gigs the week before the tour by way of a warm-up. A show at the Gallery, which used to lie on Peter Street in Manchester, was an obvious choice, but a free gig in a Stockport pub was rather more unusual, and we questioned the wisdom of it. "It's just a warm-up!" Moz kept insisting, growing increasingly irritated. "It's an opportunity to run through your set, it doesn't matter where you do it."

I can't remember exactly what was bugging Dave that night, but he was in a foul mood and it didn't bode well. Moz hadn't advertised the gig beyond the confines of the pub itself, and the audience was made up of pub regulars who'd never heard of the band before. Throughout the set, they sat drinking their beer in total apathy. John's lifestyle was seriously beginning to take its toll, and he was fucking up badly to the point where he'd just stop playing drums altogether mid-song. Dave, in his frustration, rounded on the audience, all of who were quietly and attentively drinking their pints, and delivered a barrage of insults, the like of which I'd never heard from him before. Some of the things he was shouting at the audience were quite strong. I'm amazed we didn't get our heads kicked in after the gig, but at the time it sounded hilarious and I just couldn't stop laughing. At the end of each diatribe all hostile eyes would fall back onto me as I attempted to pick up the pieces and continue with the set, only for Dave to stop again mid-song shouting, "and another thing," before launching into another torrent of abuse. This situation continued for about twenty minutes before I'd finally had enough, and I bolted for the makeshift dressing room, followed by the others. Dave continued his rant in the dressing room, and by this time I was no longer laughing. All I could do was stare at him in disbelief.

After the gig, I'd arranged to travel back down to the Midlands with Moz and rejoin Julia. The first ten minutes of the journey passed in total silence. Eventually Moz spoke, telling me that, in all the years he'd been managing bands, he'd never seen or heard anything so disgusting and offensive, and that we were arrogant and ought to be ashamed. He began attacking Dave's attitude, but I defended him: "He's right - we shouldn't be playing free gigs in pubs, it's not what we're about. We're supposed to have left all that behind us."

To be honest I was equally shocked by Dave's behaviour, but at the end of the day, he was a mate and I wasn't going to sit there and let someone trash him behind his back, especially Moz. "I was so embarrassed when I spoke to the landlady after." Moz continued. "I didn't know what to say to her. Well, I'm not going to be put into situations like that. You can find some other mug to look after you."

At once, I cheered up. I hadn't wanted Moz in the first place. "Well, you know," I said finally, "maybe you're right. Maybe you shouldn't be involved with us."

The journey descended into a tense silence once again, and I sensed that Moz realised he'd had his bluff called. He didn't speak for the remainder of the journey, until he finally dropped me off outside Julia's house and said, "Well, let's just forget the whole thing, I probably over-reacted." But I could see in his eyes he had meant every word he'd said, and how false he was being now.

Internally, we held a post mortem of the gig, and I remember being very vocal about it. I argued that it was all well and good Dave getting a cob on and attacking the audience but, as the lead vocalist, I'd be expected to pick up the pieces and carry the gig, which I thought was unfair. Dave got upset in turn and insisted that if that was the way I felt about it, then he no longer wanted a microphone on stage. He stubbornly stuck to his decision, and this was to prove the end of live backing vocals for The Chameleons.

We tried to put the incident behind us and continued writing and rehearsing for the upcoming tour. The writing was going quite well, and there was one new idea I particularly loved, which I'd titled 'View From A Hill', although we were struggling a little bit with the instrumental arrangement of the ending, something that Dave and Reg had cooked up during a coffee break in rehearsals. Still, I loved it and felt it was something altogether more interesting than the three-minute burst that was 'The Fan And The Bellows'.

CBS informed us that Steve Lillywhite had declined to produce the album and, while we were a bit disappointed, I don't recall we were that concerned about it. We were confident that another producer would be found, and if not, we'd produce the record ourselves with a good engineer. We had no shortage of confidence or ideas, and were happy with the way our music was developing. The tour was shaping up well, and we were to begin by supporting Bauhaus at a sold-out show in Manchester, setting off on our own nationwide tour the following Monday.

With only a week to go before the first of these dates, we played a final warm-up show at The Gallery. However, in the immediate wake of the debacle that had been the pub gig in Stockport, it was obvious that John was having severe problems, and we were all more than a little concerned. Even Moz, it seemed, had grown genuinely worried, so when he offered to drive John to his home after the show and have a heart-to-heart in an effort to help, we were all a bit relieved that John agreed.

Reg, Dave, and I travelled down to Birmingham to stay with Julia and Angel, and Moz offered to call us from across town the following day to tell us how John was. Sure enough, first thing the next morning the phone rang.

"Do you know any other drummers?" Moz asked. "John's quit the group."

7. SHOT BY BOTH SIDES

The first thing we tried to do was to speak with John in person, but he refused to talk to any of us when we phoned after he'd left Moz's house for home that day. Moz explained that John felt his emotional problems, combined with the deterioration in his performance, were holding the band back; that it had been a case of too much, too soon, and that he thought he was heading toward some kind of breakdown. Undeterred, we continued to try to reach John at home, but he still refused to come to the phone. His mother told us that his behaviour was extremely disturbing. "He's shaved off all his hair," she wept. "Yesterday he cleared an area of the back garden, poured petrol over his drum kit and set fire to it." Finally, Dave did get to speak with John, who wouldn't discuss his reasons with us directly except to say that there was no way he was going to rejoin the group, that he wished us luck, and that he would be moving out of the house they shared and returning to his parents.

We sat around Julia's house for a couple of days in total confusion, talking a lot but not really knowing what to do. Mixed with our concern for John was a sense of rising panic as we realised that we'd have to pull out of the tour, which was due to begin with the Bauhaus date the following week, timed with the release date of 'In Shreds'.

The single was finally released, and despite the shock and upset of losing John, I was very proud at being able to hold a copy of our first record in my hands. My father was also tremendously proud and carried a copy of it around town whenever he went out, showing it to everyone.

Eventually Moz phoned and told me that he'd managed to get in touch with Magazine's former drummer, Martin Jackson. Martin had been one of the original members of the band but had left shortly after completing their debut album, which we all felt had been their best. Singer Howard Devoto had left Buzzcocks after recording the *Spiral Scratch* EP out of a desire to do something a little more progressive, and Magazine had then produced a lively hit single, 'Shot By Both Sides', but since Martin's departure from the band they'd drifted toward the more dubious area of alternative cabaret.

Martin was a keen, confident, and proficient drummer with a considerable reputation, so we were pleased to learn that he was interested in working with us for a while. He was able to learn the bulk of our set in two days and we only had to cancel the first date of the tour. The remainder of the gigs went ahead without a hitch, and people turned up in droves.

Martin had initially agreed to join The Chameleons for the duration of that short tour but ended up working with us for about six months. He was a friendly, down-to-earth individual with a great sense of humour, and very comfortable to be around. Dave had been largely responsible for arranging the drum parts, as he had done with Scoffer, and Martin would happily take this direction without complaint. He was totally without ego, and we all retained a tremendous amount of respect and affection for him.

It was because of Martin that we did a photo session with Anton Corbijn, who Martin had got to know during his Magazine days. Anton had photographed everyone from Beefheart to Bowie during his spell as a freelance photographer with the *NME* and *Rolling Stone*, as well as being in constant demand by various record companies and artists. He's still regarded by many, myself included, as one of the finest portrait photographers in the world. The photograph that he finally chose to submit, featuring the band crouched behind the base of a large tree stump overlooking Derwent Water in the Lake District, is one of my favourite Chameleons photographs, despite the sad absence of John.

Tony, as a budding amateur photographer, benefited from watching Anton work up close, and the entire shoot was relaxed and good natured. Anton would often be very specific about how he wanted to utilise light and shadow, which resulted in varying degrees of body contortion as he zeroed in on his close-ups. Tony, meanwhile, would step back and also shoot the subject in full view and so, taken out of context, some of these contortions would look ridiculous and would have us all screaming with laughter. Over the following year Tony took most of the promotional photos that we used, and developed a great talent for candid shots.

The venues for our first full national tour were, for the most part, university halls and refectories dotted up and down the country - the same gig circuit on which U2 had cut their teeth a couple of years earlier. We had our own sound engineer for the first time, a guy named Paul who had previously been a resident PA tech at one of our regular venues, the Gallery in Manchester. He was rather straight-laced by our standards, but he seemed very down to earth. Our initial impression of him was to change dramatically, though, following a gig in Cambridge.

After the show we returned to the hotel and, as usual, a few of us began to party a little. Initially Paul seemed fine but after the laughing, the joking and the partaking of party substances had gone on for about an hour, he suddenly revealed a taste for the more obvious clichés of rock and roll indulgence and set about vandalising the room. Alarmed by this unexpected turn of events, we tried to stop him, but he was a big bloke and not very easy to control. Finally we were able to calm him down, and we made our excuses and prepared to leave - the object of the exercise being to get Paul out of Martin's room and try to get as far away from this maniac as possible. Unfortunately, Paul was just warming up. He got more and more boisterous, and it took us the best part of an hour to lose him in the narrow streets of Cambridge. Somewhat relieved, Martin decided that it was time he turned in for the night and so, with great vigilance, he made his way back to his hotel room. He got ready for bed and settled down to read the *NME* before getting some well-deserved sleep. He read for about an hour, discarded the paper and switched out the light. Suddenly the door of his wardrobe burst open and Paul came flying out. "Ha-ha!" he exclaimed to a terrified Martin, leaping onto his bed. "You didn't expect that did you?" He'd spent all this time hiding in Martin's wardrobe, silently preparing for his moment of triumph. Paul was off the tour the next day.

Anton Corbijn and Mark, 1982.   Photo: Tony Skinkis

A week later we played in Oxford, and were so impressed with the house technicians and their PA rig that we promptly hired them for the remainder of the dates, and they continued to work with us for quite some time.

Later on the tour brought us back to the Derby Hall in Bury, and it was strange to play there again in the light of everything that had happened since meeting Danny and Richard the previous year. The single had received more good reviews than bad, and by now we were attracting quite a bit of attention. Midway through one of the songs I happened to glance down at a guy who was sitting on the edge of the stage with his back to the PA stack, rolling a joint. I immediately recognised him as a fellow pupil of ours at Hollin High School, whose name was Mark, although none of us had seen him for years. I was only vaguely acquainted with him despite knowing him since around the age of eight, but I remembered him because of a very strange and terrifying dream I'd had, and which I never forgot.

Occasionally on warm summer afternoons, which seem to have been much more numerous back then, some teachers would take entire classes out for a ramble into the woods opposite Hollin Infants School and point out various types of trees, flowers and butterflies, and in my dream, my class had been taken on such a ramble. We all followed the teachers, hand-in-hand, graciously humouring their irrational desire to label everything, when I suddenly turned to see that the child whose hand I was grasping was Mark. After a while though, he began tugging my hand, indicating that he wanted to stop for a while, and soon we became disentangled from the rest of the class, none of whom seemed to notice this. I kept tugging at the boy who was now preventing us from keeping up with the others, but he proved stronger than I expected and we found ourselves lagging further and further behind. Eventually we both stood on the shore of a huge lake, which in reality didn't exist but in the context of the dream lay on a large expanse of land behind the house that the boy actually lived in, although in the dream the houses weren't there. I noticed, as we both inspected the lake, that the rest of the class were now specks on the horizon and I could faintly hear them singing, "Mad Jack, don't look back. Mad Jack, don't look back." At that moment Mark was pulled into the water by some unseen force, and he vanished beneath the black surface. I began to panic because, at the time, I couldn't swim and had a profound fear of deep water. Although I could still faintly hear them singing, the rest of the class were now much too far away to hear my shouts for help, and so I just sat down on the edge of the lake, desperately trying to come up with a plan.

Suddenly, something broke the surface of the water. I instinctively tried to scamper away, but two arms shot out from beneath the surface, got a firm grip of my calves, and began to drag me back toward the lake. I kicked and struggled, frantically trying to grab hold of the rocks and the shale that littered the beach, but the arms were too strong and they continued to pull me in. I could now feel the freezing cold water on the lower portions of my legs. The singing in my head was growing steadily louder although the rest of the class were nowhere to be seen and the grip on my legs was now so strong that they were becoming numb due to lack of circulation. Suddenly, a head broke the surface of the water and I tried to scream, but the sound was caught in my throat. It was recognisably Mark's face and yet it had been transformed into the grinning, leering face of a monster with wide staring eyes and, between fits of stifled laughter that sounded more like choking, he was mouthing the words to the taunting melody that was now so loud inside my head I thought it would burst: "MAD JACK, DON'T LOOK BACK. MAD JACK, DON'T LOOK BACK"

It was just a stupid dream, triggered by God knows what. Nevertheless it had made an impact on me, and after it I always felt a little uneasy when he was around. Still, this was almost twenty years later, I was no longer a child, and in the intervening years a number of myths had developed around this guy. He'd move to Moorclose Senior High and then suddenly dropped off the radar after attending the annual Deeply Vale Free Festival. Legend had it that he'd fallen in with a band of travelling hippies and never returned home, and that was the last any of us had heard of him, until now.

The show had been a particularly good one, and the usual dressing room piss-up went on for hours. Later on, Mark invited the band back to his house for a smoke and a chance to catch up on old times. Moz was with us that night, and he discreetly asked us if it were possible to buy one or two grams of amphetamine sulphate. This genuinely surprised me, because it was the first time he'd ever given the slightest indication that he used drugs. "Oh no, it's not for me, it's for my wife," he hastily explained. As it turned out, our old friend sold speed, amongst other things, so we were able to sort something out. Moz refused to come into the house, choosing instead to wait outside in his car with the engine running. Over the course of the next few months we saw more of Mark, although, as I say, I never really felt entirely at ease in his company.

One afternoon, Dave called me. He wanted to buy some hashish but it seemed that all the usual sources had dried up. This sort of thing had become a real problem for him, in as much as he exhibited very intense mood swings if he couldn't get stoned. Naturally, Dave knew that our old school friend, Mark, was a dealer, but there was a problem. Being somewhat paranoid, Mark didn't use a telephone, and it was a long, arduous journey by bus, fraught with danger, over many miles of hostile country. The only sensible option, therefore, was to get a cab, except if he went alone the fare would screw him. Dave reasoned that if I were to buy some hashish too, we'd both get a better deal and we could share the cab fare, hence the extremely rare phone call. Of course, it had taken a while for Dave to actually get to the point, but I'd always found him as easy to read as Dr. Seuss.

About an hour later we were at Mark's house, and as we sat in the kitchen making small talk, things rapidly became strange. Also crowded into the tiny kitchen was a small band of rather desperate looking individuals, all of whom were twitching nervously, hungrily eyeing Mark's every move, like dogs watching the roast, and it took me all of two seconds to register that they were Mark's more exclusive clientele.

To compound the embarrassment, one particular guy seemed to be hiding at the back of the queue. Dave spotted him, against all the odds, as his eyesight has never been very good, and it turned out to be a former friend of his from his college days. Dave was obviously surprised to see him, but showed no indication that he'd twigged what was going on here, somewhat naïvely asking his friend how he was. His friend, red faced, seemed to be wishing he was somewhere else; sadly, the poor guy looked pretty far gone.

Mark continued with the small talk and casually began making tea. One of the guys actually pleaded with him to get around to sorting them out. Mark rounded on him, telling him to shut the fuck up. Feeling extremely uncomfortable to say the least, I whispered "For fuck's sake, sort them out will you?" Mark looked at me with an expression of amused contempt for a moment, and then proceeded to throw his scraps to the strays.

Later we were sitting in his living room. The phantoms had now departed, and we were rolling joints. Dave went off in search of a telephone box from which to call a taxi, and it was then that Mark started his relentless sales pitch, exalting the virtues of heroin. He told me that as far as he was concerned there was nothing that could touch it, not sex, not music, not art - no other buzz could compare. All other hits and highs were a visit to the dentist by comparison. At one point, he took a book from his shelf and covered the bottom of the front cover with his hand. It read:

IT'S SO GREAT YOU DON'T EVEN WANT TO TRY IT ONCE!

He moved his hand to reveal:

HEROIN IN PERSPECTIVE

The room, which up until Dave's departure had been a breeze of strong hashish and groovy music, was now quiet except for the stifled giggling of an old face from school. My eyes rose from the book cover, and I saw in front of me the face of the monster from my nightmare.

Mark couldn't have known the real cause of my horror, instead thinking that the wraps of heroin on the table had induced the fear, and this seemed to cause him even greater amusement.

"I'd like to turn the whole world onto it," he said between whispering fits of laughter, "you know, like the hippies who used to dream of putting acid in the water supply." The air around me was so heavy I thought it would crush my skull and it struck me that suddenly even the music didn't sound right, as if I'd somehow slipped sideways into some misshapen, warped version of reality where only this wraith and I existed.

Suddenly there was a knock on the door and, in a flash, Mark removed the wraps of heroin from the table. He walked to the door, peeped quickly around the window curtains, opened the door, and in walked Dave. The monstrous grin on Mark's face had vanished. Dave, oblivious to all this, casually announced that the taxi was on its way. Mark now seemed totally rational and natural, and I would have been tempted to think I'd imagined the whole thing had it not been for the conspiratorial smiles he threw me whenever Dave's back was turned. When the taxi arrived I was first out of the door, and I never went back.

Some time later, I heard that the guy had been arrested for dealing heroin and had gone to prison. A local priest, new to the area, had taken it upon himself to wage war on heroin by targeting the dealers and, amazingly, he'd met with a large degree of success. He'd even managed to provide regular full time work for reformed addicts via a concert PA company, which the priest owned and had formed specifically for the purpose. As far as I know, Wigwam PA still thrives today.

With such a heavy touring schedule it was inevitable that some of us would get drawn into the usual excesses that exist around young rock bands and, unfortunately, there was no-one around to point out the dangers. As a result, things began to get a little out of control. The warning signs had begun in Birmingham one night when I was alone with Julia and Angel. Angel was stressed out because she had exams coming up and she'd wanted to take some speed, but then Julia stepped in and refused to allow her to have it. I found myself caught in the middle as they fought, feeling rather confused and embarrassed because I'd been taking speed fairly regularly since my teens. I can honestly say that while I enjoyed the effects of the narcotic, I wasn't addicted to it, but when Angel suddenly burst into tears and began begging for the speed, I felt a sickening realisation that the evils of amphetamine sulphate abuse, which up until that point hadn't really dawned on me, were as real and as pathetic as any other addiction.

I also came to realise that, under the influence of speed, our performances had become ragged, edgy, and brash, and that the drug was making me feel increasingly paranoid. The situation came to a head one night during a gig at The Gallery in Manchester. The place was packed and there were about fifty other people outside trying to get in, most of them badgering me to put them on the guest list whenever I came within earshot. The support band that night was a local affair named Gammer And His Familiars and, to the consternation of most of the audience, they were still playing after a full two hours. Thankfully, someone eventually took control and was able to get them off, and thirty minutes later we were practically thrown onto the stage[1].

Towards the end of our set something was thrown from the audience and I felt it hit me in the chest. For some reason, I got it into my head that it was a glass or a bottle, not that I had bothered to check, and that it had been thrown from the side balcony. I couldn't pinpoint anyone in particular because of the spotlight shining directly into my face, but I began pointing at the approximate area and shouting angrily. I even thought about climbing up the lighting rig to find them at one point. Later I discovered that the object was nothing more than a copy of a fanzine, and that the silhouette I'd been bellowing at behind the lights was actually our old mate Joe, who had been seriously freaked out by my behaviour.

Not so long after I was to have another unpleasant, amphetamine-related experience. Having been unable to secure any speed from a regular source, an acquaintance of mine stepped in and took me to a filthy flat on a housing estate in a neighbouring town. There was a young girl there, desperate for speed but without had the money to pay for it. Consequently she begged a guy, who himself was cranked high on the drug, to allow her to lick the perspiration from his dripping face in the hope of picking up some residue.

Over the next few months I came to realise the effect that drug abuse was having on me, physically and mentally - I was beginning to look gaunt, scrawny and washed out. In the end I gave up taking narcotics altogether for a very long time, although I fell short of giving up illicit substances entirely. Still, I was at least able to abstain sufficiently to ensure that it wasn't a frequent, daily habit.

---

1. Later that year, Dave and I had been on our way to London late one evening and had missed our train. With a couple of hours to kill until the next one, we sauntered down to The Gallery to see who was playing. Outside was a blackboard that read: 'Gammer And His Familiars PLUS Performance Art'. Oh no, we moaned, not them again! At that moment, it started to rain, so we paid our two quid and went in. The singer had an operatic voice of immense power and beauty and a commanding stage presence. We were both completely stunned. His music veered from highly humorous to soulfully sad in the space of sixteen bars. As we left the venue to catch our train, I found myself walking backwards out of the venue in order to catch as much of the set as I could, and subsequently became a great admirer of Gammer. I treasure his records to this day.

Another Middleton face that I knew quite well, whose name was Chris, had stopped inhaling his amphetamine and had progressed to injecting it with a hypodermic syringe. The change in him was dramatic, and before long he was barely recognisable. His transformation was akin to some kind of possession. I called round to see him one night and he was in a foul mood. He had no money, and no-one would give him any, so he hadn't been able to buy any speed. Suddenly, noticing I was wearing a small, silver cross around my neck, he demanded to know why. Actually, I wore it for no other reason than it had been the first gift Fenella had ever given to me, but this explanation didn't satisfy him. "It'll take more than some myth about a bloke with holes in his fuckin' hands to convince me there's anything in this world that's worth a shit!" he snarled.

Less than a month later, after suddenly losing his father to a fatal illness, Chris broke down in tears in Jubilee Park in Middleton and, the way he tells it, was instantly cleansed. From that moment on, he became a born again Christian and immediately gave up cigarettes, alcohol and drugs. I saw him about a week after it had happened, unable to believe the rumours. Now, having chastised me for mistakenly believing I was Catholic a few weeks earlier, he was now berating me for living a sinful, wasteful life, and urged me to repent while there was still time. "I can't win with you, can I?" I remember telling him over a coffee. After studying at bible college, Chris became a missionary and, as far as I know, continues to travel around spreading the gospel to this day. Meanwhile it seemed that heroin was suddenly everywhere, and was starting to take a foothold locally, mainly because it was cheaper and more readily available than hashish. This was to become a disturbing and continuing trend over the following few years.

That summer I fell foul of the drug squad during the Notting Hill Carnival, after a group of us had stopped off at James' flat en route to Holland, where we were planning to spend the weekend with some friends in Den Haag. On the Saturday afternoon everyone except Julia and I wanted to walk around Notting Hill to take in the carnival. It was a hot day, and we were both rather tired, so we arranged to meet up with them later. After a while, as I sat there building the first joint of the day, there was a knock at the front door. Thinking that one or two of them may have changed their minds I opened the door and saw four straight looking men in raincoats. "Mr Lipton?" one of them asked me.

"Well, no," I replied, eyeing them nervously. "He's out enjoying the carnival, I'm just staying with him for a couple of days."

He reached inside his coat pocket and pulled out some identification, and an official looking document in very small print. "We're police officers, and we have a warrant to search the house," he said, smiling.

I stalled them for as long as I could in the hope that Julia would hear and somehow get rid of anything incriminating that we might have left lying around, which thankfully she did. They began by searching our things, and the officer in charge pulled out a small shaving kit that contained a mirror, which I'd often used in the past to cut and dice amphetamine. Faint traces could still be seen around the edges of the glass and he held it up. "Coke?" he asked.

"Speed." I replied, "but you're wasting your time, it's long gone."

"At least you're up front about it," said the officer. I had no reason not to be, I knew neither I nor Julia had anything heavy and it looked at least as though Julia had managed to stash the hash. In any event, we had less than an eighth of an ounce, which wouldn't have been enough to build much of a case on.

He went on to explain that they intended to systematically search the flat, and that I would have to accompany them from room to room so that we wouldn't be able to claim later that anything they found had been planted. Julia remained in the living room, providing the same function there, while I was led into James' bedroom. After a while, they began rummaging through his laundry. Rather you than me, I thought! Suddenly one of the officers pulled a pair of clean socks from the drawer and wrapped inside was a wad of bank notes, around £2,000. He looked up at me. "Where did he get this, and what is it for?" he asked me.

"How should I know?" I snapped. "I'm a guest here, not his house keeper."

The officer continued to sift through the rest of the drawers. As he flicked through the pages of a diary, a wrap of paper fell to the floor. On examination, it contained around a gram of cocaine. "Bingo!" he said, and we moved on to the kitchen, although this provided little in the way of anything incriminating. One officer pulled a jar of raw, magic mushrooms from a shelf.

"What are these?"

"No idea, they look like mushrooms. Why don't you rustle us up an omelette, and we'll find out?"

The officer laughed, tagged the jar, and handed it to another officer. Another policeman walked into the kitchen carrying some apparatus, enamelled in pale blue, which he dismantled. Inside it were residual amounts of white powder. "This is used for grinding down cocaine." he explained. "It looks like your friend is a cocaine dealer."

Skimming through James' passport, he gave me a curious look. "Is your friend a diplomat?" he asked.

"As far as I know he works for an advertising agency," I shrugged.

"Well this passport is valid for twenty years. Even I can't get one of these, it's a diplomatic passport. How did he get it?"

"I haven't the faintest idea," I sighed. "When he gets back you can ask him, can't you?"

"Right!" he said. "Well, I think we have enough to be getting on with. I'm afraid that both of you will have to accompany us to the station, where you'll be held until such time as Mr. Lipton is taken into custody."

"You can't do that," I stated flatly, although I had no idea whether they were legally entitled to or not.

"I'm afraid that we can," he replied. "For all we know, you may be aiding and abetting."

Julia and I were escorted to the local police station, where we were placed in separate cells and held for around four hours. Eventually we were released, and as we were escorted out I saw an ashen-faced James being interviewed by another officer, but I wasn't given an opportunity to speak with him.

After he'd been charged and released on bail, we were able to piece together what had happened. James, having decided to travel with us to Holland, had offered to buy a large quantity of cocaine for some work colleagues, thereby increasing the buying power for all of them. Apparently James did this on a semi-regular basis. Someone, however, must have held a grudge, and had made an anonymous call to the police. The blue-enamelled apparatus found during the search had indeed been used to grind down the cocaine before he passed it onto his friends, but after the police had taken it away for analysis, they discovered that the residue therein had amounted to around a gram. This, in addition to the gram found in his diary, meant that the police could only bring the relatively minor charge of possession. Had they waited until his return from Holland to raid the flat the situation would have been very different, and he could have been facing three to five years in jail for smuggling and dealing cocaine. As it was, his lawyer told him to expect a fine and a caution and, in the end, this proved correct, although the fine stood at £50 plus court costs, which were minimal. None of us could understand how he'd managed to get away with such a tiny fine, and we kept asking him, but he refused to be drawn and would only say that he was lucky. Of course, James was forbidden to leave the country until the case could be heard in court, so we had to proceed to Holland without him. I asked James how he had come to have a diplomatic passport, and he would only say that the policeman must have been mistaken. He hadn't been, though, because I'd seen it with my own eyes. I never was able to get a satisfactory explanation from him.

While in Den Haag, enjoying the effects of some rather splendid acid, we decided to go to a tiny venue called the Trojan Horse to see a relatively new band from Australia called The Birthday Party. We didn't really expect much as we knew almost nothing about them, so we were totally unprepared for what we saw. They were the oddest collection of individuals I'd ever seen together on a stage. One guitar player performed with his back to the audience the whole time while the other, a lit cigarette perpetually in his mouth and eyes wide and manic, shook like a junkie as he hammered his guitar. The bass player was a huge man in leather trousers and a cowboy hat, with a bass guitar almost as big as he was. He would thrust his groin and gyrate with every beat of the bass drum, sometimes falling onto his back and continuing his contortions across the floor. The lead vocalist was mesmerising. Dressed immaculately in what appeared to be a tailor made suit, silk shirt, and black tie with a diamond dagger pin, he gave a performance of such staggering intensity that Dave and I had to walk outside repeatedly to catch our breath. "Who the fuck is that?" Dave kept asking.

"Maybe it's the devil," I joked.

It was, of course, Nick Cave.

Having more or less kicked the speed habit, I found that LSD was also losing its attraction. I had come to realise the euphoria I'd experienced with the others that night on Tandle Hill was about as good as it was ever going to get. What had initially seemed wonderful and new began to feel perverted and washed out, so once my rather substantial personal supply had been exhausted I gave that up too. I continued to smoke cannabis on a regular basis - and would occasionally take a little speed or some magic mushrooms when they were in season - but the days of wanton excess were over, and I now approached the taking of drugs with a lot more respect.

My state of mind wasn't helped when, later that month, I suffered an embarrassing and painful injury. Julia and I had been making out one night when something altogether strange and unpleasant happened to me. I'll spare you the details but it left me in a lot of pain around the groin area, and to compound the problem we had a gig the following night at the Illuminated 666 Club in Manchester with The Blue Orchids. Hoping that the problem would right itself, I decided to go ahead with the gig - but unfortunately it didn't. By the time I walked onto the stage my groin had swollen considerably, and each time the body of my bass brushed against it I would feel a jolt of pain throughout my entire body. I managed to get through the gig, and afterwards sat in a quiet corner to catch my breath. As I looked up, a rather beautiful, older woman was walking past. She stopped and regarded me for a moment as if she wanted to say something, but then thought better of it and walked away. She looked very familiar but, at first, I couldn't place her. I know that woman, I thought to myself. Of course I did; it was Nico.

We still hadn't managed to settle on a producer for our first album, and consequently CBS were being vague as to when we could start work on it, but at least we were able to air new ideas by way of radio sessions, one for Capital Radio and a second session for Radio One, this time for Dave 'Kid' Jensen's programme. We were to record this at a studio in Hulme which had formerly been home to *Top of the Pops* before the programme had relocated to London. Unfortunately, the producer of the session turned out to be a dimwit. He didn't seem to have a clue what he was doing, and looked a little too much like Cliff Richard for comfort. Having worked with BBC sound technicians in London, the contrast was startling, and to our ears, the finished recordings sounded awful. As we listened back to 'View from a Hill', we heard the sound of a door slamming over the instrumental ending to the song. We pointed this out to him but he just told us that it wasn't worth the effort of re-recording it. He appeared very bored, and quite obviously had no interest in the music we were making. We were disappointed, but at least the recordings served as a useful demo in our on-going search for a producer. In the meantime we continued to write new material, and 'Nathan's Phase', 'Paper Tigers' and 'Up The Down Escalator' were added to our gradually expanding set.

The full title of 'Escalator' had been one of Reg's bizarre suggestions for the name of the band. Obviously, we'd rejected it, but I'd liked it so much that, when the opportunity arose, I used it as a song title. The song's themes - a general dissatisfaction with the way our society was heading and a feeling of being hopelessly trapped on life's treadmill - evolved from the title itself.

In an attempt to find original ways to promote the band, we produced our own fanzine. It was titled *The Planet Earth Society Review*, and everyone involved with the band contributed a page or two. Tony and Ali's contribution, for example, proposed the theory of a lost epoch called the Wood Age. "We know about the Stone Age, the Iron Age and even the Bronze Age," their article argued, "but what about the Wood Age?" The overall result was a chaotic blend of jokes, cartoons, lyrics, insight and plain lunacy, printed on different coloured sheets of paper and featuring a great cover illustration by Reg of Barry Manilow plucking out his own eyeball. We then lovingly stapled all the sheets together and handed them out for free at gigs.

We continued to play wherever we could in support of the single, but found ourselves with a couple of days off in Middleton between shows. Rather than have the PA equipment sitting in the van doing nothing, we threw together a free gig at Cleworth Road Youth Club where both Years and The Clichés had played a few years earlier, complete with a full lighting rig. The kids that frequented the club had never seen or heard anything like it, of course, and the place went berserk. I felt it was one of the best gigs on the tour.

Over the previous year, Dave and I had our share of minor disagreements, but this escalated to a higher level one night during rehearsals. We'd been playing through 'View from a Hill', but midway through the instrumental section I stopped. This had been about the third time I'd done it, and Dave was clearly irritated, so I tried to explain that there was something about the ending that just wasn't working for me - it was meandering without seemingly going anywhere, and it just hadn't felt right. Without any warning, Dave unhooked his guitar, a rather beautiful old Burns that he'd bought some time before, and smashed it to matchwood across his amp. Everyone just stared at him, stunned. "What the fuck did you do that for?" I shouted at him.

"If I hadn't smashed it against the amp, I would have smashed it over your head," he shouted.

When confronted like this I lost all sense of reason, and, unhooking my bass, I flew at him. Then I felt Tony's arms around my chest pulling me backwards.

"Don't criticise the songs," Dave kept saying to me over and over.

"Well if I can't, who can?" I shouted back, trying to wrestle myself from Tony's grip.

Finally, I gathered my scattered wits, packed away my instrument, and stormed out of the room. I dropped my bass off at home and headed back towards town, intending to have a drink somewhere, when our van pulled over. Everyone was inside, and Tony opened the door. Dave sat sheepishly in the front seat. He offered me a handshake - without looking into my eyes however, which should have spoken volumes - and apologised. I was still very upset and badly shaken, not least because I'd thought that our friendship ran deeper than that. We made our peace, but something fundamental had broken. Our relationship gradually deteriorated from that point on.

We continued to play just about everywhere, and for the most part, - despite my gradual estrangement from Dave - when it came to touring I was having a relatively good time. I don't think I'd ever drank wine in my life, but Martin Jackson introduced me to its virtues, and we ended up clearing about three bottles following a gig in Fulham, carrying on where we'd left off at Bath Moles the following night. I started the gig only to have the bass amp break down on the first song. We didn't carry a spare, and were only able to continue when a bass player in the audience went home and brought us his own amp!

Martin even joined us on a trip to Loch Ness that year, after Moz had suggested that a colleague of his, a film-maker, photograph the band with a view to compiling a video of stills to accompany a new song we'd written called 'On The Beach'. The lyrics were vaguely inspired by my experience at Loch Ness the previous Easter, so it seemed logical that we should go there to shoot it. With the benefit of hindsight, I suspect that this was little more than a ploy on Moz's part to swing some paid work for his mate, but at the time it had struck us as an interesting idea and a far more original approach than the silly storyboard videos that were the norm at the time.

For me, the highlight of that week was a trek up the backbone of a mountain that rises high above the shores of Loch Ness. The film-maker had learned that there was to be a partial eclipse of the sun that afternoon, and thought it would provide a good visual backdrop to one of the sequences. It took us around three hours to ascend the mountain, and the climb proved tiring, even for our relatively young legs. From the summit the view was spectacular, and we were able to see practically the whole of Loch Ness - some twenty-three miles in length - spread out below us, with Inverness on the horizon and the sea beyond. We were so tired by this time, however, that we all fell asleep in the warmth of the afternoon sun, and completely missed the eclipse. Fortunately it wasn't a total loss as the photographer got some brilliant shots looking over Reg's shoulder at the panoramic view.

Although the film seemed to take an age to complete, once we saw the finished results it seemed to work quite well. However, the photographer became very strange about ownership rights, and made unreasonable demands in return for allowing us to actually use it. Because of this, the film idea was discarded, and there are very few copies of it around, which is a shame.

Dave, Reg and I were rather enraptured by the idea of having a big record label behind us, even if the on-going struggle to find a suitable producer for the album was beginning to cause friction. Martin, on the other hand, was highly disillusioned with the music business in general, believing that he'd been badly ripped him off during his time with Magazine.

One afternoon in London, I had gone with Martin to the headquarters of Virgin Records. Having concluded his business, we were both walking away when, all of a sudden, Martin whirled around and began savagely insulting this guy who had just passed us on his way in to the building. "YOU THIEVING TWAT!" he bellowed. "YOU FUCKIN' CROOK!" The guy just stood there staring at us, mouth wide open and his face bright red with embarrassment, before he finally turned away and dashed into the building. At first glance, I hadn't really paid him much attention but, taking a closer look, I saw that it was Richard Branson.

Martin was drifting more toward electronic, computer-generated percussion and was very excited by the rapid advances in the technology and its potential. One afternoon at rehearsals, we walked in to find him setting up a Simmons drum module, which was connected to a series of hexagonal, plastic drum pads. The idea was that you played the pads exactly as you would play a drum kit, and the act of striking the pads would trigger pre-programmed drum samples in the module. As the year progressed they caught on in a big way, and a lot of electronic bands and many recording studios were using them. Unfortunately, this new approach didn't fit in with our guitar sound, or the general feel of the band. I could see Martin was disappointed, because he felt strongly that it was a more interesting direction for him to take, so it was mutually decided that perhaps his tenure with the band was ending. He agreed to finish the next set of dates and, in the meantime, we'd try and find a permanent replacement. After all, Martin had only ever joined the band on a temporary basis, and he'd performed above and beyond the call of duty. We would always be grateful to him, and continued to hold him in high regard. After his departure from the group I'd bump into him from time to time, and it was always good to see him. I was particularly pleased for him when he eventually earned huge success with Swing Out Sister, although his discontent with the machinations of the music business would blight him for the rest of his career.

Our final show with Martin was at Manchester Polytechnic, if I remember rightly. We decided that it would be imprudent to attempt to find a replacement until all the gigs with Martin had been completed. None of us relished the task of having to hold auditions for another drummer, and no obvious candidates had presented themselves. I remember coming off stage feeling depressed; during the performance I'd lifted my new, and rather expensive, bass guitar over my head and smashed one of the machine heads on the exceptionally low ceiling.

As I was milling around backstage, I heard Dave's voice behind me. "Mark! Look who's here." I turned, and there was John Lever. He was quiet, and it was obvious that he was a little nervous, but he looked well. He told me that he'd been quite ill, and that the ordeal had been a nightmare experience for him. Eventually he'd suffered a complete nervous breakdown, and was still taking prescribed medication. He went on to say that his mother had bought him an antique shop in Glossop, a quaint little town situated at the foot of the Pennines. John had always had an interest in antiques, and used to make money on the side buying and selling items to dealers and market traders. He hadn't even told us he was coming to the show, but instead stood watching us from the shadows. Once in conversation, it didn't take long before the subject of John returning to the band was raised. I was very unsure about this, though - I felt at the time we'd been badly let down. That said, John had been ill; he hadn't just fucked off on a whim. Reg and Dave said that things hadn't felt right with the band since he'd left, which I could understand, and that coming back to the band would be the best thing for John; better than hiding in an antique shop in Glossop, anyway. Who was I to argue?

Unfortunately, his mother didn't exactly see it that way and I got a call from her within days, screaming at me down the phone. I tried to explain that it had been John's decision, that I'd had little to do with it, but nothing could halt the onslaught. "John's told me what you lot get up to," she wailed. "You're all on drugs!" I felt terrible.

We debated the best way of going about telling CBS that John was back in the band, and decided that simply phoning them up and telling them would be too boring. With this in mind, we hit upon the idea of disguising John, taking him into the offices and introducing him as the new mystery member of the group. We bought him a full rubber mask from a novelty shop, and marched him into the CBS offices in Soho Square. Annie and Muff were somewhat bemused, but I think we raised a smile or two. John stood there silently under his mask as we introduced him. "That's John Lever!" Annie said immediately.

"God, how did you suss that so quickly?" Dave asked her.

"I just had to look at his feet," she retorted. I glanced down at John's size twelve trainers. "Only John Lever has feet that big."

In our naïvety, we thought that CBS would be happy that John was back, but we couldn't have been more wrong, and the signs were immediately obvious. What we didn't know (and didn't find out until much later) was that by re-recruiting John, we'd really set the cat amongst the pigeons, not only as far as CBS was concerned, but also Moz.

John told us that it had been Moz who had suggested that his deteriorating mental state was holding us back, that Moz had told him he was voicing concerns on our behalf, and that he'd actually persuaded John that leaving the band would be the best thing for everyone. We were completely mystified. Why on earth would Moz do that? It eventually transpired that by leaving the band, John had presented CBS with the opportunity to drop the band at any time, while negating any claims we might make for compensation. A small clause in our contract stated that if one of the original members of the band were to leave for any reason, CBS would have the right to terminate the agreement. On hearing about John's problems, CBS had encouraged Moz to put pressure on John to voluntarily leave the band, thereby presenting them with a get-out should things not work out the way they hoped. By bringing John back, then, we had unwittingly foiled their plan.

From this point on, our relationship with CBS deteriorated rapidly. Much to our chagrin, we were no nearer starting work on our debut album, and our dialogue with the label consisted largely of arguments. Muff cited our drug usage as being worrying enough to delay investing in serious studio time. "Rushing away from gigs as soon as you're off stage, and buying drugs in dodgy suburbs of Manchester!" he bleated. I knew immediately that he was referring to the Derby Hall gig, and I also knew that the only source of this information had to be Moz - he'd clearly been telling tales behind our back. "He's a responsible, professional manager and such concerns are part of his remit," wailed Muff.

"Who does he work for?" I asked him angrily. "You or us? Did he tell you that the drugs we went to buy were for him?" I continued. Of course, he hadn't.

Further revelations came to light when we noticed that money was going out of our account for unknown purposes, or for purposes that seemed unrelated to the band. As an added security measure, we'd chosen someone we trusted to countersign all of the cheques issued by Moz. What we learned was alarming:

"There were no names on the cheques. Moz would just tell me he needed a cheque issuing for this or for that, and I'd just countersign it."

"Let me get this straight," asked Dave, stunned. "You've been countersigning blank cheques to Moz?"

"Well, yes. Why, don't you trust him?"

On checking our bank account, we weren't surprised to find that the band was all but broke.

After further debate, we decided not to even bother confronting Moz with this information, preferring to simply terminate our agreement with him. Ultimately, the money was gone and we had more urgent, immediate priorities. The last thing we needed was to get into complicated litigation with our business manager. John's revelations concerning his departure from the band were reason enough to part company with Moz, as far as we were concerned, so we felt it would be better to cut our losses and get shut of him. This we did, with a single phone call.

We called a meeting with CBS and reminded them that, under the terms of our contract, we had the right to choose who we wanted to work with and where, and that if progress wasn't made soon in finding a suitable producer then we would hire a good engineer and proceed without one. Having now sacked the manager they'd urged us to hire in the first place, thereby denying them further means of manipulation, this was merely further provocation. Muff told us that Nigel Gray - who had previously produced albums for Siouxsie And The Banshees and The Police, amongst others - was interested in meeting us, and so, as a last resort, we agreed.

Nigel was working out of his own studio in London and, although it was small, it was reasonably impressive. When we discussed the project, however, we found his ideas unacceptable. He wanted to edit the arrangements so that all the songs would be three to four minutes long. "Look at the length of some of these songs," he said, laughing. "'View From A Hill' - around six minutes, 'Second Skin' - seven minutes. You'll never get these tracks on the radio unless you cut them down. That ending, for example, on 'View From A Hill' - it's totally unnecessary."

We were summoned back to CBS. "He wants to cut the songs down, and we're not having it." Dave told them.

"Well we're out of options, so it's him or no-one." Muff replied.

We reminded him of our contractual rights regarding how and where we record our album. "We know a great engineer up north," I told him: "We'll produce the album ourselves."

"And where do you propose to do it?" asked Muff, condescendingly. I thought for a minute.

"Oh I don't know, maybe we'll go to Abbey Road?"

Later that night the phone rang and after a few minutes, James came into the room, looking very sombre. "That was CBS," he said. "You're off the label."

It seemed to take an age to work out the terms surrounding the termination of the contract. In the meantime, we were still playing live, and I remember a show at the Venue in London within days of this happening. It had been Hank Marvin's birthday and, as the curtains parted across the stage, we began the set with a one-minute version of the Shadows' 'Apache', before launching into 'Don't Fall'. We were in the dressing room when Danny from Virgin Music showed up. As the band's publishers, they'd been notified of our departure from CBS, and he came over to see how we were dealing with it. In all honesty it had come as something of a relief; we all had a tremendous belief in our music and talent, and working with CBS hadn't been the most enjoyable of experiences.

CBS cited John's temporary departure as grounds for terminating the contract, but had we challenged it they wouldn't have had a leg to stand on and, what's more, they knew it. They offered to pay the band the balance owed on the advances, which ordinarily we wouldn't have received until the album had been delivered, in return for our signatures on an unconditional release that couldn't be challenged at any point in the future. In the short term, at least, this meant that the band remained solvent.

In the wake of our sudden departure from CBS, the first order of business was to decide who would replace Moz as manager. One surprise candidate had been Ian Wilson, our agent at Wasted Talent. He drove to Middleton to see us one day and told us he wanted to manage the band. As he described his vision for the group, however, we all thought it so ridiculous that we actually started laughing. He'd envisioned that the band would adopt a kind of bandit, Sergio Leone look and write anthems to storm the stadium circuit. We declined, and he later acquired another group of young hopefuls, in the form of Seventeen. I'd seen this band at the Hereford Tavern a couple of years before; they were desperately trying to latch on to the power-pop scene, and sported red Slazenger jerseys, side-parting haircuts, and nauseating Beatles poses. With Ian Wilson at the helm and taking his vision to heart, they changed their name to The Alarm, and the rest, as they say, is history.

Dave was in London spending some time with James, when he rang me at home and suggested that James could replace Moz. James had always struck me as a smart, intelligent man with meticulous taste. Since moving back to London from Manchester, he'd been working as an executive manager for a graphics company called Yellowhammer, situated on Baker Street. On the surface, Dave's suggestion seemed to make a lot of sense. James was articulate, had a wonderful record collection that reflected a great sense of taste and style, and always presented himself well. He also had the advantage of living in central London, which has always been the hub of the British music business. Dave handed the phone over to James and we spoke about the practicalities. James was extremely keen to get involved. His work at Yellowhammer was fine for paying the bills, but he found it tedious, and relished the opportunity to get into something a little more exciting. I'd come to regard James with a great amount of affection and I could see that he genuinely cared about all of us, although I knew that sometimes my brazen humour could make him feel rather insecure. Overall, then, I felt good about this development, pushing aside matters of inexperience, lack of contacts, and his more discreet recreational habits. I asked him if he had any ideas about whom to approach with a view to recording, and he told me that both he and Dave had thought about approaching Statik Records[2]. I thought this was a sensible idea, although I knew nothing of the label as such, so I told them to keep me posted.

Within a week they'd set up a meeting with Dunn, Statik's owner. Dunn hailed from Australia and had previously been MD of Virgin Music Publishing. He eventually left the Virgin Group and struck out on his own, although Virgin continued to distribute Statik product. The meeting went well, apparently, and James informed me that Dunn wanted to meet the rest of the band with a view to recording a single, after which he'd assess whether or not Statik would be interested in the album. He also told me that Statik had European distribution, and that he was in talks with a couple of major companies in the United States with a view to setting up a licensing agreement there.

Statik commissioned a one off single, which we decided to record with Colin Richardson at Cargo. We debated the choice of song at some length, and decided to use one of our most recent numbers. None of these had actually been recorded before in any form, and it's to Dunn's credit that he put us into the studio without having heard the songs. For us, the freshest of the three was 'As High As You Can Go', despite being lyrically downbeat, reflecting as it did the mood of the moment. For the B-side we chose 'Paper Tigers' and another relatively new song, 'Pleasure And Pain'. Lyrically, the latter was an attempt to express how the band and its music made me feel amid all the ups and the downs - which were always there, no matter what happened.

Cargo was a great place to work in its day, despite the run-down state of much of the hardware. There was always a very special atmosphere about

---

2. Statik had issued the compilation album Your Secret's Safe With Us the previous year, to which we'd contributed 'Here Today'.

the place, and Colin had a tremendous enthusiasm and keen instinct. For the first time we incorporated a keyboard into the songs - albeit a pocket Casio - which we fed through a chorus echo, resulting in a very eerie sound. Dunn was pleased with the overall results and our second single's release was scheduled for early 1983. We chose one of Tony's photographs for the front sleeve, a silhouette of a statue of the Madonna that serves as a gravestone in Middleton cemetery.

As Christmas approached, our future was as uncertain as ever, but I took some satisfaction in noting that 'In Shreds' made Peel's Festive Fifty that year.

Sadly, I'd felt the need to end my relationship with Julia earlier that year, without any warning to her, and for a while she was devastated. I couldn't even say with any degree of clarity why I was ending it. The weirdness of the previous summer, in addition to my drug abuse, had made me very unstable. At the time, I felt I'd needed a firmer hand and that Julia was a bit too passive. Consequently I was spending more time in Middleton, I'd started seeing more of Fenella, and by Christmas we were back together.

On New Year's Eve, rather than squeeze into one of the many pubs around Middleton, Fenella and I took a bottle of good brandy and climbed to the top of Tandle Hill in time to see the fireworks over Manchester which always mark the beginning of the New Year. It felt strange to be standing there again, and I recalled the night that Dave, Reg, John, Tony and I had sat in that very same spot, looking out at the world, ready to embrace it. I remembered the thoughts I'd had as we sat around the conference table during that first week with CBS. "Where's the story?" I'd asked myself. It had barely begun.

8. MEN WITHOUT HATS

Once James took on the mantle of rock 'n' roll band manager, the change in him was not only startling but also somewhat comical. He saw this radical change of occupation as an opportunity to redefine himself, and dispensed with his familiar smart, hip business suits in favour of a motorcycle jacket, baggy trousers, and little pink pigtails. No-one in the band could claim to be a fashion guru, least of all me, but you didn't have to be Gucci to realise that he looked rather silly. Occasionally, in those early weeks following our migration from CBS to Statik, we'd meet with Danny and Richard at Virgin Music to discuss the transition, and I could almost see cartoon thought-bubbles over their heads, saying "What the fuck have we got here?" It has to be said that James' new image did little to enhance our credibility.

The first hint that things might not work out with James at the helm came when I was sent to London to approve the final artwork for the single. Nothing could have prepared me for what I was about to see. The photo for the front sleeve looked every bit as good as we thought it might, especially the proof for the twelve-inch format. What shocked me was the choice of typeface. Alongside the sleeve, sideways on, was the name of the band in bright yellow, rendered in the most tasteless, ugly font I have ever seen, a sort of bulbous, flowery affair that wouldn't have looked out of place on an early 1970s chocolate bar. I stood dumbstruck for a minute with my mouth wide open after the young designer had placed the proofs front of me. "What on earth possessed you to choose a font like that?" I asked her incredulously.

"I didn't choose it," she protested. "I think it's hideous. Your manager chose it."

I turned to James in stunned disbelief.

"What's wrong with it?" James asked me, in all honesty.

"What's wrong with it?" I echoed. "What, you mean apart from the fact that it looks so obviously, totally crap?"

"Well, maybe you should show the others before you make any sudden decisions," offered the designer. I explained that this wouldn't be necessary because I knew exactly what Dave and Reg would say when they saw it. The back of the record sleeve was fine - she'd been given a relatively free hand without any hindrance from James - and so I suggested that she lift the same type face that she'd used here and place it on the front of the sleeve. This became the band's typeface on almost all our subsequent records for Statik. It hadn't taken long for my confidence in James to be shaken. "I think you can trust my judgement when it comes to these sorts of things, I do work for a professional advertising company you know," said James. I said nothing, but wondered to myself how he'd held down his job for so long.

'As High As You Can Go' was released by Statik in February 1983, and although the reviews were mixed, it did well enough to persuade Dunn to commission an album. Statik wanted three albums, in return for which they agreed to an advance against future royalties to be paid in monthly instalments. However, feeling that Statik were too small an operation to sign our North American rights to, we insisted that this territory be excluded from any contractual agreement. Statik didn't have a US licensing agreement in place anyway, and so it was agreed that, while we'd consider any reasonable offer regarding the release of our records in America, we'd be under no obligation, and would remain free to pursue a more lucrative offer should one materialise. Statik, meanwhile, were free to license our material in all remaining territories, and we were granted full artistic control over our music, subject to budgetary considerations. Our decision to exclude the United States from our contractual agreement was to prove very significant indeed.

Not long after the single was released, we were asked by Statik's Belgian licensee to promote our new single on a TV music show. Having since flown hundreds of times, it's odd to recall how excited I was about my first journey on an aeroplane. I remember feeling the force of acceleration deep down in the pit of my stomach as the plane surged forward and left the ground, banking sharply over the city far below, and how London had seemed almost like a model city as we ascended into the clouds. These days, flying bores me to death.

We found Brussels less than interesting, but the novelty of being abroad together for the first time compensated for that. The experience of pretending to play our instruments and miming the song seemed ridiculous to us, but we came through it with our credibility intact, despite the performance being rather wooden. We knew that television - and video in particular - were important tools for promoting the band, but neither medium ever really interested us. A video was made later on, but the production company engaged by Statik were, frankly, inept. We had expected to play the song live, and have the soundtrack time-locked later, but we were disappointed to find that, instead, we were expected to mime to the record again. Out of a sense of duty we played along, but we were all clearly unhappy with the situation, and the results were less than satisfactory. I remember getting a call from the director, who was desperate to have another try. Following discussions with Dunn and some of the licensees, he'd been able to get a verbal agreement on quite a sizeable budget. "It'll be great!" he said. "We'll film in Paris, right? And we'll have you on top of the Eiffel Tower, yeah? With a really pretty French bird? And then we'll have a one hundred and eighty degree helicopter shot and..."

I cut him off, stifling my laughter. "I think you should take the idea to Duran Duran," I said, and put the phone down.

We began work on our first album that spring at Cargo with Colin Richardson as engineer. The prospect of producing ourselves after having worked with one of the best producers in the world should have been quite daunting. Still, we'd learned a lot over the previous year, and had confidence in ourselves and in Colin who'd recorded the demos that had initially excited the record companies. We knew the record wouldn't have the massive sound of 'In Shreds' or 'Nostalgia', but at least now, unhindered by record company interference, we were free to make the music we wanted without having to compromise. We compiled a list of songs from those we had accumulated so far, but discarded some of the earliest tunes in favour of ideas that still felt fresh to us. We intended to re-record all the songs we'd chosen rather than include any of the earlier, already released versions. We didn't think it was fair to have people paying for the same recordings twice, and besides, we felt we were improving all the time and that the album should document this.

We recorded and mixed the entire album in just over four weeks, working seven days a week. We started by re-recording 'In Shreds', but realising that the original couldn't be bettered, we abandoned this idea. We tried to strike a balance between some of the earliest songs, like 'Here Today', 'Monkeyland' and 'Less Than Human', and the more recent songs, some of which were still in development. Consequently, lyrics and titles for the newer songs were improvised as we went along. For example, we were sitting in a café having a break one afternoon, and I'd been racking my brains trying to think of a title for a new song we were working on. Suddenly Dave, who'd been reading a newspaper turned and said, "How about this?" He handed me the paper and pointed to a tiny cartoon man with a speech bubble that read, "A person isn't safe anywhere these days." It suited the theme of the song perfectly, so that's what we called it. This sort of thing was happening all the time.

All the songs evolved to some degree during the sessions, and none of us really knew what the others would add until it was done. I'd been desperately searching all corners of the studio for the whirly pipe that we'd used on our recordings in the past, but it had vanished. Since the fad had passed, they were impossible to find in any toy shops and I'd given up hope of getting hold of another one, until someone mentioned that there was a fairground nearby, and that they'd seen the tubes on one of the game stalls amongst the prizes. John and I immediately dashed over to the fairground, leaving Dave to get on with laying down his guitar tracks. Sure enough, on one of the stalls amongst the tack were a number of whirly tubes. I explained our situation to the vendor, and asked if we could simply buy a couple from him, but he refused, telling us we'd have to play for them. The game consisted of throwing darts at mounted playing cards, and it took us around thirty minutes to notch up enough wins. We arrived back at the studio just as Dave had finished his guitar parts. Colin played the track back, and John and I just looked at each other in wonder. The song was 'Up The Down Escalator', and Dave's new guitar harmonies sounded nothing short of majestic. I knew at that moment, irrespective of whether the album sold or not, that we were making a classic.

This was typical of the entire session, as some new guitar line, percussive event or vocal would, in turn, inspire someone else to come up with something equally special. We were constantly trying to find new sounds and textures to incorporate into the recordings. At one point, while recording the drums on 'View From A Hill', we realised that we had eight bars too many at the beginning of the song. "No worries!" Colin said. "I'll just edit them out." As he was setting up to make the edit, he slowed down the tape speed to find his reference and, as a result, the track sounded strange and unworldly.

"We've got to use that!" I said as we all sat around laughing, and so we eventually used it to open the second side of the album.

I also loved the tiny accidental touches that can hardly be heard on the vinyl edition. One day, while we were working on 'Pleasure And Pain', Colin decided that he needed a different vocal sound for the sake of variety, but we'd already exhausted all the rooms in Cargo, including the toilet, where I recorded the vocal for 'Second Skin'. Cargo had an access door which led from the live room out onto the roof. "I'll set a microphone up on the roof and you can do it there, the sound should be quite dead and it'll give it a different tone," suggested Colin.

As I stood in front of the microphone and began to perform the song a blackbird came and perched itself on the mantle of the door over my head and joined in. "Did you get the duet?" I asked Colin when I'd finished the vocal take.

"Yeah, it sounded great," he said, "see if you can get it to double-track." It's just about audible on the finished recording, along with the sound of a car accelerating up Drake Street.

During the session, friends would drop by to hear how it was going and we always seemed to find them something to do, either percussively or on the mixing desk. One afternoon we were in the process of mixing 'View From A Hill', and a few people were sitting in on the session. Whilst piecing the arrangement together, we'd thrown everything we could think of into the ending, but I still felt that it meandered, rather than having any dramatic impact. I was pondering what to do about this, when I was suddenly struck by an idea. Without explaining, I leapt up and asked Colin to take note of what I was about to do. I asked the others, including one of our guests, to place their fingers over as many of the mute buttons as they could reach and, on the count of four, to release them. Everyone humoured me and, on my count, we dropped out the instruments leaving only those tracks we hadn't had enough fingers to reach - a keyboard line, a tambourine, and the sound of distant thunder. "Now what?" someone asked.

"Drop them back in again on the count of four."

I counted out the time again, and everyone pushed the buttons. All except Reg, that is, who dropped his guitar in early to give the break a more natural feel. After a few more rehearsals, we refined the idea and executed the dropouts for real. We all agreed that not only had we devised the perfect ending for 'View From A Hill', we'd also found the perfect conclusion to our album.

By the time the album was finished it was almost an hour long, which is about as much music as you can fit onto a 12" record without serious loss of quality. Because of this, the album was quieter than most, so the sleeve included instructions to the listener to crank up the volume. Dunn came up to the studio to check our progress and to discuss the possibility of a second single ahead of the album release. We decided that the follow up to 'As High As You Can Go' should be the brand new 'A Person Isn't Safe Anywhere These Days', which was a little heavier - and that we'd use another relatively new song, 'Thursday's Child', as the B-side. The title of 'Thursday's Child' was taken from an old nursery rhyme:

> Monday's child is fair of face,
> Tuesday's child is full of grace,
> Wednesday's child is full of woe,
> Thursday's child has far to go...

A problem lay in the fact that we needed an additional song for the twelve-inch single format, but we didn't want to pull another track from the album, and none of us were particularly keen to use any of the older, discarded material. For one thing, we'd been playing them for so long that they were no longer fresh, and sounded dated compared to the more recent compositions. In addition, to re-record and mix a complete song from scratch with a full backline would have taken three or four days at least, interrupting the flow of the album sessions. Dunn needed something that he could take away with him that day so he could begin the process of planning a single release. "Why not do something now, and just make it up as you go along?" Colin suggested. It was an interesting idea, so we decided to have a try. We began with a drum machine playing a single bass drum beat and then, hooking up the pocket Casio keyboard through the chorus echo, we layered piano lines over the top of it. I'd always been fascinated by the idea of taping random pieces of dialogue and using them on a recording, so I suggested that we get the TV set from the lounge and tape the dialogue as someone changed channels. In the end we had around four or five minutes of mixed dialogue, but no real idea of what it consisted of, so we decided to just randomly punch the voices in and out and leave it to chance. After repeated run-throughs we got to know which snippets of dialogue we wanted, and where they occurred in the flow.

Finally, we added a single acoustic guitar, but rather than use one of the band's accomplished guitarists we asked Tony to play it, which seemed totally in keeping with the spirit of the thing. The resulting piece, 'Prisoners Of The Sun', is one of the most unusual tracks we ever did together. We also used one of the voice samples from this track to open the album, and many people have asked me over the years where the sample came from. I always have to tell them I had absolutely no idea, as it had simply been recorded from the TV at random.

Another development during the recording of the album was the use of keyboards on some of the tracks. It wasn't so much a case of writing keyboard melodies; rather we used the string or horn sections of the keyboard to enhance melodies that we could hear within the harmonics already present in the guitar parts. Dave, Reg and I could all play keyboards to some extent, although Dave had shown the most talent. We all played on the album, as did Ali, and on 'Second Skin' we even performed a string duet. The question of how we would replicate this on tour was answered when Ali volunteered to step in as our live keyboard player. He was adamant that he wouldn't join the band officially or sign any contracts, though, which simplified things greatly and suited us all just fine.

As pleased as we were with the finished result, the album sessions weren't without their frustrations. Cargo's reputation had been built on the plethora of bands that had recorded there in the late seventies: Joy Division, Gang Of Four, The Fall, The Teardrop Explodes, and many others. Since those days though, hardly any money had been spent on the studio's upkeep, and the electronics were falling apart. More than once we'd groan in frustration when, at the tail end of a particularly complicated mix, a fader would crackle as it was moved, forcing us to begin the whole process again. This was before the days of automated mixing desks or total mix recall, and so mixing a track involved setting stereo panning, fader levels and effects in real time, meaning that no two mixes could ever be exactly the same. In this sense it was more like a live performance than a studio process, and therefore hugely frustrating when the 'perfect' mix was lost due to a studio glitch. During the mixing of the album's opening track, 'Don't Fall', the studio's multi-track tape machine mysteriously slowed down at the same point midway through the song, so we were forced to mix the track in two halves and splice them together afterwards.

During the session, Colin would tell us stories about his experiences working at Cargo that would have us howling with laughter. My favourite story involved a band from Holland that had been lured to Cargo by the studio's reputation. The weekend had cost the band all the money they had, and they didn't have anywhere to stay, so they'd all turned up expecting to sleep in the back of their van. At the conclusion of the first day's recording Colin, having got to know them a little better, said that they could take their sleeping bags into the live room, but on no account where they to let the owner know about it as it could cost Colin his job. Once safely installed, he said goodnight to the band and locked up the studio for the night.

The next morning he arrived to begin work and asked them if they'd had a good night. "Oh yeah," said the band's singer. "Very nice, better than Amsterdam." After Colin had left for the night, another engineer had turned up with a young lady and had taken her into the control room to show her around. The live room was in total darkness, so he was unable to see the Dutch band huddled in their sleeping bags, but as he turned on the lights to the control room, one by one they'd all awoken. After a few minutes, the couple began to undress and proceeded to have passionate sex over the mixing desk while the band, now seated behind the darkened windows, lit a joint and enjoyed the show. The band's clapping and whooping in the sound-proofed live room went unheard by the lovers next door. When the couple were done, they dressed, turned out the lights of the control room, and left none the wiser. Some bands have all the luck.

Tony provided the cover photograph for the new single. He'd taken it outside Rochdale Parish Church using Reg as the subject in a double exposure, rendering him as a ghostly presence in front of the building. Reg would provide original artwork for the album cover, and I titled it *Script Of The Bridge*, from one of the scribbled notes I'd made at Tandle Hill the previous year.

Reg drew the illustration over three nights while we were all staying with James at his flat in London and it was fascinating to watch the illustration come together and to recognise all the elements that had made up our strange odyssey. I would sit opposite him at the table meditating on the sleeve notes, and I remember at one point he hadn't been able to decide whether he should draw the lightning tree with its roots in the ground as it actually was, or suspended in the air, which is how he eventually drew it. I know that he was a bit freaked out to find that in later months the tree, after standing in the same spot for many years, had suddenly been uprooted.

We were all very pleased with the sleeve and happy that Statik had agreed to include a folded insert featuring some of Tony's photographs of the band. We felt that, as unorthodox as the sleeve was - especially in context with the times - it really stood out as being original and different. Unfortunately the press didn't agree, one journalist writing that, although she quite liked the record, it had been in spite of the chocolate box sleeve. We met her and she was a dick, anyway, so her opinion didn't really bother us at all.

We were pleasantly surprised to learn that our reputation for being a great live band had spread to the European mainland, and that year we played our first concerts there. The earliest show I can remember was in Amsterdam at the Melkweg. Natives of Amsterdam tended to avoid the place because it was primarily a tourist haunt, but the venue itself was great. Inside was a labyrinth of coffee bars selling cake laced with cannabis (amongst other things), theatres, a cinema and a couple of gig venues, and there was something going on in all of them.

After the gig I broke the promise I'd made to myself, and decided to buy a little amphetamine sulphate, as we only had a couple of days in Amsterdam and I'd wanted to make the most of it. I made some enquiries, and was directed to a young guy standing on the steps of a building quite close to the venue. I approached him and cautiously asked if he was selling speed, and he said that he was. As I was speaking with him, out of the corner of my eye, I spotted a uniform. Trying not to appear too startled, I turned my head and saw a Dutch policeman standing directly next to me. The policeman said something in Dutch to the guy, who then handed him a wrap of paper, and the policeman skipped into the building. Laughing at my confusion the guy told me that the building was a police station, and that he supplied many of them with speed as they turned up to work the night shift. That was the first indication I had of just how out of control Amsterdam was.

The second indication was even more of an eye opener. Prior to our departure, we'd been advised by a friend in Middleton that we should head for a place called the Bulldog and buy our marijuana there. Heeding his advice, with the exception of Reg and Dave, who wandered back to the hotel, we all climbed into a taxi and made our way there. The bar was divided into an upstairs and downstairs area. Upstairs there was a bar that sold alcohol-free drinks, while downstairs there was a circular arrangement of couches facing a TV set, and in the middle of the room there was a huge, brass ashtray. We were handed a cannabis menu from which we were invited to choose. This was an entirely new experience, and I remember we were all exchanging nervous giggles as we tried to take it all in. After rolling and enjoying a generous joint of sensimilla, it suddenly occurred to me that John, who was sitting upstairs, no longer smoked cannabis and the bar didn't sell alcohol. Reasoning that he must be feeling rather bored, I went upstairs to see how he was, and found him sitting at the bar drinking an orange juice. Taking the bar stool next to his I asked him whether he'd prefer to move to another bar and get a Heineken or something. "No!" he said quietly, smiling and shaking his head. "I'm fine where I am." I noticed that he was staring across the bar and at first, I thought he was eyeing up a pretty girl who worked behind the bar. As I followed his gaze though, I noticed that on the far wall there was a window looking out onto an alley that ran behind the bar, and directly opposite another window was illuminated in a soft red glow - in which a beautiful young girl was sitting on a stool in her underwear.

I looked back at John with my mouth wide open and, seeing the look on my face, he started laughing and arching his eyebrows. I went to fetch the others. They followed me back to where John was sitting and I gestured in the direction of the window. We all agreed that this deserved further investigation, so we went outside and peeped around the corner of the building down the alley. Along its meandering length were more of the soft red lights and, with as much nonchalance as we could manage, which wasn't much in our highly stoned state, we began to walk down the alley. We were nervously grouped together in a very tight bunch which must have looked comical to the hookers behind the each window, although they were probably well used to it. We didn't so much as walk down the alley as shuffle, our eyes darting from left to right and back again. Due to the potency of the cannabis I'd been smoking, I imagined I could hear the song of the siren reverberating inside my head. The girls looked like they'd climbed fresh out of a glamour magazine, alluring and unreal.

We stopped at the end of the alley to catch our breath, laughing in disbelief. A few minutes later we began the return journey only this time, having regained some composure, we walked at a much slower pace, feigning a macho confidence that probably looked even more ridiculous to the watching girls than our first pass had. As we walked along, I suddenly noticed that John was missing. I turned around and saw him midway down the alley peering intently through one of the windows. I approached him and was amused to see that his face was so close to the glass that his breath was forming condensation on it. "Come on man, you can't afford her," I was whispering, trying in vain to pull him away from the window.

"I know, I know!" he insisted. "I just want to look for a bit."

As I tried to pull him away, the object of John's fascination was now inviting us both inside. I smiled nervously and nodded a greeting as I continued to pull John away. Finally, he relented and we joined the others outside the bar. "Reg picked the wrong night to go to bed early," Tony laughed, as we took stock of the situation.

The new single was finally released that June, again to mixed reviews, and at this point we acquired the tag of Manchester Miserablists. One *NME* writer quipped, "What does this band do for laughs, pull their own arms and legs off?" If only they knew. We continued to tour around England, and made our debut at London's legendary Marquee, though the audience was made up largely of Japanese and American tourists. Nevertheless, they went completely berserk and a few even followed us to other venues.

That was also the week Dave and I became vegetarians, having had long discussions about it at James' flat. I forget how we got on to the subject of animal rights but the more we debated the subject, the angrier we became, and ultimately we made a pact. This wasn't as easy as you might think, because in 1983 vegetarianism was most definitely a fringe issue. It was nigh on impossible to find vegetarian food in shops, or vegetarian menus in restaurants, other than cheese products and salads, and I'd never really cared for cheese. Out of pure necessity, my gastronomic skills improved overnight.

Reg also became vegetarian, though at times his dietary ideas could be rather extreme. At one point he said to me, "I'm thinking of becoming a fruitarian."

I gave him a sceptical look. "Reg, that doesn't sound very healthy. I mean, you can't exist on a diet consisting entirely of fruit, can you?"

"Oh yeah!" he assured me. "I've read about it."

While the fruitarian flirtation failed to materialise, Reg's eating habits did become strange. On one trip to London we were all going out for pizza, but Reg declined. "No, I'm alright," he told us, "I'll have these." He held up a glass bottle, containing a quantity of grubby looking beans that he'd been growing. "These are all you need to survive," he assured us.

"Do they taste good, Reg?" Dave asked him, giggling.

Script Of The Bridge was released that August and we continued to tour. We played throughout the UK and returned to mainland Europe for gigs in France, Spain, Germany and Holland. Our first few exploratory gigs on the European mainland had been very successful, due in no small part to John Peel's regular broadcasts on the BBC World Service and British Forces Radio. Consequently, most of Statik's European licensees took on *Script Of The Bridge*, and a full European tour was set up that winter to promote the album.

The long drive from London to our first show in Munich was particularly hard. Tony was a truly great driver, once you got used to his unique style. He'd driven us the length and breadth of the country and, if he'd given us all a few grey hairs, he'd never had so much as a bump and was able to make progress through London traffic faster than anyone else I know. As we made for the Dover ferry, however, he displayed his usual impatience with a car in front, which was cruising idly down the central lane, by driving within inches of its rear bumper. All of a sudden there were blue flashing lights in the rear view mirror and the police pulled us over. The policeman slowly walked up to the driver's side window, inspecting the vehicle - as they invariably do in the hope of nicking you for a faulty tyre or a spot of rust - and then began to lecture Tony on the dangers of driving too close to the vehicle in front. Tony was the epitome of politeness and calm as he patiently listened to this diatribe. Finally, the policeman told him that, by way of a future reminder, he would like Tony to display some road safety stickers on the bus and handed them over. We looked at the stickers, which read 'KEEP YOUR DISTANCE' in bold, bright red letters. Tony was thrilled with them and immediately stuck them on the back of the van. "Yeah, I'm having that!" he kept saying as he continued to tailgate every car that dared to impede his swift progress. "Keep your distance! Keep - your - fuckin' distance!"

After a brief stopover at the offices of Statik Records, Tony drove us all the way to Munich, barely stopping once. The only respite was the sixty-minute ferry crossing, which had us rocking and a-rolling in a very high swell. The boat was packed with British soldiers returning to Germany and most of them were throwing up in every available nook and cranny of the ship.

In those days, stringent customs checks were required each time we crossed any border and, inevitably, a rock band would be subjected to close scrutiny. Crossing into Germany was particularly unpleasant; the customs officers were determined to find something illicit secreted in some small crevice of the bus. On this occasion we were marched into the main building and given a thorough search which, thankfully, fell short of the dreaded finger. Meanwhile, all the guitar and amp cases were opened, laid out on the tarmac and exposed to the rain, despite our protests. All this took place in the very early hours of a freezing morning, and the continual baying from the dogs was giving me a headache. Half an hour later, we climbed back into the bus and were allowed to continue. After we'd been driving for a few minutes Spin, one of the road crew, said, "Right! I might as well skin up then!"

We all looked around in total amazement. "Where the fuck did you hide the hash?" someone asked him.

Spin just displayed his usual broad grin: "Don't ask."

Munich Stadium, 1983.   Photo: Tony Skinkis

By the time we arrived at the hotel in Munich it was late evening. The long, arduous journey had taken its toll and we were all in a foul mood. Just as we were checking out our rooms a young, blond head came peeping around one of the doors. "Hello Chameleons," he said.

Tony turned and gave him that quizzical look that was so typically Tony. "Who are you?" he demanded.

"My name is Dirk Burghardt, I am your German tour manager. I am thinking you might possibly want to be eating something."

It was the start of a long-lasting friendship. Within thirty minutes of arriving, Dirk (or Dirkenouzen, as he became affectionately known) had us comfortably installed in a nearby restaurant, eating pizza and swilling huge glass tankards of German beer, and our spirits lifted immediately. We had most of the following day to recover from the long drive and took in some of the local sights, including the Olympic Stadium where we posed for pictures, poised in the sprint position on the running track.

The venue in Munich was large, and the gig was surprisingly busy. Despite the great reaction to the band, though, I felt a wave of depression bearing down on me which grew increasingly more intense as the night wore on. By the time I arrived back at the hotel my mood had worsened, and I was deeply depressed. I had no idea what could have triggered such a savage mood swing, and I kept telling myself that it was probably the effects of the long drive, combined with nervous exhaustion from the gig. However, this hadn't been the first long drive with a gig at the end of it, and although I always felt anxious to some degree before or after a show, it had never manifested itself like this. In an attempt to shake it off I took a walk, but the black feeling just kept getting worse. In the end, out of the way of the others, I just burst into tears without having the slightest idea why. I managed to sleep that night, but the episode had left me badly shaken and, although I was feeling better the next morning, when I came down to breakfast I was in a strange, quiet mood. Dirk asked me if I was feeling all right, after noticing that I looked pale. I told him about the previous night, not really expecting him to understand something that I barely understood myself, but he surprised me. "Ah yes," he said, "I've seen that once or twice before when I have been working with bands here. This hotel is very close to Dachau concentration camp. The feeling you describe is common to outsiders here."

I was stunned. I was familiar with the subject of the Holocaust, but such a notion would never have occurred to me.

"I've been there." Dirk continued. "It's very strange, no birds sing there. If you like I will take you."

I thought about it for a second, but felt that emotionally I wasn't ready for that, so I politely declined.

"Perhaps it's better," he told me. "When I was there, I saw many Japanese tourists having their pictures taken, smiling and chattering in front of the old furnace sheds. I found it quite offensive."

The highlight of the German leg of the tour for me proved to be a gig at The Loft in Berlin, and it remains one of my all-time favourites to this day, although the entire experience was far more intense than I could ever have imagined. Dirk, who at all other times appeared completely calm and unflappable, was visibly nervous as we passed through the Soviet checkpoint that marked the beginning of the long corridor through East Germany that led to West Berlin. The granite-faced border guards stared at us relentlessly through the windows of the bus, machine guns poised, and we found this incredibly intimidating. Throughout the journey we had to maintain a constant speed of sixty miles an hour, while on either side the dull, featureless terrain that ran to the distant horizon made the journey seem all the longer. "The road doesn't pass or overlook any East German towns, because they don't want westerners to see how poor they really are," Dirk explained. At one point we were flagged almost to a halt as a number of heavily armed guards strolled alongside the bus, examining us all closely before finally waving us on our way.

A recent development had been the introduction of a single restaurant stop, so we decided, against Dirk's wishes, to pull over. It didn't take long for us to see why he had been keen to press on. As Tony parked the bus he didn't quite manage to get it inside the white painted parking space, and as we climbed out of the van a couple of East German guards walked across and promptly fined him on the spot. We were incredulous. "They will always find something to fine you for, at least once on the way in and once on the way out. They just want western currency and to flex their muscles," Dirk told us.

The restaurant itself was a grim affair, yet also comical. Inside there were two eating areas: one was a sparse, basic cafeteria, while the other seemed to be a high-class, silver service restaurant, and displayed outside each one was a menu. We looked at the menu for the posh restaurant and it seemed in keeping with the vibe, except that it was intended strictly for East Germans only. Dirk explained that nothing on the menu was actually available; they simply displayed it in a feeble attempt to impress westerners and kid them into thinking that life for East Germans was grand. "You can order anything you like in there, as long as it is cabbage soup," Dirk remarked dryly.

Although the café designated for westerners was basic, there was waiter service. Things became a little heated when I noticed Dirk's obvious irritation with remarks the waiter was making in response to our order. He explained that we were being derided because we'd asked for vegetarian food. "Vegetarians are not good communists," Dirk explained patiently, "and now they are questioning your sexual orientation." The food consisted of boiled vegetables, and was inedible. We checked out the shop, then beat a hasty retreat to the bus, eager to get the journey over with. I bought a bottle of Polish vodka, but found it undrinkable - it was far better suited to fuelling my Zippo lighter.

Finally we approached the checkpoint that would lead us into West Berlin and, with a huge sigh of relief and some slight disorientation, we joined the busy traffic that flooded what appeared to be a perfectly normal West German city. On arriving at the hotel, I was fascinated to see that a large window in the hall on the floor where our rooms were situated overlooked the Berlin Wall. Beyond the wall on the far side was a desolate wasteland of derelict buildings and large open spaces, and in the growing darkness I could make out tall observation towers staffed by soldiers who continually swept searchlights along the wall's perimeter. By stark contrast, on our side of the wall, rush hour was in progress, as streams of large Mercedes saloons and trams packed with evening commuters drifted by. It was a surreal sight.

The venue itself was very cool. The high stage, low ceiling, and wooden floors promised a great sound, and didn't disappoint. The PA was state-of-the-art, and much better than we were used to. The dressing room area was lavishly supplied with food and alcohol, and I spied a list on the wall of bands that were scheduled to play there over the next six or seven months. As I perused the list I noticed that The Fall were due to play there. As my eyes continued down the list I noticed they were playing again; and yet again a third time. Other notables making multiple visits included The Birthday Party. "I think this place is going to be all right," I remarked to the others. "It seems no-one can stay away."

I heard a welcoming voice behind me and turned to see a beautiful, mature woman dressed in black punk attire who told us that her name was Margaret, and that this was her venue. She asked if we'd had a pleasant journey, and laughed when she saw our faces. "Well, you're here now," she said warmly. "You'll have a good time here; everyone knows what a hassle it is for bands to come and they really appreciate it. In the meantime, you can relax for a bit." She opened a silver cigarette case containing a row of beautiful, hand rolled joints of the finest marijuana I have ever smoked.

I particularly enjoyed the opening band that night, an Italian band called The Savage Circle. Over the years I tried in vain to track the band down, but I never heard anything from them again.

We felt so good that we decided to improvise the final song, a half-written idea which didn't even have a title yet, let alone finished lyrics. I could sense the band's apprehension as we approached the song's finale, because no-one had a clue what to do when we got there. As it turned out we were feeling inspired, not only by the audience reaction, which was exceptionally good, but also by the events of the entire day, and we were able to improvise an interesting ending to the set. We were happy to discover that our sound engineer, Stevo, had recorded our set, so when we came to finish the song properly, calling it 'One Flesh', we had a reference.

Sadly we had to leave Berlin the next day, and I was disappointed not to be able to take in a little more of the city. Before leaving, we bought a tin of red spray paint, much to Dirk's alarm, and decorated a piece of the Berlin Wall with a large cartoon face under which we wrote, "The Chameleons - a Chapter of the Planet Earth Society".

The journey out of Berlin was every bit as tense as the journey in. We waited patiently in the van for our turn to pass through the checkpoint and, without thinking, I casually flicked a cigarette stub out of the open window. Dirk went berserk. "Are you stupid?" he bellowed. "They will arrest you immediately if they see you." Only two weeks before, he explained, a West German had been arrested for a similarly minor offence, and had mysteriously died while in police custody. Half way along the Berlin corridor we were stopped by the police, who this time handed Tony a fine for failing to adhere to the speed restrictions - not because he was exceeding the sixty miles an hour speed limit, but because he had been driving slightly below it. Further along we were brought to a halt again, while soldiers combed the underside of the bus with long mirrors to make sure no-one had been attempting to escape the East by clinging to the axles of the bus.

Bidding Dirk a temporary farewell, we next travelled to France and, as with Germany, I was surprised by the degree of enthusiasm with which we were greeted. My favourite French gig was at The Bikini Club in Toulouse, a venue we would visit regularly over the next couple of years. The owner was a generous Frenchman in the grand tradition, and it always seemed to work out that a gig at the Bikini would coincide with one of the band's rare rest days. The weather was always great whenever we were there, and I have fond memories of smoking very good marijuana by the club swimming pool, and being given tours of the city in an old, open-top Citroën. Our driver on these occasions was invariably the venue owner's mother, who had one of those beautiful, classic French looks that seems to be impervious to the weathering effects of time.

Once across the border into Spain, a problem with the van saw us stranded briefly on a lonely road that ran through a deserted sandy region, miles from the nearest town. Someone had the bright idea of flashing SOS at passing vehicles using the bus headlights but we were puzzled to observe that, if anything, vehicles tended to accelerate away. Eventually Tony was able to fix the problem and we arrived at the venue in Madrid to meet Susan, an English girl working as a tour manager and interpreter in Spain. We told her what had happened and she suddenly laughed and pointed out that we'd had the Morse code message the wrong way round. We'd actually been spelling out the letters OSO which, in Spanish, means bear. "That's it!" Tony exclaimed. "That's why they were all accelerating away. They obviously thought there was a bear around!"

In Barcelona I was particularly impressed with the architectural work of Gaudi, the expansive, open paved areas, and the many lavish water fountains that are typical of Spanish cities. We were told that the young people of Spain were still celebrating the passing of the repressive Franco regime, and consequently they were partying vigorously. However, on the day of our scheduled show in Valencia, disaster struck when I found myself croaking ominously. The venue at Valencia was a huge, beautiful arena with a massive stage and, at the soundcheck, we were running through an instrumental version of 'Second Skin' to save my voice, when suddenly the far doors opened and hordes of elderly Spanish couples entered and began waltzing elegantly around the room in time with our music.

By the end of the soundcheck, my voice still hadn't returned and the promoter was seriously concerned. I was handed a huge glass of brandy, which I swallowed gratefully with a single gulp. It certainly improved my mood, but did little for my voice. The promoter beckoned me down from the stage and began jabbering with his companion in frantic Spanish and, still reeling from the effects of the brandy, I was escorted out of the venue and bundled into the back of a very small Fiat. A fast drive through the streets of Valencia brought us suddenly to the hospital where I was ushered

---

1. "What if there's a bear around?" became something of a catch phrase with Tony ever since he learned of a local Manchester character named Psychotic Ted. For some unknown reason, Psychotic Ted would become extremely nervous and paranoid whenever he was in close proximity to any expanse of dense vegetation, such as a forest. When asked why he was so uptight he would invariably throw worried glances and reply, "What if there's a bear around?" Later Psychotic Ted took to wearing a sheet of tinfoil on his head whenever he went outdoors in order to prevent satellites or aliens from zapping his brain, although from the sound of it he may have acted too late to save himself.

into the presence of a doctor who, after examining my throat amidst many "ums" and "ahs", proceeded to prepare an injection of what I assumed at the time were antibiotics. I tried in vain to warn the doctor that I'd just consumed rather a lot of alcohol, but he continued to inject my rear. Within a few minutes I was as high as a kite. Whatever it was I'd been injected with, and I came to doubt very much they were antibiotics, they worked - and later that night I sang like a lark to an audience of around three thousand people.

Afterwards the venue continued to treat us as though we were The Rolling Stones, and the usual kinds of excesses littered the dressing room. I headed for the shower, but was taken by surprise when a very beautiful young girl, accompanied by a photographer, followed me into the shower room and locked the door. In broken English the photographer then made it very clear what he expected. I was to have sex with the girl, while he took photographs. Laughing, I tried to explain that I wasn't going to be photographed having sex with the girl, as beautiful as she was, but he was insisting. "She do anything you want. A-n-ee-thing you waannt. She suck you, a-n-ee-thing." All the while, the girl was smiling sweetly and lunging toward me as I backed away. So this is the life of a rock 'n' roll star, I thought to myself. Not bad.

The next day my voice had deteriorated even further, and we still had the final show in Madrid to play. I was disappointed when a repeat of the previous day's injection failed to materialise, and instead I was given a packet of pills, a pot of honey, black tea and a throat spray. I struggled to take the pills, which were unusually large and shaped rather like torpedoes, and they tasted terrible. At the second attempt, I coughed the pill back onto my plate. Tony was looking at me with an amused expression. "You barm pot," he said, laughing. "They're suppositories."

"They're what?" I asked blinking.

"You're supposed to stick them up your arse, not swallow them!" he explained, still grinning from ear to ear.

'Honestly!' I thought to myself. 'The things I have to do for this band'.

In fact, none of the remedies worked. The throat spray, which I used in desperation just as I was walking out onto the stage, actually numbed my vocal chords, which made matters even worse. Despite all this, the audience were absolutely brilliant, and it turned out to be another memorable night.

After our adventures in mainland Europe, shows in England began to feel depressing. To begin with, with the exception of a few cities, attendances were disappointing, and tended to be lacklustre affairs after all the excitement the foreign gigs had generated. The press, too, was less than enthusiastic, and what had originally been a mixed response was gradually becoming openly hostile and cynical. We found ourselves constantly compared to bands that we had absolutely no interest in, and to add insult to injury, the same writers kept insisting on citing these bands as major influences when nothing could have been further from truth. It was lazy journalism and we knew it, but by this time, electronic pop duos were all the rage and the music press - most notably the *NME* - was heralding the death of the electric guitar. In cities where the band was popular our reputation continued to escalate, but it was always confusing when, for example, we'd play a sold out show in Manchester one night, only to find around thirty people turning up the next night in Liverpool.

From day one, Liverpool was an arduous city to play for The Chameleons. The first time, we were puzzled to find we'd been booked to play quite early in the afternoon in a college refectory. Despite the bizarre surroundings, enhanced by a rather large lighting rig that had been hired to counter the daylight seeping in between drawn curtains, the audience had been quite responsive. All except one young girl who pulled up a chair, placed it directly in front of me while I was performing and began reading the newspaper in a very bored fashion. I found this to be particularly insulting, and so on impulse I crept over to her unseen as she read the paper then snatched it from her hands, screwing it up and throwing it at her. Afterwards she sent a few of her rugby-playing pals over to solicit an apology, but I wasn't having any of it, big as they were. Dave was at my shoulder instantly to back me up, and in the end they walked off with a flea in their ear, which is better than a Doc Martin boot, in my view.

On another occasion we arrived at the venue to find a PA system that was in a dangerous condition. We tried to continue with the gig as best we could, but glancing at the back of the stacks we were horrified to see that mains cables had been jammed into plug boards by their bare wires, and that the PA itself, some two and a half thousand watts, hadn't been earthed. In the end I received an electric shock from the microphone that almost knocked me off my feet. I was particularly disappointed because I'd seen Pete Wylie, a performer we admired greatly, watching from the bar, but in the interests of self-preservation we were forced to abandon the gig. Curiously, the following week we received one of our few positive reviews.

Our last attempt at playing Liverpool wasn't life-threatening, but was nevertheless thoroughly unpleasant. I have never seen a worse venue in which to play a gig; the tables in the centre of a dance area that led off from the main room had been designed to resemble an ancient Egyptian barge, and this seemed particularly apt because the floor was completely drenched to the extent that water splashed around as you walked across it. Tony had driven the bus to the rear of the club and I made my way backstage to help unload the equipment. As I walked out into the rear alley, I had to cover my face due to the stench of rotting refuse which was lying around in mountainous, rat-infested piles. Later, after the equipment had been brought in, I made my way down the alley. It was around 3pm, but as I passed a fire exit it was suddenly flung open and a young guy wearing a Hawaiian shirt fell out of what appeared to be a packed disco in full swing. Clearly very drunk, he collapsed into the alley and immediately began throwing up. What a fuckin' place!

Other gigs, while not unpleasant, were equally strange. We arrived at a club called The Palm Grove in Bradford to find that it was a West Indian reggae club, and the small number of people that turned up to see us, totalling around thirty or so, told us that many of their friends had wanted to go but had been inexplicably wary of doing so. As it turned out, this small audience were treated to one of the best sets we played that year, and the Rastafarians that ran the place were particularly impressed. After the gig they led us into the club's inner sanctum and handed out some first class marijuana. I spent the rest of the evening getting very stoned in a small carpeted room that had lots of bass speakers arranged around the four walls, enjoying some of the best dub I'd ever heard.

In the immediate wake of the album's release we visited as many of the regional record shops as we possibly could, taking with us promotional posters, empty record sleeves and copies of the record. Shop managers usually only met sales reps from distribution companies, and so they responded well to meeting a band in person. Consequently we were able to secure display space for the album where otherwise this probably wouldn't have happened. There were many more independent retailers back then than there are now, and we signed quite a few of the copies that the shops had already bought in. In addition to the advantages of calling in person, it was an interesting thing to do.

That summer we were invited to record another John Peel session. This time the venue was the state-of-the-art Maida Vale studios, and it was to be my first experience with Solid State Logic (SSL) equipment and, to be honest, I hated it. I thought this new direction in studio technology, which seemed to be spreading throughout every studio in the land, was depressing. SSL gave us a harder, much brasher sound, and the results lacked the warmth of our earlier recordings. SSL didn't seem suited to capturing acoustic instruments at all, although I could see how it would improve production when working with electronic instruments such as keyboards and drum machines.

This time around the chief engineer was Mike Robinson, who later that year would also produce our Janice Long Radio One sessions. He was a true character and great fun to spend time with, and again we were rather proud to see that all semblance of clock-watching vanished once he got to grips with the material. On the Janice Long session he became so enthusiastic that he wheeled out a rather antiquated device for sonically rendering a stereo signal in such a way that it seemed to revolve around the room, or rather the stereo field, in a circular fashion. He spent ages setting it up and, in stereo, it did sound impressive. However, we felt compelled to remind him that Janice's programme was transmitted in mono. "Ah, yes! That's true, but one day this stuff will be released on a record, and then they'll hear it," he said triumphantly[2].

During those days at the BBC we also worked with John Porter, and he, too, was impressed with the group. "When this goes out, there are going to be considerably more people interested in what you're doing," he whispered to me at one point during a mix. In later years I bitterly regretted the fact that we hadn't thought to ask John Porter to produce the follow-up album. He was such a joy to work with, and quite brilliant, as he was to prove later when he went on to produce one of The Smiths' finest singles, 'What Difference Does It Make?'

As *Script of the Bridge* continued to gather momentum, Statik decided they wanted to release yet another promotional single. At first we weren't that keen, as we felt we'd pulled enough tracks from the album already, but Dunn explained that the single was meant for the licensees on mainland Europe and wouldn't be widely available in England, so finally we relented and 'Up The Down Escalator' - along with 'Monkeyland' and 'Prisoners of the Sun' - was released that autumn.

On the back of that single we returned to Germany for another spate of gigs, and were reunited with Dirk. The first show was at a venue called The Odeon in the college town of Münster, and we'd arranged to meet Dirk there. However, we reached the town centre of town during rush hour and, amidst the chaos, we couldn't find the venue. We tried asking a few people for directions but were hindered by an inability to speak German. Eventually our roadie, Spoonhead, rose from his seat. "Ee-are, I'll ask someone!" he said and wound down the window. Standing outside a high street store was a

---

2. Mike Robinson would eventually go on to produce the now legendary BBC Live Aid broadcast, amongst a great many other things.

guy who looked approachable. Leaning out as far as he could, in his best German-pidgin-English Spoonhead asked, "Ell-o, doo yoo know za vey too za Odeun bitter?"

The young guy looked at him for a moment before replying, "Ah, well, you see, am not from round ear, am just waitin' for mi mam," in a stiff Yorkshire accent.

The tour brought us a departure from our usual itinerary by way of another couple of television appearances, although, once again, we were duped. The first was a return to the show we'd appeared on earlier in the year in Brussels, this time miming to 'Up The Down Escalator', and I was pleased to see definite improvements over our earlier appearance. The second TV spot, this time in Germany, was a case of bad communication. Our German agent had asked us if we would agree to appear, and we said yes on the understanding that we'd play live. "Oh yes!" they said. "You can perform live, the whole show is live in front of a large audience."

We turned up at the location, which was set in the grounds of a large country house, and immediately we noticed that there didn't appear to be a sound rig. "Oh no," the producer told us, "It's play back." We realised to our horror that we were expected to mime live on television in front of about two thousand people and to a television audience of millions. Once we relaxed, however, we started to have a good time and realised that the trick was not to take it very seriously. Throughout the day we had a couple of run-throughs in front of the crowd and laughed and joked with them, so that, by the time it came to doing it for real, we got an almighty cheer as we walked out. The song the producer had chosen for the live broadcast was 'Don't Fall', and I realised that the lyrics contained the word 'fucking' and that the show aired live at 5pm. No-one else, it seemed, had noticed, so I thought the best thing to do was to keep quiet and hope that the TV channel wouldn't get flooded with complaints from irate, English-speaking parents.

The highlight of the show was a special appearance by Howard Jones. I rarely got to see a real-life, mainstream pop star up close, so I was quite excited, but it wasn't destined to happen that day either. The helicopter (!) that brought Howard Jones landed some distance away, and he began to mime his hit immediately on climbing down, while the helicopter (!) waited for him close by. He was surrounded by an adoring throng throughout his entire performance, and the only thing I was able to see was a little white tuft of hair sticking up over all the other heads. When the song finished the little white tuft of hair climbed back into the helicopter (!) and away he flew. Oh well!

Along with the usual type of gigs, this particular visit offered up something different. Our agent in Germany was organising a large outdoor festival headlined by Simple Minds, who were enjoying massive success in Europe with the album *New Gold Dream*, and he invited The Chameleons to join the bill. It would prove to be the biggest show we ever played, and by the time we walked out on stage at around 3pm, we were told there were around 30,000 people out front. Rising to the occasion we stormed the gig, managing to piss off Simple Minds' management in the process as I leapt spontaneously onto Jim Kerr's catwalk during a song, and ran along its length, flirting with the crowd.

Marillion were also on the bill that day. Their bus was parked directly next to ours, prompting Tony, who was sitting alongside Reg, to open the sliding window and yell at the top of his voice, "Hey Fish, you're a fuckin' dick!" Tony then ducked out of the way as Fish, the lead singer of the band, turned his head toward them, leaving Reg sitting there looking like the culprit, his face crimson.

During Simple Minds' set, their crew informed us that no-one was allowed to stand at the side of the stage. I was disappointed, as I'd wanted to hear the set through the stage wedges rather than the PA system. The others went to find a place out front, but as I stood there with Dirk (who that day was tour manager for Simple Minds rather than The Chameleons, at their insistence), he brushed off the crew's efforts to evacuate me, and we spent the entire set grooving along from the side of the stage. They were brilliant that night. As one of my favourite Simple Minds songs started up, 'Someone, Somewhere In Summertime', it began to rain gently and, through the impressive lighting rig, it looked fantastic. I can't hear that song now without thinking of that moment: Dirk and I smiling happily, gently jigging to the music as the band played to approximately 50,000 people.

The tour ended in Amsterdam, this time in a more respectable venue called The Paradiso, a huge, converted, deconsecrated church. By now Christmas was almost upon us, so we decided to do some shopping before catching the boat home. Having agreed at the outset that everyone would return to England together in the bus, our sound engineer was suddenly insisting we pay for him and his assistant to return by plane, which, owing to the fact that it was almost Christmas Eve, was too expensive a proposition. As a result, a huge argument erupted between us, resulting in a lot of tension and bad feeling. The tour had been quite a long one, and the bus was too small a space to share with people who sulked a lot - and this guy sulked a *lot*. He'd even threatened to have some friends of his, a gang of

Dutch Hells Angels (or so he claimed) meet us in Amsterdam and show us what's what, and the situation became quite ugly.

The Paradiso was only about half-full but the gig itself was great, and afterwards we were all in high spirits and looking forward to getting the boat back. When we went outside, though, we had a shock. Someone had broken into the van and had made off with all they could carry, including a couple of bags and most of the Christmas presents. I'd been lucky, all my stuff had been tucked under a seat at the rear of the van and hadn't been touched, but a few of the others lost theirs. Tony was unluckiest of all; he carried a flight case containing his cameras and photographic equipment and the case now lay empty and broken on the pavement. To make matters worse, both Reg and Ali had broken the golden rule and left their passports in their bags, both of which had been stolen, meaning that, unless we could sort something out, they would be stranded in Amsterdam over Christmas. On the plus side, the thieves had missed a considerable amount of cash that, for some reason, had been left in the bus, nor had the rather expensive cassette player been ripped out. Still, as I looked at Tony's empty flight case lying there in the rain I felt sick. Meanwhile the sound engineer, hovering around like some bedraggled hippy beggar, kept saying. "Can you pay us, Tony, so we can get off to catch our plane?" How Tony kept his temper in check I shall never know, but he did. He paid the guys and I don't think we ever saw either of them again.

Getting Ali and Reg back to England proved easier than we'd dared hope. As it was almost Christmas Eve the local police couldn't be bothered with all the paperwork, so they immediately issued them with a stamped document that would satisfy English immigration. Most of my personal, essential Christmas shopping was stuffed into my jeans, and had the customs officer at Harwich simply asked me to empty my pockets I'd have been looking at about five years in prison. As I'd hoped, this being Christmas Eve, he was eager to get home, and on seeing a minibus jam-packed with musical equipment he groaned, asked for the paperwork, then allowed us to pass with the minimum of inspection. The ride home was long and grim but, over the holiday, my special groceries at least ensured that I got invited to all the best parties.

9. ANOTHER GREAT ROCK 'N' ROLL SWINDLE

With the coming of the New Year, we were delighted to hear that *Script Of The Bridge* was actually doing very well. Granted, the reviews had been mixed, and the album hadn't charted in the UK, but it was a big favourite on the US college radio network and was selling well there, despite only being available on import.

Script was also attracting attention in mainland Europe, and in January 1984 we were invited to fly to Lisbon to play two consecutive shows there. We spent the evening before the flight at The Columbia Hotel, which had become something of a haunt for rock groups staying in London, so we weren't surprised to learn that New Order were also staying there prior to their show the following evening at Brixton Academy.

As we were leaving for the airport, we walked outside to be greeted by a uniformed chauffeur and seeing our guitar cases he politely enquired. "Are you the band from Manchester?"

Tony said that we were, and we were led to a large Jaguar limousine. "Fuckin' 'ell," remarked Tony, "the album must be doing alright!"

We all agreed that it was very nice of Statik to lay this on, and that it made a pleasant change from Swan Taxis.

"Where to?" the driver asked.

"Gatwick, mate," came Tony's reply.

"Oh, I thought we were going across town. OK, not to worry," and he then proceeded to drive us to the airport. "Yes," said the driver, making polite conversation, "I've heard your record on the radio, very nice."

"You have?" we asked incredulously. "Are you sure?"

"Oh yes!" he insisted. "Just the other day, what's it called? Black Sunday or something?"

Suddenly we realised that The Chameleons had waltzed off with New Order's limo. "Oh, you mean *Blue Monday*?" I said, keeping up the pretence.

"That's the one!" said the driver. "It's got a great beat."

"I'd love to see the faces on that lot when Swan Taxis turn up to take them to Brixton Academy," laughed Tony.

We clambered down from the plane at Lisbon airport in sweaters and trench coats, only to be greeted by bright sunshine and a temperature of around 22°C. When asked what we'd like to do with the day, we immediately asked to be taken to a beach. "The beach? In winter?" We discarded our winter attire, and spent the first day breezing around the colourful streets and cafés of Lisbon. The people were good-natured, humorous, and beautiful, the sun shone on everything, and the food was out of this world. A local music journalist offered to act as guide, and we were all in such high spirits that she decided to stick around for the weekend, driving us everywhere.

Both nights had sold out, and I remember the audience being exceptionally animated. One guy directly at the front of the stage repeatedly leapt high in the air and then grabbed the tuning keys of my bass, twisting them and sending the instrument out of tune. At first, I was tempted to hit him with it, then realised it was just a mad expression of his passion, so I just got on with it.

The following night's show was even better than the first. The promoter set the tone when, having no support act with which to open the show, he projected a video of Public Image Ltd's *Live in Tokyo* onto a giant screen before we went on, which certainly put me in the right mood - I loved it. I was also enamoured with the steady supply of high quality weed that came our way, again courtesy of the promoter, who told me it had come specially from Morocco. We very much enjoyed our time in Lisbon, and I'm only sad I never had the opportunity to return.

By now the Manchester music scene was evolving rapidly. The remaining members of Joy Division had gone on to form New Order, and were making some outstanding records and breaking into the mainstream. Flush with the proceeds of their new-found commercial success, the band and their label opened a brand new club in Manchester - The Haçienda. no-one had ever seen anything quite like it, and even the most cynical had to concede that the interior design was both impressive and radical, with its motorway-chic hazard signs, walls awash with pale blue and grey, raised polished wooden dance floor, and cat's eye reflectors illuminating the perimeters.

We had our first proper look at the club's interior when we were invited to take part in one of their local band promotions. I remember we drove the van straight into the club and parked it by the edge of the dance floor. Sitting there with its hazard lights flashing, looked to all the world as if it were part of the club's faux-industrial design theme. The Smiths and James had also been booked to play in this series of concerts, and we were quite proud when, not being part of the Manchester clique, nine hundred people turned up at our show. Despite this impressive turnout we were paid just £50, and the following week we received the worst review we'd ever had. This came courtesy of the NME, who derided us for alleged on-stage antics that bore absolutely no resemblance to reality. These bad reviews would inevitably follow anything we did, but we'd already realised that this antipathy was motivated by something other than an honest appraisal of the band. In any event, whoever was behind it was wasting time, energy and copy space, because both the band's reputation and audience numbers continued to rise steadily.

We took part in two large outdoor events that year. The first was on the German - Belgian border I think, and despite our optimism, it turned out to be something of a disaster. Also on the bill that day were China Crisis, Southern Death Cult, Talk Talk and The Cure. We had the use of Stefan's red, 1950s Mercedes bus, and it looked really stylish amongst the more modern, bland-looking tour vehicles on parade. It was certainly a superior dressing room to the awful Portacabins supplied for the purpose.

Someone who worked for the promoter turned up with some exceptionally strong dope, and consequently some of us were very stoned as we walked out onto the stage. I felt as though every ounce of energy had been drained from me before we'd even begun, and the set turned into a lacklustre nightmare. Wrong drug, wrong day!

To compound matters, Southern Death Cult, pumped up on coke and eager to let fly, were the next band on and duly blew us off the stage - the only band ever to manage this feat. Top of the bill were The Cure and, while I enjoyed their set, the atmosphere in front of stage, and indeed around the whole event, was practically non-existent. I've never attended a more boring festival in all my life and I hope I never will again. After the show I was introduced to Robert Smith, but found him to be a rude, arrogant poseur of the worst order and didn't stay long. However it was nice to meet Phil Thornalley again, who we hadn't seen since he'd engineered 'In Shreds' two years earlier.

The next day we were due to fly back to England, but Stefan said that he wanted to drive us to a beach he knew so we could relax for a couple of hours before our flight. Unfortunately the journeys to and from the coast took a lot longer than anticipated, and with dawning horror we realised that we were going to miss the flight home. Tony is convinced to this day that this had been intentional on the part of the promoter, who had some grievance or other, and despite a two-year association we never worked with him again.

We were carrying a lot of equipment and no alternative flights were forthcoming, so, we had little alternative but to head for the boat train. Fairly soon we were boarding the ferry to Dover and we were joined by an army of touts who had been following The Scorpions on a tour of mainland Europe. They'd made a killing selling tickets and bootleg T-shirts, and their pockets were stuffed with rolls of banknotes. When they learned we were a band from England they made it their mission to get us as pissed as humanly possible. One of them, I was amused to see, was Spivey, who I'd met all those years ago outside a T. Rex gig in Manchester.

The train guard came around to check tickets at one point, and Tony dutifully produced ours for inspection. "You didn't buy ticketsh, did ya?" Spivey exclaimed in amazement. "We never buy ticketstsh, doo wee lads" He then proceeded to bribe the train guard. They made no secret of the fact that they ripped bands off. "We'll rip you off too, if you get really big," they boasted.

The gig we'd been racing back to England to play was the York Rock Festival, on 22nd September. This saw us billed alongside The Redskins, Spear Of Destiny, Sisters Of Mercy and Echo And The Bunnymen. On arriving at the venue we pulled into the parking area, where the only other vehicle present was a shiny black van with heavily tinted windows that wouldn't have looked out of place in an episode of Scooby Doo. We drew alongside it and began gathering our bags and jackets, when the side door of the black van slid open. In my imagination, I heard a whoosh of air and saw a cloud of dry ice emerge from the interior, but instead a mad-haired, lanky figure, dressed completely from head to foot in black, emerged from the van and slowly encircled our bus. The door of the black van was still open and I could see that the interior had been carpeted in what looked like black sheepskin. As the shadowy figure continued his inspection, we remained in our seats and watched him. Having now completely circled the van, he approached the driver's side and Tony rolled down the window. "Nice van, man," said the figure.

"Thanks!" said Tony, grinning.

After a moment's thought, the figure added: "It'd be better if it was black though," and walked off. That was our first and only encounter with Andrew Eldritch of The Sisters of Mercy.

In 1984, due largely to the post-punk Goth movement, black was very much in vogue when it came to just about everything. We noted and debated this development numerous times and so when it had come to designing a Chameleons T-shirts, to be sold at the York festival, we decided to rebel against this rather tiresome trend and turn in something we felt represented the antithesis. This would have been an excellent plan were it not for the fact that none of us could come up with a suitable idea - or any idea, for that matter. Tony had been watching all of this with increasing frustration until he finally exclaimed, "Ee-yar you lot, give us those pens, I'll design a fuckin' T-shirt."

Grabbing a sheet of paper and the day-glow felt-tips that were on the table, he scribbled and doodled away for no longer than thirty-seconds until he triumphantly threw down his creation. We sat and gazed upon the drawing in silence, for what seemed like an age. Tony had drawn a crazy, grinning hippy with a daisy growing out of his head, wearing a garish stripy tie. It was Reg who finally broke the silence: "I like it."

"I like it too," I echoed, laughing.

"I like it too," added a tittering Dave.

"That's it then, post it off."

On the day of the York festival we strolled over to one of the merchandise stalls to inspect our new T-shirts, but they were nowhere to be seen amongst the thousands of black Bunnymen, Sisters Of Mercy and Spear Of Destiny items on offer. At last, we identified the company that was supposed to be marketing our new shirts. The guy was very apologetic but sadly explained that it was felt that they just wouldn't sell. "No-one's going to buy these." he insisted.

"Why not?" Tony barked.

"They're not black," came the reply.

We carried off a bag full of them and over the following months we handed them out to whoever wanted them. We liked them, and wore them very proudly. In fact, with a suntan and the right amount of magic mushrooms, they looked stunning. The postscript to this tale is that years later, during the acid house craze, I was walking through Manchester and saw a very young looking guy wearing one of these mad-hippy Chameleons T-shirts. After doing a double take, I stopped him and asked where he'd bought his obviously new Chameleons shirt. "My what, mate?"

"Your Chameleons shirt?"

"Chameleons?"

"Yeah, you know, the shirt you're wearing."

Seemingly confused the guy looked down at his shirt and sussed what I was talking about. "Oh," he said. "My shirt! I don't know what Chameleons is, I just bought it from Affleck's Palace 'cause I like the colours."

Affleck's was an alternative clothes market in the city centre, and, feeling curious, I made my way over there. Sure enough, amongst all the other apparel on offer, were our mad-hippy shirts. The guy told me that he'd bought them from the company who'd printed them for the York festival five or six years earlier, and they were now selling like hot cakes; all the acid house kids were snapping them up. He happily gave me a few for my friends, all of whom were very pleased with them. That's The Chameleons all over, I thought, years ahead of our time!

During our set at York a rainbow appeared over the stage, which I thought was quite nice and surprisingly inexpensive for such an elaborate lighting effect. That night was the first time I'd seen Echo And The Bunnymen since they'd appeared at the Factory in Manchester. They'd recently released *Ocean Rain*, and I thought they were brilliant that night. Any misgivings I'd previously had about them were swept away by their performance. Their set ended on a rather sour note, however. The security guys at the front of stage had begun to get a little too heavy handed and, on noticing this, Ian McCulloch protested - but his repeated objections were ignored. Clearly tired of this, he belted one of them lightly on the back of the head with his microphone stand. When the band finally came off stage, a gang of security guys were waiting for them and set about him; later I saw him being dragged back to his dressing room by his own people, his white shirt covered in blood.

Since the release of *Script Of The Bridge*, we'd started to receive a growing number of letters, and I was surprised to see that the bulk of the mail was coming from the college towns of North America. This was surprising because our records hadn't been officially released there, and it hadn't occurred to us that people might be picking the record up on import. Quite a few people were though, so much so that we came to the attention of *Rolling Stone* Magazine, which requested a short interview and a photo session to form part of an article on the British pop invasion. They were heralding an American renaissance of British acts, which, they claimed, was unequalled since the arrival of The Beatles in 1963. We were told that The Smiths, one of the few British bands of the day that we had any respect for, would also be featured. We dutifully turned up in Soho to have our picture taken, and felt proud to have had a mention in *Rolling Stone*. They even sent us copies, which we were delighted to receive.

The year was to be tinged with sadness, however. The Planet Earth Society, having already lost Ken to Oxford, now lost its second founding member. Ali was becoming increasingly uncomfortable with the direction we were taking, feeling that we were too compromising in pursuit of our aims within the industry. This surprised me, because, if anything, it felt like we were a band determined to go our own way no matter what, but Ali was justifiably cynical about making a business out of music, although he was happy to receive a wage, regardless of whether the band was working or not. Ali was still regarded as an employee, rather than a full member of the group, by virtue of the fact that he had absolutely no role in the writing of the material, nor did he accept any of the responsibilities that came with signing contracts and the like. As the year progressed, his enthusiasm for The Chameleons seemed to diminish. I recall Dave, in particular, getting quite vocal about it during rehearsals. He felt that Ali was using the band as and when it suited him and wasn't really committed, which was true to some extent. In an attempt to calm the situation, I agreed to have a word with Ali, but it didn't go well. He was difficult to communicate with at the best of times, and it took a couple of hours of hard work to get anywhere at all. My reasoning was simple - surely getting paid to play music was better than toiling in a factory, or signing on? Sadly Ali didn't agree, and we found ourselves looking for a new keyboard player.

We had to look no further afield than Middleton for Ali's replacement. Andy was a member of Melodramene[1], an electronic band very much inspired by Depeche Mode and OMD, who had supported us on a couple of occasions. We'd all got along very well, and so we invited Andy to join us for our upcoming Spanish tour. Almost immediately, though, we came to realise that Andy was a little too young to be performing with The Chameleons. In a well-meaning attempt to increase the band's visual impact, he would leave his keyboard and strut to the edge of the stage, clapping his hands over his head, encouraging the audience to do the same. I found this hilarious, but Dave was not amused. "We're not a fuckin' teenage pop group," he grumbled. Andy refused to be deterred and continued regardless. In the wake of this, and in the absence of an obvious replacement, we dispensed with a keyboard player for quite a long time.

It was suggested that we visit Strawberry Studios in Stockport and record a track with Chris Nagle. Dave I had been mightily impressed with the raw production of The Smiths' 'Hand In Glove', which Nagle had engineered, so we were very keen on the idea. However, the session was strange from the very start, with Chris being very uncommunicative and distant. In fact, he'd looked very poorly. After failing to get our ideas across for most of the day, we were beginning to feel that the guy hadn't the slightest interest and that we'd made a huge mistake in hiring him. He kept whispering in conspiratorial tones about his 'little problem', and we assumed that he was a junkie. Half way through the session he suddenly turned

---

1. Fronted by Gary Lavery, who would later work with Dave and Reg as a member of The Reegs.

completely white and collapsed. It transpired that his 'little problem' was diabetes, and that he'd neglected to take his insulin that day. Nigel, a trainee engineer, stepped in to finish the session, and while he was a lot more enthusiastic than Nagle, we felt that the results were unusable. Another of the house engineers, a striking young guy named Chris Jones, introduced himself, and there was an immediate connection between us all. We swapped phone numbers and promised to stay in touch.

When we'd originally signed with Statik, we had compromised on a three-album deal, but stuck to our guns when it came to omitting the American market. As we continued to play across Europe that year, some of the European licensees hinted that we were selling a lot of copies in the US[2] and I realised that an American tour was a real possibility. The rumours and whisperings evolved quickly, and we learned that *Script Of The Bridge* might well get a domestic US release within the year.

As exciting a possibility as this undoubtedly was, the warning signs began to flash immediately. We walked into the Statik office one day to be presented with three or four alternative sleeves for the proposed US release of *Script Of The Bridge*. MCA Records seemed to be the leading contenders for Dunn's licensing arrangement, which he told us would include the best of his roster: ourselves - his words not mine - The Sound, Jeffrey Lee Pierce and Tom Robinson. However, MCA had wanted to ditch Reg's cover illustration in favour of some of their own designs. Most of them were too banal to recall, but the two they were pitching hardest included one depicting chameleon lizards on a chess board, and another that featured a badly drawn illustration of a woman with four pink poodles on a leather leash. It was the best laugh we'd had in ages, but the moment we realised that Dunn was deadly serious the laughter stopped abruptly. We told him, and an American MCA executive, that there was no way that we would agree to such a repackaging of the album. The artwork on our records was as important to us the music; it was an additional reflection of who we were, and we took meticulous care over every detail, not only the illustrations, but the type faces, the text, the colour of the centres, the spine - even the scratched messages in the disc's run off area. Love it or hate it, every aspect of the record indelibly bore the band's stamp.

In his frustration, Dunn continued to argue MCA's corner. We refused to compromise, suggesting instead that he cut a deal for the rest of his roster and we'd make our own arrangements. Of course, he could do no such thing. We were to discover later that The Chameleons were the band

---

2. We subsequently learned that this figure was around the 60,000 mark.

that MCA desired the most, and Dunn was using us as leverage to try to get all his records released by MCA in America - no Chameleons, no deal. We held an ace that we didn't even know was in the deck, but had no way of capitalising on it. We didn't have the contacts, the resources or the knowledge to secure an American deal on our own, and Dunn knew it.

The real surprise came when Dunn informed us that he wanted to extend the length of our commitment from three albums to six. We discussed this proposal and turned it down, not really thinking that it would be a massive problem. Statik Records was a very small set-up that had yet to really establish stable distribution networks, either within the UK or beyond it. The label's resources were barely adequate, and we felt that to tie ourselves to Statik for what was potentially the duration of our career would be a mistake. Dunn became very unhappy and increasingly persistent that we should agree. At one particular meeting, irked by our non-compliance, he barked, "The Chameleons were *nothing* until you came to me, you ungrateful bastards!" Tony and I set him straight on a few things, but we were still shocked at this vitriolic outburst.

The advances from Statik, which were paid monthly into the band's bank account, suddenly stopped arriving on time and in the end, ceased to arrive at all. Once all the excuses had been exhausted, Dunn delivered the sucker punch. He would resume payments on our original advances, providing we agreed to extend the contract. This amounted to a breach of contract on Statik's part, but, in our impoverished state, we were in no position to sue. From this point on, our relationship with the label would deteriorate rapidly. Things became so difficult that some of us had to sign on, even though, technically, we were still under contract to Statik. Tony had gradually assumed more of a managerial role since James' departure and this was to be a very hard time for him.

All our attempts to reason with Dunn came to nothing, resulting in stalemate. Imagine our surprise, then, when we learned that MCA had gone ahead and released *Script Of The Bridge* in America without our consent. Fortunately they hadn't seen fit to replace Reg's sleeve with one of their own hideous ideas, although they did add transparent, yellow cellophane and an ugly red sticker. However, we were horrified to find that they'd taken it upon themselves to completely rearrange the running order of the album. To add insult to injury they axed four tracks from what they felt was an overlong album, including one that had been linked, by way of the whirly tubes, to another. One of the songs so unceremoniously excised by this act of butchery was 'View From A Hill', the album's grand finale. Finally, for marketing reasons - or so they said - the title of the chosen single, 'Up The

Down Escalator' had been changed to reflect the nearest thing the song had to a hook, 'There Must Be Something Wrong Boys.' *Too fucking right* there was something wrong!

This monstrous betrayal proved to be the last straw as far as our relationship with Statik was concerned, and heralded one of the most depressing periods we ever had together. Having been dropped by Virgin some time earlier, we'd sold our publishing rights to Taktik Music. This company was also owned by Dunn, so not only did we have no money, but we couldn't officially write or record new material, even if we'd had the resources, for fear of Dunn claiming ownership of it. Tony did his best to steer the ship through the storm, and the fact that we were able to survive that year really was all down to him.

By now there was no communication between The Chameleons and Statik Records, and there was no alternative but to engage lawyers. Statik simply ignored the letters that were being sent by our legal team, and our dire financial position meant that we would have to apply for legal aid before any further action was possible. To make matters worse, we discovered that Dunn had licensed all the demos we'd recorded for CBS. He planned to combine these recordings with the songs from the 'In Shreds' single to form an album called *The Fan And The Bellows.*

Dave was livid, and demanded we take legal action to stop the release immediately. Tony and I tried to explain that if Statik had already pressed the record there was little point in pursuing Dunn through the courts, as this would only drive the existing copies underground, thus increasing the rarity value and Dunn's profits in turn. Dave remained adamant that something had to be done, however, rightly arguing that we'd probably never earn anything from the release anyway and so we applied for an injunction preventing Dunn releasing the album. The injunction was duly obtained, but Dunn was experienced and quite clever. The album had indeed been pressed, but Statik was claiming it was a US release. If we wanted to block this, it would mean seeking a further injunction in an American civil court, which was well beyond the remit of our legal aid award.

Thwarted in our attempt to stop the release of *The Fan and The Bellows*, we turned our attention to MCA in America. We were furious at the way they'd mishandled the release of our debut album, and on behalf of the band I told them that they had no contractual right to release the record in the United States. The voice on the other end of the phone went quiet for a moment before telling me that, on the contrary, they had the band under contract for six albums! I insisted that this was impossible: even Statik could only lay claim to three years, so how on earth did they think that they had the right to six albums? The truth of the matter was that Dunn didn't even have a signed agreement to cover the US for the records we'd already delivered to him.

What followed were a number of frantic phone calls from the president of MCA Records in California, and gradually the picture became clearer. MCA had wanted The Chameleons in the wake of our healthy import sales and college radio airplay, so they agreed to some form of licensing deal based on the signing of The Chameleons. The only stumbling block had been that MCA had wanted a minimum commitment of six albums, not three. Dunn simply told them this was no problem, contracts were exchanged, and the sum of $60,000 changed hands. SIXTY GRAND - and most of us had been signing on the dole because his payments weren't arriving. Of course, our refusal to extend the Statik contract to six albums presented Dunn with a real problem, because he'd already signed the MCA contracts and banked the money.

The president of MCA flew to Manchester to review and clarify the situation. We were happy to show him our existing contracts, along with the letters from our lawyers. MCA desperately wanted to work with the band and were trying to find ways in which this could happen, but they'd already paid Dunn for the group and were loath to have to pay out again. We, on the other hand, were not prepared to sign to the label for nothing just because their business department had fucked up. Meanwhile our desperate financial situation continued to grow steadily worse.

Tony and I met regularly to discuss the proposals and examine the MCA contracts, and he would keep the others informed, but despite our best efforts, there didn't seem to be any way we could make it work. Although Dunn was clearly in breach - there was evidence of fraud - we simply didn't have the resources to fight him in the courts and free ourselves from Statik Records. MCA were reluctant to give us those resources and we had no-one else we could turn to. By now, all band activities had pretty much ground to a halt. In theory, the avenue of playing live was still open to us, but we lacked the finances to cover the expenses incurred in setting up gigs and tours.

One welcome distraction from all of this came in the form of an American management company who were interested in representing us in the United States. Given our ongoing problems, we were naturally reticent to commit to an agency about which we knew precisely nothing, but we did put them in the picture regarding our situation and opened a dialogue. Their representative, Will, suggested we come to America and play a few gigs around the 1984 New Music Seminar in New York, an industry event intended to stimulate the emergence of fresh talent. Will said his company would cover the airfares, which would then be recouped from the band's fees, and it would be a good opportunity to play to practically the entire American recording industry. The Chameleons were finally heading to New York!

My initial reaction to playing in the US for the first time was "What a fuckin' madhouse!", but once I'd recovered from the initial culture shock, it struck me how much easier it was to tour in America than in mainland Europe. For example, an average European tour by The Chameleons would take in around twenty-eight cities in thirty days and typically involved leaving and re-entering the same country in a single day at various points of the compass. This meant dealing with all the heavy customs procedures, unloading, presenting and stripping down all our equipment for inspection (usually uncovered, in the pissing rain), being sniffed in sensitive places by mad Alsatians, filling out forms in quadruplicate and getting into arguments with officials in languages we couldn't count to ten in. Then there were all the different national currencies. In those pre-Euro days, it seemed that, regardless of how organised I tried to be, I never managed to have more than a few pounds in the relevant currency in any of the countries I found myself in - and woe betide me if I happened to fall asleep at the border and miss the exchange. I didn't carry a credit card, international debit cards and cash dispensers were virtually unknown, and changing currency in a bank was as much a pain in the arse back then as it is now.

The daily routine of an average tour of Europe would go something like this. We'd be awoken at around 9am and given a continental breakfast, which usually consisted of a fist-sized bread roll that you could have cracked a skull with, packets of butter and jam the size of postage stamps, a piece of string with a tea bag on the end of it and a cup of lukewarm water. The rooms would have to be completely vacated by 10am and we'd usually be back on the road by eleven. We'd then drive six or seven hours before arriving at the next hotel. It was common for promoters to work out some kind of special deal with a hotel chain, so often the hotel that you'd just spent all day driving to would look exactly like the hotel you'd left behind that morning. The hotel staff would all be wearing identical uniforms and the same coloured carpets would adorn identical looking reception areas, corridors and rooms, usually looking exactly like the carpets on the floor of the Black Lodge in *Twin Peaks*.

The rooms would have the same layout and the same framed prints on the walls, and the showers would invariably fail to work properly, suggesting that they all employed the same firm of plumbers. An hour later, we'd set off to the venue and the inescapable soundcheck. The PA crew would always be behind schedule so we'd have to spend ages hanging around the venue, eventually concluding the soundcheck about half an hour before the doors opened. Finally, four nervous wrecks would amble onto the stage to perform the set. After the gig there was the wind-down, and the inevitable frantic search for something to change into that was both dry and clean - by far the day's hardest task. Then we'd head back to the hotel for 2am, be in bed by 3.30am, followed by mad giggles until around 4am and up again at 9am to repeat the entire process.

No doubt many will pour scorn on my complaints, but it's worth noting that when many of our contemporaries were touring around they were probably carrying enough amphetamine or cocaine to fill a bin-bag. We, on the other hand, were not. Having about as much in common with The Rolling Stones as I have with Benny Hill, five weeks of this was enough to do me in. So if you're one of those who always wondered why The Chameleons didn't tour more often, now you know! All that said, for the ninety or so minutes a night when we were actually playing, all the sufferance, ordeals, inconvenience, sleep deprivation and all the rest of it was worth it a hundred times over.

However, we were about to find out that touring the US was a different brand of lager altogether. The preparations ahead of the trip were somewhat complicated and involved each of us presenting ourselves at the American Embassy in London to hand in our applications for a tourist visa and work permits. The forms requested information on everything regarding our background, political persuasion and the colour of our skin. I was asked whether or not I was any relation to Guy Burgess[3], and I truthfully answered that I wasn't.

We flew to the United States on the newly formed Virgin Atlantic airline, from London Gatwick to Newark in New York state. Inevitably we were stopped at immigration, and our hand luggage was inspected. Reg happened to have a lemon in his bag, which caused quite a stir, and the immigration officers barely stopped short of drawing their pistols before deciding that the fruit was docile enough to be allowed through. This exchange left me thanking the Lord that Reg hadn't brought his bottle of home-grown beans.

We were met at the airport by Will and his colleague Josh, and after gaping at all the sky scrapers and *Starsky and Hutch* backdrops, we were promptly installed in a very shady hotel just off 42nd Street in Manhattan.

---

3. The infamous British diplomat turned spy who defected to the Soviet Union in 1951.

It was a bit grim to be honest, but we'd stayed in far worse places. This being my first ever trip to New York, I spent very little time in the hotel anyway. Due to the high temperatures, the cockroaches were out in force and they seemed to be everywhere. On returning to my room at dawn one morning, I opened the door to see cockroaches not just scatter in different directions, but also take to the air and start flying around the room as the rest of the band slept blissfully on.

Mark in New York, 1984. Photo: Tony Skinkis

The New Music Seminar, an industry festival of parties and showcase gigs, was in full swing by the time we arrived in town. As part of the festival we were billed to play alongside The Danse Society and The Sisters Of Mercy at the Irwin Plaza. On arriving and completing the soundcheck we were told that we'd be performing first, at around 9pm, which suited us because it left plenty of time later to enjoy some of the local culture. Our set that night wasn't one of our best. It was much shorter than usual due to the time restrictions placed on us, but it was OK, and afterwards we grabbed a few beers and watched The Sisters perform an enjoyable set. Next up were Danse Society, who we'd also shared the bill with on a previous occasion, and whose music we also quite liked. As they took the stage, the place emptied out and they were left to play to about thirty people. We stayed for the entire set, and were quite shocked to see what had happened and genuinely felt for them. Josh explained that unfortunately, Danse Society had hit the stage at around midnight, which was just about the time all the best hospitality parties began around Manhattan. Consequently, the audience, being made up largely of record industry liggers, had all shot off in the pursuit of free cocktails. What's more, Danse Society had their national tour pulled from under them the day they arrived and so this was to be the band's only performance in America that year. I noticed that two of the band hadn't seemed that concerned, though. As we made our way back across town they were both laughing hysterically in the middle of the street, apparently high as kites, mock bullfighting in the traffic amid frantic car horns and shouts from irate motorists. Good for them!

Seminars were in progress in the conference areas of the hotel, and a lot of people spent a lot of time talking a lot of crap. Tony and I quickly got bored and wandered around the corridors of the Sheraton for a while, and it seemed there was a party going on in every room. We walked into one of the suites, which was packed full of people, and on the far side an army of bartenders were handing out free, giant Margarita cocktails. Naturally we helped ourselves for a couple of hours, admiring the view from the huge windows overlooking Central Park, marvelling at the sudden change of fortune that had brought us to such a sublime moment.

We were all invited to dine with MCA that night and, gathered accordingly around a long table in a Manhattan restaurant, a loud record company executive did her best to impress us. Unfortunately the conversation consisted of dull, music industry bollocks and some story about a movie star shoving a hamster up his arse, which I found a bit vulgar for dinner table conversation. She was pretty though, and although she spoke and laughed continuously, seemingly without the need to draw breath, at one point I was very tempted to slide beneath the long table, make my way discreetly along to the chair she was sitting in and gently bite her ankles. What can I say? I was stoned. A young girl who we'd befriended on the German *Music Convoy* TV show the previous year talked me out of it amid much giggling, whispering and punching of shoulders.

Our short visit to the States took in Washington D.C.'s 9:30 Club, which I'm happy to see is still going strong. We played a great gig to a packed house that night. We even had time to take in some of the sights: the giant, bleached white statues, pillars and occult temples, monuments to the formation of the United States, the Smithsonian Museum, and the White House. We even posed for a picture with the then President of the United

States, Ronald Reagan. Well, OK, it was a cardboard cut-out on a tourist photographer's stall, but it looked impressive from the right angle, and it had every bit as much character and intelligence as its real life counterpart a block away.

Our final show was back in Manhattan at a club called the Danceteria, which I was told had quite a cool reputation. The booker was a very beautiful and charming New Yorker named Ruth Polsky, who would later go on to discover Madonna. The Danceteria show was by far the best of the tour, and the hospitality we received was warm and generous.

While in New York we hung out with a young local by the name of Jack Rabid, who wrote and distributed his own fanzine, *The Big Takeover*. He gave us a copy of the latest edition, which comprised four or five double-sided handwritten photocopies stapled at the corner. Jack was a likable guy and we became quite good friends during our short time there. I was immediately struck by his passion and integrity whenever he spoke about his fanzine, his own aspirations, or music in general, and he genuinely seemed to like the band. I remember wishing that there were a few more editors and journalists like him working in the mainstream music press. Over the years, Jack continued to develop *The Big Takeover*, earning considerable respect and an impressive circulation. The magazine, published three or four times a year, is today regarded by many as the ultimate authority on the underground music scene. We never did make it to the front cover though!

Finally it was time to fly home, and we were happy to learn that Ruth would also be flying to England the same day. She told us how much she'd enjoyed working with us and that she hoped to be able to set up a full, national tour of the US sometime soon. Ruth Polsky was very cool and I liked her a lot.

Back home, everyone was eager to hear how our visit to America had gone. For the most part, I could only smile distantly and shrug my shoulders. It was such a massive difference in culture, sights, sensations and experiences that it took a while for it all to sink in, and it had passed so quickly that it was hard for us to believe we'd even been there at all. For me it had been rather like climbing into a TV set, then boarding a rollercoaster fun ride with a cultural theme, and I was eager for the more prolonged taste of America that a full national tour would offer.

After all the excitement of our first American visit, returning home to the same contractual and financial problems we'd left behind threw us into a deep depression. We did continue to write, albeit unofficially, but there was a definite lack of enthusiasm. A lifeline came from John Peel's producer, who called unexpectedly to offer us a new session, giving us the opportunity to air new material for a very welcome fee. Having said that, while I remember very little about the session itself, I do recall that it was all we could do to lift ourselves. Again, the song ideas were so new that I'd improvise all the lyrics, but no-one seemed to either care or notice. The songs we chose were 'Intrigue In Tangiers', 'One Flesh', 'Perfume Garden' and 'PS Goodbye'. This was the first time any of them had been recorded, having had no opportunity to record demos. 'Intrigue in Tangiers' took its theme from an ex-serviceman who shared the same retirement home as my grandfather. This old merchant seaman had been confined to a wheelchair, having lost both of his legs, and as we talked, he'd describe life at Broughton House, a retirement home for ex-servicemen in Salford, as rather like being buried alive. Once I came to trust him more I'd take out the occasional joint, and we'd both get stoned together sitting on the front lawn.

'One Flesh' became an anthem dedicated to women and the outmoded notions of marriage that still prevailed in the society I grew up in. I always found it rather sad to see these beautiful women that had somehow been reduced to the point where they no longer gave a fuck about anything, or had completely lost all semblance of self-belief, because of a relationship that had probably begun amid so much romanticism. 'Perfume Garden' was about leaving the institutionalised environment of school for some perceived freedom that lay beyond the school gates. I'd been thinking of the group of boys I'd seen that afternoon at Moorclose Secondary Modern, dancing across the playground at the end of their last day there, joyous that the nightmare of school was finally over. Finally, 'PS Goodbye' most accurately reflected my mood at the time. I honestly felt that the band was nearing its end, and the song became an expression of this idea. Despite the difficult circumstances in which it was conceived, I believe that this Peel session was the best of the three.

Although we couldn't tour as such, we did perform occasional one-off gigs, but the frustration was evident and we found ourselves snapping at each other with increasing frequency. On one occasion I'd even threatened to leave the band altogether after coming to feel that everything was slipping away to a ridiculous degree. My anger had been sparked by an incident during a performance when one of the roadies, in an effort to prevent the monitors from sliding around at the front of the stage, had walked directly in front of me mid-song carrying a hammer and two pieces of timber and began nailing the timber to the stage. Good idea, but slap-bang in the middle of our most popular song was perhaps not the best time to do it and I glanced over at Tony, stage right, to see him swigging on a bottle of wine, shrugging his shoulders at me helplessly.

This had merely been the final straw amongst a sack full of straws laid across the poor camel's back. Fortunately, the situation was defused, and I was persuaded not to leave the group. But it was becoming increasingly difficult to see the point of trying to continue under these conditions.

10. A TALE OF TWO TONYS

One afternoon, we received a phone call from a guy whom, for the sake of this narrative, I'll refer to as Hal. He was a senior partner in a promotion and management company that I'll refer to as KES. He told us that he'd heard about the difficulties we'd been having, and that he might be able to help sort them out. Their offices lay in a rather nice suburb of south Manchester and we could see immediately that they were the real deal. On the wall was a photograph of the company's senior director, sat with a smiling, good looking young band called The Beatles, taken sometime in the early sixties. KES had promoted The Beatles since their first headline theatre tour in 1962, and had subsequently promoted many of the Manchester copyists that had emerged in the wake of Beatlemania. KES gig promotions were now legendary, and they were equally at home staging massive events at Wembley Arena as they were in Manchester's many theatres and clubs.

During the afternoon Hal explained how The Chameleons had come to his attention, that he'd made various enquiries about us within the industry, and outlined how he saw his future involvement. Throughout this, he remained refreshingly optimistic that a solution could be found to all our problems and that we could get the band working again. While it was true that KES existed in a different world from us - more in tune with the redundant rock excesses of the past - they were quite powerful and well-respected within the industry, and it became obvious that, if anyone had the means to take on Dunn, then it was KES.

We were given to understand that ultimately, once our publishing rights had been sorted out, they'd be seeking to buy them, and that they were looking for some kind of management contract. True to their word, they had us working again as soon as we'd reached an agreement, and by way of a modest allowance they even began to advance us money to live on.

One of the first gigs that I remember playing after joining KES was at the Ritz in Manchester, which KES jointly promoted alongside Piccadilly Radio. The station hyped the gig for weeks and it was with a great deal of satisfaction that we learned that the show had completely sold out, despite our lack of activity over the previous six months.

The Ritz is a rather beautiful old venue that had originally been designed for ballroom dancing, the kind of place that has sadly disappeared over the years. It has the rare quality of having a spring-assisted dance floor, which puts a literal slant on the term 'a bouncing crowd'. Paddy, a local artist and close friend of ours, offered to lend us a huge abstract canvas he'd painted to use as a backdrop. Unfortunately, Spoonhead hung the canvas upside down, although Paddy was the only one who noticed. As I stood alongside Spoonhead admiring the backdrop, he was lamenting that the venue didn't have any black cloth to drape behind it, when a bloke standing behind us joined the conversation. "How much do you need?" he asked.

Spoonhead told him and, within seconds, the stranger was chatting into a mobile phone.

"It's coming over from the Apollo Theatre," he said. "It'll be about ten minutes."

I was impressed - as a Chameleon I wasn't used to this level of efficiency. Our new friend told us that he worked as a production manager for KES, and that his name was Tony Fletcher.

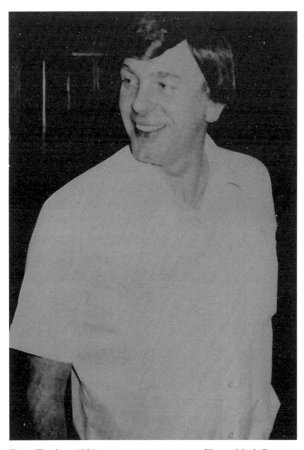

Tony Fletcher, 1986.   Photo: Mark Burgess

Fletch was introduced to the others, and soon we were all laughing and joking together in the dressing room. He hadn't seen or heard The Chameleons before, but he'd been asked to come down to the venue by Hal and make sure we had everything we needed. During the course of the evening, I noticed that he carried a laminated Australian $100 bill, and asked him about it. He told us that once, on his way home from Australia, a call had come over the airport PA system requesting that he phone the office urgently. At the time he'd been making for the departure gate, already late for his flight, and so he was cursing. He managed to find a phone booth, but didn't have any change, and for some reason it hadn't been possible to reverse the charges. All he had was a $100 bill, but no-one nearby was able to change it for him. By this time, the airline had closed the gate and Tony missed his flight. No longer in a hurry, he returned to the airline desk, and explained to the booking agent what had happened, and they let him use their phone. Having now dealt with the emergency, he booked another flight for the following day and checked into a nearby hotel. The next morning, he saw on the news that the plane he should have been on had been lost over the Pacific. No survivors were found. Subsequently, he had that $100 bill laminated and carried it around as a lucky charm.

The gig itself rates amongst my favourites, and I don't think we'd ever seen such a frenzied reaction to our set. Throughout the show, the small stage area was under constant threat of being swamped by the capacity crowd. Afterwards we were whisked off to take part in a live radio interview, and the reaction from callers was ecstatic. Fletch was hugely impressed by the gig - he hadn't realised that the band were that popular, and what he'd seen and heard on stage had made a profound impression on him. We were due to fly out to Paris almost immediately, and he told us that he'd do his best to make it to the show.

True to his word, Fletch had a car waiting to take us to the soundcheck, and then on to a French television studio where we were scheduled to give a live performance - no playback this time! The car was a stretch limousine, and on seeing it, crowds began to form outside the venue. We were rather embarrassed by this, and asked the driver to drop us off around the corner so we wouldn't be seen emerging from it. Fletch thought this was hilarious. Apparently, encountering such modesty from a young rock band was a first for him. We didn't have our own lighting engineer for the show, so Fletch demonstrated another string to his bow by filling in.

When we got back, we were told that a satellite television company wanted to film a live concert for broadcast in mainland Europe. The chosen venue was Camden Palace, which had been a haunt of the new romantics in the early 1980s, although by this time it was regarded as being somewhat passé. We were housed in the notorious Columbia Hotel, which had a policy of not closing the bar until the last customers had retired to their rooms. Providing you didn't get too rowdy or out of control, the staff were always very relaxed and easy going. That night we shared the bar with one or two other bands, and made rather a late night of it.

Two bands were being filmed, with us going on first at 6pm. The tickets for the gig were free, so as to ensure a good crowd at such an ungodly hour. Everything was going to plan, except that I had not yet recovered from the previous night's excesses and felt really ill. In desperation, I began to drink again - 'hair of the dog' and all that - but hadn't eaten anything, so all this achieved was to get me leathered again. As a result, I got a bit carried away and used more than my fair share of expletives and told too many bad jokes. Granted, this probably wasn't wise, but I wasn't that worried about it at the time. What I didn't know was that the rather generous fee included the sale of the commercial rights. Some time later, I was horrified to see that a video of the gig was being marketed. This was a first for the band, and most of my extended family rushed out to buy it - even my parents demanded copies. When they heard the language they were as horrified as I was, and it was ages before I could face any of them.

The other band being filmed that day were glam rockers Wrathchild, and they had us in hysterics from the moment they turned up to the soundcheck, wobbling unsteadily in stiletto-heeled boots and wearing huge, blonde Dolly Parton wigs that, all told, made them seem about seven feet tall. They threw in every cliché in the book, including massive racks of Marshall amps which weren't even wired up. Unfortunately the only exit from the dressing room was by way of the main stage, so once they began playing there was no way for us to get out. We were trapped there for their entire set. Absolute torture!

We received some good news that night when Hal told us that the negotiations with Dunn were going well, and that they may have found a solution. Dunn was asking for one more album and the publishing rights on any new songs we provided for it, in return for an unconditional release from both the label and any obligations regarding future publishing. The idea of giving Statik any more of our music wasn't attractive, but at least that would be the end of it and we could then get on with being a band again. Dunn gave us a choice of studio, a respectable budget and agreed to pay all costs regarding the demos for the album. We agreed, and immediately thought of Colin Richardson at Cargo, but we discovered that

Cargo had been sold to Peter Hook of New Order and re-christened Suite Sixteen. We went over there to check it out and were surprised to see Chris Jones, the guy who'd helped us when we'd run into difficulties with Chris Nagle at Strawberry. CJ, as he preferred to be known, had left Strawberry to become the resident engineer at Suite Sixteen. The idea of working here was rejected by the rest of the band, though, as they deemed the sixteen-track recording facilities insufficient.

During one of our many trips to Loch Ness, we'd discovered a recording studio built in the grounds of a large manor house just north of Inverness. As we loved the area so much, it seemed like a natural choice. The studio was a well-equipped twenty-four-track residential facility so we reasoned that, if we could track down Colin, we could record the album there.

It turned out that Colin had moved to the north east coast of England, and was working as an engineer in a small studio in Bridlington. After discussing the project with him, we decided to go there to record the album's demos. I don't remember much about the actual recordings, but by the end we felt we had an album's worth of fresh material to record, consisting mainly of songs that hadn't made the first album, songs from our recent Peel session and one or two new pieces to keep the session fresh. We didn't want to give Dunn more than a few new songs at most, considering the way he'd treated us. I found it hard to motivate myself. Rather than being excited at the prospect of recording our second album, I came to regard it as a matter of contractual obligation.

The owner of the Inverness studio had built the entire facility with the proceeds from a single song he'd written in the sixties. At that time, he'd had six different versions of this song in the Japanese top ten simultaneously. I think the song is called 'It's A Beautiful Day'. He also wrote 'Blue Is The Colour' for Chelsea Football Club in the seventies. His resident engineer was a talented guy called Ian Caple, who would commute by plane from London to Inverness whenever there was a recording session. The studio was situated some miles north of Loch Ness, off an isolated stretch of road, but we still had our van, so we didn't feel that the remote location would be much of a problem. In actual fact it did become a problem, and within a couple of weeks we all began to get cabin fever.

Colin seemed very different once the session got under way. He had definite ideas as to how he wanted to produce the record, and would dismiss many of our ideas out of hand. Compared to the free and relaxed manner in which *Script Of The Bridge* had come together, this session was a stark contrast. He and Dave would sometimes have blazing rows over certain aspects of the production, and I would inevitably get drawn in. But with the benefit of hindsight, I came to feel that we really should have listened to Colin more.

At weekends, we'd try to relax by driving into Inverness to trawl the pubs in search of a party. On one occasion we did find one, and were taken to an isolated farm cottage up in the hills. There, we were greeted by a small group of hippies, huddled together in self-made, rainbow-coloured woollen sweaters, handing out bowls of pea soup. Although this was very nice, it wasn't really what we'd had in mind. Meanwhile, Dave decided to go home for a week, leaving the rest of us to get on with it. He'd consumed all the cannabis he'd brought with him and needed to buy further supplies. A welcome distraction came by way of our regular German tour manager and friend Dirk, who turned up for a visit midway through the recording of 'One Flesh'. We gave him a tour of Loch Ness and the snow-covered Highland countryside, then we handed him the whirly tube and he joined in on the track.

Sadly, our working relationship with Colin Richardson worsened, and on the morning we were scheduled to leave we were still rushing through a remix of 'Perfume Garden'. By now the atmosphere had grown incredibly tense, so I did my best to smooth things over. On the long drive back to England, Colin and I discussed the mastering of the record. Colin had in his possession the tape containing the samples and sound effects which we were intending to use to link the album's tracks together at the editing stage. The plan was that he would arrange the specific items we wanted, and bring them to the mastering suite. After Colin left the bus, however, we never saw or heard from him again. In the end, we were forced to master the record ourselves, without the links.

Once again, Reg turned in a great illustration for the front cover. I'd been unsure of it at first because all he'd had initially was the central figure, a surreal portrait amid swirling depictions of vinyl records and hovering doves. I'd felt that it lacked a context, that it needed something else, but was unsure what. Dave saw the problem immediately and placed the image against a backdrop of blue sky with clouds. I came to feel that not only was it our best sleeve to date, but that it was the best thing about the entire record. As a departure from the first album, I wrote a poem in place of sleeve notes, and with that we duly delivered the album. The title, *What Does Anything Mean? Basically* was borrowed from the scribbled phrases in my notebook from that night on Tandle Hill. We signed the releases from both Statik Records and Taktik Music and looked forward to the future with a great sense of relief - but disaster struck immediately.

Tony Skinkis had done his very best to help steer the band through the recent crises, but he'd grown increasingly distant throughout the rather troubled album sessions. Since the arrival of KES, our immediate financial concerns had been taken care of, but I believe the problems and woes of the previous months had soured Tony's enthusiasm for what we were doing. Since KES had got involved, Fletch had spent much of his time looking after the band on a daily basis, and I got the feeling that Tony had felt he was being pushed to one side.

Dave's latest financial panic exacerbated the situation, and proved to be the final straw for Tony. He had hammered on Tony's door, while yelling through his letterbox, "Tony! I know you're in! Help me sort my fuckin' rent out!" Tony, however, had stubbornly refused to open the door. Dave came round to see me and told me what had happened. I arrived at Tony's house to find all the documentation that he had for the band in a plastic carrier bag, along with the keys to the bus. I remember him telling me once that, after getting signed by CBS, we'd all have a good time for a couple of years and that would be the end of it. For Tony, it seemed, that day had come. As far as I was concerned, The Chameleons had just lost their most cherished member.

It took me a long time to come to terms with losing Tony, and I'm as confused when I think about it now as I was then. I was inclined to suspect that KES saw Tony as an obstacle to the management deal they wanted, and were exerting pressure on him behind the scenes to bow out. We lost touch for many years, but we're very close and I love him very much. When we talk about those days now, we talk about the good times, the many deeply profound moments that we had, and the hours of hilarity. Tony Skinkis is one of the most intelligent, funny, down-to-earth guys I've ever met, and one of my dearest friends.

Over the following months our relationship with Fletch continued to deepen, and we came to rely on him more and more. We also became aware of just how much respect the man had from all quarters of the industry, which was nothing short of colossal. Everyone who worked with him came to love him, and many of the mainstream acts that KES worked with insisted on Fletch's involvement as a prerequisite. I've never seen anyone work so hard on behalf of a company or an artist, and it seemed that he hardly ever stopped. He didn't use answering machines, and would never switch off from those who came to depend on him - Fletch would answer his phones day or night. He was always available, and his common-sense, calming nature could mute the blast from any explosive situation. He often told me how refreshingly down-to-earth he felt The Chameleons were, compared to many of the artists he'd worked with, which didn't surprise me judging from some of his more extreme stories. One internationally famous client always insisted that, during his walk to the stage, any person standing in the corridors had to turn and face the wall as passed, or risk getting fired. On another occasion, Fletch had entered the dressing room of a world famous teenage boy-band of the seventies to find their manager mounting the band's most recent recruit, a seventeen year old Irish lad, from the rear.

In the weeks leading up to the release of the new album, KES had set up a European tour, and despite my great sadness in losing Tony Skinkis, I have to say it was without doubt the most enjoyable tour we'd undertaken. Fletch was able to hire a sleeper bus, a vintage model from the sixties that had once belonged to The Rolling Stones. The bus had its own kitchen area, and a number of bunks that ran either side of the central aisle. These were fitted with curtains, thereby allowing the sleeping passenger a degree of privacy, and each bunk was linked to the vehicle's sound system through a set of headphones. Our road manager, John, had been handpicked by Fletch, and was great fun to have along. I still laugh sometimes as I recall his dire warnings, delivered in a heavy Birmingham accent, whenever we would approach a border. "Ryte, awwlll ya dope an' rowches, owtt da winda..." The ashtrays would immediately be emptied, and all evidence of cannabis smoking would be hurled from the bus skylight. One particular night we were leaving Amsterdam en route for Germany, and naturally we'd bought more weed than it was possible to smoke in the time we had. John came stalking down the bus, calling out his usual refrain, and with great reluctance, we offered up our respective stashes. Dave, being completely stoned, had already retired to his bunk by this time. On hearing John's shouted warnings, however, he crawled out again, red-eyed and practically on all fours for one last series of tokes before the entire stash was thrown out into the Dutch night. Our tour manager told me this was a regular occurrence with touring bands, and I remember thinking that this particular road to the German border must have been very popular with hitchhikers.

As with the first album, the new record featured quite a lot of keyboard overdubs, so we revived the idea of hiring an additional keyboard player for the tour. John had suggested his friend Andy Clegg, who played in a struggling Ashton band called Music For Aborigines. Clegg was a good-looking young guy, and the banter between him and John was often genuinely hilarious. It centred mainly on John's jealousy of Andy's ability to cop off with beautiful girls, regardless of the situation. "How does he do it?" John lamented one night as we all trailed off to eat after a soundcheck, accompanied by Andy, who had about five gorgeous women in tow. "Look at him, he's a fuckin' sex dwarf!" It has to be said that in this area of human endeavour, he showed extraordinary talent. On our way to Spain we picked up a couple of female hitchhikers, and Andy had one of them in his bunk within ten minutes of them boarding the bus.

The show in Madrid was exceptional, although the soundcheck had been more chaotic than usual - even by Spanish standards - and in the end we abandoned it altogether, expecting the show to be a complete disaster. The stage was very high above the audience, which only compounded my feelings of foreboding, but as it turned out the atmosphere was electric, the stage sound impeccable and for a long time it rated amongst my top three favourite gigs. Madrid has always struck me as being one of the coolest cities in the world, and I remember at the after-show party I was introduced to some of the most gorgeous women I'd ever seen.

The fact that the gig was a success after such a disastrous soundcheck shouldn't have surprised us, really, because it was ever thus when playing in southern Europe. They had such a relaxed way of going about things that you could be fooled into thinking that their seemingly chaotic approach would result in a disastrous show, but at the final moment everything usually fell into place.

I did get into a little hot water with a local journalist, however. The topic of conversation drifted onto politics, and I remarked that I felt the world would be a much better place if we just turned the whole lot over to the women. This obviously offended his macho sensibilities because he suddenly rose in a huff, snatched his tape recorder and dashed angrily toward the exit, muttering to himself.

We arrived in Barcelona the following day for the second of the Spanish dates, and I was forced to sacrifice one of my rare days off to do the rounds of press and radio interviews. Meanwhile, everyone else got on with sunning themselves on the colourful Catalonian streets. The venue for the show was a converted slaughterhouse and the owners had retained the theme of death in the club's interior design, which featured macabre paintings hanging from every wall in the place. They'd even christened the club '666,' a number that I'd encountered regularly, eventually reaching epidemic proportions, invading my perception on a daily basis. The set was to be filmed by a TV crew for a music show called *Arsenal*. Watching the pre-gig interviews again now, it's obvious that we were all stoned. All the same, I was pleased that the gig had been a good one, and we were all happy with the results when we viewed the rushes in the monitor van. Some years later it was released commercially on video, and while some of it made me squirm with embarrassment, the gig itself was the best on film thus far.

The next venue was in Valencia and came as rather a surprise to us. For one thing, it stood in the middle of a great, flat, desert plain with just a few simple settlements visible in the far distance. A spacious, empty car park stood next to a large round building painted in pastel shades of pink and blue, resembling a giant birthday cake. The floors featured mosaics depicting red dragons and mythological scenes; matching painted wooden banisters bordered a balcony that ran around the circumference of the interior, while upstairs black leather sofas and recliners were scattered around for revellers to relax in. The lighting rig above our heads could twist and gyrate at the push of a button, and when activated, looked like the UFOs from *Close Encounters Of The Third Kind*. The dance floor in front of the stage was a huge expanse of polished timber. It was without doubt one of the coolest and most beautiful venues I've ever seen, and it must have cost a fortune to put together. But who, we asked ourselves, would come here?

The other big surprise of the day came when John had handed me his mobile phone, telling me that Fletch was on the line. I started talking to him, believing him to be in England, when he walked into the stage area. We were all very happy to see him, and he'd brought various home comforts for each of us, delighting the road crew with a bag full of frozen Holland's pies for them to cook in the microwave on the bus[1].

After the soundcheck we were driven to our hotel to shower, change and relax. When the time came to head back to the venue, we found that the approach roads were totally choked with traffic and we couldn't get anywhere near it. After a frantic phone call to the promoter, we were treated to an escort through the thousands of cars trying to get to the gig. By the time we took the stage we were supremely relaxed and in a great mood, and all this helped us turn in a blinding set. The venue had a license to run throughout the night, so we joined the fray and didn't leave until daybreak.

We then headed back into France and found ourselves in one or two places we hadn't been to before. One such destination was Montpellier, where we were presented with an entire case of champagne after the gig. The French record company had wanted me, as the band's singer, in Paris as soon as possible for a number of press and radio interviews. I don't know why so many of the European music media always insisted on the singer being present for interviews. My hatred of doing them never left me and, as I say, it usually resulted in everyone else getting the day off while I was

---

1. I knew where the crew were coming from on that score. It's probably different these days, but back then, being vegetarian, I had a hard time finding food in Spain, and for the whole six days we were there I'd been living on a diet of omelettes.

trundled around town on promo duty. This time I didn't mind so much, because it meant a break from the daily routine of long hours on the bus. Instead, I'd be whisked away by high speed train to Paris where I'd be met by a label representative, taken to my hotel, treated to dinner and then chauffeured around Paris to do the honours. Sometimes being the singer in did have its perks.

On this particular occasion it was decided that John would travel with me, and we were met in Paris by the label rep. She and John got on particularly well, and gradually I began to suspect that her reasons for seeing so much of the band had gone beyond the professional. She was a very cool, beautiful Parisian girl and I was pleased for John, who naturally loved all the attention she gave him. Sophie was obviously serious about John, and I always felt she would have been good for him in the long term if he'd chosen to pursue a relationship, but he didn't.

The Paris show turned out to be extra special, because Fletch had escorted both mine and Dave's mothers out for the show. It was strange to see my mother step into the world of The Chameleons, a world that was light-years away from our lives in Middleton, and one that she'd had no direct experience of before. This was her first experience of overseas travel since a school trip to Brussels at the age of fourteen, and her excitement was obvious. The sold-out gig was in one of the most prestigious venues in Paris, with balconies and crystal chandeliers, and she was extremely impressed. They stayed with the tour, catching another show the following night, but this didn't go so well. My mother had been greatly angered by some incident in the crowd and she'd had to be restrained from taking action. Finally, fearing that my father would accidentally burn the house down in her absence, she went home with Dave's mother and Tony.

While on tour in Europe, *What Does Anything Mean? Basically* was released and we were very gratified to see that the record had charted, albeit briefly. That was a first for us. We'd agreed that immediately after the tour, we'd play a benefit show for the Socialist Worker's Party at Middleton Civic Hall, but once our tour schedule had been completed we found we had only two days to make the show. Rather than pull out, we hit the road for a frantic drive home with only the minimum of stops between Berlin and Manchester. We drove directly to the venue so we'd make it in time for the soundcheck and everyone was exhausted by the time we arrived. We were greeted by the promoter, a local socialist from Middleton, complaining about the fact that he was expected to find the band something to eat and some fresh towels with which to shower. "Who do they think they are," he retorted at one point as Fletch argued with him, "rock stars?"

With the tour now over, the album launched and all commitments to Statik met, the question of whom we would record for next arose. KES decided to put the band back into the studio, at their expense, to write and record new songs which would then be used to get the band a new recording contract. We decided to return to the now fully refurbished Suite Sixteen, booking some bulk time there so we could write and arrange new ideas. We also used this opportunity to rehearse for what promised to be, for me at least, one of the most exciting shows we'd played yet. We'd been invited to headline a gig at the Free Trade Hall as part of that year's Manchester Festival. We were to be given control of the entire night, and told we could choose our own support acts.

Our first choice was the newly reformed Alternative TV, fronted by Mark Perry. One of their earliest songs, 'Splitting In Two', had been a regular feature of our set for quite some time, so I was pleased when their manager told me that they were up for it. I also suggested that we approach a local comedic character called Frank Sidebottom to perform a short set between bands after seeing a promotional postcard from the man on Fletch's desk in his office at KES. I'd heard Frank on local radio a few times, covering Queen's 'Bohemian Rhapsody' on a banjo, and thought that his humour might appeal to our audience. Frank was the brainchild of Chris Sievey[2], formerly the front man of The Freshies, who'd had a hit with 'I'm In Love With The Girl On The Manchester Virgin Megastore Checkout Desk'. Frank had a huge papier-mâché head, and the basis of his act that night was the introduction of Little Frank, a tiny replica glove puppet of big Frank. The audience were treated to what was a very surreal ventriloquist act indeed. Finally we invited The Membranes, a progressive and exciting band from Blackpool fronted by punk scenester and fanzine author John Robb, after having seen them play a great set alongside The Fall some months before.

The soundcheck at the Free Trade Hall was a proud moment for me, recalling the night I'd stood on that very spot embracing Alex Harvey at the age of fouteen. During the encore that night, Mark Perry, along with one of the newer members of ATV, joined us on stage for a blistering version of 'Splitting In Two', and I remember being very sad that Tony Skinkis hadn't been there to relish that particular moment.

The Free Trade Hall gig had been a welcome diversion, but afterwards it was back to work at Suite Sixteen. However, we hadn't been back at work

---

2. Tragically, Chris died in 2010, aged 54. Frank, his best-known creation, is commemorated by a life-size bronze statue erected by fans in Chris' (and Frank's) home village of Timperley – JL.

long when there was another, very welcome, break in our routine. An A&R executive from Geffen Records had contacted KES to say he was interested in meeting the band with a view to signing us. His name was Tom and he'd been working with another of his new signings at Air Studios, on Montserrat. He suggested that I, being the band's singer, fly out there for talks. I was intrigued by the idea, but had to tell Fletch that if Tom was seriously interested in a deal, then he should speak to the whole band, rather than just the singer.

In response, Tom revised his offer and agreed to fly myself plus one other member of the band to Montserrat. Again, I reiterated to Fletch that it had to be all of us, or none at all. Fletch had anticipated this, however, and worked out that it was possible to fly the four of us, with Fletch, in economy class for the same price as the two first class tickets on offer. The only condition was that we would have to stay there for a week, which didn't seem like too much of a hardship! The weather in Rochdale was particularly grim in the week leading up to our departure and the guys at Suite Sixteen were envious, but I promised to try and bring them back some Caribbean marijuana by way of recompense.

On arriving in Antigua, where we would spend the first three days of our stay, we were taken to a rather plush hotel on the Atlantic side of the island. Fletch rented a jeep and we were able to do quite a bit of exploring in the time we had. I was a bit disconcerted to note that - despite the relatively high cost of living on Antigua - the majority of the population seemed to exist in a depressing state of poverty, housed in poorly constructed shanties. Wherever the money was going, it certainly wasn't going to the people who made the place tick. Their impoverished circumstances didn't seem to affect their demeanour, though, and they rate amongst the most relaxed and friendly folk I've met anywhere.

I don't remember ever being as relaxed as I was during this trip. Each morning I'd wake at around 6.30am, which back then was very unusual for me, and I'd dive immediately into the pool to swim for an hour before breakfast. Fletch taught Reg to swim, which was remarkable because Reg had never got over his fear of deep water. Previously, a pride of ravenous lions prowling the beach would not have coaxed him into the sea, yet Fletch had him swimming confidently within a couple of days of arrival.

From Antigua we were taken to Montserrat in a very small plane - too small for the rest of the gang's liking. I think I'm the only one among us that has never had any fear of flying; everyone else freaked out whenever we had to do it. This time, the pilot frequently craned his neck around to have conversations with us during the flight, much to John's consternation.

"He should keep his eyes on the, erm... on the sky, when he's driving," grumbled John.

We were met at the airport by a representative of the studio and driven on the back of a four-wheel drive pick-up truck to the far side of the island where the studio lay. Tom Zutaut was a young American with striking looks and long blond hair. I hit it off with him almost immediately, and the more we talked, the more we found we had in common. We shared the same birth date to the hour, albeit a year apart. Coincidentally, we'd both independently bought a copy of the same obscure paperback to read at the airport on our way to the island. The others had very little in common with him, and he became the butt of many of their jokes, mainly revolving around his American accent, his appetite, and his not inconsiderable bulk. This kind of behaviour disgusted me, having seen so many people bullied at school for the same kind of reasons, so I tried to distance myself from it as much as I possibly could. Tom and I had our disagreements, but they were professional matters and we were always able to get past them.

The American band he was working with at the studio were so cold and anonymous I don't even remember their name. Their music was as bland as their personalities, and for some reason they weren't very friendly. On one occasion we were invited to call by the studio and the other band were in the process of sitting down to a huge banquet. We were all very hungry and eyeing up the feast, but we weren't invited to join them. At one point, when they were finished eating, I caught Reg about to sneak something from the table but I stopped him. The other band obviously knew the score and I didn't want to give them the satisfaction. In the end Elaine, the studio manager, had the chef prepare us something and joined us while we ate and we all became great friends. Elaine and her husband were originally from the north of England so we had a lot in common and she seemed very charmed by our down-to-earth attitude.

Montserrat is a volcanic island, so much of the beach coastline is composed of black sand made by the ash from the volcano mixing with the natural sand on the beach. Apparently most tourists prefer their sand flawlessly white, which means that the black sand beaches are usually empty. This was perfectly fine by us, and I spent most of my time in the water snorkelling with Tom amongst the coral, eyeing the hundreds of species of tropical fish and the occasional stingray. I spent most evenings sitting on the veranda outside the house, watching the fireflies dance around the garden and smoking huge amounts of excellent cannabis. I'd bought the weed from one of the guys that worked at the studio. He'd asked us for the local equivalent of about ten quid and then turned up with a huge paper bag stuffed with so much marijuana that he needed to keep his hand over it to stop it from spilling out onto the floor.

By the final day, the bag was still over half full and I was lamenting the fact that I'd have to leave it behind. In the end, I just couldn't do it. I had an empty tobacco tin with me, which I filled with weed. When I'd finished, the tin was so full that not a single grain more would have gone in and I simply put the tin in my pocket and set off for the airport. Apart from anything else, I was determined to try to keep my promise to the guys back at Suite Sixteen.

In Antigua, I presented myself to airport security, taking the tin and holding it in my hands as I outstretched my arms to be searched. I was dutifully frisked and then allowed to continue. At Manchester Airport I casually walked through the green zone at customs and that was it, I'd just imported a tin of the finest weed I have ever smoked.

Later that night I decided to go out for a beer in Middleton, and called at Dave's flat to see if he wanted to join me, but as I approached his front door I could hear pandemonium coming from inside. It transpired that he hadn't been able to find any cannabis anywhere, which particularly galled him considering the amount of top notch weed we had left behind in Montserrat. Smiling, I pulled the tin out of my pocket and opened it. The weed was practically glowing green in the twilight and Dave lit up like a floodlight. "Just give it back to me tomorrow at the studio," I said, and left him for the night.

The following day, I made my way to Suite Sixteen and was exalting the merits of this weed to the guys all morning. "I kept my promise and brought you some back," I told them, "Dave has it."

Dave finally arrived and I asked him for the tin. "Oh yeah," he said and handed it to me. I opened it and saw that it was practically empty, save for a few crumbs, barely enough for a single cigarette paper.

I looked at him incredulously. "Where's the weed?" I barked.

"Oh, some friends came round," he said, sheepishly.

Between them they'd smoked the lot.

11. SIGNS OF THE TIMES

As 1986 gathered momentum, I entered what I came to regard as the strangest period of my life to date. While some may have considered me delusional, I genuinely believe that something altogether deeper and truly mystical was taking place. It is my opinion that I came into contact with what some call the Godhead, or perhaps what Aleister Crowley referred to as his holy guardian angel, or maybe a phenomenon further along the spiral of Colin Wilson's hierarchy of selves. I am absolutely convinced that something was intent on guiding me down a certain path, and to do this it used a symbol - the number 666. Robert Anton Wilson writes of a similar experience in *Cosmic Trigger*. In his case, the symbol was the number twenty-three and he refers to the phenomenon as '23 Skidoo'.

At this point, however, I hadn't yet come across either the author or the concept, so I simply noted the phenomenon, hardly daring to speak of it, and allowed events to unfold. I wouldn't say that I followed the path of least resistance. Had I done so, I believe I would have experienced a far less traumatic year. By the time I realised what I was supposed to do, I resisted, and this defiance, in turn, endangered my sanity.

The entire surreal odyssey began in the wake of the strange events we'd witnessed at Loch Ness four years earlier. Over the next couple of years, I began to notice that the number 666 seemed to be following me around. I don't remember exactly when this started, but a couple of instances spring immediately to mind. I first discussed this subject with Tony Skinkis in New York during our 1984 US tour. At precisely the moment I'd finished telling him about it, the door to the dressing room closed, revealing the number 666 scrawled on the back in black ink. Naturally, Tony brushed it off as nothing more than a coincidence, and suggested I put it down to stress. He proposed that we spend the following day sightseeing in New York, so we decided to take a tour of the Empire State Building. As we walked around the observation deck, enjoying a perfect view of the New York skyline, I was suddenly stopped in my tracks. Directly in front of us, in huge, red digits on a neighbouring skyscraper, was the number 666. Tony was speechless. From this point on this phenomenon not only continued, but gradually intensified. I would see the number on car licence plates as I travelled up and down the highways and byways of Britain and Europe. Tape counters would repeatedly and inexplicably stop at 666 as I worked. I would receive bus tickets and cash receipts with the number stamped clearly and boldly on it. It became an everyday occurrence for me to see telephone numbers, TV advertisements, addresses, and hotel room numbers containing the number.

I tried to rationalise these events by looking for a simple explanation. Maybe I was actively seeking instances of the number, and due to my state of mind, was attaching a mystical significance to it. While plausible, this theory simply didn't hold water: once this phenomenon eventually ceased I continued to look for the number, but have only ever seen it once or twice since.

Following our trip to Montserrat, we signed to Geffen Records for six albums, with our first release on the label being a four-track maxi-single. This was in spite of a disastrous showcase gig at the Electric Ballroom in London when, after a show in Brighton the previous night using a PA the size of your average ghetto-blaster, my voice failed. I couldn't continue, and the show had to be abandoned after just three songs.

During the recording of the demos at Suite Sixteen, we'd been playing around with one or two pieces of equipment that belonged to New Order. Peter Hook often produced bands there, and we would use some of New Order's gadgets and equipment from time to time. Amongst all this stuff was a keyboard called the Emulator II, which loaded samples from a floppy disc. We were amused to find many of the sound effects that had been used on New Order's 'The Perfect Kiss', and were very impressed with the string quartet samples. Using these, Reg, Dave and I improvised and recorded a new piece of music on the spot. 'String Quartet 1' and 'String Quartet 2' were not released at the time, but later emerged on the retrospective release *Here Today... Gone Tomorrow*.

The same afternoon we found the drum sequence that had been used on 'Blue Monday', and were playing around with it when suddenly Reg pushed a button and the programme disappeared. "Reg!" we screamed in laughter. "You've just erased the drum programme for the biggest selling twelve-inch single of all time!" Reg turned bright red and began to panic, and was extremely relieved a few minutes later when CJ was able to retrieve it.

We all felt we had the foundation for a strong four-track EP as a forerunner to an album, so our thoughts turned to finding a producer. Tom suggested we consider Dave Allen, long-time co-producer of The Cure. They'd just completed *The Head On The Door*, the first album of theirs I'd liked in ages.

Tom at Geffen made no secret of the fact that he expected to be heavily involved with every aspect of the record's development, and initially we had no problem with that. His studio of choice was usually Air in Montserrat, and he hinted that this would probably be his choice this time around too. By way of a trial run, Geffen chose Westside Studios, one of the most expensive in London, in which to record the EP, with Dave Allen at the controls.

I'd only just arrived in London when I got a phone call from my mother telling me that the vet had examined my dog and diagnosed terminal cancer. San had been suffering quite badly over the previous few days, and they'd had no choice but to administer a lethal injection. I wept openly for hours in my small bedroom in Earl's Court, while Reg, Dave and John looked on in silence. I felt embarrassed crying in front of the others, but San had been my closest friend for thirteen years and I was beside myself with grief. Ultimately I did the only thing I could, finding the missing theme for what I felt was the strongest of the new ideas, which I titled simply 'Tears'. Fletch, who had taken San to the vet in my absence, brought his body back to my parents' home, and in spite of the heavy snow, buried San in the back garden. This simple kindness elevated Fletch to the status of a saint in my eyes.

The pre-production took place at a nearby rehearsal studio, and although it became obvious that John, in particular, was going to benefit from working with Dave Allen, I felt that we weren't being given sufficient time to arrange the new songs properly. 'Tears' felt overcomplicated, with too much emphasis on turning it into a radio-friendly single, and everything was moving so rapidly on such a tight schedule that there was no time to rectify this. Once we would have been happy to sit together and meticulously refine the arrangements, but these days the others were less enthusiastic and just seemed to want to get on with it.

The flat that had been provided for us was in a rather depressing area of central London, and I found Westside Studio a characterless and sterile working environment. The facility had two studios back-to-back, and encamped in the other were Depeche Mode. Their company lightened the mood somewhat; they were a very likeable bunch of blokes, and over the following weeks we shared more than a few drinks and jokes.

We felt that a lot of money was being wasted at this stage. Instruments would be hired in - not by us - only to be left in a corner for a week, before being returned unused. I couldn't understand why we appeared to have no say in how our budgets were spent. American record deals differed from British ones in that a certain amount of money would be agreed to fund the production and manufacturing process, and then whatever was left at the end - if anything - would go to the band. That said, everything was recoupable, even the cost of pressing the records, so the labels would be acting as little more than a bank, then reaping most of the profits. Had these profits been translated into interest percentages, the label's rate would have been enough to turn the face of even the most ruthless loan shark green with envy. Furthermore, Geffen would pay the studio's invoices immediately without bothering to query their accuracy. Because of this we were being charged for twenty-four-hour lockouts that we didn't actually get[1].

What we *did* get was a very talented engineer by the name of Mark Saunders. Westside was Mark's first premier studio placement, and a couple of years earlier he'd had a true baptism of fire while working as tape operator on David Bowie and Mick Jagger's 'Dancing In The Street'. The track had been specially recorded as a fund-raiser for Live Aid, and the producer had asked Mark to operate the tape machine for David Bowie's vocal overdubs. It had always been my impression that Bowie was a performance vocalist, in that he delivered the vocal from start to finish and then simply chose the highlights of each take, which is the way I like to work. Apparently, this isn't the case, and Bowie 'dropped in' on the track, recording the song line by line. Poor Mark could hardly stop his hand from shaking, dreading the possibility that Bowie would give them the thumbs up on a particular line, only to discover that he had been a micro second too early or too late with the drop in, in which case his first major session would probably have been his last. Fortunately, Mark survived the experience and even had the good fortune to work with the great man again when Bowie returned to Westside to record the vocals for 'Absolute Beginners'. This time around he was more confident, and during a respite in the recording, Bowie switched to doing impressions of how he felt certain other singers would approach the choruses. Mark had discreetly switched on a tape recorder, and later we were all treated to a recording of Bowie doing impressions of Iggy Pop, Elvis Presley, and Mick Jagger. Mark steadfastly refused to let us have a copy, though, which is a shame because it was truly hilarious.

Mark also told us an amusing story that Bowie had related to him during that session, which concerned the filming of the promotional video for 'Ashes To Ashes'. For those that have never seen it, Bowie appears in the video dressed as a classic French clown, complete with full facial make-up.

---

1. A 24-hour lock-out means that no other client can come into the studio when you've finished for the day and use it, changing all the effects and desk settings.

They were filming on a deserted beach, and had almost finished when an extremely irate man walked across and began shouting that they were trespassing on a private beach. After arguing with the guy for twenty minutes and getting nowhere, out of sheer desperation the producer said, "Listen mate! Don't you know who this is?" gesturing towards Bowie.

The guy had stared at the singer, blinking silently, before replying, "Yeah, some cunt in a clown suit."

We returned to Westside after the Christmas break to add another new song to the session. Reg had been playing around with a fresh guitar idea that we'd all liked immediately. After turning it around in my head for a while, an arrangement started to take shape and it quickly developed into my favourite Chameleons song thus far. We gave the song a working title in keeping with the ambience of Reg's opening riff - 'Swamp Thing' - and the title just stuck. It was the killer song we'd been waiting for.

One of the most vivid memories I have of the session involved one of those tragic and poignant events that tend to define a decade. The others were in the control room stamping their feet up and down on a piece of hardboard in time to the bass drum intro of 'Swamp Thing'. Meanwhile, I was settling down in front of the TV to watch the latest Space Shuttle launch. I'd been fascinated by the space program, ever since my mother had dragged me out of bed in the early hours of the morning in 1969 to witness Neil Armstrong's first tentative steps on the lunar surface. By this time, NASA were launching the Space Shuttle on a regular basis, and I would always try to catch the launches on TV whenever I could. On this particular occasion - 28th January 1986 - the envy I felt towards the young teacher, chosen from thousands to be the first civilian in space, turned to horror as Challenger suddenly exploded in a cascade of smoke. I continued to watch, speechless, as the spiralling debris fell back to earth, along with the doomed crew.

My working relationship with Dave, already strained, took another turn for the worse at this point. Dave had been grappling with a personal tragedy as his youngest brother Colin had begun to display symptoms of schizophrenia. We'd all been fairly close to Colin over the years and it saddened and worried all of us, but we were powerless to help him. Naturally, Colin's mental deterioration was demanding all of Dave's attention. Each day, Colin would turn up at rehearsals and his manner became increasingly bizarre as the days went by. Ordinarily, we would have postponed all activity and given Dave space to work things out, but if we'd taken a hiatus we would have lost our producer for six months. Consequently, we were being urged by all around us to stick with the schedule, come what may. Fletch recommended that the band relocate to the Lake District for five weeks to work on the material. He went on to suggest that Colin could visit periodically, and that this might even do him good. Dave, somewhat reluctantly, saw the logic of this and agreed to go.

Fletch rented a house in the tiny village of Hawkshead, which lies on the edge of Grizedale Forest in Cumbria, and here we set up a four-track tape recorder. Our backline equipment was also set up at a church hall two miles down the road. Unfortunately, being away from Middleton did little to allay Dave's fears: everything he was hearing on the phone seemed to confirm that Colin was heading for some kind of breakdown, and none of his family or friends knew what to do.

It was proving very difficult to get Dave to the church hall, and when we did, he rarely stayed long, spending most of his time in the nearby phone box instead. Sometimes Colin would turn up at weekends, along with the regular crowd, and this definitely helped, but once they'd left the tension would resume and it was a struggle to get anything done. Eventually Colin's family sought professional help, but during consultations Colin would seem lucid and rational. Faced with this, the psychologists would shrug their shoulders and tell his family that he seemed to be fine, if a little odd. Having successfully deceived the doctors, Colin's weird behaviour would resume, and none of his immediate family, it seemed, could get through to him.

Between Reg, John and myself, we managed to get a few ideas off the ground, and when Dave did strap on his guitar things happened, but I had serious doubts that the material would be ready in time at the rate we were going.

The strange and claustrophobic atmosphere of Hawkshead only added to the strain. I quickly came to feel that if I had to look at one more Beatrix Potter souvenir, I'd be joining Colin in the grip of madness. The attitudes of most of the people there were provincial to say the least, and they'd rarely disguise their disapproval of the scruffy looking rock band that had come to live amongst them. The nearby Sun Inn provided respite from their sanctimonious airs and graces during daylight hours, but more often I would drive to the nearby town of Ambleside to take in a film, or to eat alone in one of the restaurants - anything to get some distance. With the tension, the lack of stimulation, and the pressure to finish the writing, we all suffered more than a little bout of cabin fever, but it reached its peak one afternoon when Dave and I almost came to blows. Reg's girlfriend had discreetly told me that Colin had been going through other people's pockets and stealing things. I had no idea whether this was true or not, but decided after some thought that Dave ought to know about it. Even if it wasn't true, it was a particularly ugly rumour to be flying around behind a person's back, and Dave was the best person to broach the subject with Colin. A few days later I arrived at the hall to be greeted by Dave, screaming into my face and telling me that in future I'd better get my facts straight before accusing his brother of being a thief. At that moment, I lost all reason and I flew at Dave. John leapt in and averted a disaster, and I angrily climbed back into the car and returned to the house. I came close to throwing in the towel that day. Reg tried to calm the situation down, and managed to get Dave and me back on speaking terms. I couldn't bring myself to trust Dave after that, though, and over the following year our relationship pretty much came to an end.

Fletch suggested that I speak with Tom Zutaut at Geffen, as he was keen to know how we were progressing. Tom is no fool, and he could hear in my voice that all was not as it should be. During our conversation he told me that if we could get the writing done by the end of the month, then we could definitely go to Montserrat to record the album. I passed this message on to the others and it gave us the motivation to buckle down and get the work done. When we finally took stock of the situation, we were confident that we had enough ideas to produce something genuinely interesting. We even found the title of the album on our last weekend in Hawkshead. Someone had brought a videotape of the televised Barcelona concert from the previous year, and it had been the first time any of us had seen it in its entirety. During our performance of 'Splitting in Two', I'd begun to improvise, "we're living in strange times."

"Mark!" Dave exclaimed turning toward me. "That's the album title right there. *Strange Times*!"

The night before we left for home I began writing out working titles in a small notebook and transferring the four-track tapes to cassette so I could listen to them on my Walkman. The result was a rather odd collection of tunes: a reworking of a song already recorded on the earlier demos which, remembering my nightmare all those years ago, I titled 'Mad Jack'; an odd little tune I'd done on my own using just bass chords, which I called 'Seriocity', a riff that John and Reg had been jamming out together, which eventually evolved into 'Childhood', a reworking of one of the first tunes we'd ever come up with, the long-discarded 'Dear Dead Days', which now became 'Soul In Isolation', a guitar riff over which I'd played a very uncharacteristic bassline in waltz time, which I'd given the working title 'Caution' for some reason, and finally, one of the first tunes I'd ever written on a six-string acoustic, which Reg and I had jammed into an arrangement called 'Time'. This, together with the as-yet-unrecorded 'In Answer', a newly proposed treatment of 'Tears' and a remix of 'Swamp Thing', added up to what I felt was something very encouraging. I could only hope that our producer would agree, and that we'd find ourselves jetting off to a well-earned five week recording session in the Caribbean sun.

12. JACOB'S REST

With our new songs now arranged and approved, the next task was to book the studio. Immediately things were thrown into confusion. I took a call from Elaine at Air Studios in Montserrat who told me that she was really looking forward to seeing us again and that everything had been arranged. A few days later, she told me the session had been cancelled, and asked if I could clarify the situation. It transpired that Dave Allen, having initially agreed to record the album at Air, was now insisting that we work at Jacob's Studio in Surrey so that he would be able to commute to the studio each day. I was incensed, because his agreement to work at Air had been a prerequisite. My first reaction was to suggest we find someone else, but Geffen were adamant they wanted Allen to produce the record. I felt cheated and manipulated, believing that I'd been used by the label in their urgency to get the writing finished. The others agreed to the new plan, but I remained angry and resentful, so much so that Hal promised me a plane ticket to any destination I chose if I would acquiesce. Thus pacified, I finally agreed. As it turned out, recording at Jacob's Studio was to be one of the most enjoyable experiences I would have with the band, despite the fact that The Chameleons were on the brink of total disintegration.

Jacob's was two studios in one, both housed in a former stately home. Studio One, where we were based, boasted one of the best live rooms in the country, and had only recently been vacated by The Smiths, who had been recording *The Queen Is Dead* there. One afternoon while rifling through a drawer for a pen I came across a cassette labelled simply *Smiths*, which contained instrumental backing tracks from that as-yet-unreleased and greatly anticipated new album. We passed a couple of hours doing Morrissey impersonations over them: "And you've got one and I haven't got one, but I never wanted one anywayyyyy," that kind of thing.

Studio Two was designed for the electronic brigade, although the rock band Nazareth was using it while we were there. This was a rare treat for me, because, as a fourteen year old, I'd gone to see Nazareth play the Free Trade Hall whenever they came through. They had been close friends and label mates of The Sensational Alex Harvey Band - and now here I was, tearfully reminiscing about old Alex with Nazareth's lead guitarist Manny Charlton. Studio Two was the permanent haunt of Ken Thomas, producer and collaborator with Psychic TV, an innovative multi-media project fronted by notorious occultist and renegade artist Genesis P. Orridge. Ken and I would have long, passionate discussions about music, and we became quite good friends. At one point he wanted me to perform guest vocals on his then-current project, but his Parisian collaborator, having never heard of me, vetoed the idea.

The four of us had arrived at Jacob's ahead of the producer to tighten up a couple of the arrangements - 'Caution' needed an ending, and 'Soul In Isolation' needed a beginning[1]. Jacob's was an incredibly relaxed environment, more akin to a health farm than a recording studio, and the staff were a great bunch of characters. We got on so well with everyone there that the session was a talking point amongst them for a long time after. The only blight was Dave, who continued to be a pain in the arse. He and I had often argued about our music in the past, and while these discussions could be heated, they could also be very healthy, often resulting in something we were both a lot happier with. This changed after the incident in Hawkshead, and the nature of Dave's grievances became more personal, hinting at something bitter and altogether more unpleasant. I pushed myself to the limits during my time at Jacob's, but it seemed that nothing I could do would please him, and I began to feel more than a little unappreciated.

Despite this obvious tension, I'd never felt better. Having smoked since the age of fourteen, I'd been off the cigarettes for the best part of six months and found my increased energy astonishing. During periods at Jacob's when I had relatively little to do except prepare lyrics, I decided to fast, and subsequently ate nothing for two weeks, drinking only mineral water. For the first few days I felt weak, but by the fourth day I was fine, and by the end of the first week I felt euphoric. During the second week of my fast, in response to Bob Geldof's second Live Aid appeal, I swam one hundred lengths of the studio swimming pool, having got everyone at the studio to sponsor me. I would have continued for longer had Dave Allen not jumped into the pool and stopped me, lest I cost everyone more of a fortune than I already had! My thought processes were clearer than I could ever remember, and the general feeling of serenity I was experiencing had me wondering whether Tiggy, the studio chef, had been putting bromide in the

---

1. Quite a few people have asked me over the years if it's true that the Jack London novel *Star Rover* influenced the song 'Soul In Isolation'. Actually it isn't. After I'd recorded the vocal for the song Dave Allen asked me if I'd ever read it, as he felt the themes were somewhat similar and I told him I hadn't. He then gave me his copy of the book, which is now amongst my favourites.

food so we wouldn't get amorous with the female staff! Not that this was our style at all, but I just hadn't known what else to put it down to.

The studio was fully residential, and we'd been given a number of rooms in the main house. Everyone knew that I hadn't written any lyrics for the album, but Dave Allen didn't seem unduly troubled by this. I was so relaxed that it never felt like a pressure, and I felt rather spoilt when I was given a detached cottage in the studio grounds so that I'd have the peace and space to get the lyrics finished. Despite this, I spent most of my nights on the big leather couch in the control room, only to be awakened at 6am by Chrissy, the cleaner, vacuuming next to my head. When she'd finished, we'd have breakfast together, then I'd patch the previous day's work through the main speakers while I waited for everyone else to wake up.

One of the many interesting innovations at the studio was the CD player. Compact Disc was a brand new medium, and the machines were still extremely expensive, tending to be the sole province of the hi-fi geek. The studio had a few CDs, and so I'd spend most evenings alone in the mixing room listening to them after work. Eventually I began buying some of my own; this habit started after I'd bought a vinyl copy of *Glassworks* by Phillip Glass. I'd been particularly excited to find a copy of this rare record, only to discover later that it was badly scratched. I immediately returned it and asked for a replacement, but was told that this had been the shop's only vinyl copy. However, the shop assistant informed me that they did have it on the new CD format. I paid the price difference and was absolutely struck dumb by the improved quality; it sounded as if the musicians were in the room. I could even hear Glass breathing, and the sound of the piano pedals. Over the next month I went back to the shop regularly, adding Kate Bush's *The Hounds Of Love*, The Smiths' *Hatful Of Hollow*, David Bowie's *The Rise And Fall Of Ziggy Stardust And The Spiders From Mars* and Talk Talk's *The Colour Of Spring*. Dave managed to find a CD copy of *Script Of The Bridge*, and this too was a revelation. The CD sounded much better than the vinyl and cassette versions, and we could now hear many of the record's subtleties that had been previously lost to the inefficiencies of the medium.

While I enjoyed the enhanced sonic qualities of CD, I was less impressed by the reduced size of an album's artwork, and missed the lush, large format of the vinyl record sleeves. One of the pleasures of listening to an album for me was to peruse the sleeve notes or the printed lyrics, but in CD booklets the text is so tiny, and the artwork so poorly conceived that, half the time, I just can't be arsed any more. I think the reduced size of the art represents the sad loss of an intrinsic part of the overall piece of work.

Most of the themes for the new songs we were recording were bouncing around in my head, so I wasn't really concerned that I had little on paper. Over the preceding months I had bumped into a number of kids I'd been to school with after having not seen or heard anything of them for years. These chance encounters became my main themes for *Strange Times*, and, in accordance, I even reverted to my school nickname, Birdy, on the sleeve credits. Sadly, most of my old schoolmates exuded the boredom and frustration that comes with a general lack of direction, or displayed attitudes more in keeping with men approaching middle age than of boys in their mid-twenties. A few had become junkies as cheap heroin, half the price of weed, began to flood the town. Of course, what a person decides to put into his or her body is entirely their own affair, but it was particularly upsetting to see once smiling, carefree faces in such a state of social disintegration, to the point where they were barely recognisable.

I did scribble the occasional note as and when thoughts came to me, but for the most part I tended to improvise the vocal performances. 'Caution' was by far the trickiest when it came to this approach. The backing track had evolved into a rather dark, intense piece and, naturally, I'd wanted the vocal performance to capture and enhance this, but I didn't feel that any of my ideas did it justice. When the time came to deliver the vocal I took a bottle of wine with me into the vocal booth, turned out all the lights, drew the curtains across the control room windows and simply let it happen. After four or five takes I was a little unsure of the direction, but when I heard the producer say he thought we'd got it I could tell we had something special. I was momentarily confused by the surprised look on the engineer's face when he came in to pack away the microphones, until I realised that in the darkness I'd broken a wine glass and superficially cut myself. My hands and the front of my shirt were covered in blood, and it was obvious that he thought I'd been mutilating myself in the name of art.

The next day I was eager to hear what Dave thought of what I considered to be my best ever studio performance for the band. I was most disappointed to receive little by way of encouragement, save for a lecture on how good Morrissey's approach was with The Smiths, and how good the Wedding Present's records sounded.

Welcome diversions came by way of a few cover versions that we recorded for use as possible B-sides or additional tracks for future singles, although all but one, a rockabilly take on Bowie's 'John I'm Only Dancing', failed to capture the excitement of our live treatments. The latter was recorded in about three hours and John, rather than spending ages setting up and soundchecking his drum kit, ended up playing the song on his drum cases at the suggestion of Dave Allen. I was even able to elicit a rare smile from Reg when I threw in the line, "Reg, I'm only dancing." Reg's human beat-boxing on 'Seriocity' was particularly entertaining and, even now, many people don't realise that it isn't a real drum machine. I was particularly pleased by how well this track turned out as I felt it marked a genuine maturity in our songwriting, although I'd had to fight to get the song included on the recording schedule. The piano part was played by Becky, a seventeen year old trainee working at the studio. I was so smitten by her charm and natural charisma that I wanted her to join the band full-time on keyboards, but the others eventually vetoed this. The song title came from a jumble word that Fenella often used. "You're such a seriocity," she'd sigh.

One profound memory I have is of the evening we recorded the acoustic version of 'Tears' with the engineer, after Dave Allen had left for the night. John's musical percussive part was inspired, as was the engineer's harmonica-like effect, and, as the track came together, the atmosphere in the control room became very special indeed. Even Dave, who had initially opposed this new treatment of the song, graciously conceded that it had been worth doing.

The album's closing track was to be a beautiful instrumental that Dave had written, although we all contributed to some degree. I loved it, and I remember when it was finished I asked Dave what he intended to call it. He gave me a really hateful look and sneered, "I'll remember," before walking away.

"What the fuck was that about?" asked a giggling Dave Allen.

I told him I hadn't the faintest idea.

In mixing the record it seemed that we'd created a bit of a problem for the state-of-the-art, computer-based SSL recording system. Side two of the album now ran as one continuous piece, linked together by various sound effects and riff continuations, but this had proved to be too much work for the computer to handle, what with all the various stereo pans, drop-ins, drop-outs and EQ adjustments. It felt more than a little like the old days as we positioned ourselves around the mixing desk, pushing buttons and flicking dials at vital moments. I have to admit to being rather pleased that, for all its bells and whistles, such a sophisticated and expensive recording system still couldn't deal with your average Chameleons record.

Once the mixing was completed, Tom turned up to hear the results and he immediately began talking of changes and remixes. For once, our feelings were unanimous - the recordings were exactly how we wanted them, and we didn't want to start remixing tracks. Additionally, it became obvious that the others were beginning to resent Tom's constant meddling in the creative process. "Do you actually play a musical instrument, Tom?" Dave Allen asked him one afternoon.

"Well, yeah," stammered Tom, "I was a child prodigy."

"Really?" asked a bemused Dave Allen. "What instrument?"

"I was a child prodigy on the tuba," Tom replied.

I can still see the look on everyone's faces.

I suppose we'd always felt poles apart from record companies when it came to opinions and attitudes. We were artists, and therefore idealists, whereas the power within record companies rested with accountants, business managers and marketing executives. That's where the A&R person comes in, to mediate between these two extremes and get the record made to the satisfaction of all concerned. It's an unenviable role when you think about it, which probably explains why so few of them last very long.

Jacob's gave me the space to completely re-evaluate every aspect of my life, especially considering my increasing estrangement from the others. I came to think of it more as a retreat than a working environment. Dave was now openly antagonistic most of the time, Reg was simply uncommunicative, and while John's humour went some way to lightening the mood, I never really had that much in common with him. I always liked him, but we were very different people. I'd share a joke with John, and make music with him, but I would never confide in him, nor he in me.

Despite feeling very misunderstood. I was extremely comfortable with myself. I'd tried over the course of the previous year to describe some of the stranger elements of my thinking, but got little in the way of advice, support, or understanding. In fact, it got to the point where conversation on anything but the most mundane of topics would be ignored or, better still, avoided altogether. I think the quasi-spiritual aspects of where I was heading frightened them to death, and I simply stopped talking about it.

I genuinely believed that our civilisation was heading in an extremely sinister and evil direction, and that the signs of this were everywhere, for all to see. In spite of this, we seemed to be evolving into a society of zombies, lulled into a trance while our world was systematically being corrupted, poisoned and destroyed. Of course, any attempt to voice these concerns is futile, because you're simply perceived as a paranoid nut. Over the years I came to realise that if people couldn't see the way the world was heading by now, they probably never would - that it's something that has to be recognised unaided and you can only really talk about it with others who have similarly opened their eyes. At times like this, I'm reminded of the proverb derived from a short story by H.G Wells: "In the kingdom of the blind, the one-eyed man is king." However, in practice it's inaccurate, and obscures what Wells was driving at: in the kingdom of the blind, the one-eyed man is a freak. Even if I *was* going mad, it didn't seem to concern the others that much. The only thing they required was that I continue to function within the band, to fulfil my role and keep my mouth shut. There didn't seem to be the slightest residue of respect or affection, and looking back, I'm not sure why I stuck it out for as long as I did. During the *Strange Times* session I felt I'd dug deep within myself and produced my best work for the band to date; and so I was bitterly disappointed when Dave later told me that he thought side one of the record was so depressing he couldn't even listen to it.

So it was that my role within the group, my relationship to those closest to me, and the general pattern of my life all came under the microscope, and I knew that there were going to be some major changes - providing I had the courage to make them. Living at Jacob's was like living in a protective bubble. Working out the right course of action was one thing, but once that bubble burst and I was back in the real world, having the strength to do what I believed was something else entirely.

After four years together (during which time we'd actually got engaged), my relationship with Fenella was also in crisis, and this was driven home to me during my five weeks at Jacob's. Something very deep was stirring and, suddenly, the idea of getting married and settling down in Middleton was ridiculous. As much as I loved Fenella - and I did - I didn't love her enough. She would always come second to whatever was driving me - if not The Chameleons, then something else. In addition, I had a nostalgic encounter with Julia. Reg had taken an excursion into London and had bumped into Angel on the London Underground. Angel was thrilled to see Reg and had a cordial afternoon talking about old times, and she suggested he pass on Julia's phone number to me, urging me to get back in touch, which I did.

I drove up to London where Julia was now living and we spent a beautiful afternoon together in Regent's Park. We bought champagne and strawberries, and in the bright, warm sunshine of a summer's afternoon, took in an outdoor performance of Romeo and Juliet. Not surprisingly given our closeness, we found we'd been discovering the same musical and literary jewels, and we spoke longingly of the past and our doubts, fears, hopes, and aspirations for the future. However, it was obvious that I'd hurt her very deeply and the scars were still evident. I was full of remorse and regret for the way things had turned out. I talked of my doubts concerning my engagement to Fenella, and while she wasn't surprised, she withheld judgement and was able to impart a great deal of valuable advice. I was never to see her again after that summer, but I knew that she'd always have a place in my heart. I still think of her affectionately to this day, and often wonder what became of her. In any event, I had finally come to the realisation that that any kind of domestic future with Fenella was unthinkable.

Now that the bulk of the work was done, we were due to leave for home the following day. What would I do next? Hal had promised me a ticket to any destination I chose in return for agreeing to record the album at Jacob's, but where would I go? The answer came suddenly and forcefully into my mind: I would travel to Jerusalem. I'd buy a one-way ticket: no two-week package tours, no safety net. I'd go with the flow of events and see what happened.

I remember laughing out loud at such a ridiculous idea, thinking that, were I to tell anyone, no further evidence would be needed that I was losing my mind. Yet I'd never felt more lucid in my whole life. I was getting regular updates on Colin's condition and his treatment at the hands of the psychiatric unit, and I had no intention of following him down that road. I was convinced that if anyone suspected the kinds of things that were racing around my head, I'd be sectioned right along with him. I could imagine what I'd be saying:

"Well, you see it all began on Easter weekend four years ago, when I saw a bright shining figure with its arms outstretched at a ruined castle at Loch Ness. Since that night, I've had a growing feeling of unease, I mean a BAD feeling for no apparent reason, and I started seeing this number, 666, everywhere, practically on a daily basis, and I've got it into my head that this is a sign, something I'm meant to notice, something that's guiding me somewhere, although I don't know where or why exactly. More recently I took to fasting for a couple of weeks and began experiencing a kind of inner illumination, combined with feelings of elation and serenity, and the other morning in the shower I suddenly felt compelled to turn my back on my career and my colleagues and buy a one-way ticket to Jerusalem, though I have no idea why. So, Doc, what do you think?"

If I *was* suffering from mental illness then I have to say it did wonders for my personal well-being. My mind was racing, every thought coherent and I was absolutely brimming with energy and a passion for everything. My thought processes seemed crisp and sharp. What's more, others around me had begun to notice. Fletch commented numerous times about how calm and focused I seemed to have become during my time at Jacob's.

Before I left for Jacob's, Fenella and I had decided that once the new album was finished, we'd take a holiday together in Cornwall. Instead, she had to absorb the shock that I was ending our relationship. Naturally, I'd imagined our trip would be cancelled, but Fenella insisted that we go ahead with it. I think she saw it as an opportunity for her to try and come to terms with what was happening.

We made for a place that I knew quite well, having holidayed there with my parents as a child - the small fishing village of Padstow. The coast features a plethora of little sandy coves and secret surfing beaches, and the clear blue Atlantic gives the shoreline an untamed, dramatic feel. At the right time of year, before the crowds start arriving from London and the southern counties, many of the beaches are practically deserted, and you can turn up almost anywhere and instantly find accommodation, or at least you could back then. Despite the heavy, emotional drama of breaking up, the trip was great for both of us and there were one or two humorous moments. We booked into one bed and breakfast hotel to find that the bathroom was located down the hall. The next morning I went to take a shower and Fenella, thinking I'd already gone down to breakfast, locked our hotel room and went to the dining room. Of course, I wasn't there so she sat down and ordered breakfast. Meanwhile, I returned to our room to find it locked and so, with my hair still sopping wet, wrapped in a towel, I had to walk into the packed dining room to retrieve the key.

All attempts at trying to convey what I was feeling, however, failed miserably. At one point I was telling her about a book I'd read that had become very dear to my heart, Richard Bach's *Jonathan Livingstone Seagull*, explaining that I saw it as a metaphor for spiritual and creative freedom unhampered by material desires. Fenella didn't really get it. "Let me get this straight," she mused sarcastically, "You're ending our relationship because you want to be a seagull?"

I shouldn't have been surprised that she didn't understand, as I was trying to explain - but also skirting around - what was really going on with me. In the end, I told her I was planning to undertake a pilgrimage of sorts to the old city of Jerusalem. "Come with me!" I blurted out, "It'll be a real, genuine adventure."

To say that such an invitation was unrealistic would be something of an understatement. Fenella had never been further than the Cornish seaside in her entire life and typically, she hadn't had to think twice. "What for? To find God? I don't need to go traipsing round the world to find God, I know where God is, He's here!" she said angrily, thumping her chest.

She was right, of course, but I wasn't to be pacified. "Well, I believe that God, whatever God is, or something at any rate, is telling me I have to go there."

"Then go!" she said.

Fenella's outburst left me unexpectedly in the grip of uncertainty, and the more I thought about it, the more I came to doubt my own convictions. We were sitting in a café in Falmouth making small talk, and outwardly I was calm, but my mind was in a whirl. I didn't really believe all this nonsense I was spouting, did I? Surely it was all bull - wasn't it? Was I seriously contemplating running off into the blue in search of God knows what? What the *fuck* was I thinking? Surely, I reasoned, if I was expected to believe that there was something to all this, then I could expect some sort of guidance, some reassurance... *something*? Give me a sign, right here, right now and I'll accept that this isn't just the product of madness, or an over-active imagination.

I laughed to myself as I shrugged this thought off. Fenella shot me a glance as if to enquire what it was I suddenly found so funny, and I made some excuse about recalling the incident earlier in the week when she'd locked me out of the hotel room. Glancing around the café, I noticed that there was a rack on the wall offering a number of second-hand books and I walked over to have a look. One title immediately caught my attention: *Illusions, The Diary of a Reluctant Messiah* by Richard Bach. Underneath was a bright orange sticker with 50p scribbled on it. Hardly able to believe this rather unlikely find, I opened the book at random and saw that the page contained a few lines of verse:

> *A cloud does not know why it moves in just such a direction and at just such a speed. It feels an impulsion [...] this is the place to go now, but the sky knows the reasons and patterns beyond all clouds, and you will know too, when you lift yourself high enough to see beyond horizons.*

That was good enough for me. I promptly took the book to the counter, paid for it along with the more expensive and not half as nourishing sandwich, and for the next few hours Fenella didn't get a peep out of me. She seemed deaf to my insistence that finding the Bach book in a backwater café in Falmouth was anything other than an odd coincidence, and in the end I just gave up. We headed back to Padstow where we intended to spend the last four or five days before returning home. A small band of musicians was playing on the quayside, so we stopped to listen for a moment. Suddenly from behind me, I heard a man's voice say, "So this is how you spend all those royalties, eh?" I whirled around but saw only a group of impassive faces nodding to the music. The owner of the voice failed to make himself known.

As a matter of routine, I telephoned my mother to ask how things were. Fenella was right outside the phone box so she knew immediately that something was wrong. "Your nana has died," my mother said. "How soon can you get back?"

"We'll leave first thing in the morning," I told her.

13. THE DEVIL'S DAM

I was greatly saddened by the sudden death of my nana, and deeply disturbed by the unresolved issues between us, which meant we hadn't spoken for some time. Even my father's tales of how she proudly carried around the band's press cuttings hadn't cut any ice with me, and now it was too late for any reconciliation. This was to be a valuable lesson, though I sincerely wish I could have been spared it. She was a real character, and I could fill a book with anecdotes about her alone. She'd always been partial to Guinness, and whenever I'd called round to see her as a child she'd try to get me to drink it with her, claiming it was very good for children, much to my mother's annoyance. I'd always decline as I found the taste too bitter, although my younger cousin Wayne seemed to love it and would drink it by the beakerful, draining it in a single gulp while nana sat chuckling. One day she'd needed to visit the doctor who diagnosed iron deficiency and he advised her - off the record - that in his opinion the best thing would be to drink Guinness. Of course, he'd meant perhaps a glass a day, but to Nana this had been as good as divine vindication, and she began drinking it by the crate-load. By the time she died, she was so huge from drinking all that Guinness that it had taken an army of bearers to lift her out of the bedroom, and every male member of the family had been needed to carry the coffin.

Despite my over-riding urge to go racing off to the Holy Land, I couldn't ignore my responsibilities to the band, regardless of how strained the relationships between us had become. The music business treadmill is such that a new album invariably means another spell on the road, in this case a tour of the UK and Europe, followed by our first coast-to-coast tour of the United States. The possibility of the latter became apparent following a rather curious and mildly amusing incident. Fletch called one afternoon and asked if I'd meet him, along with our friend Ruth Polsky - who was now acting as our American agent - for lunch at the Britannia Hotel in Manchester. Apparently, a rumour was circulating in America that I was dead, following a knife attack in Ireland. Ruth was now having difficulty in convincing US venue managers that this wasn't the case, so she couldn't get them to book the dates. We had a very enjoyable lunch, after which I was photographed holding that day's newspaper by way of proof that I was still very much in the land of the living!

After such a cathartic experience as Jacob's, I was getting extremely restless hanging around Manchester with little to do, so when Fletch rang and told me he was in Birmingham organising a Rod Stewart show and suggested I drive down for it, I agreed. I decided I'd drop by, see Fletch at the show, and then drive to London and call on my friend Sally, who lived in Battersea. I'd visited Sally a few times during the *Strange Times* sessions, taking rough mixes of the new record to gauge her reaction. I would also call on her when the band was playing in London, glad of an alternative to the inevitable all-night benders in the hotel bar.

I drove down to Birmingham early on Friday evening for the show at the NEC. Fletch was run off his feet, as usual, so we had very little time to chat, but he gave me a pass for the press pit at the front of the stage. I had to admit that Rod Stewart was still a dynamic performer, and, despite the enormous venue, it felt quite intimate, and not at all as dull or pompous as I expected. After the gig I headed down the motorway to London, but had only driven fifty miles or so when I noticed another car matching my pace on my right-hand side. The driver was making no apparent effort to overtake, although there was no other vehicle in sight. I glanced across and saw the driver turn his head and grin at me. The car appeared to be a taxi and the name of the firm - A-Z Taxis - was stencilled across it, along with the phone number, which completely covered the car and had a 666 area code. Finally, after a few moments, it accelerated away. I'd only driven a few miles further when I heard a sharp rap on the windscreen, and a couple of minutes later the glass shattered. Fortunately, the motorway was still deserted so I was able to veer across to the hard shoulder and stop. As the car came to rest, I noticed that the odometer now showed a mileage of 66600.

Eventually I was able to call for assistance and get the windscreen replaced, but by the time I reached Battersea, no lights were visible at all in Sally's house. Unable to see any signs of life, I spent most of what remained of the night sleeping in the car. Eventually I heard a knock at the window and saw Sally peering in. That afternoon, I gave her a lift across town on my way to meet another friend, and as we talked, she took me completely by surprise. She asked me what I planned to do next, and I explained my plan to visit Jerusalem. "Aren't you nervous about going on your own?" she asked me.

I thought for a moment and decided that honesty was preferable to macho posturing. "Fuckin' terrified, to tell you the truth!" I laughed.

"I'll come if you like!" I glanced over at her, not really knowing whether to take her seriously or not.

"What? You'd travel to the Middle East with me on a one-way ticket?"

"Anything's better than this!" she sighed, staring out of the window at all the London traffic.

"Well, we've got a new album coming out, and they're talking about a big tour to promote it. I can't just walk away, so it probably won't happen." Even as I said the words I could feel my stomach churn, and my instincts were screaming at me to sack it all and just go.

The big summer event in Manchester that year was a two-night stand at Maine Road by Queen. The concerts were organised by KES, and Fletch was the man responsible for every aspect of the production, from the building of the stage to the arrival of the band. For Fletch it was to be a crowning moment. Of all the stars in the pop firmament, there were two in particular he had always dreamt of working with: the first was David Bowie, and the other was Freddie Mercury of Queen. I drove over to see Fletch and found The Chameleons' road crew already busy erecting the dressing room area. Fletch told me he needed an errand boy and asked if I'd consider doing it in exchange for a couple of seats in the Director's box. Relishing the idea of seeing such a big production come together up close, I jumped at the chance.

Knowing I was a passionate Manchester City fan he took me on a guided tour of the ground, which included the manager's office, where he sat me down behind the big desk. I even got to fulfil a childhood ambition of my own that first day. The goalposts and netting hadn't yet been taken down, and during a kick-about with some of the stage crew I scored a goal at the Platt Lane end and celebrated wildly in front of an empty Kippax Street stand, thereby outdoing my own father at last in the football department.

Fletch was a Manchester United supporter, and it amused me to note that he could be introduced to the biggest pop stars in the world and not bat an eyelid, but introduce him to a member of the Manchester United first team and he'd be reduced to a stammering wreck, shaking like a leaf, his face crimson. During that week, while on a brief visit to the office, I substituted a poster of the Manchester United squad, which hung proudly by his desk, for a picture of Manchester City, and it was over a week before I finally got a phone call from a laughing Fletch: "You crafty bastard!"

Before the end of the show I was summoned backstage by one of Fletch's assistants, and I was rather disillusioned with what I saw there. Each member of the band had insisted on a separate stretch limousine to take them to the show, and each - I was told by Fletch - occupied an entire floor of the hotel in Manchester. I was introduced to the band by Hal, at his insistence, and was rather nervous but - with one exception - they were very sweet, especially Freddie. After a while, the senior director of KES turned up to present the band with a specially framed golden concert ticket to mark the event - and well he might. I was reliably informed that his net profit from the shows had been around £1,000,000. However, during the presentation he didn't even deign to introduce Fletch to the band, despite the fact Fletch had done all the work. Naturally, he was extremely upset at being robbed of a major highlight of his career. "Fuck him!" I heard Fletch mutter under his breath.

The reason I'd been summoned backstage was because Tom at Geffen had requested I join him in New York for the mastering of the record. From there we would fly on to Los Angeles where I could oversee the final preparations for the artwork. I certainly had no problem with jet-setting off to the States. "When do they want me to go?" I laughed, as Fletch relayed the news.

"You're booked on a plane first thing tomorrow morning!" he grinned.

I hastily gathered some clothes, and within hours I was half way across the Atlantic.

New York summers are notoriously humid, and I found myself taking a shower and a change of clothes around four times a day. I was booked into a plush hotel on the south side of Central Park, in room 66, which was, of course, situated on the 6th floor. I immediately called a photographer friend of mine, Bonnie, who I'd met during our first visit there in 1984, and over dinner surprised myself by confiding more about my current state of mind than I'd intended. She was fascinated, and insisted that we embark on a quest to find the mysterious 666 building, which I'd seen from the viewing deck of the Empire State. We soon found it, and I was amused to see that it was close by a church dedicated to St. John the Divine, the alleged author of The Book of Revelation. Finding a suitable vantage point, Bonnie photographed the neon numbers glowing an ominous red at the building's summit, promising to post the photos off to me. However, in true Omen style, when the film came back all the exposures of the building had been fogged. Bonnie also gave me a large print of the photo she'd taken of the band backstage at the Danceteria in 1984, which I'd asked if we could use for the back cover of *Strange Times*.

Eventually I met Tom at the mastering suite as arranged, and was introduced to George Morino, whose clients included the Rolling Stones. I soon learned why they used him. When he'd finished the re-mastering, *Strange Times* sounded twice as good to my ears as it had before. I'm sure George's services didn't come cheap, but then this was typical of Tom's diligence and extravagance. Further evidence of the latter came on the day of our departure to LA when, after climbing into the back of a white stretch limousine, he complained bitterly to the driver because the car had been shorter than he'd wanted. "How big does a car need to be to take you to the airport, Tom?" I joked.

He saw the funny side but added ruefully, "Well, I ordered a twenty-five foot stretch and they've given me a twenty. I'm not fucking paying for it, I'll tell you that."

We were met at LA International airport by another stretch limousine, and driven directly to Tom's house on the edge of the Hollywood Hills. Tom's brother Brad also stayed at the house, and he offered to act as guide and companion while his brother worked at the Geffen offices. Brad was trying to break into acting, having studied drama under Steinberg, no less, and exhibited a warm, generous, down-to-earth nature - a blast of cool air in an otherwise dry, sterile environment.

I was immediately struck by certain aspects of LA's culture. Everyone drives everywhere, all the time - even if it's just down the road for groceries or cigarettes. Public transport is looked down upon, often regarded as dangerous and only fit for peasants. I was extremely uncomfortable with this attitude, and it seemed to me that the average Angeleno's idea of peasants equated to Mexicans, who seemed to comprise most, if not all, of the municipal workforce. It disturbed me to see so much racism directed at the Mexican population, and I did my best to buck the trend. Brad held no such racist notions, being as openly cynical and hostile with regard to such attitudes as I was.

Brad introduced me to the virtues of what is possibly Mexico's finest contribution to international culture - the Margarita, a cocktail comprising tequila, triple-sec - although some prefer Cointreau, lime juice and crushed ice. He was particularly amused one evening when, after an extensive bender, I'd stood up in the living room amidst the assembled throng and said, "Hey, let's get more Margaritas," before immediately collapsing to the floor unconscious.

Tom's record collection was huge. It ran the length of the entire house, and kept me occupied for days. I was massively impressed that he'd managed to track down all these releases, given the rarity or obscurity of some of them. Amongst them was the very first pressing of the debut single by The Wedding Present; I put it on the turntable and cranked up the volume. Tom's house was a large, modern-looking detached property and happily, blasting out loud music in the middle of the day wasn't a problem. As the record played, I was stuck by a wave of nostalgia as I recalled those far-off days I'd shared with Gedge, Solowka, Dave, and Reg at Hollin High School. Who could have imagined back then that such a moment would come?

I continued to see the number 666, on this occasion whilst browsing the stores along Hollywood Boulevard, noting the street numbers over the shop doorways: 6661, 6662, 6663… It was at this point that I found that Tom had notions of his own, ones that made mine seem quite mundane by comparison. These ranged from the collapse of the current social systems to Atlantis, reincarnation and ancient Egypt. Brad introduced me to his small circle of friends which included Danny, a script writer, and Danny's sister Laurel. She was a beautiful woman who had aspirations of being an actress, and earned a crust in an upmarket bookstore. Danny had yet to sell a major script. He was extremely witty, and the banter between him and Brad was priceless. It was obvious that he was in love with Brad, but they were content to simply flirt around it, Brad being heterosexual and involved in a long-term relationship with a major Hollywood make-up artist.

Brad, Danny and I would rove around town getting drunk and making nuisances of ourselves in every decent Mexican bar, including those in the notoriously dangerous area of downtown Los Angeles, much to Danny's consternation. "You don't understand," he whined one evening as we sat at the bar, a Mexican joint that Brad had recommended as serving the best Margaritas for miles. "They fuckin' shoot people!"

A rather large, heavy-looking Mexican guy sitting by my left shoulder was obviously irritated by Danny's protestations. He leaned over and whispered in my ear: "Where you from, man?"

"I'm from England," I told him.

"You've got nothing to worry about," the Mexican guy assured me. "We only shoot Americans," and he bought me another Margarita.

I've always found the Mexican people to be among the warmest, most generous people I've met. One evening while sitting at the bar in a Mexican restaurant, I'd been watching the owner's wife make tortillas, in the hope of gleaning how it was done. Noticing me, she invited me behind the counter and taught me how to make them.

On another occasion, Tom and I were discussing where we felt the world was heading. During the conversation the Mexican bar tender, who was listening to all of this, kept filling up our Margarita glasses, unprompted. When it came to settling the drinks bill the guy refused to accept payment, giving us God's blessing as we left.

My meeting with the art co-ordinator at Warner Brothers had been mildly frustrating, but I felt we'd got there in the end. I showed her the black and white band photograph and told her how Bonnie was to get a credit for the picture. In addition I explained how I'd wanted it placed, adding that I wanted the image in high contrast with the same colour we'd used on the border of the front sleeve washing through the white portions of the image. "Got it?" I asked. "Got it!" she replied emphatically.

"Sure?" I asked.

"Yes," she said, shaking her head decisively.

When I received the finished product I found Bonnie's credit missing, and her photograph hidden within the black of the back sleeve, making it almost invisible. Some have commented to me on the cleverness of this, pointing out that it's a photo of The Chameleons blended into the background. Oh yes, very good. It wasn't meant to be that way and I was furious about it.

Next in the band's schedule were rehearsals for the European tour to promote *Strange Times*. By now it seemed that most of our time was taken up with things which had little, if anything, to do with the business of actually playing. Regardless of the tensions building up within the band, rehearsing usually made me feel a whole lot better about everything, and getting together for gigs usually made me feel like we were brushing aside all the bull and getting down to the real business of making music. Things were different this time, though; it was as if I had my own personal raincloud hovering overhead, ominous and oppressive.

The tour started brightly enough on 6th September 1986 at Darlington Arts Centre, and I have a vivid recollection of the soundcheck. The room contained the usual smattering of venue staff, a few fans that had gathered early and members of the support band. As the soundcheck reached its conclusion we decided to end with 'Caution', the first time we'd ever played it in front of anybody since recording it at Jacob's. By now the sound had been sorted to everyone's satisfaction and the band sounded huge. Following the song's rather sudden conclusion there had been complete silence in the room for a few seconds, until an anonymous voice at the back of the room rang out: "Fuckin' 'ell!" The whole room cracked up with laughter.

On the whole I was very uncomfortable on that tour, and I remember a friend from Jacob's who turned up at the London Town and Country Club being quite shocked to see how edgy and stressed I'd become. I tried to explain that I felt trapped by what I was doing and that I desperately wanted to be free of it. I had a very bad feeling and just wanted to get away as soon as possible. The following gig at the Bierkeller in Bristol had coincided with one of the worst race riots Britain had ever seen, and we had to be diverted around the periphery of the city by an army of policemen to avoid getting caught up in it.

At Manchester International we were pleased to find that advance tickets for the show had broken all previous records, a fact that impressed us because the venue had played host to some very high-profile bands in the past. During the show they were forced to open all the fire exits, not only to alleviate the overcrowding inside the venue, but also to pacify a very large number of people without tickets who were threatening to kick the doors in.

Following our show in Leeds we had some shocking news. Ruth Polsky, our US agent, had been hit by a taxi in New York and killed instantly. She'd been trying to hail a cab outside the Limelight Club in Manhattan when a taxi had lost control and ploughed into her. I was completely devastated, and our US tour was postponed indefinitely.

The European leg of the tour went badly from the outset. To begin with, KES had hired a normal coach for the entire tour, rather than a sleeper. This was probably a cost-cutting exercise, but most of the shows on that tour were sold out, and we weren't paid a penny. Given that, due to some insane routing, we'd be expected to spend ten or twelve hours each day on this bus, we were all shocked. It wasn't so bad in the beginning, but after a while the reality of the situation began to kick in - we had nowhere to sit and relax, no table to congregate around and nowhere to change. Because of this, the atmosphere on the bus rapidly became tense and ultimately, unbearable. We would have been better off doing the tour in our old Transit van, but sadly that had long since been sold off.

The tour took in around thirty-two cities over thirty-five days. At the first show, in Rennes, we finished the soundcheck and congregated at the hotel as usual, and after asking the tour manager how much time we had and being told we had plenty, I went to my room to shave and shower. When I returned, the lobby was deserted and so, assuming everyone had opted to do as I had, I waited in the lobby - and waited - and waited. Finally, I asked the concierge to bell the rooms to tell them I was waiting, only to be informed that all the keys had been handed in and our party had left without me. This was in the days before mobile phones, and I hadn't yet been given a detailed itinerary listing the venues and contact numbers, so I was powerless to do anything other than wait and hope that the tour manager would return soon. Time passed, and it became apparent that he wasn't coming back. Finally, in desperation, I headed out into the night in search of a promo poster for the gig. Luckily I found one, and it provided me with the address of the venue. I stopped a young French lad and, in my best high school French, persuaded him to take me there, paying him two hundred francs along with a promise to get him into the show. He got me to the venue with around ten minutes to spare, whereupon I was greeted with five or six blank faces all asking me where I'd been. From that point on, things grew worse. The atmosphere on the bus was intolerable and the hours on the road, as we zigzagged our way around the continent, seemed endless.

In Barcelona, I was again forced into giving up one of my rare days off to go traipsing round town with the promoter, doing interviews for the local media. This had been particularly awkward as I hadn't had a chance to change any money at the border, and was intending to do it that day. The tour manager told me that he'd be organising a cash float later that afternoon and that he'd change some money for me, but in the meantime I was to do the scheduled interviews. John offered to come with me by way of moral support, and reluctantly I climbed into the back of the diminutive Seat, the small-time Spanish concert promoter's vehicle of choice, and was once again shunted round from pillar to post.

We'd been invited to lunch by a friend of the promoter, who had once been a very famous Spanish musician, and who now owned a restaurant. After the meal, he made us a present of a large bottle of Spanish brandy, which meant that John and I spent the remainder of the day's interviews in slightly better spirits. By late afternoon I could feel a headache coming on, so, once back at the hotel, I asked the tour manager to give me a few hours to sleep it off and then call my room.

I awoke around 8pm, and it was immediately obvious from the splitting headache and my parched throat that I was suffering from acute dehydration, thanks in no small part to the brandy. I wandered out into the hallway and rapped on a few doors, but there was no reply from any of them. With a heavy sigh, I walked down to the lobby, expecting to find a message explaining where everyone was. The receptionists looked at me blankly as I tried to make myself understood, and it eventually transpired that there were no messages for me. I asked for a bottle of drinking water and as it was handing it to me, I indicated to the receptionist to put it on the room tab. He immediately snatched the water back again, insisting that I had to pay for the water there and then. I tried to explain that I didn't have any Spanish currency, but it didn't seem to matter to him. My throat was now badly swollen and I began to get rather animated, which antagonised them even further, and finally, I withdrew, before a bad situation turned downright ugly.

That night was probably the worst I'd ever had in all the years I'd been on the road with the band. In fact, I don't think I'd ever felt so friendless and so utterly alone in all my life. At one point, I wrote a letter to Fenella, in which I apologised for putting my career and the band before our relationship, and begged her to meet me in Amsterdam, which was still about ten days away. For some reason I had a growing feeling of dread about the gig in Amsterdam, but no idea why. I screwed the letter up and threw it away, but now that I'd expressed the thought, I couldn't shake it. Suddenly the reality of the approaching show in Amsterdam seemed ominously dark and heavy, like a huge, oppressive shadow lurking in the corner of the room. I tried to sleep, but sleep was impossible. My headache was excruciating, and my throat was on fire and I was finding it difficult to swallow. I read somewhere that this is what a hangover really is; massive dehydration, so dying of thirst in the desert is really a case of the hangover that kills you. I wondered if it was possible that I would die from dehydration right there in the hotel room. Earlier I'd consumed most of a litre of brandy, and I'd been perspiring in the Spanish heat all day.

I lay there for hours, with thoughts like these my only company, until finally, at around 3am, I heard the sound of the others returning to their rooms. I walked out into the hallway, as they filed past, not saying anything until finally the tour manager approached. "Where the fuck have you been?" I croaked. He seemed genuinely alarmed and told me that the promoter had taken them all out to a bar for dinner. "So you left me here for over eight hours with no money, no drinking water, and no word as to where you were or how I could find you?" I was shouting now, despite my swollen, parched throat.

"I'll get you some water. Calm down!" was all he could say, and he walked off towards the desk. He returned with a bottle of mineral water, which I took into the room I was sharing with Reg. I was waiting for Reg to say something, anything, but he just lay there. I began taking mouthfuls of water and spitting it out onto the far wall. "Are you all right?" Reg asked, finally breaking the stony silence.

"Well, no, not really, Reg. I mean, what the *fuck* were you thinking?" I knew that in all probability they weren't thinking at all, at least not where I was concerned.

In Madrid, disaster struck again after the road manager offered to organise a laundry run for the band. By this time, I'd used every decent stitch of clothing I owned at least twice and so, gathering it all together, I handed him the bag and off he went. When he returned, everything in the bag was sopping wet. He'd thrown all the clothes in the washing machine, but only discovered afterwards that none of the dryers in the launderette were working. Our schedule was such that we didn't have a chance to dry them for around three days, by which time most of my clothes were ruined.

By now the strain I was under was becoming unbearable, and as we drove through the outskirts of Paris, I suddenly recognised where we were. Jumping up from my seat, I barked at the driver to pull over and grabbing my bag, told them I'd meet them at the next show in Holland. I was off the bus and down the road before the tour manager had even realised what was happening. I telephoned a Parisian journalist friend and she collected me from a nearby metro station. That evening she took me to dinner at an excellent Mexican restaurant. I spent the night on her sofa, and it was all she could do to persuade me to carry on with the tour. In the morning she drove me to the station, and I dutifully boarded the train to Holland.

The next night in Den Haag was no better. I was edgy, and the mood on stage was tense and awkward. The Trojan Horse was a prestigious venue to play but, as usual, everyone was smoking too much cannabis and the whole thing became leaden and uninspired. Similarly, the gig in Rotterdam was a disaster, although I can't remember why exactly. I just recall Dave ranting at everyone in the dressing room. Finally, Reg shouted at Dave to shut up, something I'd never seen before in all our years together.

Finally, the dreaded Amsterdam show arrived. The venue was the already familiar Paradiso in the centre of town, although its façade had changed since our previous visit there. Now the exterior was completely covered in black paint, and, in an attempt to satirise the building's previous incarnation as a church, a blue neon cross had been placed high above the roof of the building, teetering to and fro in a precarious manner.

After a rushed soundcheck I left the main hall and was surprised to find Sally with a young friend of hers named Steve. They'd decided to travel to Amsterdam for the show, on impulse. I was almost totally overwhelmed at seeing a friendly face, someone I could trust. Sally could see immediately that I was under a great amount of strain and we retreated to a nearby bar, where I related everything that had happened on the tour.

The audience was filled with impassive, stoned, staring faces and it immediately struck me, as I stood looking out over the hall, how utterly blank these expressions were, almost as if the audience were an army of zombies. Suddenly, as if a switch had been thrown, I experienced the worst attack of paranoia I've ever known. It was as if there was some kind of indescribably dark presence staring at me through all those pairs of eyes, and my body felt ice cold. We were midway through a song when it happened and I just stopped playing. I turned to look at Dave, Reg, and John in turn, trying to gauge if they were experiencing the same feeling that

I was. It's very hard to explain what I saw. Their faces were only vaguely familiar, as if they wore masks that were based on caricatures of their actual likenesses. It was obviously them, and yet at the same time it most definitely wasn't. It was as if something else was looking out from all those pairs of eyes, their owners oblivious. I wasn't oblivious though, I was aware of it. And my skin crawled with the sudden realisation that it was aware of me.

The atmosphere - a kind of mocking malevolence - was unbearable, and dropping my bass onto the floor, I turned and walked off the stage. A Hells Angel-type guy, Serge, a friend of Fletch's who had driven out on an errand, was standing at the side of the stage, and I remember him shouting into my face, "I feel it too, man! You're alright! You're okay."

All I could do was stare at him in total confusion, dimly aware of what was happening, but paralysed. The others had followed me off the stage and I was relieved to see that they now looked and sounded normal again. I heard Dave shouting, "Splitting in two! Splitting in two, then off." This was so typical of Dave. The fucking world could be ending in the middle of a set, and he'd still be primarily concerned with saving the gig. Just this once, however, it was a healthy approach, because I was suddenly able to snap back into focus.

"The gig!" I remember thinking to myself, "We're playing a gig. Finish the gig."

I nodded to Dave, walked back out onto the stage and took the microphone for what would be the final song of the set. I didn't make it to the end of 'Splitting In Two' though. It's as impossible as it is futile to even attempt to describe the moment. The only thing that would come anywhere close would be to say that it suddenly felt as if I'd touched minds with something utterly horrible. The next thing I remember, I was lying on the floor, the microphone discarded and I was screaming. And I couldn't stop.

14. THE ROAD TO DAMASCUS

I think it was Serge who picked me up from the stage floor. It was certainly he who bundled me down to the dressing room, shaking me in an effort to quell the shock and stop me screaming. I remember hearing the jabbering conversations that were going on around me, conscious that it was all going backwards, like a tape being played in reverse, and I kept shaking my head as if this would somehow dislodge the glitch in the circuitry. After another couple of minutes, words seemed to reorganise themselves in my mind as Serge held me. "That wasn't nice, was it?" he kept saying to me. "That wasn't nice at all."

I was still trembling violently when I heard a familiar voice at the dressing room door. Sally, having witnessed this from the audience, ran immediately to the backstage area and demanded to know how I was. The instant I saw her, I bolted for the door and asked her to get me out of the building. By this time, a crowd had assembled outside the stage door, and I was vaguely aware of their curious stares as Sally led me into the street. Suddenly the promoter, a huge bearded bear of a man, appeared directly in front of us. "That was weird, man!" he was saying. "That was fuckin' weird!" Someone had called a cab and with Steve's help, Sally got me into it, and we all went back to their hotel. Sleep was impossible for me, though I felt completely exhausted. As we talked, I was relieved to hear Sally and her friend say how strange the whole place had seemed, and that they'd also been aware of the extremely sinister atmosphere.

The next morning I was still in a deep state of shock and doubted I'd be able to continue with the tour, but Sally talked me round. I wearily accompanied Sally and Steve to the rallying point. The rest of the entourage just seemed embarrassed, and nothing was said. By this time Fletch had arrived, although whether this was a scheduled visit or not I have no idea. Fletch and the road manager took me to one side and explained how important it was that I finish the tour. Pulling out now would cost a lot of people a great deal of money and damage the reputation of the band, they said. By this time, I couldn't have given a flying fuck about the reputation of the band, but I cared deeply for Fletch, one of the few people I genuinely trusted. I could see he was extremely worried, so I agreed to finish the tour, providing that Sally agreed to stay also.

I remember very little of the remaining gigs. Sally's friend Steve only had a temporary British passport, the kind you could pick up at any UK post office back then for a few quid. It was sufficient for most EU countries, but wasn't adequate for getting him through the Soviet sectors that led to Berlin. Sally had a full British passport and was adamant that she wasn't leaving me alone, so Steve waited patiently in a nearby West German city, arranging to meet up with us after the Berlin show.

We entered Berlin from a different route than on previous visits, passing through the eastern sectors of the city, and I was struck by the stark contrast in cultures between these two political ideologies. University campuses and libraries were decorated in huge red, black and white banners depicting granite-faced silhouettes of communist party luminaries, while at the roadside, rows of crouching figures in woollen trench coats shovelled snow. The antiquated architecture looked as if it was about to collapse, as we drove past wall after wall of faded, crumbling plaster riddled with mortar fire and bullet holes, perhaps a legacy of the city's liberation by the Allies in 1945.

Having no idea what living under such conditions was like, I was fascinated, and lamented the fact that I wouldn't have time for a closer look. The contrast was even more apparent later that afternoon when, having crossed the checkpoint into West Berlin, Sally and I found ourselves drinking bad coffee in a modern fast-food joint amid row upon row of empty, garish yellow tables, staffed by pale-faced teenagers in matching uniforms and silly paper hats. As we watched the passing traffic - a seemingly endless flow of shiny Mercedes Benz - I was struck by the blandness of West Berlin and modern western culture in general. I gazed at the grey, concrete wall that separated all of this from its doppelganger; an island of freedom in a sea of Soviet totalitarianism, or a dangerous spot of cancer in the body politic, depending on your viewpoint.

I remember nothing of the show - or any of the shows in the wake of the Paradiso for that matter - although I'll never forget the horror of that night in Amsterdam, the shock I felt in its wake, and my state of mind. Afterwards, I was amazed that I'd been able to climb onto a stage and perform at all.

I knew that there'd be some kind of post-mortem following the tour and that I'd have to confront the others eventually, if only to clear the air. Thus it came as no surprise when, the following week, I was summoned to a meeting at KES. I was the last to arrive. As soon as I entered everyone fell silent and it was obvious that a lot had been said already. I knew that Fletch would be absent; he was off somewhere working on a show.

We danced around the issues, making banal conversation for ten minutes, and then the meeting began in earnest. Hal wanted to know what was going on, so I attempted to summarise the situation as I saw it. As usual, John and Reg remained silent throughout, while Dave and I gravitated towards another argument. The consensus seemed to be that I was losing my mind, which I conceded was probably true, but I argued that the grievances I had were genuine, and that I resented the accusation that they amounted to nothing more than petulance or paranoia. At the very least, I argued, I would have expected them to recognise that I was in deep trouble psychologically and to support me, rather than regard me as an object of scorn and derision.

The arguments grew increasingly heated, until finally I'd had enough. I told them I wasn't going to risk going down the road Ian Curtis went, especially for the likes of them. "That's it, I quit!" I said, then stormed out of the room.

I was told later that Hal had been the first to break the silence: "Does anyone know any singers?"

As I reached the car park Reg caught up with me. "So what are you going to do now, then?"

"I'm going to Jerusalem."

"Jerusalem? Why?"

"Because I have to."

"What will you do there?"

"I don't know," I mused. "Pick fruit or something, I suppose."

"When are you coming back?"

"I don't know that either," I told him, laughing at the sound of my own words, "maybe a month, maybe a year, maybe never. I'm buying a one-way ticket and I'll see what happens."

I heard nothing more from them over the following weeks, and spent my time getting ready for the trip. Ken was still around, preparing to leave for Rome where he'd found a job teaching English, and I spent quite a bit of time with him. Naturally, our conversation turned to the immediate future. Ken seemed to regret not continuing with music in some form, and felt a little let down by Oxford, which seemed to be less rewarding than he'd hoped.

He was very surprised to hear that I'd quit The Chameleons, and at one point even suggested reforming The Clichés. This touched me, but all I could do in response was smile nostalgically. He was even more surprised when I began to tell him of my plans to travel to Jerusalem, though he remained typically good-humoured and cynical. "You're not turning into one of those born-again nuts are you?" he asked. Ken had been raised in a Catholic household and, as is so often the case among the intelligentsia, it had left a very sour taste in his mouth.

I assured him that I wasn't about to embrace orthodox Christianity and start selling it door-to-door. "I don't know what I'm feeling," I concluded, "but something is happening to me, and I'm determined to find out what it is. How about you?" I asked.

Ken told me that he and his girlfriend Anne had been accepted by a private English language school, and had found a flat in the centre of Rome. "I'll give you the address before I go," he said, "you can drop by and stay for a while if you like. We could even go and see the Pope, set him straight on a few things."

Sally and I kept in close contact during the weeks that followed, and she remained adamant that she wanted to make the trip to Jerusalem too. I did little to dissuade her, being glad to know I would have the company. I spent some time researching Israel, and despite the many political disputes with their neighbours, the Palestinians chief among them, the situation seemed fairly stable. I was bemused to find that there were many discounts available for those aged between eighteen and twenty-five, regardless of student status, but as I was already twenty-six years old, I was told that I wouldn't qualify. Sally was six years younger - she was born on 2nd June 1966 - 02/06/66 - so she did qualify, and thus we were able to save a little money. We decided to pool what funds we had, but discussed the possibility of joining a Kibbutz community if things got tight. Neither of us relished the idea; it seemed to us that working on a Kibbutz amounted to little more than slave labour, though a communist interpretation made it sound kinder. Participants were not given a great deal of choice as to where they would be deployed, and we heard rumours that Europeans would often be sent to the least popular or most volatile locations. Neither of us had any previous experience of backpacking or this kind of travelling, so in many ways we were babes in the wood.

Fletch called and asked to meet with me. I was expecting him to try to talk me into staying with the band, but he surprised me and was totally supportive about my trip. Until Amsterdam, I don't think he truly realised just how close to the edge I'd been pushed, and I told him I believed that everything up to and including Amsterdam had happened because I'd gone against my instincts. Now, in the wake of Ruth Polsky's death, with all talk of the US tour abandoned, there was nothing stopping me. What did I have to lose?

Finally the time came to leave, and, even before we arrived in Israel, I was struck by the strangeness of some elements of the Jewish culture. A group of religious mystics dressed in black robes and hats, their hair plaited into curls, and with long beards, were checking in at the desk. Midway through the flight they all rose from their seats, around eight or nine strong, walked to the door of the cockpit, and placing their heads against it, began wailing. Suspicious that they knew something about the plane's mechanics that the rest of us didn't, I shot an anxious glance at a passing stewardess. She explained they were attempting to put themselves as physically close as possible to the Wailing Wall in Jerusalem, to offer up their daily prayers.

By the time we landed at Tel Aviv it was quite late, and we made our way to the transfer bus beneath a darkening sky. Before I was allowed to board the bus, however, we were stopped and questioned by Israeli security. What were we doing in Israel? Where were we making for? Where would we be staying? How long were we intending to remain, and were either of us Jewish?

We decided to head for a youth hostel we'd heard of in the centre of Tel Aviv, and then travel on to Jerusalem by train the following day. As we stood waiting for the bus we met a young English guy. After talking for a while, he told us that he'd bought a one-way ticket to Israel, that he'd eventually be making for Jerusalem and that he'd come because he'd simply felt compelled to do it. "I'm just going to see what happens," he said. I fleetingly wondered if there was some kind of psychic epidemic going around.

My guidebook had hinted at the unreliability of the single train service that ran between Tel Aviv and Jerusalem and, sure enough, we found that travelling to the city by train would be impossible unless we were prepared to wait another four or five days. I was disappointed because I love travelling by train and I'd been looking forward to it very much. We'd resigned ourselves to this and were heading for the bus station when, suddenly, we were kidnapped. Perhaps that is too dramatic a word for being cajoled into a taxi bound for a city we had no wish to go to, but that was how it felt. A Palestinian taxi driver accosted us, jabbering on about the very reasonable fare, and threw our bags into the back of a Mercedes van, despite our protestations. The guy wouldn't take no for an answer and so, laughing at the absurdity of the situation, we climbed in and found ourselves on our way to the city of Haifa. An old Jewish gentleman fared even worse, having been similarly accosted at the railway station, except he also suffered the indignity of being physically carried to the taxi and thrown inside. Understandably, he complained about this very loudly and bitterly every inch of the way to our destination.

Haifa seemed to be an interesting, bustling city, but we were eager to reach Jerusalem so we paid it scant attention, asking instead to be dropped at the bus station. Tensions were obviously high, and we saw armies of young Israeli conscripts walking around with machine guns. Even young girls weren't excused from this, and, as we waited for the bus that would carry us on to Jerusalem, I was mildly amused to see young women in army fatigues, toting M-16s and using their ammunition pouches as vanity cases, periodically pulling lipstick or eyeliner from them. This was well before the eruption of violence on a massive scale, of course, so the situation was tame by today's standards. The feeling was more akin to sitting on top of a gunpowder keg; danger was in the air, and it seemed that it wouldn't take much to ignite the region into fury, which is exactly what happened, eventually.

Hippies, buskers, and backpackers were in abundance, and as we climbed from the bus in New Jerusalem, we found no shortage of touts offering cheap places to stay. Our first choice was conveniently close to the bus station, but it was dreary and characterless, so we resolved to find a place within the Old City walls as soon as possible. We entered through the Jaffa Gate and I immediately saw something that stopped me dead in my tracks, causing me to drop my bags and stare in amazement. Directly before me, just inside the gates, stood a row of about ten Mercedes taxi cabs and every one of them had a 666 number plate. "Well, at least I'm still on the right track," I murmured to Sally, reaching for my camera.

"What?" she asked.

"Let's get a drink or something," I said. "There are one or two things you need to know."

Finding yourself thousands of miles from home in a strange country on the brink of civil war with a limited amount of money and no immediate escape route is probably not the best time to find out that your only travelling companion, the person on whom you depend, is a paranoid nut. Sally took it very well. The depth of trust and belief she placed in me was a great gift, and being able to openly talk of things I'd felt forced to keep hidden for so long was nothing short of liberating. She was able to provide me with a means of putting everything into perspective for the first time, and kept an open mind throughout. As I talked, something inside me clicked. Although I wasn't able to fully understand what was happening to me, I suddenly felt, for the first time in years, that I was exactly where I was supposed to be and that, somehow, Sally was part of the equation. The plan now was simple: to go with the flow, trust the instincts that had brought us to this place, and embrace the experience.

Enclosed within the walls of the Old City are four districts, the Jewish Quarter, the Christian Quarter, the Armenian Quarter and the Muslim Quarter. The sights, sounds and sensations of Old Jerusalem were an onslaught on the senses, and we spent the first couple of days just trying to take it all in. Our immediate task was to find somewhere to stay, and after consulting the tourist information office we were directed to a cheap yet clean hostel in the district of St Mark's, which acts as the boundary between the Christian and Jewish quarters. We immediately began to explore the districts and found each one unique. The Jewish Quarter was the most affluent - restoration work had been extensive, and all the sandstone had been blasted clean. Throughout this Quarter, beautiful illuminated glass spheres had been erected to light the way at night, and most of the buildings and fortifications were floodlit. Narrow walkways wound their way through subterranean passages and huge shop windows had been inserted into cavern walls displaying expensive religious artefacts, solid gold candlesticks and *objets d'art*.

This Quarter is also home to the Wailing Wall, where thousands of devout Jews congregate daily to offer prayers. The wall lies at the base of the Temple Mount and the Dome of the Rock, the third most sacred place in the Muslim world, which had originally been the site of the Jewish Temple at the heart of ancient Judea. This temple was the gravitational centre of the Jewish religion until the Romans sacked it in 70AD as an act of retribution following a failed uprising, and the Jewish nation subsequently scattered. Unfortunately for the Jews, the very same place also marks the spot where, according to the Islamic tradition, the prophet Mohammed - during a particularly intense religious experience in the company of the Angel Gabriel - ascended into heaven, and over the centuries it become a major place of worship for the Muslim world. Consequently, the Wailing Wall is as close as worshipping Jews are allowed to get to the site of their old temple.

The Muslim Quarter is made up mainly of narrow cobbled streets, vegetable market stalls, and souvenir shops selling everything from Christian icons to olive wood chess sets and gold jewellery. It was impossible to walk a single yard without being accosted by eager salesmen. Some of them tried to physically drag us into their shops, undeterred by our protestations and pleas of poverty, although, as time went by and our faces became more familiar to them, this ceased.

Palestinians owned all the shops and businesses here of course, and they were by far the friendliest and warmest inhabitants of Jerusalem, compared to the Jewish fraternity who, it has to be said, were consistently cold and distant, and sometimes downright rude and hostile. Illuminated by the bright sunshine, the scenes within the Muslim Quarter took on the quality of a Tintin comic strip as the inhabitants conducted their daily business, leading fully laden donkeys through the streets toward the markets, or balancing wicker baskets filled with tangerines on their heads, bartering with neighbours and potential customers alike at such a speed it made you breathless just listening to it. Whenever we walked through the district, all these impressions would invariably cause me to break into a beaming smile. They were all so alive, so very much in the present; even the most normal and mundane tasks and routines seemed to be fresh and dynamic.

The Armenian Quarter had little to endear it to the curious, save for the rather interesting sandstone architecture. It seemed to me at the time to consist mainly of modest private dwellings and I always had the feeling I was intruding, so I tended to spend very little time there, usually passing through it on my way somewhere else. The people inhabiting this quarter were generally retired, elderly folk who seemed to spend their time chatting or playing backgammon. The churches and chapels here were rather simple, modest structures, and it was by far the quietest area of the Old City.

Finally there was the Christian Quarter, which I found somewhat depressing. The architecture was consistent with what you'd expect to find in the Middle Ages, probably a legacy of the Crusades when the European Christian knights had controlled the city before it was retaken by the Moors. At the centre of this Quarter is the Holy Sepulchre, alleged to be the place where Jesus of Nazareth was crucified, and the interior is very dark with only the barest of soft lighting to illuminate the gloom. It's decorated with the customary Christian themes of death and suffering, and it felt strange for me to find myself standing at the very centre of the Christian world - although Catholics would no doubt argue that this dubious honour belongs to Rome. I was informed that every Christian denomination had access to the Sepulchre, although during the entire period of my stay in Jerusalem I only ever saw Mass conducted by the Greek Orthodox Church. The sight of the Greek priests conducting services in their black tussocks and handsome beards, their hair banded in short ponytails as they wafted giant incense burners before them, sat better with me. I felt more of a connection, despite being unable to understand a single word, and their rituals seemed to exhibit a higher degree of mysticism compared to the more perfunctory Anglican or Catholic services that I was used to.

My favourite time of day in Old Jerusalem was the evening. All the bazaars and souvenir shops had closed, leaving the cobbled streets practically deserted save for the massive cat population, which could be very vocal after dark - especially if they happened to be fighting, and falling into your path from the rooftops. The back streets were always blissfully free of revellers, and even the bars were hidden; if you didn't know the exact location of a particular bar, you could easily walk by without spotting it. These streets, largely unchanged for thousands of years, provided a resonant ambience, and it wasn't difficult to relate to Jerusalem as the holiest city in the world, regardless of which faith touched you. Sally and I would often walk these streets for hours discussing theology, philosophy, magic or mysticism; it was something we never tired of.

Mark and Sally, Jerusalem 1986.

While sitting in the courtyard overlooking the Wailing Wall for the first time, we were approached by a plain clothes Israeli security agent who quizzed us on our reasons for being there. We would often be challenged in this manner whenever we ventured into the Jewish Quarter, and the first question was invariably, "Are you Jews?" Answering negatively seemed to be an open invitation for rudeness, something that never ceased to irritate us. Each occurrence seemed unwarranted and completely unprovoked, although one can never tell what the true circumstances are behind such behaviour. Maybe they'd had bad experiences with backpackers? Theft, perhaps? Or maybe something worse. Notwithstanding, the relentless antipathy we endured was wearing. On one occasion, we walked into a tobacconist's to ask for directions to a nearby bank, whereupon the old man behind the counter became quite violent, seizing his walking stick and waving it at us. "I'm telling you nothing!" he screamed. "Get out of my shop, get out before I call for the police!" When it came to rudeness, public servants and bank employees were similarly consistent, and they, too, would seriously tax our patience. Neither of us forged a single, lasting friendship amongst the Jewish community during our stay in Jerusalem, and Israel is the only country I have visited where this has been the case.

There is a recognised psychiatric condition, generally referred to as Jerusalem Syndrome, which, at its most extreme, can manifest itself as a form of religious mania. Consequently some people, allegedly under the influence of this condition, have been known to attack the sales vendors who hover around the entrance to the Holy Sepulchre during the afternoons, shouting things like "Moneychangers! Blasphemers!" I hung around there myself in the hope that I'd see it happen for real, but I was unlucky.

One deluded young American Jew even tried to re-take the Temple Mount single-handedly, and was almost shot dead in the process. It's easy to understand how people could get carried away. The ambience within the Old City walls was extremely powerful - history and myth seemed to scream at you from the very walls. Beyond those walls and out across the western hemisphere, religion had become something of a dead, dry husk to most, corrupted by politics and the desire for authority and control, yet here, the heart of God - in a variety of guises - was still beating, and the reverberations of that heartbeat were all around to see. Passions ran very high in such an atmosphere, and the prejudices between Jews and Palestinians, in particular, ran deep.

Just how deep was brought home to me one afternoon after Sally and I decided to pay a visit to the Chapel of the Holocaust on Mount Zion. Although I was familiar with the subject of the holocaust and the many horrors around it, nothing I had previously encountered was sufficient preparation for the harrowing experience of the Chapel itself. After ten minutes I had to leave the building, and I sat weeping while the custodian, silent in his understanding, looked on.

Later that afternoon, in a rather sombre mood, Sally and I were sitting at the summit of the Mount of Olives looking down on the Old City. The view across Jerusalem was spectacular, and we'd come to frequent this spot to the point where we became known by the Palestinian regulars. This particular afternoon, noticing that I was more subdued than usual, some of the locals seemed concerned and asked what was wrong. I told them that I'd been to the Chapel of the Holocaust and it had badly shaken me. "Six million people!" I sighed, shaking my head.

One young Palestinian - a churlish, unpleasant kid who was always beating his donkey with a stick - looked at me, grinned and said, "They should have killed them all." While this is perhaps an extreme example, it illustrates the depth of hatred that exists for the state of Israel in some quarters and on practically every border.

Israel, on the other hand, had allowed matters of defence and security to make it into exactly the kind of fascist state that had almost brought about the extinction of its people in Europe. The regular treatment of the Palestinians at the hands of the patrolling soldiers was nothing short of outrageous. By way of illustration, Sally and I came out of the hostel one morning to find a large crowd of Palestinians chanting outside the local police station, which lay directly by the Jaffa Gate. Apparently, a family of Palestinians had been killed the previous night when their house had been set on fire in revenge for the murder of an Israeli student the week before, and every shop and bazaar in the city had been closed in protest. Finally, tiring of this peaceful, albeit passionate demonstration, the officers sent troops in, who then proceeded to disperse the unarmed civilian protesters by chasing them through the narrow streets, beating them with batons, and then forcing them to open their shops or face immediate arrest.

Despite such tensions, Sally and I felt quite at ease in our new surroundings and continued to explore the city. One afternoon as we approached the Via Dolorosa, the route that marks the twelve Stations of the Cross established by Jesus on his execution march, an elderly Palestinian gentleman who was touting himself as a guide approached us. We patiently explained that we weren't the sort of tourists that could afford to splash out on a personal guide and that we were quite happy to find our way around by ourselves, but he wouldn't take no for an answer[1].

After ensuring he understood that we could pay him little, if anything, we finally agreed to let him lead us around. Our personal tour turned out to be a very enjoyable afternoon, and he'd learned his script very well. Eventually, he led us onto the sacred mount where the Dome of the Rock stands, and we finally got to see what all the fuss was about. A huge mosque with a domed, copper roof that can be seen for miles (known as the

---

1. Whenever you pleaded poverty in the face of a person's insistent effort to sell you something, they either didn't believe you, or it seemed that the concept of having little or no money to chuck around was hopelessly beyond them. Not wishing to appear ruder than necessary, we would accelerate away at a brisk pace, but sometimes even this ploy was unsuccessful, as they'd simply follow and badger us until you caved in.

Mosque of Umar, after the Caliph who inspired it) marks the Dome of the Rock. The outside is covered with beautiful mosaic tiles, while the interior is carpeted with the finest woven Persian rugs.

After removing our shoes, we went inside and saw the piece of sandstone that is allegedly the very spot from where the Prophet Mohammad ascended to heaven. Unfortunately, it is also alleged to be the very spot upon which Abraham, the father of the twelve tribes of Israel, built the stone altar on which to sacrifice his son Isaac at God's behest, only for God to stop him at the last minute and tell him it had merely been a test. Abraham was then shown a vision of the city that would one day occupy the place where he stood, and eventually become the centre of the Jewish world.

As I examined the sacred rock, walking beneath it by way of a specially constructed cave, I was astounded that something no larger than your average grand piano could be the cause of so much strife and anguish, and I found myself almost wishing that someone would blow it to smithereens once and for all.

We'd spend most of our evenings engrossed in conversation in the ancient olive groves by the gardens of Gethsemane at the foot of the Mount of Olives, beyond the Old City walls. One afternoon - after taking some photographs of the Church of the Magdalene, with its Russian-style domed spires resplendent in the afternoon rain beneath the curves of a rainbow - we decided to walk to the summit. It had been a rather steep climb to the top, but the view from the observation area made the effort worthwhile, and it was as we sat looking down on the Old City that we had our first encounter with Ali.

Ali was a young Palestinian, around the age of twenty, with a quick wit, a fine sense of humour and a warm, friendly manner. Over the following week we saw rather a lot of him. He invited us to dine with him one evening, suggesting that we build a fire on the mountainside at a spot he knew, and he was as interested in our reasons for being there as we were to know what growing up in the shade of the Holy City had been like. We were never short of topics for conversation, and very soon a great affection began to blossom between the three of us - though as usual, on discovering that Sally and I were travelling as close friends, it was Sally who attracted most of the attention. As he came to know us better Ali made a point of taking us around his village, which was situated on the far side of the mountain's summit, and introducing us to members of his family, all of whom greeted us warmly and invited us to drink or eat with them. His grandfather was a wise, grand looking old man, and on learning that my philosophies were intrinsically Christian, he was keen to engage me in conversation - much to Ali's irritation, who kept trying to steer the conversation away from religious topics. When it comes to religion, I have no prejudices whatsoever, and I'm always comfortable discussing matters of a theological nature. As such, each discussion I had was relaxed, congenial and good-humoured, even where there was disagreement, which is as it should be.

Not everyone I met could be taken at face value, however. Other members of Ali's extended family included two cousins, an older, cannier man who called himself Mike who was something of a community leader amongst the younger element, and his constant companion, Walid, a huge bear of a guy who, despite the constant heat of the sun, only ever wore a brown leather box jacket and collared shirts. I don't recall exactly how we happened to be introduced to them - we were sat talking with Ali on the mountain and suddenly they were there. From that moment on, they were a constant presence. As we gradually got to know them better, they gave us wider tours of the village, taking us to local bars and cafés, and Mike even invited us to his home. He lived in a large, detached house complete with microwave oven, large-screen TV sets and a very expensive looking Technics hi-fi system, all of which he proudly showed off. I was curious to see hung on the wall a framed photograph of Mike shaking hands with the late King Hussein of Jordan. When I asked him about this, though, he became somewhat less demonstrative. Mike would offer his services as a guide to many of the tourists that regularly stopped at the summit, but I could see that this work was far from steady, and I wondered how he could afford the kind of lifestyle he seemed to enjoy. That was until I discovered he supplemented his meagre earnings by selling smuggled contraband to the UN troops stationed on the Mount of Olives.

They were all very interested in hearing about what life was like in England, and were particularly bemused by the notion of the dole and state benefits. "Wait! Let me see if I understand you! If you don't work, the government gives you money to buy food and pay your rent? Is that what you're saying?"

Smiling at his apparent astonishment, I told him this was true, but that it wasn't quite as simple or as idealistic as it sounded.

"And you wanted to leave? Why?"

This of course was a very tricky question to answer so I spoke of the wider implications of living in Thatcher's Britain, the Americanisation of our culture, mass consumerism and so on.

"Things are much simpler here," he mused. "If you don't work, you starve."

It transpired that Walid was a US green card holder, and that he regularly made trips to and from the United States, where his wife lived. I was a little confused as he proudly showed off his ID cards and the photo of his American wife. "I met her when she came over on a holiday a few years ago," he beamed.

"Why don't you live with her there?" I asked him, unable to restrain my curiosity.

"I have responsibilities here," he stated flatly.

"So why then hasn't she moved here?" I persisted.

Walid laughed. "What good would that do us?" he said, and the others joined the laughter - all except for Ali, I noticed, who was unusually quiet and reserved.

Mike introduced me to the dubious virtues of Arrack, a kind of Schnapps that tastes like Pernod, though much stronger, and I ended up drinking a little more than was good for me. On impulse, I suddenly darted off down the mountain toward the Old City, only to be caught by Ali about a yard short of a sheer cliff face. I didn't touch Arrack again.

One or two of the guys began singing Palestinian folk songs, then they indicated that it was now my turn. Not really knowing anything traditional, I opted for an old ballad from my childhood. Everyone present listened attentively and appreciatively and they were very complimentary when the song was done. I was surprised to see, however, that Ali was crying.

By now the mountain was in darkness, and as I gazed down at the neon lights of Old and New Jerusalem, I couldn't help making a comparison with Tandle Hill, remembering the night I'd spent with the others that summer five years before. I noticed that, as that night, we were a company of six, albeit a different complement altogether, and I laughed gently to myself as this thought struck me. Who would have thought back then that I would be standing here now, gazing down on the Holy of Holies?

I'd been somewhat concerned to see Ali in tears, so I discreetly asked Sally to take him to one side and make sure he was all right. I turned my head to see that Ali was now standing next to me on the wall of the observation point as I gazed down at Jerusalem. He was no longer crying but he seemed serious and deeply troubled. "She is a very beautiful girl," he said to me suddenly, breaking a silence that wasn't uncomfortable. I agreed that indeed, she was. "But you are not lovers?"

"Well, I love her as a friend, Ali. She's a close friend."

"She loves you very much too, my friend," said Ali, now looking directly into my eyes.

"I know," was all I could say in response.

"Listen to me, my friend - you must not stay here. You must..." Ali was interrupted by the arrival of Walid laughing loudly at some joke or other, his head darting between each of us in turn, and Ali clammed up.

The time came to say goodnight, and Walid dutifully offered to drive Sally and I back down the mountain in his car, letting us out at the Jaffa Gate, and from there we made our way back to our lodgings. We found ourselves spending more and more time with Mike and Walid in the days that followed, it seemed that every time we turned around they were there. However, we were never to see Ali again.

15. A STRANGER IN THE DARK

The next morning over breakfast, Sally and I discussed the events of the previous night. We'd left Mike and Walid at the Jaffa Gate, thanking them for what had been a memorable night, but now our thoughts were of Ali: how strangely upset he'd seemed, and the cryptic things that he'd said. Sally told me that during their conversations alone he'd also said one or two strange things, although again he had refused to elaborate on what it was exactly that was upsetting him.

In truth, our friendship with Mike, Walid and the rest of the Mount of Olives posse had begun to intrude on a very pleasant routine. Whenever we were in their company, they always seemed to make a point of arranging appointments for the following afternoon or evening. Sally and I were loath to decline, not wishing to be rude in the face of such open generosity and warmth. Eventually we did start declining their invitations, but our excuses always seemed rather lame, and would invariably be met with a vigorous insistence that was extremely difficult to disregard.

The backpackers' hostel where we were staying served its purpose as a cheap place to lay our heads and stow our clothing and bags, but otherwise we spent very little time there. With so many people coming and going, it was inevitable that some would be less than scrupulous, and after I noticed one or two things had gone missing, we began to seriously consider finding alternative accommodation. On hearing this, Mike suggested that we consider renting a house on the mountainside. He went on to say that he knew of at least two Americans who had done the same thing, and that rents, when converted to western currency, were amazingly cheap. Furthermore, he could probably arrange both a suitable house and a discount on the rent, thanks to his family contacts. Sally and I agreed that this seemed an attractive proposition, so I told Mike we that were keen to proceed.

By now we were spending so much time in Mike's company that Sally and I began to miss our evenings together, walking the streets of the old city or sitting in our favourite spot by the Garden of Gethsemane. All our questions regarding the whereabouts of Ali were at first met with quizzical expressions and a feigned failure to understand. Later, all we'd get by way of a response were dismissive grunts, or vague explanations of how Ali was off somewhere visiting a sick relative.

At the same time, their questions to us became more probing. What airline were we flying with? Did our families know where we were and what we were doing? Had we sent any postcards home? Mike told us that he had relatives living in London; it wouldn't be a problem to deliver a present to them on our return journey home would it? Save him the cost of the postage? I just smiled politely and kept my thoughts to myself. It did beg the question, though: what it was about Sally and I that they found so fascinating? Why, of all the backpackers and western travellers that constantly came and went, had they chosen to take us under their wing? What had we done to deserve their constant attention and generosity?

One obvious answer had been staring me in the face, but I'd been too naïve and carried away by our little adventure to see it. Sally told me of the physical advances Mike was making towards her whenever my attention was drawn elsewhere, and how she had to constantly fend him off, though the full extent of Mike's nuisances didn't become clear until much later. In truth, Sally had only hinted at Mike's behaviour, not wishing to worry me unduly. She'd lived alone in London for quite a long time, and despite her seemingly naïve demeanour, knew how to handle herself. Nevertheless, I promised myself that if we did end up staying on the mountain, I'd be a lot more vigilant in future.

The next day I suggested to Sally that, rather than meet Mike as arranged, we stay within the vicinity of the Old City. We spent most of the afternoon taking photographs. The best and cheapest falafel around was sold at the bus station, and we made our way there by way of the Golden Gate. As we drew near the Gate, however, we ran into another of the mountain summit regulars, a guy named Mohammed who we'd met once or twice while in the company of Ali. Mohammed was a young Palestinian who had been born deaf and was practically mute, though he had learned to speak a little English.

He immediately recognised us, and in his usual combination of sign language and barely audible articulation, kept insisting that we follow him to the bus station and take the regular bus up the mountain. Sally and I preferred to walk, and we had new film for the camera, so despite his vigorous insistence, we steadfastly declined. During this frantic discourse, Mohammed repeatedly pointed to the cross that I wore around my neck, the one that Fenella had given to me for my birthday, and as he did this, the words "Christian! Christian! Me too! Me too!" were just about understood.

Having failed to persuade us to catch the bus, Mohammed next tried to guide us towards the road that led to the mountain, seemingly unable to grasp the fact that we intended to use the rougher, less well-known track up the slope. There was no getting rid of him, either, so Sally and I eventually resigned ourselves to his company.

The track eventually led to the summit through an ancient, Christian graveyard where Ali had taken us one afternoon before his disappearance. I asked Mohammed if he knew what had become of Ali, but this was met with a grunt and a shrug of the shoulders. Once at the summit we encountered Mike, who was engaged in conversation with a small band of UN troops. He embraced us both and then, in turn, Mohammed, but he wasn't quite quick enough for me not to notice the money that he very discreetly placed in Mohammed's hands, whereupon Mohammed walked happily away.

We walked to one of the village taverns to drink Turkish coffee. Neither of us had been there before, and again, as we sat at the large table with Mike and one or two others, I was aware of the stares our presence was attracting from the other customers. These were mainly directed at Sally, and a cursory glance around revealed that she was the only girl in the room. Later, we strolled around the village and began to notice that there seemed to be a concerted effort to split us up, but having observed it, we made sure that they failed. During our conversations the subject of renting a house for the next few months came up again, but by this time I was growing less sure that I wanted his help. I think he sensed this, because he suddenly told me that he would introduce me to someone who could assist in this regard the following night, and made us promise to meet at the foot of the road that lay on the edge of Gethsemane.

That afternoon Mike was commissioned to act as a guide to a coach full of tourists, so after visiting the nearby Church of the Ascension, we made our way back to the Old City. Once there, we re-established our routine of walking the narrow streets and visiting some of our favourite places, before finally returning to our lodgings. As we entered the hostel, our landlady, who was seated at her kitchen table with a few members of her family, suddenly became quite animated. She beckoned us to sit down, asking where we'd been. "Some men were here looking for you," she told us in hushed, dramatic tones. "They asked for you, they knew your names."

Sally and I exchanged glances and I explained, after listening to her descriptions of the men, that they were our friends from the mountain.

"How did they know we were staying here?" Sally asked me, which stopped me short. We certainly hadn't told them. When they'd given us a lift down the mountain the previous week, they'd dropped us outside the Jaffa Gate, well away from the hostel.

"They search everywhere!" our host replied on hearing the question. "They search every hostel in the Old City looking for you, I know because I see the other women every day at the market and some of them know these people. You must be careful. How do you know these people?"

I was mystified. Why would they go to such trouble just because we'd failed to meet them that morning? Furthermore, why hadn't Mike mentioned it when we had eventually made our way to the summit? In the days that followed, there was a subtle change in our landlady's demeanour. Her tone became a little frostier, and although she never outwardly displayed a desire that we should leave her hostel, it was implied by her manner and the way she would examine us as we came and went.

In retrospect, it is as if a veil had been placed before my eyes, blotting out the light of logic and reason. I loved being in Jerusalem. I didn't want anything to interfere with the calm and the spiritual lucidity that roaming the streets of Jerusalem invoked. Sally felt exactly the same way, despite one or two unwelcome advances, which hadn't seemed that serious a concern at the time. We both agreed that we'd never felt more alive, so connected with the world. One day in Jerusalem felt like a week in any other place, such were the mad, chaotic and exciting sensations that were cascading all around us.

Pushing aside our doubts, Sally and I sat by the Garden of Gethsemane where we'd arranged to meet Mike, and again we discussed the possibility of renting a house on the mountainside. By now, the notion had taken a grip on my imagination and I was eager to find something suitable and move out of the hostel. We decided to ask Mike one more time if he'd made any progress in this regard. If he hadn't, then we'd make our own enquiries. It was as we sat discussing this that something curious happened.

Neither of us heard the man approach. He spoke, we turned, and there he was. Dark was fast approaching so it was hard to see him clearly in the shadows, but I could make out enough to think that he looked oddly out of place. He was obviously wearing robes of some kind, which seemed to be a mixture of wool and cotton, but they were unlike the usual attire I'd become accustomed to during my time in Jerusalem. Then there was the hat or hood that partially covered his face, which looked Peruvian rather than Jewish or Arabic. I could also discern, despite the fading light, that he was completely clean shaven, when practically every man in the Old City, myself included, was bearded, or at the very least sporting a thick moustache. His voice was unusually gentle, and he expressed himself in flawless English without the slightest trace of an accent.

Standing on the edge of the shadows, he introduced himself as Isaac and asked what we were doing in Gethsemane after dark - not in such a way as to suggest we were trespassing or breaking any rules, but as a civilised, polite enquiry. In kind, we explained that we were there to meet friends. "Ah yes," he said, as if he'd known this all along, "your friends." Without elaborating, he continued, "I'm thinking that perhaps it's time you left Jerusalem." I told him that, on the contrary, we were hoping to find a place on the mountain where we could settle for a few months, but he very politely swept this aside. "No, the right thing to do is to leave, now. Make for Haifa, rather than Tel Aviv, you won't get out that way. Yes, Haifa, there are many English-speaking people in Haifa. There's a festival in progress there right now, you'll blend in well. Don't tell your friends though - allow them to believe you're continuing with your plans, and leave before dawn. Don't take a taxi - leave as discreetly as you can."

Surprisingly, neither of us uttered a word of protest, nor did we curtly suggest that the stranger mind his own business. We simply accepted this advice as if it were the most natural thing in the world, and for a long time after I bitterly regretted that I hadn't previously been able to snap out of what, with hindsight, had seemed like a mild form of hypnosis. Bemused as we were, neither of us thought to question him further, instead we simply thanked him and said we'd think about it. "Yes, well, good," he concluded. "And if you need me I live here, well," he paused, "over there," and waved his arm in the vague direction of the olive groves behind him.

The strange thing is, afterwards neither of us could remember seeing him walk away, so we were left with no idea in which direction his dwelling lay. As quickly as he had approached, he was gone. "What the fuck was that about?" I asked Sally, laughing, and, joining my laughter, she replied that she hadn't the faintest idea.

Mike and Walid arrived about twenty minutes later than arranged, and we climbed into the back of the car as usual. Mike asked us if we'd been waiting for very long, and without going into detail I remarked that we'd just met a rather curious local who went by the name of Isaac. I might as well have suddenly announced that I was an undercover operative for Mossad, such was the frenzied reaction that my casual remark provoked. They exchanged heated words with each other in Palestinian, interjecting occasionally to question us both in English. "Someone met you by Gethsemane? Someone spoke with you?"

"Yes."

"What did you say?"

"We just told him that we were meeting you."

"What did he look like?"

We gave them our vague description.

"He lives locally?"

"So he said!"

"Where?"

We told them we weren't sure, but that he'd indicated that he lived close by, perhaps in one of the small houses that lay on the roadside leading to the summit. They told us this was impossible, they knew everyone there, and no-one by the name of Isaac, or indeed, bearing any resemblance to the figure we described, lived in those houses. "Why is it so important?" I asked.

Pausing for a second to examine my face, as if a switch had been thrown, in total contradiction to their previous reaction, Mike stopped short. "It isn't!" he said, waving his arm dismissively, before changing the subject. This didn't silence Walid though, who continued to jabber at Mike in Palestinian.

Despite not knowing a single word of Palestinian beyond 'thank you', 'you're welcome', 'hello', and 'goodnight', I experienced a feeling of quickening dread. I knew immediately that Mike and Walid's heated exchange meant that Isaac's advice was to be heeded. It seemed to me that our companions were most concerned that someone wholly unfamiliar to them (and, therefore, beyond their control) had engaged us in conversation. Furthermore, it was highly likely that, not only would this person remember the encounter, but also that we'd told him specifically we were there to meet them.

Of course I said nothing beyond the boundaries of polite, casual conversation and I was careful not to let Sally see that I was troubled, lest she became frightened. But inside my mind was racing, and deep within me, I could feel a torrent of energy slowly building; like water behind a dam that was about to burst. In spite of all this, I was determined to maintain a facade of absolute calm.

As we sat there yet another procession of people, torches blazing, passed somewhere below us on the hillside. "Another moonlight ceremony?" I asked, carefully masking the cynicism in my voice. Mike gave the procession a cursory inspection before firing a quick glance in my direction. "Yes," he said, dismissively, and began conversing with Walid in Palestinian again, as the car's cassette player droned on - 'The Final Countdown' by Europe. I'll never forget it, they played the track over and over again.

This time, however, I caught a glimpse of the casket the procession was carrying. It was indeed a ceremony - a funeral, but what sort of funeral takes place in the middle of the night? I sensed that the interment taking place was at best covert, and at worst illegal. I told Mike and Walid that we were eager to get out of the hostel, and if we'd found nothing suitable by the following weekend then we would head north, to Nazareth. Again, it was as if a bombshell had been dropped and they both erupted into frenzied discussion, which my mysterious internal Babel fish obligingly interpreted as "it's now or never". Mike leapt from the car, while Walid tried to smile at us reassuringly. Mike returned a couple of minutes later.

"We go now to see someone!" he announced and fired up the engine.

We drove a little way from the Old City, along a winding road on the far side of the mountain, before turning onto a secluded dirt track that led to a recently constructed, featureless, grey concrete house. At the door stood an elderly man who, judging by his appearance, had dressed in rather a hurry. His hair was uncombed and dishevelled, the garment he wore looked more like a nightshirt than a robe and hadn't been buttoned correctly, and on his feet were a scruffy pair of old carpet slippers. The old man seemed extremely nervous and ill at ease. Mike did most of the talking, and as usual, they conversed in rapid-fire Palestinian. I watched them intently and while the detail eluded me, it wasn't difficult to get the gist of what was being said. I was used to seeing and hearing Palestinians haggle, and this was something different. The two of them were desperately trying to persuade the old man to agree to whatever it was they wanted of him, presumably the use of his empty house, but the old man seemed agitated and disturbed. I wondered to myself if he was worried that his compliance might well lead to a visit from the Israeli security forces. However, the old man's vocal expression and body language led me to believe that he was torn between his fear and respect for Mike, and his fear of officialdom.

The discussion continued, and it seemed that Mike was winning the war of words. After a while he turned to us and said that the old man had agreed to rent us the house for just $60 a month. This seemed insanely cheap, even by the standards of Israel's devastated economy, and I said as much, but Mike explained that the old man was a close friend of the family and was doing him a favour. The old man didn't look like a close friend of the family to me, however. He looked like someone who was scared out of his wits. I turned to face Sally and noted the flicker of alarm and concern as I told them that the arrangement sounded wonderful, and that we'd begin making preparations to move in immediately. Obviously I had no intention of doing any such thing, but I was determined that our hosts would not sense even the slightest note of doubt in my voice. Once we were on the move again, I thanked Mike and Walid for their help, but said that I was feeling the effects of too much sun that day and had decided to return to the Old City earlier than we usually did, asking Sally if that was all right by her, and she silently nodded. Mike and Walid drove us to the Jaffa Gate but, unusually, they parked the car and accompanied us all the way to the hostel, even leading the way to the entrance. They embraced us as we said goodnight, and then turned and headed back toward the car. While they were still only a few steps away, I asked Mike how he'd known we were staying at this particular hostel? He turned and I caught a flicker of hesitation as he pulled the first explanation he could think of from the air. "You told me the night you drank the Arrack."

"Oh yeah, course I did." I smiled and waved goodnight. We waited in the lobby of the hostel until I was sure they were gone and then I suggested that we talk over a beer. There were things we urgently needed to discuss.

The bar, which lay a little further down St Mark's on the edge of the Jewish Quarter, was very busy but we were able to find a free table in a quiet secluded corner. Once the beers arrived, I started to lay it all out and when I did, it came like a torrent. The well of energy inside me seem to burst its banks and it felt almost as if I was relaying the information, as opposed to joining the dots myself.

What had happened to Ali? I didn't believe that any harm had come to him - he was a member of the community and was surrounded by his extended family, but he had tried to warn us of something, although probably because he was family to most of these people, he hadn't been prepared to elaborate. Still, I believed that his affection and concerns were real, especially for Sally. Why, then, if he wished to warn us without alerting his family, had he not discreetly passed us a note? The explanation for this was simple - while Ali spoke very good English, he couldn't write it. I wouldn't go as far as to say they suspected Ali of trying to warn us, but they may have considered it a possibility. Once Ali had unwittingly drawn us there, they manoeuvred him out of the picture and moved in to manipulate the friendship.

Who was Mike *really*? We knew that he ran a lucrative black market with the UN troops at the nearby base, while masquerading as a tourist guide. Mike was clearly wealthy, then, yet wasn't extravagant in the way he lived. He dressed modestly, and apart from the usual trappings of western decadence - a hi-fi, a large-screen television set and the like - he hadn't seemed much different to many of the other locals scratching a living from tourism around the Old City. He didn't own a car either - the rusty old Chrysler belonged to Walid. What did he do with all the money, then? It was possible that he was one of those types that enjoyed making money for money's sake, squirrelling it away for less profitable times or for his retirement and not flaunting his hidden wealth - but I didn't think so. I can usually spot those types from a mile away, and Mike certainly didn't strike me as one of them. Besides, his situation would demand a great deal of discretion. Israeli intelligence were no fools when it came to spotting suspicious locals - all Palestinians seemed to be miscreants as far as they were concerned. Large amounts of western currency going in or out of bank accounts would probably be noticed.

    I came to believe that Mike's insistence on dealing only with western currency was the key, and it went beyond securing a thirty percent discount in a hi-fi store. My newly invigorated instincts told me that this was his role, and what's more, it was a role he was proud of - he could never resist an occasional boast, which, until now, had passed me by. Eventually, I reasoned, all this foreign currency would then be spirited away over the border to the Lebanon or Syria. You couldn't buy serious shit with shekels, and serious shit was exactly what was needed to fight the underground war against the Israeli occupation. Weapons! Our friend Mike was an errand boy for Hamas. What did he ask us one time? Would we mind delivering a present to some family members in London and save him the postage - after enquiring what airline we were flying with. Yeah, right! The kind of present that went tick-tick boom! Mike had been fishing from the beginning, all the while trying to ascertain how these two naïve travellers could best serve the greater purpose. Let's face it, you don't get your photograph taken shaking hands with King Hussein of Jordan unless you have significant political connections or influence.

    And what of Walid? He and Mike were practically inseparable. Wannabe? Hopeful sidekick? Hardly! The man was a Green Card holder, he could travel to and from the US at will. He did this regularly, and it's worth noting that plane tickets to America didn't come cheap. He kept a wife and a house there, and that didn't come cheap either. Domestic bliss was the perfect cover, but a cover for *what*? Was he part of an active cell? Or maybe, like Mike, he was involved in raising funds for the cause? Even the most loving wife would find it difficult to tolerate such prolonged absences on the part of her husband. He didn't love her, that was obvious - he'd even joked about it when I asked if he planned to bring her to Jerusalem. "What good would that do us?" Quite! They had no children together or any semblance of a life, and yet they weren't separated as such. It was conceivable that she, too, was a sympathiser. In any event, it was clear that their marriage was a sham. Once in possession of a Green Card, there was no telling how many people had been able to use it to set up shop in the States.

What could they want from us? Their encroachment on our budding friendship with Ali had emerged from little more than curiosity. Once they realised the depth of our apparent naïvety, however, Mike had mused upon ways it could be used to his advantage, hence the probing questions that Sally and I had earlier been subjected to. He'd become especially interested when we'd entertained the idea of renting a house on the mountain for a few months. Anyone capable of doing that had to be carrying around a fair amount of currency. Of course, he had no idea of how much money we had, and he wasn't going to come right out and ask us. He may also have been unaware that the western currency I did have was in the form of travellers cheques, I certainly didn't tell him. Even if he had been aware of this, I doubt it would have presented much in the way of a problem once he had his hands on my passport. Manipulating passports and bypassing currency security restrictions were child's play to these people, especially if the original owner was no longer around to blow the whistle.

In the light of all this, what had Mike planned for us? Obviously we were meant to disappear, but the sudden evanescence of western visitors would very likely lead to swarms of Israeli soldiers descending on the community like ants. This was not the sort of attention Mike and Walid would have relished. In any event, making us disappear while we were free to wander around the crowded city of Old Jerusalem every day (under the watchful gaze of every street vendor in town) would have been problematic at best. Better to coax me out to the far side of the mountain, where they could keep tighter control on the situation.

Then there was the matter of our landlady at the hostel. She'd initially been friendly and concerned, but she was a Palestinian, and her subtle shift of attitude from friendly to wary in the wake of the enquires about us told me she knew who these people were, and that theirs was unwelcome attention. She wouldn't readily co-operate with Israeli security against a local Hamas cell. Ultimately, backpackers come and go every day - she could credibly deny all knowledge of us with total impunity.

And then there was Mohammed. It was possible, of course, that Mike had simply been rewarding him that afternoon he'd accompanied us up the mountain, for running some minor errand in town. However, it was equally possible that he was paying Mohammed for finding us and delivering us to the mountain summit after we'd missed our appointment, his search of the hostels having failed to yield results. Meeting Mohammed at the Golden Gate that afternoon may not have been a coincidence. The Golden Gate lay fairly close to the bus station, and having spotted us, he'd stayed with us every inch of the way to the summit. Until, that is, Mike had walked over to us, after which Mohammed had happily left, clutching his wages.

What of Sally? She was a very beautiful girl, as they had all pointed out on numerous occasions. She was barely twenty years old, though with her doleful brown eyes, flawless complexion, silent and alluring manner - concealing a sharp interior - she looked more like a girl in her early teens. A girl like her could be a valuable commodity in some quarters, one that would fetch a handsome price. I think they'd planned another fate entirely for Sally. Furthermore, I think that Ali suspected it, which is why he was in tears that night on the summit. Sally stared at me, thunderstruck. I could see that she was feeling the reverberations of the logic in my words. I carried on.

The old man at the house had been genuinely afraid of Mike, I had no doubt of that. He knew who these people were, and may have known what they were planning to do. Indeed, they might have done it before. Had I gone to an agency to rent a house, or answered advertisements, then this would have alerted more people to our intentions, so they'd stalled me until they could make the necessary preparations. Palestinian mouths were easy for Mike and Walid to silence, but by approaching an official agency we may have presented them with a much trickier scenario to deal with.

Except that now, something had happened - something they hadn't expected. We'd unwittingly fallen into conversation with a local man of whom they had absolutely no knowledge, possibly an informer, or even an Israeli security operative. At the very least, this person was a witness to our existence and presence in Old Jerusalem - someone beyond manipulation or coercion. It was because of this they'd felt the need to move so fast, especially as I was already talking of flying the coop. Who was the stranger? How had he known of the danger we'd placed ourselves in? I had absolutely no idea. It was possible that he was Israeli security, although I personally doubted this. Someone in that line of work would make it their business to blend in, and there wasn't anything typical about this person in the way he dressed or spoke.

Obviously, I had no proof of any of this. There was no real way of knowing whether the thoughts I'd just laid out before Sally represented paranoia, an over-active imagination fuelled by a series of coincidences, or the truth. At any rate, we were not going to hang around long enough to find out. Sally is one of the most intelligent, level-headed companions I've ever had, and I trusted her judgement completely. Acting as a soundboard, she would interject with observations of her own and occasional questions, and by the end we were in agreement. "What are we going to do?" she asked.

"We're leaving!" I stated flatly, "We're going to take the stranger at face value and we're going to do what he suggested." He may only have been the catalyst that set the alarm bells ringing, the gentle nudge that had been needed, but this in itself seemed significant to me, and we were going to act immediately!

The stranger had said we were to leave discreetly, avoiding the taxis. I knew that during the very early hours of the morning the taxis by the Jaffa Gate would be gone, and there would be very few vehicles around. Our plan was to leave before dawn, while it was still dark, and make for Haifa. As an added precaution we would avoid the bus station too, and try to hitch-hike our way to the coast.

Well before daybreak the next morning, we awoke and silently gathered our things. Our account had been settled with the landlady for the rest of the week as I always paid her in advance, so we had no further obligations. Quietly letting ourselves out, we entered the deserted streets of Jerusalem. We slowly made our way to the outskirts of the city, and gradually the number of vehicles we were seeing began to increase. Once we reached the major highway we attempted to hitch-hike, but it proved futile. My guidebook had already hinted that this wasn't a normal way of getting around the country as bus fares were ridiculously cheap. We received many curious stares from drivers as we tried to thumb a lift, but had no takers. They must have reasoned that if we couldn't even afford the meagre bus fares we must have been poorer than the poorest beggars, and not the type of passengers they wanted in their cars.

As we made our way parallel to the highway we saw the distant lights of a large complex and were happy to see a supermarket where we bought bread, cheese, pickles and fresh drinking water for breakfast, before resuming our journey on foot. Soon dawn broke fully into what was to be another hot, dry day, and we finally entered a neighbouring township. Feeling that we'd put enough distance between ourselves and Jerusalem, we headed for the bus station and boarded a bus to Haifa.

Haifa is the major port that serves as Israel's connection to Greece and the Mediterranean, and it's a sprawling, bustling community. After wandering around for about an hour we finally found our way to a tourist information office and enquired about inexpensive places to stay, but were told they were thin on the ground in Haifa and were given a choice of two. The first was a fairly typical backpackers' hostel on the edge of town, while the second was a Christian hostel called Bethel, which was nearer, around thirty minutes walking distance. The woman behind the counter gave us the street plan and marked both of the hostels on the map.

Despite the street map, we found the city unusually difficult to navigate. After about an hour we gave up, and as we were standing on a busy intersection I flagged down a taxi. As usual it was a taxi-share and three others were sat in the back of the cab. I pointed out the place we wished to go and the driver nodded, so we placed our bags in the boot and climbed in. As I did so, I fleetingly caught a glimpse of the taxi's license number, which contained the digits '666'. On seeing this, my paranoia kicked in and I would have changed my mind, had our bags not already been in the car. This had become a bad omen and I was filled with foreboding. As I was to discover, though, it was just one more sign on a trail of breadcrumbs. One by one, the other three passengers disembarked. I noticed that the car was heading for the outskirts of Haifa, which confused me, because according to our information the place we were seeking lay within the city centre. Finally, on a stretch of road that ran parallel to the beach and the sea beyond, the car stopped. The driver climbed out and placed our bags at the side of the road and I paid the fare. "This is Bethel Hostel?" I asked him, doubtfully.

"Yes, Yes," he kept saying, "hostel, yes," and he climbed back into the taxi and drove away.

"Maybe he's brought us to the other hostel," Sally said, looking around, but although we examined the street names and the buildings closely, they resembled nothing that was marked on the street plan.

By now it was getting dark and we were no nearer to our destination, or anywhere else that might offer us a bed for the night. I suggested we go over to the beach, gather our thoughts, eat and drink something and try again later, and Sally agreed. Despite the events of the preceding days and our tiring day roaming around Haifa, we felt relieved now that we were away from the oppressive vibe we'd experienced in Jerusalem. Our spirits rose and we joked a little about our predicament, feeling like undercover agents fleeing enemy territory, waiting for the submarine that would whisk us away from the beach to sanctuary. Glancing around, I noticed a number of what seemed to be observation huts that had been built high above the beach at the summit of iron stairwells, presumably erected as a defence precaution before or during one of Israel's many conflicts with the neighbouring Arab countries. Climbing atop one of them, it crossed my mind that if the hut wasn't locked then we might spend the night there and resume our search for Bethel the next morning.

I was pleased to see it wasn't padlocked, but as I reached for the handle I suddenly experienced an inexplicable feeling of absolute dread. I felt Sally's hand grasp mine and tighten. "What on earth is that?" she whispered.

"What?" I whispered back to her in the darkness.

"That feeling, that horrible feeling." she hissed back. "What is it?"

"You can feel it too?"

"Yes!"

"Let's go."

We turned and climbed quickly down the steps, but instead of subsiding, the dread we experienced intensified to the point where we were on the verge of panic. In a sense I was relieved that Sally could feel it too. However, this suggested that whatever was happening to me was contagious - that it was a part of some wider reality, and that was very worrying.

We began to walk back towards the main road, which by now was quiet, when suddenly we were illuminated by a pair of headlights on full beam. We turned away and began to walk along the beach, whereupon the car started up and began to crawl along parallel to us. Try as I might, I couldn't make out any of the occupants in the darkness. Meanwhile, the car maintained its slow progress, by now keeping its distance but still following at walking pace. Eventually we were relieved to see the lights of what appeared to be a cafeteria ahead of us, so we darted straight inside, bought coffee and settled at a table with a view of the door. The car swung into the cafeteria car park, and stopped. No-one got out.

Unsure of what to do next, I returned to the counter to order more coffee, and a young Israeli engaged me in conversation. His family had moved to Israel from England, he was keen for news of home, and soon the three of us were chatting at the table. He told us that he and some friends from Haifa had been attending a festival in the town the previous night, and he was now making his way home to Tel Aviv in his van. To our great relief, he agreed to give us a lift. Finishing our coffee, we followed the young man to the café's rear exit, and I was pleased to see his van was out of sight of the main car park, around the corner. As we drove away, I could see three dark figures sitting in the car, but they didn't pay the van any attention, and very soon the café was out of sight. The young man obligingly dropped us off at the airport, and we said our goodbyes.

After everything that had happened, Sally and I were relieved to be finally leaving the country. We made our way into the airport to organise our flights home, but the stranger had said we wouldn't get out that way - and he was right. Being only twenty years old, a cheap ticket home was no problem for Sally, but for me, having turned twenty-six, it proved far too expensive. I insisted that Sally buy her ticket and go back to London. My chief concern was for her safety. I profoundly believed that my naïvety had almost got us into serious trouble, but she absolutely refused to go without me.

I'd been led to believe that at the airport currency exchange I'd be able to convert travellers cheques to western currency, but found that, on the contrary, they would only issue shekels. I was exhausted and fed up, and the cashier's rude, unhelpful demeanour made me extremely irritable. "Give me a hundred dollars in shekels, then." I snapped at him. However, I'd pre-signed the entire book of cheques, and I suddenly realised, to my horror, that the cashier had converted all of them. I desperately tried to stop him before he could complete the transaction but he just ignored me and continued anyway. There was no persuading him to cancel the transaction and, feeling totally dejected, I made my way back to Sally.

Somewhat demoralised, we made our way back to the hostel in which we'd spent our first night in Israel. Now that flying home was no longer an option, we learned it was possible to catch a ferry bound for Greece. Once there we could catch the Magic Bus to London. This was sounding like a plan, but when we reckoned the fare, we found we were now short of the amount needed to get to London. We did, however, have enough money to travel as far as Rome, where I could telephone Ken and borrow the money we needed to get us home. There was only one small snag though - the next boat from Haifa didn't leave for another four days. As we'd just used practically all the money we had for the tickets, we had precious little for accommodation and food for the boat journey to Greece. What's more, the journey to Greece consisted of two days travelling deck class, with a further overnight sea voyage after we'd boarded the bus in Athens for Rome.

We walked back into central Haifa, and while Sally seemed relaxed, I was feeling extremely dejected. I was at my lowest ebb since the adventure had begun, and inwardly I was furious at myself for bringing Sally along. As we walked the streets I suddenly stopped in my tracks, sat on a nearby wall, put my head in my hands and came the closest I had ever come to praying for guidance. What had I done bringing us here? What on earth was I thinking?

Sally sat a few feet away, and I could feel her eyes on me as I desperately tried to come up with a plan, when again, out of the blue I felt a rising surge of euphoria and began to receive guidance from the deepest core of my instincts. I found myself compelled to reach into my bag for my copy of the King James Bible. This was a small leather-bound edition that had originally belonged to my grandmother, presented to her when she was a young girl as a prize for writing an essay in Sunday school. When my own mother was young, my grandmother had given it to her, and she'd written her own name and age inside the cover. Finally it had come to me, and I'd carried it around on my travels for a number of years, more as a good luck talisman and family heirloom than as a source of spiritual inspiration. Despite the circumstances and events of the previous months, I'd barely taken it out of my bag during the whole trip. Suddenly I felt compelled to consult it. I opened the bible at random and found myself gazing at the opening chapters of *The Book of Kings*. Again, as before, instruction came as strong impressions rather than words. I wasn't hearing voices in my head; it was more an abstract form of guidance. I stared at the first page. I wasn't travelling alone, was I? No, there were two of us. Turn to Chapter Two, Verse Two; and this is what I read:

> *And Elijah said unto Elisha, tarry here I prey thee; for the Lord has sent me to Bethel. And Elisha said unto him, as the Lord liveth, and as thy soul liveth, I will not leave thee. So they went down to Bethel.*

I was thunderstruck! However, my mysterious guardian angel wasn't finished. Your Christian name is Mark, isn't it? Yes. Turn to the Gospel of St. Mark. What is your favourite number? The number you always connect with? Ever since my childhood obsession with *The Prisoner* this had been the number six. I turned to chapter six. What's your birthday? May 11th. I traced Verse Eleven with my finger and read:

> *And whosoever shall not receive you, nor hear you, when ye depart thence, shake off the dust from under your feet for a testimony against them. Verily I say unto you, it shall be more tolerable for Sodom and Gomorrah in the day of judgement than for that city.*

I closed the Bible, placed it into my bag, and sprang to my feet. "I know what to do!" I announced. "We're making for the Christian hostel in Bethel." When Sally rightly pointed out that we barely had enough shekels to feed ourselves, I confidently told her, "It doesn't matter! I know what to say to them if they refuse us."

Sally saw instantly that my depression had lifted, that I was now full of purpose, and I talked again of the strong instincts that I felt guiding me along the road I'd chosen to follow. On the beach, she'd experienced something of this herself and she spoke of it now, the reality and the horror of it. I told her that in some ways it had been similar to the feeling I'd had that night in Amsterdam, although then it had felt a hundred times more intense.

After walking for only a few minutes we came to a crossroads, and checking the street plan we saw this was the very junction we'd failed to find two days earlier, before the cab had whisked us away to the coast road. Very soon we were standing before the doors of the Bethel Christian hostel. We waited nervously outside while I gathered my thoughts. As sure as I was that we'd been guided here somehow, I'd wanted to psych myself up before I began quoting biblical scripture to people who knew it a hundred times better than I did. Finally, taking a deep breath, we entered and approached the desk. Behind it sat a tall blond guy reading a magazine. I hesitated as his eyes met mine, but as I did so, he said "You're in Haifa to catch the boat, but it doesn't leave for another four days and you don't have money for a place to stay."

I grinned. "This must happen a lot."

"Actually no," he smiled, "but when I looked at you I just knew."

"So you'll help us then?"

"Of course," he replied, still smiling warmly. "It's what we're here for. All we ask is three hours work a day in the garden for the duration of your stay."

Sally and I looked at each other in silent agreement, totally bemused. "Deal!" I said and held out my hand.

"My name's Mark", said the blond guy.

"So is mine, and this is Sally."

The sense of relief was overwhelming.

16. IN THE FOOTSTEPS OF SAUL

Over the next few days, most of our time was spent restoring the dilapidated gardens at Bethel. We worked well beyond the three hours a day expected of us, despite our hosts' attempts to dissuade us. Working in the sunshine felt good, and the improvements we made to the garden were immediately evident. We began making friends at once, as the long-term residents gradually introduced themselves, and each had interesting background stories to tell. There was Eric, an American cop who was taking an extended sick leave. He'd been forced to fire his weapon at a fleeing suspect, wounding him fatally. This had been the only time he'd had to use his sidearm outside a firing range, and he was now trying to reconcile himself with his actions, seeking some kind of redemption through his pilgrimage to the Holy Land.

Then there was Vincent, a young American trying to reconcile his homosexuality with his devout Christian faith. Mary, a young Irish girl, had rejected the dogma of her Irish Catholic upbringing and was attempting to explore her faith on her own terms, much to her parents' consternation and confusion. I remember she was particularly nervous because her parents were due to visit her in Bethel for the first time. They'd convinced themselves that she was in the hands of a religious cult and couldn't be dissuaded unless they could see for themselves. Nothing could have been further from the truth. The long-term residents, along with the young American couple who had established the hostel, were a well-balanced group, undoubtedly deeply touched by their passion but at the same time projecting a semblance of cool that I've found sadly lacking amongst Christians in general. There wasn't the slightest degree of piety or intolerance towards others, nor did they exhibit the need to ram their message down anybody's throat. They did make us promise to return and visit them again one day, but sadly it's a promise I've not yet had the opportunity to make good on.

The gardens around Bethel now completely restored, we stood among the small company reviewing our work. Everyone was delighted with what we'd done. As a parting gift, Sally and I were each given a small envelope, but were told not to open them until we were on board the ship bound for

Greece. I was surprised at the affection we were shown as we said goodbye, as more than a few tears were shed by our hosts. In ways beyond our understanding, ways that Sally and I weren't even aware of, we'd made a deep impression, and in the years since, I've often thought of that too brief a time, of the fine looking lemon tree that stood in the corner of the garden that we'd spent hours pruning and weeding, and the free spirit of community that existed there. Given the volatile atmosphere and violent uprisings that would eventually erupt across the Holy Land, I came to think of them as frontline Christians.

On board the ship, we roamed the lower deck looking for a place to settle. It was fortunate that we boarded early, because at least this allowed us to secure a fairly comfortable spot beneath a stairwell ahead of the other backpackers, many of whom were forced to spend a very uncomfortable couple of days sleeping upright on tatty chairs. In our quiet corner we had it better, and were even able to fashion a bed of sorts. As we settled in, we remembered the small envelopes we'd been given as a parting gift. We opened the then to find two small Christian booklets, and tucked inside the cover of each was a $20 bill. This was more than enough money to feed us adequately all the way to Rome without having to touch our precious travelling money. The Bethel Christians were definitely the real deal!

Finally we felt the ship lurch and realised that we were leaving Israel at last. Despite the warm, welcoming embrace of Bethel, I wasn't sorry to be leaving as I began to reflect on recent events for the first time in days. I couldn't shake the notion that Mike had been planning something not altogether pleasant, though exactly what we shall never know. It was as if we had been saved by our very own guardian angel, working from the depths of our own instincts, and I contemplated this now, taking the small black bible from my bag.

At the back of the book was a coloured political map, depicting the region during New Testament times. As I traced the faint red lines from Israel to Rome, I was interested to see that we were now following the path of Saul, who, following his dramatic conversion to Christianity, ultimately became St. Paul. The ship would be calling at the same group of islands where he had stopped on his journey to Athens, and then Rome, where, as a Roman citizen, he'd insisted on being tried.

The voyage was largely uneventful, and after two days at sea we docked at the Greek port of Piraeus - a bustling, thriving harbour. We were carried along with the general throng to the main station where we boarded the train to Athens, less than forty-five minutes away. On arrival, we sought out the offices of the Magic Bus Company, only to be told that the bus wouldn't be leaving until around six that evening. It was still early in the morning, so we would have to hang around the city for an entire day. Our first impressions of Athens were not good. It was the most chaotic city I'd ever seen, and the air hung heavy with engine fumes. We abandoned any notions of sightseeing, but continued to stroll towards the centre.

As we walked, I began to notice illustrated handbills that had been fly posted around the city. Eventually, I stopped to examine one closely, but couldn't read any of the printed text - it was all Greek to me - but I noted the central illustration, which comprised a drawing of a multitude of people marching behind an illuminated cross. Soon we arrived at a main square, and found ourselves in the midst of what we took to be some kind of industrial dispute. People had congregated outside a rather drab concrete building and were shouting angrily in Greek, brandishing placards. As there were a number of benches in the square we decided that this would be as good as place as any to while away the warm afternoon, talking, reading and watching the world go by.

Once seated, my eyes were drawn to two large, illuminated symbols facing each other across the square. Both were letters from the Greek alphabet. Alpha, the first letter of the alphabet, was illuminated in blue on the roof of one building, while on a roof on the far side of the square was Omega, the last letter of the Greek alphabet, lit up in red. The first... and the last. Why did this seem so familiar? Then I remembered that it was a passage from *The Book of Revelation*, which I'd been reading during our sea voyage. "I am the Alpha and the Omega," it ran. "The first and the last. The beginning and the end." I was reminded again of all the events of the preceding months, the strange trail I'd felt compelled to follow and how I had seen the number 666 everywhere. It had been the first sight to greet me as Sally and I had passed through the Jaffa Gate in Jerusalem, and the bizarre chain of events since then had led us to the centre of Athens, having fled Jerusalem and bound for Rome. I knew that, ultimately, I would come to value these experiences greatly, but in that moment, all I could do was marvel at the utter futility of it. It all stops here, I thought to myself. This bullshit stops *now*.

Late afternoon arrived, and we noticed that the chanting we'd first heard outside the building that lay across the square was getting louder. Obviously, the dispute was gaining some momentum. The growing throng was proving to be more than a minor nuisance to motorists, who expressed their frustration by blasting their horns as the city centre became increasingly clogged with traffic, and soon the sound of police sirens entered the fray. It seemed that protesters were on the move, and sure enough, they gradually began emerging in their thousands to march upon the city centre. What had initially seemed like a small protest had become a full-blown demonstration, and the disruption this was causing was evident. We realised it was time to go and board the bus that would take us, by way of another sea voyage, to Rome. Outside the Magic Bus booking office, there were a number of backpackers and travellers of various nationalities waiting to depart, but there was no sign of the bus. Fortuitously, I happened to overhear two English-speaking lads talking with a Greek police officer. The reason for the delay, the officer explained, was the massive demonstration that was taking place in the city, and he went on to tell them what the demonstration was all about. I listened incredulously, unable to believe what I was hearing. When he'd finished speaking, I asked him if he wouldn't mind repeating what he'd just said to Sally. I wanted her to hear it from him rather than from me. The policeman agreed and followed me over to where she now sat. "Get a load of this!" I laughed, and stood back. The police officer repeated what he'd said, that the bus was going to be an hour late due to the traffic jams caused by the marching crowds, who comprised the various factions of the Christian church that existed in Athens. They were marching in protest at the Greek government's plans to stamp every new passport with the number 666 on the inside cover. It transpired that the grey municipal building we'd passed that morning was the passport office, which is where the protest had begun. The posters strewn around the city were intended to rally Christians to the cause. I noticed one now and went over for a closer look. Amongst the Greek text, too small to have been noticed straight away, were three small numerals – 666.

Of all the things that had happened during our adventure, it was obvious from Sally's expression that this single event freaked her out the most. She just stared at the police officer, her mouth wide open in amazement. Whatever the cause or reason, a symptom of madness or some weird, mystical design, I'd been following a trail of breadcrumbs around the world, signposts that had been screaming at me from the remote boundaries of my consciousness with increasing urgency, for years. As a result, a chain of events had been set in motion that had led me here, to this place, at this hour, in these circumstances. I could have been anywhere in the world that day, absolutely anywhere. Every choice we'd made, regardless of its basis, had brought us to this place. I suddenly realised that it no longer mattered whether my suspicions in Jerusalem had any basis in reality or not, they'd served their purpose in leading us here. Our paranoia on the beach at Haifa that night and the lift to Tel Aviv were also part of the same equation. Even the loss of half my western currency at the airport in Tel Aviv had been significant, forcing us to take the only route that would have placed us in the centre of Athens on that particular day. And here we now were, surrounded by one of the biggest public demonstrations, the policeman went on to tell us, that Athens had ever seen, and at the centre of it, the very cause of it, was the same symbol that had prompted me to embark on this journey in the first place. I was speechless.

A Magic Bus representative arrived, apologised for the delay, and told us that the bus would arrive shortly, in plenty of time to make the boat. Within thirty minutes we were on our way to the coast, and finally boarded the ship that would take us to Italy.

Despite the onset of December, the day had been hot and the evening pleasantly warm. Sally and I found a corner of the upper deck and made a sheltered camp with a wonderful view of the ocean and the setting sun. After dark, we drew my heavy, army surplus overcoat over our heads, making a canopy for ourselves by securing it to some deck iron, and eventually we fell asleep.

On landing, we rejoined the bus and headed for Rome. We finally arrived in the city at around 4.30am and sought refuge from the morning chill in a large church, the only building open. At a more respectable hour I called Ken from a public phone, and his excitement was both refreshing and uplifting. He knew the street where the church lay, and suggested a nearby café, telling us he'd be there soon.

Ken duly arrived and took us back to the flat he shared with his girlfriend Anne. To be together with Ken in such a contrasting, exciting environment as Rome bordered on the surreal, given our history together, and it was immensely enjoyable. He was happy to lend us the money we needed to complete our journey home, and we purchased the bus tickets the following day. The Magic Bus left only once a week, so he invited us to spend the remainder of the week taking in the sights of Rome.

Ken and Anne worked for a private English language school. They both wanted to spend time in Rome, the job was simply a means to that end, and while Ken loved Rome, he told us that he found the job rather boring. The main clientele seemed to consist of equally bored, rich, middle-aged Italian women with too much time on their hands, and he found the whole situation unsatisfying. "I didn't work my way through Oxford to end up teaching English to a group of apathetic old women," he remarked, ruefully.

Despite having to work most days Ken did find time to accompany Sally and I on a few occasions, including a trip to the Vatican City, where I discovered Michelangelo's *Pieta*, the most beautiful sculpture I have ever seen. By this time, sadly, it had been completely enclosed behind bulletproof glass. Only a short time previously, an Islamic extremist had climbed over the ropes and attacked the sculpture with a hammer. Fortunately he was only able to inflict minimal damage before being apprehended, and they'd been able to repair it.

Sadly, it wasn't possible to view the roof of the Sistine Chapel because it was undergoing restoration, so we went on to San Pietro to see Michelangelo's *Moses*. This is an extremely impressive sight, particularly without protective glass. The story goes that when Michelangelo had completed the sculpture, he was so pleased with the perfection of the work that he tapped the likeness lightly on the knee with his hammer, thus chipping it, and the flaw is still clearly visible. I remember remarking to Ken that it would be funny if the real Moses had had a scar on his right knee.

Soon we were able to find our own way around the city. Ken's apartment was within easy walking distance of many of the most interesting places, and although our time in Rome was short, it was a case of love at first sight. To this day, it remains one of the most beautiful, exciting cities I've ever been to, and I threw my three coins into the fountain to ensure my eventual return.

The Roman Coliseum was a totally unexpected revelation. The atmosphere within seemed charged, a vibrant ambience screaming at me from down the centuries. Originally constructed at a time when the inhabitants of Britain were still running around in wolf skins painting their faces blue, the Coliseum, like Jerusalem, gave me a fresh perspective on history. So many people travel to England, especially from America, to savour a sense of its rich history. Here however was true antiquity. The guides told us that, contrary to popular belief, no Christians were martyred at the Coliseum. It was specifically a sports arena, hosting gladiatorial battles and chariot races. I was also surprised to learn that the reason the Coliseum is only half standing today is because, during the reign of Mussolini, there was a shortage of hardcore stone; material urgently required for use as road foundations. Consequently, the order was given to tear the required stone from the Coliseum - otherwise it would still have been relatively intact.

Rome is resplendent with beautiful fountains of marble, stone, and cascading water, which we found attractive despite the December chill. The city was preparing for its Christmas celebrations, and I was sad that we weren't able to savour it during the summer when, as I was told, hordes of Italians, hand in hand with their lovers or spouses, would stroll around in the warm, evening haze and sit by these fountains sipping fresh, Italian wine.

Finally the time came to board the bus for London and we parted company with Ken, arranging to meet up over Christmas when he would be visiting his mother. The journey back was practically non-stop to the French coast and we slept most of the way, although I do remember glancing out of the window one evening as we crossed the Swiss Alps, driving through some villages in heavy snow. Fairy lights hung from every pine lodge, shop front and church, as children made their way on skis, pulling sledges behind them. It was rather like being inside a living Christmas card.

The bus boarded the ferry at Calais and we spent the sixty minute journey on deck gazing at the rapidly approaching cliffs of Dover. It was hard to believe that our adventure was almost over, and this was the only time in my life that returning to England came as something of a relief. We boarded our bus to Manchester from Victoria coach station in London, and by 6pm that evening, I was home.

17. THE DEAD CAN DANCE

Whatever lay at the heart of the madness that had sent me racing across continents in search of Christ knows what, there was no doubt in my mind that the adventure had done me good. I returned to Manchester healthier in mind, spirit, and body than I'd ever previously been. The myriad of strange encounters, numerical omens and other such nonsense ceased following the crescendo that had greeted us in Athens, along with the irrational inner compulsions and paranoia. Some would argue that, in such states, we create our own belief systems and seize on innocent coincidences with which to reinforce them in our minds. All I can say is that, despite the close examination of countless bus tickets, car number plates, telephone numbers, graffiti and the like in the immediate wake of my return home, the proliferation of the number 666 as a constant presence in my life had come to an end. My horizons had been so broadly expanded that, despite the relief of being home, I knew I would never again be content with the distractions of a small town in the north of England. Life, which hitherto had seemed little more than a series of random experiences en route to the grave, suddenly seemed full of meaning, and I found very little comfort in the routines I'd grown up with. While I'd been travelling I'd never felt more alive and so utterly connected. When you step into the world, shrug off the mind-numbing boredom, televised sedatives and all the other modern elements that cut us off from reality, you find that life is every bit as profound, mystical and meaningful as the great poets profess. The final entry of my diary, written immediately on my return, illustrates some of the insights the experience had given me.

Wednesday, December 24th, 1986.

The Israeli-Palestinian conflict is a powder keg waiting to be ignited, and when it finally explodes, the blast will be felt the world over. It's almost as if what we have here is a microcosm of a conflict that is growing between the eastern and western forces of the world; a culture clash of cataclysmic proportions. The region is a melting pot of bitter intolerance born of injustices - real and imagined - racist intolerance, religious intolerance and economic greed. I can see a time in the not too distant future when Islam and the so-called Free West come into violent conflict. Christian fanatics, such as those that provide a power base for the likes of Ronald Reagan, will no doubt see it as a holy war, a new crusade; while on the other side the fanatical forces within Islam will see it in terms of Jihad, the holy war against Satan. Of course, just as there is good on either side, there is also great evil. These are not black and white issues, and deciding where we stand will not be easy. It's as if we're being herded, rather than led, but herded towards what?

I believe that gradually, by degrees, the world stage is being set for a form of global government. As old enemies are swept away, new enemies will replace them; tools with which to manipulate the masses. What sort of order will be established to replace the old? The signs are that it will be a world of few alternatives, a world in which economic and social trends and strategies will be adopted globally, rather than nationally. It will be a world in which moral decency is bartered, bought, and sold like a commodity. It will not be a world to be poor in. It will be a world gradually herded towards global government. Tin-pot despots will be bulldozed away, clearing the path for tyrannical combines, free from opposition, whose true faces we shall never see. It will be a world of diminishing individuality, variety of culture and racial identity; a prison of technological marvels where technology is king, satisfying the most base lusts and desires but with counterfeit delights, bland, without substance. A world where money holds sway over military might; Ronald McDonald succeeding where Hitler's Panzers failed.

Winston Churchill once said that the only thing we learn by looking back at history is that ultimately, we learn nothing. Whatever it is that's driving us, however, IS learning; it is learning to crush resistance, to kill hope and extinguish love and ultimately God, the wellspring of love. It feeds on death, disease, and violence and we fuel its greed; it regards our world as something to shit on, and humanity as little more than cattle to be herded to the slaughter. As a friend of mine so eloquently put it recently, "we think World War Two was bad, but that was the just the birth pangs."

I've seen its signs and I've seen its number; and it is legion.

In the weeks that followed our homecoming, I received the occasional phone call and letter from Sally. She'd returned to London and was working as a volunteer for Shelter over Christmas, and had moved back in with her parents for a while. Although I did see her occasionally over the following year, there wasn't a great deal of contact. At the time I really didn't know why this was - it wasn't deliberate. I think we both needed time to pick up the loose threads of our lives and weave them into some kind of pattern, establish some form of order from the chaos. It seemed to me that, up to this point, I'd been living my life for other people. Relationships of one kind or another had always been the gravitational centre of my life. Now I wanted time and space to do the things I chose to do, without complications.

I didn't ring anyone to tell them I was home, and I don't remember seeing Dave, Reg or John during the whole Christmas holiday. I was so spaced out by my trip that it didn't occur to me. In any event, when they did make contact it was through Tony Fletcher, and this, too, was tinged with a degree of strangeness.

Shortly after Christmas, I experienced a very vivid dream. I was in a large theatre, and through a set of double doors I could hear the familiar preparations for a band's soundcheck, so I decided to investigate. The theatre was one of those old opera houses that, sadly, are quite rare these days, and apart from the bustling activity on the stage, the theatre was empty. I walked down the centre aisle to the middle of the stalls and took a seat midway along one of the rows, curious to know which band was playing. I watched the crew, none of whom I recognised, busily checking the vocal and drum microphones.

Suddenly .I was aware of someone sitting on my right hand side. Turning, I noticed it was Ruth Polsky, although the fact she was dead didn't immediately occur to me. "Who's playing?" I asked her.

She looked away for a moment, seemingly embarrassed, and then replied, "Well, I'm hoping you are."

"First I've heard about it," I said, throwing anxious looks towards the stage and wondering why I didn't recognise any of the crew.

"Mark, I don't have much time," she said, placing her hand on my shoulder. "I worked very hard on this US tour, it's a great tour, and I'd like you and the band to play it. All the dates are in place, there's someone else taking care of it now, but I set it up and you have to see it through."

I turned to face her again, trying to explain that the band was no longer together, but she cut me off. "Will you at least think about it?"

"Of course I will Ruth, but..." Only then did it dawn on me, "But Ruth, they told me you were dead?"

She half-smiled. "I am," she replied and, with that, I woke up.

A few days later, Fletch rang and asked if I'd meet him for a drink. After I'd given him a sanitised account of my trip, he got down to business, telling me exactly what Ruth had said in my dream earlier that week. The tour she'd been working on was still in place and was now being handled by another US tour company. Fletch had spoken with the others, who were all eager to play, and Geffen had agreed to back the tour financially as a means of promoting *Strange Times*. I told him I'd give it serious consideration but, in truth, I didn't have to think about it for long. The dream was very much at the forefront of my mind, although I didn't discuss it with anyone.

I was summoned to a meeting at KES, during which Dave hardly said a word. It would be fair to say that all the negative events of the previous year were glossed over, but I didn't mind that. In the light of my experiences, I'd calmed down considerably too, realising that everything that had occurred had been vital for the journey I'd had to make. Everyone seemed genuinely excited about the prospect of a full US tour, and the conversation was very upbeat and positive.

It was decided we would co-headline the tour with The Mighty Lemon Drops, who also had a new album to promote. I suspect that this arrangement was conceived as a way of saving money. At any rate, everything was agreed, and the tour was set for February 1987. The Mighty Lemon Drops were a likeable, down-to-earth bunch of lads and we all got on very well. Whenever we met again over the years, we always spoke of that tour as something very special, a once in a lifetime deal, which of course, it was. The tour took in around twenty-three shows in just over a month by road and air, most of which are a blur now. I can recall that the show in New York City, at The Ritz, was one of my top three Chameleons shows of all time. I don't think I'd ever felt so high after a show, and it was a totally natural high. By this time, the only thing I indulged in when performing was strong black coffee, and even afterwards, during the wind-down, it was rare for me to smoke so much as a joint. Even the cigarettes had been discarded, and my voice was stronger than ever.

There were also a lot of laughs along the way, many of them too lurid to relate here, but I have some fond mental snapshots, including one of Keith, the Lemon Drops' drummer, sitting on the baggage carousel, gliding along and filming us with his camcorder as we waited for our luggage. The morning after the New York show, the Lemon Drops had elected to drive to Niagara Falls, setting off at around 6am so they'd be able to return and resume the tour. The whole trip would take around fourteen hours, so the rest of us, wisely I think, declined to join them. When they eventually returned I asked Keith, "So, what was it like then?"

He looked away for a second, and then in his broad Wolverhampton accent, replied "It was crap."

In Buffalo we were met at the airport by an eager young promoter who presented us each with a gift upon disembarking from the aircraft. I don't recall what everyone got, but he gave me the collected works of Pablo

Neruda, which I've treasured ever since, and he gave Reg a book of Escher prints. He was so impressed with the band that he stayed with us as far as Toronto, or possibly even Detroit, sharing my room at one point. His name was Jon Donahue, and he would go on to front the excellent Mercury Rev.

The tour took us to Canada for the first time, and I was amazed at how great the reaction was, considering we'd never played in the country before. Montreal was a real education in every sense, and I was very sad not to be able to spend more time there. I came to feel it was one of the coolest places I'd ever visited, although my French left a lot to be desired. The following evening in Toronto, someone in the audience taped the show. Years later, when a recording turned up via our friend Jack Rabid, we found that the quality was so good that we made it one of the band's few official live albums.

In California, John could be heard complaining loudly about Andy Clegg's apparent ability to pull girls regardless of the situation, while John, obviously more attractive (or so he kept telling us) struggled. "Look at him, go on! Go and look at him." He bellowed to us all one morning. I strolled down the corridor to the room they shared. The door was open and Andy was lying belly down on the bed stripped of his shirt, while a beautiful blonde Californian girl sat astride his back wearing practically nothing, administering a massage. Meanwhile Andy was smoking the biggest conical shaped joint I think I've ever seen. "Alright?" he croaked in greeting as he saw me stood in the doorway, his face beaming with pleasure.

The LA show at the Vanity Arts Centre was one of the hardest gigs on the tour. The sound on stage was appalling, which created a lot of tension. We were at the end of a long jaunt, and all on the brink of exhaustion. Reg became so frustrated with the situation that he threw down his guitar at the end of the set and stormed off, which was unprecedented for him. When a crew member brought the guitar to him, Reg saw the headstock had cracked and split, and he was distraught and furious with himself. The crowd couldn't see this, of course, and I know there were a lot of unhappy people who were very angry that we didn't return to play an encore.

The tour ended in Long Beach, California at a venue called Fenders, but I don't remember anything about the show. I think the gig was rather unremarkable, which is a shame, given the fact that it was to be the last Chameleons show for fifteen years.

Following the tour, we were told that there wouldn't be a CD release of *Strange Times*. The president of Geffen had said that the minimum order for a CD pressing was 20,000 copies, which was deemed too a high a number. I argued against the ridiculousness of this situation. Statik, a small independent label, had successfully issued our albums on CD, so why couldn't a major concern like Geffen manage it? It seemed we'd made a terrible mistake in signing to a big company. I pointed out that some labels were issuing recordings on CD simply for the prestige of innovation, and perhaps Geffen, who seemed to pride themselves on being a progressive major player, ought to follow that example. Sadly, none of these arguments carried any weight whatsoever.

We were also told that there wouldn't be enough money to pay the band anything, as the entire budget had been spent on the production of the album. Nor were we to be paid anything for the US tour, which we were told had made a loss, despite most of the dates having sold out. This was depressingly familiar territory for us. The salt in this particular wound, however, came by way of Hal from KES. By this time he had come to think of himself as the band's manager, although we had no written agreement with KES to this effect. In reality, Fletch had done all the work. Hal kept moaning that he wanted to be paid his percentage, saying that he was getting grief from his wife, who wanted to go to Melrose Avenue to buy herself a new dress, so could they get a move on and pay him please? I was incredulous. Despite having just played nearly thirty sold-out performances in almost as many days, we weren't to be paid anything. Meanwhile Hal, who'd done absolutely fuck all, was about to be handed fifteen percent of the gross.

When we protested about this situation, it was pointed out that KES had been advancing money to individuals within the band for quite some time to meet day-to-day living expenses. None of us had an overview of what the total was, though Fletch told us it wasn't as high as KES was making out. In this respect, we would never be recouped. It's an old trick, still very much in practice today. Keep the band in the dark about how much money is being spent so that ever after, you can claim that the band never earned enough to recoup those amounts. If a band goes platinum of course, their success is clearly visible, nobody cares and everyone makes money; but if a band's sales fall short of that, it seems that they're destined to be forever shafted.

In the end, Fletch did manage to swing some cash our way, and while it wasn't a great deal of money it wasn't bad either. I was less than eager to high tail it back to the hotspots of Middleton, and suggested that a few of us head south for a short while, maybe across the border into Mexico, where a little money can go quite a long way, but none of the others were keen. They'd just finished a hard tour of the States and wanted to get home, which was totally understandable. Andy Clegg, who'd been having the time of his life, shared my sentiments and, in the end, we compromised on keeping our hotel suite for an extra week.

Before that week was out, though, the novelty of Hollywood began to wane, and the atmosphere became a little too strange and sinister for me. One evening we were sitting in our suite with quite a sizable entourage, including a small group of friends I'd invited to the LA show. Initially the atmosphere had been relaxed and quite humorous as we sat around drinking Margaritas and sharing a few joints. Then Andy suddenly interrupted the flow of conversation. He leapt to his feet and pointed at the television set, which had been on in the background, laughing wildly. "I love this show," he giggled. "It's so totally, utterly crap!" He then began mercilessly slating the show, telling us how its crapness verged on the humorously surreal.

Everyone sat there smiling, until finally Danny said, "My father wrote it."

The show in question was *Police Woman* starring Angie Dickinson. I can still see the frozen smile on Andy's face. Danny eased Andy's obvious discomfort by going on to say that, while show *was* crap, the money from the show had put both his sister and him through college.

I immediately hit it off with Danny's sister, Laurel, and we quickly grew closer. She was a beautiful Californian girl with a great sense of fun and a highly refined taste in all things. Her company in such an oppressive place was a relief, and I was sad to say goodbye when the time came to pack up and go home. Over the following weeks we talked on the telephone on a regular basis.

Back in the UK, the national music press was awash with double-page features on how The Mighty Lemon Drops had just completed a sell-out headline, coast to coast tour of the US. Of The Chameleons, however, there wasn't a single mention. Furthermore, not a single review of *Strange Times* had appeared in the national press; the only British one we found was in the Middleton Guardian. By way of contrast, the same day that we read the Middleton Guardian review, we received another glowing critique of our album, which compared *Strange Times* favourably with The Beatles' *Revolver*. This one was in the New York Times. That afternoon I voiced the obvious question. "What the fuck are we wasting our time here for? Let's go back."

We felt that our major problem was the lack of strong management. Fletch worked wonders in an unofficial capacity, but his hands were effectively tied. Hal regarded himself as manager of the band, and believed that a signed agreement sealing this arrangement was only a matter of time, but he was hopelessly out of touch with the modern requirements of band management. Fletch was under increasing pressure to persuade us to sign a contract, but although he was loyal to KES, having worked for them for a very long time, he didn't want us suffering the same problems other bands had in their dealings with the company. Fletch had developed a deep affection for us all and didn't feel that signing such an agreement would be in our best, long-term interests. Consequently, he would continually stall KES' requests for a signed management contract. We often asked Fletch to take over the personal management of the band, as had many other successful bands he'd worked with in the past, but he would just smile and brush it off out of a sense of loyalty to Hal and the company. In a way, I understood where Fletch was coming from on this. Despite my anger at Hal taking fifteen percent of the gross on the US tour while we got nothing, I did feel that we owed Hal quite a lot as a band. Not only had he steered us clear of the messy relationship with Statik and kept us working and solvent, he'd also come through numerous times for me personally, and I still held much affection for him.

We'd already agreed with Tom at Geffen that we'd start writing material for the next record straight away, so with this in mind, we convened at Middleton Civic Hall with our guitars and recording equipment, but it wasn't long before an argument flared up. I'd re-stated my position that we should be focusing our energies on America, but Dave didn't agree, and as usual, the discussion became heated. In the midst of all this, the door opened and in walked Fletch. As always when he paid us a visit, our disagreements and bickering were replaced with welcoming smiles. Fletch hadn't told us he'd be dropping by so it was a pleasant surprise, but he had an even bigger surprise in store. Having given the matter a great deal of thought, he'd decided that he would, after all, take on the personal management of the band. We were all overjoyed. There were conditions attached to his offer, however. First, we couldn't just cut Hal out of the picture, regardless of what the band thought about him. Fletch reminded us that Hal had continued to support the band financially from his own resources within KES, and that couldn't simply be set aside. As far as Fletch was concerned, it wouldn't be honourable. Besides, Hal had picked up the band first, and fair was fair. Fletch proposed that we set aside a small percentage of his management commission for Hal, give him the title of Management Consultant, and involve him in a minor, peripheral way.

The second condition was that we all agree to work solely in the US for no less than two years. His plan was to embark immediately on another tour to promote *Strange Times*, this time as a single headline act, followed with yet another tour in larger venues not long after. We'd also be expected to finish the writing and recording of a new record over there. Fletch explained that this was the only practical way to break into the American market significantly, with the additional aid and support of college radio stations, which we knew we already had. If we were all prepared to commit to that, he'd manage the band full-time. I asked him about KES' involvement generally and he said that apart from the publishing, which KES now owned via its subsidiary company St. Anne's Music, there would be no further involvement, aside from our arrangement with Hal. "I'm leaving KES!" he told us. We were stunned. What had happened?

Fletch's predominant role within KES was to take personal care of the many artists that the company represented. Gradually, his sphere of responsibility had widened to include organising some of the bigger events these clients would stage at huge venues, such as Wembley, the NEC and, later on, Maine Road in Manchester. He was so efficient and so trusted by the clients that he soon became indispensable. One of these clients had been an internationally famous soul singer who Fletch had worked with during his UK visits for many years. As was the norm with Fletch, they'd become trusted friends. This performer had recently agreed to appear at a KES promotion at Wembley Stadium, but as usual, it was on the condition that Fletch personally took care of the event, which naturally, KES agreed to.

Following the performance Fletch, along with the client, went to a bar for a drink and the client asked him if he wouldn't object to a personal question. Fletch didn't mind, so the client went on to say that as far as he could determine, Fletch didn't dress extravagantly, didn't drive a fancy car, and lived quite modestly in a small flat in a suburb of Salford. His question therefore, had been this. What did Fletch do with all the bonuses he'd been handing him? Fletch was dumbfounded. What bonuses? The client went on to explain that when all the accounts were settled, he would set aside around ten grand and hand it to KES' Managing Director as a bonus for Fletch, and that he'd been doing this for years. In all that time, Tony had never seen a penny of this money. Fletch had been a vital component of that company for the best part of fifteen years, on a modest salary, and the big chief had fucked him over. It was unbelievable.

Fletch told us to say nothing of his plans to anyone at this stage. In the meantime, John and I began dismantling our lives in England. Although leaving the UK for America was a difficult decision, we all agreed that it was also the right one.

Our immediate task was to prepare material for a new record, but after the buzz of playing such a successful tour of America, Middleton seemed a less than inspiring place for us to birth our new songs. Fletch and I suggested that the band withdraw to its spiritual home, Loch Ness, and spend a week mapping out new ideas. Everyone seemed to be cool with this, even John, who'd never accompanied us to Loch Ness before. Countryside retreats were never really his thing - he much preferred the distractions of the city, with its bars, clubs and restaurants - but in the end even he seemed keen to go. A date was set, and Fletch hired a couple of chalets that were situated just off a single-track road on the mountainside, high above the Loch, a place we knew and loved having stayed there numerous times over the years.

The night before we were due to leave for Scotland, however, we had some very disturbing news. Something had happened to Fletch and he'd been admitted to hospital in Manchester. I immediately contacted KES to find out what had happened, imagining that our trip to Scotland would now be cancelled. I wanted to visit Fletch immediately, but they told me that while it was worrying - Fletch had suffered a mild heart attack, apparently - it wasn't dangerous. The medical staff had said it was a warning more than anything else, and that he was being kept in for observation. They told us that Fletch wanted us to go up to Scotland as planned, do the work, and he'd see us on our return.

We left for Loch Ness the following day. Naturally, Fletch was the central topic of conversation, and under the shadow of his sudden illness the mood was somewhat tense and awkward. It didn't help matters when we finally arrived at the chalets to be greeted by a flurry of snow. I remember thinking that, if this were how the weather was going to be, at least we'd get some work done, because there wouldn't be anything else to do. Sadly, nothing could be further from the truth. It took considerable effort to pry Reg and Dave away from the TV set long enough to record anything. Reg would sit quietly, saying very little and watching the box all day, while Dave would sit beside him, eating bowl after bowl of breakfast cereal and complaining loudly about everything under the sun. John complained the loudest though, mostly about the boredom of the place. Each evening he'd have our chief roadie, Spoonhead, drive him to Inverness in the minibus so he could eat a curry or a Chinese meal at one of the restaurants or drink beer in one of the city pubs. However, our time there wasn't totally unproductive. I threw in a song of my own that I'd written on guitar, which I called 'The Healer', and Reg contributed a couple of ideas which I loved instantly. As usual, all of Reg's ideas, even though they were often little more than a couple of guitar loops, were saturated with inspiration. One of them would eventually evolve into possibly my all-time favourite Chameleons song, 'Is It Any Wonder?'

We regularly telephoned KES to get updates on Fletch's condition, and each time we were told that he was going to be fine, and that we shouldn't worry. Yes, they were still keeping him in for observation, but he sent his best wishes and he would see us when we got back. Despite these assurances, I remember feeling very uneasy.

Eventually, John's frustration with Loch Ness reached the point of no return. "Let's fuckin' do something," he shouted to everyone. "I know!" he suddenly exclaimed. "We'll have a game of hide and seek, all of us." Running around in the pitch dark was absolutely the last thing I was in the mood for, so I abstained and watched instead from a chair on the veranda. One by one, the others went out to join John, but barely five minutes had gone by when there was a tremendous yell from the darkness. A short while later Spoonhead emerged, supporting a hobbling John, who, in the pitch darkness, had not seen a particularly large and ugly looking boulder in his path. He'd ran headlong into it and injured himself. Spoonhead drove him to the infirmary at Inverness and returned a few hours later with John on crutches, sporting a heavily bandaged leg. He spent the remainder of his stay housebound and on the verge of total insanity.

The following day I walked to the nearby phone box and rang KES to enquire about Fletch. Once again I was told that he was doing fine and would be allowed home any day, and to crack on with writing the new material. I asked for information on the hospital - which one had he been admitted to? What was the phone number? KES fobbed me off, saying they didn't know. Frustrated, I told them that I intended to visit Fletch, and asked how I could find out which hospital he was in, only to be told that visitation was restricted to family members only. I decided that all this secrecy only made sense if Fletch was in a lot worse condition than KES were letting on, so I told the others I intended to go back to Manchester immediately and see Fletch for myself. In the end, we decided we'd all travel back together.

The journey home was long and tense, and I didn't get home until quite late in the evening. Nevertheless, I immediately phoned Hal, intending to wrestle the address of the hospital from him so I could bluff my way in by pretending to be Fletch's cousin or something. I left a message on Hal's answering machine, and sometime around 11pm, he rang me back and told me that Fletch had suffered another series of heart attacks, and that these had proved fatal. Tony Fletcher was dead.

Dave's flat was situated around the corner from my parents' house, but by the time I got there he'd already heard the news by telephone from Tony's distraught live-in companion, who hadn't even been allowed access to Tony, not officially being a member of the family. KES had already booked us into the studio to begin recording demos early the following week. The day after we got the news, John phoned. "I don't know about you guys," he said, "but I'm going into the studio and setting my drums up, because I honestly don't know what the fuck else to do, and if I don't do something I'll go mad." It was a sentiment we all shared.

The atmosphere in the studio was heavy and oppressive. CJ again took the helm at the mixing desk, and after running through the scattered ideas we had on our eight-track tape recorder, we started work, beginning with 'The Healer'. How we managed it, I really don't know, but gradually the recordings began to take shape, although most of the time I was in a total daze. The bickering began almost immediately. At one point Dave had been struggling to get a satisfactory guitar sound and his complaining was driving everyone, including the ever-patient and mild-mannered CJ, totally mad. CJ emerged from behind the mixing console at one point and quietly pleaded, "Get him out of here, this is horrible."

Once the bulk of Dave's work was on tape, he ceased to turn up altogether, and John, in particular, began to get frustrated. On one occasion, Dave telephoned the studio asking if John could pick him up at home in his car. John dutifully set off to Middleton to collect him but didn't return to the studio until around five hours later. I asked him where he'd been, and blazing with anger he told me he'd been sitting in his car outside a flat in Hulme while Dave partied with some friends inside. Dave's excesses were beginning to worry all of us. Later that week he failed to show up yet again. We'd been working since 10am and the hour was growing late when he finally turned up, whereupon he consumed an entire gram of cocaine in one go, right in front of us, and almost asphyxiated.

The next day I decided to call for Dave and escort him to the studio, but when he answered the door he was in a foul mood and launched straight into a relentless, breathless tirade, so, yet again, I turned up at the studio without him. His main gripe was a lack of money. "How can I go to work at the studio every day when I haven't got any fuckin' money?" he yelled at me. He may not have had any money, but he certainly had plenty of cocaine, and I knew that didn't come cheap.

During that first week we were visited by KES' accountant, a rather gruesome, suspicious character who looked more like an undertaker. He reminded us of all the things Fletch had done for us, how hard he'd worked on behalf of the band, work that had driven him to having a heart attack, no less. He said it was our duty to honour him by continuing with the band. I found this particularly galling, knowing what I did about the circumstances of Tony's imminent departure from KES, but naturally, I wasn't able to say anything about that. Instead, I had to bite the bullet, sit there and take it, a sick, churning feeling in the pit of my stomach. "I know how hard Tony worked for you," I sneered, barely able to conceal my disgust. "And I know what made him ill, so please - no lectures," and we left it at that.

During the second week Tom from Geffen Records flew in to review the tracks we were working on, along with his brother Brad. 'Is It Any Wonder' had turned out beautifully and I knew then that it was the best lyrical work I'd turned in yet. As cynical as we were about Tom's desire to constantly involve himself in the mixing process, I had to admit that some of his ideas, such as fading elements of the backing track leaving only Reg's guitar audible on 'Is It Any Wonder', were inspired. I remember thinking that if these tracks were any indication of the band's overall direction, we might well have a masterpiece on our hands. I especially loved Reg's ending to 'The Healer' which, in the space of a few seconds, managed to perfectly encapsulate the atmosphere of my time in Old Jerusalem.

Tom held a similar conviction that the ideas we were working on had the makings of a classic album, and told us he was looking forward to starting work with us in the US later that year. But I could already sense that, regardless of what had been decided initially, it was going to be a contentious issue. Tony's death had changed everything.

Work continued with the addition of another new song, 'Denims and Curls'. Lyrically, the song became a kind of anthem for those who tend to hide from the world, battling with their insecurities, but who at the same time yearn to break out, explore the world and take life on. Again, this had been inspired by my journey to Jerusalem.

The final track of the session had been something that Reg and I had jammed out in a few minutes during a period of relative inactivity in the studio, which Dave had then typically elevated. I improvised a vocal initially just for reference purposes, venting my frustration at the general situation, tinged with some cynicism towards the US Presidential election, which was then in full swing. I titled the track 'Free For All', in honour of one of my favourite episodes of *The Prisoner*, which dealt with the fallacy of the democratic process.

While I was recording the vocals, Dave came into the studio for a chat. He told me he was worried about his recent excesses, and that he was determined to get things under control. I was relieved to hear this, because I don't think I'd ever seen his habits so utterly out of control. Having said that, I understood to a certain degree. It was a very hard time for everyone.

I'm amazed we were able to go into a studio and get anything done, so utterly overwhelming was our sense of loss.

Fletch had very little time for his family, and we began hearing stories of just how deep this mutual resentment went. His family dealt with the funeral arrangements without having any real idea of who Fletch was or what he'd truly meant to people, making it a somewhat frustrating affair. The service was a cremation and the chapel was crammed with people, many of whom were forced to take part from the adjoining hallway of the main entrance through lack of space. The priest chosen to conduct the service hadn't the faintest idea who Fletch was - obviously embarrassed, he hardly knew what to say. People had flown in from all over the world to attend, and among them, an entire troupe of Scouts, their banners and flags held aloft. Fletch had been involved with their movement for some time, working to give underprivileged kids a chance to go on adventure trips, showing them there was more to life than the back streets of Salford, with its crime, poverty and deprivation.

"Well, erm, I didn't know Tony Fletcher personally but I can, erm, see from the size of this congregation that he was a greatly loved man," stammered the priest. I was hoping that someone would take the podium and offer us something relevant, half imagining leaping up there myself, but that's the stuff of television drama, and in reality it was unthinkable. I consoled myself with the fact that such a massive gathering was, in itself, the only expression of love necessary, and left it at that.

Over the next couple of months, Dave and I started to argue more and more, chiefly about America and our plans to relocate. I was still keen for us to go, while Dave, somewhat understandably, felt that without Fletch it couldn't work. I couldn't really see any future for the band in the UK and told him so, while he argued that leaving his life behind and moving to America was inconceivable. Of course, by this time, John and I in particular had gone some way towards dismantling our lives in the UK, and the thought of doing a U-turn now and continuing as we had been was particularly hard to take. "So what are the alternatives then, Dave?" I remember asking him during a particularly heated discussion on the matter, "We stay in Middleton for the rest of our lives, do a gig occasionally, and sit around getting stoned, talking about when we used to be in a band?" It was obvious that a very serious rift was developing between us, and without Fletch's calming influence, there was no knowing how long we'd able to continue working together.

Towards the end of the recording session, Peter Hook asked if we'd meet with him at Suite Sixteen. New Order had just returned from a US tour, and apparently there were a couple of things he wanted to tell us. We dutifully turned up at the studio, making our way separately. The first thing I saw was Dave smoking a hash pipe in the studio manager's office. It seemed that all the talk of the previous week, about curbing his excesses and taking more control of his life had been forgotten. Peter eventually arrived and told us that The Chameleons had created quite a stir in the States in the wake of our visit earlier in the year, and a lot of people were forecasting big things for the band. "I've never seen such a buzz about a band in all the time I've been going there," he told us. "You've got to get out there as soon as possible."

A few hours later, I was drinking coffee alone in a café near the studio, when John arrived. It was obvious he was very agitated. After I'd left the meeting, things had finally come to a head. Dave was now saying that he wasn't prepared to go to America. John had come to tell me that he'd had enough, and was leaving the band. I'd heard John talk this way before and I'd always been able to calm him down, but I saw a fresh determination in him this time, and he emphatically insisted that this really was the end. I felt that John had sacrificed the most when we'd initially made the decision to go and work in America. His relationship with his girlfriend had ended when she'd been unable to accept his decision, feeling the band was more important to him than their relationship, which, it has to be said, was true and evident. Despite the fact that Dave's change in attitude was both inevitable and understandable after Tony's death, for John in particular, it was hard to take.

As a parting shot, John delivered another shock. "You have no idea what Dave's been saying about you to everyone behind your back for ages," he continued, "calling you a freak to anyone who'd listen."

He refused to elaborate further, saying only that the name-calling had been "really bad." "Dave's never been your friend," he told me. This was nothing new. I'd given up on our friendship a long time ago, but it was still a shock to hear John say these things.

I realised that I had a lot to think about. This, on top of losing Fletch, suddenly seemed too much. I'd already told the others that I'd planned to take off for a couple of weeks' holiday. I felt I needed to put some distance between myself and the group, Tony's death, KES and everything else. During one of her regular phone calls, Laurel told me that she was planning a trip to England to participate in a healing workshop organised by a small group of Native Americans. The group was planning to hold some open lectures in Glastonbury that summer and she'd been invited to take part. Consequently, she was planning to be in the UK for around four weeks, and she invited me to join her. This couldn't have come at a better time. The first phase of the recordings was now complete, so there wasn't anything to stop me.

John drove me to the airport to meet Laurel. He told me that there were some things he wanted to discuss, and the journey would be a good opportunity. Mostly the conversations revolved around the future, but contemplating the immediate future was exactly what I was hoping to avoid for a while, so I didn't really say much. I had to tell him that, things being what they were between Dave and me, I couldn't really see one.

The next day we made our way north. We had plenty of time to kill before the seminars were due to begin, so Laurel and I kicked our heels around Manchester for a while, planning to take a trip to Scotland before finally heading for Glastonbury. Around the same time, I received another phone call from John. He told me he and Andy Clegg were forming a new band, and that they wanted me to join. I told him I thought it was a bit premature to talk about forming new bands, but that I'd think about it. I seem to recall he phoned another couple of times and in the end, I agreed to meet him and Andy Clegg to talk it over.

While out walking with Laurel, I bumped into Dave outside a shop. He told me he'd been spending his time helping a local band, The Monkey Run, in the studio and he was excited about the results. "Have you been listening to the stuff we recorded the other week? I asked him. "What do you think of it?"

"It's all right," he answered dismissively, "But I think we've got to get away from KES and Geffen, because Reg and I don't want to go to America."

I understood and even agreed with his sentiments regarding KES, although at the time I was happy to stick with Geffen and told him so. I also tried to explain that what he was talking about, breaking away from both companies, involved months if not years of legal wrangling with absolutely no resources or proper representation. I felt it would be a hundred times worse than the Statik fiasco. The idea of having to go through all that again totally depressed me. There was no way KES or Geffen were simply going to allow us to walk away clean. I asked him if he'd heard that John had left the band, and he said he had. I then told him that John had invited me to join a band with him and waited for a reaction. Dave was just staring into space nodding his head with that familiar faraway look. "I'm seriously considering it, Dave," I continued. There was still no reaction. "Did you hear what I said?" I asked again. "I'm seriously considering leaving the band with John."

Whether it was Laurel's presence or whether it was something he just didn't want to hear, I can't say for sure. I told him I'd see him when I got back in a couple of weeks, and said goodbye. Laurel and I drove up to Scotland in a camper van I'd borrowed from my father, and we spent a week exploring the Highlands. There's nothing quite like camping with someone for getting to know a person better, and my short time with Laurel proved to be quite an education. Obviously we were attracted to each other and had even begun to fool around, but I was reluctant to let the situation go too far. I didn't feel ready to jump into another relationship, especially with someone I hardly knew. I saw the trip as an opportunity for us to get to know each other, and wanted our time to be as relaxed and uncomplicated as possible. Laurel, on the other hand, was very keen, and before long we were having quite a few intense conversations. Another worry was that I didn't carry contraceptives, but she assured me that it was something she'd already taken care of and I needn't have any worries about it. I was still very hesitant, determined not to let things get out of hand, but Laurel was a very beautiful woman and not easy to resist. We toured around Loch Ness for a while and then drove south to hook up with her Native American friends at Glastonbury. We were having a wonderful, intense time, and after a particularly brilliant few days around Glastonbury town we fell into each other's arms, and that was it.

The trip to Glastonbury culminated in a ceremony at the Tor, and once this was over we said our goodbyes. The van was conveniently parked off a secluded road, and we were able to spend the night there. It was at this moment that Laurel decided to drop her bombshell: she told me she'd lied to me about using the contraceptive pill. Furthermore, she was actively hoping to become pregnant. I stared at her in disbelief. During our long conversations by phone, she'd always struck me as having quite a deep wisdom and a level of understanding well beyond her years. This was absolutely the last thing I expected, or needed. I asked her what she would do if it turned out she were pregnant. "I'd have the baby, of course. I mean, I could never get rid of it."

I was so angry all I could do was pace up and down outside the van for a while. If she had accidentally become pregnant I would have felt very differently, after all no form of contraception is one hundred percent reliable, but to actually plan it from the outset was irresponsible, unforgivable and unacceptable. She told me it was her hope that I would move to California to be with her should she conceive, but even if I wouldn't, she'd still want the baby. "I just wanted you to be the father of my child," she said.

Once Laurel had returned to California I headed back to Manchester, where I received another phone call from John. His and Andy's innocent enthusiasm for wanting to get together and write some songs was contagious, and seemed relatively uncomplicated in the wake of all the hassles of the past two years. Andy Clegg and Andy Whittaker had a band of their own, Music For Aborigines, but Andy told me that, following a final gig that week in Manchester, they planned to disband. I told them I'd be there. The gig was at The Venue on Whitworth Street West, a few hundred yards along from the Haçienda. As I cruised around the audience, I bumped into Reg, and this seemed like a good opportunity to find out where we stood with one another. I told him I was bitterly disillusioned, specifically concerning my relationship with Dave, which was at an all-time low. I asked him to confirm some of the things John had told me and he did so. I asked where he stood in all of this. He told me that as far as he was concerned, his only issue was with Hal and KES, saying that he didn't want to continue with them. I accepted that, but waved it aside for a moment. I was primarily concerned with the personal aspects of the band. "In light of the way I was treated, Reg, and with everything Dave's been saying behind my back, give me one good reason why I should stay with the band?"

Reg just shook his head and said nothing.

I told him that John and Andy had invited me to collaborate with them on a new project, that I'd been seriously considering it and that unless he could give me a good enough reason not to, I was going to go ahead. All I'd wanted to hear from Reg was that I should stay because he and I were mates, that he wanted to continue to play in the band with me. That would have been enough - after all, Reg was the real reason I'd joined the band in the first place. But he merely reiterated what he'd said earlier about KES being the only issue. "Is that all you've got to say, Reg?" I asked him again, barely able to believe what I was finally about to do.

"Yeah, basically, it's just about Hal and KES as far as I'm concerned."

"That's it then," I told him. "I'm out."

I left the venue before the show was finished and caught the bus back to Middleton. It would be some years before I saw either Reg or Dave again.

18. THE SUN AND THE MOON

Over the years that followed, Dave Fielding would maintain that I left The Chameleons without telling anyone - that I went away that summer and never came back. Many people found Dave intimidating, but I never did. I'd never baulked from telling him exactly what I thought, and therein lay the problem. Unlike Reg and John, I was never prepared to fall in line for the sake of a quiet life, which is why there was always so much friction between Dave and me. The major difference between us is that I've always been prepared to listen to others. If Dave was surprised when I left The Chameleons, it wasn't because I didn't tell him. It was because he couldn't hear what I was saying, despite the fact that, when I was saying it, I was standing less than a foot away from him.

Others have commented on how quickly I became involved with something else. The insinuation being, of course, that joining another band so soon after leaving The Chameleons was a callous and unfeeling act of betrayal. People love to gossip almost as much as they love to stick the boot into someone they've been jealous of for a long time, and there was plenty of that going on back then.

In the months following the break-up I had no close friends, only manipulative people who wanted something from me. In my grief at having lost Fletch, I felt that sharing a few beers with some uncomplicated people, picking up guitars and writing a few songs, was probably the best therapy I could ask for. It's a sad fact that such activity was no longer possible within The Chameleons. Towards the end, the quality of our work had been of the highest order, but the hassle and the drama in getting it together, the pace at which things moved and the lack of mutual respect meant that being in The Chameleons was more of a nightmare than a dream come true.

When I accepted John and Andy's invitation, I knew that Tom at Geffen would want to hear what we were doing, and that if he liked what he heard we'd probably get to make a record. At the same time, I was aware that this was something the rest of the band wanted more than I did. For me, it was more a case of trying to recapture something I'd lost since those early days at the Railway Inn, which today strikes me as being a little pathetic. But unlike Dave, Reg, John, and Tony Skinkis for that matter, I'd grown up without siblings. My relationship with these people was the closest I ever came to experiencing any kind of brotherhood - five guys in the midst of an adventure. Looking back now, it's hard for me to believe I could have been so naïve.

John and Andy suggested we enlist Andy Whitaker, Andy Clegg's partner from Music For Aborigines. This surprised me initially, because Andy Whit had always fronted his own band, and, like me, was a bassist, but they told me that he was also a great guitar player and was keen to join. I liked him, so I had no objections.

None of this was contrived. There were no plots, no career plans, or any high ideals involved. John and I were still under contract to Geffen, so it was inevitable that they would take an interest in what we were doing, but in all honesty I couldn't have cared less whether they went for it or not. As it turned out, after hearing the initial recordings, Tom was sufficiently impressed to install the band at Rockfield Studio in Monmouth to demo the songs properly.

We worked with the resident engineer there, an amiable chap named Paul Cobbold. Paul introduced me to the idea of using a cello bow on a Höfner violin bass - similar to the one made famous by Paul McCartney - and the effect was a revelation; it was like an EBow, but much smoother and more natural-sounding.

I was also inspired by the possibility of having three good vocalists in the band, as this would give a much wider scope for harmonies and backing vocals. The Chameleons' sound didn't encompass backing vocals to any great extent, not because the rest of the band wasn't capable - all of them had fine, natural voices, they simply lacked confidence on the microphone. So enthusiastic was I at this development that some of the arrangements ended up a little over-elaborate. Still, it was something of a novelty for me - as a huge Beatles fan, I really enjoyed those three-part harmonies.

Rockfield was undoubtedly a great studio, but it wouldn't really have suited us in the long term. The place was too tranquil and lacked tension. 'I Love You, You Bastard', had turned out well although I wasn't keen on the way it had been mixed. Similarly, I felt the same way about 'A Picture Of England' - well recorded, but the wrong approach.

Our new, as yet unnamed, band had a completely different writing style from that of The Chameleons. Most of the original material we worked on at Rockfield had acoustic origins. Despite the similarities in the way the two guitars interacted, this was a completely different band. We had potential, but given the level of expectation in the wake of The Chameleons, would we be given the grace to develop it? The Chameleons had been a great band, and would be a hard act to follow. I was under no illusions that it was going to be tough on everyone. To a certain extent, I was blind to the reality of the situation: Geffen had invested heavily in The Chameleons, and were eager to pay for an album, regardless of the quality of the songs, simply because it offered them a chance to claw some of that money back.

I'd insisted that the new project be treated as something completely separate to The Chameleons with regards to a recording agreement, and Tom assured me that it would be. As usual, we wrestled with suggestions of what to christen the band, and after a great deal of debate we decided on The Sun And The Moon. I can't remember why, only that I preferred it to the other front-runner, The Bicycle Thieves.

The Sun And The Moon, 1998.

Having abandoned Rockfield, we opted for the considerably cheaper, handier and far more comfortable Suite Sixteen, with regular Chameleons' engineer CJ at the desk. The bulk of the songs were written in the studio, on the fly. For me, the most interesting track on the album was 'A Matter Of Conscience', and its theme and lyrics came by way of yet another major head fuck.

Since Laurel's return to the US she had been in regular contact by telephone, and she had been trying, unsuccessfully, to persuade me to relocate to California. During the album sessions, she phoned again and told me that she'd taken a pregnancy test and that the result had been positive. While I was still trying to come to terms with this, she dropped her second bombshell: she'd subsequently panicked and had an abortion.

I carried this around inside me for a very long time, never sure whether I believed it or not, but with a grave feeling of shame and remorse all the same. There was no-one that I felt I could turn to, and it began to rip me apart. The others could see that something was wrong with me, but were at a loss as to what to do about it. This, combined with the surroundings of Suite Sixteen with all its memories, began to drive me over the edge.

As a reaction to these circumstances, I chose the issue of abortion as the theme for 'A Matter Of Conscience'. I remember the day we were jamming out the idea. I stood listening to the guitar riffs that Andy Clegg and Andy Whit were playing for a moment or two before spontaneously launching into the bass line. Andy Whit suddenly stopped playing and stared at me. I stopped playing and stared back. "What's the matter?" I asked. Andy was shaking his head,

"Sorry, I was just stunned. That's fuckin' great!"

Everyone just fell about laughing.

As the song developed, Andy Whit contributed lyrics of his own, running with the abortion theme, and the result was one of the most challenging pieces of music I'd collaborated on thus far.

I became so distraught about the possibility that Laurel was telling the truth that, with absolutely no-one else to turn to, I broke down in tears one afternoon while sharing a coffee with my father. He was very supportive, and said even in the unlikely event that it was true, I shouldn't blame myself for it. By this time, the Sun And The Moon album had been out for a while, so, after our chat, I dropped in at the Post Office to collect some mail from the P.O. box that I'd continued to maintain after the break-up of The Chameleons. As I sat in the sunshine in the centre of town, flicking through the mail, one letter in particular stopped me cold.

Dear Mark,

Just a note to say thank you for your music and thoughts but most of all for A Matter Of Conscience. I had just bought The Sun and The Moon album and was listening to it for the first time while my wife Amanda and I were talking about her being pregnant with our second child. We were thinking of abortion due to lack of money and prospects, but when that song came on and I read through its lyrics I felt a tear come to my eye and we decided to keep the baby there and then.

She's 2 months old now, born on the 28th April. We've called her Katie. Thanks Mark she's brilliant.

The timely arrival of this letter was little short of miraculous, and helped me in ways I couldn't even begin to adequately express. I felt as if a huge weight had been lifted from me, that somehow I'd been absolved, and that some sort of balance had been restored. Over the years many people have asked me whether I'm bitter about the fact that my music, in whatever guise, didn't have a wider impact. What they really mean, of course, is that I've never had my face bandied about the media, or made millions of pounds in royalties, or stepped up proudly to receive a Brit award. In response, I ask, what is a gold disc on the wall compared to a letter of this magnitude? The Sun And The Moon may never have scaled the dizzy heights of stadium rock or hung out with Sting and U2, but we changed the world with a single song. As far as I'm concerned, everything - and I mean everything - I went through to make that happen was entirely justified.

Early on in the band's life, the business side of things began to create tensions when I refused to sign a new publishing agreement with KES. I'd wanted to consult a lawyer before I signed anything with anyone - especially them - but it was only a week before Christmas, and nobody had any money. Hal turned up at the studio waving advance cheques in everybody's face, knowing we were all practically broke. Consequently, a great amount of pressure was put on me to sign. With The Chameleons now defunct, KES had nothing on any of us contractually, and after everything that had happened I was keen to make a break. Having said that, Hal had changed quite a bit since Fletch died, and I remembered what Fletch had said about not wanting to ditch Hal. It was the Managing Director of KES, not Hal, who'd shafted Fletch. As for the two Andys, this had been the first time anyone had offered them anything for their music, and I wasn't entirely unsympathetic. I did say that we should at least have the agreement looked at by a solicitor, but they didn't want to listen. Everyone was already eyeing Hal's cheques, dreaming of a white Christmas. In the end I relented, but it was with a very heavy heart.

Having once again signed with KES, I knew that it was going to be more important than ever for us to find strong personal management. A guy named Paul, who ran a lighting company and had often worked alongside Fletch over the years, had been involved in a minor way with The Chameleons at Tony's request, chiefly as road manager. We often met with Paul following Tony's death. He was trying to look out for all of us because he felt that this is what Fletch would have wanted of him. He would often refer to himself as Tony's heir apparent, adding that others also saw him in this light. I didn't - I knew that people like Fletch came along maybe once or twice in a lifetime, but I genuinely liked Paul, and so I humoured his delusions of grandeur. Paul dropped by the studio when the album was almost finished, offering to act as manager in much the same way as Fletch had. This pleased me because I was starting to feel that the whole burden of running the band was falling on my shoulders. I was the only one in the band that Tom and Geffen would deal with, so being able to turn up for those meetings with a competent manager at the helm would be a great help. He told us he'd be happy to do that, and I set up the meetings accordingly.

This time I travelled in the company of Andy Clegg, first to New York to master the record with Tom Zutaut and George Marino, and then on to California to meet with Geffen and discuss the marketing of the album. Andy and I were booked into the same suite at the Franklin Plaza in Hollywood where we'd previously been housed at the end of The Chameleons US tour the previous year. As we signed the register, the receptionist informed us that our car was in the basement car park, and handed me the keys. "Car?" I asked him, confused.

"Yeah, the hire car that Geffen Records have supplied you with," replied the receptionist.

I feigned understanding: "Oh, the car! Yes, thank you."

On the way up to our rooms we quickly established that neither of us had a driving licence. Giggling at the situation, we made our way down to the hotel car park to inspect the vehicle - a brand new Chevrolet, complete with automatic transmission. Climbing in, we sat there beaming at each other for a moment before it occurred to me that I'd never driven an automatic car before. I noticed a guy on the other side of the car park, so I called him over and asked him how it was done. "Oh it's easy," he smiled, and proceeded to show me the ropes. It was indeed easier than driving a normal car, and we spent the next couple of hours cruising around Hollywood, Ray-Ban sunglasses on, windows wound down, blasting out the *Charlie Brown* soundtrack. Welcome to the Hotel California.

I telephoned Paul in England, and he told me he was still intending to fly out for the meetings with Geffen. Accordingly, I confirmed the meetings with Tom, but as the days went by all we got from Paul was one excuse after the other, and I ended up having to reschedule the meetings. Ultimately it became obvious that he wasn't coming, despite his constant assurances, and we were forced to continue without him.

Everybody seemed pleased with the results of the sessions. We hammered out a schedule for the release of a maxi-single, and discussed ideas for the artwork. Whilst at the Geffen offices we were introduced to Edie Brickell, who'd just completed her first album for them. The president of Geffen had been so impressed by her album that he'd personally ordered that no tape copies were to leave the building. She was extremely shy and pleasant, and she told me she'd liked *Strange Times* very much.

Later, after returning to the hotel to meet up with Andy, I walked into the room and found him chatting with Edie, who happened to be staying in another suite down the hall. Andy was listening to her new album on a Walkman and invited me to listen to a track, 'Circle', which was destined to become a hit the world over. I loved it at once, and so she broke Geffen's rules and handed me a cassette copy of the album, which I still have along with the vinyl copy that I picked up much later. She left for home the following day, but not before leaving a rather lovely note, thanking us for being there and wishing us well.

We used the car to tour the Pacific Coast Highway, stopping off at various surfing beaches along the route. We drank a lot of tequila with Tom's brother Brad, and even managed a visit to Universal Studios. Andy and I shared a passion for film, so we joined the official tour around the film sets. The tour was interesting, if sedate - pretty much what one would expect, but it hadn't been enough for us. We were more interested in the entrance gate, and the road beyond which led down to the main studios. After a short debate, we threw caution to the wind and casually strolled right in. We'd just walked onto the closed set area of Universal Studios. We did our best to keep a low profile, and took in all the bustling activity that was going on around us, until finally we hit on our greater purpose: we decided that we wanted to see the Bates Motel from Alfred Hitchcock's *Psycho* a little bit closer than the official tour had allowed. We could see the building in the distance and made directly for it, even managing to peer in through the windows before being challenged by a security guard. Despite looking rather intimidating - armed as he was with a very large revolver - he was humorous and good natured, and after a brief conversation pointed us in the direction of the main exit to the lot. "They have the right to shoot you, you know, for trespassing on the lot," he informed us. We decided not to test this and did as he asked, content with having done something that, as far as we were concerned, was legendary. After all, that's exactly how Steven Spielberg is reputed to have broken into Hollywood.

Back in the real world, we reconvened in Manchester to discuss the various developments. Paul apologised for letting us down in America. He explained that he felt it would have compromised his position with Dave and Reg, to whom he also had a commitment. That was fair enough, but it would have been better had he said so in the first place. Also at that meeting was Rob Brown, who I didn't recall meeting before, but who told me he'd been to numerous Chameleons gigs and was a fan. The other members of the band knew Rob well, however, and nominated him for the position of personal manager. I liked him immediately: he was a witty, intelligent and humorous individual who most definitely appeared to have his head screwed on properly. His background was in the financial sector, but he was obviously very passionate about music, and he seemed an ideal candidate. Paul suggested that we'd also benefit by having a secretary of sorts, who could help with the day-to-day organising of the band. We couldn't immediately think of anyone that fitted the bill, until Paul suggested Sally. Paul had been impressed with the way she'd pitched in to help sell Chameleons merchandise on the last European tour. Sally and I hadn't had that much personal contact since the previous year, but I knew she was living in Bury again, staying with her parents. She'd given up on the dreary London scene after some bad experiences with the people she'd been sharing a house with in Battersea. "We could go over and see her tonight, and ask her," Paul suggested, and I agreed.

By this time, I'd taken to riding a motorcycle, despite the fact that I didn't have a license. I simply hadn't been able to resist the machine in question, a Honda 250 Super Dream US Custom, after seeing it in the window of a shop just up the road from Suite Sixteen. It was a commuting bike suitable only for carving a path through inner city traffic, but it was quick around town. I'd fallen in love with it immediately. I rode to Bury while Paul followed in his car, and we made our way over to see Sally at her parents' house. It's very hard to describe what happened next. When I saw her, I felt I'd been hit by a thunderbolt. It was rather like the clichéd legend of Cupid's arrow: I was completely smitten, as if I was only seeing her truly for the first time. Furthermore, it was obvious that Sally was feeling the same way, and clearly Paul felt awkward at finding himself in the middle of this. He made his excuses and left, and we continued talking until the early hours of the morning. She told me how disillusioned she'd become with London and how she was looking to make a fresh start at home, while I talked about the pain of losing Tony, the break-up of the band, the crazy situation with Laurel, and how being in Middleton after walking out on The Chameleons had become unbearable.

Soon Sally and I were seeing each other on a daily basis, and knowing how depressed living in Middleton was making me, her family invited me to move in with them at their house in Bury. It was obvious to them that Sally and I were deeply in love. Why it should suddenly strike me at that point, rather than earlier when Sally and I were travelling together, I have no idea. In retrospect, I think that it was simply a question of timing. My life had been complicated in so many ways, Sally had been in a similar predicament, and I just hadn't been ready to contemplate another serious relationship. Now we'd both cleared the decks of our old lives, and suddenly our feelings for each other had come into perfect alignment. Once we began living together, aside from a couple of weeks here and there, we were in each other's company twenty-four hours a day, seven days a week for the next ten years.

The Sun And The Moon made its live debut on 6th May, 1988 at Legends in Warrington. This was a warm up show for a higher profile appearance at The Ritz a few days later. We had decided to dedicate the gig to the memory of Tony Fletcher, donating all profits to a local charity he'd been involved with. The gig was a sell-out, and I was very nervous about playing a completely new set of songs with a new band in front of such a large audience. The support act that night was an impressive young band from Manchester called New Morning. They had a strong blues influence, fused with something very dynamic and fresh, and we all became good friends over the following year or so. Much to our relief, the gig was a huge success, but my favourite moment came right at the end as the PA was being packed away into the waiting truck. I turned up with some paper cups and a bottle of rum, and together with the security guys, crew and band, drank a toast to Tony Fletcher.

In the wake of this debut, it was time to think about a national tour in support of the impending album release. There were a few contenders eager to set something up, but Rob had been particularly impressed by a young promoter called Simon Moran. Simon had yet to book his first national headline tour, but Rob reasoned, correctly in my view, that his relative lack of experience came second to the man's obvious enthusiasm and hunger for success. Eventually Simon went on to form SJM Enterprises, which today is one of the biggest promotion agencies in Europe.

The two dates I remember most clearly were those at the London Astoria and Manchester's International 2, again supported by New Morning. At the International, we were so amazed by the audience reaction to the show that, by way of an encore, we played a version of 'Don't Fall', and the response was euphoric. Afterwards in the dressing room Keni, the singer of New Morning, introduced me to a rather sombre looking guy in black clothes and black Ray-Ban sunglasses. His name was Bryan Glancy, a local acoustic singer-songwriter who, by way of a demonstration, performed one of his songs for everyone in the dressing room.

My relationship with Sally deepened, so much so that I proposed to her. I'd never felt such a profound love and harmony with another human being in my life and it seemed exactly the right thing to do, although it would be a long time before we would set a date. In the meantime, we were content just to tell our family and closest friends.

The new album, simply titled *Le Soleil, La Lune*, was well received by the UK press, and John and I finally enjoyed a positive album review in the NME! College radio and much of the independent music press in America were also very enthusiastic.

I became concerned with developments on the business side when I learned that Geffen were seeking to directly recoup some of their claimed losses on the *Strange Times* album, now that The Chameleons had broken up, from The Sun And The Moon, thereby reneging on the agreement I believed I'd struck with Tom. To compound the problem, now that the album had been delivered to them, Geffen were refusing to release the remainder of the recording budget as agreed. The reason they gave for this was that Andy Clegg and Andy Whit were not yet signed officially to the label, and as such, this negated any prior agreement. They immediately proposed another scenario, which gave Geffen the right to recoup Chameleons losses from royalties and monies owed to the new band, which I felt was totally unfair.

The situation was further complicated because a budget of around $150,000, originally earmarked for a Chameleons record, had been diverted to the Sun And The Moon album. The actual cost of pressing and packaging the record would be deducted from this; however, the cost of recording the album at Suite Sixteen had been £7,000 at most. You didn't need to be an accountant to work out that we should have had a considerable sum of money coming our way, but Geffen were reluctant to hand it over. The situation was further compounded by the fact that we now had some outstanding debts to cover, incurred whilst the band were rehearsing for our first shows in London. At the same time, our personal finances were beginning to look somewhat precarious. KES called us in to discuss the situation, and Hal proposed that I travel to California personally to try and sort it out.

The entire trip was a lonely, dispiriting experience, and I began to get a real sense of just how desolate and soul-destroying Los Angeles can be. Tom was busy preparing to launch his latest signing on an unsuspecting world, a local LA band in the same vein, or so he told me, as the original Alice Cooper band. I'd loved Alice Cooper when I was a child, so on an earlier visit to L.A., when Tom had invited me to see his latest discovery, I'd been keen to go, especially when he told me that he'd also invited Bob Ezrin, the former producer and co-writer with the Alice Cooper band. Tom wanted Ezrin to produce his latest discovery, while I was simply thrilled to be having dinner with him, discussing the work he'd done with Alice Cooper. We got on so well that after I'd told him that my copy of *Killer* had been stolen during a party, he offered to try to find me a replacement. Sure enough, about two or three weeks after getting home, a personally autographed copy was delivered along with a note saying that he was letting me have his own copy because he hadn't been able to find another.

After dinner, we'd gone to The Roxy on Sunset Boulevard to check out Tom's new band. We were less than impressed, and afterwards Ezrin asked me what I'd thought of them. I told him that any comparisons with the Alice Cooper band were exaggerated, but that if Tom said that they were going to be as big as the Rolling Stones then I believed him, because Tom was the best A&R man I'd ever met. Tom seemed to appreciate this and squeezed my shoulder affectionately. Ezrin looked thoughtful for a moment, and then told Tom he'd think about it, eventually deciding to pass on the project. I sincerely hope that what I said had no bearing on his decision. The band in question was Guns N' Roses. While In Tom's company I met Axl Rose a couple of times and I found him to be a polite, warm, charming and intelligent man, something which doesn't exactly come across in his public persona.

Later on, I returned to LA to discuss our situation with the president of Geffen Records. By this time, Tom had managed to sign Guns N' Roses to Geffen and had begun to cultivate their public image. Despite my punk sensibilities, I was deeply shocked by what I saw. Geffen were gearing up for a national promotion campaign for the band, and the guys in the mailroom were proudly showing off the new T-shirt that had just come in. On the front of the shirt was a garish drawing of a young girl lying in an alley, her face bleeding and her clothes ripped from her body, the obvious implication being that she'd just been gang raped. On the wall just above her, sprayed in a graffiti style, were the words 'GUNS N' ROSES WAS HERE.' Everyone in the office thought the shirts were a hoot. I was physically sickened, and said so.

The meeting with the president of Geffen didn't go well either. I carefully and patiently explained the situation: we were now in dire need of financial assistance, having laid out thousands of pounds on rehearsal rooms, with the added complication that neither Andy Clegg nor Andy Whitaker was signed to the label. As Geffen were using that fact to withhold the funds, I told him that Andy Clegg and Andy Whitaker should be considered session musicians and that Geffen should hand over the outstanding funds to John and me. This was merely a ploy on my part to get around the loophole that Geffen had brought into play. This scenario hadn't occurred to Geffen, but their legal department wasn't overly concerned. They knew that we would need to have considerable resources at our disposal in order to mount a legal challenge, something they knew we didn't have. Furthermore, I went on to tell him how ashamed and disgusted I was to be with the company after seeing the Guns N' Roses shirts downstairs. Not the most diplomatic thing to say to the president of Geffen Records, I grant you, but it was my honest reaction.

"I'm releasing you from your contract to us," he said simply, and that was that.

Far from being upset, I can honestly say I was relieved to be off the label. Geffen Records had the reputation of being a progressive, enlightened independent major player. Secretaries would hang wind chimes and crystals around the offices, or burn incense at their desks. To some extent, I suppose Geffen's progressive reputation was due to the company's past association with John Lennon. This had been the chief attraction for me - I'd known that David Geffen and John Lennon had been close friends and been very impressed by that, but personally, David Geffen hadn't impressed me at all. When I'd been overseeing the artwork for *Strange Times*, I came to think he was a bit of a dick. He'd been berating me over something I'd written for the sleeve notes, in which I said that if the listener couldn't afford the record, then they should either tape it or steal it, the important thing being that they hear it. "I can't advocate piracy and theft on one of my record sleeves!" he wailed. No, but he could advocate a management staff that were happy to turn a blind eye while artists used recording budgets to buy heroin instead of using it to record demos - even justifying it as being a hip rock 'n' roll attitude. Geffen made massive amounts of money, and like most major corporations, their priorities were fucked up beyond all recognition. For all its pretensions, Geffen Records had proved to be no better than any other major record company, and through their dubious marketing of Guns N' Roses, and one or two other skeletons in the closet that I knew about, I felt they'd stooped lower than any of them.

Eager to be done with L.A., I hastily rearranged my return flight, said my goodbyes to Tom, and returned to England. I made directly for the centre of Manchester in order to meet with the others and give them the good news. As I expected, they were less than thrilled. I sympathised, because I knew how much a major record deal had meant to them after years of struggling for recognition, but I felt I had to stand by my own convictions too. I suggested that we could form a label of our own and might even make some money that way. Equally, if they wanted out, then I'd understand. Everyone agreed to stick with it, at least in the short term.

A little while after this, my motorcycling days came to a sudden and almost fatal end. I'd arranged to ride over to our manager Rob's house, and by the time I set out it was dark, and the roads were quiet. I was about to negotiate a roundabout when, suddenly, the bike stalled. It had developed a tendency to do this whenever the engine grew hot, and I had meant to fix it but it kept slipping my mind. I tried to restart the engine and barely noticed the slow-moving, articulated lorry that crawled past and now headed off along the stretch of dual carriageway that I was intending to take. At last, the engine fired and catching up with the truck that had just passed me, I began to overtake on the outside lane.

At that moment, a car shot out in front of me travelling very slowly, from left to right, intending to make a right turn. He'd obviously checked the flow, and on seeing the approaching truck, had reasoned that he'd make it across safely before it reached him. What he hadn't realised was that I was in the process of overtaking in the outside lane, hidden from his view. When I saw him, I had less than a hundred yards in which to stop from sixty miles an hour. I remember realising the gravity of the situation just seconds before the impact, and was firmly convinced that I was about to die. I collided with the car, the front forks taking the brunt of the impact, and I was thrown over the handlebars. My left foot shattered the driver's side window, caught on the lip of the door, and sent me into a forward somersault. I rolled on my shoulder across the roof of the car and landed deftly on my feet on the other side, minus my left shoe, without suffering any significant injury. I was aware of the driver shouting, incredulously demanding to know where I'd come from. I was pointing gingerly ahead but he was yelling that there was no way I could have come from that direction on a dual carriageway. I looked around for the bike but it was nowhere to be seen, and it was then that I realised I'd passed right over the car. I walked around the car past his white-faced, horror-stricken wife and picked up the bike. Sitting astride it, I pressed the starter and the engine fired. A nearby taxi driver had witnessed the whole thing. He ran over to me, urging me to dismount, saying that he'd already called the police on his radio. I was in shock, laughing uncontrollably, and I remember thinking, "The police? Oh no! I'm not legal!"

A few other witnesses helped push the wrecked car and the motorcycle off the road, by which time two motorcycle policemen turned up. After I'd calmed down, one of them took me aside and I tried to explain what had happened to the best of my recollection. I was also forced to tell him I wasn't legal, which he appreciated, because at least I hadn't tried to waste his time. After speaking with the witnesses and taking statements, they told me they would be prosecuting the driver for driving dangerously, and that I would also be prosecuted for riding a motorcycle without a license or insurance.

I phoned Sally first, then my parents to tell them what had happened, and I had to promise my very distraught mother that I wouldn't ride a motorcycle again for a while. A kind uncle with a van offered to come out and retrieve the bike. Not that I still had one; my bike was as good as dead as the front forks were bent at a forty-five degree angle. One of the police officers asked what I'd intended to do when I'd climbed back onto the machine earlier. "Ride off, I suppose," I mumbled.

"Ride off?" the officer exclaimed, laughing, "Have you looked at it?"

On closer inspection, I could see his point. Had the taxi driver not stopped me I would have gone wobbling off up the road at around five miles an hour, like something from a Warner Bros. cartoon.

We decided to go ahead and form our own label, which I named Glass Pyramid, inspired by a present Sally had given to me. Hal agreed to finance a week at Suite Sixteen to record a maxi-single. I had argued that, armed with this, we'd be in a better position to shop around for a new record deal or, even better, an independent distribution deal. Hal had recently invested in a buy-out of a recording studio in Bury, and he offered us the use of this to prepare some new songs. I was able to contribute a couple: a love song titled 'Adam's Song', and 'C'est La Vie', a commentary on my feelings regarding the Geffen split. Both arrangements were then augmented and improved upon. Further rehearsal sessions produced the song 'Arabs And Americans', and finally, a version of Alice Cooper's 'Elected' was added, in honour of my encounter with Bob Ezrin earlier in the year.

This was to be the last recording by The Sun And The Moon, and I believe it was our finest, which is always a great way to go out. Having completed the recordings, I was surprised when Rob Brown told me he'd received an offer to take the band up to the Shetland Islands for a concert. I remember the local promoter there had written to me some years earlier asking if it would be possible to bring The Chameleons to Shetland, but when I'd raised the subject with the others they'd greeted the idea with total derision. The guys in The Sun And The Moon had no such prejudices, happily, and everyone decided they wanted to do it.

That weekend was one of the most memorable, enjoyable and funniest trips I've ever undertaken. None of us had a clue what to expect. After a short flight of around an hour we were met at the airport by two of the locals: a guy who would only answer to the name of Catnap, and a strikingly beautiful young girl whose name was Mandy. Mandy was the live-in girlfriend of Geoff, the local promoter, and she immediately took Sally and me under her wing. She discreetly told us that it would be better for us to stay at the house, and installed us in one of the spare bedrooms. The others, meanwhile, were quickly engaged in a game of Shotgun. This involved a deck of playing cards and a seemingly bottomless bag of canned lager. A single card would be dealt to each person face down. A player then had to choose whether to stick with the card they had, or to swap the unseen card with the person next to them. Eventually, everyone turned their cards and the person with the lowest value card lost the round. The forfeit was a shotgun, which consisted of having a full can of beer placed at the mouth. With the ring-tab still sealed, the can would then be punctured and the resulting air pressure would fire the beer down the loser's throat with great velocity. The Shetlanders, besides being very robust drinkers, are also exceptional card cheats and in no time at all every member of the band, including the manager, was legless.

At the end of the game, the others staggered away, sleeping bags in hand, to spend the night at a flat belonging to Geoff's brother Mike. The following day, a vaguely familiar bunch of Manchester musicians and their manager ambled in for breakfast, looking withered and more than a little hung-over. "How was it?" I asked Rob.

He told me he'd dreamed he'd awoken in the middle of the night and had come face to face with a giant rat.

Just as he finished telling this tale, Mike stopped and said, "Ach, no mate, that weren't no dream, that was my rat. He lives under the floorboards."

Rob's face was a picture.

We were due to play two shows over the space of a weekend. The first venue was little more than a community centre, some miles out of the main town of Lerwick. Geoff, who in his spare time fronted a punk band, opened the show, and his energy was unbelievable. As a promoter too, his energy was boundless; he was seemingly everywhere at once, and nothing was too much trouble. I was rather confused by the venue because it seemed to be very remote, but I was assured that there'd be a sizeable crowd, and in the end that proved correct. I remember standing in the crowd watching Geoff perform with his band, when a young guy next to me yelled "Geoff, you fuckin' wanker!" He then hurled a freshly-opened can of beer directly at the singer's shaved head, scoring a direct hit. The can ricocheted away at an angle, but Geoff didn't flinch - he just laughed casually into the microphone and carried on regardless.

At one point I went outside to get some fresh air and noticed a car pulling up outside. A young boy, around fourteen years old, got out of the car and his mother was telling him she'd be there to collect him at around 2.30am. "Aye mam, aye mam," the boy kept repeating in response to what was a fairly typical parental lecture. No sooner had the car rounded the bend than he pulled a litre of vodka from his coat, took a sizeable swig, and ran inside to join the fray.

Walking back inside I bumped into Andy Whit on my way to the dressing room. "Look what someone just gave me," he laughed gleefully, and opened his hand to reveal about an eighth of an ounce of black hashish. As far as I knew, Andy Whit smoked neither tobacco nor dope. I told him to be careful with it, and he wandered off.

Unfortunately, he didn't heed my warning, and elected to eat the hash, and was now totally fucked up. As a result our set was awful, and when we came off I went ballistic. On reflection, I completely overreacted, but for me it was a little too close to Dave's antics for comfort. Afterwards a few of the locals were trying to reassure me that it hadn't been as bad as I imagined, and that this sort of thing happened every time a band came to Shetland. In the fullness of time I came to realise that Lerwick was in fact the party capital of Europe - forget Amsterdam!

The following morning I awoke and went down to breakfast to find Geoff preparing to leave for the venue we'd played the night before. Apparently, consent for the show had been given on the condition that he organise the clean-up the following day. Having nothing better to do with the morning, I chose to drive over there with him along with one or two other volunteers. I remember being asked to retrieve something from a large cupboard that stood in the hallway. Opening the door, a small boy, still sleeping, spilled onto the floor. "What time is it?" he croaked, squinting in the bright sunlight that was streaming through the windows. I promptly told him. "Fuck!" he shouted, and getting to his feet, he bolted through the doors and was off up the road.

I made some good friends in Shetland during my short time there, and a few of them have remained close friends to this day. Mandy worked ceaselessly taking care of us all. I remember watching her working at the house where we were lodged, and was reminded of a latter-day Cinderella. Then there was Colin, or Beanz as he was known back then. On my first visit I didn't get to speak with him for long because he was due to fly to London the following day to give evidence at the Old Bailey in a murder trial.

Our final night on Shetland was marked by a party at Mike's flat. We were booked on a very early flight the following morning, so I declined to take part in the drinking binge. Mike asked me what I wanted to drink, and I asked him if I might have a cup of tea.

"TEA?" he barked, a very confused look on his face. "Aye, okay," and off he went to organise it.

Ten minutes later, he came back and handed me a large, foul-tasting cup of tea, but not wishing to offend him I politely drank some as if nothing was amiss. After a while I was still sipping from the cup, when he asked, "How's the tea?"

"To be honest, Mike," I replied, "it tastes a bit weird. Is the milk off?"

"Och no, it isn't the milk," he grinned. "That'll be the mushrooms."

"MUSHROOMS?"

I tipped the cup and peered into it and noticed that the bottom of the cup was lined with a pulped mess of magic mushrooms. I think it took me ten minutes to stop laughing. After that, I had no option but to join the party. Sally and I were the last to leave, after everyone else drifted off to sleep in other rooms. Somehow, we made it back to our lodging with barely four hours left before we had to leave for the airport. When the hour arrived I was so tired, drunk and still under the influence of mushrooms that I hadn't wanted to move. "Just leave me here!" I was groaning, as both Mandy and Sally struggled to get me to my feet.

Over the following months, cracks within The Sun And The Moon began to show. Our relationships began to fragment, culminating in the eventual departure of Andy Whit. I forget the exact circumstances. I remember becoming increasingly disillusioned with what we were doing and the direction we were taking, although I was very much in the driving seat, and I remember the others becoming increasingly frustrated with me. I was extremely idealistic and dreamed of working independently as much as possible, rather than playing the corporate game or falling in with the machinations of the music industry. I felt that the others, Andy Clegg and John in particular, were still dreaming of those big contracts and plush, record company offices, not that I blamed them for this of course. Looking back, I'm surprised we took it as far as we did. The band should probably have ended when Andy Whit left, which in effect, it did.

Initially Andy Whit's place was taken by our chief roadie Aky, although the association was short-lived, and he went on to have greater success with another Manchester band, Molly Half Head. The Sun And The Moon's final record, a maxi-single titled *Alive; Not Dead* was released shortly after our return from Shetland. The recording had been financed by KES with the help of Rob Brown, and we'd managed to license the record in France through a company called Midnight Music, even though they were based in London rather than Paris. When UK distribution began to get complicated, Midnight Music offered to release the record in the UK too, and so in the interests of getting the record into the shops we agreed. They achieved this by importing the French copies into UK shops - which is why the sleeve notes on the record are in French!

The record did surprisingly well, reaching the top ten in the independent singles charts, but it seemed even Hal and KES had finally lost patience and we were notified that the company had dropped us. This meant that I was now effectively free of both Hal and KES without having to run up huge legal bills, which pleased me immensely. To the others, of course, it was just further evidence that they'd backed a losing horse.

The fact that the record charted suddenly meant we had London interest and that week we were asked to attend meetings with RCA and EMI. The latter offered us a publishing deal, but having finally been released from KES, there was no way I was signing with another company. John in particular was very unhappy about this as he'd sniffed money in the form of advances, but I was adamant and so, finally, John bailed too. Rob did his best to hold things together, but he was fighting for a lost cause. I'd been writing some new material for the next record, but neither Andy Clegg nor Aky were very impressed with it. Nor was I with theirs, to be honest, which sounded exactly like every other jingly-jangle guitar riff I'd ever heard.

I'd been getting quite involved with local street artists and buskers who were organising themselves into a kind of co-operative and doing regular gigs at venues around Manchester. This enterprise was promoted by a passionate, eager and lovely guy called Chris Coop, who I'd met through

Keni. Andy Clegg, in particular, was extremely cynical. I understood his point of view. To Andy, busking meant standing in the freezing cold, playing shit cover versions and making around £1 an hour. I had a much more romantic view of what Chris Coop and all the artists involved were trying to do, which was lift the profile of alternative cabaret and street performance. There were some seriously talented people getting involved, and some very respectable names from Manchester's underground scene lent their names to it, such as Manchester beat poet Lemn Sissay, Vini Reilly from Durutti Column and the comedian Frank Skinner. While it would fall short of anything permanent, it was an exciting thing to be on the fringe of, certainly better than what I'd been doing with The Sun And The Moon. I found the honesty, integrity and raw talent of these people extremely refreshing after the bullshit of Geffen, Hollywood, Hal, KES, and the rest. I believed then and I believe now that Chris Coop and his fine band of artists and friends were a far more positive influence on me than any of the other folk I'd been involved with until then. I certainly became a better musician by getting involved. The whole notion of being in a performing band had changed for me, or more accurately, my old passions had been re-kindled. The acoustic underground was far more interesting to me than anything else that was going on at that time, and would remain so until the emergence of The Stone Roses and The Happy Mondays over the next couple of years.

Rather than feel depressed about not having a record deal, a publishing deal, or a management deal, for the first time in years I felt liberated. I was free to explore directions for no other reason than because they interested me, without the slightest pressure to fall in with the whims of others. With the benefit of hindsight, I came to realise that The Sun And The Moon had never really stood a chance in the long term. The memory of The Chameleons was too fresh in people's minds, and the level of expectation too great. We did go through the motions of auditioning new drummers, and entertained one guy who had previously played with James. I played him some of the ideas that I would eventually go on to develop alone and he liked them a lot, but it was obvious we were on the brink of disintegration, so nothing came of it. We held a final meeting at which The Sun And The Moon disbanded and that, as they say, was that.

19. THE GREAT ADVENTURE

Over the next two years I was to forge new relationships of an altogether higher and more sincere order. Amongst these was my friendship with Keni, whose humour, optimism and honesty were a constant source of inspiration.

Most of my musical ideas had, until this point, been developed on the bass guitar and then augmented by the musicians I'd been working with at the time. More recently, though, I'd switched to acoustic guitar, on which I started to develop ideas rejected by The Sun And The Moon towards the end. While not exactly original - drawing on the work of Mike Scott and similar, lesser-known songwriters for inspiration - it did represent a shift in style for me.

The highlight of the summer of 1989 was a journey to Glastonbury Festival, after we'd learned that one of our favourite bands, The Waterboys, were playing. We had neither money nor tickets but, undaunted, Sally and I decided we'd cycle to the festival, camping wild as we went. As luck would have it, it turned out to be one of the hottest summers on record. There wasn't even a hint of rain during the whole of the journey, and most of the farmers we approached were only too happy to allow us to camp in their meadows. The journey took us about a week, following the old Roman roads along the Welsh border, and on into Somerset and Avon. It really was a case of rediscovering our own countryside - hamlets, villages and woodland worthy of Constable that lie hidden from the A-roads and motorways that bypass them on every side.

We arrived at the festival site about three days ahead of the event itself, but already the masses were congregating, and security around the main entrance was tight. Riding past the site towards Glastonbury town, we veered off and followed a farm track for a couple of miles, which we estimated ran roughly parallel to the festival site. We cut across the countryside until, at last, we saw a ramshackle arrangement of tents on the far side of a makeshift fence. We debated whether to wait until nightfall, but in the end simply hoisted our gear over the small fence. A young guy was sitting by his tent, so I asked him if we were actually on the festival site. Beaming, he confirmed that we were. "Well done mate, you're in, nice one!" he laughed. By the start of the festival a higher, more impenetrable fence had been erected, but our early arrival had neatly circumvented this problem.

Beanz, one of our Shetland friends, had been in touch and told us that a crowd of them were coming to the festival too, and that he'd try to find us somehow. By Saturday afternoon there were around 50,000 people camping at the festival, plus hordes of day-trippers from London, and I didn't hold out much hope of him finding us. Somehow, though, he did. We were sitting by the tents in the early afternoon when I heard a voice say, "Ah, there you are!" Craning my head, I saw the beaming face of Beanz.

Beanz was a tall, slightly built individual. He was highly intelligent, with a knowledge of drugs that bordered on the encyclopaedic. He told us that they'd driven down in a large van, parking it some distance from the site, and that they'd stopped off in Hereford and bought an entire keg of scrumpy. Unfortunately, it had been too heavy to carry to the site, and so they'd left it in the van. I suggested that, as they'd bought tickets for the festival and had wristbands that allowed them to come and go as they wished, they use my bike to carry the barrel onto the site. Beanz thought this an excellent idea and so we both set off with the bike towards the main entrance. He subsequently returned with the brown plastic barrel strapped onto the bike's carrier, and we made our way back to the tents, where another surprise awaited us. Sally was sitting at the door of our tent, laughing so hard her face was red. Someone was attempting to erect an adjacent tent from the inside and struggling badly. Eventually a head emerged, and there was young Alex, whose arrival represented an even greater miracle than that of the Shetlanders.

I first met Alex at The Duchess of York in Leeds, while touring with The Sun And The Moon. I walked into the venue to be approached by a kid asking me I was Mark Burgess - although he pronounced it Mark Bur-jess. I guessed, correctly as it turned out, that he was around fourteen years old. His short frizzy hair and large glasses gave him an almost cartoon look, and he seemed both well-educated and intelligent. When I told him that I was indeed Mark Burgess, he immediately demanded to see some form of identification, having apparently been the victim of a wind-up earlier in the day. He told me that although he lived with his mother and stepfather in Leeds he attended Carmel, a rather exclusive public school in the south of England, and was hoping eventually to study medicine and become a doctor. Having successfully established my identity, he then asked me for an autograph. I remember him turning up at a couple of concerts after that, and on one occasion we were invited to visit him at his mother's house in Leeds.

Over the following year, Alex kept in touch and we'd bump into him here and there. During one conversation, he overheard me saying that Sally and I were thinking of going to Glastonbury and asked if he could accompany us. I had to gently refuse, explaining that we were planning to cycle to the festival, that it wasn't really a place for a fifteen year old boy to be wandering around and that, quite honestly, it was more responsibility than I wanted to take on. We agreed that if he were to make his own way there he could camp alongside us, never dreaming in a million years that it would happen. Occasionally, he'd telephone me and ask if he ought to pack spare underwear, or if we knew how often the bus ran, but I honestly thought that was as far as his plan would progress.

To a hardened Shetlander like Beanz, Alex was even more of an oddity. I don't think Beanz knew what to make of him, and the banter between the two of them was nothing short of hilarious. Having very little money, Sally and I had hit upon the idea of making hundreds of multi-coloured friendship bracelets and selling them around the site. We were great at making them, but far too shy to walk around selling them. Typically, Beanz leapt into the fray. "Give 'em here, I'll fuckin' sell 'em for you," he grunted, and seized the board on which we'd fixed them. He'd stride over to someone, thrust the board into their faces and then, in a manner that suggested that they would be very unwise to decline, grunted "Wanna buy one of these?"

Alex watched all of this with a rather bemused expression, tut-tutting to himself at Beanz's less than subtle approach. "You'll never sell them like that," he kept saying, until finally Beanz thrust the board at him and barked, "Go on then smart arse, you sell 'em." Alex was in the process of choosing a likely looking customer, when Beanz pointed to a Mike Tyson lookalike who was discreetly offering various drugs to the passing revellers. "Go on, try him!" Beanz insisted, obviously out to sabotage Alex's efforts. I did my best to dissuade him, but Alex brushed my protests aside and walked over. From our safe distance, we could see Alex going into his sales pitch. The guy looked down at Alex as if he'd just arrived from another planet. Alex was now holding the ribbons against the man's forearms while the man stroked his shaved scalp in confusion. Suddenly, the guy reached into his pocket, bought six of them and tied them all together at his wrist. Smiling, Alex triumphantly returned to where we were standing and handed the money over to Sally. Beanz insisted that this had been a mere fluke so, rising to the challenge, Alex went off again in search of more customers, and in less than an hour he'd sold the lot. Humble pie does not usually form part of Beanz's daily diet, but he ate plenty that afternoon.

Alex was somewhat disconcerted when he realised we'd be spending some of the money on marijuana, but I was able to keep him happy for a few minutes with a visit to a music stall at one of the markets. The stall specialised in bootleg live tapes, and Alex's soon spied an entire section featuring his favourite band, The Chameleons. The stall-holder recognised me immediately and was obviously embarrassed. "What the fuck's this?" I barked.

The guy shifted awkwardly, "Well, you know how it is Mark." I did indeed know how it was, and suggested that he let us have a few copies by way of recompense. Smiling broadly, he invited Alex to take his pick. As far as I was concerned, this was a very equitable arrangement. Oh, the magic of Glastonbury.

The true nature of the Glastonbury Festival, however, was only just beginning to dawn on young Alex. That evening, as we gathered around the campfire, he sidled up to me and asked if he might have a quiet word. I drew him to one side and asked him what was wrong. "I think you ought to know, Mark" he said, with a rather troubled expression, "that I suspect one or two people around us may be taking drugs."

"Alex," I whispered, "I suspect that around 50,000 of the people around us are *definitely* taking drugs."

Alex was keen to know what kind of drugs people were taking. We told him that the vast majority were probably taking LSD, and tried to explain what effect this had on people's senses. He looked thoughtful for a moment, and then asked if he might be able to buy some.

"OH NO!" I bellowed, "absolutely NOT! There is *no way* that I am going to allow you to take ANYTHING, let alone acid - absolutely NO WAY!"

Alex laughed, "No, it isn't for me, I thought perhaps I could put it into my stepfather's tea. I HATE him!"

The festival wrapped up on Sunday night and we said our goodbyes. Alex was expected back at school, and Beanz, along with the rest of his posse, was making for Stonehenge for the annual confrontation with authority that always occurred around the summer solstice. Beanz told us that he might well turn up in Bury on his journey north, and we told him we'd look forward to seeing him then.

By Monday morning, the vast majority of the revellers were making their way home. The roads were predictably clogged with hikers and traffic, and by the time we reached the town of Shepton Mallet we were in desperate need of respite. We bought some food and headed for the park, intending to wait until the traffic had died down. As we sat there, a young guy pushing a bike that was stripped to the frame of all but the barest necessities, approached and asked if he might join us. We motioned for him to sit, sharing what we had. After a while, he asked if we might enjoy some wine and returned a short time later with a bottle and some paper cups. He told us he lived in a small village near Wrexham, and that he'd cycled to the festival as we had. I was amazed because he carried nothing on his bike - no sleeping bag, no cooking gear, not even a water container. I remarked on this and he smiled, "If I want water, I ask and it's provided, I don't really need to carry anything." He was so relaxed, pleasant and charming that we hung out together for the rest of the day.

Our young companion invited us for a drink at a nearby pub, shrugging off our protests that we really didn't have money to spare for such things. It was good to get out of the summer heat, but the beer went straight to my head and I was feeling more than a little tipsy. It was now too late to begin the ride north, so the three of us decided to head back to the festival site and camp there until morning. The guy introduced himself as Mark and told us he was a wizard. He went on to say that there were only two things in the whole world that he desired: the first was a pure emerald, which he said would augment his wizard's powers, and the other was to one day perform music at the Glastonbury Festival.

As we returned to the site, we came to a shallow gully bridged by a narrow plank of wood. In my slightly drunken state I foolishly elected to try and ride across the plank without dismounting, losing my balance, and the bike fell from beneath me. The full weight of our packs landed with some considerable force on the back wheel, buckling it horribly. My embarrassment aside, this was a real problem because we didn't have money for a new wheel. Mark told me not to worry, and that he'd have a look at it. He held the wheel up to the diminishing light, and then, placing the wheel on the ground, applied some weight to one side of it. He repeated this procedure, and then picked up the wheel and spun it on its axle. The wheel was now perfectly true, rotating without even the slightest waver.

The following day, Mark told me that while he believed the fixed wheel would hold, it would be better not to chance it, and that we ought to think about an alternative way of getting home. I wasn't brimming with enthusiasm for a five-day journey north by bike now that the festival was over, but the problem was lack of funds. "Don't worry about that," he told us, "just do exactly as I instruct you, and you'll be home by tonight." Naturally, we were cynical, but he told us that if we waited a while, he felt sure that something would happen that would at least get us as far as Bristol. Sure enough, as we stood idly by the side of the road, a large van pulled over and offered us a lift into the city. By the end of that day we were back home in Bury. The wizard had made us solemnly promise never to reveal to anyone how it was done, and to this day, neither Sally or I have ever done so.

Beanz, as promised, stopped off to visit us on his way back to Scotland. Sally and I were hankering to take on another bicycle tour, and when Beanz suggested we meet up in the Highlands, we vaguely arranged something along these lines. I was encouraged by two letters I received shortly afterwards: the first was from our friend Mandy in Shetland, who wrote that she'd migrated to Edinburgh and moved in with her new boyfriend, Harry, the singer with a Scottish band called Swamptrash. The second was a fan letter of sorts, from a guy called Xander, enquiring about the possibility of me playing a show in his village. The letter was extremely charming, and came with a hand-drawn map indicating where the village, Loanhead, was situated, on the outskirts of Edinburgh. I was far from confident enough to contemplate performing solo, but I told him I'd think about it, and soon a plan was forming in my mind. We could load up the bikes, travel to Edinburgh by train to stay with Harry and Mandy, visit Xander in Loanhead, and then meet up with Beanz in the Highlands.

As the weekend drew nearer, I telephoned Harry and Mandy. Harry answered the phone, and immediately I was confused. His voice sounded very gentle, unquestionably English, and very well-educated, completely unlike the raving Cajun I'd heard on the Swamptrash tape Mandy had sent me. Harry told me that Mandy had suddenly moved back to Shetland. I was quite disappointed and, sensing this, Harry suggested that Sally and I come anyway. "I've heard a lot about you," he said, "it'd be a shame to waste the opportunity." Harry was very warm and charming on the phone, so we agreed to go anyway.

Unfortunately, the timing of the trains was such that we didn't arrive in Edinburgh until quite late at night. Harry had told us he'd be there to meet us, but the station was deserted as we wheeled our fully laden bikes to the main entrance. After only a few minutes, however, a figure, draped in a long flowing black coat and hair down to his waist, emerged from the mist and came toward us. He instantly struck me as someone you'd expect to see in a seventeenth century oil painting. His movement was elegant, and his speech extremely refined.

Harry led the way through Edinburgh's cobbled streets to his flat. It was Friday night so he still had to work. His main source of income came from drawing the weekly political or satirical cartoons that appeared in the Scotland On Sunday newspaper. I was worried about us intruding, but he waved this aside. Harry was a brilliant artist in every sense, and could do these cartoons in his sleep. We talked about a whole myriad of subjects as he drew at his desk. He told us how much he was missing Mandy, and how deeply hopeful he was that she'd decide to return. He lived in a rooftop apartment in an old part of Edinburgh, just a few minutes' walk from Princes Street and the city centre. His apartment was tiny, and crammed with all sorts of strange, interesting artefacts: glass cases containing the skulls of birds, various species of exotic looking butterflies, stone simulacra, framed caricatures of people both real and imagined, antique ink wells and feathered quills, Napoleonic hats and hundreds of books and records. Despite this, it didn't feel cramped or claustrophobic in the slightest, and reflected a sophisticated, highly refined taste. Harry, besides providing the lead vocals for Swamptrash, also played banjo, and his instrument was saturated with character, featuring drawings in coloured inks and phrases written out in beautiful, old-style handwriting. He played some of his own compositions, which included a song called 'Jake's Lift' that I loved immediately, and I was able to pick it out and accompany him on my guitar.

Initially Swamptrash had struggled to find gigs and, as their music had developed a strong Cajun flavour, they hit upon the idea of pretending they were a visiting American band. This ruse proved more successful, and from this point on, they regularly played to packed houses. Bar owners were suddenly inclined to give them gigs, and the fictional origins of the band subsequently became an in-joke amongst the audience. Harry's discourse between songs became increasingly exaggerated and ridiculous: explaining for example, in a feigned Louisiana accent, how his brother had been struck dumb after having seen a relative eaten by a 'gator', or relating how he'd helped Mama bury Pa in the back yard in the driving snow following a heavy diphtheria epidemic. To compound the joke, elements of the music business hadn't realised it had been a wind-up, including a major London record label that only abandoned negotiations at the last minute when the truth dawned. Harry was the absolute master of the wind-up, as I would eventually discover for myself.

Deciding that we should visit Xander and see if the gig he was proposing was possible, we temporarily said goodbye to Harry and made our way by bike to the suburbs of Edinburgh. Loanhead had at one time been a mining village and had a rather hard, heavy ambience, so the two hippy-like characters on mountain bikes, one with a guitar strapped to the back of it, drew more than a few curious stares. We parked the bikes at a pub in the centre of the village and phoned Xander. He was thrilled when I told him I'd be interested in playing an acoustic set in Loanhead. "Great!" he raved. "When?"

"Well, it'd have to be this afternoon or not at all," I calmly told him. There was a moment of silent confusion before I finally told him where we were.

The village of Loanhead was very small, and word travels fast. Before long we were surrounded by excited, laughing faces and I'd be a liar if I said I wasn't enjoying the attention. It transpired that quite a few people in the town were Chameleons fans, and I made some long-lasting friendships that afternoon. Xander took me to the home of a guy who was a massive fan of the band. The guy had no idea I was in town, and his face when he opened the door was an absolute picture. From his point of view, a very strange day had just got even stranger. He'd taken some magic mushrooms earlier and was now tripping mightily. He just sat there wearing a dazed smile the whole afternoon while I played some songs for them on the guitar. Quite a few of them played guitar too, and so the day evolved into a jam session, after which we all retreated to the pub, where Sally and I were plied with drinks for the rest of the night by way of wages. For us, it was a special and unforgettable experience. Eventually, we said our goodbyes and made our way back to Harry.

The following day, Beanz, who'd somehow managed to track us down at Harry's flat, rang and gave us some bad news. He wouldn't be able to meet us in the Highlands as planned. He'd just received news that his mother had died suddenly at home in Shetland. He told us he'd have to go there directly to help his brother with the arrangements for the funeral and settle her estate. We decided we should return to Manchester, try to get some money together and visit him in Shetland, if possible. We knew from our conversations that Beanz didn't really get along with his brother that well, and despite having many friends in Lerwick, we thought he might appreciate some additional support. Beanz was thrilled with the idea. Later that day he rang again, this time to say that he'd flown to Shetland, and was sitting with some of the people we'd met when The Sun And The Moon had played, and that everyone was excited about the possibility of us paying them another visit. With this in mind, they'd organised a collection and raised enough money to pay for our boat fare. The money had already been sent by registered letter and should be with us the next day. Sally and I agreed to go, leaving the bikes with Harry in Edinburgh.

Beanz had two friends in Aberdeen, Chiz and Frankie, who were both members of a very fine punk band called Toxic Ephex. They'd agreed to meet us in Aberdeen and see us safely to the boat that would carry us to Shetland. We'd never met them before, but they were extremely likeable characters, and a long and enduring friendship developed that survives to this day. We were fortunate to have very calm weather during the night crossing from Aberdeen to Lerwick on the legendary St. Clair, which has sadly been decommissioned after making thousands of crossings. It was reminiscent of the ferry crossings we'd made a couple of years earlier returning from Israel, and we spent most of the early evening on deck looking for dolphins, but were disappointed not to see any.

The following morning, the boat docked at Lerwick, and Beanz put us up in a spare room at his mother's house. His brother did indeed seem rather strange and standoffish. During that first day, he'd been sat reading a book and so, later, trying to make conversation, I'd casually asked what he was reading. "Oh it's great!" he beamed, "It's science fiction - Iain M. Banks - this guy's suspended in a glass container that's slowly filling up with human shit." I think those were the only words he and I exchanged during my entire stay there.

We spent that first morning sitting around a kitchen table with a few familiar faces, including Mandy. Inevitably - always one of the nicest things about travelling up to Shetland - I was asked to get my guitar out and give them a tune. I chose The Chameleons song 'Time' with Mandy in mind. After the song was over, she was a little tearful. She asked us what our impressions of Harry had been and we told her we liked him very, very much. Not long after that, Mandy decided to go back to Harry in Edinburgh, and they were married in Shetland a year or two later.

My most immediate problem was figuring out what to do next. We'd had enough money to cover the travelling expenses, but other than that we were penniless, and I had no desire to sign on the dole in Lerwick. Beanz had anticipated this, and told me he'd arranged for me to work alongside him on a building site in town. The hours were long, but the money was very good and he told me that all they really needed was someone to make breakfast and organise shop runs for lunch for the rest of them. I agreed at once, but during that first day I had very little to do, while those around me seemed to be working very hard. In the end, I asked the foreman if I might be given other labouring jobs to do around the site, but soon wished I hadn't.

I didn't find out until much later, of course, but it transpired that a book was being run on as to how long I could stand working there. Each day the foreman would work me harder, the idea being that eventually I'd quit and someone on the site would make a great deal of extra money. But I stuck it out, made some friends, and gained a lot of respect as a result. After that first week, things eased off and the work got easier, but my hands were a mass of sores and blisters. It was a while before I could even lift a guitar, let alone play it. Shortly before her return to Edinburgh, Mandy invited us over to her parents' house. Leaving the island to move in with an Englishman had taken some courage on her part, and she'd had to deal with resentment and hostility from some quarters. Behind the house was a narrow bridge spanning a small river and she told us that her favourite Shetland poet, Vagaland, had featured this very spot in one of his poems. Back at the house, she read us the poem from a book, written in the original Shetland brogue, a dialect that's now sadly in decline. It was one of the most beautiful sounds I'd ever heard, and I said so. I knew then that someday I had to record Mandy reading that poem. A couple of days later Mandy caught the boat back to the mainland to be with Harry. Sally and I escorted her to the dock to see her off, and I'll never forget the sight of Mandy standing at the ship's stern, waving to us until she was finally out of sight.

Each day Beanz and I would leave the house for work at around six in the morning, and wouldn't usually finish until around nine in the evening. By this time, almost everyone on the site had befriended me, save for the chief foreman who seemed to have a chip on his shoulder regarding Englishmen. One time he was screaming at me at the top of his voice in front of everyone, but his accent was so strong I couldn't understand a word of it. After this had gone on for over a minute I turned to one of the men and said, "What the fuck is he saying?" The entire site erupted in laughter, including the foreman, and after that I had no further problems with him.

Another thorn in my side came by way of a junior foreman nicknamed Monster. I tried my best to get past his constant, bad-tempered attitude, but nothing seemed to work. One afternoon we'd both been sent to clear a patch of waste ground some distance from the actual building site. The day was intensely hot, and at one point Monster had stopped working and was lamenting the fact we had nothing to drink. "Why don't we just ask at one of the houses?" I suggested, but he just grunted and looked confused.

Throwing down my tools, I walked over to a nearby house and asked the woman who lived there if we could have some water. Not only did she supply us with this, but she also threw in a few chilled cans of lager for good measure. However, now feeling that he'd had his intelligence insulted by this dazzling display of lateral thinking, Monster's attitude worsened.

Things finally came to a head one afternoon after he'd instructed me to clear plaster from a small stone room just off the main hall. As I was working, one of the bricklayers came over and explained that someone hadn't turned in, and would I climb the scaffolding with him and help him out? Naturally, I went along and worked alongside him for the rest of the afternoon. Suddenly, I heard violent shouting from below. Craning my head over the edge of the scaffolding, I saw an enraged Monster, screaming insults at me for abandoning the task he'd set. The bricklayer calmly took all this in until finally, he seized a breeze block from a nearby stack and hurled it at the angry foreman below. The block shattered millimetres away from Monster, and his face turned white. The bricklayer told him that his aim was true, and if he didn't fuck off immediately the next one would land squarely on the bridge of his nose, and if he ever heard about him speaking to me like that again he'd personally kick Monster's arse.

Despite the wild parties at weekends, over those first couple of months I did manage to save a little bit of money, so when the opportunity came, I decided to hand in my notice and see a bit more of Shetland. A little bonus came by way of Rob Brown, who called to tell me that he'd taken a job in London with Midnight Music, and that the company was still very keen on commissioning a solo album at some stage. He went on to say that a contract had already been drafted and he'd had it checked out. It covered just a single album, was relatively uncomplicated, and even offered something by way of a small advance, so we did the whole deal over the fax machine.

Shetland has always had a very fine musical tradition, mostly Celtic and traditional music, and has produced some of the best fiddle players in the world. Keen students from the mainland have, over the years, flocked there specifically to learn from the locals, who can often be heard jamming together at places like the Thule bar on a Sunday afternoon, where an invitation to join in is open to everyone, regardless of skill or experience. In such company, my guitar playing improved very, very quickly.

Pete, another friend of Beanz's, invited us to his parents' place for the weekend, situated on the island of Unst at Shetland's most northerly point. His parents were away, so we'd have the house to ourselves. During our stay, Pete took us out in the family boat and gave us a tour of the smaller islands, one of which was owned by his family, although there was nothing there, save for a solitary camping shack stacked with tins of tuna and the like. Pete explained that his family sometimes vacated the house on Unst and came here to get away from it all. "Get away from what?" I asked incredulously. Unst was hardly a sprawling metropolis, enjoying one of the most desolate, albeit beautiful, landscapes I'd ever seen.

Our tour of Unst also took in a rather secluded and remote bird sanctuary among the cliffs. Such was the force of the wind that it hadn't been possible to stand at the cliff's edge for fear of being blown off, so I had to crawl to the edge on all fours in order to peer over. At first I thought the cliffs were composed of chalk, but when I gazed through binoculars it became apparent that the cliffs were white because they were completely covered in bird shit. Hundreds of different species of birds gathered there, including a family of puffins - the first we'd seen - and they all whirled around, soaring and diving about the sky as if they were participating in some perfect aerial ballet.

On our return journey to Lerwick, I had my strangest encounter yet. We were sitting in the car waiting for the ferry that would carry us across to the main island, when I noticed a single post office and grocery shop some yards away. Feeling mildly hungry I made the mistake of asking whether anyone else wanted anything from the shop, and was bombarded with orders for crisps and the like. I dashed over and bought far more packets than I could carry properly and, on hearing the horn that marked the arrival of the car ferry, dashed outside trying very hard not to drop any. As I rushed out of the shop, I collided head on with a girl on her way in. I dropped packets of crisps everywhere and I immediately stooped to retrieve them, mumbling my apologies. Rising, I came eye to eye with her for the first time and was amazed to see she was my cousin Diane.

Diane served in the Royal Navy and was married to a fellow officer, and they'd been stationed together at a Navy base on Unst. I had no idea, of course. She was equally amazed to see me there, and I quickly tried to explain the circumstances. She proudly showed off her baby daughter and told me she was making her routine weekend shopping trip in Lerwick.

Finally, we prepared to say goodbye to Shetland. The guys I'd worked alongside on the building site made us presents of very high quality Shetland wool sweaters. Sally and I were invited to a farewell dinner by a family whose daughter, the mother told us, was a big fan of The Chameleons, and who'd just taken up the guitar herself. It was a very special evening, and I impressed her mother by throwing in a rendition of 'The Partisan' on my guitar, a song made famous by her favourite songwriter and performer, Leonard Cohen.

Beanz took me completely by surprise when he asked if I would write a verse for his mother's gravestone. He seemed very happy with what I handed him:

Sun and moon, stars and sea, unlock this cage and set me free.

Beanz was due to begin his studies at Sheffield University at the end of the summer, so he hired a van and Pete offered to drive. Sally and I offered him a place to stay until the new term started, and extended the invitation to Catnap when he decided he was coming too. "Nothing fuckin' going on here, so I might as well," he lamented ruefully.

From Aberdeen, we drove to Edinburgh and stayed overnight with Harry and Mandy. Eventually we hit the road for the Isle of Skye, stopping to camp in the grounds of a large pub that lay along the route. The speciality of the house was a cocktail that they called Camouflage, which seemed to consist mainly of Bailey's Irish Cream and crème de menthe. By the end of the evening, they weren't even bothering to reckon up the cost anymore and were pouring them out for free. We must have sunk dozens of them, and despite the rather sickly concoction, we all managed to hang on to our suppers.

The Isle of Skye was a revelation that summer. Its sharp mountain peaks were worthy of Middle Earth: silver veins of water running down the slopes and rivers illuminated by the sun. We were supposed to stay at a hippy-type commune, but when we arrived our host was nowhere to be seen. He'd fled to the hills after a very strange woman had suddenly turned up and begun freaking everyone out. She fancied herself as some sort of witch, and was revelling in the fear that those present seemed to have of her. Beanz and I quickly saw through this, and after spending about ten minutes alone with her, she realised the game was up and fucked off sharpish. Mission accomplished. We then spent the day hiking to our host's hiding place to tell him it was now safe to return home. After a long walk to a very remote location, we found him housed in a bothy, a small shelter traditionally used by sheep farmers when they're out on the fells tending the flocks. Our host thanked us for exorcising the witch from his house. I told him not to mention it, and that it had been so easy I was thinking of taking it up professionally.

Eventually we made our way back to England and home. Sally and I had left for a weekend in Edinburgh - only to return some three months later. Pete bade us farewell and drove the van back to Shetland, while Beanz and Catnap took up temporary residence in the spare room, eventually making their way to Sheffield where they settled for many years. There would never be another summer quite like it, but then that's what makes great summers so precious.

20. TRIPPING DOGS

Having moved to Rochdale with very little money, Sally and I tried to make the best of it, but our financial plight meant that furnishing our new home proved difficult. Consequently I had little choice but to sell off my instruments, including my beloved Fender Jazz bass, bought with the first advance from Virgin Music. With a heavy heart, I took it to A1 Music in Manchester, who gave me a paltry £250 for it. We set aside £200 for a second-hand cooker and fridge, and with the remaining £50, Keni and I found a pub and got stinking drunk.

He, too, was in a similar financial predicament at the time, and decided to vacate his house in a neighbouring suburb. Sally and I offered him the spare room rent-free, and he lived with us over the following year. In the meantime I carried on developing the songs and ideas I'd been accumulating since the break-up of The Sun And The Moon. Rob Brown continued to encourage me and arranged for me to record new demos, under the auspices of Midnight Music, at a local studio. This session benefited from the presence of Keni on additional guitar and backing vocals. Although I was now writing predominantly on the guitar, I only knew five or six chords, and the idea of performing to audiences on the guitar was a frightening one. Keni urged me on, and he'd often invite me to go out busking with him on the streets of Manchester or Rochdale.

I found this to be the fastest and most efficient way of improving my guitar playing, and also one of the most nerve-wracking experiences I'd ever had. That said, there was something undeniably pure about playing your guitar for a few hours in some bustling shopping centre with an empty pocket and walking away with ten or fifteen quid, though busking alongside Keni was far less intimidating and much more enjoyable than playing alone. With the addition of harmonies, and eventually one or two other instruments, such as harmonica or banjo, you could transcend mediocrity and draw more attention. People were more inclined to pause for a moment and watch a small group of buskers enjoying themselves, and were more inclined to tip you something too. Occasionally John Burr, a friend I'd met through Keni, would join us on blues harp. John was a brilliant yet modest guy, who was studying for his doctorate in quantum mechanics at Leeds University. Having always been interested in advanced physics, I relished the stimulating conversations we shared on the philosophical implications of various discoveries. John, however, much preferred playing his blues harp to immersing himself in the world of quantum physics, as it was a world about which he'd become somewhat disillusioned and cynical. "When I see a particularly spectacular sunset," he once told me, "I want to appreciate it for what it is, rather than get bogged down in the physics of it as so many of my colleagues seem to do." Only the previous year, John had become the official blues harp champion of Britain, and over the following year he joined me on one or two recording sessions. I nicknamed him Quantum John Burr, and the name stuck for a while.

Another regular busking companion was Mick, an ageing gypsy who lived on the fringe of a local housing estate. Mick had parked his caravan, a traditional wooden affair with a green canopy roof and real gold leaf inlay, on some nearby waste ground alongside a more modern caravan that served as a living room and bedroom for his youngest daughter Diane. While not Romany himself, he'd adopted the life at the age of fouteen, eventually marrying a Romany woman, and had brought up five children on the road, though these days he travelled less. Keni and I met him one day when he'd been busking with his banjo in Rochdale town centre.

Mick Darling, Mark, John Burr, Mark Kennedy, 1989.   Photo: Sally Altana

It was Keni (along with Bryan Glancy) who introduced me to Paul Fallon. Paul worked at Johnny Roadhouse Music in Manchester; Keni had taken me there when I needed to buy a new guitar tuner. Apparently I'd met Paul once before during my Chameleons days, but couldn't recall this. The band had played a sold-out gig at Salford University, and Paul had turned up without a ticket. Consequently, he had approached me, and I'd arranged to put him on the band's guest list. While I didn't remember this incident, Paul did and it proved to be, albeit unwittingly, the best investment I ever made. I left the shop that day with not one, but three tuners, on a trial basis. "I have loads of them," he told me, "so just hang on to them for as long as you need." Paul is an extremely energetic, tireless soul who will go to tremendous lengths to help a friend, and is one of the most selfless individuals I've ever known, very much in the vein of Tony Fletcher, whom he knew well. Over the years, he's supported my work more than any other person I've ever met. On many occasions, it would have been impossible for me to accomplish some of the things I did without his help, and I regard him as a very dear and special friend.

I hadn't seen Bryan Glancy since The Sun And The Moon concert at the International the previous year, until Keni brought him over to the house one afternoon. Of all the friends I made during this period, Bryan was the most curious. He was a charming and talented guy, and his tales of adventures in Israel cemented our friendship. In some ways, his experiences reflected my own and I quickly came to regard him as a fellow mystic, a kindred spirit. The first time I ever saw Bryan play live was unforgettable. He looked extremely cool indeed, dressed entirely in black, complete with matching Ray-Ban sunglasses. A hushed silence fell across the room as he took his seat and, strumming his guitar, reached across to the amp to adjust the volume. At that moment, having reached too far, the stool slipped from beneath him and both Bryan and his amp went sprawling, and the theatre erupted into hilarity. To his credit, Bryan recovered well, turning in a beautiful set that had the audience cheering for more.

While in Rochdale we ran an open house and welcomed an endless stream of visitors. Carlo was Dutch, although he lived and worked in Germany, and I met him for the first time when The Sun And The Moon played at the University of London. He'd driven from Germany with a small contingent of friends especially for the show, and was quite a fan. He led me over to a window and invited me to inspect his car, which was parked directly below, and I saw he'd painted the logo of our band on the bonnet, much to the bemusement of British customs officials at Harwich. He was an immediately likeable, charming guy, and I did something that I rarely do

- I handed him my home telephone number. That summer he rang and asked if he might stay the weekend during a trip to Manchester with another friend of his, and, after consulting Sally, I told him there was no problem.

On their arrival, Carlo introduced us to his friend. The guy's name was Thies and he was rather a cool-looking individual with blonde hair, dressed in a leather jacket with a yellow and black polka dot scarf tied around the sleeve, and dark glasses. We spoke for a while and he offered me a cigarette, which I took and then ignited with my Zippo lighter. He immediately leaned forward, lit his cigarette from my outstretched hand, and thanked me. Carlo and Thies were in high spirits as we walked, Thies gripping Carlo's jacket and jabbering in German, sometimes hauling himself up and down on Carlo's shoulders. Soon we reached the house and I introduced them to Keni. In the course of our conversation, Keni asked Thies if he'd seen a particular television programme, and Thies then stunned us all, with the obvious exception of Carlo - by telling us that he hadn't, because he was completely blind.

In retrospect, I came to think that it was very cool of Carlo not to say anything about this in advance, and to allow Thies to eventually tell us himself. Nothing in his behaviour had given us the slightest hint as to the reality of the situation. Thies explained he'd been a passenger in a car with a friend, who had taken a bend at too high a speed. The car had left the road, ploughing into a tree and causing severe damage to his cranium and facial bone structure. Thies was nineteen years old at the time. He'd spent his time since the accident recovering from surgery and coming to terms psychologically with what had happened to him. "What was I going to do?" he told us soberly, "I was nineteen, I had my whole life in front of me. I wasn't going to give up." Thies had gathered his courage, and here he was, on his first major adventure away from home since the accident. We listened in stunned admiration to the guy's fortitude. In Germany, the yellow and black polka dot scarf he wore alerted the general public to the fact that he was blind, but most people in the UK would be oblivious to this, as we had been. I remember feeling quite ashamed as he went on to tell us that, during a British Airways flight, the stewardess, on trying to give Thies his in-flight meal, had become irritated when he'd failed to take it from her or even acknowledge her presence.

"Fly Lufthansa next time," mumbled Keni ruefully.

Another memorable visit was by the veteran punk band Toxik Ephex from Aberdeen, including our friend Chiz on drums and Frankie on guitar, whose acquaintance we'd made on our trip to Shetland the previous year.

The band was in the midst of a national tour and needed a place to stay for a few days, so Sally and I invited them over to the house. After going along to see them at Manchester's Swinging Sporran, we'd been so impressed that we'd jumped in the van and gone along to their next show in Bradford, but arrived to a rather unwelcome surprise. During our time in Shetland, we'd heard the legends that surrounded Mad Alec, a crazy Glaswegian who sometimes frequented Shetland, leaving terror and chaos in his wake. Some of the stories were so horrible I refuse to relate them here, suffice to say that he once hurled an axe through the window of a Shetland bus because he hadn't liked the expression on the face of one of the passengers. As we entered the venue with the rest of the band I saw Chiz turn away, screw his eyes shut, shake his head and mutter, "Och no, Mad Alec!"

Alec had only recently decided to take up the drums, but was already playing in a touring band. I didn't really know what to expect, but as his band soundchecked I was stunned. Whatever else he was, Mad Alec was a brilliant drummer - so good that you'd think he'd been playing for years.

After the show, Alec came over to the guys from Toxik and finagled some of the money they'd been paid for headlining. It was barely enough to cover their expenses, but Alec was a guy you didn't argue with. I found myself talking with him for a few minutes, which is probably one of the bravest things I've ever done, and I found him to be quite a charming, almost calm, individual. I told him I'd been very impressed by his drumming and he thanked me, telling me that he'd taken it up as a form of therapy, and that subsequently he'd calmed down quite a bit. At one point during their set he'd impressed me further when he'd left the kit to play guitar on a couple of songs and, again, he was very proficient. He told me that he'd only been playing the guitar for a few months. He was undoubtedly a prodigy. More recently I heard he'd become a Born Again Christian. If this is true, then no greater proof of God's miracles would ever be needed by the faithful.

Eventually Keni moved to Leeds to start a new band with Quantum John. On the one hand, it was pleasant to have the place solely to ourselves for a bit, on the other we came to miss his warmth, humour and energy, though happily he remains one of my closest friends.

An interesting diversion came my way one afternoon while I was perusing a local bookshop. While browsing a few paperback books on the subject of UFOs, I came across a business card inserted between the covers of one of them, advertising the Rochdale UFO Society. The group met regularly at our local pub, so Sally and I decided to attend the next meeting. The co-ordinator's name was Mike, and it turned out that he was also our regular postman. He had an in-depth knowledge that reflected a twenty-five year fascination with the subject, having allegedly seen a so-called flying saucer back in the fifties. His eccentricities included a shoulder-length pageboy hairstyle and an obsession with Neil Diamond, which I was never able to reconcile with his more esoteric interests. Above all, he was a warm, friendly, humorous man, completely devoted to his partially sighted wife Patricia, and Sally and I became extremely fond of both of them.

After attending their meetings regularly over the next couple of months, I offered to produce a newsletter for the group on my computer. After years of relative apathy, Mike had welcomed this enthusiastic contribution with absolute joy. I presented him with the first issue, compiled from snippets of current news and UFO sightings gathered from various sources throughout the month, eventually inviting other members of the group to contribute.

Some of Mike's regulars were even more eccentric than he was. Ian, for example, was a partially-sighted bear of a man with bad body odour and an even worse sense of fashion. He was obsessed with traditional English folk music and would only answer to the name Ufolkie. Patrick, an old Irishman, would spend most of his time sowing the seeds of discord between fellow group members or rival research organisations. He would circulate lies and rumours wherever he could, then sit back and gleefully observe the resulting fireworks. There were also one or two middle-aged women who'd convinced themselves that they were being regularly abducted in the middle of the night and subjected to all sorts of unspeakable experiments, after having read books on the subject by the likes of Whitley Strieber. During our monthly meetings, these women would invariably say things like, "I knew they were watching me in the kitchen because Freda - that's my cat, she's Persian - would keep meowing at the wall above the sink and she NEVER does that normally."

Despite the group's lack of investigative depth, it did rekindle my interest in the subject, and after having been recommended to a national Scottish newspaper editor by my friend Harry, I agreed to write an article around a high-profile conference on UFOs and crop-circles that was due to be held in Leeds that summer. This opened the door to one or two very interesting opportunities, as I found myself conducting telephone interviews with some of the leading lights of British UFO research, including renowned expert and author Timothy Good, and the founder of *UFO Magazine* and *Quest International*, the late Graham Birdsall.

I'd arranged a phone interview with Pat Delgado, one of the so-called experts in crop circle research, who, along with his co-author Colin

Andrews, had written a number of books on the subject. Delgado also lectured extensively at international conferences and within the British and North American media. Both men had been raving for years about the intricate and evolving complexity of design exhibited in crop circles, which had been appearing mysteriously overnight in fields across the south of England. They claimed these circles had been constructed in such a way that made it impossible for human beings to replicate them, the inference being they had to be the work of extra-terrestrial intelligence. The designs that appeared were of increasing complexity, peaking with the appearance of a formation depicting a Mandelbrot Set, a geometric pattern associated with computer fractals and chaos mathematics that measured over one hundred and fifty feet across.

On the evening of the interview, Pat answered the phone and told me in a very downcast voice that something had come up and asked if we could postpone the interview. I agreed, and arranged to ring him again the following week. The next morning, however, the subject exploded in the media.

Delgado had received a call from the editor of the *Today* newspaper. The editor rather excitedly informed him that a particularly impressive crop formation had appeared in a farmer's field, and asked if he would verify that the formation was genuine. A car was sent to collect him, and Pat dutifully went to inspect what turned out to be a large and complex pictogram in a wheat field. Pat made a hurried inspection, and told the reporters he'd need more time to be sure, but they pressed him for an answer, citing deadlines. Pat went on to tell them that, in his opinion, the formation was genuine and represented one of the most impressive examples he'd seen to date. Upon this, two old men, Doug Bower and David Chorley, came forward and told Pat they were personally responsible for all the crop circles that had been found in the south of England over the past fifteen years, including the one Pat had just verified as genuine for the benefit of the journalists from *Today*. The whole thing had been a set-up, and poor old Pat had fallen for it. What followed was a week of public humiliation, claims and counterclaims in the media, and the total discrediting of the phenomenon in the eyes of the public. Pat had been manipulated into authenticating a hoaxed crop formation and in doing so had destroyed the credibility of the entire subject. Sadly, his colleagues and contemporaries abandoned him in droves, desperate to preserve their own respective cottage industries. The entire episode was sickening to behold.

At the height of all this I was contacted by a researcher at Granada Television, and was subsequently invited to take part in a discussion programme on the subject. The live debate was less than a satisfactory experience, however, the only redeeming feature being a chance meeting with *Red Dwarf* star Craig Charles. He'd been drafted in to perform some stand-up comedy in the middle of the programme, and I chatted with him over coffee in the Green Room, laughing at some of the cranks that had been assembled for the debate. Patty Caldwell, one of the presenters, lamented when I told her that in my view, crop circles were the work of hoaxers. "I want it to be true!" she wailed. For me, the whole subject was placed squarely in perspective by the focus of the first half of the programme, a debate concerning a woman who had been sent to jail for killing her husband in self-defence after years of abuse at his hands. After such disclosures, silly patterns in a crop field seemed trite to the point of inducing nausea.

In the following months, I found myself involved in a couple of other journalistic endeavours. The gathering of research and background material and the coverage of press conferences relating to the Rochdale satanic abuse case was one such assignment; providing background material for an international conference on the JFK assassination was another. Finally, I was asked to report on a lecture that David Icke was scheduled to deliver at Manchester University. The previous year Icke had quit his job as a television sports commentator, declared himself directly related to Jesus Christ and was forging a new career as a New Age, apocalyptic prophet. After the lecture, I'd turned in a fairly neutral article and was quite pleased with it, but was then asked by the editor to revise it because it wasn't scathing enough. I refused.

To be honest, new age rhetoric aside, much of what Icke had to say about how our culture had evolved and where it was heading made perfect sense to me. I found the core of his message to be very positive. As luck would have it, Jon Ronson, another journalist friend of mine, was accompanying Icke on his lecture tour, along with a documentary film crew. On seeing me at the Manchester lecture, Jon asked if I'd like to meet him David in person. David and I spoke for about twenty minutes, after which he kindly recorded a greeting for Mike's wife Patricia, a huge fan of his, on my Dictaphone. While I found some of what he had to say dubious to say the least, I had to admit that he was a charming, seemingly lucid and highly intelligent individual. I still believe there are many elements of Icke's message, shape-shifting reptilian members of the Royal Family notwithstanding, that are highly perceptive and positive. Consequently, I refused to deliberately trash the man or his ideas for the sake of getting an article into print, which is what the editor was asking me to do, and as a result, my brief flirtation with journalism ended.

Later that summer I received a phone call from John Peel's former producer, John Walters. He told me that Strange Fruit, a label established primarily to make John Peel's session recordings commercially available, wanted to compile all The Chameleons' BBC radio sessions and release them as an album. John told me he'd already been in contact with the other members of the band and had managed to get a tentative verbal agreement, but he needed all of us to provide written consent before proceeding. I told him that I'd welcome the release. In the meantime, he offered to send me a copy of the standard contract.

Such retrospective interest in the group didn't really surprise me, given that I still received a great amount of fan mail at the Chameleons/Sun And The Moon post office box. With this and John Walters' phone call in mind, a possible solution to our current financial plight began to crystallise. Strange Fruit's proposal didn't offer anything by way of cash advances, but it could pave the way for fresh product, and so my mind now turned to the unreleased material that lay on a shelf at Suite Sixteen. This comprised a live recording of a rehearsal for a concert at The Free Trade Hall in the mid-1980s, and the final four tracks that the band recorded in the wake of Tony Fletcher's death. Through our mutual friend Alan Duffy at Imaginary Records, I suggested to Dave and Reg that we release this material on our own label, but these overtures were immediately rebuffed. Dave and Reg were very keen that I agree to sign the Strange Fruit agreement, as this would ensure income for the band in the short-term, but didn't seem to be interested in anything else beyond that. I therefore decided to use this as a bargaining chip. I would agree to sign the Strange Fruit contract immediately, in return for an agreement to put out the unreleased material at Suite Sixteen at some unspecified future date. Dave met with my manager, Rob Brown, and this compromise was duly agreed. I dutifully signed and returned the Strange Fruit contract, and thought no more about it.

A week later, I got an extremely rare phone call from Dave. This had been the first contact I'd had with him in some years, and it was typically hysterical. Now that he had what he wanted, he told me I could go and "fuck myself" with regard to any other agreements that might have been reached. Naturally, I was extremely angry and insulted, feeling that this reaction was rather uncalled for. Additionally, it was very frustrating. I knew that the release of this material would be extremely lucrative for all of us, and that financially we were all in the same boat - without a pot to piss in. After giving the matter a great deal of thought, and consulting Alan Duffy, I decided to go ahead and release the material anyway. Alan couldn't be directly involved, given his relationship to Dave and Reg, but he did put me in touch with a distributor that would be willing to help. The only problem now, of course, was how to get hold of the tapes.

This proved to be not such a problem after all. I telephoned Suite Sixteen and told the studio manager that I wanted to copy some Chameleons master tapes. The manager replied that he first had to check with the studio owner to confirm that the tapes had been paid for, which he did, and I was then told there would be no problem. I booked the studio, and with the help of the resident engineer found the material I needed, and copied it at a CD quality sample rate. I then had him write out a receipt for the work: Mark Burgess - copying of Chameleons masters - paid in full. Later on, when Dave Fielding and the studio owner publicly accused me of stealing the material, I was able to produce this receipt and show this up for the nonsense it was.

The business of releasing the records was an education. Like many recording artists, I'd always been quite ignorant of the processes involved. Consequently, I'd never seriously contested any of the claims of costs and expenses that seemed to prohibit bands or artists from receiving a fair share of the proceeds.

The distributor offered me what they told me was a standard agreement. They would take thirty percent of the gross, in return for which they would cover the costs of manufacturing, artwork preparation and distribution to retail outlets. A whopping seventy percent would then be paid to the record label. The record label in this case existed in name only and had relatively few overheads. This meant that after publishing royalties had been paid to the copyright owners, the remainder would be split equally four ways, to Dave, Reg, John and me. Additionally, as we were also the composers, some of the publishing money paid to the copyright owners would find its way back to us. For the first time in our careers we stood to make a significant return on our own records.

Now that I had the material in my possession and a distribution deal organised, the next task was to secure publishing licenses from the copyright holders. The material would constitute two separate releases. The first release would be the live rehearsal tape, and this consisted of material owned by Virgin Publishing Ltd. On contacting them I was told that for such a small number of pressings - around 3,000 in mixed formats - I didn't need one. All I had to ensure was that the royalties were paid once the record began to generate income, and, upon submitting the titles to the

Mechanical Copyright Protection Society, an automatic license would be granted. I was unsure as to whether or not KES held the rights to the four unreleased tracks, but to be on the safe side I obtained a letter from the Managing Director stating that I had permission to release the material providing that mechanical royalties were paid. I subsequently commissioned artwork, titling the live record *Tripping Dogs*, with the unreleased tracks appearing on an EP titled *Tony Fletcher Walked On Water* in memory of my late friend. We were all set. Some months later, I took delivery of a small quantity of stock, and forwarded half of it to Imaginary Records for Dave, Reg, and ultimately John. It was at this point that an awful lot of shit hit a very large fan.

By the time the others had received their copies, *Tripping Dogs* had already been sent to the retailers, all of whom had pre-ordered the release, so the entire pressing had sold out immediately. The *Tony Fletcher* EP had been held back until we could gauge the reaction to the album. While the mechanical royalties were safely set aside in lieu of collection, the bulk of the income remained with the distributor. Dave and Reg wasted no time in alerting the Mechanical Copyright Protection Society, who immediately placed an injunction preventing further distribution, but by this time it was too late. The only result of this action was that the distributor froze all payments until the situation was legally clarified. Anticipating this, I made sure that my share was paid ahead of this action, so while this was unfortunate for Dave, Reg and John, who hadn't been part of the legal action, and was simply caught in the crossfire, it didn't affect me in the slightest. While my actions could be construed as being ethically questionable, I have no regrets about it, nor did I feel any guilt. As far as I was concerned, if anyone had been fucked-over regarding The Chameleons it had been me. Dave had been motivated by selfishness and spite, and it was this attitude that had condemned us all to relative poverty while a veritable goldmine of music, some of which comprised the best work I'd ever done, gathered dust on a shelf at Suite Sixteen. Reg had meekly followed Dave's line, while I later discovered that John had applauded my initiative.

Verbal and legal recriminations weren't the only forms of flak I was forced to dodge. A worried Alan Duffy phoned one day to warn me of the imminent danger of an altogether more evil kind. An acquaintance of Dave's, I was told, was very close to a notorious band of Middleton gangsters, and Alan had heard I was due to be paid a visit. The people in question were a serious bunch of characters, and while I tried to play it down, I was fearful of what might happen should they call when Sally was alone at the house. Fortunately, my own family are very well-connected and respected in the town. After alerting my father, he was able to make some enquiries and was told that these people had no interest in getting involved, and were, in fact, upset that their name was being bandied about in such a fashion.

One afternoon a retailer friend of mine, who had a business in the Midlands, told me that a sales rep from the distribution company had covertly offered him a quantity of the unreleased *Tony Fletcher* EP at an exaggerated price. It later transpired that unscrupulous individuals at the warehouse, having been made aware of the high black market value, had been taking copies and selling them at hugely inflated prices. I removed every remaining copy from the warehouse, putting as many as I could into circulation. Most were given away, some auctioned for charity and some I used as currency to help fund tours and suchlike. This didn't prevent copies from eventually turning up on the collectors' market, of course, but at least it significantly lowered the asking price from £100 a copy to around £10.

It was around this time that Sally and I travelled to Glasgow to attend a wedding, a trip which ended with another long-term house guest for us. While attending a party with our mate Shetland Pete, we were introduced to a young Indian girl. Shobu was an actress who had just finished a successful run in a Glasgow play. Subsequently, she was contracted to perform with the M6 Theatre Group, based in Rochdale, but was struggling to find somewhere to stay in the area. This may have seemed a rash offer to make to a stranger, but Sally and I shared a good instinct for people and were rarely disappointed, and ultimately, we all got on so well that Shobu opted to remain for the duration of her contract with the M6 Theatre Group.

Eventually she migrated to London to take an acting job there. We stayed in touch, and were surprised and delighted when she rang to tell us that she'd landed a major character part in EastEnders. The show wasn't something we watched ordinarily, but it became pleasantly strange to watch our friend on prime-time television twice a week. The scale of the show's impact didn't really dawn on us until the day she phoned to say she'd be coming to town and wanted to meet up and spend the day with us. Sally and I went to meet her train and arrived to see Shobu and a couple of her friends, surrounded by an excited group of autograph hunters. One of her friends was a fellow-cast member, and they had both been instantly recognised. It simply hadn't occurred to us that EastEnders was at that time the second highest rating TV show on air, and as celebrities, they were bound to cause something of a stir. The constant stares that came our way throughout the day took some getting used to, and by the end of it, Sally and I had a fairly clear picture of just how much major celebrities have to put up with. It isn't enviable, believe me. I always imagined that confusion amongst viewers of a popular television show was something of a myth, but it was frightening how many people confused Shobu with her on-screen character, offering her unsolicited advice on how to save her TV marriage, or filling her in on what her fictional husband was really up to.

I continued to work finishing the songs that would comprise a brand new album, but it proved to be heavy going. The biggest problem was the label, Midnight Music. Rob Brown had become disillusioned working for label manager Nick Ralph, who was probably one of the most slothful people I've ever encountered. All Rob's attempts to seriously organise the label were fruitless and, out of pure frustration, he returned to his old career as a financial consultant. This now meant that communication with the label, such as it was, became even more difficult. I was only to meet Nick once or twice, but it was enough to recognise that Rob's assessment was totally correct. The most frustrating incident came after I'd used a studio he'd bought in Rotterdam to record additional demos for my album. I'd wanted to go because I felt a change of ambience might prove inspirational, and I was right. I invited Keni and Bryan Glancy to join me for the session, and we spent a week there together. Initially, Nick had told me that, while he was pleased that I'd wanted to work there, it was really only fit for acoustic sessions, so I didn't bother recruiting a full band. The resident engineer had been surprised I hadn't brought a drummer along, and when I told him what Nick had said about the studio, he was rather insulted. As it turned out, Nick couldn't have been more wrong, and I was left to lament that I hadn't planned a more elaborate session.

We'd planned to record three songs in total. The first was an acoustic version of The Chameleons song 'Paradiso'. Keni played guitar while Bryan played a Spanish guitar, and the result was fairly agreeable. Next came a song I'd written with Keni that we'd titled 'Restless Children'. This became one of my favourites, though it would be years before it saw the light of day. The third song was little more than a half-formed idea, and I invited Bryan to collaborate on a duet. It was to gain an altogether unexpected dynamic when we enlisted a local drummer to play on the song. We had a finished arrangement within a couple of hours, which we titled 'When Harmony Comes'.

By the time we came to mixing the three tracks, I seriously began to feel we had something special, an opinion endorsed by Carlo and Thies, who, having heard we were in Holland, had driven from Germany to see us. I soon began thinking in terms of a single. Not a chart single, obviously -

the recording was much too raw for that - but a single in the classic sense: simply a great record. Indeed, all of us, including the engineer, were buzzing with enthusiasm for the energy that the tracks seemed to capture.

On our return journey to England we had to drive by Midnight Music's home town of Watford anyway, so I decided to call on Nick and play him the tapes. The phone call should have set warning bells ringing in my head. I told him very excitedly that Rotterdam had been a great experience, that we had something we were very eager to play him, and would it be all right if we came over. "On a Sunday?" he moaned into the telephone, "Can't it wait?"

This was not exactly the response I'd been hoping for, but I explained we were just down the road and the next day we wouldn't be, and we were very eager for him to hear the tapes.

"Oh, all right then," he moaned in a whining voice very reminiscent of a Robert Smith vocal, "come over."

This was the first time I'd met him face to face and it was less than a happy experience. He was one of those individuals who seems to suck all the positive, vibrant energy out of people like a vampire, but rather than utilise the energy, he allowed it to evaporate as though it had never been. We played the tape to him, which I suppose was rather unfair. It isn't easy to objectively judge a piece of music while the artists sit there staring at you, waiting for a response. However, circumstances being what they were, I had no other option. I didn't want to leave the master tape with him, but in the end I was forced to do exactly that when, suddenly, he asked where it was. Keni, not reading the situation well at all, blithely handed over the only copy. "Well, I'll make some copies, play it to a few people and see what they say," moaned Nick.

We all drove back to Manchester with the wind having been sucked out of our sails somewhat, and the following day Keni said his goodbyes and headed off home, while Sally, Bryan and I went into Manchester in search of Rob Brown, who was now managing a finance office. Rob was about to take a lunch break, so we dragged him out into Albert Square armed with a ghetto blaster and played him 'When Harmony Comes'. He was smiling the whole time as we all danced around, drawing amused looks from passers-by, one of whom asked us if we were filming something. Rob was in hysterics when we related our first impressions of Nick. In essence, Nick's attitude was precisely the reason Rob had decided to bail out of the company and head back to Manchester.

Bryan suggested that we play the tape to Paula Greenwood, a friend of his who ran Playtime Records, who were chiefly responsible for discovering

Manchester's latest sensation, Inspiral Carpets. She loved it too, telling us that, if Nick decided he didn't want to put it out, then she definitely would. I think if I'd had the master tapes with me, I would have handed them over to her there and then. As it turned out, Nick didn't want to put it out, nor did he want anyone else to. He kept the master tapes, which we never saw again, and from that point on my relationship with Nick Ralph and Midnight Music worsened.

I quickly realised that it had been a huge mistake committing to Midnight Music, especially now that Rob was no longer there to mediate. Unfortunately, by this time I'd already recorded a lot of music, and had run up some serious studio bills. This included a session at a studio in Edinburgh that Harry had recommended on which he, his wife Mandy and a cellist named Joe had all contributed. I'd finally been able to persuade Mandy to recite the Shetland poem for me, marrying it to another pet project, a cover of Phillip Glass' *Facades*. I was particularly proud of this piece because, apart from Joe's cello, I played all the instruments myself. The thought of losing control of these recordings, or having to re-record them due to disputes of ownership, was very depressing. Other recordings included a duet with Bryan on one of his compositions, 'Beat the Boat', which also turned out well, and we'd both seriously talked about forming a band together and taking things further.

A possible solution to this situation came by way of a phone call from a guy named Jeff, who was an A&R representative at A&M Records in California. He told me he'd been an avid fan of The Chameleons for years, and he was very interested to hear the solo material I'd been working on. Having supplied him with a tape, he became quite excited and urged me to meet with him in California. Despite my situation, I was rather sceptical of American record labels after my experiences with Geffen Records and besides, I was now working very closely with Bryan Glancy. This didn't seem to make much difference to Jeff however, who told me I was welcome to bring Bryan along too, at A&M's expense. Bryan was extremely excited by this development, seeing in it a chance to sign for a major label, and was urging me to accept. I, on the other hand, was far more cautious. I knew that contracts with major American record companies ran to five or six albums, and could become extremely complicated if things should go wrong. In the end, swept along in the current of Bryan's enthusiasm, I agreed to go and meet with A&M. I was rather hoping seeing the industry at such close quarters would open Bryan's eyes, and he would come to understand me a little better. Sadly, this was a forlorn hope.

While Jeff and his immediate colleagues seemed genuine and friendly, having been shown around, I found the general ambience of the A&M offices depressingly familiar, and it only strengthened my resolve to have as little to do with that side of the business as possible. Bryan, however, had a different view of it. If anything, the glamour of Hollywood completely enraptured him. I think he would have stayed behind if he could. Jeff said that A&M might be prepared to help me free myself from the Midnight Music agreement and negotiate a fresh deal with me, but I had to tell him that I wasn't interested. The situation with Midnight Music was frustrating, but joining a major corporation without the protection of strong management would have been too much like leaping from the frying pan into the fire. I told Bryan that I'd decided against having any involvement with A&M, and he was visibly disappointed. This was as close as Bryan had come to the major league and he saw it as his big chance, but he respected my reasons.

By far the highlight of the year was my marriage to Sally. This had been something we'd already committed ourselves to, but for one reason or another we hadn't got around to tying the knot. Now we were resolved to making it happen, and we decided that we wanted to be married in a place that had become sacred to both of us - Loch Ness.

I wrote to Scottish Heritage, who own Urquhart Castle on the shores of Loch Ness, asking about the feasibility of holding a wedding ceremony there. I expected it to be well beyond our means, but was pleasantly surprised. In return for a very modest donation, they were happy to grant permission, and would even provide a custodian to oversee the arrangements. A friend in Aberdeen put us in touch with a local minister who agreed to officiate the ceremony, and we sent out the invitations. Thirty or so friends and assorted family members convened for our wedding at Urquhart Castle, some of them camping at nearby Borlum Farm, where Tony, Reg, Ken and I had stayed on our very first visit to the area some ten years before.

As I stood before the congregation and watched Sally approach in bright sunshine beneath a cloudless sky, I was reminded of the night of Easter Sunday, 1982, when, standing on practically the very same spot, I'd seen the sky inexplicably erupt with colour, and in that moment I wondered if I'd been granted a premonition of a greater moment to come.

By the year's end, Bryan had tried his best to help me extricate myself from the Midnight Music agreement, introducing me to lawyers and barristers of his acquaintance, but the more it went on, the more stressed I became. Ultimately, these rising stress levels began to affect my health. I started suffering from heart palpations and had to take medication. As if this wasn't enough, both the local recording studio and the studio in Edinburgh told me that Midnight Music hadn't paid the outstanding invoices for the sessions, and that unless they were paid immediately the tapes would be wiped and the masters disposed of.

In addition, Sally and I were becoming increasingly depressed living where we were. Having very little money didn't really bother us that much, but we reasoned if we were going to be poor then we might as well be poor in a more pleasant environment. Vandalism, drug-related crime and alcoholism were rampant, and all sense of community and social responsibility had seemingly vanished. Mike, our postman, was attacked one morning, his sack stolen while he was delivering the morning mail.

Eventually we resigned ourselves to moving on, and tried to think of a way we could make it happen. The obvious choice was Scotland, as we already knew and loved the country and its people. By this time Harry and Mandy had left the flat in Edinburgh and had bought a house in the Borders, and they told us the region offered many affordable properties for rent. Of course, even if we were able to find something that was affordable, the question of how we would support ourselves in such a relatively remote area would need to be addressed. Still, it seemed an encouraging place to begin looking.

The situation regarding Midnight Music didn't improve, and as the threats from the various unpaid studios intensified, I reached my wits' end. It began to look very likely that I would lose all the work I'd done thus far. Rescue came by way of Alan Duffy, who turned up at the house one afternoon wanting to discuss the frozen royalties that were still being held by the distributor of the *Tripping Dogs* album. Apparently, Dave and Reg had asked Alan to mediate on their behalf. Of course, I was more than happy to accommodate them. It was always my intention that they'd receive their full share of the royalties. I signed the relevant paperwork, and was pleasantly surprised when Alan told me that I hadn't received all my share. Once i'd complied, the others received their cheques relatively quickly, and apparently they'd been pleasantly shocked at the amount they received. The royalty cheques put an entirely different complexion on things as far as Dave was concerned, and he now requested that I allow Imaginary Records to acquire and release more retrospective Chameleons material. This confused me initially. Having fought my attempts to release the material to everyone's benefit, he was now asking that I allow him to do the same thing, but in such a way that it meant signing off fifty percent of the band's share of the profits to Imaginary Records, who used the same distributor on the same terms as I had. By my method, the band received one hundred percent, because the label I'd set up existed in name only, for the benefit of the distribution deal. In short, Dave had unnecessarily cut our returns in half. Dave's answer, of course, was that I couldn't be trusted, although the only reason the others had needed to wait a year for their money was because of his stupidity. Wearily, I told Alan that, providing I was accounted to, I didn't care what they did and was content to let them get on with it. Not only did I now have the money to pay off the recording studios and rescue my tapes, but also, with the future advances on the proposed Imaginary Records releases, we'd have the means to move to Scotland.

That summer we drove up to the Borders in search of a suitable house. Eventually we reached the town of Berwick-upon-Tweed, where Sally bought a local newspaper, reasoning that we might find a property being offered for rent in the classified section. Sure enough, we came across a small private advertisement from someone who was seeking a reliable couple to occupy a cottage, which was being offered rent free in return for a few hours a day working to help renovate a small estate. Although no specific address was provided it did mention it was located very close to the village of Duns, so we went to look. The area seemed idyllic and was situated only half an hour or so from where our friends Harry and Mandy lived. Having arranged to stay with them for a few days, we made our way there and they encouraged us to write to the P.O. Box number quoted in the advertisement. On returning home I wrote a letter in response to the advertisement explaining our situation, our desire to relocate to Scotland, the circumstances that had led to this decision and my hope that I would find somewhere relatively peaceful where I could continue my writing. A couple of weeks later we received a reply asking us if we could attend an interview.

Russell was a very charming, well-spoken individual who, despite his obvious affluence, showed not the slightest hint of snobbery. He worked in the city of London and kept a flat there, but he'd previously visited Caldra House often and had come to love it. The estate had grown increasingly dilapidated over the years, something he'd noted with a great degree of sadness, and so when the opportunity came to buy the property he hadn't hesitated, and had since devoted himself to restoring the house and the grounds to its former glory. The house, boasting around fifty rooms, was set amongst sixty acres of private woodland on the banks of Blackadder Water, although much of the woodland surrounding the house was completely overgrown. Russell told us that in return for our help in the gradual restoration of the grounds, he was offering the use of the gatekeeper's cottage that marked the entrance to the estate.

Caldra Lodge looked idyllic. The entrance was situated at a discreet distance beyond the main gate by way of a hidden track, and the cottage had its own private garden. During the summer months it was alive with the riotous colour of flowers of every description. The prospect of being able to live in such a place, under such an arrangement, had exceeded our wildest expectations, and without hesitation we told Russell we were definitely interested. He told us that the cottage wouldn't be available until the following November, which was ideal as it gave us plenty of time to wind up our affairs in Rochdale and organise the move. After chatting with him a little longer, Russell gave us a tour of Caldra House and finally he told us that he'd contact us should our application be successful. We said our goodbyes and returned to Harry and Mandy, gushing with excitement. As it turned out, we didn't have to wait too long. The very next day, Russell rang Harry and Mandy's house and told us that, having considered it overnight, he definitely wanted us to take the cottage. Unbelievable!

That summer, Carlo asked me if I'd assist with the production of his band's debut album, *Counting The Stars*. I'd got to know Carlo's writing partner and guitarist Jo-Jo Brandt, and was impressed with their new songs, so I agreed to join them for the recording session. Most of the backing tracks were already recorded, needing only a few additional overdubs ahead of the final mixing. The work took around a week, and I was able to bring much experience to bear, contributing to what I felt was a fine debut record. The work also served to further cement my relationship with Carlo and Jo-Jo, and we've remained good friends. This was to be the first of two albums I would produce and mix for The Convent, and I was rather proud that both of them were the best-received of the band's career.

November arrived at last, and we vacated our house on Greengate Close and moved into Caldra Lodge. I think most of our friends thought we were mad to leave Manchester; I remember that Bryan, in particular, was rather bemused by our decision. He'd sportingly offered to help with the move, and had driven with us to the cottage that first weekend. The following day, as we unloaded the rest of our furniture from the truck, he asked how I expected to continue with my career from such an isolated backwater. I told him that I really didn't care much about a career, which was true, and extolled the virtues of living in such a quiet, peaceful location. No sooner had I said this than a Royal Air Force Tornado jet fighter roared over our heads, less than a thousand feet above the tree line. Bryan just looked at me. "Peace and quiet!" he mumbled, "You've got to be joking, Burge!"

The cottage had two bedrooms, a living room and a fully-equipped kitchen. The only source of heating in the cottage was a large open fireplace, fuelled from a woodpile that lay outside the front door. Behind the fireplace was a boiler that heated the water. With winter approaching, we set about laying carpets and setting the cottage to rights. The previous tenant, a young man with only a large dog for company, had neglected it, so restoring our new home became a full-time job in itself. As winter tightened its grip, the cottage would become very cold indeed. Looking back, I'm amazed that we were able to handle it, given that we'd been living in a modern, centrally-heated house for the past two years. However, we weren't daunted in the slightest - in fact, we were so excited to be there that we never really gave it a second thought.

Russell was on hand to meet us that first weekend, and he was keen to help us in every way, lending us tools with which to work on the house, an axe so we could split the firewood, and even offered us the keys to his Land Rover should our trusty Morris Minor suffer the winter blues. For Russell, Caldra House was truly a labour of love, and in the short time he'd owned the place he'd worked wonders. He would have preferred to live at Caldra full-time, but his work in London simply didn't allow it. The best he could manage was weekends and the odd fortnight throughout the year. The rest of the time, Sally and I had the whole place to ourselves, and we were very proud at the level of trust that had been placed in us. In the early days, I'd sometimes walk up to the house to play the beautiful baby grand piano that lay in one of the larger ground-floor rooms.

Most of the work we did for Russell was in the grounds. At the end of each weekend, he'd take us through some of the things he wanted us to do - it would then be entirely up to us when we did them. A great deal of our time was spent clearing and reseeding areas of grass, cutting back rhododendron trees or re-establishing walking paths through the wood, which over the course of time had become lost or overgrown. Aside from the farm opposite, our only other neighbours lay in the village of Caldra, two miles away on the opposite banks of Blackadder Water; it would be months before we met any of them. The nearest large settlement was the small town of Duns, four miles away in the opposite direction.

We spent some time exploring the area, and would often drive the fifteen miles to the coast and walk the long stretches of beach. Our dog Adam loved the beach best of all, and seemed to benefit the most from our move to Caldra. Adam was a Bedlington Terrier, and he'd previously spent a considerable time as a stray living on the streets, so when he'd first come to live with us he was in rather a poor condition. His coat, which on a Bedlington is closer to wool than hair, was heavily matted, and we'd been forced to cut most of it away, despite it being the depths of winter.

Consequently, we'd taken Adam to a local pet parlour to find him an overcoat, but on seeing the state of him the manager had exclaimed, "What on earth have you done to this poor animal?" Once we'd explained the circumstances, the guy began showing us photographs of how Bedlington terriers were supposed to be groomed, resembling small lambs with pleats dangling from their ears. Adam, having spied a standard poodle supported in a truss having its coat blow-dried, was standing with his head firmly against the exit. This was understandable - to Adam's eyes, the place must have resembled some kind of torture chamber. The fact is, Bedlington terriers had been bred in the north-east of England specifically as working dogs, to keep farmland free of rabbits and rodents. The Bedlington is a highly intelligent, fearless breed of dog that boasts an armoury of razor-sharp teeth. Despite a gentle temperament where human beings are concerned, in matters of territoriality they're prepared to fight to the death.

When it came to interacting with other dogs, Adam had seemed almost psychotic, and it wasn't hard to understand why. Initially, the only food we could get him to eat was from the Chinese takeaway, a fact we discovered accidentally one evening shortly after his arrival. Adam must have kept himself alive by eating the discarded scraps thrown down casually on a Saturday night outside the many takeaways to be found on suburban high streets. He was a mass of cuts and grazes, earned from fighting with other dogs. When we lived in Rochdale, it was common for people to allow their dogs to run free all day. Amongst these street dogs, hierarchies would form, and rites of passage established for the crossing of neighbouring territories. However, a stray has no territory, nor does it have a strong human scent, so when a stray attempts to cross another's territory, all the house dogs that form a particular hierarchy will come together to drive it away. Consequently Adam found himself fighting for his life every day.

In the tranquil surroundings of Caldra House, Adam seemed to calm down considerably, and from that time on we had no further problems or worries concerning his behaviour. He'd spend most of his time exploring the woods, chasing the many rabbits that lived there. Occasionally, despite his deteriorating eyesight, he managed to bring one or two rabbits down, after which he'd proudly drag them back to the cottage. Adam even managed to pull his weight when he successfully chased off a roving pack of rats that had attempted to move into one of the storage barns behind the main house. Eventually Adam's more relaxed nature manifested itself by way of an idiosyncrasy that I have never seen in any other dog. Whenever he was in a good mood or particularly pleased to see you, he'd grin broadly, his lips drawn back in a wide, toothy smile. Sally and I never did find a cure for his bad breath, however.

During our first six months at Caldra I hardly made any music at all. For one thing, there always seemed to be so much to do around the place, and the novelty of our fresh surroundings was, at the very least, distracting. For another, my old life as the frontman in a rock 'n' roll band seemed a universe away. Instead, Sally and I focused on managing the estate under Russell's guidance and instruction, and gradually we took on more and more responsibility, not because we felt compelled - Russell's attitude was remarkably relaxed - but simply because we enjoyed and appreciated being there so much. I came to think that the circumstances were rather ironic. Russell was obviously a very successful, wealthy man, although we never did discover what he did in London. He rarely talked about his work and we didn't ask, figuring that if he'd wanted to talk about it he would have. Yet his commitments were such that he was able to spend precious little time enjoying the estate, while we, on the other hand, with barely a penny to our name, enjoyed all the benefits of Caldra on a permanent basis. Still, Russell was obviously happy with the situation, feeling that he had people on hand that he could genuinely trust, and in all our time at Caldra we never received so much as a single complaint. He made us feel totally appreciated, and was more like a close friend and neighbour than an employer.

One of the great delights of Caldra was the abundance of wildlife that coexisted all around us. The estate was an island of woodland amid miles of open farmland, and still boasted a colony of red squirrels. In most areas of Britain these have been completely wiped out, due to the arrival of the larger and more aggressive North American grey squirrel at the turn of the century. A pair of goshawks lived in one of the surrounding fields - at that time there were only around six pairs left in the wild in the whole of Scotland.

The only blight came by way of the Duns Hunt, which met periodically to charge around the countryside on horseback, dressed in red tunics, accompanied by a large company of baying hounds. However, they very rarely, if ever, managed to catch a fox. There was one local fox in particular that had managed to evade these morons for the last fifteen years. Sally and I saw him one evening down by the river, having disturbed him in the process of trying to catch one of the wild ducks that nested on the riverbank. We were alerted to a sudden splashing sound from the river's edge, and caught a glimpse of him as he climbed the opposite bank, pausing to check us out before vanishing amongst the hedgerows on the far side.

During the winter months Adam's arch-enemy, a stoat, would take up residence in the cavity walls of our cottage. In winter, the stoat's fur would turn white, making him much harder to see against the snow, though we could always hear him scurrying behind the walls as he came and went through a small entrance beside our front door. No matter how vigilant Adam was, he was never able to catch the rascal. Eventually the stoat took to stealing the occasional egg from our hen house, and I'd watch him roll the egg to his summer den, not begrudging him one iota.

The hens were a present from Harry and Mandy who sadly, during our second year at Caldra, decided to move back to England. The circumstances surrounding Harry and Mandy's departure were rather sad. One of the many things we had in common was a love of Scottish rural life. Apart from the obvious attractions of the idyllic rural surroundings, there was also the warmth and fine character of the locals who, largely, tended to accept people at face value regardless of their origins. We hadn't the slightest desire to impose our values or interfere with their way of life. However, it seemed we were just ahead of a rising wave of city dwellers who began descending on the area, bringing with them attitudes that reflected an intolerant and unpleasant nature, the very things the four of us had tried to escape.

As Harry was an artist and an author working from home, they'd chosen a relatively secluded cottage with this in mind. It had once formed part of a working farm which had long since been broken up, sold off, and converted into cottages. Initially, the location gave Harry the space and the solitude he needed to work, but gradually others from the cities, eager to escape the disadvantages of urbanisation, had snapped up adjacent cottages at bargain prices. These were typically English families from Newcastle, who would then commute each day to work, or retired southerners looking for a cheaper, rural alternative to the home counties. Generally, these people would fail to demonstrate any empathy for the workings of daily rural life, and impose their petty, redundant values on everyone around them. I began to notice a shift in Harry's normally relaxed manner to one of extreme agitation and stress, and very quickly I came to realise that his new neighbours were slowly driving him stark raving mad. He was bombarded with complaints on a daily basis, ranging from where and how he chose to park his car to the volume and quality of the music he chose to play as he worked in his study. One particular thorn in his side was a middle-aged woman who would always begin her diatribes with the same words: "Now, I don't wish to be a pain and I don't want to complain but..." delivered in a whining Essex accent. She would then launch into a tirade on the day's chosen subject. During one heated exchange she'd complained about his hens, which ran freely about the property. After arguing with her for about half an hour, Harry sarcastically offered to gather the hens and kill them all by wringing their necks. Completely oblivious to his sarcasm, the woman initially appeared shocked by this somewhat violent solution, and after only a slight pause, asked him if it might not be more humane to kill them by lethal injection.

Having no immediate neighbours, Sally and I were generally spared this kind of thing, although this was not always the case. One day a neighbour from the village called to ask if she could use my computer to design a flier, and asked us to sign her petition. Her name was Lisa, and together with her husband, her eighteen year old daughter and sixteen year old son, had migrated to the Borders from Canada by way of an extended journey across Africa, finally settling in Scotland so that their children could be educated there. We'd met them at a New Year's Eve party hosted by Russell, after which they'd tried to force Sally and me to integrate into local village life. Privacy and the desire for seclusion seemed to be a concept that was hopelessly beyond her. Lisa was intrigued by the fact that Sally and I had no children, and sought to investigate the reasons for this at every opportunity. We were as polite and as friendly as the circumstances allowed, tolerant and patient in the face of every intrusion, and would often have our friends in stitches as we related their latest antics.

"What's the petition for?" I asked her.

She told me that a local farmer was planning to sell a portion of his land to a developer, who was then going to build a small number of modern, detached houses.

"How many houses?" I asked her.

"Four!" she exclaimed loudly, as if to emphasise that it would be as many as that.

I told her that I didn't think this constituted much of a problem and, judging from the Ordnance Survey map she was thrusting at me by way of illustration, they would lie at the edge of the village anyway. "It isn't as if they're going to be blocking your view of the river or anything," I reasoned.

Undaunted, Lisa went on to complain that such a development would completely alter the character of the entire village and that she was determined to stop it by any means available, including the presentation of a petition to the local authorities calling for a district enquiry and debate. Initially Lisa had told us that she and her family planned to move on in a year or two, and I now reminded her of this. Here she was, seeking to dictate to a family that had lived there for many generations - and who would probably continue to live there for many generations to come - what they could and could not do with their own land. I told her that, out of neighbourly duty, she could use my computer, but that I had no intention of signing her petition.

Lisa's husband Ken was the manager of a large, prestigious hotel some miles away, where he would spend most of his working week. Ken played soprano saxophone and was a great lover of jazz music. Unfortunately for him, he'd never been able to make a living from it. He told us he'd been forced to abandon his musical aspirations to put his children through school, something which seemed to fill him with a great deal of resentment. Ken didn't really care much for my music, and I didn't care much for his, so much so that on our first social meeting, having played me some of his own compositions - which seemed to consist of hundreds of high-pitched soprano notes reminiscent of a cat with its tail caught in a thresher - I was actually sick. I diplomatically explained that it must have been something I'd eaten.

The family had a large dog, an Old English Sheepdog named Dill. Obviously a fellow-music lover, Dill would leap on Ken, barking frantically each time he attempted to take his saxophone out of its case. Even locking the dog in another room didn't help, because she continued to complain at a competitive volume level until Ken stopped playing. Sadly, one afternoon Lisa phoned to tell us that Dill had died suddenly, and invited us to attend a funeral for her in their back garden. I dutifully helped lower poor Dill into the freshly-dug grave and we all stood there in a moment of contemplation. "Maybe I should play a lament for her on my saxophone," whispered Ken.

"Not unless you want her to jump out of her grave and bite your arse," I replied.

Having long since mastered the limited capabilities of my computer, I decided to buy a modem and launch myself onto the internet. Back then, the internet was still an obscure phenomenon, practically unrecognisable from what it is today. The World Wide Web was little more than an interesting idea, although there were one or two web browsers around. I was playing around with one of the first browsers, Mosaic, but with hyperlinks and HTML coding still very much in their infancy, it had limited appeal and hardly any practical value. I had to use separate software applications for each function I wished to perform: an email program, Telnet, for connecting to remote UNIX networks, FTP for downloading files and applications from remote servers, and Newsgroup readers for browsing and posting. The standard connection fee with Demon Internet Services - I was amused to discover that every access number contained the numbers 666 - was around £25 a month plus phone charges! In preparation for my first foray into cyber-space, I had to plough through a textbook the size of your average telephone directory.

Imagine my surprise then when, whilst in the process of trying out a new search engine, I entered the name The Chameleons and was rewarded with an instant hit. One result pointed me in the direction of an American university FTP site where I found a folder containing some of my lyrics, some Chameleons biographies and a few international press cuttings. A young American student named John Caruso - who also ran an email list devoted to the band - hosted the site, and it wasn't long before we were corresponding. Eventually he flew out to Scotland to visit us, and though he seemed rather bemused by our lifestyle, I seem to remember that we had a good time.

Although I did occasionally play my guitar during that first year at Caldra, I hadn't been actively involved in music at all. The situation began to change following a phone call from John Lever, who was interested in the possibility of forming a band and performing Chameleons material. Based on the amount of correspondence I continued to receive, I knew that the demand was there, but had to think long and hard about it. The more we talked, however, the more interested I became. Many of the people who were writing to me were only now discovering the band, and had never had the opportunity to hear us perform this material. I was concerned, though, that we'd need an exceptionally gifted guitar player, and no-one came immediately to mind. It was at this point that John told me that he'd had a brief spell drumming for a band called The Chrysalides, a band formed by a Corsican musician who had migrated to Manchester. He was called Yves Altana, and John felt that Yves might be the missing piece in the jigsaw.

I was vaguely familiar with this curious individual, having encountered him once or twice during our time in Rochdale. The first time had been when my father rang and told me that a visitor had called at their home asking for me. On hearing Yves' accented English, my parents had mistakenly believed that he'd travelled there especially to meet me, so after telling him that I no longer lived there they offered to call me, and invited him in for a cup of tea. "What's he doing now?" I asked my father,

"He's sitting with your mother going through an old photo album," my father replied.

Yves had been trying to track down a copy of the *Tony Fletcher* record without much success, which wasn't surprising, considering it was unreleased, and the bulk of the pressing was sitting in a warehouse in York. I did have a few copies, however, so after speaking with him on the phone, I offered to send him one. A few months later, as I was leaving a recording studio, I met him in person. Yves had just arrived with his band for a recording session and we spent half an hour chatting amiably. I was amused to learn that he'd been buying up our discarded instruments, a distinctive American guitar that had belonged to Dave, and an acoustic bass that I'd sold to Paul Fallon at Johnny Roadhouse Music, whom Yves had got to know well.

Around the same time, I was invited to play a solo gig at the Witchwood by a pirate radio DJ called Craig Cash[1], who was then managing a young band called That Uncertain Feeling. Craig suggested that his band open the show and, as its members were such huge admirers, they could back me at the show's finale. I accepted the invitation, and it resulted in another rapturous night.

I also used the opportunity to meet with John to discuss the idea of forming a band. Before the performance I was outside the venue, chatting to some people, when Yves Altana approached me. He'd heard that I was recruiting and said he was interested. John, however, had quit his band very suddenly and it had caused some animosity between the two of them. Happily, I was able to sort this out, and by the end of the evening, he and John were talking again. I came to the conclusion that forming a new band required resources which at the time I didn't have, so I told them that I'd think seriously about it over the next few months, and we went our separate ways.

News of my return to the stage travelled far and wide, and shortly afterwards I got a call from a young American named Rob, who asked if I would be interested in playing a similar show in LA at the Whiskey A Go-Go. He managed a young LA band that he believed would benefit greatly from filling the support slot, and he also suggested that they could join me on stage for the finale. I vaguely knew him from a previous trip to the US, so after discussing it with Sally - who would be expected to hold the fort at Caldra - I agreed.

I'd also been in regular contact with another friend of mine, Jimmy Oakes, who I'd initially met during The Chameleons US tour in 1987. Since then we'd swapped letters, photos and the odd cassette, and I'd given Jimmy and his friend John a guided tour of central Manchester the previous year. Jimmy, who subsequently became my closest friend, is an immensely relaxed, likeable, charming guy, who also writes and performs his own songs on guitar. During one of our phone conversations I told him that I'd

---

1. In the days before achieving fame as co-creator, actor and writer on The Royle Family, Craig was a long-standing presenter on KFM, Manchester's most enduring pirate radio station of that era – JL.

be playing a gig at the Whiskey and he suggested that I fly up to San Francisco and play a second show there, which he would organise and promote. It sounded like a great opportunity to hang out with Jimmy in San Francisco, so I agreed at once. I reasoned that this might offer a perfect opportunity to establish some useful contacts for the future, so I invited John Lever to accompany me and perhaps play in some capacity and, initially, he agreed. Rob gamely offered to cover John's travel expenses and made the arrangements. Unfortunately, shortly before we were due to depart, John phoned again to tell me that he'd badly broken his hand and wouldn't be playing drums for a while, and didn't want to travel to LA and not be able to do the show. His ticket had already been booked, and now it looked as if it was going to be wasted. Sally would need to keep things running at Caldra, so we couldn't both be absent. Later that week, Bryan rang to see how we were and told me that a guy in California wanted to put a single out for him. I explained the situation, asking him if he wanted to come with me and play a show, and he agreed at once.

By way of a bonus, Bryan's girlfriend Jackie, also a very close friend of ours, offered to come and stay with Sally at Caldra while I was away. And so it was that, with no small degree of excitement, I left for America - and stepped into a movie that could well have been directed by Oliver Stone, with David Lynch acting as creative producer.

21. HEAVEN AND HELL

The flight to California was scheduled to depart from Heathrow, so Bryan arranged for us to stay overnight with David Gray, a friend of his. I'd met David the year before when Bryan had brought him over to the house, and we'd all sat together, playing our songs on the living room floor. David was a quiet, reserved Welshman with an incredible voice, and he was already attracting a great deal of interest, having come to the personal attention of Peter Gabriel. He was being chased by a horde of record companies, and I remember him telling us how weird he'd found it as he attended the media parties around town. He said that he felt he was constantly surrounded by vampires, referring, of course, to the legions of music business leeches who are invariably drawn to the Next Big Thing. To his credit, Dave was able to steer a safe path through all the bullshit and develop at his own pace, finally breaking into the mainstream some six or seven years later.

We stashed our guitars and bags at Dave's flat and headed for a bar, where we spent the rest of the night trying to get into the Californian spirit by slamming tequila. We awoke with stinking hangovers, gathered our belongings, left a note for our snoring friend, and headed for the airport. By the time we'd checked in for the flight it had been too late to secure seats in the smoking area of the aircraft. This was less of a problem for me because, at the time, I hadn't smoked for some time, but for Bryan, who was practically chain-smoking, it was more stressful. As we sat on the plane watching the little LCD screens embedded into the backs of the seats in front of us, Bryan walked off down the aircraft to see if he could temporarily find a vacant seat in the smoking section, but returned some minutes later in an agitated mood. "I know you've stopped smoking," he said, "but just do me a favour. Go and sit in 53D, light up and tell me what the guy whose sitting there says to you."

I returned his stare for a moment, but he kept badgering me. Apparently he'd walked to the seat in question and found a guy trying to sleep, his legs sprawled along all three adjacent seats. When Bryan had asked him to move over, the guy had got very aggressive for no apparent reason and refused. "I mean, is it me or what?" he complained remorsefully.

With a heavy sigh, I took a cigarette from him and did as he asked. I approached the seat, and sure enough, the guy lay there sprawled across the seats covered with a blanket. He raised his head as I approached. "Mind if I take this seat for a moment while I have a cigarette?" I asked him politely.

"Sure, no problem," he said and moved his legs to accommodate me. I smoked the cigarette for a few moments and then returned to my seat.

"Well?" Bryan barked after I'd taken my place.

"Well, what?" I snapped back, "The guy was fine about it."

"Weird!" he exclaimed, and we said no more about it.

Of course, being a rabid nicotine addict and having now broken my self-imposed fast, I arrived at LAX with every nerve screaming for a cigarette and immediately bought a packet.

Rob was at the airport to meet us, and our first stop was Long Beach, where he and his band were based. The plan was to spend a few days at the house he shared and rehearse with the band. Bryan and I would then fly to San Francisco to hook up with Jimmy, play the show, hang out there for a few days, then return to LA to play the show at the Whiskey before heading home. Reece and Eric, the two guys who shared the house with Rob, were very easy-going, and having heard of The Chameleons, they were quite excited to have us there. They introduced us to Brad, the Good Egg, a giant of a man who hosted an independent radio programme in his spare time and was renowned for his astute taste in fresh, underground, independent music. The band, on the other hand, were a bunch of obnoxious southern California surfer types who didn't have the slightest interest in me or my music, having simply recognised a good opportunity to use my name to further themselves. They weren't very good, either. In any event, it was too late to pull out now, nor was dropping the band and going ahead with the gig on my own an option. I tried to make the best of it, promising myself that I'd be more cautious in future. The rehearsals went the way I expected, so I kept them short, satisfied that we could probably get away with just playing a couple of songs together, and left it at that.

Bryan and I arranged to meet socially with our mate Jeff from A&M Records. Rob asked if I'd introduce him to Jeff. I wasn't comfortable with this, but ultimately Rob was our host and I didn't feel comfortable with refusing either, so after clearing it with Jeff first, I agreed. He'd now been promoted within A&M, had left his modest apartment and moved into a relatively large, though not lavish, wooden house in the hills above Silver Lake. I doubt I'd have done the same had I been in his shoes. For one thing, the backyard overlooked the freeway, and the drone of engines and blaring horns was relentless. Jeff had erected a hammock and was telling me how pleasant it was to relax in the garden on Sundays, but I was incredulous how anyone could relax there, given the amount of din from below. In addition, there was a very creepy ambience to the entire area - nothing I could directly put my finger on, but it was as if there was something lurking on the outer edges of awareness, and it gave me a bad feeling. Anyone who's ever seen and appreciated David Lynch's movie *Lost Highway* will know precisely what I mean.

Jeff told us that he'd arranged dinner at his favourite restaurant in town, and that he'd be stopping on the way to collect a girl he was particularly eager to impress. I didn't expect to be wined and dined, but it was a typically friendly gesture, so I thanked him. The interaction between Rob and Jeff struck me as vaguely odd. From the outset, Rob had seemed very tense, almost shuffling like a junkie at one point. He seemed nervous of Jeff, as though he was suddenly in the presence of greatness. Jeff, on the other hand, spoke to him in very dismissive, almost scornful tones. I found this very odd, and not at all like the Jeff I remembered from my previous visit. Having said that, the time he'd spent in LA had definitely changed him. When we first met, the previous year, he'd seemed more carefree and somewhat childlike. This new Jeff was harder, cynical, arrogant even. I remember Rob and Jeff discussing the ticket price for our show at the Whiskey, all the while Jeff was gazing down at him, as though he were examining an insect. "Cheapest tickets in town," Jeff scoffed in answer to Rob.

"Well, that's good isn't it, that it isn't expensive to get in?" I chipped in.

Jeff explained that in L.A., if tickets were too cheap, people assumed the show wasn't worth going to.

"Not in the world I live in, Jeff," I replied, and let it go.

We all climbed into Jeff's new four-wheel drive and set off for the restaurant, calling to collect the girl, a small, attractive waif with very dark hair, who hardly spoke a word all night. If the gathering at Jeff's new house was strange, then the restaurant seriously bordered on the surreal, and was about as far removed from Caldra - with its majestic woods, shimmering rivers, flowering meadows and the sweet, scented fragrance of wild garlic - as it was humanly possible to get. The restaurant boasted huge, plate glass windows that were heavily tinted to allow the diners to look out onto the street, whilst at the same time preventing wandering bums, of which there appeared to be many, from looking in.

The restaurant staff also ran with this theme, and they too were dressed entirely in black. On the walls of the reception area hung a number of canvasses. These were white, and bore the image of giant handprints and footprints rendered in black paint. We were escorted to a large table that had been reserved for us. Drinks were ordered, and after saying that I'd quite like to have a beer, Jeff suggested that I leave it to him, as he knew a good one. The waiter arrived with a large bottle of specially imported Japanese beer, which I noticed ran to the tune of around five quid a bottle.

The menu turned out to be surplus to requirements when Jeff loudly announced that, since he ate there regularly, he'd order for all of us. The waiter returned after an eternity with a huge - and I'm talking American huge - silver tray packed to the rim with all kinds of sushi. I didn't need to request the return of the menu and undertake serious research to know that it must have cost an absolute fortune. I also noticed that our female companion, despite Jeff's efforts, remained singularly unimpressed. If our surroundings were bizarre, the general pattern of conversation grew even more so. Jeff was quizzing me about new material, curious to hear how things were progressing. Bryan, who was sitting directly opposite, would occasionally interject, as we continued to study the sushi. Jeff lamented that A&M Records weren't producing and developing a new album, and Bryan, somewhat ruefully, echoed this sentiment.

Jeff rounded on him immediately, "Yes Bryan, but it was Mark we wanted, not you!"

Bryan and I were staring at Jeff in disbelief, while Rob, seated at the very end of the table, sniggered like some demented sidekick. On the printed page it's difficult to accurately convey the venom in Jeff's voice, or the expression of contempt that his face barely concealed, suffice to say that the effect could be likened to Jeff seizing a fork from the table and stabbing Bryan through the heart with it.

"That'll do, Jeff," I said in a low voice.

The dark cloud passed over and instantly, or so it seemed, the expression on Jeff's face was replaced by a not-very-convincing, genial smile. Over the next hour or so Jeff continued in this vein, quizzing Bryan about what his future plans were, and greeting each response with a sarcastic put-down.

Bryan and I barely touched the food, and we pushed the platter away leaving at least a hundred dollars of sushi to fester. I gazed around, vaguely aware of the distant drone of chatter, disgusted by the gorging scenes that greeted me on every side, and became nauseous as I noticed our nearest neighbour dipping his sushi into mixture of soy sauce and wasabi; a thin trail of the liquid ran from the corners of his mouth to gather at the base of his chin. "Time to go!" I urged, neglecting to add, "before I throw up".

Jeff summoned the bill and produced a credit card from his wallet, holding it out at the end of an extended wrist between the thumb and forefinger of his hand, flicking it to and fro so that the holographic security stickers - a recent innovation - glimmered in the shifting light. "Compliments of A&M," he smiled.

We walked at a painfully slow pace toward the exit - in truth, I couldn't get out of the restaurant fast enough - and climbed back into Jeff's car. We dropped the girl off outside her home and she said goodnight with barely a backwards glance. I took no offence at this. Had I been her, I'd have done exactly the same thing. At last, we were back outside the shambolic, wooden house above Silver Lake. "Did you enjoy the restaurant?" Jeff asked me, smiling, as we made our way to the house. The time had come for a little, much-needed, honesty.

"Actually Jeff," I replied. "I much preferred sitting on the carpeted floor of your empty flat, eating celery and peanut butter. You know, you don't need to try to impress us with hundred-dollar dinners and a gold credit card."

Of course it had probably been the girl he'd been out to impress, and in that he'd failed miserably. My words seemed lost on him. What had living in this awful place done to such a lovely man?

We'd initially arranged to spend the night at Jeff's new house, but I was already beginning to regret it. By this time, however, the hour was late and we'd all been drinking, so crying off wasn't a viable option. Jeff put some music on the stereo and, inevitably, the tobacco box came out and I decided, somewhat unwisely given the way the evening had gone, to smoke some marijuana with them. I perused the living room with fresh eyes and they rested on a large, wooden figure of a person rendered in bright primary colours, in the artistic style of a young child. The white borders around the painted figure were scrawled with a mass of writing in a very untidy hand, and on closer examination I saw that the text denoted excerpts from *the Book of Revelation*. I asked Jeff about it, and he told me that he bought it directly from the artist, who lived somewhere in the Deep South. "They're very expensive," he explained, "That's the most valuable one. I can generally only afford the smaller pieces," and he began pointing them out to me around the room. These were much, much smaller, rendered in the same style, and denoting tiny demons. They'd been placed carefully in various locations - some were peeping from behind a speaker cabinet, others served as bookends, or were perched above the room on the ledges. The more I looked, the more I saw, hiding in discreet corners of the room with impish, mischievous expressions on their faces. "I'm flying down to see him tomorrow to buy another from him," said Jeff.

Eventually we moved to the rear of the house, which acted as a sort of conservatory. When I smoke too much marijuana, my mouth runs away with me a little. Jeff had asked how the flight had been, and I related the incident of the sleeping man in the smoking section of the aircraft. It had been a casual remark on my part, nothing more, but Jeff suddenly leapt on it. "So the guy was cool with you?" he laughed.

"Well, yeah," I laughed.

"So, HE JUST didn't fuckin' LIKE GLANCY!" Jeff exclaimed.

Bryan, who was also smoking the joints, wasn't laughing at all. The strange feeling I'd had at the restaurant came on me again. "Come on man," I said to Bryan as gently as I could, "He's just kidding."

Eric and Reece had kindly given us the use of a couple of quilts, and we'd piled them into the back of Rob's car. Now seemed like a good time to call it a night, retrieve them and get some sleep. As we followed Jeff and Rob to the car, Bryan said, "This is a weird night, Burge."

I agreed that it was, pausing to stand with him for a moment in the kitchen, but told him it was too late to change our minds now. I squeezed his shoulder and we went outside to join the others who were standing by the car. As I climbed the steps that led to the street from Jeff's kitchen door, I noticed the view of Los Angeles in the distance below us and stopped to take it in. Suddenly, from behind me, I heard a heavy thump as something hit the ground, and turning, I saw Bryan lying on his back, mumbling incoherently. Standing over him was Rob, resembling some kind of human vulture, laughing wildly, and my immediate thought was that Rob had punched Bryan, knocking him to the ground. "What did you do to him?" I shouted.

Rob, craning his head without moving the rest of his body and crouching in a wide, bent stance grinned at me. "I never touched him, I never touched him, I didn't need to touch him," he said in a whining voice. The enigmatic use of the word 'need' was lost on me at the time, though the sight and sound of Rob caused me to recoil.

I whirled around to look at Jeff who was standing by the open boot of the car. He was laughing too, but it was a choking kind of laughter, which seemed to me to be totally devoid of humour or the slightest degree of concern or sympathy, completely at odds with what I would expect from anyone who'd just seen another person collapse onto the ground. "Yeah, Glancy, yeah. Ha! Yeah, yeah," he kept saying through his laughter.

Jeff continued mocking Bryan, until finally I turned on him, "Jeff, cut that out right now and help me get him up!"

As if a switch had been thrown, Jeff's expression immediately changed. The laughter vanished and he began voicing concern, but in a fake, condescending way that I found to be even more sinister.

Bryan didn't seem to be injured and I attempted to lift him to his feet, but he was dead weight. All the time he was mumbling, but his voice was growing louder and I could now hear that he seemed to be praying. It took all three of us to manhandle Bryan back toward Jeff's kitchen door. At one point before we reached the steps, Bryan managed to throw us off and I was amazed by his strength. Having wrestled his way free, he immediately closed his hands as if in prayer and, falling backwards as if in a swoon, without the slightest attempt to use his hands to break his fall, he fell full-force onto the road. It was a miracle he didn't crack his skull on the tarmac. We managed to get him to his feet again, and this time we managed to retain our grip of him all the way to Jeff's house, flinging him inside and closing the door. The struggle was taking its toll on me, and I'm a strong guy. Bryan's mantra was now considerably louder and I could hear Jeff shouting at him, telling him to knock it off and stop fucking around. By now, Bryan was racing around the living area, discarding his clothes, as Jeff and Robert just stood there looking at him. Soon he was stark naked and, taking us all by surprise, he rushed toward the giant plate glass window looking out onto the rear of the house. I lunged at him and managed to bring him down before he could hurl himself at it. Throughout all this, Jeff was taunting Bryan, seemingly believing it to be a total sham. If it had been, it was a performance worthy of an Oscar.

Eventually Rob departed, leaving Jeff and me alone with Bryan. We managed to calm him down a little, although we weren't able to get him to dress, so he sat there on the sofa uttering cryptic biblical references, intended to ward us off. "Leave me, Piety!" he would scream at me, and at Jeff, "Leave me, Demon!" Eventually Jeff announced that he'd seen enough and was going to bed. I harboured the faint hope that, once Jeff was out of the picture, Bryan would swing back to some degree of normality, but this was in vain. Bryan was seemingly gone. I spent the whole night keeping vigil for fear that he might seriously harm himself. At one particularly alarming point, he grabbed a large French carving knife from the kitchen that I had to wrestle from his grasp. When I had retrieved it, he tried to force my arm back toward himself. "Kill me!" he kept shouting, "Kill me!"

Things continued in this vein for the whole night, and it was with some relief that I saw the faint glimmer of dawn above the city below. "Why are you trying to keep me here?" he kept sneering, hinting at a conspiracy.

"Because you haven't got any fuckin' clothes on!" I kept shouting back at him, but I may as well have been talking to the painted wooden figure in the corner of the room.

Jeff joined us some time later, and in the interests of safety we finally opened the glass doors and allowed Bryan access to the garden. "He needs a doctor, or something." I sighed wearily, "There's no sign of him letting up." Jeff told me he knew someone who might be able to help, and went off to use the phone while I kept an eye on Bryan, who was now standing motionless in the garden, still stark naked.

After a few more phone calls over the space of a couple of hours, Jeff's friend turned up, a genial young individual who was able to exude an air of calm, which was a great relief. Jeff and I wrestled Bryan back into the living area, again after no small degree of struggle, and we hurled him onto the sofa where he just sat, eyeing the stranger curiously. The guy crouched in front of Bryan placing both his hands on Bryan's knees. "Bryan," he said slowly and deliberately, in his broad American accent, "I can see you're in a very dark place, I'm here to lead you back toward the light."

My heart sank. "What kind of doctor are you?" I asked him, cautiously.

"Oh," he said, "I'm not a doctor, I work for the Screen Writers Guild. Here's my card."

"Jeff!" I exclaimed, "What the fuck are you doing?"

Jeff explained that it was true, but in his spare time the man practised holistic medicine. "In my spare time," I retorted in exasperation, "I like to read about UFOs, but I don't claim to know how to fucking pilot one."

Bryan suddenly rose and launched himself at the plate glass window once again. Fortunately, we'd left it open, so he simply darted through, returning to the garden. I decided that, exhausted as I was, I had to take control of the situation. I ordered Jeff to get me the number of a hospital, which he did and I spent the next hour trying to get Bryan admitted, and ended up speaking with three. The problem was they were asking for a credit card by way of a surety.

The only alternative they would accept was a $10,000 cash bond, and I didn't have to pat down my pockets to know how fucked-up that was. I knew that Bryan had a Visa card, but I was unable to find it. The only thing I could think of was to call his parents, try to explain what had happened and ask if they could provide a credit card number so that I could get him admitted. I was in the process of doing this when the inevitable happened. A neighbour, having seen a naked man standing in the garden next door, had dutifully called the police. There was a knock on the door and in walked two members of the LAPD, complete with Ray-Ban sunglasses and standard issue swagger. To give them credit, they took the situation very much in their stride. They told us that only a couple of nights previously, Zsa Zsa Gabor's daughter had been arrested attacking cars with a sledgehammer on Sunset Boulevard, so maybe this kind of thing happened all the time.

I explained that I was doing everything I could to get the situation under control, but they advised me that I had to do something quickly. If I wasn't able to get him admitted to a secure facility, they'd have to arrest him and he'd be placed in what they called the tank, a holding cell for drunks, dopeheads and the like. Once there, he wouldn't be released for a minimum of forty-eight hours. The tank was the last place on earth a guy in Bryan's condition needed to be. I therefore had no alternative. Despite the time difference, I had to talk with his parents - now!

Bryan's mother picked up the phone and I patiently explained the events of the previous fifteen or sixteen hours. "Has he had any drugs?" she asked. There was no point beating around the bush.

"Well, yeah, he was smoking marijuana last night," I sighed heavily.

"It's happened before," she told me. She gave me her credit card number and I was able to get him admitted into Bethel hospital in Hollywood.

Meanwhile the LAPD, having now tired of trying to reason with Bryan, had cuffed him. Bryan stood motionless, staring into the sun, apparently oblivious to all that was going on around him. Someone produced a pair of red shorts, and managed to get him into them, so at least now he was decent. We loaded Bryan into Jeff's four-wheel drive, and the LAPD set off at a slow pace and escorted us to the hospital. I signed some papers affirming I was Bryan's next of kin - a barefaced lie of course - and they dressed him in a white hospital gown, placed him in a wheelchair, and trundled him away. I was told to call the hospital the following morning.

By now it was getting quite dark, and for the last few hours, Jeff had been complaining loudly that he had a plane to catch. Once Bryan was safely within the hospital building, Jeff had left his house keys and car keys with the receptionist, along with a note of apology asking if I'd be good enough to drive his vehicle back to his house. It was only then I wished I'd paid more attention to the route we'd taken, because as I stood there, I had absolutely no idea in which direction Jeff's house lay. I drove off in the direction I believed we'd come but, to my tired eyes, all the streets looked the same. I remembered there'd been a freeway below the hillside on which the house lay, and that it was somewhere near Silver Lake. Sure enough, as I joined the freeway I thought I glimpsed a sign with Silver Lake written on it, so it seemed at least as if I was going in the right direction. After about thirty minutes, though, I began to have my doubts. As slow as our progress was, it hadn't taken that long to reach the hospital. Somehow, I'd overshot. Pulling off the freeway, I backtracked. Then, all of a sudden, I saw a diner. Strong black coffee seemed like a very good idea, and as I parked the car a thought occurred to me. Surely there would be documents in the car bearing Jeff's address? I rifled the glove compartment and indeed there was. Unfortunately, they still displayed his old address, the apartment off Melrose Avenue. Jeff had yet to update his registration document. I made my way over to the diner. At least with some strong coffee inside me I might be able to think straight, or even check the phone listings for Jeff's name and address.

The diner was practically deserted. At the counter sat a very old-looking man in a heavy lumber jacket and red baseball cap, staring without moving at a plate of what appeared to be ham and eggs. The only other customer was a craggy-faced old woman, also in a heavy coat despite the summer balm of a California evening, sitting in one of the booths staring into space. The diner's only waitress, a middle-aged, dark-haired woman in a white uniform, was standing behind the counter with a frozen grin on her face. Aw Christ, I instantly thought to myself. It's *Twin Peaks*. I sat down at the counter, and my conversation with the waitress went something like this: "Hi, what can I getcha?"

"Just coffee, please"

"What?"

"Coffee?"

"Huh?"

"A cup of coffee?"

"You want something ta eat?"

"No, just the coffee thanks"

"What?"

"Just the coffee thanks."

"Huh?"

"JUST THE COFFEE!"

"Sure thing." She poured the coffee. "Anything else?"

I gave her a ten-second stare, then just shook my head in the negative. The frozen smile never left her face the whole time.

It was then that I noticed the noise - you couldn't really call it music - coming from a speaker mounted on the wall, some kind of mad cacophony, like the sound of classical string instruments warming up, accompanied by a wailing voice of indeterminate sex. The voice wasn't wailing in the melodic way that Asian or Arabic vocalists do. It was wailing in a way I would expect a Martian vocalist to sound and was unlike anything I'd ever heard, and absolutely horrible. Apparently, I wasn't the only one who thought so.

"Do we have to listen to this goddamn awful music so goddamn loud the whole goddamn night, it's driving me goddamn bat shit," croaked - and I do mean croaked - the old woman from the booth behind me. I turned to face her. She was still staring directly ahead at nothing, an untouched cup of coffee in front of her, and as I continued to watch her, she repeated this diatribe with only slight variation.

"Whatsa matter? Don't ya like music?" the waitress shouted to her, grinning from ear to ear with an expression that was nothing short of manic. Again, I focused on the awful warbling sound and orchestral discord coming from the speaker. Music? You've got to be fuckin' kidding!

Just then I heard a deep hacking, the sound of a man who was determined to rid his sinuses of every drop of phlegm. Turning to face the old man sitting further down the counter, I was just in time to see him spit the wad into the ham and eggs on the plate in front of him, and my mouth fell open in shock. I turned to look incredulously at the waitress but she didn't bat an eyelid. I drank the coffee down and it tasted strong and hot - thank God for small mercies. Was it my imagination or was the din from the radio getting louder? And what the fuck was it? It was endless! No DJ, no weather checks or temperature reports, no evangelistic yelling urging me to shop at Big Al's, just that constant wailing noise.

As if in answer to that thought, the old woman behind me was off again. "That noise is driving me goddamn nuts, can't ya turn it down. What is it anyway? That aint music! What the hell is that?" Right on cue, the old man hacked again and spat another wad of phlegm onto the plate in front of him.

"I'm looking for Silver Lake." I shouted to the waitress.

"Huh?"

"Silver Lake, I'm looking for Silver Lake."

"What?"

"I'm trying to find Silver Lake."

"Oh!" Leaning forward, she refilled my coffee cup. "That'll do it," she beamed happily.

"That'll do what?" I asked her wearily.

"What?" she said again blankly.

"What will that do?" I asked her again.

"Keep you awake," she sang.

I gave up. I drained the second cup of coffee as fast as I could, pulled a five dollar bill from my pocket, threw it on the counter and fled before the old man could spit on his supper again. I continued along the freeway for a while, but fearing that I'd end up in southern California or something, and practically falling asleep at the wheel, I took the first main exit and found myself eventually climbing a long, steep hill dotted with houses on either side. At the summit, I pulled the vehicle over for a second and tried to gather my scattered wits. I was tempted just to switch off the engine, climb on the back seat and sleep but, of course, it was out of the question. If the LAPD were to come across me, they'd probably throw me in the tank for forty-eight hours. Far away in the distance, I saw a huge white, illuminated cross on a hillside, and in the darkness of that moment it suddenly seemed like a beacon of hope. A church! Sanctuary! Well, at the very least, I might be able to park beside it or something. There might even be somebody there. I decided, for want of a better plan, to make directly for it.

I descended the hill, rounded one or two bends, and began to climb the opposite rise, losing sight of the cross but seeing it again as I came to the summit. Here I paused at a crossroads stop sign intending to check the flow of traffic, although since leaving the freeway I'd seen nothing else moving on the roads. I glanced to my left and paused. That couldn't be Jeff's house, could it? Could I get that lucky? I turned the vehicle and pulled up beside the house. The kitchen light was on and I was terrified of seeing anyone, knowing that in all likelihood, should someone here see a stranger lurking by the window, they would probably fetch a gun and shoot me. As I drew nearer, I became increasingly certain. Maybe Jeff's house lights were on a timer or something? In any event, by some miracle, I'd found the house.

Unlocking the door I entered the living room, grabbed my shoulder bag, gathered up Bryan's belongings, and tried not to think of all the little wooden demons lurking in every nook and cranny. I snatched the phone from its cradle, and bolting back outside, sat on the front steps. I called the guys in Long Beach, and found myself talking to big Brad Thornton. He'd heard what had happened to Bryan, or a version of it anyway, from Rob. They'd been waiting by the phone for me to ring. Rob wasn't there to give Brad directions to the house, so I grabbed an addressed envelope from the kitchen and gave him Jeff's address. "Stay put, man," Brad calmly said, "We'll be right over."

The next person I called was Sally, and she listened, astounded, as I breathlessly gave her an account of the previous twenty-four hours. With rescue now imminent, I was laughing as I told her the story, but was more sombre when the phone was passed to Bryan's girlfriend Jackie, who was obviously worried. Jackie promised she'd phone Bryan's parents and put them in the picture.

Brad and Reece turned up in Brad's car about an hour later, and I threw my arms around the pair of them. Placing the two sets of keys on the kitchen table, I flicked the lock and closed the door behind me. I slept most of the way back to Long Beach. Holly-weird? Fuckin' right!

I awoke the next morning to an obvious dilemma. Do I take the plane to San Francisco as scheduled, meet Jimmy Oakes and make the gig? Or, do I blow the gig and hang around Hollywood until we can get Bryan straightened out? As it turned out, I didn't have to give it any further thought. I phoned the hospital and was put directly through to the psychiatric ward, and within a couple of minutes, I heard Bryan's voice. "Alright, mate?" he croaked. I don't think I'd ever felt such a wave of relief. I had horrible visions of Bryan being stuck in some kind of delusional limbo, and having to leave America without him. "That was some Saturday night!"

I laughed, and Glancy was laughing along with me. "Next time," I barked, "We take out some travel insurance."

Collecting Bryan from the hospital proved to be rather problematic. Having no credit card, none of the major car hire companies would give me a car at any price. Reece saved the day by taking the morning off work and driving me to the hospital to collect Bryan, after which we all drove to a local diner to eat and discuss everything that had happened.

I was in a state of deep confusion and shock. I'd seen some very strange behaviour in Rob and Jeff at the onset of all of this that I couldn't easily explain away, but neither of them seemed to be aware that their behaviour had been in any way odd. Bryan was telling me that the entire experience had been some kind of spiritual revelation, claiming his soul had been under attack by sinister, satanic forces. This was crazy, but considering everything that had happened, it did make some weird kind of sense at the time. I trusted Glancy completely, and was able to corroborate much of the strangeness that had surrounded his sudden breakdown, and the idea that he was somehow manipulating the whole chain of events didn't even enter my head. The idea that Bryan was completely delusional did enter my head, but I couldn't dismiss from my mind the sight of Rob and Jeff, giggling like a couple of demented monsters as Bryan lay on the ground. Yes, I was stoned, but I'd always found Hollywood to be quite scary at the best of times, and in such a sinister ambience it's easy to feel one is in a spiritually perilous place. One thing was sure, Bryan's paranoia was contagious, and I for one could hardly wait to get out of there.

We made directly for the airport at Burbank and flew to San Francisco, where we were met by my friend James and his friend John. They had tickets for a Roddy Frame gig, so we went along. I remember the gig was quite a pleasant experience after the nightmare of L.A., and James and John proved to be amiable, secure, sane company. Nevertheless, I was relieved when it was finally time to head to James' flat.

James lived on a small street close to the University of Berkley's north gate, where he'd been a student of English and dramatic art. His flat was tiny but comfortable, with a great vibe, and I came to really love the community feel of the small neighbourhood as we hung out in the bars and cafés that littered the area. Artists and photographers would sell their work by the roadside alongside market traders touting bootleg Ray-Ban sunglasses and jewellery. Berkley, being on the opposite side of the Bay Bridge from San Francisco, tended to enjoy much warmer summers, protected from the cold air that blows down the channel of the bay. Over the years, I developed a love affair with San Francisco that continues to this day, and dreamed for a long time of being able to live there for a while. Very few views inspire me as much as the sight of the Golden Gate Bridge spanning the bay, even if it does look somewhat neglected close up, and recently, I experienced the rare joy of cycling across the bridge. The views from above the bay are a joy too, and the steep gradients of its streets as they rise and fall dramatically are a wonder. Of course there are earthquakes too, though I've yet to experience one. Many have speculated that one day the entire San Andreas fault, along which the Californian coastline runs, will crack completely and slide into the sea. The people of San Francisco are also special. I particularly love the way one's lifestyle, regardless of how unorthodox it may be, is not just tolerated, but accepted as being a natural right of an individual to live as they please. Such attitudes are refreshing, even for a European, but especially for an Englishman.

While I've never felt unsafe or intimidated there, San Francisco can be a tough and frightening environment for its inhabitants. There was one guy who we came to affectionately refer to as Heineken Man, because it was the only beer the guy would drink. Bryan and I first met him while having lunch around the corner from James' flat, when he'd approached our table and asked if he might remove the bar codes from our cigarette packets. Apparently some company or other offered prizes, such as sleeping bags, based on the number of product bar codes an individual collected and sent to them. This seemed rather curious to us, and before too long we were buying the guy beer and chatting away. James joined us some time later, and a shadow immediately crossed his face when he saw the Heineken Man. Noticing this, I discreetly steered him to one side and asked him what was wrong. "He threatened me with a gun a while back," remarked James, a worried expression on his face.

By this time, we were all getting along very well, so as I went to the counter to order more beers, I turned to Heineken Man and said, "My mate just told me you threatened to pull a gun on him."

Heineken Man looked confused for a moment, glanced over at James, turned again, shook his head and said, "Really? I don't remember that at all!" He walked over to James and immediately apologised. I was dumbfounded. Never having belonged to a gun culture, such a blasé attitude to the use of firearms never ceases to amaze me.

The Great American Music Hall is my favourite venue in the world. The hall is an old, vaudeville-type theatre, complete with gold-etched balconies, red velvet and crystal chandeliers. The promoter had thoughtfully laid out tables, illuminated with small candles, for the audience to sit at. Glancy began the evening with a short set of his own, and it remains the best I ever saw him. James was up next, and his falsetto-style vocals and jazz chords seemed to sit perfectly with the ambience of the evening. Finally it was my turn, and as I nervously took to the stage, I was greeted by an almighty roar of cheers and applause that immediately put me at ease.

There was one moment that sticks in my memory from that evening, though. I'd been approached outside the venue by a guy who told me his name was Tony, and he imparted a familiar story of how he was trying to raise the money to buy a bus ticket home so he could be with his family. In Manchester you heard these stories all the time, ploys used on the gullible by alcoholics, drug addicts, or plain con-men. Still, while I'd never allow myself to be taken advantage of in such situations, I saw no reason to be rude or uncivil, and promised the guy that if he was still around after the show I'd be able to at least give him the price of a drink. During our conversation he told me that one young lady on her way into the venue had screamed at him when approached, "People like you should just crawl away and fuckin' die somewhere!" I thought this was a particularly hurtful and extreme reaction, and refused to let it go without comment. During the performance, I referred to this incident. "Crawl off and die?" I lamented, "I've got news for you," I announced to the unknown young lady, who was sitting out there somewhere, "You're dead already!" To her eternal credit, I was told by the guy on the street after the show that she later approached him in tears, apologised, and gave him something.

Following the show, we had another couple of days to relax around Berkley before finally reconciling ourselves to returning to LA The contrasting environment of San Francisco in the company of James and John had been a great relief, and the prospect of having to return to LA was not a happy one. James decided that he'd accompany us, and I remember pulling him and Bryan close as we waited to board the plane to Los Angeles. "We're going to a bad place, but we're a circle," I whispered, somewhat dramatically, "and nothing is going to break it."

We spent the first evening staying with a friend of James' called Mike, an actor trying to scratch out a career in Hollywood. Mike happily acted as guide, taking us to the pool hall frequented by Arnold Schwarzenegger and Sly Stallone, although neither deigned to put in an appearance that night. Obviously, they'd heard we were in town.

Back then, the Whiskey a Go Go had a gothic, vampire theme. Paintings of semi-naked female vampires stared down from every available wall, and it seemed to have affected - or should I say infected - the staff, who were less than friendly. The members of the band I was billed to play with were every bit as obnoxious as when I'd first met them the week before, but on the positive side the turnout for the show was fantastic. Again, Bryan opened the proceedings, followed by the surfer pricks, and finally me. James then joined me on a few songs towards the end. The response was ecstatic, and I was called back for a couple of encores. It was an unforgettable night.

Rob made a swift exit, after having made sure he got the money from the show as quickly as possible in order to cover the flights. The guys at the house he shared eventually tired of his bullshit and threw him out. He also collected a number of records that belonged to me, which disappeared along with him, and I never saw or heard from him again.

Eventually we said our goodbyes to the Long Beach posse and to James, and were soon on our way back to England. Somewhere along the line I'd arranged to play an in-store acoustic set at Piccadilly Records in Manchester, so we made our way directly there from the airport. It was strange, considering the week I'd had, to be met at the shop by both my parents and a store full of Chameleons fans. I was heavily jet-lagged, but did the best I could, and people still remind me today of how much they enjoyed the set that afternoon. Finally, I said goodbye to Bryan and headed back home to Scotland with no small degree of relief. It had been, without doubt, one of the strangest weeks of my life.

22. ZIMA JUNCTION

For all the advantages that rural life brought us, the biggest drawback was the cost of living. Not having to find the rent each month was an obvious bonus, covered as it was by the twelve hours a week we worked for Russell, but of course it didn't pay anything, and we still had to live. As I tried to focus on my writing or took time out to play gigs, Sally took on many of the responsibilities for running Caldra, and she was happy to contribute in this way and never complained. Still, I hated leaving her behind to hold the fort while I went off to work in Manchester, California or wherever.

During our second year there, things took a turn for the better and a number of career opportunities unfolded. The first major development came in the wake of an offer from Imaginary Records. Alan had called to discuss yet another proposed Chameleons release, and during the conversation had asked me about the tapes that were now gathering dust on a shelf in my office, referring to the recordings I'd rescued from the Midnight Music fiasco. He'd heard the songs and liked them, but I explained that I'd been unable to find a producer or the resources to develop them further. Alan was keen to release them as they were, which was a possibility I hadn't contemplated. We struck up a deal whereby he would license the tracks from me for distribution within the UK.

There hadn't been quite enough material to comprise a full album, but there was also the Philip Glass piece that featured Mandy, 'Facades', a version of John Barry's, 'You Only Live Twice', originally recorded for the Imaginary Records compilation album *1967*, and Bryan Glancy's 'Beat The Boat'. When these tracks were taken into account, the album would have a respectable running time. Harry Horse provided the artwork, and also the inspiration for the title I chose, *Zima Junction*. Over the years, Harry had produced a series of numbered canvasses with that title, which I greatly admired, depicting a lonely crossroads that, from canvas to canvas, evolved until it became a sprawling metropolis. Harry had, in turn, been inspired by Yevgeny Yevtushenko's poem of the same name, and I became fascinated by its themes. Harry agreed to allow me to use two of these canvasses, for the CD and vinyl editions respectively, and he went on to produce the inlays and sleeve notes. This had been a great deal of work for very little money and I'm eternally grateful to him, as it became my favourite sleeve design of all the records I'd been involved with. There was no cash advance on offer, but

I held all rights to my original compositions, so I could eventually expect healthy returns on the publishing royalties. Once released, the album went on to generate further licensing advances both from America and Germany.

Added to this sudden change in fortune were a few developments concerning The Chameleons. Alan, with the backing of Dave and Reg, decided that he wanted to reissue an edited, re-packaged version of the *Tripping Dogs* album, re-christened *Free Trade Hall Rehearsal,* and on this, cash advances were offered. Even more lucrative by far was an announcement from Geffen that they intended, at last, to issue *Strange Times* on CD. About a year earlier, I'd had a letter from St. Anne's Music, telling me that they'd sold all their rights to this material to EMI Publishing. In practical terms, this meant that all previous claims and debts - mainly advances that they'd claimed were never recouped - were wiped, and EMI would be accounting to the band directly, thus we would earn royalties from the release for the first time! The fan base had been crying out for a CD release of this album for years, and there was a steadily-increasing number of people who were only now discovering The Chameleons, so I knew that demand for this release would be high. Once these publishing royalties had funnelled through the system, we would all receive a bit of a windfall.

With this sudden resurgence of interest in the band, it was inevitable that a few opportunists would crawl out of the woodwork. The most notable was a guy who ran a company called Visionary Communications. His previous company had been responsible for issuing a Chameleons video, *Live At The Camden Palace*, although of course, we'd never received a penny in royalties as the release had been negotiated and handled by KES. That company had since gone bust so he had needed a fresh agreement, and he called me at home to discuss it. He had also acquired the rights to one or two other items: a Spanish TV documentary entitled *Arsenal,* and a single-camera video shot a few years earlier at the Haçienda. He now wanted to negotiate a release for all three, but given our history with his previous company, I was sceptical. Additionally, the cash advances he'd been offering were rather insulting and so I refused. A short while later, much to my surprise, Reg called me. I hadn't spoken with him in years and, at first, I'd been very happy to hear from him. I was quickly brought down to earth when it transpired that all he wanted to talk about was his and Dave's desire to sign the video agreement. With a heavy heart, I told him that I didn't think it was a very good idea, given that the guy had already cheated us on the first release, but Reg continued to press his case. I pointed out that the paltry advances on offer would hardly keep them going for long, but he was adamant. Nor was he receptive to the possibility of retrieving the rights and issuing the material ourselves. I decided that I didn't want to stand in their way if they were that desperate for cash, and so I reluctantly agreed.

Encouraged by this, the guy contacted me again proposing yet another video release, this time of a concert filmed in 1982 at The Gallery in Manchester. On this occasion, I told him to consult with the other members of the band directly, and that if he were able to secure their agreement then I'd probably fall in. Imagine my shock, then, when I received an email from a contact in New York asking if I was aware of a new video release on the Californian label Cleopatra Records. Of course I wasn't, so I contacted the label directly, but they replied that they had a signed agreement from the band's lead singer. Further investigation revealed that the guy from Visionary Communications had forged my name on the agreement. Furious, I phoned him demanding an explanation, and he was clearly shocked that I'd found out so quickly. The internet had yet to make a wide impact on the public consciousness, and he had no idea that my communications network was so extensive. He told me that he'd continued as per our verbal agreement, but of course, there had been no such thing. I knew that, in all likelihood, the stock had already been manufactured, and any attempts to block the release now would prove both expensive and futile as it would have simply driven the product onto the black market, increasing the guy's profit margin. However, forging signatures on contracts was a criminal offence, so I held a strong hand. The guy suggested that in return for not pressing charges of fraud, he would pay the band a sizeable and respectable advance on the product.

Around this time I was also to discover that the money I'd paid to the Mechanical Copyright Protection Society over the previous eighteen months, around £6,000 in total, had apparently vanished. This sum represented mechanical royalties owed on the Glass Pyramid release *Tripping Dogs*[1]. Ordinarily, this money would be collected by the MCPS on behalf of the copyright holders, which in this case had been Virgin Music Publishing. The MCPS would take a percentage by way of commission, and then pass the balance on to Virgin, who in turn would account to the artist under the terms of the publishing agreement. Not only was I essentially the record label responsible for putting out the album, my name was also on the publishing agreement, so I should have expected to receive publishing royalties from the release. Except, of course, I hadn't - nor had any of the

---

1. Mechanical royalties shouldn't be confused with the artist royalties that had been frozen by the distributor and then released to us following Alan Duffy's mediation on Dave and Reg's behalf. MCPS deals only with publishing royalties.

others. What's more, Virgin Publishing informed me that they hadn't received any money either, so what had happened to it?

My solicitor contacted the MCPS, only to be told that all the money had been spent on legal fees incurred in recovering the money from the label, Glass Pyramid. Of course, this was absolute nonsense. The total amount of legal pressure had amounted to three letters. The first informed me that I was in breach of copyright and insisted that I hand over the mechanical royalties immediately. The second letter concerned the *Tony Fletcher* EP and made similar noises, but I'd obtained written permission from the copyright holders, and had informed them that the release had been withdrawn. The third and final letter had acknowledged receipt of the mechanical royalties after I'd authorised the distributor to release them.

Taking the phone from the solicitor, I told the MCPS representative that if three letters constituted £6,000 worth of legal fees, then they should seriously consider changing their lawyers, and I requested that copies of the invoices relating to this action be sent to me immediately, by way of proof. "I don't know where you got your information about three letters," he smarmed. This idiot still hadn't grasped the fact that the record label, Glass Pyramid, and Mark Burgess of The Chameleons, were the same person. I enlightened him, asking if he wanted my solicitor to supply copies of the three letters in return for copies of any correspondence they might have relating to the matter. Finally, the penny dropped and he became extremely rude. "You're a bootlegger!" he wailed.

"Well, only part time," I answered "and only of my own material. If you want to go to court on that basis then that's fine, I have plenty of mitigating circumstances and nothing that I've done is remotely as suspicious as what we have here."

With that, the conversation ended. Within ten days, Virgin Music had received a cheque for the money owed, and it was duly distributed to the four of us. Young aspiring musicians take note: you can't trust anyone in the music business, least of all the private monopoly that was set up to protect artists from the very thing that the MCPS attempted to do here.

I now had sufficient resources to consider putting together a new band. With this in mind, I contacted John Lever and Yves Altana, and told them that, as far as our plans to tour together were concerned, we were now very much in business, and we began discussing logistics. I decided to augment our line-up with a second guitarist, Neil Dwerryhouse, who'd sent me a tape of his own music the previous year that had impressed me very much. Neil was a very strong songwriter in his own right, recording at home on an eight-track tape recorder, and I've always thought it a shame that his songs didn't attract wider attention, because I played them pretty much non-stop. He surprised me by devising a guitar arrangement for 'Swamp Thing', which in our day Dave had played on a keyboard. I was overjoyed, because it's always been one of my favourites and I hadn't thought we'd be able to perform it without a keyboard player. Neil joined me on a couple of solo semi-acoustic shows around the north of England and we'd got on very well, so when the time came to put the band together, I gave him a call.

Now that I had a full line-up, the next step was to put the band through its paces, and so I set about organising rehearsals and securing one or two exploratory gigs. Playing Chameleons material in this context wasn't as weird as I feared it might be, because John Lever was on hand to power the drums. Both Yves and Neil were familiar with much of the material, so within days we were ready to perform. I was even reunited with my old bass guitar. I was lamenting to Yves that I was struggling to find a quality instrument. "Oh, I've got one you can borrow in the short term."

I thanked him but explained that I only played Fenders.

"Yes, yes," he told me. "It's a Fender Jazz."

The next day he brought it to rehearsals and I saw immediately that it was a Bird Brothers flight case, similar to the ones The Chameleons had used. Sure enough, inside was my old black and white Fender bass.

Shortly after Keni and I had left A1 Music, Yves had come strolling down Oxford Road and gone in, as he usually did. Looking around, he'd been stopped in his tracks when he saw my bass, recognising it immediately from various photos he had of the band. When he asked how much the instrument was, the salesman turned to a colleague and shouted, "How much for the Jazz bass?"

His colleague, without really taking much notice replied, "Two hundred and fifty quid!" I can only assume that there must have been some confusion, because this is exactly how much I'd received for it only an hour before! Yves put a deposit on the guitar with all due haste, ran to the bank, withdrew the balance, and now here it was.

Our debut was at The Powerhouse in London. This was the first indication I had of how energetic, enthusiastic, and focused Yves could be. Not content with simply playing guitar with the headline band, he also asked if his own band, Wonky Alice, could open the show. Yves, however, was to receive a shock the following week. By now, he'd bought a house near Middleton, and on the day in question he'd been sitting in a café when Dave Fielding, who was now aware that Yves was playing Chameleons material in a band with me, had tried to threaten and intimidate him into leaving my band. Yves was left seriously disturbed by the ordeal. "The man was evil." he wept, as he recounted the incident to me on the phone. I was so incensed that during a visit to Manchester a short time later, I scoured the town searching for Dave. An old school friend of ours, who was working as a security guard in the local shopping centre, told me that Dave regularly frequented a café within the complex. Fortunately for Dave, on that particular day he hadn't been there.

Before the year was out we'd played shows across England, Germany and France, with a US visit looming on the horizon. I'd released the album under the name Mark Burgess And The Sons of God, in order to acknowledge some of the musician friends that had contributed to it. The name had come from a book about antiquated mythology by Thomas Lethbridge, a favourite author of mine, titled *The Legends of the Sons Of God*.

The sponsor of the 1994 US tour was a guy called Herm, who ran a record store called Vinyl Solution in Michigan. There wasn't much in the way of promotion for the tour besides the odd interviews set up through various online contacts. I employed Usenet to promote the dates, requesting that people pass the information around. This had a slightly positive effect, but in the main, the gigs were quite poorly attended, save for one or two places, most notably California. The tour had its good moments, and I met many fine people who seemed genuinely excited to hear the band, but overall it was quite a miserable experience. During the East Coast stretch, my voice gave out and I was subjected to numerous medicinal injections, while our latest recruit, bass player Karen Leatham, seemed to find the impact of American culture a little too much, and would burst into tears of depression every other day.

As superficial as it may seem, the best thing about the whole trip from my point of view was the timing. The tour coincided with the football World Cup, which was being staged there for the very first time. Yves and I had been particularly excited about that, except that by the time it came around, both France and England had failed to qualify, leaving us both equally frustrated. Despite the general apathy toward the tournament in the US, its presence was rather hard to ignore. We'd been in New York the day that Ireland had beaten Italy during the early stages, and that evening we were taken to an Italian restaurant in town. Mistaking us for Irish football fans, the food had been practically thrown at us. Toward the end of the tour, I managed to secure tickets for Brazil versus Cameroon in San Francisco, and enjoyed the carnival atmosphere that seems to follow the Brazilian football team all over the world. Stunningly beautiful women in Brazilian colours, dancing to the rhythm of samba drums, were on practically every sidewalk in the city. The match fell woefully short of expectations, and half the stadium missed the kick-off due to congestion, after the San Francisco authorities failed to make adequate transport arrangements. The legendary Brazilian striker Pele described the 1994 US World Cup Tournament as the best he'd ever attended. Of course, it had been alright for him - he'd been ferried around by helicopter. The tournament certainly hadn't been the best for Andrés Escobar, the Colombian captain, who scored an own goal in their match against the USA. The Colombians lost the game by a single goal, eliminating them from the tournament, and Escobar was shot dead on his return home[2].

Having been very impressed with Yves' talent and work ethic, I mentioned to him during the tour that I was preparing new material for a follow-up album to *Zima Junction*, and that I'd very much like him to get involved. Yves was very interested, and suggested that I get in touch on our return. Encouraged and inspired by all the activity of the previous year, I threw myself into the task of writing new material. Now that I had the resources, I set about buying some home-recording equipment and, with the help of Paul Fallon, was able to build a respectable eight-track studio in a spare room of the cottage. The ideas came quickly, but I became frustrated by my inability to contact Yves. On his return, he'd signed on as a sound engineer with a band that was touring extensively in Ireland, and followed this with a production job for another up-and-coming band in the south east of England. Consequently, he'd been recruited by this band as an additional guitarist, and joined them for dates in North America. As the months went by, he hadn't been able to find the time to reply to my increasingly frantic phone calls, so I finished the songwriting without him.

On the strength of the German release of *Zima Junction*, another contact was making an offer to buy the publishing rights on the new material. While I hadn't exactly been shopping for a new publishing deal, the offer was tempting. Feeling a little out of my depth I contacted another, more experienced, acquaintance. Steve Harrison was manager of The Charlatans, and also ran his own independent label, Dead Dead Good Records. He'd been a fan of my past work, and had previously approached me with a view to getting involved in some way. On learning that I was considering selling the publishing, he made me a counter-offer that I found impossible to refuse, so we negotiated terms and a recording contract for a

---

2. The American media did little to motivate interest in the tournament. After all, ninety minutes of football coverage with only a fifteen minute break in the middle left very little space for advertising, which from their point of view was a bad thing. "Tune in to the 1994 World Cup," ran one national television ad, "and watch the grass grow before your very eyes."

new album. On the one hand I was loath to relinquish control over my material, and knew that, in the long run, it would be more profitable to hang onto it. On the other, preparing a band ahead of touring and recording is a very expensive proposition, and I needed all the help I could get. When Yves found out that I'd gone ahead and written the material without him he wasn't too pleased, although given the circumstances he could hardly complain. In the end, I offered him the role of producer on the new record.

I'd initially planned to record the new album with the band I'd been working with, but that proved not to be an option. The departure of Karen, who opted to join The Fall, didn't worry me so much. After all, I was primarily a bass player and live performances were quite a considerable way off. It was the loss of Neil that saddened me, because as far as our live work went, he'd made a significant contribution. His sound and style, being very similar to Dave Fielding's, had complemented the older material; unfortunately it hadn't sat so well with the new songs I was writing, especially when compared to Yves' guitar work which was far more versatile and sophisticated. Wishing to secure his continued involvement, I'd switched him to bass guitar, but this hadn't worked out either, chiefly because of a sudden personality clash with Yves, who I think he found a bit overbearing and egocentric. Mid-way through the recording, Neil went his own way.

Then there was John. By way of pre-production, Yves had booked us into a rehearsal facility called the Water Tower, quite close to where he lived. The main task had been to tighten up the basic arrangements, and in this Yves was outstanding, improving them hugely over a period of five days. Because we were still working out arrangements, John struggled to know how to approach them, so we decided to map them out using a drum machine. Once done, John would have a clearer idea of what was required of him. We'd chosen a residential recording facility in Nottingham, at Steve Harrison's recommendation, and so we convened there with John and Neil. I left Yves to oversee recording the drum tracks while I got on with finishing lyrics, but during that first week we were already having problems. Progress was painfully slow, and when I quizzed the two of them, it transpired that John was recording the drum parts to an electronic click track, as opposed to a guide guitar and vocal. I was incredulous. The drums form the foundation of the track, and I was baffled as to how John expected to inject an agreeable groove when he wasn't drumming to any music. As the producer, Yves should have overruled this, but unfortunately he seemed too much in awe of John, so while he would argue his case, he fell short of enforcing it. I insisting that we record guide tracks for John, which we'd later replace with the real thing.

The session was booked in two two-week segments. During the first we'd focus on the actual recordings, break for a fortnight, and then return for a further two weeks to mix the album. Yves would be spending the interim period helping a friend in France record some demos, and he'd hired John to drum on this session too. Towards the end of the first half of the session, they prepared to leave for France, while I planned to return home to Scotland and rehearse the vocals to the unmixed backing tracks. Before I could leave, I still had some guitar to record for a track with the working title 'See You', so I continued to work alongside our resident engineer, but I was struggling badly. John's timing was badly off during one of the middle sections of the song, and the drum track was slowing down in parts then speeding up again, which made it impossible to play to. Finally I had to give up, and the track ended up having to be scrapped.

I took the remainder of the tracks away with me on a cassette, but as I worked on them at home, my heart sank. Practically every track we'd recorded during those first two weeks suffered from a similar problem and, before long, I was on the verge of panic. I think I'd already decided in my mind what the best course of action was. We'd return to the studio, erase everything and start all over again. This wasn't as crazy as it sounds; the demos that Yves and I had produced during our week at the Water Tower sounded great, despite the technical inadequacies, so I was confident that we could complete the album using the same methods in Nottingham. I couldn't discuss this with Yves at the time without alerting John, and I hadn't wanted to hurt his feelings or insult him. Nor did I see the point of panicking the record label just yet, and so declined to put Steve Harrison completely in the picture, which was perhaps a bit unfair, but seemed to me to be the only practical course. If I'd told them, it would have only increased the stress levels of everyone concerned. Eventually, Yves turned up and agreed that starting again was the best option, so that's what we did.

Having now wasted around £7,000 of the record label's money, we drove ourselves to the brink of exhaustion, engineer Ric Peet included, in order to get the work completed. The improvements were evident almost at once: "You know, I wasn't really sure what you were trying to do here exactly," said Ric, "but I get it now, this feels great." Similarly, as the tracks evolved, others wandered in to add their voices of approval. The owner of the studio was also an A&R representative for Polydor Records in France, and he was now urging us to consider the album's opening track 'Sin' as a potential single release. "It's like a Kinks record, or something," he said, beaming from ear to ear.

One or two people continued to drop by to help make the session memorable, including Quantum John Burr, who provided blues harp on a couple of the tracks, and he gave me one of my most vivid memories of the session. We'd been working late into the night, and John was positioned in front of a microphone by a large, plate glass window that looked out over the city of Nottingham. I sat in a discreet corner to listen to him play, entranced as a glorious sunrise erupted over the town, casting him in silhouette.

Harry and Mandy also dropped by the studio, and Harry played banjo on the track 'Always Want', as he'd done many times during our weekends together. Other visitors included Steve Harrison, eager to check on our progress, and he was thrilled with the results. It was at this point that I put him completely in the picture, and begged for additional mixing time, which he graciously agreed to. After a great deal of thought, and having discussed the situation with Sally, I also decided, in recognition of Yves' gigantic contribution in turning the album around and his contribution to the arrangements, to cut him in on the publishing deal I'd struck with Steve. Yves was so pleased that he rose from his chair and gave me a hug when I told and him. In practical terms, this entitled him to fifty percent of the publishing advances that were due on delivery of the record, which represented a significant sum of money - far in excess of what he was due to be paid as producer.

I hadn't yet told John that we'd been forced to replace the drums, not wishing to do this on the telephone, and so when he came to the studio to hear the finished mixes, I was in a delicate situation. To his credit, he took it very well, and couldn't dispute the improvement when he heard the finished tracks. In a private moment, he told me that he felt it had been down to a lack of preparation. His estranged ex-wife was giving him a hard time, bordering on emotional torture, and I felt deeply for him. As he told me about her latest escapades, his entire manner changed and I watched him transform from a well-groomed, calm individual to a wild-eyed, perspiring wreck in the space of a single hour. On hearing the finished mixes, John made a solemn promise to both Yves and I that he'd begin preparing himself for live work immediately. For want of a better title, Yves and I settled on *Paradyning*, something I'd jotted down on a writing pad in the control room amongst a list of other suggestions. Steve Harrison was sincere in his belief that we'd turned in a great album, telling everyone he knew in the business. Unfortunately, as far as the media were concerned, I was no longer deserving of their attention. By this time, the ethic of style over content had a greater grip on the industry than ever. One major booking agent in London had lamented to Steve on the telephone that he absolutely loved The Chameleons and my solo work, but that he just couldn't sell me in the market place. "He just doesn't project a young, fresh image," the guy had told him, "Mark's great, but he isn't Menswear[3]."

Eventually an agent was found, and we embarked on the inevitable promotional tour, starting in the UK, followed by Germany and Holland. Problems with the line-up, and a general dissatisfaction with the quality of the band, made the prospect an extremely depressing one from my point of view. It was all Sally could do to persuade me to get on the plane. However, some of the shows were genuinely good and there were a few laughs along the way, and on a more sombre note, a brush with death caused me to seriously re-evaluate my priorities.

Carlo and his girlfriend Christina travelled with us to some of the shows in Germany, and one evening after playing a gig the three of us flagged down a taxi and asked to be taken to a pizzeria. As we approached a set of traffic lights, which were on green, another car turned directly into our path. We were travelling far too fast to stop, about 35mph, and I knew in that instant that a collision was inevitable. I shouted to Carlo and Christiana, who were sitting in the back of the taxi, that they should get down and, diving into a foetal position, I braced myself for the impact, which was sudden and violent. When I rose from my seat a couple of seconds later, I saw that the whole front of the car, a large Ford Scorpio, was gone. If I hadn't reacted quickly and lifted my legs into the front seat, they would probably have gone with it. The engine block was now all over the road causing a large oil slick, and the car we'd hit was completely wrecked. Fortunately the couple that had been in it were relatively unharmed, although they were clearly in shock. I climbed gingerly from the wreckage and we awaited the arrival of the police. As I stood there, I felt a tugging on my arm and turned to see the driver. "Entschuldigen, zere is zer small matter of zer fare," he said.

In my shock, I just laughed in his face. I could imagine the scene once the driver had reported to his chief. "Well, the bad news is I wrote off the taxi while driving a client across town. The good news is, at least I got the 10DM fare."

The German tour manager proved woefully inexperienced, and he became an object of scorn amongst the others. One night, we all got

---

3. A short-lived Britpop 'phenomenon' hailing from Camden Town – JL.

particularly stoned and stopped off at a service station for cigarettes and munchies. We fell out of the bus joking and giggling, and fumbled our way around the shop, desperately trying to feign normality for the benefit of two on-looking policemen. Still under their watchful gaze, we all clambered back into the van. Yves was driving, if I remember rightly, and after putting the van into reverse, there was an almighty crunch. Everyone looked at each other in confusion and we leapt out again to investigate. Someone - and I quickly came to suspect it was Andrew, our keyboard player - had taken the road manager's aluminium utility case and placed it under the back wheel of the bus, and Yves had now crushed it almost completely flat. Unfortunately, the case had contained our tour manager's mobile phone, which was now wrecked. Predictably, he failed to see the funny side.

After three years in the Borders, Sally and I decided to move on. My work was causing me to spend more and more time away from Caldra, causing the burden of responsibility to fall more heavily on Sally's shoulders, resulting in her spending an unacceptable amount of time at the cottage alone. In addition to this, we began hankering for some of the social benefits and trappings of modern town life.

We resigned ourselves to moving back to Manchester. In the short term, we were granted the loan of a house that had belonged to Sally's grandparents, who had sadly passed away. The house was a lavish property, and in a depressed market it was proving difficult to find a buyer. However, it still needed to be heated and maintained, added to which there was the constant threat of burglary or vandalism, so the arrangement was mutually beneficial.

Russell was upset when we told him we'd be moving on, but understood our reasons, and we parted on very good terms. As it turned out, we were able to help with finding a replacement. A young Spanish couple, who had been visiting the area for the same reasons and with the same motivations we originally had, jumped at the chance when they heard the news. They both seemed very nice, so once they'd been introduced to Russell, the matter was settled. The young Catalan guy was so overjoyed that he gave me a copy of Jack Kerouac's *On The Road* by way of a thank you.

Ironically, once we were installed in the bungalow, there followed quite a period of inactivity, aside from a couple of retrospective Chameleons releases. By this time our first two albums were proving harder to come by. Consequently Steve Harrison, being a fan, took it upon himself to track down Dunn, who had long since returned to Australia. Somehow, Steve was able to get the exploitation rights back for those early albums, and re-

released them on Dead Dead Good, so we were being paid royalties on them for the first time.

By way of a diversion, I'd been helping Harry on an altogether different type of project. During one of his visits, I'd bought a computer game for the Apple Macintosh called *Myst*, and I loved it so much that I'd given Harry a demonstration. It was atypical of the sort of computer games available at the time, being fairly static and quite cerebral, but it oozed atmosphere, with its lush graphics depicting dramatic island scenery and a spooky soundtrack of wind and ocean. Harry, being an artist, decided he wanted to create something in the same vein. In the end, what he came up with was far more ambitious, and even more graphically striking. It presented an alternative history of humanity, complete with historical figures such as Isaac Newton, Leonardo De Vinci and Albert Einstein, interpolated with UFO mythology, ancient magic and popular conspiracy theory. As the story arc developed, we'd have long brainstorming sessions by telephone, and I was thrilled to see that many of my suggestions and elaborations found their way into the final script. He'd wanted me to develop the game alongside him, but at the time I was busy writing and recording a new album and preparing for promotional tours, so I hadn't been able to commit. Eventually he was introduced to a producer with contacts at Time Warner Entertainment and, having pitched the idea, they gave the project the green light and backed it to the tune of around one million dollars.

Harry then asked if I'd undertake background research for the writers and artists, so I was officially hired to do exactly that, on a very respectable salary. Harry's role was to write the story arc and provide guide visuals for the artists, who would then render the ideas into computer graphics. A puzzle architect was hired to adapt basic puzzles into interesting computer experiences for the player, and the results were quite stunning. As the project evolved I began contributing other things, such as technical dialogue for some of the actors portraying pilots or naval crew, for example, and even mock CIA and FBI documents, complete with authentic signatures and official seals. The most unusual thing I was asked to provide, once I'd proved my proficiency at this kind of thing, was a personally signed photograph of Marilyn Monroe. Not content with simply scrawling any old autograph, using my Photoshop skills I scanned a series of letters she'd written in her own hand, taken from a book about handwriting analysis, and meticulously pieced together the message using letters and phrases from her correspondence. I was so proud - it was flawless.

My most cherished memories are of Harry and I sitting at the computer together, working out various problems and scenarios. One of them had been the Newton/Einstein puzzle, which took around two hours to develop. Later, I was extremely gratified when one major online reviewer described this particular puzzle as being nothing short of brilliant. Unfortunately, the production was also beset with problems. Algy, the producer didn't seem to have a true grasp of the concept, and lacked vision; the fact that he managed to steer the project to a conclusion at all was a minor miracle, given the chaos that erupted on all sides.

Most of the people hired to work on the game didn't play computer games themselves, and this often resulted in poorly thought out programming, where the player would be forced to endure repetition that couldn't be by-passed, or the provision of too few save slots. Additionally, the coding was a little sloppy in parts, and at least four post-release software patches had to be made available, although, to be fair, it was an incredibly complex piece of programming. A second conceptual artist was hired to work alongside Harry, but again this person had absolutely no experience of the medium. At one production meeting, he'd waxed lyrical for over an hour, outlining his suggestion for a historical scenario that relegated the player to little more than a passive observer. "We're making an interactive computer game, not a BBC documentary!" Harry retorted. Eventually, on learning that this guy had been at Cambridge with the producer, we came to suspect that hiring him had more to do with the Old Boys' Network than anything else. The game was titled *Drowned God*, and it remains one of the most - if not the most - original pieces of interactive art ever created for the computer. As far as Harry and I were concerned, our chief aim was to create rich, surreal environments. Ultimately, the game did attain cult status, and this is exactly how its admirers came to perceive it. *Drowned God* is one of the most interesting, enigmatic and beautiful projects I've had the pleasure of being involved with, and it's a shame that it never reached a wider audience.

Sally and I set about the task of finding somewhere permanent to live, but it wasn't easy. Rents had soared in the Manchester area, so we decided that it might be time to take the plunge and buy a house, especially in light of the fact that mortgage repayments were around half of what was typically being asked for private rented accommodation. Still holding out for a rural location, we switched our attention to North Wales. We made frequent journeys to the area, but couldn't find anything suitable and felt that the area was depressing compared to the Scottish Border region, so we resigned ourselves to searching in the Bury area. Eventually we found a house that seemed to fit the bill, and duly bought it. It was at this point that I experienced a feeling of foreboding regarding the responsibility of a mortgage, which seemed a little contrary to my overall philosophy of life. Sally suspected this, but when she broached the subject, I rather foolishly waved these feelings away, believing that they were down to little more than immaturity. On reflection, I came to feel that in the past I'd focused far too much on my creative endeavours, and not enough on my marriage. I saw this opportunity as a means of rectifying this, and for the first time really began to think in terms of starting a family, although thinking about it was all we seemed to do - I don't recall us ever seriously discussing it openly.

To complicate matters, over the previous few months I'd been experiencing intense periods of depression that could sometimes last for weeks, and as time went by, they grew steadily worse. Sally seemed powerless to help, nor could I fathom what was at the root of the problem. Suffice to say that in the depths of these attacks, I was in absolute despair.

During one period of deep depression, I dreamt I'd been at Maine Road, in the Kippax Street stand, watching Manchester City. It's the only so-called lucid dream I can ever recall having. The fortunes of the side had been in the balance of late, and City had won the game by a very large margin, so I wondered if I'd been dreaming, which of course I was. On realising this, I found I was able to manipulate the dream and do some quite amazing things, such as levitate myself around various parts of the stadium to get a better view. In any event, the next day I felt a whole lot better. The depression of previous days having lifted, I resolved to go to a real game.

I turned up on the afternoon of the game - against Chelsea - and joined the queues. I'd only been there a few minutes when a guy turned up and announced he had a single spare season ticket for the day if anyone wanted to buy it. The seat was perfect, situated right at the back of the lower tier of the newly refurbished Kippax stand, which enabled me to stand throughout the game, something that had generally been outlawed, and it felt a bit like old times. At the interval, I wandered down to the bar and bumped into my old mate Rob Brown who I hadn't seen since my days in Rochdale, and immediately our friendship was rekindled. I also bumped into one or two old school friends who still regularly went to watch City, and despite losing the game 1-0, I felt that overall the day had been positively therapeutic, so I decided to attend a little more regularly. My next visit saw the team at home to Newcastle, but this time a ticket proved more difficult to come by. The asking price on the forecourt, where ticket touts discreetly cruised, was extortionate, and I'd almost given up when I heard someone shout my name. Turning, I recognised an old school friend, Lamby, who I hadn't seen for around twenty years. On learning I was searching for a ticket, he shouted his brother over and he agreed to let me have a Main Stand ticket at face value. That day I was privileged to watch one of the finest games of football I've ever seen at Maine Road, a 3-3 draw, and I considered the money well spent.

That evening I'd told to Sally how much better I'd been feeling generally since returning to Maine Road, but she ruefully reminded me that it was quite expensive, and that we had to be a little more careful with our finances. With that in mind, I settled down to read the match day programme and saw an advertisement stating the club needed casual, part-time staff to help in the ticket office. The more I thought about it, the more attractive the idea became - I'd be assured a ticket for the home games, and get paid at the same time! I hadn't been doing much musically for quite a while, and the ticket office work was casual, which would still leave me time to focus on other things. I wrote a letter of introduction, outlining my love of the club, explaining I had little office experience as such, but a great deal of business experience, and was summoned for an interview. A few weeks later, I received a call telling me I'd got the job.

Before I could begin working in the ticket office I'd needed to be trained in the use of the computerised sales system. The guy who was to train me was called Alex, and it had surprised me to learn that he was a devout Manchester United fan. I don't know why this surprised me so much, I suppose I just assumed that the only people who would want to work for Manchester City would be supporters, but this turned out to be commonplace. Most of the casual staff employed back then, especially on match days, were students from the local Polytechnic or University supplementing their grants, many of whom hadn't the slightest interest in football, which was just as well given the club's slide over the following few seasons.

We'd begun the training on an up-and-coming game, the big local derby against Manchester United. As Alex was explaining the process of credit card transactions, he paused. "I can't show you the entire transaction because we'd need a credit card for that," he said.

I offered him mine so he could complete the transaction, which he did before reversing the procedure and cancelling the sale.

"I'll show you again," he said, and repeated the process. This time however before cancelling the transaction he paused again, "unless you don't want to cancel the transaction?"

My eyes lit up instantly. Derby tickets were extremely difficult to come by for the casual supporter, and I knew a few people who would offer anything to get hold of a ticket for this particular fixture. "I'll take them," I beamed happily, and was instantly educated as to the kinds of perks that existed for regular staff.

Working regular hours in a collar and tie was an altogether strange and novel experience, and serving on the sales windows was a little nerve wracking at first, but I soon got used to it.

Eventually, I started to be recognised on the window by people who knew The Chameleons, and the reactions varied from mild surprise to outright shock, or on one or two occasions - such as the time Mark Radcliffe, another ardent City fan, had called to collect tickets - derision that I could have fallen so low and been forced to take, you know, a *real job*. I'd just shrug my shoulders for the most part. I hadn't taken the job purely out of economic necessity, it had simply been a way to ensure I could watch the team regularly without the hassle. Once I'd been recognised, my cover was blown as far as my colleagues were concerned, and they humorously took the piss, calling me 'superstar' and the like.

Members of the first team would sometimes stop by the office to pick up tickets. My favourite personality in this respect was Paul Dickov, who we'd signed from Arsenal that summer, and he'd always make a point of popping his head round the corner and saying hello to the young casuals working on the windows. One afternoon, Tony Book strolled in to ask me to change money for him at the sales till, and I found myself in awe of him. Tony was a hero of mine from the days when my father used to take me to matches, and had gone on to manage the team during the late seventies, taking the side to within a point of winning the championship, as well as winning the League Cup in 1976. Back then, I was the only City fan in the office that had ever seen the club win a trophy, which I suppose makes Tony Book one of the best managers the club's ever had. "It's Tony, son," he said to me, when I'd insisted on calling him Mr Book, and he was pleased when I asked him to sign my Cup Final ticket, which I'd had laminated and kept in my wallet as a good luck charm.

On another occasion, one of the senior goalkeepers Andy Dibble asked me to change a £50 note. By that time, the club was in real trouble and was languishing in what amounted to the old Third Division. The night before, he'd turned in the worst performance I've ever seen from a goalkeeper, which had cost us the game. As I handed him five new, crisp ten pound notes, he immediately dropped them and they went fluttering to the floor. I just looked at him, I didn't have to say anything. Andy was gone a few weeks later.

There was a good sense of camaraderie amongst the senior staff and casuals alike, especially the City fans in the office, and they were a good crowd of people. Unfortunately, the senior ticket office manager turned out to be a bit of a twit. I think it's fair to say that the position of senior manager can be quite unenviable in that they always seem to attract derision from younger members of staff, desperate for someone to vent their daily frustrations on. That said, Duncan gave everyone plenty of ammunition. He was a master of delegating responsibility. Every manager needs to delegate to some degree, but Duncan delegated everything to the point where no-one else in the office could work out what it was he did all day, aside from sitting in his office playing with his new personal organiser. Meanwhile outside, usually in the pissing rain, hordes of irate City fans would be gnashing their teeth, venting frustrations of their own, frittering away their dinner breaks queuing to buy their tickets at the windows. Having said that, the only time Duncan made a decision and took responsibility, it resulted in disaster.

Oasis had agreed to play two concerts over consecutive nights at Maine Road at the close of the season. Duncan was adamant that we wouldn't be accepting credit card applications by telephone, or applications by fax directly at the office. Tickets would only be sold in person at the sales windows, and were limited to two per person. Everyone was incredulous. The playing surface would, naturally, be under a protective covering and used as a standing area. With the addition of the seating sections this boosted the stadium's capacity for the concerts to around 65,000, which meant that the office was expected to handle the sale of around 130,000 tickets by direct sales at the ticket windows. Duncan was equating the situation with the normal routine of selling match day tickets. Senior management tried to point this out to him, of course, but to no avail. "Gentlemen," he droned, "I think I have enough experience of this office to know the best way to proceed." The result, naturally, was absolute pandemonium. Before long, Duncan was besieged by sales staff who were grappling with a whole myriad of problems, and finally, in a panic, Duncan retreated to his office and locked himself in. Later it transpired that during the chaos, around £5,000 worth of tickets had gone missing, and he'd been forced to telephone the secretary of the club. The conversation had gone something like this. "Hello Mr H, yes it's Duncan, yes. Er, Mr H, we appear to have mislaid some of the Oasis tickets. Er, well Mr H, I believe the figure is around £5,000. Hello? Mr H? Hello?" Five minutes later, the club secretary arrived, and the thin partition walls did little to stifle his expressions of anger. You may wonder how Duncan was able to keep his job for the best part of ten years? Well, let's just say that, in some situations, it can be advantageous to some people to have a blind man tending the shop.

One afternoon I took a phone call from a woman who was asking if we could send her printed information regarding the cost of tickets. She wanted to take her twelve year old son to a match. "His father used to take him every other week," she explained, "only he isn't here anymore, and he's got a birthday coming up." She went on to tell me that all his school friends were Manchester United supporters, but despite giving him a hard time, he adamantly refused to change his colours. The massive fame of United players such as David Beckham and Eric Cantona had done much to promote Manchester United to young children as a fashion statement, and they all wore their replica kits around school. City players played their part, touring local schools to give special coaching classes and talks, but I felt that the commercial division of the club could have done a bit more. After all, these kids were the future of the club.

The only information we had to mail out was a single sheet of printed A4 paper, crammed with badly rendered purple print outlining the pricing policy on match day tickets and Season Ticket postal applications, which could bore even the most ardent City fan to death. Each Saturday morning, on the day of a home game, the commercial department would send the ticket office a number of match-day programmes, and these would be handed around the office. However, on Saturday mornings, most of the sales staff consisted of students who were not in the slightest bit interested, and the programmes would be left behind after the day's shift and placed in a drawer somewhere to gather dust. I took the lady's name and address and promised I'd send her the information she'd asked for. The match-day magazine also contained information on ticket pricing, so reasoning that this would be far more encouraging for the young boy, I retrieved an old back-copy. As an afterthought I printed off the two complimentary tickets I was entitled to, one of the perks of the job, and enclosed those too, along with a short note on headed paper wishing the boy a happy birthday, which I signed. I then asked Peter, who sometimes came in to help answer the phones or put stamps on envelopes, to send the package off. Peter was the eldest member of staff, having retired from his previous job as an insurance broker, and was in fact a shareholder of the club. However, he was a rather shifty individual who seemed to take delight in stirring up trouble and spreading rumours of impending doom. On this occasion, having watched closely as I'd dealt with the lady's enquiry, he subsequently reported me to Duncan, who then called me into his office to deliver a dressing down. "We don't usually do that kind of thing," Duncan whined, "please check with me first in future."

About a week later I was summoned to the office again, this time in the presence of the club secretary, and I noticed Peter smirking as the call went out. I nervously entered the office and was in there for about ten minutes before returning to my post. "Had another dressing down, Mark?" Peter asked me, grinning.

"Er, no actually, Peter, I've just been offered a senior managerial position."

His face was a picture.

23. VENUS ON THE RISE

Before accepting a permanent managerial position at the Manchester City ticket office, I talked it over with Sally. She was concerned that it might interfere with my career in music but, foolishly, I waved this concern away. By now my career was at a total standstill, though I was largely responsible for that. I seemed to have lost all interest, and had little appetite for new projects, much to Yves' frustration and annoyance. Every now and again he'd call and ask when I planned to resume writing and recording the demos we'd begun some months earlier. I'd repeatedly fob him off with lame excuses about having more immediate priorities, such as meeting the monthly mortgage repayments on the house, or having too little time now that I was working so much at the office. Nor did the record label exert any pressure to continue, despite having picked up further contractual options. Steve was delighted when he heard I'd taken at job in the City ticket office. Being a fan himself, he relished having a contact in the club's engine room.

I was told that I'd still need to submit an application in writing and attend an interview for the post to satisfy one or two of the other senior executives, but that this would be a formality. Since the incident with the woman on the telephone concerning her young son, I'd fallen under the watchful gaze of the appreciative club secretary. Apparently the lady had written to him, thanking the club for its generosity in supplying complimentary tickets.

I was given my own office, and my remit included maintaining the computer system that handled the stadium seating plans, ticket sales and general accounting, and the printing and distribution of match tickets to other clubs for visiting supporters. Finally, there was the matter of administering tickets for away fixtures. With this in mind, I installed a steel cabinet in my office and began locking the away tickets in one of the drawers. My predecessor had simply kept them in a cardboard box under his desk, distributing them to the sales staff on the windows periodically. Curiously, in the wake of this change, the accounts on away ticketing suddenly began to balance perfectly for the first time in years.

I was even able to repay the favour to Lamby, who'd sold me the ticket for the Newcastle fixture the previous year. "Hey Mark! I hear you're working in the ticket office now," he enthused. "Can you get tickets for Sheffield Wednesday away?" he asked me.

"Yeah, no problem Lamby, how many do you want?"

"How many have you got?" he asked.

"About three and a half fuckin' thousand, I've just counted them, and they're sitting right here on my desk."

"Wicked," he laughed. "Get us two!"

Along with added responsibilities came longer working hours, and I'd now have to leave home at around 6.30am to get through the rush hour traffic in time to begin work at 8.30, barely getting away again before 6pm. For the seasoned commuter this was tame, of course, but for someone who'd always had the luxury of time, it was a fairly hard transition to make, and more often than not I'd have very little energy to do anything other than slump in front of the TV in the evenings. The bouts of depression eventually returned, as week by week I grew more dissatisfied with myself, gaining weight and becoming increasingly uncommunicative.

A surprising and welcome diversion came by way of a chance encounter with Dave Fielding, of all people, who suggested we meet for a drink and a chat. Despite all the antagonism over the years I'd come to view my history with The Chameleons in a philosophical light. I still received appreciative emails and letters from old and new fans alike, all eager to tell me how much our music meant to them. From my point of view, however, none of it had been worth the cost. Dave and Reg had been amongst my oldest, closest friends, and now those friendships lay in ruins. I lamented my own role in the disintegration of our relationship, questioning whether I'd done the right thing by bailing out, asking myself if I could have done more. Now I saw Dave's overtures and the sudden thaw in his attitude as an opportunity to try and set things right.

When I told Rob Brown I was having a pint with Dave, he immediately said he'd like to come along. Dave remembered him from when he'd been representing my interests concerning the release of the BBC Radio sessions some years before, and seemed to like him. What I imagined would be a tense and awkward meeting turned out to be exactly the opposite, and all past acrimony was swept aside as the three of us cracked jokes and sipped our beer, reliving all the good times. At one point Dave seemed to be dancing around the idea of us all getting back together to play a gig, but in such a way I thought I must have imagined it, so I let it go. At the football match the following Saturday I remarked on this to Rob: "Was Dave saying what I think he was saying?" I asked him, and Rob concurred. "Oh yeah, that's *exactly* what he was saying."

Around the same time, I was invited to Germany by Carlo to take part in the tenth anniversary celebrations of his band, The Convent, for a special concert at a venue called the Moderne in Bremen. I'd declined to produce their third album, *Crashed Cars And Love Letters*, in the belief that what they needed was a fresh approach. In the end I suggested they hire Yves, which they did. Consequently, Yves was invited to the celebration too, so we put together a short acoustic set and agreed to appear. Also on the bill was Adrian Borland from The Sound, who was in the middle of a European tour to support a new record. Carlo had always been a huge fan, and had collaborated with him on a side project, White Rose Transmission, producing an album the previous year.

As usual, we stayed with Carlo and Christina at their home on the furthest outskirts of the city. I think Carlo was a little surprised at how much I'd changed over the previous year, having put on quite a bit of weight, with my short cropped hair now visibly greying. He took me for a ride on the back of his motorcycle to a quiet spot he knew, and I confided in him about how I was feeling. I told him how I'd hardly touched my guitars over the previous six months, and how my new role at the offices at Manchester City didn't quite seem to fit. I talked about how disillusioned I was becoming with my life in England, and my bouts of deep depression that Sally was struggling to deal with. By this time, Carlo's business was doing well. He'd split Red Sun into two divisions: one focused on setting up a mail-order record retail company specialising in the reissuing of rare or deleted 1980s releases, while the other concentrated on supplying contractors with used cars. The car business was flourishing, and he used the profits from this to subsidise the record business, which was more a labour of love. After hearing what I had to say, he suggested that I move from England to Germany and work for him. This sounded interesting to me and, after discussing it with Sally, I told him I'd seriously think about it.

The venue was packed, and despite my despondent mood, Yves and I turned in a good set. At the end of the night Adrian Borland took the stage and I found myself increasingly impressed by him. Before he arrived, Carlo played me a recording of an acoustic set Adrian had performed on his previous visit. It had been a spontaneous decision to play the show, so there'd been little or no promotion and he'd played to around thirty people. Nevertheless, it was one of the most dynamic acoustic sets I'd ever heard from anyone. He was the lead singer of The Sound during the early 1980s, and we'd been stable mates at Statik Records, although the band's guitar sound hadn't really endeared me to them, so I'd paid them scant attention. Stripped of that, however, Adrian's songwriting ability shone through, and I became an admirer of his solo work. That night he and his band were in top form, having just completed a European tour, and they sounded great. Yves and I were invited to join Adrian and The Convent for the encore, whereupon Adrian, Carlo, and I performed David Bowie's 'Rebel Rebel', which Adrian obviously enjoyed very much. As the song ended, we were standing arm over shoulder at the microphone when he suddenly turned and kissed me full on the mouth, which I thought was a bit forward for a first date.

Adrian Borland, Ralph Kirshbaum and Mark, 1998.　　　　　Photo: Carlo van Putten

Adrian was a bear of a guy, a huge presence in every sense, with a quick wit and a great sense of humour. I also knew, however, that he often suffered from clinical depression. When I'd been writing the *Paradyning* album I'd received a phone call from Carlo. He told me that Adrian's mother had rang to tell him that Adrian was in a psychiatric hospital, and had asked if Carlo could ring him. As Carlo related some of the problems that Adrian was dealing with, I was empathising, and as soon as I put the phone down I began singing, "I know how Borland feels," to the chorus of the song I was writing at that moment, eventually including it on the album. The song was titled *Adrian Be*, and when the album came out Carlo played it to him. Adrian, confused as to why a relative stranger would write a song about him, said to Carlo. "Yes, that's very nice, best song on the album - but he does know I'm not dead, doesn't he?"

In the dressing room after the show, Adrian was in a very buoyant, upbeat mood, celebrating Tony Blair's recent election victory, and heralding the outcome as the coming of a new, golden age for British politics. It was hard not to get carried along with the euphoria that greeted Blair's victory, which ended fifteen years of rule under a right-wing Conservative government. I wasn't so optimistic, however, having long since lost the belief that power politics would ever change the world for the better.

In the days that followed I caught a glimpse of the other side of Adrian's nature when he telephoned Carlo from Holland - where he'd gone on alone to perform an acoustic set - asking Carlo to meet him at Bremen airport. Adrian was suffering a panic attack in the midst of another bout of depression. That afternoon, The Convent were due to appear at a free open-air festival in Bremen, so Carlo returned with Adrian to perform the show. Adrian, being a huge fan of Joy Division, engaged me in conversation about the late Ian Curtis. He told me how much he understood and respected Ian's decision to end his life, and that suicide was something he often thought about, having already attempted it on more than one occasion. As we spoke, I sensed the deep seriousness of this conversation - this was more than self-pity or ego talking. Later, Adrian joined The Convent on stage for a version of Joy Division's 'Shadowplay', and as I watched him, I remember thinking that this guy was a tragedy waiting to happen.

We returned to England, Sally to her nursing home job and I to Maine Road and the ticket office. It seemed I had everything, a good job, a beautiful, loving wife, a nice home and a nice car, and yet I couldn't recall ever having been so bored and miserable.

At work, the spats with the ticket office manager intensified. He came into my office one day carrying the staff season tickets that belonged to Colin Bell, probably the most legendary Manchester City player of all time. In recent years he'd been employed by the club as an ambassador of sorts, trying to encourage very young, up-and-coming players to sign with Manchester City's youth academy, and would often visit promising candidates at home, impressing their parents no end. After all, any person of my generation with even the slightest interest in football knew who Colin Bell was. Except now something had gone wrong, and the club had fired him. Duncan was now telling me to cancel his season tickets, and erase him from the system. Perhaps it was foolish of me, but the more I thought about it and the more I stared at the seating plan on the screen, the less able I was to carry out these instructions. I couldn't believe the club could be so petty as to take the man's season tickets away, but, this being the case, they could find someone else to do it. I walked into Duncan's office and asked him to get one of the casual staff to cancel the tickets. Most of them wouldn't even know who Colin Bell was, so there would be no emotional attachment, but Duncan refused. "I asked you to do it, and I expect it to be done." he drawled.

I continued to argue, but Duncan was adamant, so in the end I went back to my office and slammed the door. A little later a colleague came in and took the tickets from me. "I'll get somebody else to do it, mate," he said.

I received a call from Steve Harrison, asking for a meeting. I was expecting him to urge us to finish the new recordings, but I was surprised. He told us that one of his business partners had, somewhat unscrupulously, sold the controlling shares in the publishing and recording companies they'd jointly owned. The buyer, a major American company, had ousted Steve, and in his anger and indignation he'd sold his remaining shares. He told us that both divisions would have new managing directors appointed, and they were still keen to continue with the option of a further album from Yves and myself. This was a major setback. I'd entered into these agreements on the basis that it would be Steve Harrison in the driving seat, and had come to regard him as a friend. Suddenly Yves and I found ourselves under contract to some faceless conglomerate. I sympathised with Steve's predicament, but ultimately he had plenty of other interests and was now free to pursue them, whereas Yves and I were stuck with this situation. Gradually, my depression deepened and I became even more convinced that I'd spent the last eighteen months completely wasting my time, and that taking an office job had been a good move.

Eventually I got a call from the new head of Dead Dead Good Records, telling me that he intended to come to Manchester to review the material. Yves had continued to work on the new songs we'd been writing and recording. They were still in a rather a crude state, though I'd recorded rough guide vocals before losing my enthusiasm for the project, so they were coherent to some degree. Somewhat reluctantly I met with the new managing director, who seemed to like the work we'd done very much. I pointed out that my job left me very little time to focus on finishing the work. He suggested I finish the recordings during my holiday periods, but I dismissed this. "Listen mate," I told him. "When I do take a holiday from work, I'll be going on holiday, not spending two weeks in a recording studio." This was unfair of me, because initially I'd taken a fair proportion of the recording budget, and together with Yves, spent it on recording equipment, all of which was now installed at the Water Tower in Moston. The new guy was simply trying to protect their initial investment, but my priorities had shifted significantly and I was crying off. Yves was desperate to finish the record and continue with some kind of career, and eventually he managed to persuade me to agree to carry on working on the material, arguing I'd only be needed for the vocal takes and that he could handle the rest of it alone. We scheduled a week at the Cutting Rooms, and I would attend as and when I could to finish the vocals, leaving Yves and the engineer to finish the mixing.

That week I got a call from Carlo in Germany. Sally and I had discussed getting her a car of her own, so she could more easily commute to her own job, and Carlo, having learned of this, told us he had a car that he'd taken as a trade-in but would never be able to resell. "You can have it if you want," he told Sally, "but the problem will be getting it to you, because I don't have time to drive it over." I offered to fly over for the weekend, collect the car, and drive it back. Carlo met me at the airport and took me to the home he shared with his girlfriend Christina on the outskirts of Bremen. He told me that they'd now taken on a flat in the city centre so they could enjoy drinks over the weekend without having to worry about driving home. Additionally, he told me that our friend Daniela had needed some distance from Hamburg following the break-up of her relationship. She was now a student at Bremen University and was staying at the Carlo's full-time. I hadn't expected to be seeing Daniela on this trip. Carlo had introduced us years earlier after he'd invited her to one of our shows in Hamburg. We'd hit it off immediately and would often spend time together whenever I passed through. There was an obvious attraction, but for the most part we ignored it, both enjoying a stable relationship with our respective partners. Over the years, however, we'd grown closer and closer, so much so that some of our best friends in Germany had made a point of chaperoning us whenever we were together, worried that something might develop. Once we noticed this, Daniela and I laughed it off, but in retrospect we'd been in denial about how we truly felt toward one another.

We arranged to meet with Daniela the following afternoon, but as we cruised along the rural road that led to Bremen, I suddenly had a premonition so strong that I almost had Carlo stop the car. I knew in that moment that it was a dangerous situation, and that I couldn't push the truth of the matter aside anymore. I was a married man, and I'd fallen in love with another woman. While Daniela had been in a stable relationship, this fact had been easy for me to deny, but now the situation had changed, I could no longer trust my own feelings. Ahead of me in the distance, I saw a telephone box. I could stop the car, phone Daniela, explain how I felt and tell her that for both our sakes, I could never see her again. Or I could allow the journey to continue and let the chips fall where they may.

During our lives, we arrive at many such crossroads, but how many of us are aware of the full ramifications that come from taking this road or that? Most of us become completely enveloped in the moment, unable or unwilling to take a bird's-eye view of the wider situation. We can choose to quit our job and do something else, and see the potential social and economic ramifications of that. We can choose to emigrate, and see the possible consequences of that. But with affairs of the heart and soul, the signposts are less clearly defined. We have only our instincts to guide us, along with the choice to either obey them or reject them. Why, then, do we make these choices at all? Why not simply continue along a relatively safe path? Curiosity? An inherent desire to explore the highways and byways of life? No, it is my belief that in such situations we're governed by *desperation*. We tell ourselves that we are so desperately unhappy, that the outcome couldn't possibly be any worse, but then we have no more control over the outcome than a driver has over what lies at the end of the M62. Furthermore, we can attempt to map all the possible outcomes but, in my experience at least, the ultimate outcome tends to be the one thing we didn't consider. It's as though, by merely contemplating the possible outcomes, you somehow banish them from the field of probability, leaving only the remainder - God's loophole. Rather than use it to swindle us out of our soul, however, as his arch nemesis is traditionally reputed to do, it's the antithesis, designed to enhance our soul and teach us something profoundly important about ourselves. All of this raced through my mind as the dim light of the telephone box grew nearer. I remained silent, and we sped past.

I suspected that Daniela felt the same way towards me, but I couldn't know that for sure. The sophistication of adulthood is an illusion in this respect, which is why I suspect we all tend to revert to a childlike state when we fall in love. We'll always be those little boys from school, plucking up the courage to make our first approach, or those little girls who are left wondering, having given umpteen thousand signals, whether he will, if ever, finally get around to it. The fear of rejection always holds sway. It never really goes away.

In any event, I knew Daniela well enough to realise that she wasn't about to get involved with a married man. She and her ex-boyfriend had been together for a number of years and would obviously be dealing with the emotional turmoil of their break-up. She probably needed this kind of complication like she needed a price on her head. As for me, I wasn't going to leave my wife for another woman, but at the very least the situation would require serious re-evaluation.

The apartment lay in the old quarter of Bremen, and as we approached we saw Daniela returning from the convenience store with a bottle of red wine. Carlo and I made our way up to the flat and helped her empty it. Speaking as openly as we could in Carlo's presence, she told me how her attacks of depression had become worse, and of her boyfriend's inability to get to grips with it. Gradually, he'd become increasingly uncommunicative and withdrawn, unable to understand the root of the problem. Recognising that the relationship was no longer working for either of them, she made the difficult decision to leave.

While my own circumstances were somewhat different, we shared many of the same symptoms, and I was able to empathise, although I stopped short of telling her how I really felt. For one thing, there was Carlo's presence, and for another, I didn't wish to complicate her situation. Whenever Daniela and I were together, we seemed to exist in a timeless state, and it was like that now, until Carlo broke the spell and said it was time to leave. He'd arranged a special dinner that night for all his employees at Red Sun, and I'd been invited. We invited Daniela too, but she was due to attend a friend's birthday celebrations and, though she was tempted to cry off and come with us, in the end, she felt she had to be there. We embraced and said goodbye, promising we'd try to talk again before I left for home that coming Sunday.

The following night, we were invited to a party by a friend of Christina's and, as I got myself ready, Daniela phoned and said she'd been able to borrow her parents' car and arranged to come along. The party was held in a large, isolated house in the middle of nowhere, with great music and endless crates of beer. I went to this house a few times over the next eighteen months, and it was always as if the same party was still going on. Maybe it was? Who knows? We got to calling it the never-ending party. Daniela and I were pretty much wrapped up in conversation the whole evening, but the DJ was great and I even found myself dancing, which I hadn't felt like doing in years. I was having the best time I'd had in ages, and Daniela was able to help me reach a level of clarity that was nothing short of inspirational.

What the *hell* was I doing at Maine Road? The collar and tie and the office desk fitted me about as well as the back end of a pantomime horse. Hurtling toward middle age, which had as much to do with my state of mind as the march of time, it now seemed as if I was on the verge of embracing it with open arms: safe, comfortable, complacent - what was next? Work out an equitable pension plan? It wasn't even about the money. Despite a generous salary and Sally working full-time, it seemed we were barely able to keep our heads above water. You could work like slaves six days out of seven, and consider yourself fortunate if you could scrape enough together for a couple of weeks holiday in Malaga. We couldn't even claim we were doing it for our children. Ten years together, seven of those as a married couple, and we still hadn't got around to actually having any. I hadn't turned my back on music so much as ran away from it – the only thing in my life I'd ever truly loved doing.

My career in music, such as it was, was the very antithesis of my present situation. There was no safety or security in it, nor had there ever been, but my motivation had never been fiscal. Music hadn't brought me millions of record sales or worldwide notoriety, but I'd made a difference to the world with a single tune, and I came to believe I'd be happier dedicating my life to that. The house, the car, and the satellite TV system were all very nice, but they meant little to me. I flicked through the channels of my brain and found that, as usual, there was nothing on. Some people may feel they need these things to be happy, but for me, it's the soul that's the centre – and the centre must hold sway over everything else. Happiness, in all its varying forms, represents the foundation of life, and the desire to achieve it is probably our deepest poetic yearning. We've all felt it at one time or another – in a solitary moment on a river bank, casting a fishing rod in the moonlight, or walking from a venue, damp and exhilarated after the greatest gig you've ever seen. In every accomplishment, both private and shared, in every chorus of your favourite song or the movements of a symphony, or perhaps simply in the way your partner momentarily catches the light, what you've glimpsed are the mechanics of heaven. These things help us to transcend the mundane and trigger a wider awareness, however fleeting – a state of being that our civilisation, with all its noises, distractions and allures, seems hell-bent on drowning out. Of course, happiness is also a foundation that needs careful maintenance. You have to occasionally check for cracks, as, unchecked, they continue to widen, and can cause everything that's been built on that foundation to come crashing down.

By the time Daniela and I sat at Carlo and Christina's kitchen table after the party, exploring deeper and deeper levels within each other, little was needed to spark the fusion. Our hosts had long since retired for the evening, and the chemistry between us hung so heavy in the air that I felt I was about to combust. It would have been easy for us to have taken things to their logical conclusion, except that there would have been nothing logical about it. I was a married man who was extremely emotionally confused, and

Daniela was on the rebound and just as confused as I was. We weren't so far gone that we'd lost sight of one simple, basic fact - you can't build anything on a rotten foundation.

The following morning, I rose early and prepared myself for the long drive to Rotterdam and the ferry home. Daniela and I had not had chance to privately discuss what was happening, and I hated having to dash away leaving such tangled, emotional chaos in my wake, but I simply had no option. I had an appointment with Yves first thing Monday morning at the studio and was due back at the office on Tuesday. And, of course, Sally was expecting me home. I mention this last, not because it was less of a priority, but because it was unquestionably the heaviest. I love Sally profoundly. In all our years together she had never stood in the way of anything I did, and our support for each other was never anything less than absolute. Despite this, somewhere along the line we'd lost something, and what's more we both knew it. Each of us was stuck in a job that was making us miserable, in the name of something neither of us had wanted in the first place. There's a tendency in human nature, whenever we find ourselves on a slippery slope, to blame our circumstances, or each other, but I blamed myself. Rightly or wrongly, I felt I'd brought Sally and I to this situation. I hadn't taken enough care of the foundations, and now everything was coming apart.

The drive to Rotterdam took around seven hours, complicated by the fact that I got lost a couple of times on route, but finally I made the ferry with about five minutes to spare. I phoned Carlo and Christina, and Daniela was still there. I apologised again for having had to dash off so suddenly, promising to keep in touch. Then I started writing her a letter straight away. I had absolutely no idea how I'd even begin to explain that weekend to Sally, although I knew that eventually I'd have to. I said as much in the letter, adding that there was no way I was about to crucify Sally with this, and that I'd have to consider the situation very carefully. I placed it in a pocket of my knapsack, intending to post it from England, but I never got the chance.

The ship docked in Hull at around 6pm the following morning. Sally was already gone for the day, so after a brief stop at home to shower and shave, I made my way directly to the studio to meet Yves. Despite the heavy emotion, I was in high spirits, which took Yves completely by surprise. Having had to twist my arm to get me to finish the tracks at all, I don't think Yves expected me to be quite so eager. For my part, I was suddenly on fire, fuelled by a tremendous sense of liberation, and fresh ideas poured out of me in torrents.

The enthusiasm and the hunger to produce something interesting was not only rekindled, but also contagious. As each track came together, Yves, the engineer John and I quickly came to realise that what we had was something special, and the album soon became the focus of all our energy. We were working well into the night to complete the work in the limited time that we had, and now, freshly inspired, Yves put everything into the backing tracks. I remember him being particularly proud on that first day when, having connected our digital tape recorders to the main studio array, he patched the drum track through the studio monitors. Other engineers began to stroll into the control room to listen to this incredible drum sound. "What the fuck are you using on those drums, Yves, they sound *huge*," said one of them, craning his neck to look at the digital reverb displays.

"Nothing!" replied Yves flatly, "That's the sound of the room I recorded them in," referring to the Water Tower, the redbrick Victorian building we'd used to record the bulk of the demos.

The drum tracks themselves were impressive to our ears, given that the drummer we'd ended up hiring, Geoff, had originally been provided with very little in terms musical guidance. Once we'd rebuilt the tracks around the drums, he came to the Cutting Rooms to have a listen, and the results had been little short of a revelation to him. He immediately agreed to play live with us, should a tour materialise.

As this record had been a true collaboration between me and Yves, we decided that the project should have its own identity and that we should form a band around it. After some thought, I came up with the name Invincible. Everyone around us liked it and felt it was right, but, as things turned out, the name proved rather ironic.

Returning to life at the ticket office now seemed more alien to me than ever. I chose to get on with the job as best I could, but resolved to make some drastic changes in the longer term. One of the first steps I took was to telephone the new label manager at Dead Dead Good Records. I asked if they were still committed to marketing our new material, and he confirmed that they were. Pleased, I told him I was prepared to commit myself to the project too, and that I'd be delighted to tour to promote the album if required. This represented a complete U-turn from my stance at our previous meeting. He was extremely happy to hear it, and arranged to meet us when we felt we were nearing completion.

On the far more serious matter of how to tackle the situation with Sally, fate forced my hand. During that first week, it had been obvious to her that something was not right. For the most part, I was evasive and moody. It would be easy to put this down to simple cowardice, but it wasn't. I had every intention of sitting down with Sally and discussing all the things that were going on with me, but it wasn't something I was going to rush into - not until I had a clearer view of the situation. With few people to turn to, I sought out Yves, and would sometimes drive over to his house for a chat and confide in him. He told me he'd experienced the same thing with his live-in companion Marie-Luce, with whom he'd sadly parted company earlier that year. "If you're seriously thinking of ending it, you have to be one hundred percent sure!" he told me. "I envy what you and Sally have, I would love to find that. I've been searching my whole life."

The working hours had been taking their toll on me too, and I'd been getting very little sleep. Along with the usual twelve-hour day, I'd leave the office and go directly to the studio to work alongside Yves until 3am, finally returning home around 4am, and rising again at 6.30. By the second week of this, I was utterly exhausted.

After working late one night, I came home in the early hours to find Sally in tears. She'd found the letter I'd written to Daniela in one of the pockets of my knapsack, and naturally was distraught. I tried to console her as best I could, explaining that although it had been a close-run thing, nothing serious had happened. This is typical of a man, not to recognise that deep intimacy with another woman is far, far worse than any other form of infidelity. Frankly, I was relieved that the matter was finally out in the open, and I could express my true feelings. Having said that, it was a terrifying and painful time for both of us. Being the cause of such enormous distress to someone I love so profoundly has left me with scars that have never truly healed.

Finally, following a blazing row with my senior boss at work, I handed in my notice. "I'll stay long enough to train someone in the job," I told him, "then I'm leaving." My game plan was simple: I'd focus on finishing the album with Yves, and once we'd delivered it, both the label and the publishing company would be obliged to pay us the balance of the advances owed to us. These amounts were significant, so in the long term at least, the loss of salary would be a moot point.

In the short term, the mortgage still had to be paid, but we'd prudently taken out insurance at the outset for precisely this contingency. In addition, I sold various things I felt we no longer needed. In retrospect, I suppose I was systematically dismantling the life we'd built, although I didn't really see it that way at the time. Mentally and emotionally I was in far too much of a mess to see anything beyond getting the record finished, and re-establishing connections to my true nature - a nature I felt I'd neglected for far too long.

With the new album finally delivered to the label, I tried to take stock of everything, but found that I was as confused as ever in regards to the future. I decided that I needed some distance from the situation, perhaps a week, in order to try and get a better perspective. Carlo told me that a friend of his who ran a bar in former East Germany was a huge fan of my work, and had asked if I might perform an acoustic set. This was something I hadn't done in a very long while, but it came at an opportune time and so I agreed. Sally, while still confused as to what was going on, understood that we needed some time away from each other, as hard as that was to accept. In all our years together, we'd spent almost every hour of every day in each other's company, and neither of us had ever taken time out purely for ourselves. As it turned out, one week became three weeks, and when they were over, nothing would ever be the same again.

24. SPLITTING IN TWO

Divorce is something I had never, ever contemplated, and it's an experience I profoundly hope I'll never have to go through again. One might think that the initiator has the relatively easy role, and it's the one who's been abandoned who has the hardest time dealing with the situation. If someone is suddenly greeted by the realisation that they no longer love the person they are with, or an overwhelming urge to flee from their responsibilities, then this might be true, but my situation reflected neither scenario. Yes, I had fallen in love with somebody else and when such a situation occurs it can be horribly cruel, but my feelings for Sally remained deeply rooted in a foundation of love. Consequently, the conflicts that arose over the space of the next two years were nothing short of tortuous to me, conflicts that caused a gaping wound in my soul, and while it did eventually heal, the scar still remains. For a long time, the urge to pick at the scab was irresistible, and even today I have to occasionally trace the line. If this metaphor seems ugly, that's because it is.

I simply don't believe you can live a happy, fruitful life remaining solely true to one person, regardless of how deep the love goes. To attempt to do so is not only impossible, but also evidence of falsehood. With all the will in the world, if a person is deeply unhappy, there is no way that person can bring happiness to anyone else. You cannot give someone a gift that you don't possess, it's as simple as that. Speaking for myself, I have to say that the mystic force of love is the only thing in this world that I absolutely believe in. I cannot accept there are any circumstances in which we can justifiably slam the door in the face of love, regardless of what guise it chooses to manifest itself. To do so would be a betrayal of every dream I've ever had and every word I've ever written. I have done it, as most of us have, and in my experience, the consequences have always been negative. Fortunately, love displays the resilience of a Jehovah's Witness. No matter how many times you slam the door, it will always reappear in some form and give you another chance to hear its song in the hope that one day, you'll join in.

My first port of call in Germany was Güstrow, a small town a couple of hours east of Hamburg, where I'd been booked to play an acoustic set at a bar called The Gurruh. The bar was owned and managed by Andreas and his wife Jackie, who I got to know through Carlo. Andreas can be quite eccentric, and takes a little getting used to. His enthusiasm is little short of rampant, and he tends to greet people that he loves with childlike wonder and enormous energy. As a result one needs quite a large degree of patience to deal with him, and some handle Andreas better than others. When Adrian Borland visited the Gurruh he was driven to the brink of madness. Following his set at the end of what had been a particularly long day, he'd retired to bed in the early hours only to be awakened at 3am by an intoxicated Andreas, demanding that he bring his guitar into the bar immediately and play another set. "I'm in my fuckin' pyjamas, you freak!" Borland had screamed at him. I've never had a problem with Andreas' demanding nature, and always had a brilliant time whenever I've been invited to play there, although Daniela has sometimes been driven to distraction by Andreas' insistence that she act as translator in round after round of twenty questions. Performances at the Gurruh were more like attending a party than playing a gig, and in such a congenial atmosphere it wasn't uncommon to find me propped up at the bar with my guitar, driving my voice to the brink of total disintegration, as I enjoyed the Gurruh's seemingly endless hospitality until four or five in the morning. On one occasion, in the company of my Dutch friend Martin Bosker, and to the chant of "We'll drink the Gurruh dry!" we very nearly did. My debut at the Gurruh was a successful one and Andreas has always been generous when it comes to paying his live acts, which meant that in the short term at least, I was reasonably solvent.

However, by the end of that first week in Germany, I still wasn't sufficiently prepared to go home and face the consequences. In addition, Carlo was wrestling an emotional brute of his own. Christina had decided to spend six months in England as part of a student exchange programme, and he was feeling a little low on her list of priorities. While not unsympathetic, I saw this for the bollocks that it was. Christina had spent her entire life in the bosom of her family. Suddenly, she had an opportunity to sample something new, and thereby broaden her horizons. Deep down, I didn't believe this constituted a serious threat to their relationship and I don't think Carlo did either really, but in his more insecure moments such doubts and uncertainties would dominate his thoughts. At any rate, it seemed to help both of us to have someone to talk to, so I suggested that perhaps we go somewhere together, somewhere fun and relaxing where we could continue to help each other gain some perspective. We agreed on Mexico City, and Carlo arranged for us to stay with some friends that he had there.

By this time, I'd come to terms with the fact that stepping back into my old life was an unbearable prospect, and that my marriage to Sally was effectively over. I'd already said as much during our last telephone conversation. I hadn't wanted to deal with this on the telephone, but at Sally's urging I'd been forced to. She had questions I simply couldn't answer. An immediate return to the UK had been out of the question for me, and again I'd pleaded for more time to consider the situation, although I quickly came to realise the unfairness of this. To Sally it must have seemed as if she was being forced to endure unnecessary suffering, rather like being placed under a guillotine that could fall at any time. Yves had called round to see her and, in an effort to help her cope, had invited her to Corsica to visit his parents. They sent me a fax the following week informing me of their intentions, and while I thought it strange, I was also relieved that the pressure had been lifted a little.

Ironically, for most of the time I was away from England, Daniela was staying with Christina on England's north east coast, so the time we spent together was limited. We did talk on the telephone, however, and by the time each of us had returned to Germany, we'd accepted how we felt about each other.

On my return to England, Sally was prepared for what I had to say, as I broached the subject of divorce for the first time. She displayed a sense of calm that I found little short of miraculous, given the circumstances. What I didn't know was that she'd already accepted the situation, and had taken definitive steps towards a life without me. It seems that both Yves and Sally, each on the rebound, had taken solace in each other, and they too had fallen in love. I didn't take this news very well initially, but any anger I felt was impossible to justify, given the circumstances. Had I not taken a sledgehammer to my marriage, this would not have happened. What I was now faced with were the unforeseen circumstances of the decisions I'd made, a trump card that I never would have suspected was even in the pack. This is what happens when you play games not only with your own life, but also with the lives of others. All that said, I would not have changed my decision; what I'd done had been in the pursuit of happiness, believing it to be nothing less than a primary duty to myself. Who the fuck was I to deny Yves and Sally the same right?

I'd like to be able to say that I was able to live up to such noble ideals, but the reality is that it took quite a long time, and it was an extremely difficult road to walk. Simply quitting England and leaving it all behind was not an option. Over the course of the following year, Carlo would make good on his promise to find me work with Red Sun, but it would be occasional at best, and wouldn't provide sufficient basis for a new life abroad.

There were also my commitments to the new album, which, despite the obvious complications, I was still resolved to meet. To a certain extent I felt obligated to do right by another friend of mine, Simon Lawlor, who had recently become involved with us after hearing a rough cut of the new album. I'd known Simon for quite a number of years, ever since he initially contacted me requesting an interview. In the wake of that, we'd kept in touch regularly by telephone, engaging in long rambling discussions on a wide range of subjects. We'd never actually met in person, as he had been suffering from an illness that prevented him from travelling. However, this didn't prevent him from eventually drifting into music management, and he formed his own company. One of the bands he worked with, Shed Seven, went on to do very well. We lost touch for a while, but Simon re-appeared in my life at a most opportune time.

Pinnacle Labels, who were effectively the new owners of Dead Dead Good Records, had inexplicably rejected the new album, and under the provisions of our contract it meant that we were now free to shop the album around to other labels. Simon helped us consider our options, going so far as to provide us with financial support so that the band could continue to promote itself effectively.

Simon suggested that we use the various contacts he had in the industry to shop the album around, but also that the best and least complicated option would be to form a label of our own and distribute the album independently. Furthermore, he'd be prepared to fund the initial pressing. The distribution arm of Pinnacle - in a direct contradiction to Pinnacle Labels, which had its own, separate management structure - professed interest in distributing the album, which I found equally inexplicable. Ultimately, this was the route we were forced to go down to get the album released.

We set about putting together a band with which to tour in support of the new record. Geoff, who'd performed percussion duties on the new recordings, fell in immediately, and in turn introduced us to another friend of his, Phil, who played bass. Since my only function in terms of performance on the record had been vocals, it was felt that this was the way to go. Within the first few months, Phil apologetically told us that he and his girlfriend were expecting a baby and he no longer had the time to devote to the group, so I reverted to bass guitar and the band became a trio. With the odd exception, attendances at the gigs were fairly low, but once we began to work as a band, everything clicked into place and the audiences were treated to something rather special. Even the obligatory shouts for Chameleons songs became rare. In fact, following a particularly well-attended Manchester show, one guy told me that he'd often yearned for the day when I'd stop trying to go my own way and reform The Chameleons. "But after what I just saw and heard, Mark," he beamed happily, "fuck it! Just go right on doing what you're doing." It was nice to hear such a reaction, there's no question about that, but in all honesty I found it quite difficult, given the circumstances. I could hardly bear visiting Yves at his home. It was as if bits of my broken life had been strewn around his house. The sight of Sally bustling around Yves' kitchen was simply too strange for me. Even the sight of our dog Adam, now living with Yves and Sally, was too much to bear. By this time, he was old and almost completely blind. With my current emotional state and unsettled lifestyle I wasn't able to look after him properly anyway, and I knew that he was far better off living with Sally and Yves - but it broke my heart every time I saw him.

I'd spend the months flitting between England and Germany as and when the work demanded. In Germany, I'd stay with Daniela at the flat in Bremen until either I ran out of money or work called me home, and then I'd return to England, staying at the house until we could organise the sale. Daniela joined me there once or twice, but it was a depressing scene and while it was always great to be with her, it was as if a dense, black cloud hung over everything. The feelings of elation and liberation quickly dissipated and were replaced by emotional turmoil. I was unable to think clearly or see a way forward, and life began to resemble some kind of surreal nightmare.

Fate dealt another blow when Dead Dead Good's new owners refused to release the balance of the publishing advances, on the grounds that the label we'd set up to handle the release of the album didn't constitute a label as defined in the contract. This was nonsense, and privately they admitted as much, but again they'd gambled that I didn't have the resources to contest them, and they were right. My lawyer told me that I'd probably be able to make a case in the small claims court, eliminating the usual heavy legal costs, but he said I'd have to represent myself in court, which would have taken a tremendous amount of time and energy - neither of which I had at the time.

Our drummer Geoff was the next casualty, and under quite strange circumstances. We'd been playing a gig at the Witchwood as part of a small tour and Geoff, despite having to drive home, drank a few beers. As he and his girlfriend drove home, they were stopped by the police and questioned. Geoff hadn't been noticeably drunk, but nevertheless he was over the limit. Not content with simply booking him for drunk-driving, however, the police arrested him and escorted him back to the police station. What happened next isn't entirely clear. According to his girlfriend, Geoff was placed in a cell with a couple of suspected sex offenders, while the arresting officers looked on laughing. The following day we received a frantic phone call from Geoff's girlfriend asking if we could drive over there right away. Yves and I arrived to find Geoff in a complete mess, seemingly on the edge of some kind of nervous breakdown. His girlfriend told us that, during the previous night, he'd tried to hurt himself several times. Nothing Yves or I said seemed to get through to him, and we were both at a complete loss. Not long after that they quit Manchester for good, and it was years before either of us heard from him again.

We managed to find a replacement, and for a while we carried on, but the strain of working closely with Yves, given our situation, began to take its toll - not only on my mental well-being, but also on my relationship with Daniela, who was finding my mood swings and emotional outbursts too much to handle. As Christmas approached, she told me that, all things considered, she felt it might be best if she went her own way. By the time Christmas arrived, I was a nervous wreck, almost suicidal, in fact. I sat down and planned it. I'd drive to a remote area around Loch Ness, attach a hosepipe to the exhaust, and have done with it; I suddenly understood why it is that suicide numbers increase at Christmas. It has to be one of the most depressing times of the year for anybody over the age of ten, and especially for those in the midst of divorce or bereavement. I'd been spending that Christmas with my parents and they were extremely worried, although they seemed paralysed by the situation and unable to help. I've never been one to wallow in self-pity, and I was eventually able to push such stupid notions away, but it was, without doubt, my darkest hour. Fortunately, help came by way of a phone call from Daniela who, having realised the state I was in, took an initiative. "I've booked a plane ticket for Boxing Day," she told me. "There's no point arguing about it, it's paid for. Just get on the plane and get the fuck out of there." It was good, and extremely welcome, advice.

Still, no matter how hard I'd try to pull away and leave it all behind, something would always draw me back. Now that we'd been dumped by Pinnacle Labels, and having very little in the way of resources with which to promote the new record, work began to dry up. With barely 1,000 copies of the album pressed, Invincible proved to be anything but. Fortunately The Chameleons came to the rescue, thanks to royalties on the Dead Dead Good re-issues of our early albums and a 'Best of' compilation, so I wasn't entirely destitute. Nevertheless, I still had debts, and while they weren't outrageous, they were a little worrying. One piece of good news was that we managed to sell the house before the payment insurance ran out.

Daniela had accompanied me back to England to see to the house, but was disappointed when I told her that I didn't think I'd be able to afford to make it back in time for her birthday the following week. She returned to Bremen, dejected, having been given little more than vague promises that I'd sort something out eventually.

As luck would have it, this coincided with a rare visit from my close friend Jimmy from San Francisco. He'd come to Manchester to visit one or two other friends, and though I lamented that I wasn't able to spend more time with him, the time we did have was invaluable to me. He was able to help me reach a degree of clarity that had eluded me for months, and by the end of that day, I'd been galvanised into action. I decided there was no way I was going to miss Daniela's birthday, and took stock of the situation. The only thing I had of any commercial value, besides my instruments - which were untouchable - was the car, so I decided to ditch it and use the money to get to Germany. James thought this was a brilliant idea, and gamely accompanied me to a Mercedes dealer I knew of. Now solvent, I bought a birthday present for Daniela along with a plane ticket to Bremen, and the day before Daniela's birthday I contacted Carlo asking if he could meet me at the airport, but not tell Daniela.

Later that evening I phoned Daniela at her flat in Bremen, but I still didn't tell her I was in the country. This may have seemed like a cruel joke, but in my view a birthday surprise should be exactly that. Having no idea I was with Carlo, Daniela was extremely downbeat and I sadistically turned the screw. "I just wanted to find out exactly where you were planning to spend your birthday." I asked her.

"I'm spending it here at the flat alone of course, why?" She responded frostily.

"Well, I wanted to surprise you," I said, "I thought maybe I'd send you a birthday fax."

"A BIRTHDAY FAX!" She exclaimed, "How thoughtful of you." She told me again how disappointed she was that I hadn't managed to get back to Germany in time.

"Well, you know, I'm disappointed at your lack of faith in me, I mean, faith can move mountains you know."

"Try moving boxes!" she barked, and hung up the phone. A few moments later, she repented these rather harsh words and phoned me back at the house, but naturally, I wasn't there to answer. Reasoning that I was probably upstairs watching the football, unable to hear the phone, she gave up.

Naturally her birthday didn't begin until midnight and so I timed my arrival at the flat accordingly. Carlo and Christina took me to the flat in the car, all the time giggling and lamenting that they wouldn't get to see the expression on Daniela's face when she opened the door, but not wishing to intrude on such a private moment. We said our goodbyes, promising to get together over the next couple of days, and I climbed the stairs to the flat. I rang the bell a couple of times and waited until finally I heard Daniela behind the front door. "Who is it?" the sleepy voice behind the door enquired nervously.

"It's me!" I laughed. "Open the door!" Had I really been thinking clearly, I would have had a camera at the ready, because her face was an absolute picture as she stared at me, open-mouthed. However, it probably would have been thrown from my hands and gone tumbling down the stairs, such was the force with which she hurled herself at me, all the while laughing hysterically. We spent the night drinking champagne as she unwrapped her gift, a brooch that she'd noticed in a shop window during a recent visit to England. While there'd undoubtedly be a few more trials and tribulations along the way, I finally felt I'd taken the first step towards a new life. There really was no turning back, which, considering what I'd left behind, suited me just fine.

25. RESURRECTION

Like many central European cities, much of Bremen's unique charm had been blanded-out in favour of rust-shaded pedestrian zones and endless rows of shoe shops. The flat I shared with Daniela was situated in a more attractive part of town, at the heart of Bremen's oldest quarter, on a side street just around the corner from the Weser river and its adjacent promenade. This was a very agreeable place to live, especially in the summer, and we'd often stroll the narrow, cobbled streets, exploring the many sidewalk cafés, drinking dens and restaurants scattered throughout the area. On particularly warm days, I'd take my guitar and sit for hours on the cool, grass riverbank, watching the boats sail lazily by as my fellow citizens cruised past, either on foot, on roller-blades or bicycles. Sometimes on Sundays the waterfront would be transformed into a huge flea market, seeming to offer every conceivable used item under the sun - a sun that, more often than not during the summer months, bathed Bremen from a pale blue sky.

My parents were happy and more than a little relieved to see me in such good spirits, given the drama of the previous year. They'd met Daniela by this time and thought the world of her, and while parental approval wasn't a prerequisite, I was glad to have it. Both my parents had been fantastic throughout, supporting me in every way they could, and I regard myself as extremely lucky to have them. I hadn't really shown them much evidence as the storm had gathered, and my break-up with Sally had come as a complete surprise to them. Ultimately, I'm proud of the fact that Sally, Yves and I were able to retain close, lasting friendships, despite the emotional hardship of those first couple of years.

I was playing my guitar more often by then, although I wasn't composing much. The band I'd formed with Yves was over, and while Dave and I had discussed the idea of a Chameleons reformation, we didn't take any steps towards making it happen. However, creative activities didn't grind to an absolute halt. With the help of Carlo and his label manager Lars Fischer, I was able to issue a Sun And The Moon compilation album entitled *The Great Escape*. Most of these recordings belonged to Geffen Records, and the publishing rights were still owned by KES and St. Anne's. Consequently, I didn't earn royalties from this release, but did make some money as the owner of the record label issuing the CD. This wasn't a huge amount, but it kept me afloat. The CD was a limited edition release, with half the copies sold as advance orders, and overall it did quite well.

I continued to play acoustic shows here and there, returning to the Gurruh in Güstrow at Andreas' invitation, and on another occasion - in rather peculiar circumstances - a private performance. One evening Daniela and I had been eating at our favourite restaurant, when one of the regular waitresses suddenly asked if I was Mark Burgess from The Chameleons. I wasn't often recognised casually like this, although it happened more often in Germany than it did in England. She went on to explain that her boyfriend was a huge fan of the band, and asked about the possibility of me performing an acoustic set at an outdoor birthday party she was arranging for his birthday. I explained that I didn't ordinarily do that kind of thing, but that I'd certainly think about it, so she and Daniela exchanged phone numbers. I had done something similar the year before with Yves for a couple living in London and had a really good time, so I came to feel that it might be a fun thing to do. The waitress tentatively asked me how much money an acoustic performance would cost, but I'd already thought of that. As she was a permanent member of staff at our favourite restaurant, I suggested that she pay me with dinner for two, and she was thrilled. On the weekend of the party, Daniela and I drove in glorious sunshine and summer temperatures to a secluded, rural house on the outskirts of Bremen. When we got there, the party was in full swing, and while some of the guests knew what was afoot, her boyfriend hadn't the faintest clue; on seeing me, his face lit up. I performed to around fifty revellers who all sat in rapt attention on the lawn of the house, applauding enthusiastically. It was one of the most pleasant experiences I've ever had playing solo. As I began to sing the line "No wonder it feels like I'm floating on air," a hot-air balloon drifted over our heads, right on cue, and low enough to allow us to see its waving occupants.

I was also invited to take part in a recording session by Carlo and Adrian Borland, who were collaborating on what would become the second album for their White Rose Transmission project - a loose collection of individuals and acquaintances who gathered, whenever time permitted, to play Carlo and Adrian's compositions. I'd been a huge fan of their first album and was extremely pleased when Adrian asked if I'd play bass on the sequel, and subsequently spent a couple of weeks at the studio working on the album.

Having similar musical backgrounds, Adrian and I got on very well, and soon, besides performance duties, I found myself assisting with the mixes. Adrian had composed a song that he wanted me to perform, 'Digging for Water', but had been shy about asking me, and had to get Carlo to broach the subject. Adrian later told me he'd written the song in his head during a flight to Bremen, and I was extremely impressed, given the song's quality. That was typical of Adrian - he never stopped working on songs, or thinking about music. In a situation where you or I might be nonchalantly browsing an in-flight magazine, dozing in our seats or staring blankly out of the cabin window, this guy was composing new songs in his head. I performed the song and he was extremely complimentary about my voice: "Man, I didn't realise you could sing like that." Previously he'd only ever heard my vocals with the band, which had always sounded more like shouting than singing. He did pull me up on my Mancunian accent, however. "What's this 'warder'?" he barked over the studio intercom. "Warder? It's *water*, with a 't '!" Carlo had been even more sternly admonished during the recording of the first White Rose Transmission album, when he'd attempted to record a vocal in a semi-drunken state after consuming half a bottle of whisky. "You're not Jim Morrison, you FREAK!" Adrian bellowed, causing Carlo to fall to the floor in tears of laughter.

Adrian had the quality of being hilarious regardless of the situation or mood, to the extent that it was often difficult to take him seriously. He'd been having numerous rows on the telephone with his girlfriend that week. She'd remained behind in London and had convinced herself that he was simply partying and womanising in Bremen, rather than working hard in the studio. Ironically, the day before the latest of these heated exchanges, I'd driven him into town to pick up an engagement ring, a surprise for her on his return. The following evening, as we sat drinking a beer, he was fuming over the latest row. "Come on, man," I joked. "When you get back home and show her that ring she's going to feel really guilty about giving you a hard time."

"Good!" He barked, nodding emphatically to himself, "Fuckin' good! I hope she feels fucking shit!"

Nor did Adrian have any shame when it came to being comically two-faced. He had a bit of a jealous streak where Carlo was concerned, and hated it if Carlo ever seemed to get excited about another artist. He'd make a point, for example, of deliberately miss-pronouncing the name of another mutual friend, Marty Wilson Piper from The Church. "Wilson Mighty Puppet" was one I recall, "Martin Popeye Wilson" another. There was never any malice with him, though, and I'm sure I got the same treatment whenever I was out of earshot.

One night a crowd of us went along to a local theatre to see The Red Sky Coven, a kind of alternative cabaret show that featured Justin Sullivan of New Model Army along with his wife, the poet Joolz, and another satirical poet called Rev Hammer, among others. The show was refreshingly original and Justin's acoustic performance, in particular, was excellent. Adrian, however, seemed unimpressed, and spent the whole evening watching cynically from the bar. After the show the promoter, a fan of both The Chameleons and The Sound as well as a friend of Carlo's, invited us all to have a drink at another bar he owned across town. On arriving, we saw that The Red Sky Coven were already there, sitting at a table some distance away. Adrian was quietly scathing. "Fucking shit!" he kept saying, nodding his head violently. "All that political rhetoric, insincere bollocks! New Model Army were shit, and he's just as shit on his own." We argued to the contrary, all the time trying to keep the volume of our laughter down until, eventually, it was time to leave. I had a few words with Joolz and Rev - who told me his wife was going to be "made-up" when he told her he'd met a Chameleon on the road - and then shook hands with Justin, telling him how much I'd enjoyed the show. As I turned, I saw Adrian right behind me, and he lunged forward and held out his hand. "Great gig! Great gig! Totally enjoyed it!" he gushed in his usual, gentle voice. We were then kept waiting for twenty minutes while he and Justin chatted.

I wouldn't let it go without comment, and ribbed him mercilessly all the way home. "Well, it was alright, I suppose," he finally conceded, magnanimously.

As the White Rose Transmission album neared completion, Adrian asked me about the possibility of joining Carlo and himself on a tour of Germany to promote it, and I agreed. Carlo would set up the shows for later that year, and we promised each other we'd arrange a schedule that would allow us some rehearsal time ahead of the shows.

As was customary whenever Adrian or I recorded or produced music in Bremen, we wanted to check the mixes through Carlo's hi-fi. It had been purpose-built for him by an expert friend, and was the best sounding domestic sound system I'd ever heard. Eventually, Carlo and Christina retired for the evening and Daniela, Adrian, and I sat around the kitchen table, conversing, drinking whisky, and playing a few tunes on the guitar. As on our first meeting, the topic of Joy Division - or more precisely, Ian Curtis - had come up. Again, he emphasised how much the man, his lyrics, and the drama of Curtis' suicide had meant to him, and he became rather emotional. Rather than break down in front of us, he rose slowly from his chair and went to the bathroom to compose himself. After a few minutes, he returned and we changed the subject, but both Daniela and I were deeply touched, and it was something I'll never forget.

Adrian would never tour the White Rose Transmission album. Some months later, while working on a new solo album, he began skipping the medication he took for depression. He'd been preparing to record his vocals, and the medication made him drowsy and lethargic. During the week, his long-suffering girlfriend finally ended their relationship, and during the early hours of Monday morning, having already been forcibly returned home by the police at his mother's urging, he left the house and walked to Wimbledon train station. The CCTV video produced at the inquest clearly showed him sitting on the platform, awaiting the arrival of a train. As the train drew into the station, Adrian sprang to his feet and leapt into its path. He was killed instantly.

I'd imagined that the tour would be scrapped, but Carlo surprised me by telling me that he wanted to go ahead and play the shows as a tribute to Adrian. Initially, I was dubious about it, but I understood his logic. Carlo was exclusively a vocalist, however, and I was nowhere near competent enough to take on the guitar parts - and, by now, we barely had a week to go before the tour was due to begin. Carlo's regular guitarist had never shown much interest in the project, and it was doubtful he'd be interested. After giving the matter a great deal of thought, I realised that the best and most competent person I knew to take on the task was Yves. After discussing it with Carlo, I asked Yves if he'd be prepared to fly out, learn the parts and play the tour. Yves had also been a fan of Adrian's work during his days with The Sound and agreed without hesitation. He rose to the challenge magnificently, learning the bulk of the set in about three days, and, despite the high emotion, those shows remain some of the most satisfactory live experiences I've ever had.

In the wake of this tragedy, the following six months proved extremely turbulent. Daniela and I separated for a time, while I was brought to the very brink of a nervous breakdown. I think I was in a state of mild shock for the remainder of the year, retreating further inside myself than I had for a long time, and by the year's end I was in the grip of another depression. Clearly, I had a lot of thinking to do. We celebrated the coming of the New Year in the company of Daniela's parents, along with a gathering of friends and family at a house they owned on the island of Mors in Western Denmark, where Daniela had been born. The house lay in an isolated spot on a lonely road, ten minutes' walk from the nearby Limefjord, a wide expanse of water which leads to the open sea and boasts a couple of miles of deserted beach. Not fully able to enter into the festive spirit, I retreated to the beach, gathering driftwood with which to build a small fire, and reflected on the events of the past few years. I was looking forward, as I always do, to New Year's Eve - the beginning of a new chapter of my life, a fresh, blank page. Of course, in reality, each day of your life is like that, but there's something about the symbolism of New Year's Eve that gives the idea potency.

As I meditated by the roaring fire, it occurred to me that I'd been running away my entire life, leaving chaos, heartache, and disappointment in my wake. When school had become unbearable, I'd run away. When my most treasured friendships at the heart of The Chameleons had disintegrated, I'd run away, twice: once on some mad escapade to Jerusalem, and again when we lost Tony Fletcher. When the members of The Sun And The Moon had failed to meet my expectations, I'd cut them loose without a second thought and done another runner. In Sally I'd found a running partner, but we'd been running nevertheless - from England to Scotland and back again, and when Sally had flagged, I'd barely looked back. When she found a rescuer in Yves, rather than rise to this challenge and live up to my own lofty ideals, I revealed them to be the sham they were and promptly turned tail. Finally, I'd almost run away again, coming dangerously close to destroying my relationship with Daniela.

Still, despite this onslaught of self-pity, I wasn't ready to catch that early morning train just yet, not without at least attempting to set some things right. Daniela and I were well on the way to recovery; while the wounds would take time to heal, at least we'd made a start. As for Sally, I was convinced that all I needed was time, and I remember laughing to myself at that thought - 'I just need time' had become something of a private joke between Sally and myself, having heard the cliché uttered across thousands of soap operas. Finally, there was Dave, Reg, and John, and it seemed that, even here, I'd been handed a thread of opportunity. I would return to England and see if we could get The Chameleons back together. If not, then I'd be able to move on, content in the knowledge that at least I'd tried.

This would prove to be the longest period I'd spent in Middleton in quite a number of years, and I found that times had grown desperate for many. It had become a hard place, although within both the people I remembered and those who were new to me, there was a warmth and generosity of spirit completely at odds with the violent ambience of the town. During my first week back, I found Dave hugging a pint of cider in his usual haunt, a back room of the Brunswick. After I'd given him the 'now or never' speech, he told me he was more up for it than he'd ever been. He said that John was also into the idea of reforming the band, and wanted a meeting to discuss it. He was less sure about Reg, suggesting that I should talk to him about it in person. Of course, I intended to do just that, but I was a little nervous of the prospect, not having had any direct contact with him for years. That said, I'd always held the most affection for Reg, and I was genuinely looking forward to seeing him again. As it turned out, I needn't have been nervous at all. He put me immediately at ease, and one would have thought I'd never been away, rather than returning after more than ten years. He'd been sprawled out on the couch watching the Discovery Channel when I called round, and he greeted me with what was to become a familiar refrain in the coming months and years. "Hi Mark, wanna brew?" My new-fangled European idiosyncrasies were immediately apparent. "What? No milk or sugar? You're joking?"

Reg was still living alone in the same flat he'd occupied when I'd last hung out with him thirteen years before, although there were a few more bottles of red wine than I'd remembered, and over the following weeks I was more than happy to help him empty a few of them. Reg was always good company, and even when we touched on the past it was good-natured and humorous. Having said that, despite the welcome and the familiar banter, there was an air of sadness about the twenty-first century Reg. Not in any pathetic way, I hasten to add, but there was a hint of loneliness that went beyond his natural, reclusive state. He had a small circle of friends who would often drag him out to the pub on a Friday night, and no shortage of visitors to the flat, but I think he'd be the first to admit that he was far from happy. This made me sad. I felt that, of all of us, Reg most deserved to be happy, at the very least.

While Reg was open to the idea of doing another show together, he was also cautious. It was clear that the last thing he wanted was to become embroiled in the ugliness of another war between Dave and myself. I genuinely believed that we could all shed the baggage of the past, redeem the deepest friendships any of us had ever known, and at the same time give The Chameleons a satisfactory sense of closure. "Surely that's something worth doing?" I argued.

"I'll play the gig, but I'm not committing to anything beyond that," he said, which was good enough for me. After all, I certainly hadn't been thinking of taking it any further.

The following week, the three of us met with John, and already there seemed to be a problem. By this time John had taken a job as a social worker and his commitments would prevent him from joining us until May. This meant that we would be left kicking our heels for three months. Additionally, he was adamant that the only person he trusted to handle the show was a guy named Pod, a local promoter in nearby Ashton. At the time

I don't think I'd ever met him, although I knew of him and he had a pretty solid reputation. The problem was that, at the time, Pod only promoted shows at the Witchwood.

"The Witchwood?" I said, incredulously. "Jesus, John! It only holds about three hundred people. When word of this gets out, they're going to be flocking in from everywhere!"

John met my protests with his usual, stubborn resolve. "I only want to do it if Pod handles it! I only want to do it at the Witchwood!"

Pod, a likeable straight-talker with an extremely dry sense of humour, put us at ease immediately. He'd announce the date, but put a second night on hold, should the demand for tickets require one. Reg doubted that we could fill two nights at the Witchwood, while I just looked from one to the other, dumbfounded. Christ, are these guys in for a shock! As it turned out, so was I.

For Dave, Reg and me, the idea of going our separate ways and then reconvening in three months' time to play the show wasn't particularly attractive. This would mean that by the time we did finally come together, we'd have barely a week to prepare, and we hadn't struck up a note together in thirteen years. It was suggested by someone that the three of us play a series of acoustic shows to get back in the swing, but we dismissed this. Acoustic sets would hardly have provided a satisfactory preparation and besides, any kind of live performance as The Chameleons without John was out of the question.

Still, the idea wasn't entirely without merit, so I suggested that, instead, the three of us go into the studio and record selected acoustic arrangements of some of our songs. This way, we could get back in the swing of playing together in the privacy of a studio, whilst at the same time generating funds which would allow us to re-equip for the full reunion show. I felt that now, having matured as musicians, we'd be able to give familiar material a different slant, and rediscover our own music - the perfect preparation!

Simon Lawlor agreed to act as a manager of sorts and to provide a modest budget to fund the recordings. The album, *Strip*, would be released on our own label, Paradiso. The question of where to record *Strip* was solved when Shan Hira, who'd worked extensively with The Reegs, offered us the use of Suite Sixteen, where we'd recorded *Script Of The Bridge*. The studio was in the process of winding down for good, and most of the equipment, along with the actual lease on the building, was up for sale. Shan waved this aside, "Fuckin' 'ell," he said. "If we can't reopen for you lot, there's something wrong." Along with resident engineer Jonathan Barrett, Shan also offered to oversee the production, cutting the studio rate to the bone. Picking the right songs for the session was a hit and miss affair, but interesting nevertheless. Some of the songs we chose worked and some didn't; others were little short of a revelation. Over the years, Dave had got to grips with quite a few strange instruments, one of them being the didgeridoo, which provided a suitable tribal feel to the bridge section of 'Soul in Isolation'.

The end result is one of my favourite Chameleons records, in spite of John's absence. We were even able to add something completely new: a brilliant instrumental piece by Reg, reminiscent of something Claude Debussy might have written. Reg named it 'The Road to San Remo'. I'd first heard him play the piece fourteen years before, and had casually asked him if he remembered it. To my surprise, he did, and it's one of the most beautiful pieces I've heard on the guitar. In addition, Dave had come up with something of his own that we would eventually title 'Indian'. As I rehearsed the vocal, working to a cassette played on an old boom box, I accidentally erased a small fraction of the track. When I played it back this new flaw was perfectly in time, so I utilised this weird timing for the stops and starts that make up the arrangement. We all felt we needed some stronger percussion on the song, so, in the absence of John, Reg played the drums. Reg had been forced to record the drums to the main backing track after it had been recorded, without the aid of a click-track to help him keep time. His meticulously cool sense of timing served him well, and he performed flawlessly. Reg also came into his own when it came to his guitar parts, which, typically, he performed without any semblance of fuss. As this was a brand new idea and still largely unfamiliar, I asked him if he'd prefer to have a couple of hours alone with it to work out what it was he wanted to do. "Nah," he shrugged, "just run it and I'll see what happens." What happened was, to my ears, little short of stunning. I wasn't the only one who thought so, but Reg wasn't quite satisfied. "I'd like to do another one." We ran the track a second time, and again Reg performed brilliantly, leaving us with a bit of dilemma as to which recording we should use. They were both different, but sounded equally good.

As we were agonising over this choice, Dave, who'd been inhaling from his hash pipe at the back of the room, croaked, "Why don't you try listening to them both together?" That, we decided, was a very good idea. As we listened back, we could only look at each other shaking our heads. Reg had created a soaring duet, one rising while the other fell, saturated with the perfect rock 'n' roll feel. I knew in that moment that he was among the greatest guitar players I'd ever heard. Ignored, underrated and largely unacclaimed, he was the best guitarist since Mick Ronson and twice as original.

I'd been impressed by The Chameleons fan website *Home Is Where The Heart Is* since my earliest days on the internet, and would drop by from time to time, sometimes posting on the site's forum. It was a particular pleasure, then, to be able to announce that the band would be reforming to play two nights at the Witchwood. Word travelled fast, and within a day of Pod announcing the opening date, the two nights became a five-night, sell-out residency, as people fell over themselves in a frenzy to secure tickets. I'd expected that demand would be high, but I was still shocked at the level of excitement as people from all over the country and as far away as America, Europe and the Middle and Far East made preparations to travel to Ashton-Under-Lyne.

With John finally on board, and with barely a week to go before the opening date, we began rehearsals. Any reservations I may have had about our ability to recapture the spirit of the band were swept away that very first day. It was as if we'd simply reconvened after a brief hiatus, except that I was filled with a sense of wonder. After all these years, after everything that had gone on, it was hard to believe that this was truly happening.

Having said that, the build up to the shows wasn't stress-free. Demand for tickets was extremely high, and the small capacity of the venue restricted the number of people that could be added to the band's guest list. Family members that we hadn't seen or heard from in years were suddenly hassling our parents for tickets, along with various close – and not so close - friends. Fortunately, most of them had the good sense to let us know well ahead of time so that arrangements could be made, but a few would simply turn up on the night and expect to stroll in. While Pod did his absolute best to try to accommodate most of them, others were turned away disappointed and more than a few curses were hurled in our direction.

One incident was particularly surreal. Dave had been sitting alone one afternoon in the Brunswick, when a regular he hardly knew began demanding that Dave get him a ticket for the show. Dave patiently explained that he didn't have any, and that the guest list for the shows was full. "What?" barked the guy, "You're the fuckin' guitarist in the band and you can't get me a ticket?" and with this, head-butted Dave. After he'd followed Dave to the gents' toilets brandishing a bottle, the head barman stepped in and was able to bundle the idiot out of the door.

As we prepared the stage for the first of the shows, I happened to notice a Rastafarian guy casually watching from the side of the stage. Dave hailed him, "Alright Kwasi!" Apparently they'd been friends for years, and so I was introduced to Kwasi Asante for the first time. Having a British mother, he'd grown up in Middleton, but his father was from Ghana, so Kwasi had taken a Ghanaian name, embraced his heritage, and taken up the Rastafarian faith. One of the songs we were planning to feature that week, 'One Flesh', had an extended ending built around a dub bassline, and as we prepared to run though the song during soundcheck, Dave invited Kwasi to join in, at which point Kwasi delivered an African rap.

"Can you do that every night?" I asked him, mightily impressed.

Laughing, he said that he could, and from that point he became a regular additional percussionist and vocalist in many Chameleons performances.

When the time came, the Witchwood performances were a bit of a blur - a fusion of high adrenaline and passionate emotion. I do recall seeing a few people in tears during the opening song, 'Swamp Thing', and the ensuing sing-along raised the roof. During that week, the centre of Ashton was transformed into something that resembled an international Chameleons festival, much to the bemusement of the town's inhabitants and the local police, who regularly took to patrolling slowly past the venue, surveying the crowds that gathered outside. None of the locals had ever heard of The Chameleons, of course, though this sudden influx was welcomed with open arms - especially by the hotel proprietors and local taxi firms, who were suddenly and unexpectedly being run ragged. One young American, having been plied with drinks after he wandered into a local pub, staggered to the venue only to fall asleep, missing the performance. Fortunately he'd booked tickets for the remaining three shows, so his trip hadn't been a complete waste.

Daniela flew in for the concerts, and at Pod's recommendation I'd booked a room at a local hotel of sorts, a stone's throw from the venue. The hotel was run by an eccentric foreign woman, thrilled to suddenly find her place fully booked. We found an odd collection of individuals there, including a couple of girls with a taste for fetish fashion, a small contingent from Spain, and an Israeli doctor. The girls were sisters and lived in New York, and one of them had very definitely set her sights on Reg, although from what I could gather, she'd almost scared him to death. "What do you do in New York?" I asked her.

"I'm a performance artist," she told me.

"What sort of performance art?" I asked.

"Well, my last performance," she casually informed me, "consisted of eating birthday cake from another female performer's ass."

I resisted the temptation to try to book a private performance, and could only imagine what Reg would make of that when I finally got around to telling him.

Amongst the audience there was a leading national promoter, and before the residency was over, we were offered two prestigious dates the following month: the first at Manchester Academy, one of the city's largest venues, and the following night at The Shepherd's Bush Empire in London. These would be the biggest shows we'd ever done. So it was that on 3rd June 2000 we climbed onto the stage at Manchester Academy in front of 2,500 people, some five hundred more than the venue's official capacity. I dare say that the myth that had grown around the band in the intervening years had been largely responsible for this mass turnout, and that many were probably left wondering what all the fuss was about. Nevertheless, as the official video of the event testifies, the concert was an undisputed triumph, the welcome unprecedented, and our existence as an influential Manchester band validated. It was one of the proudest moments of my life.

"Good evening everybody, we're The Chameleons."

EPILOGUE

2000 – 2003

THANK YOU! GOODNIGHT!

The final year of the twentieth century had been a difficult time for me, but it was to be merely an appetiser for the main course. For seven years I had been the singer and bass guitarist in The Chameleons, until the band's rancorous dissolution in 1987. We'd reformed some thirteen years later, only for it to finally dissolve amidst an even higher degree of acrimony than that surrounding the first split. In the midst of all this, my wife Daniela and I experienced an ordeal of far greater magnitude. Our twin sons, who were to be named Joshua and James, died in the womb five months into the pregnancy. All I could do was stand by helplessly as Daniela endured the ordeal of an induced labour - and what should have been the proudest moment of our lives became an almost unbearable tragedy.

Five months earlier, things couldn't have been more different. I was working in England when I got the call, a message from my mother that Daniela had been trying to reach me with some exciting news. I'll never forget the euphoria I felt when she told me. The whole course of my life suddenly came into sharp focus. Every fucked-up, instinctive decision I'd ever made now radiated rightness. Sacrifices suddenly seemed justified and saturated with meaning, doubts were washed away. Man! I felt eight feet tall!

For a long time I'd been uncertain as to where exactly I was supposed to be, bouncing back and forth between England and Daniela's home in Germany, and this had put a strain on our relationship. Now it seemed that fate had taken a hand and, for the first time, I was ready to settle in Hamburg and build a life there.

A few weeks later I was in the studio in England when Daniela called again. "Are you sitting down?" she asked. I recognised the bubbling, excited slant in her voice, verging on the boundary of joy, so I knew it wasn't bad news. I only had to wait seconds. "It's twin boys!" Of course, our joy was mixed with a hint of shock. She was aware that twin pregnancies could be problematic, but you push nagging fears like that from your mind. You have to.

I walked into the studio control room, a huge, stupid grin on my face, drinking a massive whiskey and soaking up the congratulations from the producer and the guys in the band - drummer John Lever, and guitarists Reg Smithies and Dave Fielding. What a year it was turning out to be. The oldest friendships I'd ever known, friendships that I'd come to believe had been irredeemably destroyed, had been reforged - and here we were making our first studio album together in nearly fifteen years.

The Chameleons, 2000. Photo: Paul Ciff

Those tentatively-booked gigs at the Witchwood had been a runaway success, as had the sold-out shows at Manchester Academy and Shepherd's Bush Empire. That year we went on to play over forty additional shows across Europe, followed by four dates in California, and we ended the year with two nights at the Ritz in Manchester. For the first time in the history of the band, we were actually getting paid for performances.

Experience should have told me that it was all too good to be true; the cracks were beginning to show before the end of the second year. Getting the band rehearsed and into the studio had been a huge strain. Of the fourteen days we spent rehearsing the new material, Dave turned up twice; there was always an excuse as to why he couldn't make it. Consequently, the pressure of getting the new material written and arranged in time had fallen on John, Reg, and me. The four of us sitting down together and working out ideas, jamming out songs, was central to The Chameleons, as far as I was concerned. All our best work had been produced that way, and it was a bitter disappointment to me - not to mention an immense pressure - to discover that this was a thing of the past. From then on, I knew that the whole enterprise was ultimately doomed to failure. If you can't get excited about making music, then it's a waste of time even trying - you might as well stay in the pub, which is exactly where Dave was most of the time. Of course we'd already spent the advance from the record label, so we had to deliver a new record. As Reg rightly pointed out, it was futile to moan about the situation - we simply had to get on with it.

Given the circumstances, I knew that the album - *Why Call It Anything*, as it was eventually titled - wasn't the classic that everyone was hoping for, but it definitely had its moments. I particularly loved the ideas I'd developed alongside Reg, such as the epic 'Dangerous Land', which lyrically is supposed to form a kind of riddle:

> *I am the pride at the heart of a man.*
> *I am a refuge in a dangerous land.*
> *I am a wall or a line in the sand.*
> *I am a gathering. I am a stand.*
> *I am the daylight when darkness draws near.*
> *I am a signal that's heard without ears.*
> *I am the rapture and I am the tears.*
> *I am a centre, regardless of years.*

Additionally, there was 'Lufthansa', for me one of the most beautiful songs we'd ever written together, lyrically inspired by the long-distance love affair I'd been having with Daniela over the previous few years, flitting backwards and forwards from England to Germany on the cheapest ticket I could find.

To be fair, once Dave was fully focused on the task, he did deliver. It was Dave's idea to bring in our mate Kwasi Asante as guest percussionist for the duet 'Miracles and Wonders', which was based around a three-chord pattern Dave had invented. Consequently, I found myself playing and writing in a style that I was unaccustomed to, and I enjoyed that immensely. The instrumental ending to the piece, along with the soundscape that eventually came to close the album, was also pure Dave, and I could only lament what might have been had he been more involved with the writing process at an earlier stage.

The recording studio, located just a few miles from Bath, seemed sterile and soulless compared to other studios we'd used. The facility was relatively new and the studio manager was eager for the block booking, so I suppose he cut us a very competitive rate. However, he compensated by locking up the kitchen after 8pm to ensure that we didn't exceed our daily quota of tea bags. There was little to do there when not actively involved in the recordings, except watch TV or take walks. The studio lay in the midst of endless crop fields and large detached houses, and the only shop was in a small village three or four miles away. We did venture there once or twice, but by and large the village was populated by folk with minds as narrow as the roads that led there, as Kwasi discovered. He had gone to the shop to buy top-up cards for his mobile phone only to be told by a stammering, ashen-faced female shopkeeper that she didn't have any. Of course Kwasi had glimpsed a stack of them before she had chance to close the till drawer, so he knew she was lying, and continued to insist until she caved in. We didn't fare much better, having to endure stares and silences whenever we entered the shop. Meanwhile, on the street that ran through the centre of the village, nothing stirred; it felt rather like being in a 1960s Hammer horror film.

Being well-paid for what you enjoy doing is very nice, of course, and a luxury that seems to elude most of us, but even this started to frustrate me. On the one hand, I saw it as recompense for all the times back in the 1980s that we'd played sold-out tours and never been paid a penny. On the other hand, back then we'd always been cynical about capitalising on our talent at the expense of our art. Admittedly, we were younger and more idealistic, so perhaps we could afford such pretensions, but part of our reputation had been based on the idea that, despite our massive potential, we'd never sold ourselves out to achieve mass popularity, or taken the easy money. Ultimately, I'd been proud that we'd taken such an independent and forceful stance when it came to controlling our art. With the coming of the new, re-formed Chameleons, however, there was a marked shift of attitude. Suddenly, it seemed that money was the central motivation for practically everything we did, and it was an attitude that sometimes had our manager, Simon Lawlor, tearing out his hair in frustration, as he struggled to find gigs that paid the kind of fees that the others had come to expect as a matter of course. To his credit, he managed it more often than not, but there were times when he couldn't, usually for reasons of timing. Simon would constantly warn of overselling the band, but his concerns were mostly ignored. Certain elements within the band simply would not accept the situation for what it was, and ploughed on regardless. We would convene, play the shows, get paid at a progressively diminishing rate, disperse, spend the money and then panic the management into finding more - or if that wasn't possible, revert to the old standby of playing a show in our hometown of Manchester for as much as we could get, all without varying what we did in the slightest. Everyone has the right to make a living from what they do, of course, but in music there has to be a degree of integrity, and I quickly came to feel less like an artist and more like a pimp. Realising that The Chameleons had become little more than a cash cow was a bitter pill to swallow, given the pride I'd felt for our past work and the depth of love in every fucking letter and email I'd ever received on the subject.

I also became frustrated with the band's live set, which had barely changed since the first chord had been struck at the Witchwood in May 2000. The sheer volume of live work the band had taken on since then meant there had been no time to write new material, so by the end of the year the set had come to feel stale to me. During rehearsals I'd argued that in the absence of new material, we should at least introduce songs from our back catalogue that we'd rarely, if ever, played before. While I was able to get a couple of fresh songs into the set, the resultant bickering only increased the tension, so for the sake of avoiding further argument I let the matter drop. It felt as though trying any new approach required too great an effort. Back in the 1980s it wasn't uncommon for us to continue the song writing in front of live audiences, so keen were we to keep the content fresh, but that element had seemingly vanished. While it was true that we were better paid than we'd ever been before, we were far less conscientious, adventurous, and interesting - at least from my point of view. Of course, all those gripes were swept away in my euphoria at being an expectant father.

The album had yet to be mixed and, for this, producer Dave Allen chose another studio owned by a friend of his in Leamington, the very same studio that had given birth to the Ska revival at the end of the 1970s. Some additional touches were needed ahead of the mixing, so Reg and I drove to the studio together to do that. That's where I was heading when the hammer fell.

Daniela called my mobile and told me there was a problem with the pregnancy. One of the embryos had developed perfectly, but the twin, due to some biochemical deficiency, had not, and the specialist was telling us that his chances of surviving to full term were very low. The clinic was requesting that we attend as soon as possible to confer. I was completely devastated. How I held it together sufficiently to drive the car, I have no idea; Reg hadn't yet learned to drive, and was a helpless onlooker in all of this. By the time we arrived I was a wreck, and could barely finish the work. The track in question was 'Music in the Womb', and the cruel irony of that wasn't lost on anyone.

The next day we were scheduled to drive to London to play a second show at Shepherd's Bush Empire. Daniela decided to fly into London for the show regardless, saying that she wanted our babies to feel the vibration of their father's music at the very least.

A Tube strike meant that the journey to Shepherd's Bush was horrendous. After collecting Daniela from the airport, we ended up stuck in traffic for hours and arrived at the venue very late. I didn't bother trying to explain what had happened as I was still in a state of shock, but I think Reg must have relayed the news, and one or two people offered their condolences. I'd never felt less like playing a show in my entire life, obviously, but I had no choice. The audience, battling their way across London despite the Tube strike, turned up by the thousand and did us proud. We were at last able to augment the live set with fresh material, and my memory of the show, while hazy, seems to be that it was one of the best we'd played that year.

The very next day, Daniela and I rushed back to Hamburg for the consultation at the clinic and what they had to say was enough to physically sicken us. They urged us to consider terminating the ailing foetus in order to give his healthy brother the best chance of survival - otherwise, they cautioned, we might well lose them both. From a purely logical point of view I suppose it was justifiable advice. Emotionally, however, it was ripping us apart. Science and technology have undoubtedly brought great benefits to humanity, especially in the area of prenatal care, and many babies have been saved that would have otherwise perished. The flip-side is that complications such as ours are now more easily detectable, whereas in years past, this wasn't the case - nature would have to run its course, and expectant parents would not be called upon to make such a horrible decision.

A scan revealed that the boys were far enough apart in the womb to make such a procedure possible, but time was of the essence, and so we were given only a few days to make the decision. Traditionally my means of seeking spiritual guidance had been more in the way of meditation and contemplation rather than outright prayer. Throughout those three or four long days and even longer nights, however, I was praying - praying very hard that this decision be taken away from us, because I didn't believe I was strong enough for this. My deepest instincts were screaming at me to oppose the procedure, but did I have the right? Do we kill one of our babies to give the other every chance of survival - or do we refuse the procedure and risk killing them both?

455

We returned to the clinic a few days later with very heavy hearts, still undecided. Things were happening too quickly, and in our highly emotional state, we weren't able to find any clarity of thought. A second scan was conducted to determine their current condition and we were able to see for ourselves that the situation had already changed. Both babies were now very close to each other, almost embracing, and I knew before the specialist even spoke that we'd been spared from making a decision; there was no question of carrying out the procedure now. The risk of killing them both had become too great, and nature would have to take its course after all. The feeling of relief was overwhelming. Despite the problems with the pregnancy, at least now they would have an equal fighting chance, which was all we could give them.

With more gigs on the distant horizon and the final mixing of the new album still a couple of months away, there was little to do but carry on with life as normally as we could, and hope for the best. Obviously, it was a period of extreme stress for both of us, but we tried to remain optimistic. Dredging the situation for positive meaning, we took this latest development as a sign that fate had intervened. We went ahead and named the boys Joshua, who had so narrowly escaped termination, and James, whose fate was entwined with that of his ailing twin. We trawled the internet for more information on Joshua's condition in preparation for what might come, and even found a ray of hope. One child who'd been born in similar circumstances had lived as long as seven years, and our resolve was strengthened by the testimony of the parents as to the quality of life their child had enjoyed. Of course, we also suspected that Joshua's condition was of a more severe nature and, even if he should survive to full-term, his chances of living much longer would be very low indeed.

When the time came to rejoin the others for the mixing of the album, five months into the pregnancy, I hadn't wanted to leave Daniela behind. She was due to have a routine scan on the date of my departure to England, so I booked a flight that would allow me to be present for that, at least. At the clinic, I didn't need to have a good enough understanding of German to realise what was happening. The babies weren't moving. Hastily, the doctor hooked up the ultrasound and it confirmed our worst fears. James and Joshua were dead. They were the victims of an unrelated complication that, sadly, all too often occurs with twin pregnancies - asphyxiation due to a tangled umbilical cord. Additionally, the pregnancy was too advanced to allow re-absorption of the foetuses, so the only course was to admit Daniela into hospital and induce labour.

The full horror of such an experience is beyond my ability to convey, but at the same time, I saw degrees of strength, courage and dignity in Daniela that filled me with nothing less than absolute awe. Over the following forty-eight hours I didn't leave her side or sleep a wink. The head nurse on the ward of the hospital graciously housed us in a private room, so at least I didn't have to wait in the corridor with other expectant fathers, and strong coffee was in endless supply as we waited for the drugs that would induce Daniela's labour. We were so deeply shocked at the suddenness of it all that we didn't fully realise what was happening, and the consequences of this would hit us hard later. At no time were we given counselling of any kind, and the chief surgeon, while not callous, outlined the procedures in a routine manner of professional detachment.

When Daniela did finally go into labour, she was in no state to think clearly, and was simply reacting to the gentle coaxing of the nurse as I helplessly looked on. Later, I couldn't bring myself to even think about where they'd taken the bodies of our dead sons. Either from sleep-deprivation, denial, or equal measures of both, it didn't occur to me to ask. Daniela didn't even get to cast her eyes on them and consequently was denied any real sense of closure and, while some may consider that a mercy, it was something she would bitterly regret later on.

Afterwards, Daniela handled it a lot better than I did. I was in a state of almost perpetual rage. All my life I'd formulated a philosophy of meaning. I'd felt the universe was saturated with it and this philosophy was reflected in every word I'd written. Now, of course, those words, of which I was reminded daily in the never-ending flow of email from people that had been deeply touched and inspired by the things I'd written, rang hollow - it all suddenly seemed like total bullshit to me. Of course, there was no tangible focus for my anger, nothing to aim it at, no-one to blame. Life just seemed so pointless and, for a very long time, I couldn't see beyond the negative. Experience has taught me that it is futile to search for any kind of positive meaning while in the midst of an event - such insight only comes with the passing of time and the evaluation of consequences. I believed that then, and I believe it now. However, knowing it didn't help me, and I was unable to imagine ever coming to terms with what we'd been through. I just couldn't envisage a time when I'd be able to think about what had happened and see anything positive in it - and yet such a day did come. With Daniela's help, over a period of about a year, I was able to see beyond the loss and realise how much the boys' brief presence in Daniela's womb had given us. We were closer now than we'd ever been. In the midst of the trauma, we saw qualities in each other that served to deepen our mutual love and respect to an immeasurable degree. I think I can honestly say that I became less selfishly motivated. I would never have admitted to myself that before this happened I'd been in any way ambivalent about our relationship, but looking back I realised that I hadn't taken it as seriously as I should. I finally grew up a little bit during those months, and it had been long overdue.

Daniela's emotional struggle in the aftermath, like that of all mothers in this situation, was of an altogether different nature. For five months she had carried life in her womb and now, suddenly, it was gone, as if it never existed. She didn't have the closure of a casket and a gravestone, only the memory, a body geared for a delivery that would never come, and a single Polaroid from an ultrasound scan. The sadness of it broke my heart and, as I struggled with the grief, I did what was probably typical of most men: I tried to push it from my mind, to be filed away in the folder marked 'Heavy Experiences'. For a long time I couldn't discuss what had happened without erupting into bitterness and anger. I know that this aspect of my behaviour deeply disappointed Daniela and made her feel that she was alone in her grief at a time when she should have had more support.

Our final gig that year was a fittingly depressing affair on the band's home turf at Middleton Civic Hall, and I was extremely relieved to be finally boarding the plane back to Hamburg. As I walked through the arrivals gate, Daniela was there to meet me as usual, although this time she seemed a bit edgy. We climbed into a cab and drove to the flat, but then she instructed the driver to wait while we dropped our bags off, telling me that we were going on somewhere else. From there, we drove to a very upmarket restaurant that I was unfamiliar with, and we were ushered to a candlelit table by a smiling waiter, who then brought a bottle of champagne on ice. I was bemused and didn't have a clue what was coming. We ordered our food and as we sat waiting at the table, Daniela explained that she'd thought it over very carefully, that she'd come to terms with all that had happened, she felt very positive about our relationship and how would I feel about getting married? I'd broached the subject of marriage a couple of times during the course of our relationship but Daniela had never really taken me seriously, so it was all the more impressive to have her finally address the subject. I said "Yes" immediately. It wasn't the most traditional of marriage proposals, but it was totally in keeping with my nature, and thus perfect. We were married the following summer.

Toward the end of that year - the big offers having more or less dissipated - the band had agreed to play a series of semi-acoustic shows across the north of England. They were essentially pub gigs, something we would never have contemplated at the height of our success. I'd sided with our manager Simon initially, feeling that the whole thing reeked of desperation, and I was concerned about its effect on our standing within the business. Later, for the sake of unity, I would rationalise the enterprise. Stripped-down, unplugged performances can have certain appeal, and had become very popular in recent years. However, during preparations, a fresh approach seemed once again to present too much of a challenge, and we ended up delivering a show that barely differed from what we usually did. The chosen venues were, for the most part, poorly-equipped and barely able to handle the demands the band placed on the sound systems. On a few occasions, disaster had been averted only by our talented sound engineer, who we learned had the uncanny ability to make a silk purse from a sow's ear. I hasten to add that this was not due to any fault of the promoter; he'd been expecting acoustic performances, and we'd changed the parameters.

Simon and I agreed that we'd exhausted practically all the opportunities for touring the band in Europe. The new album had failed to perform commercially, and there had been no significant movement toward writing or recording a sequel. Instead, we'd continued to live on past glories, which included a live album recorded the previous year at Manchester Academy and a second acoustic album, *This Never Ending Now*. The latter had been less than a happy experience. Unable to return to the now dismantled Suite Sixteen, we'd recorded it on the cheap at the engineer's house, and the whole session felt tense and awkward. This, coupled with the cancellation of a Spanish tour barely two weeks before it was due to begin, had left us with a depressingly sparse calendar.

With European dates no longer an option, we turned our attention to the US. Since re-forming, we'd been inundated with requests to try to get the band to tour there. The problem was that the contacts we had in the business, including our own management, felt that touring America without a US label or booking agent was impossible. Considering my own experiences in America, I didn't share that view, and believed that if the band were to have a serious future, then it was vital that we play there. I discussed the situation with the others, and with Simon. He was supportive, but sceptical that we could pull it off. In the end, it was generally felt that we had little to lose by trying. After all, I reasoned, if at the end of the day it didn't make sense financially, we'd simply pull out. Everyone agreed it was worth a shot and so, equipped with a telephone, a laptop, and an internet connection, I set to work.

I began by contacting venues directly, after first canvassing the fan base by way of the band's website as to which venues in each respective city they thought might be suitable. Securing the gigs and the necessary guarantees we needed proved far easier than I'd imagined. I only had to mention the band's name to get firm offers within days, sometimes within hours. One or two were unfamiliar with the band and turned me down, only to contact me again a day or so later telling me that, after consulting other venue managers, they'd changed their mind and wanted the show after all. Over a period of about three months, I was able to put together a coast-to-coast tour of the US that also included shows in Toronto and Montreal.

The next hurdle, of course, was logistics. Touring anywhere, especially America, is a very expensive business. An affordable crew would have to be assembled, transport arranged, and accommodation found. Much of the equipment would have to be hired locally on a daily basis, as returning equipment to a single point of origin was impractical. This all seemed daunting initially, but the band generated so much excitement that people were falling over themselves to make it happen. Managers and musicians, eager to play on the same bill, volunteered to coordinate shows. Fans of the band offered to print flyers for the shows and distribute them locally. Even with all this help, it represented a great deal of work and stress and I was already exhausted by the time we convened for rehearsals. By now, I had developed a much greater appreciation of a manager's role.

In every respect, the 2002 US tour was a success. Most of the gigs were sold out, including two consecutive shows on the same night in New York, and The Chameleons remain one of the few British bands ever to play a major tour of the US at theatre level and turn a profit. The tour was a testament not only to the power of the band's music, but also to the concept of creative independence. No US record labels offsetting costs, no agents, no promotion companies - none of the usual music business mechanics - just the love and respect of our audience, and the shrewd business acumen of a few venue operators.

During the tour, a significant number of industry people approached us wishing to get involved with the band in the US. Simon and I realised that the band couldn't continue to function the way things stood; independence can work up to a point, but if we were to make significant progress in America, we'd need the kinds of resources that are only available within the US music industry. This involved touring within the US consistently over a longer period, so I, for one, was happy that we seemed to be drawing the attention of people who could help make that happen. Typically, my focus was fixed on the future of the band to the detriment of the present. Despite the industry attention, the sold-out venues, the respect and adulation of our audience, and the fact that we were actually making money for the first time, at the heart of the band there was a cancerous discontent. This began to manifest itself in all sorts of ways: irrational and erratic behaviour on and off the stage, and the spreading of rumours and lies behind my back. I was aware of it, but by the end of the tour I was simply too exhausted to worry about it.

When the tour was over, I couldn't quite believe we'd pulled it off. In every city we'd visited there had been people eager to help in any way they could, asking little or nothing in return, beyond the odd support slot or a couple of passes to the show. I tried to thank them all by way of a roll call on the band's website, but there were so many that I'm sure I must have omitted some in error. I just hope I was able to convey the depth of appreciation I felt for everyone who had helped us.

Thanks to the consistently high attendance at the shows, and Daniela's diligent handling of the band's merchandising, the tour had turned a profit. Reg was so happy when I gave him the news, he gave me a hug. John and Kwasi also took time out at the hotel on the evening before their flight home to give me a pat on the back, as did the crew: Chiz, who'd served as drum tech, Will, our stage manager and guitar tech, Shan, our sound engineer, and Kim, the road manager.

The final run of dates, in Germany, was to begin with a warm-up show at Dingwalls in Camden. The venue had rather sour memories for me - I'd never really liked it very much, but in the years since I'd last been there it had been impressively refurbished and revamped, and the show turned out to be one of the best we played that year. What's more, it was tinged with a shade of personal nostalgia in that my old friend Bryan Glancy opened the show. I remember getting quite tearful as we performed his song 'Beat The Boat' together, as part of his opening set.

I'd been dreading the German dates, feeling that by agreeing to do them we'd taken on a bit too much, but Simon and our German tour manager Lars had gradually brought me round to the idea, and the rest of the band were keen to claw in some extra income.

I thought the routing of the tour rather curious, beginning as it did with major cities that had traditionally given us warm, rapturous welcomes and ending in provincial German towns that we'd never heard of. Consequently, the latter stages of the tour seemed rather lacklustre. The gigs were well attended, but the audience didn't seem to have much inkling who or what The Chameleons were and, while they made us feel appreciated, it was a cooler response than we were used to.

Behind the scenes, everyone remained upbeat, despite the hassles. Even Dave opened up a bit and told me he was happy with the way the year had gone. We had plenty of opportunity to talk about plans for the following year. Again, I voiced concern that we were milking past glories a little bit too much and felt we'd gone about as far as we could with the established set, and everyone pretty much concurred with that. The plan, then, involved getting new material written and a new album under way. I'd been impressed with some tapes Dave had played to me in England. They were ideas he and Reg had been working on for a follow-up album by their own project, The Reegs, which had ended shortly before The Chameleons reunion. Those ideas were never used, so Dave suggested that I take them on board to see what I could make of them. I thought they were very interesting and a healthy direction for the band to take, and I was looking forward to receiving them in a workable format. Dave promised he'd send them to me in the new year and even proposed coming out to Hamburg for a while to work on them together.

Reg had been forced to re-evaluate his priorities since the arrival of his new son. At that time, Joe was barely six months old and, understandably, Reg had found it difficult to be away from his family during the US tour. Consequently, with the coming of the new year, he was worried about his level of commitment. I felt that as long as Dave and I could make a start, however, then Reg could work on the ideas remotely, and any live work that might come along could be adapted to suit his availability.

The last gig of the tour proved to be somewhat low-key, which was a shame because, although I didn't know it then, it would be the last time that The Chameleons would ever play together.

The rest of the guys left immediately after the show to catch the boat back to England, while I remained with our German tour manager, Lars, and returned to Hamburg the following day. I never saw Dave Fielding again.

With the coming of 2003, I patiently waited for the promised tapes to arrive from Dave, or to hear when he was planning to make the trip to Hamburg to start work on fresh ideas. And waited. And waited. Direct communication with Dave and John, in particular, was difficult. Both of them only used mobile phones, and John had a habit of throwing his into canals whenever he had a row with his girlfriend, which was often. This meant that John's phone numbers were out of date within days of receiving them. Similarly, Dave had an aversion to buying top-up cards for his phone and would simply carry his SIM card around with him, inserting it into a borrowed phone to retrieve his messages whenever he got the opportunity. Even though I left messages, I didn't merit a reply.

The only reliable avenues of communication were Reg and Kwasi. Reg, now fully immersed in the joys of fatherhood, had become quite reclusive.

Still, he was enjoying more contact with the others than I was, so I'd consult with him periodically, as well as with our manager, Simon. Meanwhile the months drifted by, and all activity around the band ceased. This was rather worrying for me because I realised that unless some kind of schedule was worked out, I'd be without work or income that coming summer.

I began to seriously consider my options, and was inspired after being invited to play a solo acoustic set in a bar owned by a friend of mine in Germany. I'd played the odd show for him before during the late 1990s and knew the venue well. On this particular occasion, it was to celebrate the bar's tenth anniversary, and the fee was generous, so I hadn't had to think twice about it. By way of a fresh approach, I used some music sequencing software that a friend had given me, and built two or three virtual backing tracks. The set - performed to around forty people as the venue was extremely small - was particularly well-received. I didn't give it a second thought afterwards, but some time later I was contacted by Chris Chandler in Atlanta. It seemed that someone at the show had recorded it and copies were now doing the rounds. Chris had heard it and was asking if I'd consider playing similar sets in America. I was both surprised and flattered, but told him that at that point I couldn't make any commitments because I didn't know what The Chameleons would be doing. However, I went on to say that should the band not be active that summer, then I would most definitely be interested.

In the meantime, I continued to try to galvanise the others into some kind of activity, but was constantly frustrated. I still hadn't managed to speak with Dave in person, but Simon contacted me, announcing that Dave had abandoned any intentions of coming out to Hamburg to work. "I hate Hamburg," Dave had told him. At least now I knew where I stood. Another conversation with Reg was equally frustrating. Reg told me that such were his responsibilities now to his wife and son, that he didn't feel he could contribute any time to the band. I completely sympathised with his situation (after all, but for a cruel twist of fate, I would have been in the same boat), but when you're in a band and you're saying that you can't rehearse, you can't tour, you can't record and you can't find the time to work out new ideas, it doesn't really leave much. I'd been recording a few ideas of my own and suggested that I send them over. If he liked them and could find some time, perhaps he could augment them in some way? Reg agreed to have a listen and also to pass copies of these recordings on to the others.

The only firm offer the band had that approaching winter came from a company in Greece. The organisers were eager to bring The Chameleons to

Athens for the first time ever; apparently we had a large fan-base there. They'd attempted to book the band the previous summer, but the cost of airline tickets had been too high to make the venture viable. Now the situation had changed and they'd made a respectable offer. The show would take place on a Saturday night in April 2003. The band would fly to Athens on Friday, perform the show on Saturday, and fly home Sunday evening. The organisers would look after the cost of the flights, the hire of the venue (they were a local independent record store, as opposed to agents), the hire of the backline, accommodation, the provision of as much food and drink as would be required, and then pay the band what, in all fairness, was a decent fee. All in all, a fairly sweet deal.

I put all of this to Reg and, although he was dubious at first, it would only involve him being away from home for two nights. By now we could have played our regular set in our sleep, so rehearsals ahead of the show weren't vital. Additionally, it would give us the opportunity to sit down together and work out a schedule for the remainder of the year. Reg promised he'd speak with the others and, sure enough, he reported the following week that everyone had agreed to the show, so I dutifully sent our confirmation to the organisers.

Simon had been busy with various other projects, so again, the responsibility of putting together a crew and organising the flights fell to me. Not that I was complaining - after weeks of inactivity I felt buoyant now that something was finally happening. I was pleased with the ideas I'd recorded for Reg and was looking forward to hearing his input. However, the rumblings of discontent had begun again, and they were about to evolve into the perfect storm.

The first came by way of a phone call from Simon. He'd spoken to Dave, who had heard rumours that I was planning a solo acoustic tour of the US. He was very unhappy about this, and was threatening to pull out of the Athens show. Frankly, I wasn't that concerned. I was confident that once I'd explained my situation to Dave - that I hadn't committed to anything, and that my priorities still lay with the band - everything would be fine. I spent a fairly congenial, if rather expensive, couple of hours on the phone to Dave, patiently explaining that the acoustic tour was something I was only considering should the band be out of work that coming summer. I told him that I needed to work, and while I hadn't confirmed the US visit, should we be unable to sort out a working schedule fairly quickly, I wouldn't have any practical option but to accept the offer. In the end, Dave seemed to accept this.

I asked about the tapes I'd been waiting for, but he explained that he'd changed his mind and didn't want to use ideas that were originally intended for his side-project on a Chameleons record. This was fair enough - what a guy chooses to do with his own material is entirely up to him - although I did think it strange, as he'd used ideas originally intended for The Chameleons on a Reegs record back in the late 1980s. I asked him to send anything else he might have that I could work on, but he told me that besides the odd thing he'd come up with on the dulcimer - an instrument he'd taken up the previous year - he didn't have anything that fitted the bill. I asked what he thought of the ideas I'd sent to Reg, but Dave said he hadn't seen him in quite a while. Utterly frustrated, I urged him to go and talk to Reg, and finally asked him if the Athens show was still on. Dave said he'd have to renew his passport, but assured me he'd be there.

Next came a flurry of emails asking me if I could confirm that John Lever had left the band; apparently, rumours to that effect were now circulating on the band's official website. This was completely unexpected, and presented more of a problem because it was being discussed on the band's online forum. The organisers of the show in Greece had heard about it and they, too, were seeking clarification. Again, I tracked down John's latest mobile phone number and spent an hour trying to get to the bottom of it but, as usual, John was being obtuse and it was hard work. However, he did tell me not to worry, that he hadn't left the band and that he was looking forward to playing the show in Athens, so after checking his drum requirements I got on with organising and hiring the crew. As the weeks continued to drift by, nothing happened. No-one had called on Reg to collect the ideas I'd sent him, nor had Reg found time to even listen to them. As it stood, the Athens show was the only paying gig we had. I realised that if I allowed the situation to continue, I'd be in serious financial trouble by the summer, so after discussing it with Daniela, I made the decision to accept Chris's offer and play acoustic dates in the US that coming June and July. I then posted an announcement to that effect, outlining my reasons and quashing the rumour that John had quit the band. Posting frank, open letters on the band's forum was something I'd been doing regularly for years, so I didn't think twice about it. On this occasion, however, the consequences proved fatal.

The day before the band were due to collect their tickets and fly to Athens, Reg had met the others at our rehearsal room to collect the guitars, only to find that Dave and John, incensed by the things I'd said publicly, were now refusing to play the show. Reg called to tell me they weren't coming. Naturally, I was devastated and more than a little worried. By this time, after having confirmed their intention to play the show, I'd finalised the contracts. The backers in Athens had already laid out a considerable amount of money, I'd signed the agreements, and now I couldn't deliver the band, which made me liable. I was also aware that people were planning to travel to Athens to attend the show. In fact, some had already arrived there ahead of us. Attempts to contact Dave and John directly failed - neither of them picked up their phones or responded to messages. With a very heavy heart I informed the organisers of the situation and, after some deliberation, they asked me if I'd be prepared to play the show solo. I told them that if they were prepared to accept that compromise then, yes, I would. Reg declined to join me, but Kwasi phoned to say that he at least would be there, as would the crew, and I greatly appreciated the support.

My next task was to inform the fans, and I felt deeply for those that had already made the journey. I also knew that many Athenians had been looking forward to seeing the band for the very first time and that excitement had been mounting for months, so they were in for a bitter disappointment.

We assembled in Athens to discuss our options. Our regular guitar tech, Will, hadn't been available, so I'd recruited Pete, who had previously worked for The Stone Roses. He told me he was already familiar with some of The Chameleons' best-known songs, and was willing to play some bass if needed. Our drum tech, Chiz, was also familiar with much of the set and a great drummer in his own right, and Kwasi had brought his percussion equipment as planned. We decided then to spend the Saturday afternoon putting together a set. I'd begin alongside Kwasi, playing acoustically, then we'd bring in Pete and play a few songs with him on bass. I had my laptop with me and would run the sequencer on a couple of brand new songs, and then bring in Chiz on drums for the final four or five songs.

The afternoon of the gig was very stressful as we worked hard rehearsing our set. The opening band was an Athenian outfit consisting of a couple of guys playing guitar to a computer sequencer. During the soundcheck, having taken stock of the situation, they told me that they knew how to play 'Second Skin' and asked if they could join us on stage to play the song. As you can imagine, I was more than happy to accommodate them, ultimately performing it by way of an encore.

Walking out onto the stage that night was one of the hardest things I've ever had to do. It became immediately obvious to me that the promoters had neglected to inform the audience of the change of plan for the evening. While this was unethical, on reflection I couldn't really say I blamed them, considering the amount of money they'd laid out on the show. Consequently some people left the venue immediately, although, happily, most stayed. By the end of the set the audience was going wild, and I'll never forget the look of joy on the faces of the two Athenian musicians that joined us for the encore as we played 'Second Skin'. I glanced across and noticed that one of the guys had tears streaming down his face.

After the show I felt physically and emotionally drained, as if all the drama of the previous year had caught up with me at once. I ate for the first time that day, and then proceeded to get as drunk as I possibly could. The next day, the chief promoter turned up and settled the account. Naturally, the fee had been revised once it was known that The Chameleons wouldn't be performing, but I was still able to pay everyone more than we'd originally agreed for the show, which came as a pleasant surprise to them, and allowed me to show my appreciation in a very practical way. That done, we said our goodbyes, and Daniela and I left for a few days respite on the island of Hydra, just a couple of hours away by fast boat from the Greek mainland.

Despite everything, I didn't feel that this was necessarily the end of the band. We'd had our spats before and come through them, and I didn't honestly think it would be otherwise this time. On arriving home, however, it quickly became apparent that the reality was somewhat different.

The first few email messages were very confusing and, considering how they were worded, rather alarming. "Mark! Just seen the news. We're deeply shocked and sorry, you must be feeling terrible right now." At first I thought that something truly awful had happened; that one of the others had been killed, or something equally hideous. I logged on to the band's forum to find that Dave had posted an open letter of his own, in which he accused me of all manner of things and hurled insults in every direction, incensed that the show in Athens had gone ahead without them. He finished by announcing that he, Reg and John had quit the band. This was typical of Dave, but even so, I was deeply shocked and uncertain how to react, or indeed whether I should react at all. Similar spurious accusations had come in the wake of my departure from the band during the late 1980s, and I hadn't countered them. I subsequently found that most people had been inclined to accept them as the truth until they'd got to know me personally and realised what nonsense it all was. This time I did react, but the resulting discourse rapidly degenerated and, embarrassed by such a public display of hostility, I finally withdrew, realising how futile it was.

Reg immediately contacted me to distance himself from Dave's vitriol, which Dave had claimed was on behalf of the three of them and, happily, Reg and I have remained friends ever since. Even John made his peace eventually, explaining the circumstances that had caused him to make the decisions that he had and, ultimately, I was able to come to terms with his reasons. I was never to see or hear from Dave Fielding again.

Those closest to me were concerned that I was now dealing with something unresolved, and that the longer it continued, the unhealthier it would be for me. On the contrary, I felt I had resolved something deep within myself. As justified as I'd felt in leaving the band in 1987, I'd been haunted over the years by the thought that, if I'd stayed, I might have been able to turn the situation around. I wasn't thinking about anything as mundane as a career as a member of a successful band, more contemplating the sadness of losing something altogether more profound. As the popularity and reputation of the group had continued to grow following our initial demise, I'd received hundreds of letters and thousands of emails from people who had only lately discovered our music, thanking us for the impact we'd had on their lives. Yet the band had cost me the dearest friendships I had ever known, and sometimes it hardly felt worth it.

Now all those doubts had been swept away. I realised for the first time that there was nothing I could have done, either then or now. The love I'd imagined had never really been there in the first place; it was a total sham, just as the reformation had been. Those ecstatic bursts of emotion from Dave when he would grab me in a fierce embrace in front of a joyous, cheering audience who never thought they'd ever see the day were also fake, merely the result of too much ecstasy. That's who we had become - the fucking Shameleons.

So, if I could turn the clock back would I do it again? Absolutely!

THE CHAMELEONS
DISCOGRAPHY

Singles

- In Shreds / Less Than Human (Epic 7", March 1982)

For all the following, the third track listed only appeared on the respective 12" version

- As High As You Can Go / Pleasure And Pain / Paper Tigers (Statik 7"/12", Feb 1983)
- A Person Isn't Safe Anywhere These Days / Thursday's Child / Prisoners Of The Sun (Statik 7"/12", June 1983)
- Up The Down Escalator / Monkeyland / Prisoners Of The Sun (Statik 7"/12", Nov 1983)
- In Shreds [live] / Nostalgia [live] / Less Than Human [live] (Statik 7"/12", Feb 1985)
- Singing Rule Britannia (While The Walls Close In) / Singing Rule Britannia (While The Walls Close In) [Radio 1 version] / Pleasure And Pain [Radio 1 version] (Statik 7"/12", Aug 1985)
- Tears / Paradiso / Inside Out (Geffen 7"/12", June 1986. Some copies of the 7" included a free single: Swamp Thing / Inside Out)
- Swamp Thing / John I'm Only Dancing / Tears [Original version] (Geffen 7"/12", Sept 1986)

EPs

- Tony Fletcher Walked On Water... La La La La La La La La La (Glass Pyramid 12"/CD, withdrawn before release in 1990. Not officially released until 1994. Re-issued by Dead Dead Good in May 1997)

Albums

- Script Of The Bridge (Statik, Aug 1983. Reissued by Dead Dead Good in 1995, and again as a 25th anniversary edition double CD on Blue Apple in 2008)
- What Does Anything Mean? Basically (Statik, May 1985. Reissued by Dead Dead Good in 1996, and again in 2009 as a double CD adding demos recorded immediately prior to the album)
- The Fan And The Bellows (Hybrid, March 1986. Released, quickly withdrawn and eventually released 1989. It consists largely of demo recordings made for Epic)
- Strange Times (Geffen, 1986. Later released on CD with a second disc containing the tracks from the two Geffen singles)
- John Peel Sessions (Strange Fruit, 1990. Contains all three sessions the band recorded for Peel)
- Tripping Dogs (Glass Pyramid, 1990. Recording of a rehearsal for the Free Trade Hall concert)
- Here Today... Gone Tomorrow (Imaginary, 1992. Radio sessions and demos)
- Live In Toronto (Imaginary, 1992)
- Dali's Picture (Imaginary, 1993. A collection of early demos)
- Aufführung In Berlin (Imaginary, 1993. Live recording from The Loft, Berlin 1983)
- Free Trade Hall Rehearsal (Imaginary, 1993. Edited and re-mastered re-issue of 'Tripping Dogs' with one extra track)
- The Radio One Evening Show Sessions (Nighttracks, 1993. BBC sessions recorded in 1983 and 1985)
- Northern Songs (Bone Idol, 1994. Compilation including the 'Tony Fletcher' tracks)
- Live Shreds (Cleopatra, 1996. US-only live album)
- Return Of The Roughnecks – The Best Of The Chameleons (Dead Dead Good, 1997. Early copies included a second CD containing the 'Tony Fletcher' EP tracks)
- Live At The Gallery Club (Visionary, Feb 1999. Re-issued by Cherry Red in 2001)
- Strip (Paradiso 2000, acoustic album recorded without John Lever)
- Why Call It Anything? (Artful, 2001. Re-issued by Blue Apple in 2013 as a re-mastered double CD with material added from 'Live at the Academy' album)
- This Never Ending Now (Paradiso, 2002. Acoustic album)

- Live At The Academy (Paradiso, 2002)
- Acoustic Sessions (Blue Apple, 2010. Re-mastered re-issue of the 'Strip' and 'This Never Ending Now' albums with 4 tracks from a KEXP radio session)
- Dreams In Celluloid (2013, re-mastered material from 'The Fan and the Bellows' and 'Dali's Picture' albums plus the 'Tony Fletcher' EP tracks)

Videos

- Live At The Camden Palace (Jettisoundz VHS, 1985. Re-issued on DVD in 2004 as 'Live From London')
- Live At The Haçienda (Jettisoundz VHS, 1994. 30-minute live performance)
- Arsenal (Jettisoundz VHS, 1995. 40-minute programme made for Spanish TV)
- Live At The Gallery (Jettisoundz, 1996. 55-minute live performance)
- Resurrection Live (2001, recorded in concert at Manchester Academy)
- Live At The Gallery Club & The Haçienda (Cherry Red Films, DVD 2002. Contains the two previously released VHS tapes of the same name)
- Singing Rule Britannia – The Chameleons Live (Cherry Red Films, DVD 2004. Re-issue of the 'Camden Palace' and 'Arsenal' VHS tapes)
- Ascension (Scourge Productions, 2xDVD 2006. Live recording from the Great American Music Hall, SF from October 2002)

MARK BURGESS DISCOGRAPHY

The Sun And The Moon

- The Sun And The Moon (Geffen LP/CD, May 1988)
- The Speed Of Life / The Death Of Imagination / The Boy Who Sees Everything / I Love You, You Bastard (Geffen 7"/12", June 1988. Last two tracks on 12" only)
- Alive; Not Dead EP (Midnight Music 12"/CD, November 1988)

Mark Burgess And The Sons Of God

- Zima Junction (Imaginary LP/CD, July 1993)
- Manchester 1993 (CD, Oct 1994. Live recording)
- Spring Blooms Tra-la-la (Indigo 2xCD, Nov 1994. Live recording)

Mark Burgess And Yves Altana

- Sin / Hollin High / Moon Over Kentucky (Dead Dead Good 7"/CD, Aug 1995. Third track on CD only)
- Always Want / Stephanie Weaves / Something For The Girl With Everything (Dead Dead Good 7"/CD, Sept 1995. Third track on CD only)
- Paradyning (Dead Dead Good LP/CD, Oct 1995)

Invincible

- Venus (Gethsemene CD, 1999)
- Black And Blue (Alchemized CD, 2002. Live recording)

Black Swan Lane

- A Long Way From Home (Eden CD, 2007)
- The Sun And The Moon Sessions (Eden CD, 2009)
- Things You Know And Love (Eden CD, 2010)
- Staring Down The Path Of Sound (Eden CD, 2011)

Mark Burgess

- Magic Boomerang (Indigo 2xCD, 2004. Compilation with some unreleased tracks)

ChameleonsVox

- M + D = 1 (8) (Blue Apple CD EP, 2013)

THE CHAMELEONS

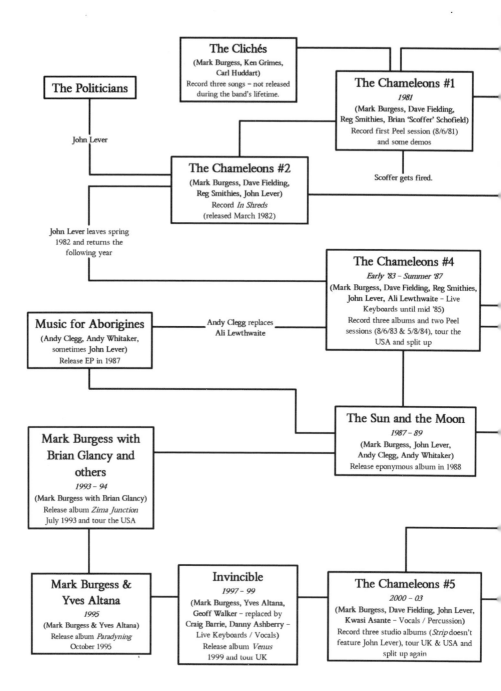

FAMILY TREE

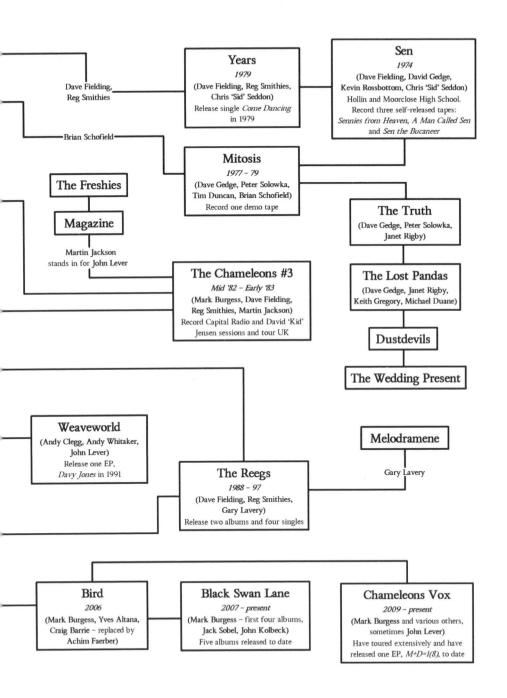

ALSO FROM MITTENS ON:

THE CITY IS ABLAZE!

Ablaze! was a notorious and outspokenly passionately fanzine published in Manchester and Leeds in the late eighties and early nineties. The zine's highlights, along with masses of archival material and new writings, have been compiled into a 320-page A4 book that captures an era where DIY was de rigueur and indie actually meant something. It's a post-punk history that could only be obtained by surfing the sliproads, sneaking backstage at a thousand shows, sleeping on strangers' floors and living to type up the tales of the sounds that defined an era.

The book includes original interviews with: The Sun and The Moon • The Wedding Present • The Membranes • The Stone Roses • The Inca Babies • Tools You Can Trust • The Bodines • Inspiral Carpets • The Pastels • Happy Mondays • King of the Slums • The Dust Devils • The Shamen • Cud • Sonic Youth • Dinosaur Jr • The Pixies • Throwing Muses • The Sundays • Thrilled Skinny • Eyeless In Gaza • Rapeman • UT • Dog Faced Hermans • Edsel Auctioneer • Mudhoney • AC Temple • fIREHOSE • Band of Susans • Henry Rollins • Live Skull • Kilgore Trout • The Breeders • Happy Flowers • Silverfish • The Keatons • The Stretchheads • Nirvana • Pale Saints • Mercury Rev • The Heart Throbs • Babes in Toyland • American Music Club • Hole • Pavement • My Bloody Valentine • Shudder To Think • Leatherface • Nation of Ulysses • Tsunami • Poster Children • Moonshake • Hood • Polvo • as well as irate letters from Morrissey and Thurston Moore.

"There are other people to condemn, Karren – aren't there?" – Morrissey
"I forgive and hope for Karren A" – Thurston Moore
"Fuck off!" – Ian Brown

"The most moving music-related thing I've read since Kristin Hersh's memoir." – Scott Creney, Collapse Board

Available from **www.mittenson.com**

ABOUT THE AUTHOR

Mark Burgess is an English rock musician and co-founder of critically-acclaimed post-punk band The Chameleons. He now lives in the USA, and is currently writing, touring and recording with Chameleons Vox.